Managing Human Resources

Managing Human Resources

FOURTH EDITION

Personnel Management
in Transition

Previously published as *Personnel Management*

EDITED BY Stephen Bach

Blackwell
Publishing

BLACKWELL PUBLISHING
350 Main Street, Malden, MA 02148-5020, USA
9600 Garsington Road, Oxford OX4 2DQ, UK
550 Swanston Street, Carlton, Victoria 3053, Australia

First edition published 1989 as *Personnel Management in Britain*
Second edition published 1994 as *Personnel Management*
Third edition published 2000
Fourth edition published 2005 by Blackwell Publishing Ltd

1   2005

Library of Congress Cataloging-in-Publication Data

Managing human resources : personnel management in transition /
edited by Stephen Bach.—4th ed.
    p. cm.
  Rev. ed. of: Personnel management. 3rd ed. 2000.
  Includes bibliographical references and index.
  ISBN-13: 978-1-4051-1850-7 (hardcover : alk. paper)
  ISBN-10: 1-4051-1850-4 (hardcover : alk. paper)
  ISBN-13: 978-1-4051-1851-4 (pbk. : alk. paper)
  ISBN-10: 1-4051-1851-2 (pbk. : alk. paper)
1. Personnel management—Great Britain.   I. Bach, Stephen, 1963–
II. Personnel management.
  HF5549.2.G7M357 2006
  658.3′00941—dc22

                                                            2005006590

A catalogue record for this title is available from the British Library.

Set in 11/13pt Bembo
by Graphicraft Limited, Hong Kong
Printed and bound in the United Kingdom
by TJ International, Padstow, Cornwall

The publisher's policy is to use permanent paper from mills that operate a sustainable forestry
policy, and which has been manufactured from pulp processed using acid-free and elementary
chlorine-free practices. Furthermore, the publisher ensures that the text paper and cover board
used have met acceptable environmental accreditation standards.

For further information on
Blackwell Publishing, visit our website:
www.blackwellpublishing.com

Contents

Notes on Contributors

Stephen Bach, Reader in Employment Relations and Management, Department of Management, King's College

Trevor Colling, Principal Lecturer, Department of Human Resource Management, De Montford University

Stephen Deery, Professor of Health Services Management and Human Resource Management, Department of Management, King's College

Linda Dickens, Professor of Industrial Relations, University of Warwick Business School

Martin R. Edwards, Lecturer in Human Resource Management and Organizational Psychology, Department of Management, King's College

Paul Edwards, Professor of Industrial Relations, University of Warwick Business School

Tony Edwards, Senior Lecturer in International Human Resource Management, Department of Management, King's College

Anthony Ferner, Professor of International HRM, Department of Human Resource Management, De Montford University

David Guest, Professor of Human Resource Management and Organizational Psychology, Department of Management, King's College

Ewart Keep, Professorial Fellow and Deputy Director of the ESRC Centre on Skills, Knowledge and Organizational Performance, University of Warwick Business School

Ian Kessler, Lecturer in Management Studies and Fellow of Templeton College, University of Oxford

Zella King, Director, Centre for Career Management Skills, University of Reading

Mick Marchington, Professor of Human Resource Management, Manchester Business School, The University of Manchester

Sue Newell, Cammarata Professor of Management, Department of Management, Bentley College

Keith Sisson, Head of Strategy Development, Advisory Conciliation and Arbitration Service and Emeritus Professor of Industrial Relations, University of Warwick Business School

Stephanie Tailby, Principal Lecturer, School of Human Resource Management, University of the West of England

Janet Walsh, Reader in Human Resource Management, Department of Management, King's College

Adrian Wilkinson, Professor of Human Resource Management, University of Loughborough Business School

David Winchester, Associate Member, Industrial Relations Research Unit, University of Warwick Business School

Figures

Tables

Boxes

Preface

This book is a direct descendant of the first edition of *Personnel Management* published in 1989, edited by Keith Sisson. This edition continues the traditions of its predecessors, while including substantial modifications, to reflect the profound changes in the context of managing human resources (HR) over recent years. This volume continues the style of earlier editions in which each chapter, in the words of the foreword to the 1989 edition, comprises 'an original essay that brings together the relevant theoretical and empirical work. Each is stamped with the views of the authors who are leading experts in the field.' The book therefore seeks to move beyond description of current HR recipes and to assess trends and differing perspectives on contemporary developments. This volume also reflects its origins in the University of Warwick's 'Industrial Relations in Context' series and it maintains much of this industrial relations orientation. In contrast to many texts which provide only cursory analysis of influences on the management of human resources that lie beyond the boundaries of the firm, this volume places the regulation of the employment relationship at the heart of the analysis. It considers the variety of contextual and institutional influences which shape the sectors and employer units in which people work, and seeks to understand the manner in which people are *actually* recruited, developed, appraised, disciplined and involved at work. The book is therefore not prescriptive as most textbooks in this area tend to be.

In addition, by exploring the particular contexts in which people are managed, it aims to contribute to debate about the state of HR practice in the UK and to shed light on a variety of contemporary policy debates. What are the consequences for HR practice of the increased internationalization and Europeanization of the UK economy? How far has HR policy altered in response to the growth of service sector employment and shifts in organizational boundaries? And have shifts in national patterns of regulation, implemented by successive Labour governments, had an impact on the skills, managerial competencies and forms of flexibility present in UK workplaces?

These questions reflect the changes that have been made in this edition. I have modified the book's title to reflect the evolution of the subject. As I engaged with authors it was clear that all contributors took HRM as the reference point for debate and engagement. HRM is considered to be a broad field of inquiry concerned with the practices used to shape the employment relationship rather than as a narrow and prescriptive set of 'best practice' strategies. This is the approach

I have adopted, which has many similarities with the term 'Personnel Management', used in previous editions, a term which is now used less frequently. My analysis of these issues and the debate about HRM is developed in more detail in Chapter 1.

In terms of the volume's content, the profound ways in which the context for managing human resources has altered is captured in the opening section which highlights the consequences of alterations in organizational structures, changes in labour and product markets, and international developments for HR practice. Two new chapters consider the impact of European integration and the role of multinational companies in altering the context in which people are managed. The chapters in the other sections are concerned with more long-standing themes: employee resourcing; employee development; pay and performance; and work relations. However, reflecting developments since the last edition there are new chapters concerned with issues of work–life balance, customer service work, and the emerging area of HR branding. The chapter on discipline has also been expanded to take account of the prominence within the HR community of concerns about the management of absence.

It proved difficult to make space for important new developments and at the same time keep the volume to manageable proportions. In some cases topics that were the subject of separate chapters in the previous edition have been integrated into several chapters. In other cases some of the chapters from the third edition had a timeless quality to them and consequently there seemed little point in asking contributors to update them for the sake of it.

A key change which merits special mention relates to editorial roles. When Keith Sisson invited me to edit jointly the third edition, he made it clear that if a fourth edition was to be produced, he would bow out of his editorial role. Despite my attempts to persuade Keith to change his mind, understandably he wished to channel his energies into other projects, especially his important policy role at the Advisory Conciliation and Arbitration Service (ACAS). ACAS's gain has been my loss, not only because of the self-evident increase in workload that halving the editorial team brought, but also because of the companionship and intellectual stimulus that is associated with joint writing and editorship. Nonetheless, Keith has maintained an active role in the volume by providing valuable guidance on editorial matters, very helpful comments on the introductory chapter, and contributing a chapter on the impact of European integration.

This book was written during the period when the obsession within universities about the forthcoming research assessment exercise (RAE) was reaching its peak. The RAE has put pressure on academic staff to focus on a narrow set of activities and has reinforced the self-serving behaviour that lurks just below the surface in most universities. Textbooks carry little weight in such research exercises, but this fails to recognize the degree to which texts are a key representation of our subject to students and other interested parties. It also undervalues the complex task of analysing and synthesizing a mass of research evidence and presenting it in an accessible and coherent manner to a non-specialist audience. I am therefore very grateful not only that all authors approached agreed to contribute, but that they took the time and trouble to produce high-quality chapters.

As well as the authors many people made this book possible. I have benefited enormously from the stimulus and support from colleagues in the Department of Management at King's College. Over the last four years, it has been rewarding working with colleagues to establish a Masters' degree in Human Resource Management and Organizational Analysis. Special thanks are due to Stephen Deery, Martin Edwards, Howard Gospel and Ian Kessler for providing me with detailed comments on the introductory chapter of this book. I am also grateful to the team at Blackwell – Bridget Jennings, Eloise Keating, Rhonda Pearce, Rosemary Nixon and Karen Wilson – that helped keep the book on track. As ever I am most appreciative of the encouragement from my wife and children, Caroline, Alexandra and Richard, who have been a constant source of support as the book moved through its various stages.

Stephen Bach

PART I

Managing Human Resources in Context

CHAPTER ONE

Personnel Management in Transition

Stephen Bach

For almost two decades analysis of the employment relationship has focused on the many uncertainties surrounding the emergence and consequences of human resource management (HRM). One approach has been to view HRM as involving particular strategies and approaches towards the management of labour, with analysis centring on the breadth and scope of HR policy. HRM has also been defined more broadly as a subject of study. This has raised many questions about the differences between HRM and personnel management both in terms of the HR practices used and also whether the underlying values and concerns of HRM are distinctive and managerialist in their orientation.

These debates have been reflected in the evolution of personnel management *practice* as charted in previous editions of this book. At the end of the 1980s there was a general recognition that competitive pressures were forcing employers to review personnel practice, but there was only the beginnings of a debate about whether personnel management was in transition and, if so, where it was going (Sisson 1989). By the mid 1990s, fundamental changes were afoot, but there were major questions about the degree to which these changes marked a fundamental break with past practice in the direction of the emerging HRM models (Millward 1994: 127; Sisson 1994). By the end of the 1990s, it became clearer that there had been a major reshaping of HR practice in the UK, but many employers appeared to be following the low road of cost minimization associated with low pay, disposable labour and outsourcing rather than the high road of skill development, partnership and mutual gains (see Kochan and Ostermann 1994; Bach and Sisson 2000).

In terms of the debate about the *definition* of HRM it is striking that in comparison to a decade ago much of the controversy has dissipated. When HRM emerged in the late 1980s and 1990s it was the definition of HRM as a specific, high commitment style of HR management, signalling 'a radically different philosophy and approach to the management of people at work' (Storey 1989: 5) that proved controversial. This normative approach to what managers 'should do' was criticized because it did not reflect actual developments in many workplaces (Bach and Sisson 2000). Increasingly, however, a broader, more encompassing definition of HRM has gained ground that downplays many of the preoccupations of HRM of the 1980s and 1990s. As an authoritative overview of the field explains:

> The notion of human resource management (HRM) is used in this book to refer to all those activities associated with the management of the employment relationship in the firm. The term 'employee relations' will be used as an equivalent term as will the term 'labour management'. (Boxall and Purcell 2003: 1)

This definition is on the right lines, but is arguably a little too broad because it becomes hard to highlight any distinctive features and values underpinning HRM, to chart changes in HR practice, or to understand why HRM has proved controversial if HRM is associated with *all* aspects of managing the employment relationship. HRM can usefully be defined in a generic sense as an approach that uses a variety of policies and practices related to the management of people, but it differs from employee relations in its dominant interest in management practice which tends to ignore employee interests. HRM as a subject of study assumes that the interests of employees and employers will coincide and is preoccupied with the end goal of organizational effectiveness that marginalizes the interests of other stakeholders such as employees. HRM is also predominantly focused on the individual firm and seeks solutions to HR problems within the firm, with an analytical focus on the motivations and aspirations of individual employees. This largely precludes the possibility that HR problems may lie beyond the boundaries of the firm and that employees may wish to combine together and act collectively to further their own interests (see Kaufman 2001: 364–6).

This chapter builds on these initial observations to provide a critical overview of the field to contextualize the detailed analysis of managing human resources considered in later chapters. First it considers the evolution of the HRM debate and examines the shift in emphasis from a focus on the meaning of HRM towards a concentration on the link between HR practice and organizational performance. Second, the implications for the personnel function are drawn out and the degree to which it has shifted towards a more strategic role are assessed. Third, the diverse patterns of HR practice are considered in relation to changes in the labour market, business restructuring and evolving patterns of corporate governance. It is the evolving institutional features of the UK employment context that continues to shape management practice. Finally the emerging 'New HR' is sketched out which arises from changes in the global, national and organizational employment context. The New HR signals new challenges for HR practice and represents a significant departure from the focus of the HRM debate over the last two decades.

The Evolution of HRM

Origins

The term 'human resource management' crossed the Atlantic in the 1980s and the UK debate has been shaped in large part by its US heritage. The antecedents of HRM originated in the study of large non-unionized US companies such as IBM and Hewlett-Packard. In these companies HRM has been associated with a particular style of people management that placed a great deal of emphasis on gaining the commitment of individual employees to organizational goals. In this unitarist perspective, management is viewed as the sole source of authority that safeguards the interests of managers and workers; trade unions are regarded as interfering unnecessarily in the harmonious relationship between employees and managers. UK employers and policy makers were receptive to this unitarist perspective in the 1980s and the resonance of HRM can therefore be linked to the political and economic context and the dominant ideological values prevailing at this time. In particular, intensified competition made the task of effective personnel management more urgent. Related pressures in the public sector arising from policies of privatization and market testing presented similar challenges as public sector managers were encouraged to emulate private sector 'best practice'. The popularity of the term 'HRM' came to symbolize not only a belief that major changes in product markets required a fresh management approach, but also that Conservative government reforms of the labour market allowed managers to exercise an unprecedented degree of 'strategic choice' in shaping organizational employment practices. With trade unionism in retreat, employers had an opportunity to decide whether to (de)recognize trade unions and to develop a more direct relationship with the workforce with the establishment of new channels of participation and involvement.

Models of HRM

The emergence of HRM was accompanied by controversy about the meaning of HRM and the degree to which normative models of HRM were reflected in organizational practice. There was recognition of the danger of comparing normative/ideal models of HRM with a descriptive model of the practice of personnel management, but Guest (1987: 507) concluded that there were significant differences between the 'stereotypes' of personnel management (PM) and HRM (Table 1.1). Storey (1989: 8) argued that interpretations of these developments were hamstrung by the conceptual elasticity of HRM. He distinguished between a 'soft' and 'hard' version of HRM which became the key reference points for debate. Both variants share an emphasis on the integration of HR policies with business planning but differ in the degree to which they highlight the 'human' or the 'resource' aspects of HRM.

Table 1.1 Stereotypes of personnel management and human resource management

	Personnel management	HRM
Time and planning perspective	Short-term: reactive *ad hoc* marginal	Long-term: proactive strategic integrated
Psychological contract	Compliance	Commitment
Control systems	External controls	Internal controls
Employee relations perspective	Pluralist: collective low-trust	Unitarist: individual high-trust
Preferred structures/systems	Bureaucratic: centralized formal defined roles	Organic: devolved flexible roles
Roles	Specialist	Line management
Evaluation criteria	Cost minimization	Maximize Utilization

Source: Abbreviated from Guest (1987).

The soft version focuses on the development of employees and emphasizes an investment orientation, in which a high trust approach results in a committed, adaptable and motivated workforce that are a key source of competitive advantage. The soft model has dominated the HRM literature and underpins Guest's (1987) model that identifies integration, employee commitment, flexibility and quality as the key goals of HRM. The orientation to the development of *internal* human resource assets and the manner in which human resource policies are combined together to ensure 'internal fit' has been reinforced by the emergence of the resource-based view of the firm. By contrast, the hard approach views employees as another factor of production and a commodity that has to be utilized and disposed of in a similar dispassionate fashion to other assets. In the hard version, HR policy is geared towards the external environment and the emphasis is on the alignment between external market conditions and the employment of labour. By implication, increasingly volatile product market conditions requires labour to become a less fixed asset via outsourcing, downsizing and other forms of numerical flexibility.

In the mid 1990s when the meaning of HRM and the prevalence of different HR policies provoked lively debate, a frequent criticism was that hard HRM was being wrapped in the language of the soft version as a means to manipulate and control the workforce (Sisson 1994: 15; Legge 1995). It was suggested that workers' acquiescence arose less from the potency of these techniques and more from the changing balance of power at the workplace in which management was in the ascendancy against a backcloth of high levels of unemployment and fears about job security. Even in so-called 'leading edge' companies including BP, Citibank, Hewlett Packard and Glaxo Pharmaceuticals, Truss (1999: 57) concluded:

> even if the rhetoric of HRM is soft, the reality is almost always hard with the interests of the organization prevailing over those of the individual.

The soft/hard dichotomy has been approached differently by discourse analysts, These commentators reject positivist assumptions about the existence of an objective reality and argue that language is crucial in framing understanding within organizations and can be marshalled to legitimize organizational policies. A sharp distinction between rhetorical language and an empirical reality is rejected because language is not just rhetorical – that is, seductive but false – but has real effects by legitimizing managerial actions that result in work intensification and other detrimental consequences for the workforce. By deconstructing the language of HRM these writers question the underlying unitarist and neutral assumptions of HRM. As Bunting (2004: 116) argues:

> Human resources . . . has taken on pleasantly democratic overtones as the 'people department'; and companies are very fond of instituting 'communities' in place of departments, while 'positions', not people are made redundant. Two of the most ubiquitous and fraudulent words are 'empowerment' and ownership.

There is no doubt that the 'linguistic turn' and discourse analysis has been highly influential. Society has become more sensitized to the use of rhetorical language; 'spin' in popular parlance. Journalists delight in pointing out how many times politicians such as Tony Blair mention 'Modernization' and 'New Labour' in their speeches and impute the direction of government policy from their choice of language. For Carter and Jackson (2004: 474) the use of managerial/HRM rhetoric contributes to the growth of organizational cynicism.

The difficulty with these types of analysis, however, is that in the absence of detailed empirical evidence, the reader is heavily reliant on the interpretation of the author. Despite Keenoy's (1999) suggestion that HRM is a hologram in which what the viewer sees is an illusion, but one that is constantly shifting depending on the vantage point of the observer, in practice these writers eschew this plurality of perspectives and claim the superiority of their own unique insights into 'HRMism'. Empirical evidence that seeks worker and management responses to initiatives such as empowerment, for example, often portray a more nuanced picture. As Edwards and Collinson (2002) highlight in their study of six organizations, the language of empowerment was not used by managers as an insidious form of labour control to mislead workers. They report that 70 per cent of workers were broadly favourable towards these quality programmes and 72 per cent of workers said that communication and participation had improved. Consequently, although discourse analysis has proved useful in sensitizing researchers to the use and abuse of HRM language, it can play only a very limited role in advancing our understanding of the contemporary workplace.

Best practice HRM

By the late 1990s debate about HRM had shifted from a concern with the meaning of HRM and whether HRM was a predominantly a soft or hard phenomenon towards an emphasis on the link between HRM and performance and the appropriate *measures* to use to capture these links. As Boxall and Purcell (2003) point out, two broad normative approaches to the HR/strategy link can be distinguished – best practice and best fit models. The best practice approach advocates a series of universal practices that are appropriate for all organizations and these practices are very much in the soft HRM mould. There are many such lists available, but Jeffrey Pfeffer's is the best known (see Box 1.1).

The assumption is that the more organizations adopt and implement these practices the clearer the pay off will be in terms of performance improvements. Although there is no definitive list of practices, there is considerable agreement that policies should be adopted which promote autonomy, commitment and opportunities to participate, especially through teamworking, indicating an emphasis on a soft, high commitment style of HRM (MacDuffie 1995; Ichniowski et al. 1996). Nonetheless, there has been criticism that wide variations exist between such lists (see Becker and Gerhart 1996). An additional concern is that best practice is invariably context specific, with US studies tending to ignore the importance of independent employee representation which is central to HR practice in a UK context (Boxall and Purcell 2003: 63; Marchington and Grugulis 2000). The influence of the best practice approach should not be underestimated, however, as policy advice from the DTI Best Practice series and the ACAS model of the 'effective workplace'

Box 1.1 Pfeffer's seven practices of successful organizations

1. Employment security.
2. Selective hiring of new personnel.
3. Self-managed teams and decentralization of decision making as the basic principles of organizational design.
4. Comparatively high compensation contingent on organizational performance.
5. Extensive training.
6. Reduced status distinctions and barriers, including dress, language, office arrangements, and wage differentials across levels.
7. Extensive sharing of financial and performance information throughout the organization.

Source: Pfeffer (1998: 64–5).

indicates (ACAS 2004: 4–5; DTI 2003). A key question, especially for policy makers and practitioners, however, remains the need to understand why relatively few firms adopt such measures, rather than become mired in a debate about the precise HR practices which constitute best practice.

Best fit HRM

In contrast to these universal models, best fit models adopt a contingency approach focused on the 'fit' with the environment. The modelling of the linkage between HR and strategy is derived from particular aspects of the organizational context. In the 1980s these studies focused on key components of the firm's competitive strategy and aligned HR policies to the external product market circumstances that confronted the firm; termed 'external fit'. There was some difference of emphasis in terms of how HR practices should be aligned to business strategy in these 'matching models'. The business life-cycle approach linked HR practices to the phase of the organization's development with differing HR priorities associated with start-up, growth, maturity and decline phases (Kochan and Barocci 1985). The dominant approach, however, was orientated to the firm's competitive strategy. Miles and Snow (1984) differentiated between three types of strategic behaviour with differing implications for HR practice depending on whether a firm was primarily geared to defending existing product markers (defenders) or was seeking market growth through innovation (prospectors). Schuler and Jackson (1987) took this type of analysis further, drawing on Porter's (1985) well-known model of competitive advantage, to specify that different competitive strategies required distinct employee behaviours. HR policies had to be designed to align competitive strategy and employee behaviour, resulting in favourable HR outcomes.

These type of contingency approaches were criticized as being too crude and deterministic in the manner in which they sought to align HR to business strategy, underplaying a variety of other contextual factors that influence approaches to HR as well as overlooking the degree to which employee interests and competencies influence competitive advantage (Boxall and Purcell 2003: 54–6). These criticisms informed more recent studies that have been more influenced by internal fit, that is, the degree to which a coherent *bundle* of HR practices can be constituted in which complementary HR practices produce superior levels of organizational performance (MacDuffie 1995). This has led to a focus on the bundle of HR practices that produces the most favourable organizational outcomes. An important influence on these studies has been the prominence of the resource-based theory of the firm which suggests that rather than adopting universal 'best practice' panaceas, firms derive competitive advantage by focusing on developing unique internal resources that are rare, non-substitutable and hard to imitate (Barney 1991).

Many studies have tested the relationship between specific bundles of HR practices, associated with high performance work systems, and organizational performance. The dominant message emerging from a variety of US studies across a number of industries suggests that there is a positive association between HR practice, firm performance and profitability, especially where HR practices are bundled together in a coherent and integrated fashion, termed a 'high performance work system' (Appelbaum et al. 2000). Practices that provide employees with more information, enhanced skills, extended opportunities for teamwork and enhanced discretion have been associated with enhanced organizational performance (Becker and Huselid 1998; Huselid 1995). The US study by Huselid (1995) has been highly influential because it concluded that the use of particular HR practices was reflected in higher organizational performance, lower labour turnover and higher labour productivity. The practices examined, which related to work organization and skill utilization, included employee participation and communication mechanisms and a focus on skills training. A second bundle of practices, which he termed a motivation index, examined data on performance appraisal and merit-based pay plans.

A very widely cited study of three US manufacturing plants by Applebaum et al. (2000) reinforced these earlier studies reporting that the use of high performance work systems – that is, a combination of teamworking, employee participation and sophisticated selection, training and appraisal systems – achieved organizational performance outcomes that were superior to traditional forms of work organization. High performance work systems elicited greater discretionary effort, more employee creativity and higher job satisfaction than traditional 'command and control' regimes. Some critics, however, suggest that higher discretionary effort may arise from work intensification rather than higher levels of job satisfaction (Godard 2004).

Although many of the research studies have been US based, in the UK one of the most striking recent studies reported an association between a bundle of high performance HR practices and lower death rates in a sample of 61 NHS hospitals (West et al. 2002). Guest et al. (2003) in their study of 366 organizations also concluded that there was an association between high-commitment HR practices and higher profitability as well as lower reported levels of labour turnover in manufacturing, but not in services. The study did not, however, demonstrate that HRM practices *caused* higher performance and the issue of causality has been at the centre of continuing controversy about the HR/performance link.

Commentators have highlighted a number of measurement and other methodological shortcomings associated with large-scale survey data used in many of these studies (see Godard 2004; Guest 2001b; Legge 2001; Purcell, 1999). The main concerns are:

- reliance on financial yardsticks of organizational performance which ignore the consequences for employees;
- the use of single managerial respondents, often situated at corporate head office, that are required to have knowledge of HR practice and organizational outcomes;
- the dominance of cross-sectional rather than longitudinal data which makes it difficult to be confident about the causal relationship linking HR practice to outcomes. There is scope for reverse causality, that is, that firms with better organizational performance are able to manage their staff more effectively rather

than that organizations become more competitive from the use of bundles of high performance HR practices;

* evidence which suggests that the low road of cost minimization may be equally effective in performance terms as the high road of the high performance workplace approach.

One consequence of this uncertainty is that HR directors are reluctant to use the evidence as a basis to persuade colleagues, especially CEOs, about the benefits of investing in high commitment HR practice (Guest and King 2004: 414). A number of responses, however, are evident, which is continuing to take forward the research agenda on HR and performance. First, there has been a greater recognition that more attention needs to be paid to the link between HRM and employee well-being (Guest 1999; Peccei 2004). This reflects the increased policy attention directed to issues surrounding the quality of working life. Second, there is increased sensitivity to context and more emphasis being placed on the institutional settings which shape strategic HR across industries and between countries. This amounts to a plea to Europeanize the HR bundles debate to bring employee interests and institutional context more fully into the analysis (Boxall and Purcell 2003; Paauwe and Boselie 2003). Third, there has been a recognition that large-scale cross-sectional survey data in isolation cannot resolve the issue of the relationship between HR practice and organizational performance and that other research methods which delve inside the organizational 'black box' and focus on how line managers actually implement HR practice is needed to advance understanding of the processes involved in sustaining better performance (Purcell et al. 2003). Finally the ambiguities surrounding the linkages between HR and performance also have significant implications for the status and influence of the personnel function.

The Evolution of the Personnel Function

Personnel management and ambiguity

For personnel specialists the debate about HRM was especially significant because it held out the prospect of a new dawn. The emphasis on the importance of the management of human resources to the competitive advantage of the organization appeared to give the personnel function the strategic dimension and status which it had been seeking, together with the means to achieve it by devolving responsibilities to line managers and demonstrating a measurable contribution to business performance. It had long battled to shake off its image as a low status function and struggled to escape the ambiguities inherent to the personnel role (Tyson and Fell 1986: 62–6).

A key source of ambiguity is the uncertain boundary between personnel management as a separate specialist function and as a description of a set of activities undertaken by all managers. From their origins in welfare work, personnel specialists have acquired a wide range of tasks including industrial relations, human resource planning and management development activities whose importance has shifted over time (Hall and Torrington 1998). The aspiration to shift from an operational to a more strategic conception of the function has encouraged the devolution of activity to line managers, but the specialist is expected to be the 'expert'. Indeed it is only by establishing expertise in operational matters that the personnel specialist is very often able to persuade senior managers that they have the capability to make a strategic contribution. The danger, of course, is that the more time and energy is spent on operational matters, the less they are associated with the strategic dimension.

A second source of ambiguity is that personnel specialists act in an advisory capacity and it is therefore difficult to identify their distinctive and measurable contribution. Their authority is both mediated and limited by the actions of line managers who may not share the same aims and priorities. For example, the emphasis the personnel specialist may put on consistent and standardized rules to reduce the ambiguities of the employment relationship and ensure procedural fairness, can appear to line managers to be unnecessary interference limiting their discretion. The other side of the coin is that managing people is an element of every manager's job; the distinct 'people' expertise of personnel specialists can be easily discounted by line managers. This is especially the case because of the difficulties of quantifying the HR contribution. The search for HR 'metrics' has therefore been a key task in attempting to overcome their ambiguous status.

A third source of ambiguity arises from the position of the personnel function. It combines a responsibility for the well-being of the workforce, and a set of pluralist values that view employees as a key organizational asset, while at the same time remaining an integral part of management whose priorities may differ from those of the workforce. By contrast mainstream management ideology is essentially unitarist, in which management and the workforce are viewed as sharing the same interests and any conflict arises from miscommunication. These frames of reference lead to differing perspectives on the management of the workforce and in the past the personnel function has often found itself in an uncomfortable position highlighting the consequences for the workforce of downsizing and other measures designed to maximize shareholder value. The response of the personnel function to this source of ambiguity has increasingly been to conform to the more strident managerial unitarism of the last two decades, placing more emphasis on business requirements. HRM has therefore been viewed as an attempt to escape the welfare straightjacket of personnel management (Townley 1994: 16).

A final source of ambiguity has been attributed to the gender bias of personnel management and the undervaluing of occupations in which many women work. This is reflected in the terminology used to describe routine personnel management roles such as 'handmaidens' and 'clerk of works' which have low status connotations, as does the general label 'Cinderella' function. Women make up an increasing proportion of personnel specialists, comprising almost two-thirds (63 per cent) of specialists in 1998 compared to one-fifth in 1980 (19 per cent). As Kochan (2004: 144) observes in the case of the USA, as more women entered the HR profession real wages of HR professionals declined by 8 per cent between 1993 and 2002.

Reinventing the personnel function

There has been no shortage of advice about how to shift towards a more strategic HR role. The most influential perspective has been Dave Ulrich's (1997) relentlessly upbeat book *Human Resource Champions* that predicted: 'the next ten years will be the HR decade' (p. viii) with the HRM agenda presenting opportunities for HR to 'add value'. This required a radical shift in thinking from a concern with 'what HR professionals do and more on what they *deliver*' (p. vii). Such an outcome is possible if HR professionals are able to fulfil four key roles:

- strategic partner;
- administrative expert;
- employee champion;
- change agent.

These roles require HR to balance short-term operational requirements *and* a strategic focus and combine the management of HR processes *and* people management. This amounts to a restatement of the ambiguities associated with the personnel function, but by developing new competencies HR professionals 'can go to heaven' (p. viii).

Ulrich's analysis is couched in unitarist terms with other interest groups, including trade unions, barely mentioned. The assumption that the goal of HR is to deliver value – that is, shareholder value – is seen as non-contentious. Ulrich's prescription has been enthusiastically endorsed by the Chartered Institute of Personnel and Development (CIPD), but to what extent has the personnel function moved towards becoming a valued business partner? An indication of the shift towards a strategic champion role can be gauged by the terminology used. Language, as discussed above, can be important. The Department of Health (2002: 3), for example, has lamented the degree to which 'human resource management in the NHS is still too often tarnished by its former role as the pejorative "personnel" function'. It is therefore noteworthy that the 1998 Workplace Employee Relations Survey (WERS) indicated that there had been a significant increase in the number of management specialists with 'human resources' in their job title. Approximately 7 per cent of workplaces with 25 or employees had a specialist with HR in their job title compared to 1 per cent in 1990, comprising approximately one-third of specialists (Millward et al. 2000: 52–4). More significantly, Hoque and Noon (2001) suggest that specialists using the HR title differ from personnel specialists in terms of being more likely to hold a formal qualification, are engaged more actively in strategic planning activities, and devolve more activities to line managers. The uptake of the HR label is therefore associated with a more sophisticated conception of HR practice and is suggestive of a shift of emphasis towards the strategic champion role.

This evidence in isolation, however, indicates little about how HR is viewed by HR professionals themselves or by chief executives and these perspectives reveal much greater uncertainty about their influence and capacity to develop a 'value added' agenda. Despite the interest in developing 'balanced scorecards' of HR performance the lack of quantifiable HR 'metrics' remains a significant barrier for the HR function in its aspiration to become a strategic partner (Bartlett and Ghoshal 2002: 37; Caldwell 2004: 201). A further dilemma arises from ensuring the appropriate balance between operational and strategic concerns. A CIPD survey of 1,188 senior HR practitioners reported that respondents spent relatively little time on business strategy in comparison to reacting to line managers' needs (CIPD 2003a: 24; IRS 2004: 11). The focus on operational tasks cannot be solely attributed to workload pressures; HR specialists recognize that their credibility depends on managing an effective operational regime. Consequently HR specialists, while espousing the language of strategic champions, focus on ensuring they are administrative experts. This bias towards an operational role is reinforced by a perception among CEOs and senior HR practitioners that there is insufficient HR talent available to fulfil the strategic champion role (Caldwell 2004: 203; Deloitte and Touche 2003: 15; Guest and King 2004: 416).

These challenges are being reinforced by the complexities associated with devolution of HR responsibilities to line managers, intended to allow specialists to concentrate on more strategic concerns. It has proved difficult to devolve a clearly defined workload and while line managers support devolution in principle they are often unwilling to undertake enhanced people management responsibilities in addition to their existing workload (CIPD 2003a: 26). This reluctance is reinforced by perceptions that HR's emphasis on procedural fairness can result in complex administrative procedures that are resented by line managers (Guest and King 2004: 420). The upshot is that a sizeable gap remains between espoused policy and its implementation which the CIPD (2003a: 6) describes as the 'Achilles' heel of contemporary HR strategy'. Although there has been much speculation about the degree to which HR outsourcing, forms of HR shared service centre and eHR can lower transaction costs and free up senior HR specialists for more strategic activities, managers have proceeded with caution. Outsourcing of HR activities was ranked 18th (out of 18) as a priority by both HR directors and a matched sample of CEOs (Deloitte and Touche 2003: 7).

In contrast to the strategic champion and administrative expert role much less attention has been directed at the employee champion role. It is important to recognize that Ulrich's term is misleading because the substance of what he proposes is focused on employee contribution, that is, the degree to which managers can enlist employees' efforts as a means to add value rather than being primarily concerned with employee well-being as an end in itself. Even in these more narrowly defined terms than the traditionally welfare orientation of personnel, the evidence is unequivocal. The HR function appears resistant to viewing itself as an employee champion and, interestingly, HR specialists have sought to move away from the welfare tradition more forcibly than CEOs view as appropriate (CIPD 2003a: 27; Deloitte and Touche 2003: 14; Guest and King 2004: 415). These findings are reinforced by survey evidence of union representatives that indicated, with the possible exception of the health service, that HR rarely acted as a buffer between management and the workforce (Labour Research 2003). Similarly Kochan (2004) in his analysis of the state of the US HR function attributes its loss of trust and legitimacy as arising from its disregard of workforce interests, exemplified by the absence of any serious challenge to soaring CEO pay levels in its failed quest for a more strategic role. Kochan's analysis provides a salutary warning about the pre-occupations of the HR function in recent years.

Summary

The debate on HRM has come a long way since the early 1980s. The controversy surrounding the meaning of HRM has largely dissipated and HRM has become defined in broader terms to describe all aspects of personnel practice rather than associated narrowly with a specific high commitment style of HR. This shift in emphasis has dampened down the ideological concern that HRM was 'an industrial version of Thatcherism' (Strauss 2001: 873). Analysis of HRM, as illustrated more fully in the next section, has continued to be shaped by the evolving political and economic context at the workplace and beyond.

The passion and controversy about HRM has therefore shifted towards the ongoing debate about the link between bundles of HR practices and performance and whether the search for the holy grail of an HR-performance link is, in Karen Legge's (2001) terms, a silver bullet or a spent cartridge. These changes have had important consequences for the personnel function as it has sought to become a more strategic HR partner. Although HR managers are better qualified than their predecessors and the CIPD has continued to increase membership; achieving chartered status for its members, uncertainty about the HR contribution remains a significant preoccupation.

The Practice of Personnel Management

It is not only the debate about HRM that has moved on significantly, there is also much more data available about the state of HR/personnel practice. The emergence of large-scale survey work, especially the Workplace Industrial/Employment Relations Survey series, has provided an authoritative portrait of the changing landscape of employment practice since 1980. Its shifting focus from a preoccupation with formal structures of collective bargaining towards a focus on management practice and its incorporation of smaller workplaces (with more than 10 rather 25 employees) has attempted to keep pace with the changing state of management practice. There has also been a rapid expansion of surveys undertaken by the CIPD, DTI and by management consultants and the posting of these surveys on the Internet has ensured much greater access to this material. The representativeness and sample sizes differ, but they contribute to the overall sense of where personnel practice is headed. In addition, the availability of large-scale data sets has encouraged academics from related disciplines including psychology and economics to focus more squarely on employment matters.

Case study research remains important in illuminating our understanding of contemporary HR practice, but there are many difficulties in gaining high-quality research access. Edwards and Collinson (2002: 280) in a study of the implementation of quality initiatives, with direct relevance for the organizations concerned, were only able to gain agreement to undertake the research from 6 of the 19 organizations approached. The resource intensive nature of case study research and the inclination of many leading academic journals to publish predominantly narrow, highly quantitative survey-based research, has led to a reduction in the availability of high-quality case study research. As Barley and Kunda (2001) point out, however, it is only by detailed observation of the workplace that our understanding of the contemporary world of work can be advanced and this type of material is also essential for teaching purposes in galvanizing student interest in HR practice. Although this knowledge gap is being partially remedied by some of the findings that are emerging from the ESRC *Future of Work Project* (Nolan 2004), it is notable that some of the most compelling, albeit largely anecdotal accounts of recent employee experience of work, have been written by journalists (Bunting 2004; Toynbee 2003).

State of play

During the last two decades there has been very significant restructuring of personnel practice and many of the long-standing features of the UK's employment relations landscape have been transformed. It is relatively straightforward to identify the shift in institutional structures and declining union presence. There has also been the growth of direct communication, employee involvement and increased coverage of performance appraisal. There is much more scepticism about the extent to which HR practices are bundled together to form a coherent and integrated HR architecture and, most contentious of all, differences remain in the interpretation of employees' experience of work.

The main trends in personnel practice can be summarized fairly succinctly. First, there has been a large reduction in traditional employment relations institutions with a decline in joint regulation by collective bargaining. The WERS series indicates that union recognition has fallen from 66 per cent in 1984 to 53 per cent in 1990 to 42 per cent in 1998. This fall in recognition was a private sector phenomenon and was attributed to lower rates of recognition among workplaces that were less than five years old rather than derecognition in continuing workplaces (Millward et al. 2000: 106–7). Workplace size is also of crucial importance in explaining the fall in union recognition because of the strong association between larger workplaces and union presence. Of course the last 5 years has been a key period for trade unions with the 1999 Employment Relation Act establishing a statutory right to union recognition, but as discussed in the next section this has slowed, but not reversed, the picture of trade union decline.

In workplaces where unions continue to be recognized their influence has declined sharply and even if formal negotiation remains in place all the indications suggest that trade unions are consulted and in many cases merely informed about a range of pay and non-pay matters (Brown et al. 2000; Oxenbridge and Brown 2004). WERS data also indicates that there has not been any increase in consultative committees which were present in 28 per cent of establishments, the same proportion as 1990.

It has been the growth of direct communication with the workforce, such as team briefings and meetings between senior managers and the workforce, that has been the clearest trend. As Table 1.2 indicates, between 1984 and 1998 the proportion of workplaces with just representative voice halved and those with direct voice nearly trebled. Unionized workplaces added complementary forms of direct communication while almost all new workplaces favoured direct communication methods without union recognition (Metcalfe 2003: 174). These trends are consistent with the WERS 4 finding that 72 per cent of workplace managers expressed a preference to consult directly with employees rather than with unions and that

Table 1.2   Changes in worker voice arrangements, 1984–1998 (%)

Type of voice arrangement	1984	1990	1998
Union only	24	14	9
Union and non-union	43	39	33
Non-union only	17	28	40
No voice	16	19	17
Representative voice only	29	18	14
Representative and direct voice	45	43	39
Direct voice only	11	20	30
No voice	16	19	17

Base – all workplaces with 25 or more employees, approximately 2000 workplaces in each year. Union voice defined as one or more trade unions recognized by employers for pay bargaining or a joint consultative committee meeting at least once a month with representatives chosen through union channels. Non-union voice defined as a joint consultative committee meeting at least once a month with representatives not chosen through union channels, regular meetings between senior management and the workforce, briefing groups, problem solving groups, or non-union employee representatives.

Source: Metcalfe (2003: 174), adapted from Millward et al. (2000).

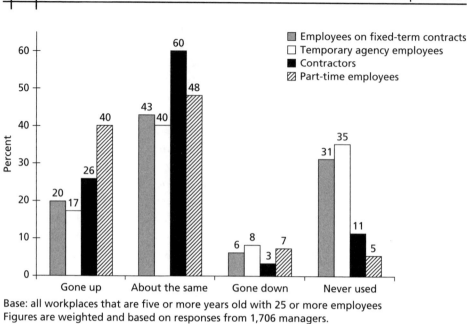

Base: all workplaces that are five or more years old with 25 or more employees
Figures are weighted and based on responses from 1,706 managers.

Figure 1.1 Changes in the use of different forms of labour over the last 5 years
Source: Cully et al. 1998

employers have become less accommodating in providing support and time off to union representatives (Cully et al. 1999: 88, 206–7).

A second major change is the growth in the different forms of so-called 'non-standard forms of employment', as indicated in Figure 1.1. Most important is the growth in part-time work which is associated with increased female participation rates in the labour market (Chapter 7). Part-time employees account for around a quarter of the workforce and they make up the majority of the workforce in a similar proportion of workplaces. Significantly, this figure is up from 16 per cent in 1990 (Cully et al. 1998: 6). A major impetus for this increase arises from the growth of private sector services which make heavy use of part-time work. More recent data from the *Change in Employer Practices Survey* conducted in 2002 also pointed to the greater use of part-time employees, especially among large establishments in the public services (Taylor 2003: 8).

Third, there has been the considerable experimentation with new management practices, but the overall growth in a range of so-called 'new' management practices has been relatively modest. The details are shown in Table 1.3, grouped according to four main areas of activity: appraisal and reward, involvement and participation, training and development, and status and security. Although many of these practices are not new, they have nonetheless come to be associated with change. In the case of *appraisal and reward*, it will be seen that just over a half of non-managerial employees have some form of appraisal. Only one in ten of these employees have individual performance pay, however, raising major question marks about the amount of attention such arrangements have received in the prescriptive literature. More

Table 1.3 Percentage of workplaces using 'new' management practices and employee involvement schemes

Appraisal and reward	
Most non-managerial employees have performance formally appraised	56
Individual PRP scheme for non-managerial employees	11
Employee share ownership scheme for non-managerial employees	15
Profit-sharing scheme operated for non-managerial employees	30
Involvement and participation	
Workplace level joint consultative committee	28
Regular meetings of entire workforce	37
Problem-solving groups (e.g. quality circles)	42
Staff attitude survey conducted in last five years	45
Workplace operates a system of team briefing for groups of employees	61
Most employees work in formally designated teams	65
Training and development	
Most employees receive minimum of five days training a year	12
Most supervisors trained in employee relations skills	27
Status and security	
Guaranteed job security or no compulsory redundancy policy	14
'Single status' between managers and non-managerial employees	41
Workplace operates a just-in-time system of inventory control	29
Attitudinal test before making appointments	22

Base: all workplaces with 25 or more employees
Figures are weighted and based on response from 1,926 managers

Source: Cully et al. 1998: table 4.

enjoy the benefits of share ownership (one in seven) and profit sharing (one in three), but they remain very much a minority. In the case of *involvement and participation*, as noted earlier the signs of activity are greater. Thus, 37 per cent of workplaces reported regular meetings, 42 per cent said they had some kind of problem-solving group such as quality circles and 45 per cent that they had used staff attitude surveys. Even so, this still means that less than half of workplaces were affected. Only team briefing, with 61 per cent affected, was practised in a majority of workplaces.

At first sight, the evidence for the incidence of team work looks pretty strong with around two-thirds of workplaces (65 per cent) in the WERS reported that employees worked in formally designated teams, only a handful (5 per cent of those with teams) had something resembling the semi-autonomous team working which has come to be regarded as the *leitmotiv* of new forms of work organization, that is, respondents said team members had to work together, had responsibility for specific products or services, jointly decided how work was to be done, and appointed their own teams leaders. Similarly, a striking finding of the 2001 Skills Survey is that although there had been some increase in team working from 44 per cent in 1992 to 53 per cent in 2001, there had been a substantial decline in task discretion. Consequently, whereas in 1992 nearly half of all team workers worked in teams with significant decision-making powers, this had declined to a quarter by 2001 (Gallie et al. 2004: 256).

The next dimension of Table 1.3 concerns *training and development*. Here, too, the evidence is hardly supportive of a major shift. Despite the widespread importance attached to training because of the association between low levels of training and the UK's comparatively poor productivity record, only 12 per cent, or one in eight, said that most employees received a minimum of 5 days' training per year. Notably only 27 per cent, or one in four, said they trained most supervisors in employee relations skills training, but it is the development of people-orientated skills which is often highlighted as an important element in any shift towards a high commitment HR approach. The final cluster to be considered involves *status* and *security*. Here it will be seen that less than half of workplaces (41 per cent) had single status arrangements between managerial and non-managerial employees and only 14 per cent, or one in seven, guaranteed job security or no compulsory redundancy policy. This last point is especially significant in terms of the spread of new forms of work organization and social partnership arrangements as in both cases it is suggested that guarantees of employment security are integral to the effectiveness of these arrangements. These findings are consistent with Kelly's (2004) analysis of partnership companies which indicated that job-security provisions are not widespread and that in sectors in which there is significant job shedding, partnership agreements may accelerate the rate of job loss.

The overall picture is in many ways even less encouraging if we look at the WERS figures for the total number of practices. The practices listed in Table 1.3 after all are viewed as standard practices which are repeatedly mentioned by the 'best fit' and best practice' schools of HRM. Moreover, the figures measure incidence only and not scope; as in the case of team working discussed above, therefore, they might be thought to exaggerate the significance. In the circumstances, the finding that only one in five (20 per cent) had half or more of the 16 practices and only one in fifty (2 per cent) had more than 10 indicates the limited uptake of high commitment HR practices. Guest's (2001a: 112) conclusion about the low levels of adoption of such practices, especially in the private sector, is stark:

> What this implies is that management is not doing a very good job of managing human resources. The popular cliché that 'people are our most important asset' is patently untrue.

In order to make sense of what is happening it is crucial to disaggregate the picture. Even taking account of broad sectoral variations between public and private sectors only takes us so far. It is variations in product market strategies alongside differences related to organizational size and patterns of ownership that have a crucial bearing on personnel practice.

Labour Market Change and Patterns of Corporate Governance

It is necessary therefore to consider changes in the labour market and evolving business structures/corporate governance arrangements to explain the diversity of employment practice.

Employment restructuring

In terms of employment restructuring changes in the composition of the workforce are associated with first, a shift from manufacturing to services and second, the polarization of the occupational structure.

The dominance of service industries

The UK, like all advanced economies, has become dominated by service industries, such as retailing and financial services. These trends have drawn attention to the HR implications of work that is centred on interaction with customers, uses emotional labour, and is often linked to the growth of call centres (Chapter 13). Service industries contribute over 70 per cent of GDP, account for 8 out of every 10 jobs, and employment has increased by over 2 million since 1997 alone. As Table 1.4 indicates, alongside the massive increase in service sector jobs there has been a rapid fall in manufacturing employment. The Department of Trade and Industry (DTI) suggests that globalization has played a part, with the largest falls occurring in industries most vulnerable to competition from low-cost producers in developing countries; accounting for the trend in textiles, clothing and footwear (DTI 2004: 47). More generally, however, successive governments have been implicated by the lack of concern they have attached to the decline of manufacturing industry. The growth of health and education services as well as leisure and retail services indicate increased demand arising from secular changes in society – ageing populations and the emergence of a 'time poor' society in which individuals use increased wealth to purchase a wider range of services.

The growth of the private service sector has had a critical effect on the age structure of the workforce. Industries with the youngest workforces included distribution, hotels and restaurants, banking, finance and insurance in which at least 40 per cent of the workforce were 16–34 year olds, while by contrast in public administration, education and health almost 40 per cent of the workforce were between 45 and pension age (Begum 2004). Trade unions face particular difficulties in encouraging younger workers to become union members. Many commentators have suggested that the values of young workers, and the aspirations that they bring to work, differ from older workers and that they are less likely to place their trust

Table 1.4   Key changes in employment by sector, over 25 years

Description	Employment (000s)		Change (%)
	June 1978	June 2003	
Increases:			
Real estate, renting machinery, computer activities	1,783	3,964	122
Hotels and restaurants	1,082	1,818	68
Health and social work	1,700	2,854	68
Other service activities	907	1,318	45
Education	1,592	2,240	41
Financial intermediation, insurance pension funding	757	1,050	39
Wholesaling and retailing	3,631	4,451	23
Publishing, printing and recorded media	323	347	7
Decreases:			
Transport and communications	1,597	1,547	−3
Construction	1,373	1,477	−11
Food products; beverages and tobacco	715	467	−35
Agriculture, hunting and forestry, fishing	418	234	−44
Electrical equipment	740	389	−47
Manufacturing	6,922	3,501	−49
Textiles and clothing	814	180	−78
Mining and quarrying	383	71	−81
Footwear and leather goods	124	15	−88

Source: DTI (2004).

in the organization and its HR policies (Sparrow and Cooper 2003). Consequently the growth of sectors of the economy that employ a higher proportion of younger workers presents challenges for HR practitioners and union organization.

A further component of this compositional effect relates to the increase in part-time workers (Millward et al. 2000: 44–5). The changing balance between stand-ard and non-standard employment is being fuelled by the shift towards a 24/7 society in which consumers expect to access services at a time that is convenient to them. Not all of the growth in non-standard employment, however, originates solely in employer preferences for more flexible working hours. The majority of part-time workers are women and the decisions within households to manage work and childcare responsibilities in an affordable manner shapes working patterns. For example, in a significant minority of households with young children women work exclusively in the evenings or at night once the father has returned from work; a pattern that is shaped by the high cost and limited availability of affordable child-care (Harkness 2003: 160).

A further consequence of the shift from manufacturing to services has been the shrinkage in the size of the workplace. As the WIRS/WERS series has indicated there is a long-standing association between workplace size and a range of personnel practices. Smaller workplaces are less likely to have a specialized personnel manager, less likely to recognize unions and the adoption of 'new' management practices is also less prevalent (Millward et al. 2000).

Occupational structure

The second dimension of labour market change relates to the occupational structure of the workforce in which a growing polarization is apparent. Over the last 25 years there has been a large rise in the number of well-paid jobs and an increase in poorly paid jobs with a squeeze in the number of jobs in the middle (Goos and Manning 2003). This has been described as the emergence of an hourglass economy in which a strata of highly paid two-earner families can be contrasted with the growth of an under-class of low wage predominantly women workers (Nolan 2004). Between 1979 and 1999 the fastest growing 'bad' jobs reflected the growth of employment in service industries (Table 1.4), especially among labour intensive tasks that are less susceptible to technological change, for example, sales assistants, waiters, bar staff, cleaners and care assistants. By contrast most of the increase in 'good' jobs has been among managers, with a very rapid growth in the number of managerial positions across all sectors. The UK stands out in Europe as having a very high proportion of managerial and supervisory employees. This picture is consistent with the evidence presented above about the limited spread of 'empowering' new management practices, highlighting the UK 'management problem' (Chapter 9). It almost certainly reflects also the increased pressure on managers within public and private sectors to demonstrate compliance with a proliferation of targets and regulatory requirements.

This polarization of the job structure is reflected in increased pay inequalities.

Pay levels are closely associated with sector and the Low Pay Commission (2003) has identified a number of industries – virtually all private sector service industries – including retail, hospitality, business services, social care, childcare and hairdressing, in which low pay is prevalent. Consequently more than 20 per cent of jobs in the hospitality, cleaning and hairdressing sectors benefited from the rise in the October 2001 national minimum wage increase. At the other end of the pay scale top managers' compensation has not risen to the stratospheric levels of the USA, in which by 2000 CEOs were typically earning 500 times the wages of the average employee – the ratio in the UK is 25 – (Stiglitz 2004: 123–4). Nonetheless, there has been considerable disquiet that directors of UK FTSE 100 companies have benefited from an increase in median salary of 92 per cent between 1993 and 2002 (£301,000 to £579,000) compared to an increase in average earnings of 44 per cent (see Iles 2004). The Labour government expressed concern that executives have been rewarded for failure as well as success (Chapter 12). For HR practitioners these trends raise sensitive questions about the degree to which employees view the distribution of rewards as fair and transparent because large variations in pay are routinely viewed in the HR literature as detrimental to teamwork and a united sense of organizational purpose.

To summarize there have been fundamental and interrelated changes in the patterns of employment which help to explain much of both the restructuring and diversity of HR practice which is to be observed in the UK. The decline of joint regulation, for example, can be associated with the reduction in the manufacturing workforce, along with highly unionized sectors such as coal, and a shrinking in the size of workplaces more generally. The growth in part-time work, much of it low paid, and the feminization of the workforce reflects the expansion in the service sector.

Nonetheless, a word of caution is needed in assuming a straightforward relationship between changes in the labour market and the practice of HR management from a single set of structural variables. There are a number of cross-cutting dimensions. A part-time female employee in a large successful retail chain like Tesco might enjoy greater de facto security and training and development opportunities than her counterpart in a small family-owned store. Less expectedly, the same is likely to be true of the comparison with male full-time employees, including managerial posts in manufacturing and financial services, that have been subject to constant rounds of downsizing and merger and acquisition activity. Much depends on the business systems, strategy and structure of employing organizations and so it is to these that the analysis now turns.

Corporate governance

Underpinning the changes in both the practice of personnel management and the patterns of employment are specific business systems, strategies and structures. A key reference point in interpreting changes in personnel practice has been the increased interest in distinctive *national* patterns of corporate governance which focuses on who controls firms, in whose interests firms are governed and the ease with which ownership of firms can be altered. Hall and Soskice (2001) who differentiate between 'varieties of capitalism' suggest that financing and ownership patterns of firms impact on corporate governance which significantly shapes employment practices. Within the UK, it has long been recognized (Sisson 1989: 16) that the most important features of corporate governance include:

- an overwhelming emphasis on shareholder value as the key business driver as opposed to the interests of other stake-holders;
- institutional share ownership by investment trusts and pensions funds which encourages a focus on short-term profitability as the key index of business performance rather than long-term market share or added value;

- relative ease of take-over, which not only reinforces the pressure on short-term profitability to maintain share price and dividend payments, but also encourages expansion by acquisition and merger rather than by internal growth;
- a premium on 'financial engineering' as the core organizational competence and the domination of financial management, both in terms of personnel, activities and control systems, over other functions.

These characteristics of the UK (and USA) termed 'liberal market economies' are contrasted to the co-ordinated market economies of more 'patient' capitalism associated with Germany and Japan. As Gospel and Pendleton (2003) point out, these differences between market-outsider and insider-relational forms of corporate governance exert pressure on the management of labour. In liberal market economies the overriding emphasis on shareholder value, an ideology that has strengthened markedly in recent years, ensures that labour is treated as a variable cost of production to be downsized if the share-price is jeopardized. The dominance of the market is mirrored inside the firm in which market-type devices – the organization of the firm as a series of business units that compete for investment – and the use of outsourcing are prevalent. Employers may also be reluctant to pursue a range of investment strategies and forms of employee involvements because it may limit management prerogatives and their capacity to respond to shareholder demands. The UK's poor training record is frequently attributed to a system of corporate governance that provides an inhospitable environment to invest in HR (Chapter 8).

Similar developments are evident in the public services. For more than two decades government reforms have encouraged the public services to mimic the organizational and management structures of the private sector. The diffusion of market-type mechanisms across the public services has put pressure on managers to alter employment practices to ensure efficient and effective public service delivery. The authority of senior managers has increased and managerial responsibilities devolved from central government to lower levels within semi-autonomous organizational units (Kessler and Purcell 1996). At the same time, however, central government has accrued unprecedented levels of control over the funding and management of nominally independent service providers through strictly enforced cash limits and demands for annual 'efficiency gains'. Systems of performance management have been intensified by the proliferation of government targets that has generated a form of short-termism. Senior managers manage upwards to fulfil ministerial targets, which act as proxies for shareholder pressure. These pressures, alongside the requirement to respond to an unrelenting stream of new initiatives, inhibited managers from developing a longer-term, more strategic conception of HR practice (Bach 2004).

This analysis needs to be qualified to the extent that employment practices cannot be assumed to follow in a deterministic fashion from the dominant system of corporate governance. Variations between firms in the UK indicate that managers can exercise a degree of strategic choice in responding to shareholder demands (Gospel and Pendleton 2003). As Bunting (2004: 49) illustrates in the case of the budget hotel chain Travel Inn, shareholder pressure to cut staffing costs led managers to place more, not less, emphasis on training because as one manager explained:

> My labour budget is very tight – I manage that, I don't complain – the key is to get people trained. Two people could have managed that situation [a busy bar and the restaurant] if they had been trained.

There is also a sense that changes are emerging in the UK's system of corporate governance that provide counterveiling pressures to arrest short-termism with employee and other stakeholder interests bolstered by EU driven reforms of employment law and the changing structure of institutional share ownership (Armour et al. 2003). At present, however, these developments have not led to a dilution of the primacy of shareholder value and the increased concentration of ownership enables investors to force changes on managers, especially when performance is poor, which continue to have dramatic effects on employment and HR practice (Pendleton and Gospel 2004).

Changing business strategies and structures

The last two decades have witnessed a period of continuous organizational restructuring that is associated with these underlying features of corporate governance. The lightly regulated character of the UK economy has encouraged high levels of inward and outward foreign direct investment. Across the whole of private sector manufacturing, the incidence of foreign ownership trebled from 7 per cent to 19 per cent between 1980 and 1998 and in private sector services the figure more than doubled from 5 to 11 per cent (Millward et al. 2000: 33–4). Foreign-owned multinational companies have therefore become an even more important source of variation and innovation in personnel practice (Chapter 3).

The UK economy has become more open with relatively few regulations, ensuring that competitive pressures have intensified (OECD 2004). These trends have been reinforced by the expansion of the European Single Market, trade liberalization alongside continuing privatization and deregulation. This context has reinforced the short-term planning horizons of companies and resulted in a continuing high level of restructuring because firms are less embedded in institutional structures allowing rapid responses to changing circumstances. One significant trend has been an increase in sub-contracting within the networked organization (Chapter 4). There have been two distinctive phases of the debate about sub-contracting. In the 1980s and 1990s, this trend was closely associated with privatization and programmes of compulsory competitive tendering in the public services, which led to many services being transferred to the private sector. These developments reflected the conventional wisdom that management should focus on its 'core' activities and divest itself of so-called 'ancillary services', such as catering, cleaning and distribution.

In the second phase of externalization, which has gathered pace since the mid-1990s, managers have been less concerned about the balance between 'core' and 'periphery' activities and have focused on more radical divestment of business activities, which has included the relocation and export of productive capacity abroad, a trend termed 'off-shoring'. A survey of Confederation of British Industry (CBI) members indicates that the pressure to off-shore is increasing and the main rationale is cost driven, with predominantly low added-value manufacturing functions transferred to Asia and to a lesser extent Central and Eastern Europe. It also appears that despite the media hype surrounding the off-shoring of call centre work, this activity is less 'off-shorable' than production of industrial goods (CBI 2004: 6). In the public sector large swathes of public provision, such as housing and social services have been transferred to the private sector and the Labour government's modernization of public services has involved an extended role for the private sector in the provision of core services (Bach and Givan 2005).

These changes have been accompanied by high levels of organizational upheaval as firms have divested themselves of businesses and acquired new ones. UK organizations are not only involved in a permanent revolution of minor structural change, but can expect major restructuring every 3 years, of which 85 per cent involve redundancies and early retirements (CIPD 2003b). This leads the CIPD to conclude that the economy is subject to the '3Rs' effect of simultaneous reorganization, redundancy and recruitment (CIPD 2004: 13). Part of the explanation for this degree of turbulence arises from the divisionalization structures of large UK companies that are viewed by managers as aggregates of separate cost business units which have to meet performance targets; set and tightly monitored by the centre. When divisions do not meet their profitability targets they are sold off and other more profitable divisions acquired. Ackroyd and Procter (1998) in their analysis of the largest 200 UK-owned manufacturing firms highlight the consequences for employment practice in which there is little investment in advanced technology or multi-skilling, but instead semi-skilled employees compete with sub-contractors to retain their employment. The upshot is that the increased use of contractors is significantly associated with work intensification (Green 2004: 731).

Summary

Changes in the labour market, patterns of corporate governance and business strategies are profoundly important in understanding why there has been restructuring, but only a very limited shift towards high commitment HR practice in the UK. Within the labour market the growth of part-time employment and the shift to service industries have been the dominant trends leading to the creation of more relatively disposable and low value-added 'bad' jobs. At the same time there has been a marked increase in job polarization with an increase in the number of well-paid 'good' jobs. These jobs are much better rewarded and include other benefits associated with higher status work; however, the pressure on managers and professionals to achieve a variety of performance targets, such as absence, has increased (Chapter 14). The scope to monitor performance has also been enhanced by the spread of performance appraisal (Chapter 11) and the wider use of information technologies has facilitated increased accountability resulting in work intensification and less task discretion (Gallie et al. 2004; Green 2004).

These changes are occurring against a backdrop of continuous organizational restructuring. The sheer pace and extent of the change in business portfolios has been a consideration in its own right. Not only has it produced massive uncertainty on the part of managers and employees alike, which is inimical to developing the long-term relationships of the high performance workplace, it has also made it very difficult to develop a consistent approach towards the management of the workforce. Indeed, organizations are littered with half-finished initiatives which have had to be interrupted because of take-over or merger or change of business direction or divestment, leading to considerable cynicism not only on the part of employees but also among the senior managers who are supposed to be implementing them.

The Emerging Directions of HR Practice

During the 1980s and 1990s the emergence of HRM was the key reference point for evaluating the evolution of personnel practice in the UK. By the time the last edition of this book was published, however, the appeal of the soft model of HRM was on the wane. The election of a Labour government in 1997 signified a rejection of the deregulation and anti-collectivism of this period and brought the language of fairness, partnership and greater engagement with the European Union to the fore (Bach and Sisson 2000: 14–15). It was not apparent, however, the extent to which these emerging currents would solidify into a new approach towards HR. Five years on, it is much more evident, especially in terms of managerial ideology and policy, even if not always in terms of HR practice, that a new HR is emerging that has started to set the debate about HRM on a different trajectory. This section sketches out the emergent direction of HR practice that is shown in stylized form in Table 1.5.

Globalization

As this chapter has emphasized it is the specific institutional features of the UK employment context that has shaped personnel practice. Successive Conservative governments used deregulation, privatization and the contract culture to increase product market competition and foster changes in personnel practice. Foreign direct investment was encouraged, increasing the internationalization of the UK economy, and it was the practices of Japanese inward investors in particular, such as

Table 1.5 Emergent directions in HR practice: From HRM to the New HR

Dimension	HRM	The New HR
Contexts		
Internationalization	• Product market competition	• Globalization
	• Focus on attracting capital investment	• Focus on attracting labour investment (migration)
	• Managers as heroes	• Managers as villains
Legal		
Goals	• Strengthen management prerogatives	• Enhance competitiveness
Methods	• Restrictive labour law	• Re-regulation and legal compliance
Employment relations	• Union exclusion	• Shallow partnership
Organizational	• Single employer	• Multi-employer: networks
HR practice		
Values	• Commitment/loyalty	• Engagement
Focus of HR practice	• Job	• Person
Orientation	• Employer	• Customer/brand

Nissan, that UK employers were encouraged to emulate (Wickens 1987). As the 1990s progressed this preoccupation with 'Japanization' developed into a broader concern with 'lean' production and the high performance workplace.

HRM therefore emerged in a context in which internationalization was construed narrowly as a concern with attracting inward investment and emulating 'best practice'. This restricted view of the consequences of internationalization for HRM practice can be contrasted with the pervasive, but highly contested, impact of globalization (Stiglitz 2004; Wolf 2004). Globalization reflects the increasing international economic integration of countries arising from the worldwide revolution in communication technologies, the growth and dominance of international capital markets, the global reach and influence of multinational corporations and an increase in labour migration. Three points are relevant in terms of the new HR. First, employment is becoming more volatile because of the coordination of stock markets and increased sensitivity to institutional shareholders. Moreover, at the level of policy and managerial discourse, globalization represents and legitimizes the sense of risk and uncertainty that pervades the workplace and which has been used to 'manufacture uncertainty' and promote more contingent work (Amoore 2004).

Second, globalization is associated with the spread of information and communication technologies (ICT) that are facilitating global production and distribution of goods and services. Inter and intranets have enabled rapid communication across time and space enabling organizations to integrate and centralize control while decentralizing production and distribution. As Frenkel (2003: 139) highlights, ICT is having a significant impact on the content of work by reducing the requirement for manual skills while fostering new kinds of work requiring higher level skills (e.g. web design) and lower level skills such as forms of customer service work in call centres. In addition ICT also changes the location of work by facilitating home-working and work across spatial boundaries with the increased use of forms of virtual teamworking. For Gratton (2004: 75) the primary impact of technology is therefore its ability to democratize the workplace:

> Software technologies have the capacity to make an enormous amount of previously restricted information available to individuals. This will ultimately support their capacity to be autonomous and insightful.

ICT has contributed to the increased complexity of jobs and the upward bias of qualifications required of the workforce, but contrary to Gratton's assumptions employees' task discretion has declined (Gallie et al. 2004). Moreover, the degree to which employers trust employees to be autonomous remains uncertain, reflected in the small numbers of professional and managerial employees that are able to choose whether to work at home (Felstead et al. 2003).

A third dimension of globalization is the increased importance of labour migration. Labour markets remain less integrated than capital markets with considerable legal, cultural and linguistic barriers inhibiting the free movement of labour. Nonetheless the expansion of the EU, labour market shortages and an ageing workforce has stimulated labour mobility. In the UK the number of inward migrants rose from approximately 300,000 to 513,000 between 1993 and 2003 resulting in a net inflow of around 200,000 per annum. The HR implications are more significant than these figures imply because migrants are predominantly young (15–34), with one-third concentrated in London, and include a net gain of professional and managerial workers (Dobson and MacLaughlan 2001; National Statistics 2004). Consequently internationally recruited labour comprises a very substantial proportion of the labour force in London and the South East and is being used to remedy staff shortages among nurses, teachers and social workers. The HR consequences for training, career progression and pay of managing a more diverse workforce, has received very little attention (Bach 2003).

Finally, the emergence of a particular form of neo-liberal globalization has become a lightning rod for a variety of disparate forms of worker and citizen disenchantment with corporations. This has led employers to pay more attention to their corporate social responsibilities and their brand image (Chapter 10). Nonetheless a profound sense of unease remains that corporations have become unaccountable and are primarily concerned to promote the interests of a small strata of top managers and shareholders. These concerns are reinforced by corporate fraud scandals, most famously the collapse of Enron in the USA, but also in more dilute forms in Europe (e.g. Parmalat, Shell). There is widespread disquiet about the withdrawal of final salary pension provision and escalating top managers' pay. A number of high profile critiques of corporate behaviour have gained wider currency through the media (e.g. Bakan 2004). Importantly unease about corporate behaviour and the creed of the market that is pivotal to contemporary forms of globalization has not been confined to traditional sources of criticism such as trade unions, but has included eminent economists, industrialists and management gurus (Stiglitz 2004; Turner 2001: 364–70; Mintzberg 2004: 147).

These emergent trends in the workplace associated directly and indirectly with globalization have the potential to empower the workforce but few commentators detect a shift towards what Gratton (2004) terms 'the democratic enterprise'. Instead there is a growing sense that power in the workplace has become unbalanced, tilting strongly towards employers and the interests of shareholders to the detriment of the workforce. In this context senior managers are increasingly viewed as villains rather than corporate heroes as they were in the HRM paradigm. For US commentators, in which these trends are more stark, the HR function has been implicated in these changes because in its pursuit of becoming a strategic partner, the HR function lost sight of its core values and supported top managements' interests while neglecting the concerns of employees. This has not led to increased credibility of HR with top managers but it has led to a profound loss of trust in corporate HR policy and practice which is reflected in a growing concern in the management literature with issues of trust, organizational justice and organizational citizenship (Kochan 2004; Peterson 2004). Before accepting such a bleak US-orientated interpretation of contemporary trends in the workplace, however, it is necessary to consider whether the harsher consequences of globalization have been modified in a UK context by the increasingly interventionist role of the state in shaping personnel practice.

Re-regulation and legal compliance

For most of the twentieth century the UK system of employment regulation has been characterized as 'voluntarist' which ensured that employment regulation was conducted primarily through collective bargaining between employers and unions and the state did not intervene to provide a legal framework of individual and collective rights to the same degree as in most other European Union (EU) countries. The emergence of HRM was premised on a decisive break away from voluntarism in which successive Conservative governments used the law to restrict the powers of trade unions and bolster managerial prerogatives (see Dickens and Hall 2003). The UK's membership of the EU provided a further stimulus to legal regulation and the growing importance of EU employment law often conflicted with the restrictive direction of Conservative government policy. By 1997 the ambitious domestic agenda of the Labour government in combination with EU initiatives signalled very far-reaching changes in the UK regulatory framework. The EU agenda has continued to play a pivotal role in extending employment rights for individuals and since 1997 EU directives have included the regulation of working time, rights to information and consultation, equal employment rights for part-time workers, increased protection for employees on fixed-term contracts, new rights on maternity and parental leave and statutory rights to information and consultation. The UK government is also in the process of implementing the EU's Anti-Discrimination Framework Directive which extends existing provision to prohibit discrimination on the grounds of religion or belief, sexual orientation, disability and age.

The Labour government's approach can be characterized, following Collins (2001), as regulation for competitiveness which stems directly from their belief in the competitive challenge posed by globalization. The Labour government endorsed much of the previous Conservative labour law agenda but it views much of this legislative inheritance (e.g. restrictions on union power) as a necessary but not a sufficient framework to ensure competitiveness. It has therefore intervened actively to re-regulate the labour market, establishing a minimum floor of rights via mechanisms such as the establishment of a statutory minimum wage. This measure is primarily viewed by the government as a means to enhance competitiveness by encouraging employers to invest in and deploy their workforce more effectively.

The Labour government's acceptance of an increased role for individual employment rights has not been matched by its support for collective employment rights, although there has been a shift from the unitarist union exclusion assumptions of HRM to an emphasis on partnership in the new HR (Chapter 16). The Labour government has fostered forms of voluntary partnership working via union recognition provisions and this altered the climate of employment relations, creating scope for more active engagement with employers, resulting in 'robust' and 'shallow' forms of partnership (Oxenbridge and Brown 2004). Partnership, however, while assigning greater legitimacy to trade unions, privileges their role as partners with employers in bringing about productivity improvements and helping to manage change in an orderly manner, but underplays the role of trade unions as independent actors in the workplace striving to bring about social justice and protect employee interests. In sectors where trade union density remains high and unions retain credibility with employers, partnership working can bring benefits for union members as national agreements in health and education on complex pay and working conditions indicates.

In vast swathes of the private sector, however, and in many public service workplaces in which unions lack influence, partnership agreements yield limited benefits for the workforce or employers. As Terry (2003: 500) argues, weak trade unions serve no useful function because they have little legitimacy with the workforce and are unable to help employers manage and legitimate change. Many of the more recently elected union leaders view partnership as an acknowledgement of weakness because it highlights the degree to which unions are engaged in a process of continuous concession bargaining with employers (Murray 2003). Union support for partnership is equivocal. The fragility of partnership is also reinforced by the difficulties that many employers have in keeping their side of the bargain, given the degree of restructuring noted above. For these reasons, while the term partnership signals a greater willingness on the behalf of employers to consult with the workforce, reinforced by the imminent arrival of the information and consultation directive, employers continue to favour the expansion of direct channels of communication and involvement with the workforce (Chapter 15). Employers therefore remain reluctant social partners and forms of shallow partnership predominate.

To summarize, the New HR signifies a subtle shift away from the primary emphasis on restrictive labour law and the strengthening of management prerogatives, which was the context in which HRM emerged. Instead the Labour government, while supportive of the overall balance of power in the workplace, has sought to establish minimum safeguards for employees to ensure managers are accountable for their actions and use labour effectively rather than simply as an asset to be sweated. However, because the Labour government has a largely benign view of the employment relationship, influenced strongly by the view that the economy is increasingly reliant on knowledge workers, and partly because of its reluctance to alienate employer interests, it has pursued a very cautious agenda of re-regulation which has led to a minimalist interpretation of the EU social dimension (Chapter 2). In the past trade unions have played a crucial role in publicizing and enforcing rights at work, but in a context of reduced union presence and the growth of individual employment rights it is not surprising that HR managers confront an increase in individualistic responses to employment problems. This is reflected in the growing number of inquiries to ACAS and the growth of cases being taken to employment tribunals which rose in the last year from 98,616 applications to 115,042 in 2003–4 (Employment Tribunal Service 2004).

For HR practitioners, the growth of legal regulation will continue to be a dominant feature of their working lives. It is necessary, nonetheless, to differentiate between the *volume* and effort required by employers to get to grips with new employment rights and their actual *effects* in terms of the protection they provide for employees. Consequently, particularly for small firms that are much less likely to have specialist in-house HR expertise, getting to grips with what cumulatively represents a substantial corpus of employment regulation contributes to a sense of burden even if the effects of regulation are more modest than they anticipate. This process is illustrated by the degree to which employment regulations, such as a statutory minimum wage, have been vigorously opposed by employers prior to their implementation, but broadly accepted after implementation as the regulatory effects are accepted as having only a small effect on employer behaviour.

Shifting organizational boundaries: towards the permeable organization

A pivotal element within HRM has been the emphasis placed on developing employees' commitment to the organization. Individual commitment arises from establishing integrated and coherent bundles of HR practice with a strong corporate culture used as the glue to bind individuals to the organization. Some workers are excluded from the 'core' and consigned to the 'periphery' employed on a temporary basis or outsourced, but the assumption of HRM is that these differing segments of the workforce are managed separately, delivering differing sources of value added for the firm (see Kalleberg 2001).

This view of the firm has been increasingly questioned. There is a shift away from an emphasis on the management of the employment relationship by a single employer who exercises control over HR practice and promotes commitment to the enterprise. Instead within the New HR there is increased recognition of the diversity of employment relationships that exist in multi-employer, networked organizations. The blurring of organizational boundaries results in a variety of employers exerting an influence on all aspects of HR practice including pay, labour deployment, skills acquisition and performance management, but in a contradictory and ambiguous manner raising many HR challenges and great uncertainty about the capacity of employers to sustain organizational commitment (Rubery et al. 2002).

There are a variety of inter-organizational relationships emerging and in manufacturing considerable attention has been directed at the HR consequences of supply chains. In the public services forms of public-private partnerships and statutory requirements to work across organizational boundaries has been an integral component of the Labour government's modernization agenda, while call centre employees frequently undertake work for a variety of clients with differing requirements of staff, creating complex HR management challenges.

The first relates to employment *status*, which distinguishes between employees and workers that are supplied by another employer on a temporary or agency basis. The assumption of the core and periphery type model, that workers employed under different employment regimes can co-exist harmoniously and their labour deployed effectively, has been questioned. In the health service the use of agency nurses to stem staff shortages has created resentment among existing staff that received less pay and had less discretion over the hours that they worked in comparison to agency staff (Bach 2004). More often agency staff are employed on worse terms and conditions of employment than directly employed staff. As Rubery et al. (2004) highlight in a call centre they studied, differences in pay and conditions did not reflect different skill or job requirements, creating resentment among agency staff that were often assigned to more intensive work.

A second dimension concerns the *presence* of multiple employers rather than a single employer within a workplace. This arises from outsourcing, the transfer of staff in mergers and acquisitions, the growth of hybrid forms of partnership working and joint ventures. These arrangements result in employees and managers being subject to a variety of management controls from many employers which also creates uncertainty about employee identification and commitment to their formal employer. Take the case of a large regional airport in which many employers are present. The airlines do not employ the passenger handling agents but indirectly exert a great deal of influence over their working practices because of their expectations about how passengers should be checked in, the timing of the process, and by monitoring passenger handlers' appearance and interaction with passengers. These staff wore the uniform of the airline they were checking in and frequently sought to transfer to employment with the airline, creating HR difficulties for passenger handling firms (Rubery et al. 2003).

The third dimension relates to the influence of the *client* in shaping the employment relationship, which highlights the degree to which customers can exert influence over staff management irrespective of whether they are the formal employer. Scarbrough (2000: 14), in his analysis of supply chain management in three engineering companies, coined the phrase 'corporate colonization' to capture this process. In one case, a car parts manufacturer (Compco), benefited from the expertise of a major car manufacturer (Carco) in improving the production line dedicated to the production of parts destined for Carco. However, Carco insisted on the implementation of a no-redundancy policy to accompany these changes which was not applied to other parts of the plant and which reduced the autonomy of Comco in shaping its HR practices. Client requirements are not necessarily accepted, however, if the employer has sufficient power to dilute client demands. In the call centre case referred to above, the main employer (TCS) refused to allow their staff to wear the uniform of their client (TruckCo) precisely because they wished to maintain control of their HR practices and wanted their staff to retain their identification with TCS (Rubery et al. 2004: 1216). Overall, the rise of the networked enterprise creates tensions in the employment relationship, increasing the complexity of managing and monitoring performance and makes it harder to sustain employee commitment.

From commitment to the employer to engagement with the customer

The final change in emphasis away from the assumptions embedded in HRM models concerns a shift from employers' concern to gain the commitment of employees' towards an emphasis on ensuring that employees are engaged and derive emotional *meaning* from work. The New HR therefore does not attempt to impose a set of managerially defined values which employees are expected to accept unquestioningly. Instead the starting point is a bottom-up focus on the personality of individuals at selection stage, which is then reinforced to ensure that the organization understand its employees and what shapes their engagement with the organization and how these personal values can be harnessed for organizational success. Understanding this shift in practice is linked to the experience of culture change programmes that were a prominent feature of HRM practice in the 1980s and 1990s.

The starting point of organizational programmes of culture change was an attempt by senior managers to instill in employees the importance of core organizations beliefs and values in a predominantly top-down manner. These initiatives had very uneven results, which is not surprising, taking account of the degree to which senior managers found it difficult to adhere to these values in a context of continuous organizational change and downsizing (Thompson 2003). Many of these trends have intensified in recent years, reflected in the degree to which there has been a continuing fall in job satisfaction in the UK since the mid 1990s. Moreover, although perceptions of job insecurity have decreased as unemployment has fallen many employees still feel insecure in the sense that valued aspects of the benefits of employment are being withdrawn, such as pensions, which reinforces a sense of distrust of employers (Burchell et al. 2002). In these circumstances, employees have proved unreceptive to senior managers' espousal of corporate values and there has been an erosion of trust and commitment to organizational values (Sennett 1998: 141). Simultaneously, many studies have shown only a weak link between affective organizational commitment and performance (Sparrow and Cooper 2003: 188), leading to a cooling among HR practitioners of the emphasis on sustaining organizational commitment.

The implications are that the New HR places more emphasis on measuring the attributes of the person and the degree to which their values and emotions 'fit' the requirements of the job (Chapter 5). In service industries, such as airlines, selection is based on ensuring staff are empathetic to customer values which are then reinforced by processes of socialization, training and appraisal (Bolton and Boyd 2003: 300–1). There is a tendency for employers to place more emphasis on the appearance, dress sense, tone and accent of voice of their employees and in some cases, for example, fashionable bars and hotels to specify appropriate body shape and size. The increased importance of emotional and aesthetic labour has contributed to the shifting definition of skill (Grugulis et al. 2004: 7).

Employers such as Tesco, the largest private sector employer and dominant UK retailer, has taken this process a stage further by identifying 'a retail gene', derived from the skills of their existing employees, and applicants are measured on the degree to which this gene is present (Overell 2003: 2). Tesco has also transferred the methodologies used to understand their customers to their employees to gain insight into their personalities and identities. This has resulted in employees being categorized into five attitudinal segments: work–life balancers; want it all; pleasure seekers; live to work; and work to live with HR practices geared towards the different motivations and aspirations of these employee groups (Gratton 2004: 119–24).

A related component of this shift in HR practice has been to reshape employee expectations focusing not on bland corporate mission statements as in the 1990s, but rather using customer expectations and values to shape the requirements of staff (see Rosenthal 2004). In the NHS, for example, the emphasis on servicing internal and external customers is reflected in job titles such as ward hostess. This development of customer-orientated skills is altering job roles away from an exclusive focus on professionally defined norms. Pay modernization is reinforcing this process by placing a premium on softer interactive competencies such as oral communication; which is defined as a core skill for all NHS staff (Bach 2004: 192). Consequently, attempts to rehabilitate the image of corporations by policies of branding and corporate social responsibility, which create personalities for companies and try and ensure that employees become emotionally engaged with them, are being combined with recruitment, selection, development and involvement practices which aim to ensure greater fit between the company and the personality of the employee.

These trends have important implications for the HR function. First, it is not self-evident that HR will necessarily be assigned a leading role, as the Tesco initiative testifies, which has been a joint marketing-HR initiative. Similarly, to the extent that communications is a central component of attempts to engage employees, the HR function confronts the risk of being hollowed out by the growing importance of corporate communication departments and uncertainty about HR's role in internal communications (Deloitte and Touche 2003: 17). In conjunction with changes in company law from 1 January 2005 that require companies to account for their human capital in operating and financial reviews, HR could increasingly be challenged by other functions seeking to control the people management agenda.

Second, the emphasis on the importance of managing the whole personality and promoting engaged employees, broadens the scope of HR practice and inevitably spills over into considerations of the balance and boundaries between work and home (Chapter 6). Employees already confront pressure to attend social events outside of work, but more fundamentally the emphasis on emotional labour draws attention to the psychological injuries of work and broadens the scope of the HR remit to address issues of bullying, violence and stress at work (Fineman 2004: 721).

Conclusion

The management of human resources is becoming a more prominent component of corporate and government agendas. For policy makers the UK's relatively poor productivity record and concerns about the quality of management practice has unleashed a stream of policy guidance and initiatives related to how employees are recruited, deployed, trained and involved. The government has intervened to reshape training provision, exhorted employers to attend to management development and issues of work–life balance, fostered forms of social partnership and cajoled employers to address problems of discipline and absence. Among employers, there is greater acknowledgement that purposeful consideration of HR issues is integral to organizational effectiveness. Moreover, in a tight labour market, with low unemployment, many employers are directing more attention to the recruitment and retention of the workforce. In addition, intangible people-related assets such as worker skills, relationships with customers, employee engagement and branding are becoming more central to organizational success and the value that capital markets place on companies.

It would be surprising, given the degree of organizational restructuring, alterations in the legal context, and the attempt to engage the workforce more fully, if HR management was not on the organizational agenda to a much greater extent than a decade ago. Nonetheless, many employees' experience of employment remains shaped by immediate work pressures reflected in concerns about job satisfaction, work intensity and limited discretion. It appears that managers are not addressing effectively the needs and concerns of their workforce in too many UK workplaces and this reflects their own sense of uncertainty about how to respond to the pressures they and their workforce confront. Top managers are more sensitive to the importance of HR issues than in the past, but this is orientated to providing improved leadership and communication rather than translated into tangible improvements in the quality of working life; indicating that people management issues are not sufficiently embedded within mainstream management practice in large numbers of UK workplaces. What does this indicate about the state of HRM in the UK today, more than 20 years after the debate about HRM first emerged?

The coming of HRM promised a new dawn for personnel management in the UK. Not only was it extremely optimistic, but here was a model that also appeared to be able to meet the demand for economic efficiency and make a significant contribution to improving the quality of working life. In the event, proponents considerably underestimated the will and ability of senior managers to make the necessary changes. The UK's business system, with its emphasis on short-term profitability, was not conducive to an investment orientation towards the workforce; while the ever-intensifying competition, far from driving firms up-market, encouraged many to follow the low road and reduce their cost base through restructuring. For the personnel function the attempt to shift from an operational to strategic role floundered and the harsher economic and political context jeopardized attempts to develop enhanced organizational commitment.

As it became clear that few organizations practised soft HRM in its fully developed sense, and as the economic and political context altered, the ideological connotations of HRM have lessened and it has come to represent a generic term for managing employees rather than a specific style of progressive high commitment management. There is still much interest in the relationship between HRM and organizational performance. In particular, the debate about HR bundles has highlighted the degree to which coherent and integrated HR policy is likely to yield more effective organizational performance and a more satisfied workforce.

As this chapter has highlighted, it is impossible to make sense of the transition of personnel practice without reference to the political and economic context, alterations in the labour market, and the degree to which an altered balance of power in the workplace has enabled employers to alter HR practice. The emergence of the new HR reinforces the extent to which our understanding of evolving HR practice requires a broader field of vision that moves beyond immediate HR practice in the workplace to take account of developments in the wider political economy. Globalization indicates the extent to which more volatile financial markets, continuous business restructuring and the more strident demands of shareholders are reshaping the HR context. Globalization does not undermine the extent to which the state remains crucial to shaping HR practice. Quite the reverse as governments attach more importance to national regulation to bolster competitiveness.

It is the response of the Labour government to these developments and its desire to improve UK competitiveness by shifting the economy from the low road of cost minimization towards the high road of skill development, partnership and satisfying work that provide pointers to the emerging direction of government policy with important implications for HR practice. There are signs of a growing impatience among policy makers and a belief that voluntary actions by employers are insufficient to address the HR challenges highlighted in this chapter. A more interventionist stance by the Labour government is evident, which is being reinforced not only by EU regulation, but also by a variety of other forms of 'soft' regulation. There has been an increase in Codes of Practice and related provisions, including statutory minimum dispute procedures for disciplinary and grievance cases that apply to all workplaces. There is also the prospect of more compulsion, via a training levy, if employers fail to meet targets for vocational training. These types of interventions and the establishment of institutions to monitor and shape employer behaviour, such as the Low Pay Commission, signal a determination by the government to intervene more actively than in the recent past to reshape employment practices.

This interventionist stance is being reinforced further by a growing awareness among policy makers of the expansion of poorly paid work in sectors like agriculture and hospitality, that utilize exploited, often migrant labour, at the margins of the labour market. These groups – the bottom of the hourglass – in Nolan's description of the labour market, have traditionally been neglected by HRM writers focused on managerial labour. They are, however, figuring more prominently in public policy debate. Although it is too early to gauge the full significance of these developments, cumulatively, they signal a decisive break with the non-interventionist, employer-led approach that has dominated the context for HR over the last two decades.

REFERENCES

ACAS 2004: *Annual Report and Resource Accounts 2003/04*, London: ACAS.

Ackroyd, S. 2002: *The Organization of Business: Applying Organizational Theory to Contemporary Change*, Oxford: Oxford University Press.

Ackroyd, S. and Procter, S. 1998: British manufacturing organisation and workplace relations: Some attributes of the new flexible firm, *British Journal of Industrial Relations*, **36**(2), 40–54.

Amoore, L. 2004: Risk, reward and discipline at work, *Economy and Society*, **33**(2), 174–96.

Appelbaum, E., Bailey, T. and Kalleberg, A. 2000: *Manufacturing Advantage: Why High-Performance Work Systems Pay Off*, Ithaca, NY: Cornell University Press.

Armour, J., Deakin S. and Konzelmann, J. 2003: Shareholder primacy and the trajectory of UK corporate governance, *British Journal of Industrial Relations*, **41**(3), 531–55.

Bach, S. 2003: International migration of health workers: Labour and social issues, Working Paper 209, Geneva: ILO.

Bach, S. 2004: *Employment Relations and the Health Service: The Management of Reforms*, London: Routledge.

Bach, S. and Givan, R. 2005: Union responses to public-private partnerships in the health service, in S. Fernie and D. Metcalfe (ed.), *British Unions Resurgence or Demise?* London: Routledge.

Bach, S. and Sisson, K. 2000: Personnel management in perspective, in S. Bach and K. Sisson (eds.), *Personnel Management*, Oxford: Blackwell.

Bakan, J. 2004: *The Corporation: The Pathological Pursuit of Profit and Power*, London: Constable and Robinson.

Barley, S. and Kunda, G. 2001: Bringing work back in, *Organization Science*, **12**(1), 76–95.

Barney, J. 1991: Firm resources and sustained competitive advantage, *Journal of Management*, **17**(1): 99–120.

Bartlett, C. and Ghoshal, S. 2002: Building competitive advantage through people, *MIT Sloan Management Review*, **43**(2), 34–41.

Becker, G. and Gerhart, B. 1996: The impact of human resource management on organizational performance: Progress and practice, *Academy of Management Journal*, **39**(4), 779–801.

Becker, G. and Huselid, M. 1998: High performance work systems and firm performance: A synthesis of research and managerial implications, *Research in Personnel and Human Resource Management*, **16**, 53–101.

Begum, M. 2004: Employment by occupation and industry, *Labour Market Trends*, **112**(6), 227–34.

Bolton, S. and Boyd, C. 2003: Trolley dolly or skilled emotion manager? *Work, Employment and Society*, **17**(2), 289–308.

Boxall, P. and Purcell, J. 2003: *Strategy and Human Resource Management*, Basingstoke: Palgrave Macmillan.

Brown, W., Deakin, D., Nash, D. and Oxenbridge, S. 2000: The employment contract from collective procedures to individual rights, *British Journal of Industrial Relations*, **38**(4), 611–30.

Bunting, M. 2004: *Willing Slaves: How the Overwork Culture Is Ruling our Lives*, London: HarperCollins.

Burchell, B., Lapido, D. and Wilkinson, F. (eds.) 2002: *Job Insecurity and Work Intensification*, London: Routledge.

Caldwell, R. 2004: Rhetoric, facts and self-fulfilling prophecies: Exploring practitioners' perceptions of progress in implementing HRM, *Industrial Relations Journal*, **35**(3), 196–215.

Carter, P. and Jackson, N. 2004: For the sake of argument: Towards an understanding of rhetoric as process, *Journal of Management Studies*, **41**(3), 469–91.

CBI (Confederation of British Industry) 2004: *Off-shoring Survey 2004*, London: CBI.

CIPD (Chartered Institute of Personnel and Development) 2003a: *HR Survey: Where We Are, Where We're Heading*, London: CIPD.

CIPD (Chartered Institute of Personnel and Development) 2003b: *Reorganising for Success*, London: CIPD.

CIPD (Chartered Institute of Personnel and Development) 2004: *Overview of CIPD Surveys 2003–04: A Barometer of HR Trends and Prospects*, London: CIPD.

Collins, H. 2001: Regulating the employment relation for competitiveness, *Industrial Law Journal*, **30**(1), 17–46.

Cully, M., O'Reilly, A., Millward, N., Forth, J., Woodland, S., Dix, G. and Bryson, A. 1998: *The 1998 Workplace Employee Relations Survey: First Findings*, London: DTI.

Cully, M., Woodland, S., O'Reilly, A. and Dix, G. 1999: *Britain at Work as Depicted by the 1998 Workplace Employee Relations Survey*, London: Routledge.

Deloitte and Touche 2003: *Aligned at the top? Survey of CEOs' and HR Directors' perceptions of HR*, London: Deloitte and Touche, www.deloitte.co.uk

Department of Health 2002: *HR in the NHS Plan*. London: Department of Health.

Dickens, L. and Hall, M. 2003: Labour law and industrial relations, in P.K. Edwards (ed.), *Industrial Relations*, Oxford: Blackwell.

Dobson, J. and McLaughlan, G. 2001: International migration to and from the United Kingdom, 1975–1999, *Population Trends*, **106**, 29–38. www.statistics.gov.uk/articles/population_trends/migration7599-pt106.pdf

DTI (Department for Trade and Industry) 2003: *Achieving Best Practice in Your Business: Maximising Potential: High Performance Workplaces*. www.dti.gov.uk/bestpractice/assets.hpw.pdf

DTI (Department for Trade and Industry) 2004: *Liberalisation and Globalisation: Maximising the Benefits of International Trade and Investment*. DTI Economics Paper No. 10, London: DTI.

Edwards, P. and Collinson, M. 2002: Empowerment and managerial labor strategies: Pragmatism regained, *Work and Occupations*, **29**(3), 272–99.

Employment Tribunal Service. 2004: *Annual Report 2003–04*, www.ets.gov.uk/annualreport2004.pdf

Felstead, A., Jewson, N., Phizacklea, A. and Walters, S. 2003: The option to work at home: Another privilege for the favoured few, *New Technology, Work and Employment*, **17**(3), 204–24.

Fineman, S. 2004: Getting the measure of emotion – and the cautionary tale of emotional intelligence, *Human Relations*, **57**(6), 719–40.

Frenkel, S. 2003: The embedded character of workplace relations, *Work and Occupations*, **30**(2), 135–52.

Gallie, D., Felstead, A. and Green, F. 2004: Changing patterns of task discretion in Britain, *Work, Employment and Society*, **18**(2), 243–66.

Godard, J. 2004: A critical assessment of the high-performance paradigm, *British Journal of Industrial Relations*, **42**(2), 349–79.

Godard, J. and Delaney, J. 2000: Reflections on the high performance paradigm's implications for industrial relations as a field, *Industrial and Labor Relations Review*, **53**(3), 482–502.

Goos, M. and Manning, A. 2003: McJobs and MacJobs: The growing polarisation of jobs in the UK, in R. Dickens, P. Gregg and J. Wadsworth (eds.), *The Labour Market under New Labour*, Basingstoke: Palgrave Macmillan.

Gospel, H. and Pendleton, A. 2003: Finance, corporate governance and the management of labour: A conceptual and comparative analysis, *British Journal of Industrial Relations*, **41**(3), 557–82.

Gratton, L. 2004: *The Democratic Enterprise: Liberating your Business with Freedom, Flexibility and Commitment*, London: Pearson Education.

Green, F. 2004: Why has work effort become more intense? *Industrial Relations*, **43**(4), 709–41.

Grugulis, I., Warhurst, C. and Keep, E. 2004: What's happening to skill, in C. Warhurst, I. Grugulis and E. Keep (eds.), *The Skills that Matter*, Basingstoke: Palgrave Macmillan.

Guest, D. 1987: Human resource management and industrial relations, *Journal of Management Studies*, **24**(5), 503–21.

Guest, D. 1999: Human resource management: The workers' verdict, *Human Resource Management Journal*, **9**(3), 5–25.

Guest, D. 2001a: Industrial relations and human resource management, in J. Storey (ed.), *Human Resource Management: A Critical Text*, London: Thomson Learning.

Guest, D. 2001b: Human resource management: When research confronts theory, *International Journal of Human Resource Management*, **12**(7), 1092–106.

Guest, D., Michie, J., Conway, N. and Sheehan, M. 2003: Human resource management and corporate performance in the UK, *British Journal of Industrial Relations*, **41**(2), 291–314.

Guest, D. and King, Z. 2004: Power, innovation and problem-solving: The personnel managers' three steps to heaven, *Journal of Management Studies*, **41**(3), 401–23.

Hall, P. and Soskice, D. 2001: *Varieties of Capitalism*, Oxford: Oxford University Press.

Hall, L. and Torrington, D. 1998: *The Human Resource Function*, London: Financial Times/Pitman.

Harkness, S. 2003: The household division of labour: Changes in families' allocation of paid and unpaid work, 1992–2002, in R. Dickens, P. Gregg and J. Wadsworth (eds.), *The Labour Market Under New Labour: The State of Working Britain*, Basingstoke: Palgrave Macmillan.

Hoque, K. and Noon, M. 2001: Counting angels: A comparison of personnel and HR specialists, *Human Resource Management Journal*, **11**(3), 5–22.

Huselid, M. 1995: The impact of human resource management practices on turnover, productivity and corporate financial performance, *Academy of Management Journal*, **38**(3), 635–72.

Ichinowski, C., Kochan, T., Levine D., Olson, C. and Strauss, G. 1996: What works at work: Overview and assessment, *Industrial Relations*, **35**(3), 299–333.

Iles, N. 2004: *Life at the Top: The Labour Market for FTSE-250 Chief Executives*, London: The Work Foundation.

IRS (Industrial Relations Service) 2004: HR roles and responsibilities climbing the admin mountain, *IRS Employment Review*, 795 (March), 9–15.

Kalleberg, A. 2001: Organizing flexibility: The flexible firm in a new century, *British Journal of Industrial Relations*, **39**(4), 479–504.

Kaufman, B. 2001: Human resources and industrial relations: Commonalities and differences, *Human Resource Management Review*, **11**, 339–74.

Keenoy, T. 1999: HRM as hologram: A polemic, *Journal of Management Studies*, **36**(1), 1–23.

Kelly, J. 2004: Social partnership agreements in Britain: Labor cooperation and compliance, *Industrial Relations*, **43**(1), 267–93.

Kessler, I. and Purcell, J. 1996: Strategic choice and new forms of employment relations in the public service sector: Developing an analytical framework, *International Journal of Human Resource Management*, **7**(1), 206–29.

Kochan, T. 2004: Restoring trust in the human resource management profession, *Asia Pacific Journal of Human Resources*, **42**(2) 132–46.

Kochan, T. and Barocci, T. (eds.), 1985: *Human Resource Management and Industrial Relations*, Boston: Little Brown.

Kochan, T. and Osterman, P. 1994: *The Mutual Gains Enterprise*. Boston: Harvard School Press.

Labour Research 2003: Is HR good for today's workplace? *Labour Research*, October, 16–18.

Legge, K. 1995: *Human Resource Management: Rhetorics and Realities*, Basingstoke: Macmillan.

Legge, K. 2001: Silver bullet or spent round? Assessing the meaning of the 'high commitment management'/performance relationship, in J. Storey (ed.), *Human Resource Management: A Critical Text*, London: Thomson Learning.

Low Pay Commission 2003: Fourth Report of the Low Pay Commission. www.lowpaycommission.gov.uk

MacDuffie, J. 1995: Human resource bundles and manufacturing performance, *Industrial and Labour Relations Review*, **48**(2), 197–221.

Marchington, M. and Grugulis, I. 2000: 'Best practice' human resource management: Perfect opportunity or dangerous illusion? *International Journal of Human Resource Management*, **11**(6), 1104–24.

Metcalfe, D. 2003: Trade unions, in R. Dickens, P. Gregg and J. Wadsworth (eds.), *The Labour Market Under New Labour: The State of Working Britain*, Basingstoke: Palgrave Macmillan.

Miles, R. and Snow, C. 1984: Designing strategic human resource systems, *Organizational Dynamics*, Summer, 36–52.

Millward, N. 1994: *The New Industrial Relations*, London: Routledge.

Millward, N., Bryson, A. and Forth, J. 2000: *All Change at Work: British Employment Relations 1990–1998, as Portrayed by the Workplace Industrial Relations Survey Series*, London: Routledge.

Mintzberg, H. 2004: *Managers not MBAs*, London: Pearson Education.

Murray, A. 2003: *A New Labour Nightmare: The Return of the Awkward Squad*, London: Verso.

National Statistics 2004: 151,000 more people migrated to the UK than left in 2003, *News Release*, November 4. www.statistics.gov.uk/pdfdir/migr1104.pdf

Nolan, P. 2004: Shaping the future: The political economy of work and employment, *Industrial Relations Journal*, **35**(5), 378–87.

OECD (Organization for Economic Cooperation and Development) 2004: *Economic Survey of the UK*, Paris: OECD.

Overell, S. 2003: Few employers find using the web meets all needs, *Financial Times: Special Report Human Resources*, 27 October, 2.

Oxenbridge, S. and Brown, W. 2004: Achieving a new equilibrium? The stability of cooperative employer-union relationships, *Industrial Relations Journal*, **35**(5), 388–402.

Paauwe, J. and Boselie, P. 2003: Challenging 'strategic HRM' and the relevance of the institutional setting, *Human Resource Management Journal*, **13**(3), 56–70.

Peccei, R. 2004: *Human Resource Management and the Search for the Happy Workplace*, Rotterdam: Erasmus Research Institute of Management.

Pendleton, A. and Gospel, H. 2004: Markets and relationships: Finance, governance and labour in the United Kingdom, in Gospel, H. and Pendleton, A. (eds.), *Corporate Governance and Labour Management*, Buckingham: Open University Press.

Peterson, R. 2004: A call for testing our assumptions: Human resource management today, *Journal of Management Inquiry*, **13**(3), 192–202.

Pfeffer, J. 1998: *The Human Equation: Building Profits by Putting People First*, Boston: Harvard University Press.

Porter, M. 1985: *Competitive Advantage: Creating and Sustaining Superior Performance*, New York: Free Press.

Purcell, J. 1999: Best practice and best fit: Chimera or cul-de-sac?, *Human Resource Management Journal*, **9**(3), 26–41.

Purcell, J., Kinnie, N. and Hutchinson, S. 2003: *People and Performance: Unlocking the Black Box*, London: CIPD.

Rosenthal, P. 2004: Management control as an employee resource: The case of front-line service workers, *Journal of Management Studies*, **41**(4), 601–22.

Rubery, J., Earnshaw, J., Marchington, M., Cooke, F-L. and Vincent S. 2002: Changing organizational forms and the employment relationship, *Journal of Management Studies*, **39**(5), 645–72.

Rubery, J., Cooke, F-L., Earnshaw, J. and Marchington, M. 2003: Inter-organizational relations and employment in a multi-employer environment, *British Journal of Industrial Relations*, **41**(2), 265–89.

Rubery, J., Carroll, M., Cooke, F-L., Grugulis, I. and Earnshaw, J. 2004: Human resource management and the permeable organization: The case of the multi-client call centre, *Journal of Management Studies*, **41**(7), 1199–222.

Scarbrough, H. 2000: The HR implications of supply chain relationships, *Human Resource Management Journal*, **10**(1), 5–17.

Schuler, R. and Jackson, S. 1987: Linking competitive strategies and human resource management practices, *Academy of Management Executive*, **1**(3), 209–13.

Sennett, R. 1998: *The Corrosion of Character: The Personal Consequences of Work in the New Capitalism*, New York: Norton and Company.

Sisson, K. 1989: Personnel management in perspective, in K. Sisson (ed.), *Personnel Management in Britain*, Oxford: Blackwell.

Sisson, K. (ed.) 1994: *Personnel Management in Britain: A Comprehensive Guide to Theory and Practice in Britain*, Oxford: Blackwell.

Sparrow, P. and Cooper, C. 2003: *The Employment Relationship: Key Challenges for HR*, London: ButterworthHeinemann.

Stiglitz J. 2004: *The Roaring Nineties: Why We're Paying the Price for the Greediest Decade in History*, London: Penguin.

Storey, J. 1989: Introduction: From personnel management to human resource management, in J. Storey (ed.), *New Perspectives on Human Resource Management*, London: Routledge.

Strauss, G. 2001: HRM in the USA: Correcting some British impressions, *International Journal of Human Resource Management*, **12**(6), 873–97.

Taylor, R. 2003: *Managing Workplace Change: Future of Work Commentary Series 5*. Swindon: ESRC. Available at www.leeds.ac.uk/esrcfutureofwork

Terry, M. 2003: Partnership and the future of trade unions, *Economic and Industrial Democracy*, **24**(4), 485–507.

Thompson, P. 2003: Disconnected capitalism: Or why employers can't keep their side of the bargain, *Work, Employment and Society*, **17**(2), 359–78.

Townley, B. 1994: *Reframing Human Resource Management*, London: Sage.

Toynbee, P. 2003: *Hard Work: Life in Low-Pay Britain*, London: Bloomsbury.

Truss, C. 1999: Soft and hard models of HRM, in L. Gratton, V. Hope-Hailey, P. Stiles and C. Truss, *Strategic Human Resource Management: Corporate Rhetoric and Human Reality*, Oxford: Oxford University Press.

Turner, A. 2001: *Just Capital*, London: Macmillan.

Tyson, S. and Fell, A. 1986: *Evaluating the Personnel Function*, London: Hutchinson.

Ulrich, D. 1997: *Human Resource Champions: The Next Agenda for Adding Value and Delivering resutls*, Boston: Harvard Business School Press.

West, M.M., Borrill, C., Dawson, J., Scully, J., Carter, M., Anelay, S., Patterson, M. and Waring, J. 2002: The link between the management of employees and patient mortality in acute hospitals, *International Journal of Human Resource Management*, **13**(8), 1299–310.

Wickens, P. 1987: *The Road to Nissan: Flexibility, Quality, Teamwork*, London: Macmillan.

Wolf, M. 2004: *Why Globalization Works*, New Haven: Yale University Press.

CHAPTER TWO

Personnel Management and European Integration: A Case of Indelible Imprint?

Keith Sisson

Introduction: Contested Terrain

The UK's role in and reaction to European integration has been a dominating political issue for more than half a century. Moreover, at the heart of the debate has been the subject matter with which this book is centrally concerned, namely the system of employment regulation. If there was a defining moment, it was the speech of Jaques Delors, the then president of the European Commission, at the Trades Union Congress (TUC) conference in 1988. In offering a vision of 'social Europe', he did not just inspire the conversion of much of the British trade union movement to the European cause, but also delivered a message that opponents of such a vision could not and did not ignore. For Delors, like Monnet and Schuman, the founding fathers of the EU, European integration was not just a market phenomenon. It was also a political and social project. Market making was intended to yield long-term wider union out of economic co-operation through the process of 'spill-over' (Falkner 1998: 8; Rosamond 2001: 71). Just as a single market would create pressures for closer political union, so it would lead to demands for a level playing field in employment matters. Certainly the proposition, first enunciated by Commons (1909) nearly a century ago, that employment relations systems follow the market has been the starting point for much academic analysis (Kauppinen 1998; Sisson et al. 1999).

The political controversy about the direction of European integration has never been far from the surface since Delors' intervention. Prime Minister Thatcher's furious response at Bruges only days later became the rallying point for those opposed to economic union becoming political and social union. Successive Conservative governments dug their heels in to the extent that other countries were forced to outflank the UK's veto with the addition of the Maastricht social chapter in 1991.

In agreeing to incorporate the chapter in the EU Treaty in 1997, the in-coming Labour government seemingly adopted a different course. Yet, in important respects, little changed. Successive Labour governments consistently opposed further developments in the social dimension, including the information and consultation Directive and the inclusion of the Charter of Fundamental Rights in the EU Treaty. They have also put themselves at the forefront of articulating the alternative neo-liberal vision to the European 'social' model based on making labour markets 'work' more effectively. Witness their support for the Lisbon agenda of 2000. In setting the goal of stretching targets of improved employment rates and overtaking the US as a knowledge economy, Europe committed itself, at least in principle, to substantial reforms of both labour and product markets.

Overall, however, the impact of European integration on the UK has been much more complex than might have been imagined. The UK has not developed the social partnership arrangements that most other European countries have and collective bargaining continues to be in decline. Yet European integration has been fundamentally important in shaping developments. The social dimension that European integration has spawned has revolutionized the pattern of regulation in ways that are almost certainly irrevocable, whatever the UK's future relationship with Europe. The much-lauded 'voluntarism' of UK employment relations is all but dead: personnel management and individual employment rights have become inextricably tied together, bringing about an increasing tendency to a legal dependency culture. European integration has also been a major factor in accelerating the reshaping of the UK's economy and, consequently, its structure of employment. Arguably, 'Europeanization' has been more important in this regard than the 'globalization' that most pundits have proclaimed. Simultaneously, in encouraging the emergence of the 'Euro-company', it has opened significant path ways for the 'Europeanization' of company policies and practices.

Critically important in these developments have been the choices UK policy makers have made and the political and institutional context within which they have made them. Far from being encouraged to move towards the European social model, the exact opposite has happened – policy makers have adopted neo-liberal policy frameworks in which institutions supposedly do not matter. They have also found it difficult to rise above the short-term tactical considerations that the UK's 'competitive' governance arrangements encourage. Consequently, the impact of European integration has been as unintended as it is profound.

The remainder of this chapter expands on this argument. The chapter begins by briefly outlining the three key dimensions of European integration that need to be considered, namely the economic, the political and the social. It goes on to consider the impact, focusing on the patterns of employment regulation and the structure of the economy. In accounting for this impact, it emphasizes the critical importance of the political choices made and the fundamental importance of path dependency in shaping and constraining them. The chapter concludes with an assessment of future prospects. In the light of the foregoing analysis, it argues that path dependency is likely to continue to be fundamentally important. Even if there are major changes in the UK's political relationship with Europe, therefore, the impact that European integration has already had will be long lasting.

Three Key Dimensions: Economic, Political, Social

The economic dimension: a regional bloc within a global economy

There is an on-going debate about the relationship between 'globalization' and 'Europeanization' (Hay and Rosamond 2000). It is very clear, however, that the economic forms of European integration are fundamentally important in their own right.

Following Tinbergen (1965), Europe's economic integration has essentially been a 'negative' process, taking the form of the removal of restrictions, tariff and non-tariff, on movements in goods, services, capital and labour, and regulation aimed at enhancing economic efficiency. 'Market making' began with the creation of the European Economic Community (EEC) in 1956. In 1985, came endorsement of the Commission's White Paper, specifying over 300 legislative acts needed to 'complete' the single market and setting a deadline of the end of 1992 for implementation. The Single European Act establishing the political competence to complete the single market, was ratified in 1987.

The 1991 Maastricht Treaty launched economic and monetary union (EMU), bringing three major developments:

- a European Central Bank (ECB), responsible for setting a single monetary policy across the 11 signatory member states from 1 January 1999;
- a single European currency (the euro), with electronic transactions taking effect from 1 January 1999 and euro notes and coins replacing national currencies in January and June 2002 respectively; and
- a Stability and Growth Pact, which severely restricts members states' fiscal freedom by establishing a 3 per cent ceiling for public deficits with fines if the fiscal excess is not eliminated within 2 years (Eichengreen and Wyplosz 1998: 67–71).

A major focus of the literature has been on the implications of the much-changed economic policy context that EMU brings (Sisson et al. 1999). The Euro zone is not, in Mundell's (1961) terms, an 'optimum currency area', lacking such essential features as a common taxation policy and the fiscal resources to secure adjustment through transferring sizeable funds from one region (country) to another. In the circumstances, the concern is that the ECB, in seeking to fulfil its remit to maintain price stability, might set an unduly restrictive monetary policy thereby triggering deflation. If so, the burden of subsequent adjustment will fall on the labour market (wages and employment) and social protection systems, leading to damaging 'regime competition' between member states (Streeck 1992).

Less attention has focused on the implications of membership of the single currency, the UK remaining outside along with Denmark and Sweden. As the European Commission (1998: 13–14) emphasizes, as well as reductions in trans-action costs and increased competition, 'All economic agents will ultimately benefit from the availability of loans or borrowings in one or the same currency on a larger or more liquid market and under conditions of transparency, equality of access and cost that are similar to those that are prevailing for the US dollar.' The key advantage is the reduction of the exchange rate risk, that is, that investment in another market could be undermined by devaluation.

The political dimension: multi-level governance in the making

In Martin's (1996: 6) words, the EU has political institutions with 'a capacity to control the process of international economic integration that is greater than in any other region'. Unlike other regional blocs such as the North Atlantic Free Trade Association, the EU does not just have a Council of Ministers and a secretariat. It also has many of the hallmarks of a national polity including a Commission with the right of legislative initiation, an elected Parliament, and the European Court of Justice (ECJ) with judicial authority. Yet capturing the essence of the EU's polit-ical dimension is a major challenge. In Delors' words (quoted in Olsen 2001: 329), the EU is an *'object politique non-identifié'*. It is more than an intergovernmental organization, but it is not a superstate. Even to conceive of it as 'something in-between' misses the mark, because relations between the EU and the member states cannot adequately be defined in hierarchical terms. The increasingly accepted metaphor is 'multi-level governance' (Rosamond 2001: 75; European Commission 2001: 34–5). In Olsen's (2001: 329) words,

> The current institutional configuration is complex, ambiguous and changing. It is multi-levelled, multi-structured and multi-centred, characterized by networks across territ-orial levels of governance, institutions of government, and public-private institutions.

As Olsen (2001: 335) stresses, the EU's configuration is the result of a history of 'informal and gradual institutional evolution' as well as 'founding acts and deliberate institution building'. The original intention may have been to yield long-term political union out of economic co-operation via 'spill-over', but the process has been far from straightforward. 'At each step, developments have been highly contested and the outcome is best imagined as the complex consequence of the acts of multiple political and economic agents with differing views about the speed and direction of development and also the destination' (Olsen 2001: 337). Such has been the nature of the EU political process that it has produced *both* a neo-liberal economic regime *and* a social dimension.

The social dimension: a framework
for a European industrial relations system

While the EU is not a polity with the powers of the nation-state, it has nonetheless developed a social dimension that constitutes our third dimension. The 1997 Amsterdam Treaty sets out the main aims of European social policy in Article 136:

> the promotion of employment, improved living and working conditions, so as to make possible their harmonisation while the improvement is being maintained, proper social protection, dialogue between management and labour, the development of human resources with a view to lasting employment and the combating of exclusion.

Following Rhodes (1997: 69–70), there are five areas of EU policy that might be described as 'social': the subsidy and income-maintenance programmes of the Common Agricultural Policy; the various funds (regional, social and cohesion) targeted at disparities between different regions; regulations on environment, product safety and consumer protection, including the harmonization of health and safety standards at work; regulatory policies for the labour market embracing worker's rights, the promotion of social dialogue and collective bargaining; and a strategy designed to improve the rates, quality, adaptability and equality of employment.

Ever since the founding Treaty of Rome, core employment relations matters, such as the right to association, the right to engage in industrial action (strikes and lock-outs) and wage determination have been excluded from the EU's competence. Nonetheless, the EU has evolved a European framework that can lay claim to principles, procedures and substantive outcomes. The principles are set out in the Social Affairs Commissioner's foreword to the Commission's first report on industrial relations and reflect the conviction that economic and social progress must go hand in hand: 'respect for fundamental social rights in a frontier-free Europe; worker's rights to information and consultation on company operations; social dialogue as a mainstay of good governance and a means of involving citizens in the European venture' (European Commission 2000).

In addition to the original Community procedures for adopting legally based directives and regulations, three processes are prominent. The first is social dialogue, which goes back to a summit conference involving the Commission and the social partners at Val Duchesse in 1985. This covers bi-partite exchanges between the social partners, with the aim of reaching common positions or agreement. It also embraces social partner consultation under the social policy process outlined below. The intention is that employers' organizations and trade unions have 'voice', and therefore influence, over issues and developments of common concern arising from economic integration. There are sector social dialogues as well as the cross-sector arrangements.

Second are procedures relating to consultation and collective bargaining under the social policy process of the 1991 Maastricht Treaty subsequently incorporated in the social chapter of the Amsterdam Treaty. These place the Commission under an obligation to consult with the social partners and provide for the conclusion of EU-level collective agreements as a method of regulation. Specifically, Article 137 requires the Commission to consult the social partners in advance of adopting legislative proposals in the following fields:

- improvement of the working environment to protect workers' health and safety; working conditions; information and consultation of workers;
- equality of opportunities and treatment at work between men and women;
- integration of persons excluded from the labour market; social security and social protection of workers;
- protection of workers where their employment contract is terminated; representation and collective defence of the interests of workers and employers;
- conditions of employment for third-country nationals residing in the EU; and financial contributions for the promotion of employment and job-creation.

In key respects, this process goes to the heart of the European 'social model' in as much as it reflects and reinforces the position in most member states.

Article 138 of the Treaty requires the Commission to consult the social partners in two stages: (a) on the need for and the possible direction of Community action; and (b) on its content. At the end of this consultation process, the social partners can present an opinion to the Commission or inform it of their intention to open negotiations. In this case, they have an initial period of nine months to reach an agreement. Where the social partners do not take the initiative, or do not reach agreement, the Commission resumes its active role.

The third procedure involves the 'open method of co-ordination' (OMC) originally associated with the EU's employment strategy. In the European Commission's (2002: 7) words:

> The open method of co-ordination means that all countries fix common objectives in a given policy area, prepare national actions plans, examine each other's performance with Commission guidance and learn from their successes and failures. It is a new way of working together in the EU – no longer only through legislation, but through a flexible yet structured co-operation among Member States.

The EU's extraordinary summit in Lisbon in 2000 formally adopted the OMC as a regulatory method. It also brought together the so-called 'Luxembourg' and 'Cologne' co-ordination processes dealing, respectively, with the development and implementation of national action plans for employment and 'macro-economic dialogue' addressing wage policy *inter alia* involving the ECB, the European Commission and the social partners.

The outcome of these processes, the so-called *acquis communautaire*, includes the measures outlined later. Further topics have been addressed in voluntary collective agreements, at cross-sector and sector levels, which are not binding. A substantial body of joint texts has also emerged from the social dialogue process. Completing the picture have been landmark decisions from the ECJ, notably in the area of equality.

Assessing the Impact on the UK

Attention now turns to the impact of these features of European integration. The discussion is evidence based, but necessarily general. Precise evaluation presents massive methodological problems. It is not just a question of unravelling the effects of different influences, such as 'globalization' and 'Europeanization'. Critically important, too, is the focus, which can be absolute or relative, depending on whether comparisons are made with other EU member states, and macro or micro, depending on whether sectors and companies are included.

Patterns of employment regulation

'Soft' regulation equals 'hard' regulation

In other EU countries, criticism of the EU's *acquis communautaire* comes predominantly from those who think it has not gone far enough. This is because, in most cases, extensive regulation already exists either in the form of national legislation or multi-employer agreements. The *acquis*, say critics, deals with minimum provisions, which means that its contents are limited in comparison with existing national regulation. It does not cover 'hard' issues such as wages, the right of association, the right to strike and the right to lockout. The bulk of the social dialogue output is 'not binding for the signatory parties' (Keller 2000: 38). It is therefore more difficult to enforce than the collective agreements of national systems – the Commission has 'no institutions or instruments of its own to implement existing regulation' (Keller 2000: 42). Similarly, the new regulatory forms associated with the EU's employment strategy, benchmarking and peer review, are seen as a pale reflection of the traditional methods (legislation and collective bargaining) and, possibly, a potential threat to them (Goetschy 2003).

Things are very different in the UK and Ireland, however, where there has been a lack of comparable regulation reflecting the tradition of 'voluntarism'. As Box 2.1 suggests, the *acquis* has touched on virtually every area of employment relations other than association, industrial action and wage determination – not to mention human rights. Listing only those areas where there has been major UK legislation gives us freedom of movement of workers; equal opportunities in terms of age, disability, gender, race, religion and sexual orientation; health and safety; collective redundancy and business transfers; working time; the proof of employment; information and consultation – both national and cross-national; maternity and parental leave; equal treatment for part-time and temporary workers (with agency

Box 2.1   Main developments in EU employment regulation

Stage 1: The 1960s and early 1970s
The Treaty of Rome contained a chapter on freedom of movement for workers (Articles 48ff/new article 39ff) and social security for migrant workers (Article 51/new article 42). Articles 119ff referred to a social chapter, but made no provision for legislative interventions. Article 235 dealt with equal opportunities for women and men. The basic framework to achieve these aims introduced in 1972 was subsequently developed and reinforced by ECJ case law.

Stage 2: The second half of the 1970s
Although the institutional framework remained unchanged, this period saw the adoption of the first labour directives and measures promoting health and safety and equal opportunities. Events prompting action included the oil crisis and restructuring (resulting in the collective redundancies directive) and the discovery of the carcinogenic effects of vinyl chloride monomer. These provisions were based on Article 100 of the Treaty, which enabled the Council to adopt unanimously directives for the approximation of such national provisions as affect the establishment or functioning of the Common Market, and on Article 235 dealing with equal opportunities.

Stage 3: The 1980s
The Single European Act strengthened the legal basis for health and safety provisions. The first indent of Article 137(1) (ex Article 118a of the EC Treaty) enabled the adoption by qualified maturity of directives laying down minimum requirements for safety and health at work. It also recognized the social dialogue at European level (Article 118b/new Article 139). A framework directive adopted in 1980, defined a strategy for dealing with all physical, chemical and biological agents at work. There were also further developments in equal opportunities.

Stage 4: 1990–1993
A number of initiatives followed the signing in 1989 of the Charter of the Fundamental Social Rights, including 15 health and safety directives, one equal opportunities directive and four labour law directives. However, the experience led to demands for a stronger legal basis for social policy. The entry into force of the 1991 Maastricht Treaty and, in particular, its social protocol (currently Articles 136ff) extended the use of qualified majority voting beyond health and safety and defined the role of the social partners at Community level. A major concern

was to give Europe a 'social face' at a time of intensifying change stemming from completion of single market and prospect of EMU.

Stage 5: 1994–1999
The social protocol attached to the Maastricht Treaty enabled the social partners to reach collective agreements as the basis of EU directives. Agreements followed dealing with parental leave, part-time work and fixed-term contracts, implemented by directives. The protocol also established a more favourable political, institutional and legal context and enabled proposals linked to the Social Charter to be followed up. But the European Works Council Directive was adopted in 1994, after a failure to agree by the social partners.

Stage 6: Since 1999
The Treaty of Amsterdam consolidated and significantly reinforced the institutional framework and instruments of social policy, ending the UK opt-out. Work focused on four areas: employment, combating discrimination, equal opportunities, and the role of the social partners (Articles 3, 13, employment chapter, 137, 138 and 141). It also signalled a shift towards new, 'softer' regulatory mechanisms, including benchmarking (Article 118) and the OMC, subsequently endorsed by the 2000 Lisbon summit. In 2002 the adoption of the national information and consultation directive completed the action programme linked to the Social Charter. In 2002 the EU social partners conclude the first agreement to be implemented through collective agreements within member states (on teleworking).

Source: Based on European Commission (2000: 25).

workers to come); pensions; employment agencies; data protection and corporate governance.

Critically important too is that the decline of multi-employer bargaining at national level means that the UK has been unable to take maximum advantage of the flexibility increasingly been built into EU legislation. In effect, the *acquis'* 'soft' regulation has been tantamount to 'hard' in its impact in the UK. Standards and entitlements have had to be laid down in law, with mechanisms other than collective bargaining, such as employment tribunals and/or the courts, ensuring compliance and redress.

The end of 'voluntarism'?

In most other member states, the EU's Maastricht social policy process has also had a significant impact on the wider context of employment relations. Most importantly, it has helped to legitimize social dialogue and collective bargaining as the main vehicles for handling change. Witness the emergence in most other EU countries of 'social pacts' at the national level and 'pacts for employment and competitiveness' at company level (Marginson and Sisson 2004: chs. 5 and 6). Ireland, which shares much of the UK's employment relations history, is an example: national agreements involving government and the social partner organizations have become a regular feature, embracing a wide range of economic and social policy issues (O'Donnell 2001).

In the UK, by contrast, collective bargaining is in decline and social dialogue a term rarely used. A key factor has been the structure of collective bargaining touched on above. The decline of multi-employer bargaining in the form of national agreements means that the machinery to ensure a wide coverage regardless of trade union membership no longer exists. Collective bargaining is increasingly dependent on trade union ability to organize individual companies, which is an uphill task given the shifts in employment structure discussed below.

Also fundamentally important has been the political context. In the 1980s and 1990s, successive Conservative governments rejected not only the tentative forms of national level social dialogue developed in the 1970s, but also the very principle of collective bargaining as the preferred means of employment governance. They dismantled national tri-partite bodies such as the National Economic Development Organization, campaigned vigorously against national multi-employer bargaining and introduced a plethora of legislation curtailing the activities of trade unions. Individualism rather than collectivism was very much the preferred route (Employment Department 1992).

The incoming Labour government of 1997 similarly set its face against systematic national level social dialogue. The prospect of social pacts has never figured in debate and, until recently, the term 'social partnership' frowned on. 'Partnership' has been seen primarily as an organization-based rather than national level activity (Taylor 1999).[1] The relative success of introducing a national minimum wage via a representative commission was not built on to develop a method of transposing EU regulation. True, the Labour government honoured its election commitment to introduce a statutory trade union recognition procedure, but it is largely a matter of choice – Labour governments have so far not been willing to promote collective bargaining as a matter of principle.

A similar reluctance to promote representative forms of participation is to be found in the approach to information and consultation. Having reluctantly accepted that it would have to implement the EU Directive, the regulations implementing it give equal weight to individual as well as representative forms (Department of Trade and Industry 2003).

The government has also done very little to promote social dialogue in the public services. Here it has adopted a rather 'macho' approach, forcing change through rather than achieving its ends by dialogue and diplomacy. This approach was reflected in the budget episode of 2004, when many thousands of civil service redundancies were announced in Parliament without prior consultation.

In these circumstances, EU support for social dialogue and collective bargaining has had little effect. Paradoxically, instead of promoting these processes, which is the intention, the *acquis* is having the opposite effect. The 'voluntarism' that characterized UK employment relations for a century is fast disappearing under the weight of the regulations implementing EU Directives. Not only has the emphasis shifted from collective to individual rights with an increase in 'juridification' in the sense of the involvement of the law and the courts in employment relations matters. More fundamentally, it is not unfair to suggest that a culture of legal dependency is fast developing.

Hard evidence for this view is available in the patterns of conflict. The incidence of 'organized' conflict, notably strikes, has dropped to an all-time low. By contrast, claims to Employment Tribunals in pursuit of individual employment rights have grown to around 100,000 per annum. Also calls to national helplines about employment legislation have rocketed. The Advisory Conciliation and Arbitration Service (ACAS) alone receives around 800,000 a year roughly divided between employers and employees, while the Citizen's Advice Bureau gets around 600,000 almost exclusively from employees.

Although anecdotal, this author's experience going round the country in 2003 and 2004 talking to a range of audiences about handling the Information and Consultation of Employees (ICE) Regulations is instructive. The focus has not so much been, as many hoped it would be, on the ways in which managers, employee representatives and employees can benefit from the flexibility the Regulations give to reach agreements that suit local circumstances. Rather it has been on what has to be done to comply with the Regulations. As representatives of Chambers of Commerce and employers' organizations very apologetically explained at one such meeting, few of their members, especially small and medium-sized enterprises (SMEs), had the experience or the confidence to negotiate their own arrangements and so did not find the Regulations' flexibility very attractive. It was contradictory, they readily admitted, given their principled opposition to regulation. But many of their members would prefer to have further and more detailed provisions that told them what they had to do.

Restructuring

Restructuring is the other main area where European integration has had a significant impact. Some restructuring resulted directly from policies promoting the rationalization of sectors such as steel or the opening up of previously closed markets to European-wide competition, as in energy, telecommunications and airlines. Much restructuring, however, has taken the form of mergers and acquisitions, joint ventures and strategic alliances, as multinational companies (MNCs) have sought to establish and/or consolidate a presence across the single European market. An initial wave of mergers and acquisitions from the mid-1980s peaked in 1990. There was another surge anticipating EMU from 1994 accelerating towards a new peak in 2000 – at which point they accounted for virtually half of all mergers (Marginson and Sisson 2004).

Two dimensions of this restructuring deserve attention. One, the internal, is the emergence of the 'Euro-company'. The other, the external, involves the impact of rationalization on the structure of employment. Consequently, new pathways have opened up for the spread of cross-national policies and practices at the same time as there has been an exaggerated shift in employment from manufacturing to services.

The emergence of the Euro-company

The emergence of the 'Euro-company' (Marginson and Sisson 1994; Marginson 2000) reflects two developments, leading to distinct European dimensions to the forms of (management) organization. One involves the response of MNCs to the economic, political and regulatory space that is being created from above, bringing the co-ordination of production and market servicing. The other takes the form of bottom-up developments. Although they continue to bear many of the traces of their national origins, MNCs are increasingly more than the extension of national companies beyond their borders. The formation of divisions that group business operations across different countries, together with European regional management structures, has not just downgraded the role of national subsidiaries and/or assumed the co-ordination role that might otherwise be exercised by global headquarters. These developments have also created a 'transnational social space' (Morgan et al. 2001) in which hybrid polices and practices are emerging. Importantly, too, this is not limited to European-based companies (van Tulder et al. 2001). US MNCs such as General Motors have established market servicing and production operations on a pan-European basis as well as EU ones such as Shell, Thomson and Unilever.

EARLY DAYS FOR EUROPEAN WORKS COUNCILS

The growth in the number and importance of 'Euro-companies' has led to the first attempt to introduce cross-national machinery in the form of the European Works Councils (EWCs) Directive of 1993. The UK, being home to more MNCs than most, probably has the largest single number operating within its shores (Hall et al. 1995, appendix 1).

Although in their infancy, one thing is already very clear. There is enormous variation in the role and influence of EWCs (Hall et al. 2003; Marginson et al. 2004). Many EWCs appear to be largely a symbolic exercise, reflecting the immense difficulties facing cross-national employee representation. But others exercise de facto rights of consultation and even negotiation beyond that envis-aged in the directive.

Two companies with significant interests in the UK falling into this second cat-egory are Ford and General Motors (GM). In Ford's case, the 2000 agreement dealt with the status, rights, and terms and conditions of employees being transferred into the Visteon spin-off. In GM's case, there were three major agreements in

2000–2001, dealing respectively with a new power train joint venture with Fiat and restructuring involving the Vauxhall and Opel subsidiaries (for further details see EWCB 2001a and 2001b).

The explanation for the differences mainly lies in the nature of the company's operations in the role and influence of EWCs and the degree to which they are integrated. In so far as international integration of operations is progressively spreading across as well as deepening within sectors, one of the pre-conditions for the development of EWCs possessing the capacity to exert influence is becoming more widespread.

BENCHMARKING TOWARDS 'EUROPEANIZATION'?

EWCs are far from being the only pathway of cross-national influence, however. Management itself is promoting 'Europeanization' of policies and practices. As MNCs deepen their international management structures at European level, there is an increasing tendency to develop transnational approaches to HRM and industrial relations, reflecting not just home country but also experiences from the melting pot that they have effectively become (Marginson and Sisson 2004). In practice, there are two main forms. In the first, the centre openly implements common policies across different countries. Some, such as team working, flow automatically from standard operating processes. Others come from the pressures for consistency of approach and/or minimization of transaction costs – the salary arrangements of senior managers, for example. A third, such as the European and sometimes global agreements that larger MNCs have entered into on corporate social responsibility, very often reflect company philosophy (Sisson 2005).

The second form, which is much more implicit, involves common policies implemented as a result of local decisions. Crucial here is the use of benchmarking to diffuse 'best practice' and/or enforce 'coercive' cross-national comparisons of performance. Methods include the regular convening of meetings of managers from different countries, rotation of managerial personnel from one location to another, compilation of manuals of 'best practice' and the setting up of task force and/or nomination of 'lead' operations with responsibility for directing change.

The paradigm case is again the automotive sector with its standardized products and high levels of integration. In the run up to EMU, Ford, GM, Mercedes-Benz and Volkswagen negotiated agreements in a number of European countries including the UK, offering reassurances on jobs in return for greater flexibility of pay, working time and work organization (Sisson and Artiles 2000). In each case the catalyst was a headquarter's review of future investment plans and existing cost structures across its businesses. Once an agreement had been concluded in one country, its contents assumed the status of 'best practice' solutions operations in other countries under pressure to emulate (Hancké 2000). The result was not only a greater convergence of costs but also the standardization of some conditions of employment from one country to another, such as overtime corridors, annual-hours agreements and teamwork.

Management's use of benchmarking has had a 'spillover' effect on employee representatives. Although they have found it difficult to make cross-national comparisons of pay because of the complexity of different payment structures and tax, national insurance and social security systems, these representatives have successfully argued that issues such as working time are valid reference points. At both GM Vauxhall and Peugeot's UK subsidiary, for example, international comparisons have successfully been used to secure a reduction in working time (Sisson and Marginson 2000).

It is management, in short, that is opening up one of the main path ways for the 'Europeanization' of employment relations. It may be informal and unintended, but it is no less important. The more companies reorganize and integrate their operations across Europe, the more 'Europeanization' there is likely to be.

Changing employment structure

In recent years the UK has enjoyed one of the highest employment rates of all the EU member countries. For present purposes, however, it is not so much the overall employment rate that is important, but the structure of employment and, in particular, the balance between manufacturing and services. Put simply, the intensifying competition that European integration has promoted, coupled with the knock-on effect of the 'Euro-company' and the decision to stay out of the single currency, has exaggerated the on-going shift from manufacturing to services. This, in turn, has had wide-ranging implications for the size of workplaces, the composition of the workforce and the prospects for trade union recognition and collective action.

As Table 2.1 shows, despite starting with one of the lowest proportions of employment in manufacturing, the UK has nevertheless experienced the largest rate of decline of major EU countries. Employment in manufacturing in the UK as a percentage of total employment declined from 20.7 per cent to 15.6 per cent between 1993 and 2002. In Germany, where it started from a much higher base, it declined from 27.8 per cent to 23.5 per cent. France saw a decline of 1.5 per cent, while Italy experienced a small increase.

This may come as a surprise since the UK supposedly has had one of most flexible labour markets in Europe with a relatively low cost base. With the UK's relatively low pay levels, however, also comes low skills and low productivity, which means higher unit labour costs and greater difficulty in moving up market (Porter and Ketels 2003). Flexibility is also a double-edged sword – it may encourage MNCs to come to the UK, but it also makes it easier for them to depart.

A further consideration is the decision to stay out of the single currency. This is significant because of the implications for foreign direct investment (FDI), which is one of the Treasury's five tests for membership. Domestically owned companies account for 80–90 per cent of UK business investment and employ some 90 per cent of British workers. But foreign-owned firms contribute more than one-quarter of

Table 2.1 Manufacturing employment in the UK and EU

	1993	1996	1999	2002
UK				
Manufacturing employment	5,267	5,036	4,858	4,428
Total employment	25,478	26,177	27,107	28,388
Manufacturing as % of total	20.7	19.2	17.9	15.6
EU-12				
Manufacturing employment	30,812	NA	NA	25,605
Total employment	138,135			127,547
Manufacturing as % of total	22.3			20.1
Germany				
Manufacturing employment	10,039	8,548	8,574	8,541
Total employment	36,111	35,634	36,089	36,275
Manufacturing as % of total	27.8	24.0	23.8	23.5
France				
Manufacturing employment	4,224	4,102	4,291	4,256
Total employment	21,908	22,195	22,755	23,885
Manufacturing as % of total	19.3	18.5	18.9	17.8
Italy				
Manufacturing employment	4,567	4,609	4,869	4,934
Total employment	20,321	20,013	20,618	21,757
Manufacturing as % of total	22.5	23.0	23.6	22.7

Source: Eurostat (1994, 1997, 2000, 2003).

manufacturing employment and 40 per cent of manufacturing investment. They also fund about one-third of total business research and development.

As Table 2.2 suggests, the trend for FDI is consistent with the worries that many individual MNC representatives have expressed about the exchange rate uncertainty that non-membership of the single currency creates. Like the other two countries outside the single currency, Denmark and Sweden, the UK's share of FDI into EU member countries has declined not only in absolute but also proportionate terms from 28.7 per cent in 1998 to 5.0 per cent in 2003.

In its most recent assessment published on 9 June 2003, HM Treasury (2003) noted that there had been a fall in the UK's share of FDI coinciding with the start of the single currency, but was reluctant to commit itself to making the causal link. The Economist Intelligence Unit, an organization sceptical about the overall benefits of membership, has shown no such qualms. Drawing on further evidence from a survey of 500 global investors, in whose thinking exchange rate uncertainty looms very large, it concludes that:

the arguments for or against membership of the single currency rest on a broader set of considerations than the impact on inward FDI. Nevertheless, the evidence

Table 2.2   Foreign direct investment inflows into the UK and EU

	1998	1999	2000	2001	2002	2003
Inflows (US$m)						
EU-15	260,322	478,659	686,012	382,638	369,544	271,285
UK	74,650	89,540	119,940	61,530	29,180	14,542
Sweden	19,413	59,385	22,124	13,084	11,829	3,576
Denmark	6,675	16,076	35,847	10,237	6,411	2,623
% share in EU total						
UK	28.7	18.7	17.5	16.1	7.9	5.4
Sweden	7.5	12.4	3.2	3.4	3.2	1.3
Denmark	2.6	3.4	5.2	2.7	1.7	1.0

Source: Economist Intelligence Unit (2004).

available for this particular test seems clearer and less ambiguous than the evidence for any of the remaining tests. The UK is likely to suffer sizeable losses of future potential FDI if it remains outside the euro area. (Economist Intelligence Unit 2004)

Wider Considerations: Context Matters

There are several points implicit in this discussion with wider relevance. In recent years there has been a general tendency to prioritize the 'universal' in explaining developments in employment regulation, with economics and psychology providing the dominant disciplinary frameworks. For many, it is axiomatic that 'globalization', in the form of the internationalization of markets and advancing technology, has not only been the dominant driver of change, but has also 'determined' outcomes. Similarly, many have taken refuge in the notion of the 'psychological contract', with the individual and their supposed needs being the starting point for understanding the implications of the much changed macroeconomic environment.

In practice, a strong case can be made for suggesting that, even in this global economy, developments continue to be massively contingent on the immediate context. To answer the conundrum that Dunlop (1958: 94–7) posed many years ago, the 'locus and distribution of power in the wider society' are at least as important as 'technological and market considerations'. Critically important are the choices that policy makers make. Not only that. In making these choices, there are very strong tendencies to 'path dependency', whereby past decisions set actors on a particular course and give some a position of privilege and strength to block change. In the language Scharpf (2000: 224) uses to discuss the importance of existing arrangements for social protection, it is the 'path-dependent constraints of existing policy legacies' and the 'institutional constraints of existing veto positions' that deserve our attention in understanding why things happen or not. Politics matters massively, in other words, and so do institutions, which is why they need to stay at the forefront of analysis.

Much of the reaction of UK policy makers to European integration can be explained in terms of ideological framework. For, despite their very different interpretations, Labour and Conservative governments alike have been firmly committed to neo-liberalism. The emphasis is on markets and making them work effectively. Institutions such as collective bargaining are largely seen as 'imperfections' in the working of markets rather than necessary to shape and give them direction. The complexities of managing the employment relationship are largely ignored as is the significance of the workplace as a key decision-making unit. The emphasis is on skills and the supply of skills rather than demand for skills and the way that they are used/misused. Public intervention can only be justified in terms of market failure. It also needs to be evidence based, which means macro-level target setting, and so the prioritization of the measurable over the immeasurable and the formal at the expense of the informal.

Fundamentally important too have been the UK's 'competitive governance' arrangements. Put simply, the UK's electoral arrangements encourage governments to focus on short- rather than long-term issues. Ironically, after 18 years out of power, Labour governments' desperation to demonstrate that they have broken with their party's 'corporatist' past has served to reinforce the tendency to path dependency overall. In practice, the much-vaunted 'third way' has meant little more than a 'pendulum approach'. Anything resembling a concession to trade unions, such as signing the social chapter or a commitment to introduce statutory trade union recognition, has quickly to be balanced by downplaying its significance and/or limiting its impact.

The then Minister of State for Employment Relation's very open and honest answer to a question about the government's opposition to the information and consultation Directive at a seminar in 2002 offers a good illustration of the significance of short-term tactical considerations. The government, he emphasized, genuinely felt that the directive was inappropriate in that it was interfering in domestic as opposed to cross-national issues. But practicalities were also important. UK employers were bitterly opposed to legislation. Many trade unions were lukewarm about employee-based arrangements. In the circumstances, it was understandable and reasonable for the government to adopt the position they had.

Short-term considerations have similarly shaped the reaction to European integration. Labour governments professing to want to be at the heart of Europe have been unable to resist the temptation to 'blame' Brussels when it has suited them domestically. But this, in turn, has fuelled Euro-scepticism, making it even more difficult to press Europe's case. The about-turn on the referendum about the new EU Constitution in 2004 is an example.

Importantly, too, the pressures on UK governments to rise above such short-term considerations have been less than in other EU member states, enabling 'path dependency' not only to assert itself but also increase its influence. The decline of manufacturing has meant that support for adopting the single currency has been less than in other countries. Staying out of the single currency means, in turn, that the government has not had to confront the monetary, exchange rate and fiscal implications that other countries have had to, although a not dissimilar monetary regime has been put in place. In giving the Bank of England, along with its Monetary Policy Committee, effective control over exchange rate, the Chancellor reinforced the sceptical camp. Expecting the Bank of England to promote support of entry in these circumstances is tantamount to asking turkeys to vote for Christmas.

Perhaps most fundamentally, the significant countervailing pressures of institutional arrangements in other countries have been absent in the UK. The structure of collective bargaining and, in particular, the decline of multi-employer bargaining has been critical on two accounts. First, unlike in other countries, government and employers did not have to weigh up the costs as well as the benefits of its demise – the machinery was broken and no significant interest group was pushing for its re-instatement. Second, the option of transposing EU regulation by such bargaining, which is one way other countries promote social dialogue, did not appear to be a realistic option. In the circumstances, and taking into account the 'social contract' experiences of the 1970s, the government's rejection of national social dialogue is understandable. But it reduced the pressure that employers in other countries have been under to compromise and so, again, made it more difficult to break with the past.

Also important is the absence of a dedicated employment or social affairs ministry. In practice, policy responsibility for the area has been fragmented between many players: No 10, the Treasury, the Deputy PM's office (with responsibilities for local government) and three departments (Department of Trade and Industry, Department of Work and Pensions, Department of Education and Skills). The DTI's Employment Relations Directorate, which nominally has policy responsibility for the area, is very much a minority group mainly concerned with implementing regulation.

Future Prospects

Looking ahead, there are grounds for thinking that European integration will not be as influential as it has been. Certainly there are issues in the pipeline that will have an impact, such as the decision on the 48 hour opt-out from the working time regulations. The reviews of existing legislation dealing with such issues as information and consultation could also lead to significant changes. The incorporation into the Treaty of the Charter of Fundamental Rights proclaimed at the 2000 Nice summit could provide the legal basis for national level activity in the form of judicial review by the European Court of Justice leading to 'hard' regulation. It could even provide the basis for further EU-level 'hard' regulation where transnational issues are involved – collective bargaining and collective action are possible candidates.

The prospects are far from strong, however. The 'shadow of the law' is, in Falkner's words (2003: 24), 'fading', with the stream of legislative proposals deriving from the 1989 Social Charter having run its course. The Commission's work programme agreed for 2003–2005 sets the pattern. It covers actions under three main themes – employment, EU enlargement and mobility. Significantly, however, these are to be implemented through a range of instruments: exchange of good practice information; recommendations and declarations; benchmarking by means of charters, codes of conduct and frameworks of actions; and agreements dealing with standards, which may be voluntary or implemented by directive (EIRO 2003a). The future, it seems, lies with 'soft' regulation to be implemented through national procedures. The 'Orientations for reference in managing change and its consequences' agreed in October 2003 are an example (EIRO 2003b).

Also significant is enlargement, which will deepen and change the character of the EU's collective action problem. The difficulties of reaching agreement have been substantial enough with the present 15 countries. The expansion to embrace 25 countries brings in many more players – governmental, employer and trade union, company management and employee representatives. This means increasing complexity, uncertainty and instability at every level of the EU's emerging multi-level governance arrangements.

Enlargement will also change the character of these arrangements. Crucially, it shifts the balance away from countries with inclusive structures of multi-employer bargaining. Among the eight CEE accession countries, multi-employer arrangements have become well entrenched only in Slovenia and Slovakia (Carley 2002; Kohl et al. 2000). It means that the European model of industrial relations can no longer unequivocally be presented as one characterized by strong interest associations, regulating the labour market through inclusive agreements concluded at sector and/or cross-sector levels, with decentralization towards the company level 'organized' within higher level frameworks. The weakness of the sector-level in a significant group of member states, combined with the underdeveloped nature of the EU sector-level, threatens to deprive the system of a key linkage integrating mechanism. The possibilities of invoking the twin principles of subsidiarity and devolution to resolve problems will become more constrained. As Meardi (2002) has argued, the accession countries could turn out to be the 'Trojan Horse' for the wider 'Americanization' of industrial relations, including the break-up of the dominant multi-employer bargaining model.

Whatever the EU's direction, however, it is difficult to escape the conclusion that European integration has had an indelible imprint. Assuming the UK stays in Europe, it will be difficult for governments to champion the European social model, even if they wanted to. Equally, going to the other extreme, if the UK leaves EU, it is difficult to envisage widespread deregulation. The 'market' state, as Majone (1996) has argued, increases the demand for regulation. For it will not just be trade unions pressing for such regulation. The Citizens' Advice Bureau is already campaigning

for a Fair Employment Rights Commission, which would encourage further depend-
ence on the law. Concerns about quality standards are also likely to be important
in sectors such as financial services and health care. In any event, it is legislation
rather than collective bargaining that will characterize employment regulation in
the UK – something that would have seemed inconceivable when the UK joined
the then European Economic Community.

NOTE

1   At the time of preparing this chapter over the summer of 2004, the immediate polit-
    ical context was set by the on-going Iraq crisis and the prospect of a 2005 election,
    with the Labour Party hoping to achieve an historic third consecutive election
    victory. Consequently the government had become much more dependent on trade
    union support. On 25 July 2004, the Labour Party's National Policy Forum meeting
    at the University of Warwick agreed a wide range of initiatives designed to promote
    'fairness at work' including a commitment to 'work in partnership with unions and
    help them grow'. The Prime Minister opened his speech to the TUC Congress on
    13 September with the following: 'So I come here to praise Warwick not bury it. To
    advocate social partnership not belittle it.' The outcome remains uncertain. If there
    is a change of approach, however, it will be further confirmation of this chapter's
    argument that context matters.

AUTHOR'S NOTE

The author is writing in a personal capacity and the views expressed in this chapter do
not necessarily reflect those of any organizations to which he is affiliated.

REFERENCES

Bach, S. and Sisson, K. 2000: Personnel management in perspective, in S. Bach and
    K. Sisson (eds.), *Personnel Management*, Oxford: Blackwell, 3–42.
Carley, M. 2002: *Industrial Relations in the EU Member States and Candidate Countries*,
    Luxembourg: European Foundation for the Improvement of Living and Working
    Conditions/Office for Official Publications of the European Communities.
Commons, J. 1909: American shoemakers 1648–1895: A sketch of industrial evolution,
    Quarterly Journal of Economics, **24**, 38–83, reprinted in 1968 in R.L. Rowan and H.R.
    Northrup (eds.), *Readings in Labor Economics and Labor Relations*, Homewood, IL: Irwin,
    60–76.
Department of Trade and Industry. 2003: *High Performance Workplaces*, London: DTI.
Dunlop, J. 1958: *Industrial Relations Systems*, New York: Holt.
Economist Intelligence Unit. 2004: Inward investment tumbles; recovery is uncertain –
    EIU views. *World Investment Prospects 2004*. London: EIU.
Eichengreen, B. and Wyplosz, C. 1998: The stability pact: More than a minor nuisance?
    in D. Begg, J. Von Hagen, C. Wyplosz, and K.F. Zimmerman (eds.), *EMU: Prospects
    and Challenges for the Euro*. Special issue of *Economic Policy*. Oxford: Blackwell.

Employment Department. 1992: *People, Jobs and Opportunity*. London: HMSO.

EIRO. 2003a: Social partners sign pact for development, *European Industrial Relations Observatory On-line*, Ref. IT0307105F.

EIRO. 2003b: EU-level social partners negotiate joint text on restructuring, *European Industrial Relations Observatory On-line*, Ref. EU0307203F.

European Commission. 1998: *Report on Progress towards Convergence and the Recommendation with a View to the Transition to the First Stage of Economic and Monetary Union. Part I: Recommendation*. Luxembourg: Office for the Official Publications of the European Communities.

European Commission. 2000: *Industrial Relations in Europe 2000*. Luxembourg: Office for the Official Publications of the European Communities.

European Commission. 2001: *Enhancing Democracy: A White Paper on Governance in the European Union*, Brussels. Available from <http://europa.eu.int/comm/governance/index_en.htm>

European Commission. 2002: Directorate General for Employment and Social affairs. *Social Agenda*, Issue No. 1 April, Luxembourg: Office for the Official Publications of the European Communities.

Eurostat. 1994: *Labour Force Survey 1993*, Luxembourg: Office for the Official Publications of the European Communities.

Eurostat. 1997: *Labour Force Survey 1996*, Luxembourg: Office for the Official Publications of the European Communities.

Eurostat. 2000: *Labour Force Survey 1999*, Luxembourg: Office for the Official Publications of the European Communities.

Eurostat. 2003: *Labour Force Survey 2002*, Luxembourg: Office for the Official Publications of the European Communities.

European Works Council Bulletin. 2001a: GM deal highlights EWC's negotiating role, Issue 33, May/June, 7–11.

European Works Council Bulletin. 2001b: GM EWC reaches agreement on Opel restructuring, Issue 36, November/December, 8–10.

Falkner, G. 1998: *EU Social Policy in the 1990s*, London: Routledge.

Falkner, G. 2003: The interprofessional social dialogue at European level: Past and future, in B. Keller and H.-W. Platzer (eds.), *Industrial Relations and European Integration*, Aldershot: Ashgate, 11–29.

Goetschy, J. 2003: The European Employment Strategy and the open method of co-ordination: Lessons and perspectives, *Transfer*, **9**(2), 281–301.

Hall, M., Carly, M., Gold, M., Marginson, P. and Sisson, K. 1995: *European Works Councils: Planning for the Directive*, London: Industrial Relations Research Unit/Industrial Relations Services.

Hall, M., Hoffmann, A., Marginson, P. and Müller, T. 2003: National influences on European Works Councils in UK- and US-based companies, *Human Resource Management Journal*, **13**(4), 75–92.

Hancké, B. 2000: European Works Councils and industrial restructuring in the European motor industry, *European Journal of Industrial Relations*, **6**(1), 35–59.

Hay, C. and Rosamond, B. 2000: Globalization, European integration and the discursive construction of Economic imperatives. Paper prepared for the Second Annual Conference of the ESRC 'One Europe or Several?' programme, University of Sussex, 21–22 September.

HM Treasury. 2003: UK membership of the single currency: An assessment of the five economic tests, *HM Treasury*, Cm 5776.

Kauppinen, T. (ed.) 1998: *The Impact of EMU on Industrial Relations in the European Union*, Helsinki: Finnish Industrial Relations Association.

Keller, B. 2000: The emergence of regional systems of employment regulation: The case of the European Union. Paper presented to the 12th IIRA World Congress, Tokyo, 29 May–2 June.

Kohl, H., Lecher, W. and Platzer, H-W. 2000: *Labour Relations in East-Central Europe between Transformation and EU Membership*, Bonn: Friederich Ebert Stiftung.

Majone, G. (ed.) 1996: *Regulating Europe*, London: Routledge.

Marginson, P. 2000: The Eurocompany and Euro industrial relations, *European Journal of Industrial Relations*, **6**(1), 9–34.

Marginson, P., Hall, M., Hoffmann, A. and Mueller, T. 2004: The impact of European Works Councils on management decision-making in UK- and US-based multinationals, *British Journal of Industrial Relations*, **42**(2), 209–33.

Marginson, P. and Sisson, K. 1994: The structure of transnational capital in Europe: The emerging Euro-company and its implications for industrial relations, in R. Hyman and A. Ferner (eds.), *New Frontiers in European Industrial Relations*, Oxford: Blackwell, 15–51.

Marginson, P. and Sisson, K. 2004: *European Integration and Industrial Relations: Multi-level Governance in the Making*, Basingstoke: Palgrave.

Martin, A. 1996: Wage bargaining under EMU: Europeanisation, re-nationalisation or Americanisation?, European Trade Union Institute Discussion and Working Papers, DWP 99.01.03.

Meardi, G. 2002: The Trojan horse for the Americanisation of Europe? Polish industrial relations towards the EU, *European Journal of Industrial Relations*, **8**(1), 77–99.

Morgan, G., Kristensen, P. and Whitley, R. (eds.), 2001: *Organising Internationally: Restructuring Firms and Markets in the Global Economy*, Oxford: Oxford University Press.

Mundell, R. 1961: A theory of optimum currency areas, *American Economic Review*, **51**(4), 657–65.

O'Donnell, R. 2001: Towards post-corporatist concertation in Europe?, in H. Wallace (ed.), *Interlocking Dimensions of European Integration*, Basingstoke: Palgrave, 305–22.

Olsen, J. 2001: Organizing European institutions of governance: A prelude to an institutionalized account of political integration, in H. Wallace (ed.), *Interlocking Dimensions of European Integration*, Basingstoke: Palgrave, 323–54.

Porter, M. and Ketels, C. 2003: *UK Competitiveness: Moving to the Next Stage*, DTI Economics Papers, London: DTI.

Rhodes, M. 1997: The welfare state: Internal challenges, external constraints, in M. Rhodes, P. Heywood and V. Wright (eds.), *Developments in West European Politics*, Basingstoke: Macmillan, 57–74.

Rosamond, B. 2001: Function, levels and European governance, in H. Wallace (ed.), *Interlocking Dimensions of European Integration*, Basingstoke: Palgrave, 305–22.

Scharpf, F. 2000: The viability of advanced welfare states in the international economy: vulnerabilities and options. *Journal of European Public Policy*, **7**(2), 190–228.

Sisson, K. 2005: International employee representation – a case of industrial relations systems following the market?, in T. Edwards and C. Rees (eds.), *International Human Resource Management: Globalisation, Multinational Companies and National Systems*, Harlow: Pearson.

Sisson, K., Arrowsmith, J., Gilman, M. and Hall, M. 1999: *EMU and the Implications for Industrial Relations: A Select Bibliographic Review*, Dublin: European Foundation for the Improvement of Living and Working Conditions.

Sisson, K. and Artiles, A.M. 2000: *Handling Restructuring. A Study of Collective Agreements on Employment and Competitiveness*, Luxembourg: Office for the Official Publications of the European Communities.

Sisson, K. and Marginson, P. 2000: *The Impact of Economic and Monetary Union on Industrial Relations: A Sectoral and Company View*, Luxembourg: Office for Official Publications of the European Communities.

Streeck, W. 1992: National diversity, regime competition and institutional deadlock: Problems in forming a European industrial relations system, *Journal of Public Policy*, **12**, 301–30.

Taylor, R. 1999: Blair 'rejects' partnership with unions and employers. *The Financial Times*, 7 July.

Tinbergen, J. 1965: *International Economic Integration*, 2nd edn, Amsterdam: Elsevier.

CHAPTER THREE

Managing Human Resources in Multinational Companies

Tony Edwards and Anthony Ferner

The primary focus of this book concerns developments in human resource management, examining issues such as the nature of the legal framework governing equality in UK employment, patterns of remuneration, and the meaning and significance of 'social partnership' in the UK context. One question that arises from this is: what is unusual or distinctive about the *national* element to the nature of human resource management? In an increasingly internationalized economy, are nationally distinct management styles still influential? Or are they converging around global norms? Multinational companies (MNCs) are one channel through which such a convergence in the nature of employment practices can take place. In this chapter we consider the role of overseas MNCs as a conduit for innovative influences within the UK system of employment relations.

The growth of MNCs has been one of the key features of globalization. The United Nations estimates that there are around 60,000 multinationals in the world economy, controlling around 850,000 foreign subsidiaries. The investments made by MNCs in countries outside their original national base have increased sharply in recent years; the stock of foreign direct investment (FDI) has risen from $513 billion in 1980 to $6,866 billion in 2002 (United Nations 2003). The influence of MNCs extends beyond the operations they directly own, also reaching the firms that have a trading relationship with them, be it as supplier, franchisee or retailer. Many observers argue that MNCs are often at the heart of global 'commodity chains' or 'value chains' in which complex webs of firms across countries are governed by powerful multinationals (see Kaplinsky 2001).

In terms of managing human resources the key issue arising from this growth is how such firms, which by definition straddle a range of national systems of employment relations, are affected by these differences. As background, the chapter considers why there are national variations in patterns of HRM, and how and why these national patterns change over time. Subsequently, it gets to grips with the core questions: how are MNCs affected by the distinctiveness of the national system in which they originated? And how does this influence from foreign MNCs shape the UK system?

To make such a task manageable we will look at two contrasting countries, the USA and Germany, and use case studies of MNCs from these two countries to develop the analysis. The focus on these two countries is justified partly because of their size and influence on the global economy as two of the key economic powers of the last one hundred years or so. It is also justified because they each represent examples of wider types of 'national business system' and of national styles of personnel management: the USA is the archetypal case of the liberalized, free-market economy in which employers act with considerable autonomy from the state or business associations; Germany, on the other hand, represents a much more regulated, partnership-based system in which firms often collaborate with others over issues such as pay determination. In addition, from a UK perspective, German and particularly US firms account for large proportions of foreign direct investment (FDI), much more in fact than the more heavily researched Japanese MNCs. Over the 5-year period from 1998 to 2002, US MNCs accounted for just over 25 per cent of flows of FDI into the UK and German MNCs accounted for a further 21 per cent (ONS 2004). Thus they have the potential to have a significant impact on the management of human resources in the UK.

The chapter has three principal sections. In the next section we examine the various types of explanation for national differences in HR management that have been advanced. Following this, the main section looks at the way that US and German MNCs manage their international workforces, using evidence from our own recent work. We focus in particular on the evidence relating to how these firms behave in the UK, thereby enabling us to shed light on the impact on the UK system of the growing presence of MNCs. Finally, we consider how the findings relating to US and German MNCs can be understood in terms of the nature of the US and German business systems and how they give rise to quite different traditions and styles of human resource management.

Why Do National Management Styles and Practices Differ?

There is a range of types of explanations as to why styles of HR management and associated employment practices differ across countries. The explanations attach importance to different sources of national distinctiveness, and their predictions concerning whether national differences are likely to persist or be eroded over time vary markedly. We highlight three main forms of explanation.

The first is what we refer to as *convergence theories*. This perspective stresses the importance of globalization in driving common approaches across borders on the part of firms. These pressures towards convergence stem in part from the influence of MNCs themselves through their ability to transfer practices across borders, but they also derive from the growth in international trade, the move towards an internationally integrated financial system, and the greater visibility of aspects of business practices stemming from improvements in travel and communications across countries. The convergence argument rests on the notion that styles and practices that appear to be linked to good financial performance are transferred across countries more rapidly than hitherto, and consequently national patterns of management are coming to resemble one another more closely. As a result of the intensification of globalization in general and international competition in particular, so the argument goes, the pace of convergence is increasing. Any differences between countries in management styles and practices are in the process of disappearing.

At a level of economic systems, there are similarities here with the core of Kerr et al.'s (1960) argument in their famous book *Industrialism and Industrial Man*, in which the authors envisaged the major economies developing along increasingly similar lines as common technological developments drove similar processes of industrial development. More recently, some authors have argued that globalization has been accompanied by a greater visibility of organizational structures and working practices across borders. For example, Piore and Sabel (1984) considered that a widespread development across countries was the erosion of 'mass production' and the adoption of 'flexible specialization' in which multi-skilled employees operated flexibly within teams to produce goods and services tailored to the particular tastes of consumers.

In relation to managing human resources, the notion of convergence arising from globalization features strongly in the literature. For instance, many observers have argued that industrial relations structures have become more 'disorganized' in that forms of employee representation have become weaker and collective bargaining has gone through a process of decentralization and contraction (e.g. Lash and Urry 1987). A further illustration of the convergence argument is Warhurst's (1995) analysis of the European airline industry. The author argued that all airlines in Europe were facing some common pressures – the volatile market for air travel, the deregulation of the airline sector in Europe, the reduction in state ownership and subsidization of national 'flag carriers', and so on – and these had led to significant, though gradual, signs of convergence around the HRM practices adopted by British Airways (BA) in the 1980s and early 1990s. In sum, the essence of these arguments is that differences across countries are only temporary and national variations are being eroded as national systems move towards similar end-points.

The convergence argument has come under strong criticism, however. One line of attack has been that convergence theorists have exaggerated the extent and influence of globalization. The evidence indicates that international economic flows (such as trade and FDI) are small as a proportion of national output and that most MNCs are in fact highly concentrated in the country in which they originate and those which neighbour it (see Dicken 2003 for a review of the evidence). The logic of this criticism is that the sources of national distinctiveness retain considerable influence and convergence is unlikely to occur.

This is consistent with a large body of work that argues that there are persistent differences in the way that national economic and social systems are configured.

For instance, in the field of employment relations Traxler et al. (2001) have shown that important national differences in systems of employment relations systems remain intact. Based on detailed comparative historical analysis, the authors concluded that 'even the strong internationalisation caused by the single market and EMU will not suffice to stimulate convergence towards a genuinely European labour relations regime' (2001: 304). Given this, what are the sources of these national variations?

One answer is contained in the second of the main sets of explanations for national distinctiveness, namely *cultural approaches*. These see nationally distinct values and attitudes as the principal source of variation across countries. This school of thought owes much to the pioneering work of Geert Hofstede whose massive study of IBM in the late 1960s and early 1970s formed the basis for his well-known dimensions of national cultures. Based mainly on the questionnaire responses of employees from more than fifty countries, Hofstede argued that countries could be distinguished along initially four, later five, aspects of culture. A full discussion of this is beyond the scope of this chapter (see Hofstede 1980 for an elaboration), but the essence of this and other work on culture is that persistent differences in the way organizations function in different countries can be attributed to the 'collective programming of the mind' that national cultures provide.

The cultural approach in general and Hofstede's ideas in particular have been widely used in international HRM research. One illustration is the use of national culture to try and explain differences in forms of labour market 'flexibility' across countries. Black (1999) used Hofstede's dimensions of national culture to construct a set of hypotheses concerning variations across countries in such things as forms of employment protection and trade union density. Based on analysis of data from the OECD countries, he found several significant associations between cultural indices and differences in labour markets. For example, he argued that countries which are considered by Hofstede to be 'masculine', such as Japan, tend to have weaker statutory protection for workers and lower levels of union density than 'feminine' ones, such as Sweden. He concludes that 'it is plausible to assert a causal relationship, with culture playing an exogenous determining role' (1999: 604). Hofstede's work is also widely used in the literature on personnel practice in MNCs (e.g. Ngo et al. 1998; Bae et al. 1998). In sum, the key to the cultural approach is that enduring differences in values and attitudes give rise to enduring differences in patterns of HRM.

In many ways the cultural approach represents an advance on the simplistic convergence theories, providing the beginnings of an explanation for persistent differences in management practice across countries and a definite shift away from assumptions of 'one-best-way' of operating. However, it too has been subject to significant criticisms. Some of these relate to specific problems with using Hofstede's work as the basis for subsequent research, such as the assumption of cultural homogeneity within countries (see McSweeney 2002 and Hofstede 2002 for a debate on the utility of the latter's framework). Other criticisms are quite different in that they argue that cultural values approaches are unsatisfactory because they do not get to the root of cultural differences. That is, the existence of differences in values and attitudes across borders simply begs a further question concerning the source of these variations: if values and attitudes do indeed differ between countries, why is this? The answer to this for some writers is the nature of national level institutions.

Thus the third of the explanations for national differences in HR management is the *institutionalist school*. This approach conceives a 'national business system' (Whitley 1999) as comprising interlocking institutions in a range of areas of economic and social life: forms of regulation of labour markets; patterns of ownership and control; the role of the state; and so on. Hall and Soskice (2001) argue that countries with particular types of institutions in one sphere of the economy tend to develop complementary institutions in other spheres. For example, countries characterized by a financial system in which shareholders and investors evaluate firms with primary emphasis on short-term financial performance tend to be characterized by labour markets that present few obstacles to laying off staff quickly and cheaply. The logic of this is that firms will seek to use frequent alterations to their labour costs as a way of trying to ensure that financial performance is in line with investors' expectations. In contrast, firms are more likely to accept and work with regulations promoting job security where their shareholders evaluate them on longer-term criteria. It is these 'institutional complementarities' that give rise to distinct national systems and provide the context within which cultures emerge.

The institutionalist approach has been used as a way of explaining how variations across countries evolve over time. One illustration is in the airline industry in which Lehrer (2001) has argued that the national context in the UK was conducive to the radical changes that BA made to its operations in the 1980s in relation to information systems, organizational structure, flight scheduling as well as its adoption of HRM practices. In contrast, the 'statist' institutional frameworks in Germany and France meant that Lufthansa and Air France responded in a more incremental fashion to the changed industry environment. Initially this meant that the latter companies lost ground on BA, and Air France in particular suffered persistent losses. However, the institutions in France and Germany were much better suited to the more stable environmental conditions of the late 1990s that called for more incremental innovations, allowing the two airlines to outperform their UK rival during this period. This offers a more sophisticated and dynamic approach to restructuring among European airlines than Warhurst's 'convergence within limits' model.

A different application of the institutionalist approach is Thelen's (2001) examination of the nature of collective bargaining structures across five developed economies. She considered whether it was really the case that a common trend is away from multi-employer negotiations towards decentralized bargaining at firm or plant level. Far from exhibiting a clear pattern of convergence, the trend towards decentralization has been highly uneven across countries; while multi-employer bargaining has practically disappeared in the UK and has never been an important feature of the USA, it remains significant in Germany, Sweden and Italy in the form of sector-level bargaining. Thelen's explanation centres on the wider institutional structures within which firms in the latter three countries are embedded which make them more favourably disposed to collaborating with other firms in the same industry.

We consider the institutionalist approach to have clear advantages over the convergence or culturalist approaches, particularly because it provides a convincing form of explaining national differences. Institutionalist approaches should incorporate a dynamic element that sees them as evolving over time, with one aspect of this evolution being the way in which they interact with each other through such mechanisms as the operation of MNCs (Djelic and Quack 2003). We adopt such an institutionalist approach in this chapter to analyse the management of human resources in MNCs.

National Business Systems and MNCs as Employers

The influences from national systems of personnel management create a range of possibilities and pressures on the part of MNCs. One possibility is for MNCs to act as innovators in the countries in which they have foreign subsidiaries, taking with them the style and practices of the home country. Indeed, organizations do not sever their ties with the institutional context in which they originated as soon as they begin to internationalize, and therefore the institutions in the home country inform the behaviour of MNCs as they expand overseas. In some cases the influence of the home country shows through in the broad priorities that the firm pursues, an illustration of which is the time-frame with which decisions on labour issues are evaluated. In other cases, a particular practice is transferred as a result of a conscious decision by managers because it is perceived as superior to alternatives operating in other countries and is seen as contributing to the firm's competitive advantage. These combined influences create a detectable 'country of origin' effect.

At the same time, distinct national traditions also give rise to pressures to adapt to national systems. Departing from established practices in host environments is unlawful in some cases. For example, in some countries there is a legal obligation to negotiate with employee representatives concerning major organizational changes. In other cases, transferring practices into a host country may be legal but would go against the grain of the national system in question to such an extent that costs would be incurred in the form of lost goodwill from staff, for example. These considerations lead to the pressure to operate in a highly decentralized way with relatively little holding the units together in terms of employment policies. This is the 'host country' effect.

There are also competitive pressures on MNCs to emulate the styles and practices of firms that originated in other countries. That is, MNCs may look to build an integrated and standardized set of operations across countries, but not see the home country model as an attractive one on which to base this. Where this is the case, the perceptions concerning the strengths and weaknesses of other national models become very influential. A good illustration of this is the extent of interest among firms in Europe and North America in Japanese-style 'lean production' in the 1980s and early 1990s. The pressure to build integrated operations internationally is strongest in sectors where competition is highly internationalized and where firms compete on the basis of a similar product or service across countries, such as in cars, electronics, fast-food and hotels. This pressure to take on the characteristics of firms based in other countries can be termed an 'emulation' effect and acts as a force towards convergence.

Evidence from US and German firms

The evidence from US and German MNCs illustrates these varying effects, and shows how MNCs of different nationalities adopt quite different ways of managing their international workforces. In examining this we use a combination of findings in the academic literature and our own case study work. This comprises two research projects, one of some forty German MNCs in the UK and the other of a smaller number of more in-depth case studies of US MNCs in the UK.[1] We cover the evidence relating to both the process of decision making on international HR issues and the substance of the resulting policies.

A large body of evidence testifies to the relatively centralized approach to international HRM taken by US MNCs (e.g. Hamill 1984). For example, Child et al. (2000) found that UK firms which had been acquired by a US parent were subjected to greater control from the new corporate HQ than were firms acquired by German, French or Japanese MNCs. Our own case study work on US firms broadly confirms these findings; a range of HR policies were mandated or recommended to foreign subsidiaries by corporate or divisional HQ, particularly in the area of pay and performance management. For example, most of the companies had global performance appraisal systems that applied to managerial and senior professional staff, though there was more flexibility for non-managerial and junior staff. This broad pattern of centralization can be seen as an extension to the international level of the corporate structures characteristic of firms in the USA. US firms developed formal management functions and control systems at an earlier stage than their counterparts in other countries, and have used these to exert strategic control over a range of operating units in diverse product markets and a large geographical area within the USA. This has given US firms both the technical means and experience to manage international operations in a similar way. Thus the close monitoring of HR in foreign subsidiaries can be seen as reflecting the extension of domestic structures in the US to the international level (Ferner et al. 2004).

In contrast, German firms appear be more decentralized in the way they manage their international workforces. Previous studies have shown there to be little systematic attempt to transfer the German-style practices in the areas of employee communication and training, for example (Innes and Morris 1995; Beaumont et al. 1990). Case study work on German MNCs has shed some light on the causes of this. Essentially, the export of elements of the German system to other countries is perceived by managers in German MNCs to be problematic because they rely in their domestic context on 'institutional supports' that are either different in character or missing altogether in the UK. This is exemplified in the case of training practices (see also Dickmann 2000). More specifically, in terms of corporate structures and relations between managers at different points within the firm, the hierarchical decision-making structures that operate within Germany have been seen as inappropriate to extend to the international level since they appear to be perceived as too slow to respond to rapidly evolving markets and technologies in internationally competitive sectors and too cumbersome to deal with the complexity of international operations. Consequently, more responsibility is transferred down to the level of devolved business units, as is commonly the case in UK and US MNCs (Ferner and Varul 2000a). Moreover, there is evidence that German MNCs use their UK subsidiaries as a source of organizational learning about how to operate in an international environment. This is because the UK, as a highly deregulated, open and internationalized business system, is a prime location for exposure to innovative practices. 'Vanguard' UK subsidiaries of German companies were the source of HR/IR innovation in areas such as international management development, the management of performance and reward, corporate 'culture', and work organization. For example, German MNCs involved UK subsidiary managers in the design of corporate appraisal and performance-related reward systems, and in the drafting of global corporate mission and values statements (Ferner and Varul 2000a).

US MNCs

These contrasting levels of centralization and roles for subsidiaries have very different implications for the substantive nature of international policies. The evidence of HR management in US MNCs suggests that many practices in the foreign subsidiaries are strongly influenced by the home country system. We highlight three ways in which the US influence on the management of labour shows through in US MNCs.

The first relates to the way in which management style in US MNCs is geared towards the interests of shareholders. The evidence from the case studies reveals the importance of quarterly reporting in framing the nature of personnel management. One apparent consequence of the need to ensure that quarterly profits are in line with or exceed the expectations of shareholders and analysts is the fluctuation in employment levels. Decisions on recruitment and also on laying off staff are governed in part by the movements in the company's fortunes over relatively short time-frames. Many of the UK workplaces of US-owned firms have responded to these pressures by developing a large workforce of temporary employees, often supplied through an agency, who work on very short contracts. The resulting two-tier workforce presents a number of challenges to personnel practitioners, such as the integration of permanent and temporary staff into teams. It also can produce some unintended consequences. For example, in an IT company in our study the lifting of hiring freezes led to a rush by line managers to recruit staff, with the result that the elaborate recruitment process designed to ensure that only high quality staff became permanent was sometimes bypassed (see Edwards and Ferner 2001).

A second distinctive feature of US MNCs is an emphasis on promoting workforce diversity. The development by US firms of domestic HR policies geared towards equality of opportunity and anti-discriminatory practices can be seen as reflecting the specific legal, political and demographic context in the US. One might therefore presume that pressures to extend such policies to foreign subsidiaries, operating in quite different contexts, would be limited. In fact, there is some evidence of transfer in this area. Many US MNCs issue quotas to their foreign subsidiaries on issues such as the proportion of women in management positions and monitor their performance against these targets. In addition, training on handling diversity issues for managers and especially those involved in recruitment is widespread. Some companies have extended policies developed in response to US domestic concerns to their international workforces, one illustration of which is Domestic Partners' Benefits in which those benefits that were previously only available to husbands and wives of the firm's employees are extended to unmarried heterosexual and homosexual partners (for a full discussion see Ferner et al. 2005).

A third area, and one that is well documented in the literature, is the hostility of US MNCs to unions. For decades, researchers in a range of European countries have examined the propensity of US MNCs to recognize unions and respect other forms of worker participation at the national level. While there is some variation in the findings, a majority of the studies testify to a clear anti-unionism in US firms (e.g. Geary and Roche 2001; Muller 1998). One illustration is the case of McDonalds which has gone to some lengths to avoid dealing with unions, national level works councils and even the comparatively toothless European Works Council (Royle 2000). In the UK, our case study evidence confirms the deep-rooted ideological suspicion of organized labour on the part of senior managers in US MNCs. This is conveyed to the UK subsidiaries in the form of campaigns to keep unions out or their workplaces and, in some cases, to derecognize unions where they are already recognized. However, the evidence also show the limits of central influence on this issue; in some of the cases studied local managers advised the parent that overt campaigns against unions were likely to generate ill feeling and possibly industrial action, and this advice often led to a moderation of the parent's influence. In other words, the more pragmatic approach of the British mediated the ideological opposition to unions of the Americans (Almond et al. 2003).

There is some limited evidence in US MNCs that the influence of managers in the foreign subsidiaries extends beyond merely adapting corporate policies to local requirements towards playing a part in the policy creation process. Our case studies revealed some instances of practices that were developed in the UK being incorporated into global HR policies. However, most of these represented minor adaptations to existing corporate policies, going with the grain of the firms' philosophy and management style. Moreover, the impact of such 'reverse diffusion' was also limited by some features of the US business system. For instance, attempts by UK managers in one company to get the parent firm to adopt a form of teamworking that had been developed in the UK were thwarted by the preoccupation of US managers with retaining non-unionized status; the apparent fear was that the practice of 'broad-banding' of pay grades associated with teamworking had the potential to disrupt pay relativities, thereby creating the danger of unions finding fertile ground for an organizing campaign (see Edwards et al. 2005).

In sum, there is strong evidence of a country of origin effect in US MNCs, with the relatively centralized approach to decision making on HR issues giving rise to a significant country of origin effect. However, this is both mediated by host country institutions in the way we have seen in relation to diversity and trade unions, and it is also strongly contested by actors in the foreign subsidiaries. Actors at this level, particularly managers, can strive to minimize the influence of Americans by using a range of aspects of the local environment as a resource. These are the pressures towards adaptation that we identified at the beginning of this section. In addition, there is some evidence of an 'emulation effect', albeit only of very limited force.

German MNCs

The evidence from German MNCs shows a less marked influence from HQ. For example, field studies by Dickmann (2000; 2003) and by Quintanilla (2002) suggest that German firms have rarely attempted to transfer concrete elements of their dual training system. One explanation for this is that practices in this area are dependent on institutional supports in the German context and they cannot easily be transferred to countries that lack the institutions that promote inter-firm collaboration, such as the more liberalized business system of the UK.

Another factor is also at play in the lack of direct influence of the corporate centre on substantive HR practice in UK subsidiaries. This relates to the nature of the personnel function itself within the German business environment. The institutionally regulated nature of the system, particularly with its statutory support for employee representation and codetermination, and the sector-based system of collective bargaining, has constrained the activity of personnel professionals, impeding the adoption of the innovative approach of their Anglo-Saxon counterparts. Operating within a strong framework of national labour legislation, and an associated network of national labour courts, the personnel function has become highly 'juridified' and reactive, with a strong focus on administering the minutiae of the system of codetermination. As a result, personnel functions in German MNCs have often not been in a position to offer strategic direction to international personnel management in the manner of their US counterparts. Where they have played an international role, it has tended to be narrow, bureaucratically focused and non-strategic (Ferner and Varul 2000b).

However, despite the lack of direct country-of-origin influence in personnel policies, a home-country effect is still discernible. German firms tend to adopt a longer-term timeframe in conducting HR, and a more stable set of policies involving largely incremental rather than radical changes. There are also more subtle influences. In training, for example, while they tend not to transfer substantive elements of domestic practices, German firms still appear to give a high priority to their training activities in UK subsidiaries (see Dickmann 2000; 2003), in some cases creating a general 'culture' of training.

A key area of subtle parent-country influence is that of employee representation. Many surveys (e.g. Beaumont et al. 1990; Guest and Hoque 1996) suggest that German companies are no more likely to adopt a collective approach to dealing with their employees in the UK than are MNCs of other nationalities. There are also some case studies of German firms in the UK that show an actively hostile approach to collective employee representation. Dundon (2002) for example, studied a German-owned steel plant which adopted an aggressive and intimidating attitude, derecognizing existing unions, bearing the costs of an unfair dismissal award in order to dismiss a union activist, and propagating its fiercely anti-union attitudes among the workforce. Among the 38 subsidiaries of German MNCs in our study (Ferner and Varul 1999), around half had no union recognition, and some others had only limited recognition. However, these findings of apparent anti-unionism in German MNCs have to be qualified.

First, the prevalence of non-unionism did not generally reflect an HQ initiative or culture (in contrast with US MNCs where companies tended to be deeply impregnated with ideologically driven non-union assumptions), but rather was a consequence of the devolution by head office of HR management responsibilities to subsidiary management. Thus choices on non-recognition were made relatively autonomously by local UK managers. Second, despite the frequent avoidance of collective representation, German companies in the UK were influenced by a typically German ethos of co-operation and consultation with their employees. Within the patterns of employment relations prevailing in the UK, a co-operative style entailed the use of *direct* communication with employees and the avoidance of *indirect* communication through union or other collective channels (Ferner and Varul 1999). This finding of a more subtle influence of country-of-origin factors is borne out by other research using survey evidence: Tüselmann et al. (2003) suggest that German MNCs in the UK are more likely than native firms to combine union recognition with 'high involvement' personnel management systems – as one might expect on the basis of the traditional collectively based systems of involvement within the German system. Moreover, even those German subsidiaries that reject collective employment relations are less likely than UK firms to adopt the low involvement, individualistic 'Bleak House' model.

The story in German MNCs appears to be one of a more modest country of origin effect than is evident in US MNCs. The German business system sets a tone for the operation of HR practices in the foreign subsidiaries in areas such as training and employee representation, but within this there is a high degree of autonomy for local managers to devise practices they view as appropriate for their context. Crucially, this is not just a consequence of reluctant adaptation to host country constraints, but is also a result of devolution to 'vanguard' subsidiaries as a part of an international learning process. This involved the encouragement of 'reverse diffusion' in areas such as performance-related pay and other forms of variable pay, something we can see as evidence of the emulation effect. As is the case in US MNCs, this emulation effect is constrained in its impact by institutional features of the domestic business system. For example, many German MNCs have emulated the 'Anglo-Saxon' practice of formal statements concerning the priority of delivering 'shareholder value', but this means something quite different in a context where shareholdings are highly concentrated among 'insiders' such as families and banks.

In sum, both sets of evidence – those relating to US and German MNCs – point to significant host country effects exerted by the UK business system, but also to considerable scope for innovation by MNCs. Within this scope, a strong country of origin effect was in evidence in US MNCs while a weaker effect was notable in German MNCs. Linked to this, there was a correspondingly stronger emulation effect in German than in US MNCs. In order to understand these findings more fully we need to appreciate some of the key features of each business system in more detail, and this is the aim of the following section.

Contrasting 'Market-based' and 'Relational' National Systems: The Cases of USA and Germany

The purpose of this section is to seek to explain the different patterns of behaviour that are evident in US and German MNCs through a discussion of some key aspects of the US and German business systems.

Corporate governance and management style

One of the key differences between the two countries concerns the ownership and control of firms. The US system of corporate governance has changed markedly in the last two or three decades. For much of the twentieth century, salaried managers in large firms operated largely without challenge from shareholders who, apart from 'insiders' such as founding families, were generally too small to exert much influence. This situation has been termed 'managerial control' (Roe 1994). However, in the final quarter of the twentieth century a number of developments occurred which changed this. Uppermost among these were the growth of institutional investors that assumed the clout to challenge managers to pay more attention to their interests and the growth of mergers and takeovers, particularly hostile ones, that acted as a disciplinary mechanism on managers. This represented a shift towards 'market control' and a key consequence was the pressure on managers to increase returns to shareholders. Accordingly, the 'effective corporate payout ratio', which measures the proportion of profits paid out to shareholders in the form of dividends and share 'buy-backs', rose from just over 40 per cent in the 1960s and 1970s to around 70 per cent in the 1980s and 1990s (O'Sullivan 2000). The shift in orientation towards delivering 'shareholder value' has a number of important implications for firms as employers.

One consequence relates to 'numerical flexibility'; the need to maintain financial performance each quarter in line with investors' expectations leads to firms looking to be able to vary the number of workers they employ on a regular basis. Many companies which had previously made a virtue out of guarantees of job security, such as IBM and Kodak, found themselves unable to maintain these in the face of pressure from shareholders to increase returns and with greater international competition in product markets. Incidents of collective redundancies are now commonplace in the US, and it is often argued that these are timed to send signals to shareholders that management is taking cost-cutting seriously. It is in this light that the fluctuations in employee numbers and the evidence of 'two-tier' workforces – the co-existence of a large pool of temporary workers alongside permanent staff – in US MNCs should be seen.

In contrast, the German system is characterized by a markedly different financial system. There is a much greater concentration and stability of shareholdings than in the US and relationships between managers and shareholders are closer. Most big German firms have one of the national banks or insurance companies as a large shareholder. These owners have commonly held the shares for a considerable period of time and their role is often greater than the size of their stakes would suggest since they control the proxy votes of many small shareholders and commonly have formal representation on the company board. Where a bank or insurance company is not a major shareholder, other bodies such as families, private foundations and the state often control a significant tranche of shares. VW's largest shareholder, for example, is the regional government of Saxony. The system of cross-shareholdings between firms and of inter-locking directorates provides a further contrast with the US system. This pattern of ownership is one barrier to mergers and takeovers which, despite a small number of high profile exceptions such as Vodafone's acquisition of Mannesmann, remain relatively rare in Germany.

There are some signs of change in the German corporate governance system, however, particularly among large, multinational firms. Many of this group of firms have become listed on foreign stock exchanges and have picked up some of the practices common in the US, such as managerial pay being linked to share prices, setting up 'investor relations' departments and adopting international accounting conventions (Lane 2001). These changes have occurred alongside a sharp increase in the value of dividends in German firms, which doubled in value between 1992 and 1998 (Beyer and Hassel 2001). In addition, a market for corporate control has begun to emerge as regulatory changes have made takeovers easier and the role of banks as major shareholders has diminished somewhat. The net effect has been to bring the German system more towards the Anglo–Saxon model, although the main effects on the market for corporate control have still to be seen to their full extent.

While the changes in the German system in general and in large firms in particular are highly significant, the dominant features of the German corporate governance system have exhibited a degree of resilience to pressures for change (Jürgens et al. 2000). Consequently, the influences on German firms continue to differ from those affecting their US counterparts, providing a quite different context for managing human resources. One consequence is the nature of commitments that management give employees concerning job security. Managers in Germany appear to be more favourably disposed to forming 'employment pacts' with worker representatives in which job guarantees are offered in return for agreements concerning the introduction of new technologies and new organizational practices (Streeck 1987). Arguably, the weaker pressures to meet short-term financial targets means that firms are more willing to seek to use job security, at least for core workers, as a way of ensuring that changes are accepted by employees. Similarly, the 'patient capital' that characterizes the system is a key support for firms to devote considerable resources to training (Culpepper 1999). More generally, the stability in ownership makes firms more likely to stick to long-term plans, to negotiate changes and to introduce them more gradually. Overall, differences in the corporate governance systems in the two countries help to explain why the priorities and orientation of US and German MNCs are distinct.

State regulation of the labour market

A further source of differences in management style and practices across countries is the role of the state. In the US the state has traditionally favoured the operation of free markets over state regulation, and consequently employers have been allowed considerable freedom to devise personnel policies free from direct state intervention. Compared with countries in Europe, the statutory protections enjoyed by workers relating to issues such as compulsory lay-offs are relatively weak, and state provision of health and social security provision is much more limited.

The one exception to this general picture of deregulation relates to equal rights legislation. The strength of the civil rights movement in the US gave rise to a range of measures initiated by federal and local government designed to ensure that firms do not discriminate against minorities or women. Faced with high financial penalties if they were to lose a legal case of discrimination and with the need to appeal to an ethnically mixed workforce and consumer market, US firms have developed a range of measures designed to produce a diverse workforce. It is in the light of this domestic context that the internationalization of diversity policies in US MNCs should be seen.

In the main, however, the US labour market is highly deregulated. Apart from the period following the 'New Deal' of the 1930s – which involved a more favourable legal climate for trade unions, the legacy of which can be seen in a small number of large firms in sectors like automotive and transportation – support from the state for unions has been very limited. Indeed, many US governments have clearly signalled their hostility to unions; key incidents in this regard were the government's determination to face down strikes in the immediate aftermath of the Second World War and the aggressive sacking of striking air traffic controllers by Ronald Reagan soon after he came to power in 1981. In comparative context an unusually large proportion of big firms are non-union. One variant of non-unionism in US firms is the paternalistic management style of firms like Kodak and IBM where job security and favourable pay and conditions for core workers within internal labour markets was part of an attempt to convince employees that management, not unions, would look after their interests most effectively. Jacoby (1997) has termed this 'welfare capitalism'. In another variant of non-unionism that is typical in sectors that have expanded employment in recent years such as fast-food, domestic services and security, management style is geared around strong pressures to minimize labour costs, with a preponderance of insecure, poorly paid jobs the result, with few opportunities for employee development and little meaningful consultation between management and employees. The harsh realities of work under this 'low-road' management style have been vividly captured in Schlosser's (2001) book *Fast Food Nation*. As we have seen, the ideological hostility on the part of management to trade unions is carried over into their foreign subsidiaries.

In Germany the contrast is marked once again. An important part of the post-war reconstruction of western Germany was the creation of the so-called 'dual' system of employee representation, giving employees a clear voice over a range of aspects of the employment relationship. Sectoral level collective bargaining is complemented by the system of codetermination through works councils that should exist in workplaces employing more than five employees and that have the right to negotiate over issues such as shift patterns, bonus schemes and new working practices. Arguably, these have acted both as a constraint on unilateral and drastic changes to management strategies, and as a facilitator of incremental change, since changes agreed by the works council tend to have a degree of legitimacy in the eyes of workers. They have also played a part in shaping the role of the personnel function in German firms; as we argued above, the role of operating this system domestically has tended to curtail the potential for the function to be involved in international HR strategy.

This distinctive regulatory framework does not present fully binding obligations on management. Many firms, particularly foreign ones such as McDonalds, have sought to minimise the effects of works councils and other bodies through a series of 'avoidance strategies' (Royle 1998). More generally, there is some evidence that the institutions of the dual system have declined in their coverage: the proportion of employees who work in establishments that do not have a works council has increased to nearly one half; union membership has fallen; innovative company-level collective agreements have risen, eroding the role of sectoral bargaining; and practices more commonly associated with the US or UK, such as performance-related pay, have become more widespread (Behrens and Jacoby 2004; Hassel 1999,

2002; Kurdelbusch 2002). While these changes are highly significant, they have not gone so far as to completely erode the distinctiveness of the German system of employment relations, and it is this system which helps explain the relative absence of HQ driven anti-unionism in German MNCs of the sort that is common in US MNCs.

The training system and employee development

The differing approaches to the regulation of employee representation are mirrored with contrasting approaches to training and skill development. The US approach to training is organized primarily around the economic motivations of employers and employees. It is left to firms to undertake the amount and type of training that they see as appropriate for their circumstances. There are few supportive structures established by the state or business associations that promote collaboration between employers in this respect, and consequently most training undertaken by firms tends to be firm-specific in nature (Lazonick 1998). It is also left to employees to undertake that education and training which individuals see as equipping them with transferable skills and which will yield a return to them in the form of higher future earnings (Estevez-Abe et al. 2001). For instance, further and higher education involves students or their parents paying large sums to cover the cost of their studies. This system has produced marked variations in levels of educational attainment and skills. Those able to attend the elite universities, which are well funded through high fees and donations from the business community and the alumni, graduate with a degree that is respected world-wide and is to some extent a passport to a successful career. On the other hand, there is a large pool of unskilled workers: 46 per cent of school-leavers possess no formal certificate or degree and 31 per cent receive no formal training after leaving school (Hutton 2002: 154).

From the point of view of employers, this pool of unskilled, and therefore cheap, labour is an advantage to those firms pursuing a 'low road' approach based on low wages and causalized labour, such as those referred to above in sectors like fast-food. The absence of broad skills and certified qualifications also suits firms in those areas of manufacturing relying on a 'Taylorist' form of mass production involving a rigid division of labour with operators performing a simple task over and over again. For firms in high-tech industries, however, this can be more of a problem; by undertaking significant training themselves, companies run the risk of losing skilled workers to other firms that rely on 'poaching' rather than training. Historically, many firms in sectors like electronics relied on 'internal labour markets' in which recruitment was mainly of junior staff at low levels with the acquisition of skills being tied to progression up a salary structure and a high level of security of employment. Such arrangements have proven difficult to sustain in the volatile and more competitive climate of the last two decades, however, and this has presented a problem for many US firms. In some regions and sectors, such as Silicon Valley, clusters of high-tech firms have given rise to the creation of a pool of highly skilled workers who are mobile between companies. In other areas and industries, the market-based system has been identified as a source of skills shortages, presenting a competitive problem for firms operating in international markets (Dertouzos et al. 1989). The evolving use of internal labour markets in the foreign subsidiaries of some US MNCs and the creation of a pool of easily disposable workers in many more are products of this system.

In Germany, on the other hand, there is a quite different approach to the development of skills. Instead of being left mainly to employers and employees to make individual assessments, there exist a range of extra-firm bodies that are engaged in the provision of training. Industry-based employer associations and trade unions representing workers across a sector supervise the administration of a training system that is publicly subsidised. Firms co-operate with these bodies and commit to undertake training to equip employees with a range of skills to agreed standards and qualifications (Culpepper 1999). Further education colleges are integral to the system since in many occupational groups young workers spend a portion of their working week at such a college. The monitoring of the system by industry-based bodies limits the extent of 'free-riding' by firms and ensures that employees have an incentive to gain the skills the training can provide because many of them have applicability in other firms.

This system is seen by some as meshing neatly with other aspects of the German business system – 'patient' capital, the regulated industrial relations system and the practice of 'diversified quality production' involving multiple variations of products to meet customer requirements – to produce a 'high-skills equilibrium' (Finegold 1991). There have been some indications of an erosion of the features of this system in recent years, notably the decline in the coverage and power of employers' associations and industry-based unions, while many foreign firms appear to be reluctant to engage with the system (Muller 1998). Nonetheless, its main institutions remain more or less intact and continue to provide a distinct context in which training and skill acquisition takes place. It is this system that gives rise to the 'culture of training' in German MNCs that we referred to above.

Summary and Conclusions

In this chapter we have argued that nationally established patterns of managing human resources have not disappeared in the face of globalization. These differences are likely to exist so long as the institutions that give rise to nationally distinct ways of organizing economic activity continue to vary. In this context, we have explored international management style in US and German MNCs, demonstrating that their approach to managing their international workforces is strongly shaped by their embeddedness in the domestic business systems.

In doing so we have adopted an institutionalist approach. We have seen that convergence theories cannot account for the persistence of systematic national differences in the way that firms are organized and the strategies they pursue. The cultural approach is better equipped to begin to get to grips with national differences but does not get to the root of these. A focus on institutions in a range of 'spheres' of an economic and social system, we have argued, provides a more convincing way of explaining how and why firms' strategies in general and their management style in relation to employees in particular continue to differ across borders.

We have used an institutionalist approach to show how the way that US firms are monitored in the financial markets pressurizes them into making frequent changes in the level of the workforce, and the lack of employment regulations and inter-firm mobility of labour facilitates this. In Germany, in contrast, the nature of ownership and the system of patient capital is compatible with a stable approach to labour management that changes only gradually and meshes with a consultative approach and a commitment to developing the skills of the workforce. Not only do they set quite different contexts within which firms develop personnel practices, but they also give rise to different patterns of internationalization; as firms become multinational, their orientation and strategies continue to be shaped by their origins.

This has very important implications for countries such as the UK. The UK system is both the home for large amounts of FDI and also exhibits a relatively deregulated labour market that presents relatively few institutional obstacles to foreign firms introducing novel practices. In these circumstances, MNCs have the potential to drive significant change in the nature of the national styles and traditions of personnel management. We have reviewed a number of important innovations in this respect, such as the focus on promoting diversity and marginalizing trade unions in US MNCs and the emphasis on promoting a 'culture of training' in German MNCs.

Where FDI in a country is dominated by one nationality of MNCs, one could argue that their innovations have the potential to shift prevailing norms and practices in the business system in a relatively coherent way. Perhaps the best illustration of this is Ireland, a country which has received an enormous amount of US FDI with US MNCs dominating sectors such as IT and pharmaceuticals. Thus Geary and Roche (2001) argue that US firms have introduced a range of practices into their Irish subsidiaries that are subsequently adopted by Irish firms. However, in the UK the situation is more complicated because FDI stems from a range of countries. In addition to US and German MNCs that have been the subject of this chapter, Japanese, French and Swedish MNCs also have a major presence in the UK. The logic of the argument in this chapter is that the innovations pursued by MNCs will vary according to the nationality of firms. Therefore, the growth of FDI is likely to be accompanied by the increasing heterogeneity of styles of HR management within the UK.

NOTE

1 Both of the empirical projects to which we refer involved the authors in wider research teams. The study of US MNCs, funded by ESRC award R000238350, involved

in-depth case studies of five US MNCs and nine additional case studies that were carried out in less depth. Around 170 interviews took place in the UK and US between 1999 and 2004 (see Almond et al. 2003 for more details). In the project examining German MNCs, financed by the Anglo-German Foundation for the Study of Industrial Society, some three dozen firms were examined. Where possible, interviews were carried out both in the UK operations and at German headquarters. Eighty interviews were conducted between 1996 and 1998 with a range of senior management respondents (see Ferner and Varul 1999 for further details).

REFERENCES

Almond, P., Butler, P., Clark, I., Colling, T., Edwards, T., Ferner, A. and Holden, L. 2003: *US Multinationals and the Management of Human Resources in Britain: Feedback Report to Participating Companies*, Leicester: De Montfort University.

Bae, J., Chen, S. and Lawler, J. 1998: Variations in HRM in Asian countries: MNC home country and host country effects, *International Journal of Human Resource Management*, **9**(4), 653–70.

Beaumont, P., Cressey, P. and Jacobsen, P. 1990: Key industrial relations: West German subsidiaries in Britain, *Employee Relations*, **12**(6), 3–6.

Behrens, M. and Jacoby, O. 2004: The rise of experimentalism in German collective bargaining, *British Journal of Industrial Relations*, **42**(1), 95–123.

Beyer, J. and Hassel, A. 2001: The market for corporate control and the internationalization of German firms, Paper presented at ESRC Transnational Communities Programme Conference entitled 'Multinational enterprises: Embedded organisations, transnational federations or global learning communities?', University of Warwick, 6–8 September.

Black, B. 1999: National culture and labour market flexibility, *International Journal of Human Resource Management*, **10**(4), 592–605.

Child, J., Faulkner, D. and Pitkethly, R. 2000: Foreign direct investment in the UK 1985–1994: The impact on domestic management practice, *Journal of Management Studies*, **37**(1), 141–66.

Culpepper, P. 1999: The future of the high-skill equilibrium in Germany, *Oxford Review of Economic Policy*, **15**(1), 43–59.

Dertouzos, M., Lester, R. et al. 1989: *Made in America: Regaining the Productive Edge*, Cambridge, MA: MIT Press.

Dicken, P. 2003: *Global Shift: Reshaping the Global Economic Map in the 21st Century*, London: Sage, 4th edn.

Dickmann, M. 2000: Balancing global, parent and local influences: International human resource management of German multinational companies, PhD thesis, Birkbeck College, University of London.

Dickmann, M. 2003: Implementing German HRM abroad: Desired, feasible, successful?, *International Journal of Human Resource Management*, **14**(2), 265–83.

Djelic, M. and Quack, S. 2003: Theoretical building blocks for a research agenda linking globalization and institutions, in M. Djelic and S. Quack (eds.), *Globalization and Institutions: Redefining the Rules of the Economic Game*, London: Edward Elgar.

Dundon, T. 2002: Employer opposition and union avoidance in the UK, *Industrial Relations Journal*, **33**(3), 234–45.

Edwards, T., Almond, P., Clark, I., Colling, T. and Ferner, A. (2005) Reverse diffusion in US multinationals: Barriers from the American business system, *Journal of Management Studies*, **42**(6), 1261–86, forthcoming.

Edwards, T. and Ferner, A. 2001: Wall Street, short-termism and the management of labour in US multinationals, Paper presented to conference entitled 'Multinational Enterprises: Embedded Organisations, Transnational Federations or Global Learning Communities', Warwick, 6–8 September.

Estevez-Abe, M., Iversen, T. and Soskice, D. 2001: Social protection and the formation of skills: A reinterpretation of the welfare state, in P. Hall and D. Soskice (eds.), *Varieties of Capitalism: The Institutional Foundations of Comparative Advantage*, Oxford: Oxford University Press.

Ferner, A., Almond, P., Clark, I., Colling, T., Edwards, T., Holden, L. and Muller, M. 2004: The dynamics of central control and subsidiary autonomy in the management of human resources: Case study evidence from US MNCs in the UK, *Organization Studies*, **25**(3), 363–91.

Ferner, A., Almond, P. and Colling, T. 2005: Institutional theory and the cross-national transfer of employment policy: the case of 'workforce diversity' in US multinationals, *Journal of International Business Studies*, **36**(3), 304–18.

Ferner, A. and Varul, M.Z. 1999: *The German Way? German Multinationals and the Management of Human Resources in their UK Subsidiaries*, London, Anglo-German Foundation for the Study of Industrial Society.

Ferner, A. and Varul, M.Z. 2000a: 'Vanguard' subsidiaries and the diffusion of new practices: A case study of German multinationals, *British Journal of Industrial Relations*, **38**(1), 115–40.

Ferner, A. and Varul, M.Z. 2000b: Internationalisation and the personnel function in German multinationals, *Human Resource Management Journal*, **10**(3), 79–96.

Finegold, D. 1991: Institutional incentives and skill creation: Preconditions for a high skill equilibrium, in P. Ryan (ed.), *International Comparisons of Vocational Education and Training for Intermediate Skills*, London: Falmer Press.

Geary, J. and Roche, B. 2001: Multinationals and human resource practices in Ireland: A rejection of the 'New Conformance Thesis', *International Journal of Human Resource Management*, **12**(1), 109–27.

Guest, D. and Hoque, K. 1996: National ownership and HR practices in UK greenfield sites, *Human Resource Management Journal*, **6**(4), 50–74.

Hall, P. and Soskice, D. (eds.) 2001: *Varieties of Capitalism: The Institutional Foundations of Comparative Advantage*, Oxford: Oxford University Press.

Hamill, J. 1984: Labour relations decision making in multinational corporations, *Industrial Relations Journal*, **15**(2), 30–4.

Hassel, A. 1999: The erosion of the German system of industrial relations, *British Journal of Industrial Relations*, **37**(3), 483–505.

Hassel, A. 2002: The erosion continues: Reply, *British Journal of Industrial Relations*, **40**(2), 309–17.

Hofstede, G. 1980: *Culture's Consequences*, Beverly Hills, CA: Sage Publications.

Hofstede, G. 2002: Dimensions do not exist: A reply to Brendan McSweeney, *Human Relations*, **55**(11), 1355–61.

Hutton, W. 2002: *The World We're In*, London: Little Brown.

Innes, E. and Morris, J. 1995: Multinational corporations and employee relations: Continuity and change in a mature industrial region, *Employee Relations*, **17**(6), 25–42.

Jacoby, S. 1997: *Modern Manors: Welfare Capitalism since the New Deal*, Princeton: Princeton University Press.

Jürgens, U., Naumann, K. and Rupp, J. 2000: Shareholder value in an adverse environment: The German case, *Economy and Society*, **29**(1), 54–79.

Kaplinsky, R. 2001: Spreading the gains from globalisation: What can be learned from value chain analysis, IDS Working Paper No. 110.

Kerr, C., Dunlop, J., Harbison, F. and Myers, C. 1960: *Industrialism and Industrial Man*, Cambridge, MA: Harvard University Press.

Kurdelbusch, A. 2002: Multinationals and the rise of variable pay in Germany, *European Journal of Industrial Relations*, **8**(3), 325–49.

Lane, C. 2001: The emergence of German transnational companies: A theoretical analysis and empirical study of the globalisation process, in G. Morgan, P. Kristensen and R. Whitley (eds.), *The Multinational Firm: Organizing across Institutional Divides*, Oxford: Oxford University Press.

Lash, S. and Urry, J. 1987: *The End of Organized Capitalism*, Cambridge: Polity Press.

Lazonick, W. 1998: Organizational learning and international competition, in J. Michie and J. Grieve Smith (eds.), *Globalization, Growth, and Governance*, Oxford: Oxford University Press, 204–38.

Lehrer, M. 2001: Macro-varieties of capitalism and micro-varieties of strategic management in European airlines, in P. Hall and D. Soskice (eds.), *Varieties of Capitalism: The Institutional Foundations of Comparative Advantage*, Oxford: Oxford University Press.

McSweeney, B. 2002: Hofstede's model of national cultural differences and their consequences: A triumph of faith – a failure of analysis, *Human Relations*, **55**(1), 89–118.

Muller, M. 1998: Human resource and industrial relations practices of UK and US multinationals in Germany, *International Journal of Human Resource Management*, **9**(4), 732–49.

Ngo, H., Turban, D., Lau, C. and Lui, S. 1998: Human resource practices and firm performance of multinational corporations: Influences of country origin, *International Journal of Human Resource Management*, **9**(4), 632–52.

ONS (Office for National Statistics) 2004: Net foreign direct investment in the UK analysed by area and main country, www.statistics.gov.uk/Statbase/Expodata/Spreadsheets/D7168.xls

O'Sullivan, M. 2000: *Contests for Corporate Control: Corporate Governance and Economic Performance in the United States and Germany*, Oxford: Oxford University Press.

Piore, M. and Sabel, C. 1984: *The Second Industrial Divide*, New York: Basic Books.

Quintanilla, J. 2002: *Dirección de Recursos Humanos en Empresas Multinacionales. Las subsidiarias al descubierto*. Madrid: Prentice Hall.

Roe, M. 1994: *Strong Managers, Weak Owners: The Political Roots of American Corporate Finance*, Princeton: Princeton University Press.

Royle, T. 1998: Avoidance strategies and the German system of co-determination, *International Journal of Human Resource Management*, **9**(6), 1026–47.

Royle, T. 2000: *Working for McDonald's in Europe: The Unequal Struggle?*, London: Routledge.

Schlosser, E. 2001: *Fast Food Nation: What the All-American Meal Is Doing to the World*, London: Penguin.

Streeck, W. 1987: The uncertainty of management in the management of uncertainty, *Work, Employment and Society*, **1**(1), 281–308.

Thelen, K. 2001: Varieties of labor politics in developed democracies, in P. Hall and D. Soskice (eds.), *Varieties of Capitalism: The Institutional Foundations of Comparative Advantage*, Oxford: Oxford University Press.

Traxler, F., Blaschke, S. and Kittel, B. 2001: *National Labour Relations in Internationalized Markets*, Oxford: Oxford University Press.

Tüselmann, H.-J., McDonald, F. and Heise, A. 2003: Employee relations in German multi-nationals in an Anglo-Saxon setting: Toward a Germanic version of the Anglo-Saxon approach?, *European Journal of Industrial Relations*, **9**(3), 327–49.

United Nations. 2003: *World Investment Report: FDI Policies for Development – National and International Perspectives*, New York: United Nations.

Warhurst, R. 1995: Converging on HRM? Change and continuity in European airlines' industrial relations, *European Journal of Industrial Relations*, **1**(2), 259–74.

Whitley, R. 1999: *Divergent Capitalisms: The Social Structuring and Change of Business Systems*. Oxford: Oxford University Press.

CHAPTER FOUR

Managing Human Resources in the Networked Organization

Trevor Colling

Business growth for much of the twentieth century has been achieved through the development of bureaucratic and integrated corporations. Subcontracting and alliances between small firms, which characterized the UK's early industrial development, appeared to have been consigned to history. As capital ownership became more and more concentrated and as plant sizes grew, 'the visible hand of management replaced the . . . invisible hand of market forces' (Chandler 1977: 1). Organizing production in these larger enterprises required hierarchies of management capable of passing information and directions from executive level to the shopfloor. This parallel growth of capitalist development and bureaucracy seemed so inevitable that they were considered practically synonymous. As Blau put it, 'strange as it may seem, the free-enterprise system fosters the development of bureaucracy in the government, in private companies, and in unions' (1966: 38). Commonly, the 'organization' has been counterposed to market relations and associated with the imposition of order and certainty on economic and social relations; 'deliberately calculated means are adopted in the pursuit of consciously selected ends' (Watson 1987: 168).

As one of the least predictable business transactions, the management of the employment relationship was subject to the extension of bureaucratic rules within organizations; research questions tended to revolve only around which kind of bureaucracy (see Gouldner 1964). This quest for order was evident in attempts to structure labour markets. Government intervention or multi-employer agreements could provide external co-ordination, to create common terms across organizations for occupational or professional workforces. In relatively decentralized economies though, like the United Kingdom, there was a focus on the internal labour market (ILM) operated at firm level. ILMs vary in terms of their scope and depth (for a summary of the literature in this area, see Claydon 2004) but they are distinguished by three organizational preferences. First and foremost, employment needs are met from internal sources rather than external ones. Existing employees receive training to enable them to fulfil management, technical and professional roles in preference to importing such skills from the external market. Second, the labour market tends to be bounded, relatively well defined and structured. Managers and employees share a sense of the boundaries of employment structures; where their current role fits, and the opportunities for mobility and development. Finally, these structures are administered through organizational norms that are clearly codified and articulated. Each of these requirements generates tasks for an established human resource function; an expert role in administering an ordered employment system. Writing on the United States, Jacoby (1997) has emphasized the historic centrality of ILM approaches to 'welfare capitalist' companies, which he identifies as the pioneers of strategic human resource management. This focus has come to predominate the HR literature and is associated strongly with the extension of HRM philosophies, including the emphasis on the resource-based view of the firm.

Any such consensus is now open to question (Purcell 1998; Rubery et al. 2002). Bureaucracies are being fragmented deliberately in the attempt to limit risk within the firm and to develop tighter accounting and performance controls. Joint ventures and strategic alliances produce economies of scale without the complications attending full company mergers. In project environments, such as large 'roll-outs' of new information technology and complex engineering construction, consortium bidding for projects by groups of companies offers similar benefits. Under public–private partnerships, new hospitals, schools and prisons are built increasingly by private companies and leased back to public authorities with various aspects of buildings and estates management. Within organizations, franchises permit low-risk growth by requiring investment from franchisees bound by organizational norms. Devolution to strategic business units, sometimes misleadingly termed 'autonomous businesses', has similar effects. Particular services such as IT helpdesks are often 'in-sourced' now, rather than developed internally. Others previously delivered 'in-house' are increasingly 'outsourced', transferred to specialist third-party suppliers and delivered subject to contracts.

The novelty of this organizational innovation is easily overstated; sub-contracting has always been a feature of capitalist growth, for example. Nevertheless, the development of so-called virtual, networked, or extended organizations undoubtedly carries important ramifications for the employment relationship and for those in the personnel/HR function charged with overseeing it. Employment relations in these settings are 'externalized'. This process is most apparent under outsourcing arrangements, where employees are 'transferred' to a third party, beyond the boundaries of their original employer. Where such a process has not taken place, and employees are recruited directly into a 'networked' environment, externalization is manifest in the amalgam of inter-firm influences on the employment relationship. In one catering firm studied by Colling (2003: 380), for example, representatives from client companies were involved in discussions about pay awards for the contractor's employees, and since the catering services were delivered on the client's premises, they retained a role too in workplace discipline (for similar examples, see Rubery et al. 2003).

For some time, the model of the 'flexible firm' (Atkinson 1986) provided a fig leaf, obscuring the challenge of all of this to HRM practitioners. So long as change affected only 'peripheral' employees, their externalization may facilitate deepened management consideration of the remaining 'core' workforce, in the way envisaged by the burgeoning HRM literature. Thus, for much of the 1980s, 'contracting-out' was aimed only at ancillary or support functions, such as cleaning, catering, and estates maintenance, and organizationals were able to 'stick to their knitting' as the consultants put it (Peters and Waterman 1982). Gradually, though, these core-periphery distinctions have become harder to draw, as more central groups of staff have been drawn into this greater variety of 'networked' relations. Public–private partnerships often involve key professional employees, like teachers, health specialists, and air traffic controllers, either working directly for private sector employ-ers or alongside them. In the private sector, consortium-based bidding in sectors like engineering and construction means that projects are staffed by blends of highly skilled professional and technical staff from different companies (see Colling and Clark 2002).

Much of the management literature on networked organization has a unitarist feel, a presumption that everyone benefits from the organizational flexibility being sought; 'it is now perceived as a route to improve business performance and com-petitive strength' (Moran, cited in Oates 1998: 6). Often though, 'the employment relationship all but disappears' in these discussions (Earnshaw et al. 2002: 5). Externalization disrupts ordered employment relations based on administrative systems within the firm, since networks are, 'more readily decomposable or redefinable than the fixed assets of hierarchies' (Powell, cited in Sennett 1998: 23). This might enhance career prospects for employees, opening opportunities to gain experience in a greater variety of positions beyond the boundaries of the firm. To return to the contract caterer discussed above, for example, chefs and kitchen staff were able to move frequently between different contract sites as new opportunities arose in more complex or prestigious catering operations (Colling 2003). Many commentators, though, draw more negative inferences. The attraction of networks, it is said, lies primarily in the potential to vary labour costs and to defray risk asso-ciated with maintaining employment security in the context of volatile demand. Citing Holmes, Blyton and Turnbull (2004: 82) suggest that, 'sub-contracting can be used to accommodate not only structural and temporal instability in product markets, but also establish different levels of "minimum efficient scale", and respond to the structure and nature of different labour supply conditions'.

Current controversies about 'offshoring' illustrate the potential employment impact of organizational innovation. The externalization of support functions accomplished so far within national borders has now attained an international dimension. Service provision through call centres, for example, has been transferred to cheaper loca-tions abroad. Offshoring of this kind has been at the centre of policy debate in the US and the UK (see Department of Trade and Industry 2004), where it is expected to displace up to 200,000 jobs over the next 5 years in the financial services sector alone (Scullion 2004). Consequences in terms of process are equally important as these outcomes. Where firms have been famed previously for their co-ordinated approach to employment, externalization will generate shocks to the psychological contract between the firm and its employees, which may well foster adverse reactions. Witness here the phenomenon of Marks and Spencer, previously an icon of strategic human resource management, being taken to an employment tribunal by employees alleging fundamental breaches of their employment rights during outsourcing (Mesure 2004: 37). Difficulties arise because it is unclear which management agents are responsible for which parts of the employment relationship. At what point in an outsourcing process does the transferee (the body to whom the function is being transferred) assume management responsibility from the trans-feror (the body transferring the function)? In environments where staff from dif-ferent organizations work alongside each other, who has the authority to direct and discipline employees? Quite fundamental issues such as the day-to-day exercise of control and duties through the contract of employment come into question; in short, 'who is the employer?' (Earnshaw et al. 2002; also see Deakin 2001). Disrupted lines of accountability carry key consequences for the fortunes of the HR function itself. To the extent that ordered labour markets provide an obvious rationale for a well-resourced and influential HR function, the re-entry of market relations may well preclude any such strategic roles. Indeed, HR services are themselves frequently the target of insourcing and outsourcing of various kinds (see Chapter 1).

This chapter examines these important issues. It focuses on outsourcing or contracting-out under which key functions or support services are transferred to third-party firms to deliver via contract. It is not the only form of networked organ-ization, or the most novel, but such a focus is justified by the fact that it is its simplest manifestation and as such is often an elementary building block in other forms. In building new hospitals and schools, public–private partnerships may grow through entirely new investment and employment but they may also involve out-sourcing and employment transfers where they replace existing facilities (UNISON 2003).

The first section explores some of the evidence indicating the spread of out-sourcing. In theory, at least, the consequences for employment are not fixed. Much depends on the dynamic of contracting processes and the kinds of relations established between firms. These in turn are influenced by the regulatory context governing business and employment relations. In the UK, the motives of buyers engaged in outsourcing tend to perpetuate low-trust relationships between firms, with important ramifications for employment and the effective operation of the HR function. These themes are explored in the closing sections, using an illus-trative case study of outsourcing in the IT industry.

Incidence and Character of the Networked Organization

When this chapter was first published, in the preceding edition of this book, con-troversy was raging about the extent of organizational change. Prophetic voices,

Table 4.1 Workforce jobs by manufacturing industry (Man) and financial and business services (FBS), December 1979–December 2003 (millions)

	1979	1982	1985	1988	1991	1994	1997	2000	2003
Man	7,027	5,582	5,312	5,303	4,635	4,392	4,523	4,151	3,689
FBS	2,980	3,019	3,499	4,120	4,336	4,593	5,081	5,674	5,851

Source: Office for National Statistics (2004).

speaking about the emergence of the 'boundaryless' firm, vied for space in journals with more sceptical ones, asserting the durability of hierarchical and bureaucratic forms. A few years on, something can be taken from both propositions.

First, there is now very little doubt about the rapid extension of outsourcing. Table 4.1 indicates growth in employment in financial and business services. The sector is of interest because it covers firms active in outsourcing markets. Trends here can be backlit by considering them against those in manufacturing industry. At the end of the 1970s, the financial and business services sector was dwarfed by manufacturing industry, which employed twice as many people. By 2003, that position had almost reversed, with business services employing nearly twice as many people as manufacturing.

These figures are not conclusive in themselves. They include financial services (such as banking, insurance and investments), which have also grown through the period. Corroborating evidence is available, however. When it was first established in 1956, members of the Management Consultancies Association reported a combined turnover of £6 million and employed 1,500 people. Now the turnover is around £6 billion and around 40,000 people are offering their advice services to businesses (Caulkin 2004: 1). Outsourcing is closely implicated in these trends. Advice on the issue is providing a rich vein of fee income across all sectors, now accounting for around one-half of the annual fee growth and around one-third of income overall. Public sector employers have proved to be particularly voracious consumers of such advice. They accounted for 13 per cent of consultancy income in 2003, at a time when fees from private sector sources were actually in decline. During the 1980s, the number of business transfers across the European Union member states doubled every 3 years (Cooke et al. 2004: 276). Research in the late 1990s found take up extending to new parts of the economy, 'sectors like metal casting, pharmaceuticals, and printing, which did not outsource in the earlier periods, have now been doing so' (Croot in Oates 1998: 3). In the Workplace Employee Relations Survey, 90 per cent of organizations subcontracted one or more functions, with slightly more companies in the private sector doing so than in the public sector (Cully et al. 1999: 34). Manual or ancillary services (such as buildings and grounds maintenance, cleaning and transport) were most likely to be outsourced but relatively skilled tasks including training were also apparent. Moreover, the survey confirms the growth of the practice; 28 per cent of firms reported having outsourced a function in the preceding 5 years that had been performed previously by direct labour (ibid.).

Outsourcing, then, is making a significant contribution to the growth of net-worked organizations. But it does not follow necessarily that hierarchy is in decline. As Sennett notes (1998: 56), 'challenging the old bureaucratic order has not meant less institutional structure. The structure remains in the forces driving units or indi-viduals to achieve; what is left open is how to do so.' Work in the networked organ-ization is likely to be structured by the contracts between the respective businesses. Indeed, to the extent that these are closely specified, work may well be still more circumscribed than previously. What matters, is the nature of the interaction between businesses and how this conditions work organization and employment relations.

Character of networks

Theoretically, a range of contractual relationships is possible with variations fostering different implications for employment within them (see Felstead 1993; Sako 1992). At one end of the spectrum, low–trust or 'distanced' relationships will be evidenced by an emphasis on competition between potential providers, the close scrutiny of contractual terms, and the predominance of cost and risk issues in bid-evaluation. Contracts are allocated primarily on the basis of price and security of tenure is weak, since buyers prefer short contract periods to allow for frequent market testing. At the other extreme, 'engaged' models infer a different set of inter-firm relationships characterized by some degree of mutual dependency (Beaumont et al. 1996). Market mechanisms are less important and may be virtually absent where buyers select firms as 'preferred suppliers'. A broader range of attributes than price alone will be con-sidered during the evaluation of bids – though this may still be important. Contracts are augmented by joint approaches to strategic and operational issues manifest in anything from mixed project teams to shared equity arrangements. As bureaucratic and financial ties are increased, the formal content of contracts diminishes, is less prescriptive in nature, and is relied upon less in day-to-day management.

Between these two poles lie a variety of motives for proceeding towards extern-alization. Objectives can be mixed and are rarely proclaimed publicly, but five key reasons for outsourcing can be deduced (Harrison and Kelley 1993; Hunter 1998). First, 'capacity subcontracting' refers to situations where demand is charac-terized by extreme peaks and troughs. Where it outstrips the capacity of in–house resources but only for short periods, additional production will be sourced through external suppliers so as to obviate the expense of incurring fixed employment costs. Second, 'specialization subcontracting' may be adopted where the complexity of services required increases beyond the capacity of the in–house function, as it stands. Professional and technical services will be covered primarily by these sorts of arrangements. Third, 'power subcontracting' refers to attempts to bypass internal obstacles to change by rendering these 'someone else's problem' (Atkinson 1986). Outsourcing has been threatened or used to weaken employee resistance to restructuring in the public sector, for example. Early instances of privatization, involving refuse collection in the London Boroughs were explicit attempts to restructure industrial relations (Ascher 1987; Colling 1995). Fourth, though often related to 'power subcontracting', cost-reduction can be a distinct motive. Vendor firms are able to realize capital savings unavailable to buyers; large catering firms, for example, extract preferential purchase terms from food producers and retailers and may undertake to pass part of the savings on to the buyer. In labour intensive services, though, wage and employment costs are a primary target. Finally, fads and fashion undoubtedly play a part and many have begun to point to an 'outsourcing bandwagon' (Lonsdale and Cox 1998: 55). Consultants have played important roles in spreading the practice, persuading clients of the merits of outsourcing by referring to the promise of cost savings and undertaking to take fees only as a proportion of savings achieved.

Regulatory context

Choices between these options are not made in a vacuum, they are conditioned by 'existing social, structural and cultural constraints and facilitators' (Lane and Bachman 1994: 3). Preferred contractual models are promoted actively in some countries (Lane and Bachman 1997: 243) but, in the UK, minimal state involvement in commercial and employment practice has long been the norm, permitting a focus on power and cost reduction motives.

Commercial law in the UK provides a relatively permissive framework for outsourcing activities. These are subject to various statutory influences, including the Restrictive Trade Practices Act 1976; Supply of Goods and Services Act 1982; the Unfair Contract Terms Act 1977; the Contracts Applicable Law Act 1990; and the various mechanisms through which public sector contracting are governed (Arnold 1995). Statutes set elementary standards in terms of fair dealing but stop well short of advocating or requiring particular contractual models. Rather, law has developed with the priority of protecting individuals from the unreasonable use of power by the state. The rights of individuals to contract as they see fit has been interpreted as a critical index of such freedom and firms have been left to arrive at voluntary agreements with suppliers and business partners. Consequently, standard terms are less common in the UK than elsewhere. Reflecting specifically on outsourcing contracts for IT services, Arnold notes that, 'differences of style . . . are great' (Arnold 1995: 18).

Neither has employment law provided particularly powerful standards or requirements. Historically, the rights of employees provided no barriers at all to the disposal of businesses, or parts of them. Under common law, employment contracts simply ended with the sale of the business (*Nokes v Doncaster Amalgamated Collieries Ltd* [1940] AC 1014 HL). New owners were therefore free to decide whether or not to take on existing employees and to determine the terms and conditions on which they did so.

More recently, European law has encroached upon this absolute freedom. The Acquired Rights Directive (ARD) was developed explicitly in recognition of the growth of the networked organization: 'economic trends are bringing in their wake both at a national and Community level changes in the structure of undertakings, through transfer of undertakings, businesses or parts of businesses to other employers' (preamble to the ARD, quoted in McMullen 1996: 287). It seeks to protect the terms and conditions of staff affected by business transfers. For precisely this reason, UK governments during the 1980s and 1990s were unenthusiastic about the measure, viewing it as alien to the UK's legal tradition and antithetical to the spirit of entrepreneurialism they were seeking to instil (see Hardy 2000). In particular, the directive potentially constrained reform of public sector industrial relations through the use of externalization strategies, including Compulsory Competitive Tendering (CCT) and market testing. When transposing the Directive into UK law, through the Transfer of Undertakings (Protection of Employment) Regulations 1981 (TUPE), the government amplified widely held beliefs that the Directive did not apply to outsourcing in general and the less widely held view that the public sector was excluded (no such exclusion is apparent in the ARD, or subsequently since 1993 in TUPE).

The ARD has become increasingly central to outsourcing processes in the UK, largely as a consequence of cumulative judicial activism and the statutory reform this has required. Because these rights stem from a Directive, there is a require-ment upon courts to interpret them purposively; that is, to ensure their effective operation in every circumstance where there is no compelling reason not to do so. The European Court of Justice has made it clear that the ARD and TUPE applies to outsourcing, thereby binding the decision making of UK courts on the issue through case authority. Jurisprudence has since been consolidated in revisions to the Directive in 1998 and 2001. In September 2001, the government announced plans for revisions to TUPE to comply with the new directive, and consultation on the issue was concluded in February 2003.

At the time of writing in Autumn 2004, new general regulations have yet to surface but changes have been implemented separately for the large public sector workforces so ravaged by contracting-out in preceding decades (see Davies 2004). For example, important reforms in local government were introduced in 2001 and 2003. Authorities were permitted to consider the employment consequences of contracting out and to extend to workforces protections beyond those avail-able under TUPE, as extant (Local Government Best Value [Exclusion of Non-Commercial Considerations] Order 2001). Continuing budgetary pressures place limits on the inclination to do so, but some 'TUPE-Plus' contracts have sub-sequently been agreed (see UNISON 2003). Since 2003, The Best Value Code of Practice on Workforce Matters has reduced the scope for 'two-tier' workforces; that is the division emerging post-transfer between staff retaining TUPE protected contracts and newly recruited staff lacking those protections. Under the code, new employees must be offered terms and conditions which are 'overall no less favour-able' than those of transferred employees (on public sector transfers in general, see

Bach 2002; Fishbacher and Beaumont 2003; Grimshaw et al. 2002; Hebson et al. 2003).

The TUPE regulations carry deep consequences for employment and employee relations affected by the outsourcing process. They place upon employers a duty to consult employee representatives about the fact that a relevant transfer is to take place; approximately when; the reasons for it; the legal, economic and social implications for affected employees; and the measures that are envisaged to take place in connection with the transfer. As on other similar issues, consultation must be with a view to seeking agreement to any proposed changes. They also confer some degree of employment security, since dismissal or redundancy related to transfer is automatically unfair. Finally, the contractual rights of individual employees are protected. Continuity of employment is protected by passing to the transferee all obligations carried through the contract of employment by the transferor immediately before the transfer. The scope for new employers to vary terms and conditions for transferred staff is constrained correspondingly. Dismissal of an employee who refused to sign a new contract 2 years after the relevant outsource has been found automatically unfair and variation may be invalid even where the employee agrees to it (*Taylor v Connex South Eastern Ltd* [2000] WL 1480025 EAT/1243/99; *Martin v South Bank University* [2004] ECJ IRLR 74). Finally, rights to union representation are preserved; where the transferor has recognized a union, '(it) shall be deemed to be recognised by the transferee to the same extent' (TUPE 1981 s. 9(2)(a)) and the transferee is similarly bound by any collective agreements in existence.

In the context of minimal legislative intervention overall, however, it is important to acknowledge the limitations of this single element. Important swathes of outsourcing, particularly in the public sector, proceeded unchecked as a consequence of that confusion over the scope of the directive. Though the trend of jurisprudence tends now to be towards purposive application, business transfers outside of some public sector operations are still not covered automatically. Under the directive, protections apply where there is the transfer of an 'economic entity which retains its identity'. Each case must be judged on its facts, according to a series of interlocking and complex tests:

> including the type of undertaking or business, whether or not the business's tangible assets, such as buildings and moveable property, are transferred, the value of its intangible assets at the time of the transfer, whether or not the majority of its employees are taken over by the new employer, whether or not its customers are transferred, and the degree of similarity between the activities carried on before and after the transfer and the period, if any for which those activities were suspended. (*Spijkers v Gebroeders Benedik Abbatoir CV* [1986] 2 CMLR 296, at para. 13)

Numerous stratagems are available to companies wishing to loosen the restrictions required by the directive and consultancy advice on which of these to use and how to implement them is plentiful. Even where TUPE has formally been applied, it often does little to prevent changes to terms and conditions of employment. Despite the blanket application of the regulations to transfers in the civil service, one-third of civil service staff affected during the 1990s reported that changes had been made to their terms and conditions of employment (Cooke et al. 2004: 277). This is because TUPE does not prevent variation of terms and conditions *per se*, as is often assumed. That would be to offer protections over and above those available to workforces more generally. Only those changes imposed *as a consequence of the transfer* are unlawful. Employers may seek the consent of employees prior to transfer, possibly making their acceptance a condition of the contract proceeding. In this way, the new terms and conditions become the protected ones since these were in operation 'immediately before the transfer' (see Cooke et al. 2004: 279). Dismissals are still possible too, where they are due to economic, technical or organizational (ETO) reasons not related to the transfer. This diminishes the force of the regulations in practice since it provides a justification that employers can present within the organization, which is likely to be exposed only in the limited number of cases where employees choose to challenge it at law (see *Wilson and others v St Helens Borough Council, British Fuels Ltd v Baxendale and Meade* [1998] IRLR 706 HL). Finally, and perhaps most important of all, TUPE protections are relatively narrow, limited primarily to contractual terms alone. Cooke et al. (2004: 277) note, 'it is likely that workers' experiences in areas such as work reorganization, skill levels, work intensification, career structure, and opportunities for retraining may all have been substantially altered'.

In short, within the UK, there are few statutory incentives to high-trust, engaged contracting models. Underlying the variety of contractual expression is a common objective of capturing all aspects of commercial relations in enforceable terms, rather than leaving them to trust: 'the differences in wording that account for the differences of length are the result in bespoke contracts both of leaving nothing to implication and of spelling out all obligations' (Arnold 1995: 17). Strategic considerations relating to capacity or innovation tend to lag some way behind the objectives of intensified budgetary control. Nearly half of all companies (48 per cent) embark on subcontracting processes to cut costs (Cully et al. 1999: 36): 'the primary reason given to explain the outsourcing trend is simple: cost efficiency' (Lacity and Hirscheim 1995: 13). Even this may understate the case since it appears that organizations realize cost-savings even where this has not been an explicit or primary objective. More than 50 per cent of organizations outsourcing information technology services cut costs as a result and the figure is even higher (83 per cent) in the public sector (Pritchard 1998: 14).

Challenges of the Networked Organization

Important consequences follow for the human resources function. General emphasis on cost reduction is likely to impact directly on the employment contract. Even in functions that are relatively capital intensive, like information technology, employment costs are a critical controllable budget. One-third of local authorities delivering Best Value projects reported workforce reductions already but two-thirds expected to make them in the future (Geddes 2001: 503). In this section, we evaluate the challenges posed to the human resource function by processes of this kind. The principal argument is that these are substantial and not easily overcome by normative models of good practice predicated on ordered labour markets, or at least the agreed need to order them. In the context of quests for cost savings, externalization puts the HR function in an unenviable position and weakens its ability to pursue its traditional concerns.

All other things being equal, human resource professionals are likely to have a series of priorities. Their traditional welfare role means that they may be expected to support employees through the process and to answer their concerns. Effective consultation, required by TUPE, depends upon the early identification of those employees likely to be affected. Information needs to be gathered on the outsourcing process and on any proposals for change and imparted straightforwardly to employees: 'the whole emphasis should be on the provision of maximum information to reduce, if not wholly eliminate, the fear of the unknown' (Institute of Personnel and Development 1998: 12). Critically, with one eye trained on the TUPE legislation, advice generally emphasizes the need to prepare carefully for any changes to terms and conditions or to headcount.

The outsourcing context just discussed generates three key tensions within those general principles which, at the extreme, may compromise even such modest models of good practice. First, and most obviously it is likely to disturb employee morale. The process of 'externalization' may well induce a sense of rejection among staff, since the firm is effectively telling them that their skills are no longer required directly. Any change in the identity of the employer not initiated by them may also produce a sense of powerlessness and perceived threats to their terms and conditions of employment may be well founded. Arguably, effecting change in such a context should not be an insurmountable challenge. Initiation, variation and termination of employment contracts are 'bread and butter' to the HR professional, even where the overall tone of the discussion is negative rather than positive.

A second element heightens the challenge, however, in that the component tasks will be shared by at least two organizations; the transferor and the transferee and, possibly, other potential vendors that have been involved in the tendering process prior to selection of the transferee. This is something often overlooked in models of good practice which tend to focus on human resource practice in one organization or the other. Advice from the main professional body, for example, 'deals mainly with the role of the client organization' (Institute of Personnel and Development 1998: 1) but the information needed to reassure employees necessarily will be pooled. The transferor organization can share its information with employees on the process and the reasons for it, since these decisions fall primarily to them. In most cases, though, future developments in the employment relationship will be within the bailiwick of the transferee. At the very least, there is a need to co-ordinate the dissemination of this information but this may not be possible. Outsourcing is often a complex process of negotiation. Important outcomes influencing employment decisions may not be anticipated until quite late in the process. Where distanced or arm's-length relations prevail, organizations may not be willing at an early stage to share information. A transferee organization, for example, may not want to discuss in detail their plans for operating the putative contract for fear that they will be shared with competitors or simply adopted by the transferor.

Finally, the discussion so far presupposes that the HR function plays a prominent role in the outsourcing process and subsequent to it but this may not be the case. There is a tension within outsourcing processes between the needs of the business and the needs of employees. Where the emphasis on varying labour costs is particularly marked, business needs will tend to eclipse those of employees to a considerable extent. Key issues are likely to include how capital assets are divided; the services required and responsibilities for resourcing them; and the level of reward and liability payable subject to contract performance. These are not necessarily for the HR department to determine and 'much of detailed administration and contract law that is involved is not specific to the personnel function' (Institute of Personnel and Development 1998: 1). Further, the logic of outsourcing, and of the networked organization in general, is to identify, isolate and control costs. Particularly where price is a central consideration, overhead costs will be a primary target in bid evaluation producing pressure to minimize the costs of support functions. As Legge notes of personnel management in 'financial controllers', 'a personnel function would be likely to be defined as overhead and, as such, a waste to be eliminated . . . If this approach to leanness is adopted, it is difficult to see any significant, proactive role for personnel specialists' (Legge 2000: 63; see also Armstrong 1989). Normative arguments supporting a substantial role for HR can certainly be advanced; TUPE might generate expedient pressures at the very least. But practical accounting pressures arising from the outsourcing context may diminish the size and authority of HR within organizations, undermining further any capacity for the complex inter-organizational liaison required.

Examining the issues in practice: strategic outsourcing in IT

This section examines some of these issues through the experience of one critical case of outsourcing information technology (IT) functions.[1] There are good reasons for such a focus. Though there is a vast literature on IT outsourcing, most of it looks at the technological implications and relatively little is known about the employment issues. It also offers the opportunity to explore the impact of outsourcing upon skilled professionals, rather than the ancillary and support functions covered often in outsourcing studies. A different contracting dynamic might be expected here, based on the transfer of specialist knowledge, rather than the cost-reduction strategies that usually predominate, and this may generate more positive consequences for employment: 'IT specialists . . . may well ultimately relish the idea of moving from a department where they are by and large peripheral to the main business to an organization where they are surrounded and understood by fellow IT professionals' (Oates 1998: 135).

The transferor company in this case, Pharma Co, is a major multinational involved in drugs research and manufacture. It has a presence on several sites in the UK, including a large IT function. Historically, parts of the function played an integral role in the company's research activities. Highly skilled programmers worked closely with research scientists to devise proprietary software and maintain secure databases. IT Co, the transferee company, has shifted substantially from the manufacture of computer products into business services worldwide, including outsourcing. The Global Services division has recently become the largest single business stream, accounting for 40 per cent of the company's business and about half of the UK workforce.

Discussion over the shape and boundaries of the outsourced workforce, how these various functions were to be divided between the two companies, developed throughout 2000 and the transfer took place in February 2001. These discussions provided an important backdrop to the way that changes in the employment relationship were planned. On the one hand, retaining influence over the function became a critical concern for Pharma Co and was manifest eventually in the preference for keeping some elements in-house. This was in tension to some extent with IT Co's ultimate commercial objectives. Clients are offered several levels of service, help desk support to on-site system maintenance and, ultimately, integration of client databases. In this ideal latter scenario, mainframe operations are transferred to server based ones that can be managed remotely using IT Co technology from IT Co sites. Benefits to IT Co include stability; since clients become more technologically reliant they will sign up again at contract renewal because, as one manager put it, 'they are so *bolted in* to your way of doing things' (emphasis added). Integration also offers scope to realize economies of scale. Sites from all over the world can be maintained using a 'follow the sun' strategy. Systems are usually running during the daylight office hours, so most maintenance work is done in the evening and at night. Shifting this work between time zones on a daily cycle permits a 24-hour service at lower cost by, for example, eliminating the need for premium payments for night working.

Ultimately, this scenario was not achieved in Pharma Co. Price and control became key considerations in the award of the contract and conditioned markedly low-trust relations between the companies. IT Co became the preferred supplier only after another previously selected company had withdrawn. Pharma Co's requirement that the contract price remain at the level previously agreed was matched then by IT Co's insistence that the division of responsibilities should be redrawn; 'IT Co then hooked out loads of stuff out of the bid, some of which should have stayed in, so that they could achieve the price that Pharma Co would go for.' This had the effect of lowering the level of service IT Co provided to Pharma Co and the degree of integration between the firms. Important groups of specialists remained direct Pharma Co employees and others transferred to IT Co continued to work mainly on Pharma Co projects and from their premises.

This background carried three sets of consequences for the transfer. First, in the early stages, it disrupted effective HR planning. Right up to the point of transfer, exactly which employees would be transferring and how remained unclear. Second, which model prevailed also conditioned the employees' experience post-transfer. Integration clearly carried the most risk and disruption, but also potentially broadened career prospects. Third, low-trust relations stemming from those initial uncertainties proved resilient, and employees became defensive and unwilling to offer the flexibility that was a prerequisite for integration. These themes are now explored in more detail.

The HR function: status and role

The process of externalization transformed the relationship between these employees and the HR function. In Pharma Co, they had enjoyed the benefits of a classic internal labour market administered by a prominent, accessible and paternalistic HR department. HR in the new outsourced arrangements was less prominent, difficult to access directly, and employment systems were more 'market-oriented'; 'it's down to you, you go as far and as fast as you want to but don't really ask for any help along the way', as one employee described it.

Conventionally, management of the outsourcing process is split into three stages (Hunter 1998: 44): the tendering stage; the transition stage; and the post-transfer stage. HR involvement in the first one was limited, eclipsed largely by the negotiations between operational managers about the shape of the contract. Turning to the critical transition stage, three points need to be made. First, HR responsibility overall was not the sole or obvious prerogative of one party or the other, with consequences as we will see for the management of specific tasks such as consultation. Second, as a consequence of the prominent cost-reduction imperatives, Pharma Co HR had become distanced from the employees prospectively involved in the transfer. Their role shifted from the traditional welfare orientation to a more commodified one focused on effectively dismantling contractual commitments to staff. One employee involved in the transfer consultation referred to Pharma Co's HR representative as 'a big problem': 'we perceived his interest to be get the best deal for [Pharma Co], not for the staff, that was the perception we were left with from the engagement that we had'. Rather than transferring contracts of employment as they stood, Pharma Co restructured labour costs by varying the contract: 'Pharma Co were effectively saying (to IT Co), "this is going to be the cost . . . these are the terms we are giving these staff, do you want to sign this contract or not?"' A number of premium payments and allowances were consolidated into basic pay along with a lump sum compensation for a reduction of annual leave entitlement. Basic pay increased consequently by approximately 4 per cent. Completion of the transfer became conditional upon the explicit acceptance of the new terms by a majority of the transferees. 'You had to agree to them all together. You couldn't individually agree or disagree, it had to be a quorum of like 80 per cent agreement otherwise Pharma Co and IT Co might have to go back and re-negotiate.'

Third, the transition stage provided a rationale for active and more positive HR involvement from the transferee, but it was a rather instrumental and ephemeral one. This stage is vital for the transferee. The organization needs to learn quickly about the technology and procedures already in place so that the handover goes smoothly. Close and positive relations with key staff are vital to this, particularly where information flows between the organizations to that point have been less than open: as an IT Co manager put it, 'they're your inside information to build your procedures and things, if you haven't got much information from the company'. These processes were managed by a 'transition team' involving key operational staff but also HR representatives. For most employees, these first contacts with IT Co were seen positively. They seemed eager to welcome staff and to tell them about the benefits likely to accrue from their transferred employment: 'I think [IT Co] actually did a pretty good job on those sessions in terms of the pitch that was made, the level of people that were brought in . . . they seemed to get the right senior people in to give a good image of IT Co.'

Significantly, though, this prominent role for IT Co HR evaporated during the post-transition phase; 'the first six months they put the HR in, so you had people who were proactively looking after you but all the time really warning you that, "we're not here for very long"'. The function's role in the broader networked organization was much more remote. Reflecting the need to restrain overhead costs, HR did not maintain a presence within the contract sites but was concentrated in one centre on the South Coast, several miles away from Pharma Co, and operated on a call-centre basis. As one employee put it, 'it's the way of the people in our Ivory Towers to keep away'. Most contact was channelled through websites, which was a problem for recently transferred employees since many were not given access to IT Co's internal systems for several months.

The experience of externalization was manifest strongly in a more distanced and market-oriented employment relationship. Manifestations of paternalism vanished quickly following the transfer. IT Co pointedly did not attempt to replicate the Christmas parties and Summer barbecues hosted annually by Pharma Co for employees and their families. As one employee remarked wryly, 'they're not reaching out . . . the onus is on the employee to find the love that this company has! [laughs]'. Market relations were apparent particularly in the requirement to submit weekly timesheets, allocating their working hours to chargeable codes for accounting purposes. Recognition and development within the firm was also said to depend on employees' ability to 'market' themselves through the appraisal system. Employees who were used to relying on tacit recognition in Pharma Co found that this did not work in a virtual context, where line managers could often be located several miles away: 'you just naively think, "well I worked bloody hard and I did some brilliant things and everything else, you know about that? No? Oh well." ' Rather, employees found they had to demonstrate and document closely their individual contribution. One described learning this only gradually by observing the approach of other IT Co employees, used routinely to collecting written affirmations of their contribution for use during appraisal; 'sort of . . . "can you send this note to me saying how good I was?" "Excuse me, I worked on that project, can you just confirm I delivered?" And all of this stuff, which is alien to the way you did it in Pharma Co.'

Communication and consultation

Consultation mechanisms required by TUPE were established. Elected represeatives met formally with Pharma Co managers on a regular basis and IT Co initiated a series of communications 'roadshows'. But the primacy of operational and cost issues, noted above, and the division of information between the transferor and transferee, undermined the ability to consult fully with staff, and provided some powerful operational incentives not to do so, with important ramifications for employee perceptions and their trust in managers.

The decision to outsource was first announced to staff in February 2000. It demonstrated an evident instrumentalism which set an unfortunate tone for subsequent discussions.

> The woman who made the announcement . . . latterly known as the Wicked Witch of the West, announced that they had made this decision about the volume and style of the outsource some months ago but weren't going to tell anyone in case it pissed off a whole bunch of people prior to the millennium roll-over. *Which kind of impressed us all!* (emphasis added)

The quality of information imparted to staff subsequently was diminished by uncertainty about the shape of the contract. Horse-trading between IT Co and Pharma Co, described above, was exacerbated by lobbying by key Pharma Co departments to ensure that their IT staff were excluded from the transfer: '[They] had ringfenced their people and other parts of [Pharma Co] . . . and said, "whoah, yeah but you are not having ours!"' But it was the low trust relations between the firms that really narrowed the flow of information to employees. Pharma Co's approach to IT Co was affected by experience with a contractor preferred previously, which had withdrawn from the process during the transition process, shortly after discussion of key operational matters with employees.

> They then realized the size of the issues like the . . . the count of servers, some of the systems that were involved, the fact that some of the systems were validated systems, and a whole bunch of other IT issues, hadn't really been brought to much attention in the prior phases and the phases in the contract negotiation prior to the due diligence phase.

In subsequent negotiations with IT Co, Pharma Co expressly prohibited contact with technical staff on operational issues until the transfer was completed: '[IT

Co] didn't know on day one what they were getting.' In this context, IT Co limited the supply of information to transferring staff and, as important, suspicion permeated Pharma Co's approach to consultation too.

> The transfer of information was zippo. We were told pretty much . . . the minimum they could get away with telling us. I suspect at the time because there were still on-going negotiations with IT Co that they were just playing it very, very cagey, because they didn't want information getting across to IT Co.

Reward and performance

This focus on cost was sustained into the contract following transfer, with consequences for the management of reward and performance. Connections between them remained rather limited and were structured entirely by the operational need to vary wage costs downward to match levels prevailing in the rest of IT Co.

Pay for employees transferring into IT Co frequently reflected the internal labour markets in the companies from which they came. In the case of Pharma Co, pay for IT specialists was conditioned by labour markets for the scientific and research staffs they worked alongside. Pay relativities within IT Co were consequently disrupted by outsourcing processes that brought in workers on protected salaries.

Yet the networked context militated against thoroughgoing restructuring of pay systems. The regularity of inward transfers would make this an almost constant requirement. Further, complications arose from TUPE protections since they prevent variations to terms and conditions, including pay, attributable solely to the transfer. Instead, piecemeal adjustments predominated. While the initial salary uplift for Pharma Co staff (see above) sweetened the experience of transfer, it also removed annual incremental progression. Subsequent pay rises notionally were performance based and awarded following an annual pay review. In practice, though, the performance ethic was displaced by practical pressures felt by operational managers to 'normalize' salary levels. Pay for most transferred staff effectively remained static until IT Co salary bands rose to that level. As one transferred employee complained, 'IT Co have really screwed us on salary in the bandings and everything else. Like I haven't had a rise since I have been in IT Co and an awful lot of ex-Pharma Co people haven't.'

Recruitment, development and organizational flexibility

Employee development was a critical issue for IT Co, permitting the integration of new staff into the broader organization. But this was constrained in this case because the lack of trust between transferred staff and their new managers made employees unwilling to abandon the protections of their TUPE contracts.

IT Co's outsourcing functions had very little scope to recruit staff in the open market. Because TUPE was applied to a majority of outsourcing contracts, as one manager remarked, 'every time a new account comes in it seems, our perception is, that we are going to catch a couple of heads from it'. In this context, the capacity to broaden skills and move staff into new roles appropriate to the IT Co's business was critical both to cost structures and to the broader employee resourcing strategies. This mode of recruitment did not offer IT Co the skill sets that it needed. Managers perceived a tendency for companies to retain their core technology expertise for themselves, 'a business that is outsourcing a part of its business is not going to let the best people go – they will dump people to some degree'. Even talented individuals required development before they could move into integrated operations, because of their necessarily narrow experience of technology in specific organizational settings: 'these people come in used to running one processor, one image with one tape mount a week and all of a sudden they're expected to look after fifty different images, doing all sorts of things they have never done before.'

Initially on transfer, staff had understood this process and expected to see career opportunities open out for them. IT Co was seen as 'a very big organization, lots of other strings to their bow'. The scope to access roles in other accounts, following development and integration was welcomed because, 'that's got a far better career opportunity for most people'. But staff soon learned that this was dependent on a willingness to transfer from their TUPE protected contracts to pure IT Co ones. Managers strongly encouraged selected staff to do this. Project managers in particular reported regular exhortations to become IT Co accredited and to sign new contracts. Positive inducements were relatively rare, however; rather it was the risk of not doing so that was emphasized. Remaining as part of a substantially non-integrated operation meant that, if the contract were to be re-tendered, 'they run the risk of being TUPE'd again'.

But development was slowed by the general atmosphere of low trust relations stemming from experience of the transfer and this was compounded further by the rapid experience of rationalization in the account. While recruitment difficulties left chronic shortages in some key areas, the availability of economies of scale created sustained potential for workforce reductions overall. At moments of crisis, IT Co pursued these aggressively and Pharma Co transferees were implicated in one such exercise soon after their transfer. One employee recalled, 'it was, "every department will lose 5 or 10 per cent or whatever". That is going, there is nothing you can do about it. Don't argue about it, don't seek to influence it. It is going to happen and it did.' Selection for redundancy was done very quickly on the basis of technical criteria: 'if they are going to get rid of people, they get rid of them'.

Such rationalization quests and the way in which they were managed affected the orientation of remaining staff towards their new employer. As one employee recalled, 'I was a bit surprised that they came into an account and very early on started reducing numbers because I would have imagined that they would have priced the account with a realistic number of people and there wasn't overstaffing here.' The contrast with Pharma Co's more paternalistic approach to rationalization, in which affected employees were given opportunities to apply for other jobs and to retrain over a 2-year period, was stark. While some expressed admiration for IT Co's ability to take and implement decisions quickly, others were shocked by the experience, 'I can't accept it. I don't think it is an acceptable part of industrial relations.'

This did little to encourage flexible approaches to development opportunities, rather a marked instrumentalism and reliance upon contract was evident. Employees reported that colleagues had left the organization but, outside a small group of senior managers and technical specialists, most employees retained their TUPE contracts: 'there's not that many people moved off the Pharma Co account, to my knowledge, into the wider IT Co'. Managers acknowledged employees' understandable insecurity; having being forced into a transfer in the first place, 'they're sick of it'. Retaining a TUPE-protected contract offered some sense of control to employees where so much else was patently beyond their influence. But employees also perceived in their substantive terms strong incentives to retain their TUPE contracts. Several commented on dilution of their pension entitlements occasioned by the variation of their contracts on transfer; 'they were probably doing the best job they could under the pressure at the time in the short space of time, etc, etc, but they were nearly lying to us'. Since employees had not understood fully the implications at that moment, because of the quality of information available to them, they were suspicious about invitations to go through the exercise again: 'If I want to go and work for [account of a named High Street Bank], they will make me sign another contract which will be much more [pure IT Co]. That might be better in some ways, it might be worse. It would kill my pension rights, I am pretty sure.'

Conclusions

Organizational innovation is changing relationships within firms and between them with important consequences for HR practice. Devolution to business units and franchises, joint ventures, and public private partnerships do not necessarily atomize control based on hierarchical bureaucracies, but they do disrupt and reconfigure them. Subject to relations between the firms in question, a wider range of actors are implicated in managing the employment relationship and on terms which are not always clear. For employees, the experience of 'externalization' may open new opportunities for career development beyond previously bounded internal labour markets, but they also bring the risk of changing authority relations and rationalized employment structures. These themes have been explored in this chapter and illustrated using a critical case study of outsourcing in the information technology sector.

In networked contexts, developments in the employment relationship are conditioned principally by relations between the firms and the motivations behind organizational innovation. Objectives may include eased access to established sources of information or expertise or the opportunity to share risks involved in product development. Heightened competitive pressures may also lead to attempts to maximize employment flexibility and to drive costs savings through economies of scale available to specialist suppliers. These objectives may well be mixed in particular circumstances; significantly, they carry some potentially positive consequences for employment but also some adverse ones.

Choices between these options are conditioned by the institutional framework, particularly the structure and content of the law. In the UK, the law provides a basis for judging fair dealing in business contracts between firms, but it stops short of prescribing particular contractual forms or inter-firm relations. Employment law has traditionally done little to circumscribe this freedom either. The Acquired Rights Directive, transposed into UK law under the TUPE regulations, has impinged increasingly on the transfer of staff and is gradually being strengthened. Its impact in practice has been qualified by the scope afforded to companies to navigate around key provisions. In consequence, there are relatively few barriers to 'low-road' approaches to networked employment relations.

Possible consequences for employment and for the HR function emerge from the case study considered here. Care is required when interpreting findings from single case studies and it is not claimed that this episode is necessarily representative of outsourcing in every instance. Yet it does throw into sharp relief some of the tensions associated with the process. It demonstrates in particular how relations between the organizations permeate the process of transfer. Low-trust negotiations about the shape and price of the contract narrowed the information made available to employees and the initial contact between them and their putative employer. A strong focus on cost-constraint also carried ramifications for the role of HR in managing this change. Prospective labour costs were altered in this instance by the transferor and Pharma Co HR was given the key role in varying contractual terms for those staff to be transferred. Alongside a rather constrained process of consultation, this did not provide the foundations required for supporting employees in the way anticipated by normative models of best practice. Equally important, though prominent roles for IT Co HR were generated by the need to ensure a smooth transition of staff between the companies, overhead costs within projects were minimized and access to HR was to become rather remote. Thus, for these employees, the process of 'externalization' ejected them from the paternalistic environment of a strong internal labour market within Pharma Co, and exposed them fully to an employment relationship founded prominently on market relations in which they had to account for their time and market themselves to the organization. Perhaps the most important finding here, however, relates to the response of employees to these unfolding circumstances. Faced with a broader context of limited information flows, job cuts, and cost-constraint that impacted directly on their pay, employees responded defensively. Relatively few were prepared to give up their TUPE protected contracts as the price of entry into IT Co's broader employment structures. In this case then, while organizational innovation delivered cost savings, it also generated a marked instrumentalism among employees that militated against the employment flexibility needed by IT Co and often associated with the networked organization.

NOTE

1 Data considered here were generated during fieldwork exploring human resource management in multinational companies, supported by the Economic and Social Research Council (award number R000238350). The project team consisted of Phil Almond, Ian Clark, Trevor Colling, Anthony Ferner, and Len Holden (De Montfort University); Peter Butler (University of Leicester) and Tony Edwards (Kings College, London). This case draws on 14 interviews conducted with managers in IT Co; IT Co employees; Pharma Co transferees and their employee representatives.

ACKNOWLEDGEMENTS

I am particularly grateful to Tony Edwards, with whom I worked on gathering the views of transferred employees in IT Co, and to all those managers and staff who spoke to us with such candour.

REFERENCES

Armstrong, P. 1989: Limits and possibilities of HRM in an age of management accountancy, in J. Storey (ed.), *New Perspectives on Human Resource Management*, London: Routledge.

Arnold, C. 1995: *Outsourcing Contracts: A Specially Commissioned Report*, London: Richards Butler International Law Firm.

Ascher, K. 1987: *The Politics of Privatisation: Contracting Out Public Services*, London: Macmillan.

Atkinson, J. 1986: *New Forms of Work Organizational*, IMS Report No. 121, Brighton.

Bach, S. 2002: Public sector employment relations under Labour: Muddling through or modernisation?, *British Journal of Industrial Relations*, **40**(2), 319–39.

Beaumont, P., Hunter, L. and Sinclair, J. 1996: Customer-supplier relations and the diffusion of employee relations change, *Employee Relations*, **18**(1), 9–19.

Blau, P. 1966: *Bureaucracy in Modern Society*, New York: Random House.

Blyton, P. and Turnbull, P. 2004: *The Dynamics of Employee Relations*, 3rd edn, Basingstoke: Palgrave.

Caulkin, S. 2004: Working with management consultants: Goodbye industry, hello government, *The Observer*, 25 April, 1.

Chandler, A.D. 1977: *The Visible Hand: The Managerial Revolution in American Business*, Cambridge, MA: Harvard University Press.

Clawson, D. 1980: *Bureaucracy and the Labour Process: The Transformation of US Industry 1860–1920*, London: Monthly Review Press.

Claydon, T. 2004: Human resource management and the labour market, in I. Beardwell, L. Holden and T. Claydon (eds.), *Human Resource Management: A Contemporary Approach*, 4th edn, London: Prentice Hall.

Colling, T. 1995: Renewal or rigor mortis? Union responses to contracting in local government, *Industrial Relations Journal*, **26**(2), 134–46.

Colling, T. 2003: Managing without unions: The sources and limitations of individualism, in P.K. Edwards (ed.), *Industrial Relations: Theory and Practice*, Oxford: Blackwell.

Colling, T. and Clark, I. 2002: Looking for Americanness: Country of origin, sector and firm effects in Process Plant Construction, *European Journal of Industrial Relations*, **8**(3), 202–324.

Cooke, F.L., Earnshaw, J., Marchington, M. and Rubery, J. 2004: For better and for worse? Transfers of undertakings and the reshaping of employment relations, *International Journal of Human Resource Management*, **15**(2), 276–94.

Cully, M., Woodland, S., O'Reilly, A. and Dix, G. 1999: *Britain at Work: As Depicted by the 1998 Workplace Employee Relations Survey*, London: Routledge.

Davies, R. 2004: Contracting out and the retention of employment model in the NHS, *Industrial Law Journal*, **33**(2), 93–120.

Deakin, S. 2001: The changing concept of the employer in labour law, *Industrial Law Journal*, **30**(1), 72–83.

Department of Trade and Industry 2004: *Making Globalisation a Force for Good?* London: DTI.

Earnshaw, J., Rubery, J. and Cooke, F.L. 2002: *Who is the Employer?* London: Institute of Employment Rights.

Escott, K. and Whitfield, D. 1995: *The Gender Impact of CCT in Local Government*, London: HMSO.

Felstead, A. 1993: *The Corporate Paradox: Power and Control in the Business Franchise*, London: Routledge.

Fischbacher, M. and Beaumont, P. 2003: PFI, public–private partnerships and the neglected importance of process: Stakeholders and the employment dimension, *Public Money and Management* (July), 171–6.

Geddes, M. 2001: What about the workers? Best value, employment and work in local public services, *Policy and Politics*, **29**(4), 497–508.

Gouldner, A. 1964: *Patterns of Industrial Democracy: A Case Study of Modern Factory Administration*, New York: The Free Press.

Grimshaw, D., Vincent, S. and Willmott, H. 2002: Going privately: Partnership and out-sourcing in UK public services, *Public Administration*, **80**(3), 475–502.

Hardy, S. 2000: The Acquired Rights Directive: A case of economic and social rights at work, in H. Collins, P. Davies and R. Rideout, *Legal Regulation of the Employment Relation*, Amsterdam: Kluwer Law International, 479–90.

Harrison, B. and Kelley, M. 1993: Outsourcing and the search for flexibility, *Work, Employment and Society*, **7**(2), 213–55.

Hebson, G., Grimshaw, D. and Marchington, M. 2003: PPPs and the changing public sector ethos: Case-study evidence from the health and local authority sectors, *Work, Employment and Society*, **17**(3), 481–501.

Hunter, J. 1998: Selling disempowerment: The impact of outsourcing upon staff in the IT industry, unpublished MA thesis, De Montfort University, Leicester.

Institute of Personnel and Development 1998: *The IPD Guide on Outsourcing*, London: IPD.

Jacoby, S. 1997: *Modern Manors: Welfare Capitalism since the New Deal*, Princeton: Princeton University Press.

Lacity, M. and Hirschheim, R. 1995: *Information Systems Outsourcing: Myths, Metaphors and Realities*, Chichester: John Wiley.

Lane, C. and Bachmann, R. 1994: Risk, trust and power: The social constitution of sup-plier relations in Britain and Germany. Paper presented at the 'Work, Employment and Society Conference', University of Kent, 12–14 September.

Lane, C. and Bachman, R. 1997: Co-operation in inter-firm relations in Britain and Germany: The role of social institutions, *British Journal of Sociology*, **48**(2), 226–54.

Legge, K. 2000: Personnel management in the lean organization, in S. Bach and K. Sisson (eds.), *Personnel Management in Britain: A Comprehensive Guide to Theory and Practice*. Oxford: Blackwell.

Local Government Management Board 1992: *CCT Information Service: Survey Report No. 6*, November, London: LGMB.

Local Government Management Board 1994: *CCT Information Service: Survey Report No. 10*, December, London: LGMB.

Lonsdale, C. and Cox, A. 1998: Falling in with the outcrowd, *People Management*, 15 October, 52–5.

Lonsdale, C. and Cox, A. 2000: The historical development of outsourcing: The latest fad? *Industrial Management and Data Systems*, **100**(9), 444–50.

McMullen, J. 1996: Atypical transfers, atypical workers, and atypical employment structures, *Industrial Law Journal*, **25**(4), 286–307.

Mesure, S. 2004: Store detectives take M&S to employment tribunal, *The Independent*, 7 April, 37.

Oates, D. 1998: *Outsourcing and the Virtual Organizational: The Incredible Shrinking Company*, London: Century.

Office for National Statistics 2004: Employment 5: Workforce jobs by industry, at http://www.stats.gov.uk/downloads/theme_Labour/LMS_FR_HS/tableOS.xls, consulted May 2004.

Peters, T. and Waterman, R. 1982: *In Pursuit of Excellence: Lessons from America's Best Companies*. New York: Harper and Row.

Pritchard, S. 1998: Outsourcing – the insider guide, *Independent on Sunday*, 2 August.

Purcell, J. 1998: In-sourcing, outsourcing, and the growth of contingent labour as evidence of flexible employment strategies, *European Journal of Work and Organizational Psychology*, **7**(1), 39–59.

Rees, G. and Fielder, S. 1992: The services economy, subcontracting and the new employment relations: Contract catering and cleaning, *Work, Employment and Society*, **6**(3), 347–68.

Rubery, J., Earnshaw, J., Marchington, M., Cooke, F.L. and Vincent, S. 2002: Changing organizational forms and the employment relationship, *Journal of Management Studies*, **39**(5), 645–72.

Rubery, J., Cooke, F.L., Earnshaw, J. and Marchington, M. 2003: Inter-organizational relations and employment in a multi-employer environment, *British Journal of Industrial Relations*, **41**(2), 265–89.

Sako, M. 1992: *Prices, Quality and Trust: Inter-Firm Relations in Britain and Japan*, Cambridge: Cambridge University Press.

Scullion, H. 2004: Offshoring's ills, *Morning Star*, 24 May, 8.

Sennett, R. 1998: *The Corrosion of Character: The Personal Consequences of Work in the New Capitalism*. London: Norton.

UNISON 2002: *Best Value and the Two-Tier Workforce in Local Government*, London: Best Value Intelligence Unit, UNISON.

UNISON 2003: *Guide to Best Value Code of Practice on Workforce Matters in Local Authority Service Contracts in England*, London: UNISON.

Walsh, K. and Davis, H. 1993: *Competition and Service: The Impact of the Local Government Act 1988*, London: HMSO.

Watson, T. 1987: *Sociology, Work, and Industry*, London: Routledge.

PART II

Employee Resourcing

CHAPTER FIVE

Recruitment and Selection

Sue Newell

Increased global competition coupled with enhanced customer expectations means that the growth, or even survival, of a firm is difficult. It is no longer sufficient to be effective in selling a particular product or service or to rely on past reputation. Organizations need to respond to a rapidly changing global environment. Continued success is, thus, dependent on attracting and retaining high-quality individuals who can respond effectively to this changing environment. This implies that there can be 'wrong' people; individuals who are a liability rather than an asset because they do not contribute to organizational success and may even harm the organization. This occurs because there are differences between individuals, which influence how they perform particular jobs. For most jobs, it is the psychosocial differences between people that are crucial in relation to organizational performance – differences in terms of abilities, personality, motivation and emotions that influence how people behave and cope with the demands of particular jobs. In other words, given that jobs and organizations differ in terms of what they require, some individuals will be more suited to some jobs and organizations than others.

Hiring competent people is of paramount importance and this is dependent on effective recruitment and selection procedures, which aim to select the 'right' individuals and reject the 'wrong' ones. The importance of this should not be underestimated because a poor recruitment decision can cost an employer an amount equal to 30 per cent of the employee's first-year earnings (Hacker 1997). These costs can include: lower productivity; potential loss of clients; training costs; advertising costs; recruitment fees and redundancy packages (Smith and Graves 2002).

One of the earliest management writers, F.W. Taylor (1911) bemoaned the typical way in which individuals were selected, based on 'who you knew' or who was first in the queue. Ability to do the particular job was not, at that time, systematically assessed. Taylor introduced the idea that people should be selected for their particular skills and abilities which should be tested prior to the selection decision. Despite this early emphasis by Taylor, many organizations still fail to adopt even the most basic recruitment and selection procedures which would allow them to attract suitable candidates (recruitment) and then make good predictions about the likely 'fit' between particular individuals and the organizational and job requirements (selection).

Recruitment and selection involves making predictions about future behaviour so that decisions can be made about who will be most suitable for a particular job. Predictions must always be couched in terms of probabilities because the future is unpredictable. However, informed judgements can be made (like actuaries deciding insurance premiums), rather than uninformed guesses (like crystal ball gazers). This requires a systematic process of assessment of both individual differences and organizational requirements.

Traditionally, recruitment and selection has been viewed as a process by which the organization tries to accurately match the individual to the job and can be compared to completing a jigsaw puzzle. Recruitment and selection is a process of selecting the correct jigsaw piece (the 'right' individual) from the incorrect pieces (the 'wrong' individuals) to fit into a particular hole in a jigsaw puzzle. I will refer to this model as the 'psychometric' or traditional approach to recruitment and selection. It focuses on the 'job' and presents the recruitment and selection process as a systematic and objective process which follows a logical sequence of events. The key is to find selection methods which are able to predict 'good' employees from 'bad' employees; that is, methods which have sound psychometric properties of validity and reliability.

The psychometric approach, fitting the person to a specific job, is the dominant perspective in practice and underpins the good practice model of recruitment and selection. This approach espoused, for example by the UK Chartered Institute of Personnel and Development, states that: 'Care should be taken to use techniques which are relevant to the job and the business objectives of the organisation. All tools used should be validated and constantly reviewed to ensure their fairness and reliability' (http://www.cipd.co.uk/subjects/recruitmen/general/recruitmt.htm).

The approach has been adapted to the current structure of employment. For Taylor it was the physical skills required of workers in a particular job that were crucial to assess. The growth of the service sector has ensured that more emphasis is placed on social or 'soft' skills (Crouch et al. 1999; Redman and Matthews 1998). This is because in service sector jobs it is social competencies that are seen to be essential to ensure an effective interaction between the employee and the customer. It is this interaction that is crucial to customer satisfaction. For example, Callaghan and Thompson (2002) found in a detailed case study of call centre recruitment, that the key criteria were 'personality traits, communication (especially verbal) skills, and with less emphasis, technical skills' (p. 239). In particular, the stress in this case company was on finding employees with a 'good attitude to customers'. This was seen by the recruiting managers in this firm to stem from personality rather than being something that could be taught and so the recruitment and selection process was heavily oriented to assessing this 'good attitude'.

From this psychometric perspective, jobs are defined in terms of their tasks (job description) and the characteristics of the person who will be able successfully to

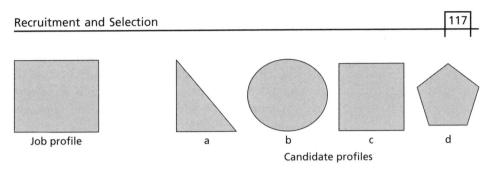

Figure 5.1 The traditional psychometric view of selection

carry out these tasks (person specification) is then developed. Recruitment is a process of attracting individuals who might meet this specification. Selection is the process of measuring differences between these candidates to find the person who has the profile which best matches the person specification as indicated by the job profile or description. In Figure 5.1, candidate C would be chosen, being the best match for the particular 'hole'. This process resembles an obstacle course with the organization putting up increasingly difficult obstacles for the candidates to overcome. The individual who can demonstrate the greatest number of essential and/or desirable competencies (jump over the most obstacles) is given the job.

The first part of this chapter is concerned with examining the recruitment and selection process as viewed from this dominant psychometric approach. This approach is highly prescriptive – defining a 'best practice' method for recruitment and selection. Based on this approach, the key stages in the recruitment and selection process are outlined and the different methods of recruitment and selection assessed. The limitations of the psychometric perspective are examined in the context of increased uncertainty and competition facing organizations. In the final section, the advantages of viewing the recruitment and selection process from an 'exchange' perspective are discussed, which sees the recruitment and selection process as the outcome of a process of exchange and negotiation between the potential recruit and the recruiting managers, rather than as a race judged solely by the organization's managers.

The Recruitment Process

Organizational review and job analysis

Recruitment is the process of attracting people who might make an organizational contribution to fill a particular role or job. Recruitment is often stimulated when an existing employee leaves. The organizational response is often to try and replace the individual with a replica of that person. However, a more systematic response would involve reviewing the post and possibly reallocating some responsibilities to empower other staff. There are also circumstances where recruitment might be necessary, even when no one has left the organization, for example because of organizational expansion. In other words, it is better for organizations to proactively decide when to recruit, rather then merely react to the departure of an employee. Thus, in relation to recruitment decisions it is important to take a helicopter view of the situation and ensure that there are not better alternatives to recruitment (e.g. automation).

So, the first stage in the recruitment process involves a systematic review of the organization's requirements. Following this review, a thorough analysis of the requirements of the job should be established, often termed *job analysis*. This is necessary because even in those situations where an individual is simply being replaced, there may still be changes in job requirements, especially if the individual being replaced has been with the organization for some time. There are a number of techniques that can be used for undertaking job analysis (see, for example, Greuter and Algera 1989), but essentially they all require the collection of systematic data about the particular job from existing incumbents and colleagues. This usually involves interviews, questionnaires or diaries. Recently, the focus of research has been on understanding the sources of variance that are evident in using these different techniques (see Morgenson and Campion 1997 or Prien et al. 2003).

First, using interviews, job holders may be asked to describe their main tasks and responsibilities. There can be a bias in what is recalled using this method because job analysis is used for a variety of purposes, including salary decisions, so that job holders may have a vested interest in inflating the worth of their job. Another interview technique is to focus on *critical incidents*. Job holders are asked to recall specific incidents of either good or poor job performance. This provides an indication of the most important aspects of the job and provides an insight into how good and poor job-holders are differentiated. Another commonly used technique is the *repertory grid*. There are many versions of this, but a common one is to ask respondents to think of five or six job incumbents they have worked with on an anonymous basis. The five or six people are assigned letters, A to E, for example. The interviewer asks the respondent to choose three of them and describe how two are similar, and one is different from the third, in the way they work. For example, 'A and B are willing to work through their lunch times to complete an urgent task, while the other person, C, doesn't', might be a typical answer. This information forms a 'construct'. Later on, respondents rate A to E in terms of overall effectiveness at the job. For example, if A and B are rated more effective performers than C, and other respondents provide similar examples, then it is reasonable to conclude that a key competence which distinguishes good from poor performers has been established – work commitment.

Second, structured questionnaires have been developed to collect data about specific jobs. The most well-established is the Position Analysis Questionnaire (PAQ) developed in the USA by McCormick et al. (1972), which consists of nearly 200 items which are categorized under six headings: information input; mediation processes; work output; interpersonal activities; work situation and job context; and miscellaneous aspects. Saville and Holdsworth (1995) have developed a similar structured approach in the UK, called the Work Profiling System (WPS).

Third, job holders can be asked to keep a diary recording their activities. This overcomes problems of incomplete memory, but can be very time-consuming. Finally, in contrast to other methods which rely on self-reporting by the job holder, it is helpful to carry out some direct observation to reduce bias and inaccuracies. While observation itself may alter the behaviour of people, as demonstrated by the classic Hawthorne Studies (Roethlisberger and Dickson 1939), it can nevertheless provide additional data and provide the job analyst with a better understanding of what the job entails. Moreover, although the job holder has the most intimate knowledge about what the job involves; peers, subordinates and superiors can be valuable sources of information and provide an alternative perspective, as the vogue for '360 degree' feedback illustrates (see Chapter 11). Data from these other sources can be collected in similar ways to those obtained directly from job-holders.

Job description, person specification and competencies

Once the job analysis data has been collected, the next stage is to develop a job description. This describes what the job involves: the purpose of the job; the tasks that are to be undertaken, together with an outline of the expected performance standards; the duties and responsibilities; reporting relationships and details of remuneration. The job description identifies the particular demands of a job and emphasizes those aspects which are crucial to success. In some cases a distinction is made between a *job description* and a *job specification*. The job description is job-orientated, focusing on the work itself, while the job specification is worker-orientated, focusing on the psychological and behavioural requirements of the job. Ideally for the selection process, both a job description and a job specification should be drawn up and reviewed against the job. This practice appears to be common at least in the UK (see IRS 2003a) with many employers reporting that they always review the job description against the aims of the job before proceeding to the recruitment stage, in line with best practice.

The job description and job specification provide the necessary information to move to the next stage of the job analysis process, which is to develop a person specification. This converts the job specification into human terms, specifying the kind of person needed to perform the described job. Inferences are made about the psychosocial characteristics that are necessary for a successful job holder. There are two frameworks, which are well established, to help with this process. The oldest is the Seven Point Plan, developed by Rodger (1952) which provides seven headings under which to categorize those personal qualities considered to be essential or desirable. An example is shown in Box 5.1. A similar framework was developed by Munro Fraser (1978) and consists of five categories: impact on others; acquired knowledge or qualifications; innate abilities; motivation; and emotional adjustment.

Box 5.1   Personnel specification for a secondary-school head of English (following Rodger's seven-point plan)

1. Physical make-up: no specific requirement (teachers come in all shapes and sizes).
2. Attainments: good honours degree in English plus a teaching qualification; at least 7 years teaching experience in secondary schools, preferably including some managerial experience.
3. General intelligence: good general intelligence.
4. Special aptitudes: high verbal ability plus an ability to impart knowledge to students working at a variety of levels; leadership ability to coordinate the members of the English department.
5. Interests: in the arts generally and an interest in enthusing students and staff to take an interest in the arts.
6. Disposition: dependable and sociable to both students and staff.
7. Circumstances: no specific requirement, although must be prepared to work some evenings both for parent consultations and staff meetings.

These two approaches are still commonly used by firms in the UK. Both stress the need to relate the personal characteristics specified to the prior identification of job demands and both can be used as the basis for designing a structured interview approach (see below). More importantly, however, both suffer from a heavy reliance on personal judgement to determine what human qualities are associated with successful performance. So they are not politically or socially neutral (Watson 1994). Because of this inherent difficulty, an alternative approach has been gaining prominence, which emphasizes job competencies rather than personal qualities.

Job competencies focus on behaviours rather than personal characteristics (IRS 2003b). Organizations adopting a competency approach seek to define a series of effective individual behaviours, usually in the context of promoting superior organizational performance (Boam and Sparrow 1992; Dale and Iles 1992). So, for example, it is not a question of determining that the job demands someone with 'self-confidence', but that the job requires someone who can perform in front of 120 MBA students and deliver a lecture which is well received. While this specific behaviour need not have been demonstrated before, the key is to identify other situations which can be used as evidence that the individual possesses the competence to successfully engage in this behaviour. A well-known example of an attempt to use such an approach is the case of British Petroleum (BP). Faced with major challenges to its business in the early 1990s, BP sought to identify the key behaviours to support high performance and a shift in the corporate culture. The competencies which emerged from repertory grid and other analyses identified 67 essential behaviours which were clustered into a framework termed OPEN: Open thinking, Personal impact, Empowering and Networking. These competencies fed into graduate recruitment and other personnel practices (Boam and Sparrow 1992).

While in theory this competency approach looks significantly different from the person specification approach, in practice there is considerable overlap. This is because there is still a translation process, which moves from the specific behaviour required to its root source in terms of the subsequent identification of traits, motives, attitudes, skills and aptitudes; which still requires subjective judgement. Thus, a behavioural competence has been defined as 'an underlying characteristic of a person which results in effective and/or superior performance' (Boyatzis 1982). As such a competence consists of 'all work related personal attributes, knowledge, experience and skills and values that a person draws on to perform their work well' (Roberts 1997: 6). So while the difference lies essentially in the premium that is placed upon observable behaviour, nevertheless the problem – that the under-lying causes are rooted in psychological make-up – remains the same. Consequently, traditional psychometric instruments may be used to obtain evidence of these competencies during the selection process (Sparrow 1997; Callaghan and Thompson 2002). Moving from behavioural competencies to personality traits is certainly not straightforward (Fletcher 1992), nevertheless competency approaches are well established with most large organizations using a competency framework which they use for selection and other HR practices like 360 degree feedback. The introduction of a competency based recruitment process can help to improve workplace performance by allowing managers to assess candidates more objectively (Farnham 2000).

Recruitment Methods

Once the job analysis phase is completed and the job specification or behavioural competencies are identified, the next stage is to consider how to attract people who meet the requirements. Effective recruitment is crucial to organizational success (Barber 1998). A key decision is about whether to recruit internally or externally. Internal recruitment may have a number of potential advantages. Recruits will already understand something about how the organization operates and so socialization and learning may be significantly reduced; it will be cheaper because expensive advertising and recruitment consultancy fees are avoided; it may provide an opportunity to relieve an organizational problem of too many employees in another area; and it may provide motivation to existing employees who can see new opportunities available within the wider organization. Given this motivational advantage, internal recruitment is more common among organizations that are keen to develop and nurture their own internal talent, along the lines advocated by proponents of a 'soft' human resource management approach. For these reasons it is not surprising that many employers routinely attempt to fill vacancies from internal sources before seeking external applicants. There are disadvantages, however, of relying on internal recruitment because it prevents the organization bringing in 'new blood' with outside experience and it may leave a gap elsewhere in the organization. In addition, internal recruitment can be potentially unfair and discriminatory, since it tends to perpetuate the existing workforce, reinforcing existing organizational inequalities. Internal recruitment is therefore less common in the public sector, where concerns about discrimination tend to be a higher priority than in the private sector (Harris 2000).

External recruitment brings in individuals from outside. The advantages of internal recruitment are basically the disadvantages of external recruiting. However, as organizational boundaries become more permeable with the rise of interorganizational networking the definition of internal versus external recruitment becomes less straightforward. Take the case of an individual who worked as an outside contractor or a consultant for a number of years prior to being recruited by the same organization in a similar job as they were previously doing. This would be classed as external recruitment, even though the new recruit was in many ways already an 'insider'.

Sources of external applicants

Because internal sources are often not sufficient to supply a suitable pool of applicants, most organizations make use of external sources. There are many such sources, including employee referrals, employment agencies, 'walk-ins', and going direct to educational establishments. When existing employees are encouraged to find future employees this is termed 'employee referrals'. This may be merely asking them to inform relations, friends or acquaintances, or it may involve a financial reward for the existing employee if a new recruit they have encouraged to apply, is offered and accepts a job. The advantage of this method is that the new recruits are likely to have a better understanding of the culture and values of the organization, and the nature of the work on offer than the average recruit. The socialization process may, therefore, be shortened for these recruits so that employers can benefit more quickly from the knowledge and skills that these workers bring with them to the organization. In addition, these recruits may be more amenable to management control, not least because the existing workforce may take on some of the responsibility for ensuring the effective performance of those workers they have recommended (Manwaring 1984). As Ram's study of small Asian-owned firms in the West Midlands clothing industry shows, for workers faced with very limited job opportunities, this form of recruitment avoided having to go through interviews or other formal recruitment methods (Ram 1994: 76–7). It should be noted that reliance on referrals may run up against equal opportunity laws if certain groups have a less than equal chance of hearing about vacancies. However, this is less of a problem where employers are seeking out disadvantaged (and cheap) sources of labour.

Employment agencies have been a very popular source of recruits. Recent survey evidence, however, suggests that their use has declined as recruiters have turned instead to using Internet sources to directly recruit new employees rather than going through an intermediary (Murphy 2003). Frequently cited reasons for using agencies include for hiring staff with specialist skills, for hiring temporary staff or in situations where a vacancy needs to be filled quickly (see Rankin 2004).

Employment agencies vary in their size, degree of occupational specialization and geographical spread. Some specialize in temporary help while others search for more permanent placements. Head-hunters will often search and select, that is, draw up a short-list to present to their client, who has the final say on who should be appointed. There are also public employment agencies in many countries, including Britain. Many recruitment agencies are web-based, such as monster.com (www.monster.com), where you can search jobs online, post a resume (CV) online to let employers search candidates, and get careers advice. Many other online recruitment agencies exist, both general and specialist.

'Walk-in' is where an applicant simply walks into the employer's premises, often as a result of seeing an advertisement in the window. Many shops and fast food outlets recruit in this way. Like employee referrals, it is quick, cheap and can be very effective in terms of retention. Employees often stay longer than do those who come via different routes (Decker and Cornelius 1979). As with employee referrals, care needs to be paid to the issue of equal opportunities.

Increasingly, organizations are targeting recruitment towards particular educational institutions. This may be in addition to other methods. Companies that recruit graduates, particularly those in short supply such as software engineers, or where the market is fiercely competitive, such as accountancy, often set up good relations with university departments in selected universities. This helps them to advertise their company as well as to be able to position themselves to recruit early and 'the best'. In addition, the services of university careers offices and the facility to conduct interviews on campuses are well known and much used by frequent recruiters of graduates.

Methods of attracting applicants

To increase the pool of applicants, organizations use local newspapers, which were used almost universally by employers in the mid-1990s (IRS 1997: 8). This contrasts with national newspaper advertisements which were used by approximately three-quarters of employers, mainly for professional and managerial posts (IRS 1997: 9). Preparing advertisements, particularly for managerial or professional jobs, is a specialist skill. For this reason, many organizations outsource this work to advertising firms or recruitment agencies, rather than attempt it themselves. Radio and television are expensive methods and are far less frequently used methods, but do reach a large audience. Occasionally British universities have advertised for students with prime-time television advertisements. This is a more common approach in the USA where many colleges use radio and TV adverts to attract students.

Firms are increasingly turning to online forms of advertising, through online newspapers and magazines, but even more so by direct recruitment through their own websites. Thus, 82 per cent of employers were found to be using corporate websites to attract applicants and advertise vacancies (Czerny 2004). The Internet is therefore playing a more important role in recruitment. It advertises jobs and serves as a place to locate job applicants. One of the earliest examples of using the Internet for recruitment was provided by Cisco Systems Inc. in the USA, which set up the world's first recruitment website. It set up an 'opportunities page' to advertise all vacancies. A tailored search program was developed which enabled users to enter key words describing their desired positions and to apply via e-mail. Cisco indicated that one of the major advantages of using the Internet was that it could reach candidates who were not actively seeking work. It resulted in quicker and less expensive recruitment. The opportunities page received 64,000 visits in 1996, resulting in several thousand applications. More recently, HMV used online advertising to attract 12,850 applicants for its temporary positions that it needed to fill over the Christmas holiday period (Personnel Today 2004). Using online advertising is very attractive because it is a cheap way to attract large applicant pools. For example, Smethurst (2004) reports companies that have reduced their recruitment costs by 85 per cent by using online recruitment advertising and data collection where candidates can apply directly for a particular post.

Websites can provide Internet users with information on the type of work the company is involved in and the job opportunities that are available. Interested parties can respond by e-mail, reducing paperwork and turnaround times. The Internet allows an organization to reach a larger and broader range of applicants than traditional methods. Thus, if the Internet is used sensitively it has been shown that it can increase an organization's access to candidates that traditionally have not applied and so can boost diversity initiatives. Smethurst (2004) reports on how British Gas successfully developed its recruitment site in order to attract candidates from ethnic minorities, women and older people.

While the Cisco example was relatively novel in the mid 1990s, using the Internet to recruit has become common practice. For most companies the decision is not about whether to use the Internet for recruitment, but how to fully utilize its potential (Williams 1997). The Internet can provide potential recruits with a much broader array of information about a job and the company, as well as providing a fast and effective way for sending in candidate applications, gathering applicant data, and making initial pre-selection decisions. For example, the Washington Department of Personnel has developed an internet tool (http://hr.dop.wa.gov/statejobs) to provide hiring managers with 'virtually instant certification of highly qualified candidates for employment' (Bingham et al. 2002: 53). The system allows people to submit applications online. Applicants take a number of screening tests as part of this application process and these tests are automatically scored. Based on this data, the eligibility of candidates for the job is assessed and those candidates fulfilling the eligibility criteria are automatically referred to the hiring manager for a subsequent interview. This has reduced the recruitment cycle from several weeks to 1–2 hours.

While many companies are reporting the success of their online recruitment campaigns, it is clear that there are problems, in particular in terms of the sheer number of applicants often attracted (Czerny 2004). This can be partly offset by incorporating some form of online screening to remove unsuitable candidates. Many companies, however, do not supply enough information about particular jobs on their websites which encourages people without the requisite skills to apply. Providing more detailed job and company information can therefore help to offset the problem of too many unqualified people applying.

Evaluation of the applicants attracted by different recruitment methods is considered best practice (see Carlson et al. 2002). They argue that the first phase (attracting candidates) is the most important to evaluate since if good candidates are not initially attracted this cannot be remedied at selection stage. In undertaking this evaluation they stress that it is important to measure the quality as well as the quantity of applicants attracted. Unfortunately, very few organizations actually do this in practice, despite the benefits that it can bring (Grossman 2000; Millmore 2003).

Both because of skill shortages and to improve customer services, some organizations have looked beyond the usual pool of candidates. Both B & Q, the UK 'do-it-yourself' chain of stores, and Tesco, the UK food retailer, for example, have targeted an older age group, the over 50s, as employees. Both have found that these recruits are more conscientious, more reliable, and are better with customers than younger staff. Forward-looking employers try to see recruitment from the applicant's point of view and choose methods that are likely to attract and retain suitable employees by adopting equal opportunities initiatives (Chapter 7) or by allowing flexible working hours (Chapter 6).

The Selection Process

Following the recruitment of a pool of applicants, employers need to make a choice between candidates. The most common method used to make this selection decision remains the interview (see Figure 5.2). However, increasingly firms are recognizing the importance of selection decisions and are applying other methods that can improve the effectiveness of the process, even though there are still frequent concerns expressed in the literature about the continued use of traditional interview methods (Smith and Graves 2002). In evaluating which methods are effective, three basic criteria are normally applied, at least when seen from the traditional, psychometric perspective. These are reliability, validity and usefulness.

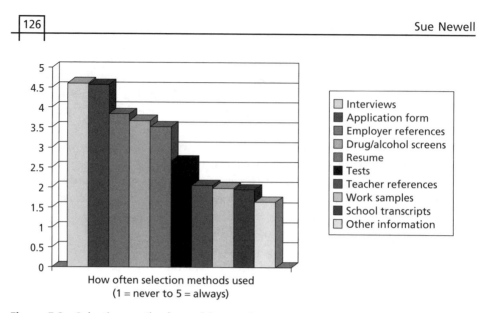

How often selection methods used
(1 = never to 5 = always)

Figure 5.2 Selection methods used by employers
Source: Adapted from Wilk and Cappelli (2003)

Reliability

Reliability essentially refers to the consistency of a method used to select individuals. While there are numerous types of reliability three are most important when considering selection methods. The first comprises 'testee' reliability. For example, if a person uses a tape measure to measure a desk, it needs to be reliable and give the same reading each time. It would be of little value if the tape was made of a material that was highly sensitive to variations in temperature, yielding different readings as the temperature changed. The same is true of any selection method – if they are going to be of value, they need to provide the same information over time. Thus, if the results of a personality inventory indicate an extrovert personality, it should generate the same result six months later. If there is consistency over time then the inventory can be said to be measuring this trait reliably. This type of reliability is commonly referred to as test-retest reliability.

Secondly, there is 'tester' reliability. Using the tape measure analogy again, the measurement process can only be described as reliable or consistent if two people measuring the same desk come up with the same answer. If one person finds that it is 80 cm in length and the other 85 cm then the measuring process is not very reliable. Similarly, in terms of selection, if two people interview a person for a job, but one concludes that the candidate is suitable while the other concludes that she/he is not, the selection method is not reliable.

Thirdly, there is 'test' reliability. Sticking with the tape measure, if it is a reliable instrument, there should be consistency in relation to the distance between 3 and 4 cm and between 7 and 8 cm. That is, any part of the tape measure, which indicates a centimetre, should be the same as a different part of the tape measure which measures a centimetre. The same logic applies to a personality measure. If there are a number of questions which all relate to the assessment of the personality dimension of 'extroversion', all these items should have the same (or at least very similar) scores for the measure of extroversion to be reliable.

Reliability is typically presented in terms of a correlation coefficient, r. That is, the correlation between two scores, whether these are the scores of the same individual at different points in time, the correlation between the results of two testers, or the correlation between two items on a test which measure the same underlying dimension. A perfect positive correlation would provide a score of $r = 1.0$. This would mean that there was a totally predictable relation between the two scores. For example, taking a group of individuals, all of their scores might differ on a particular personality trait, but if for any given individual the scores on one of the measurements (scores on a personality scale at time 1), were identical to the scores on the other measurement (scores on the same personality scale at time 2), the correlation would be 1.0 and the trait could be said to be measured reliably. In reality, in the domain of human behaviour, such perfect correlations do not exist. Nevertheless, what is required are significant deviations from randomness (total randomness being indicated by a score of $r = 0$) so that employers can be confident that the assessments used to make selection decisions are reasonably reliable or consistent.

Validity

There are a number of different types of validity, but in considering selection methods, the most important is predictive or criterion-related validity. That is, establishing the relationship between the predictors (the results from the selection methods used) and the criterion (performance on the job). For a selection tool to be considered valid it must discriminate between candidates in terms of subsequent performance on the job. Those candidates who were predicted to be 'good' potential employees, on a selection method, should subsequently perform well while those predicted to be 'poor' should perform less well. So again, a correlation is required but this time between the predictor (the selection method) and the criterion (the job performance). The 'pure' method of establishing this relationship is to measure applicants during selection and, based on whatever method(s) are being used, make predictions based on this, about future performance. However, applicants are not chosen on this basis, but either all or a cross-section of applicants (i.e. those predicted to be poor performers as well as those predicted to be good) are taken on. This is necessary in order to be certain that those who were predicted to be 'poor' actually are weak performers on the job. Then, after a period in the job, performance is measured and the correlation established between the selection method prediction and the job performance criterion measure. The two graphs in Figure 5.3 demonstrate the relationship between two different selection methods and subsequent performance. The aim is to avoid the selection of either

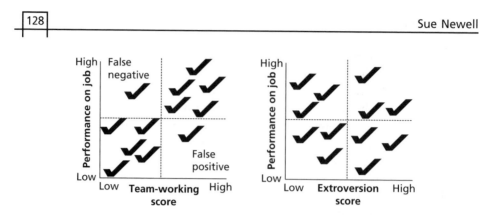

Figure 5.3 Comparison of the validity of different selection methods

'false positives' – people predicted to be 'good' but who were subsequently 'poor' – and vice-versa, that is, 'false negatives'. In Figure 5.3, the team-working score, derived from a group exercise used during the selection process, is a fairly good predictor of subsequent performance. This is because those who were given high marks on this exercise subsequently did well on the job while those who were given low marks did poorly, and there are few either false positives or negatives. On the other hand, the extroversion score, derived from a personality measure, bears no relationship to subsequent job performance. There are as many false positives and negatives as there are true hits, that is, high scorers who subsequently did well and low scorers who subsequently did poorly.

There are practical difficulties with this process of validating selection methods, such as the need to get results from a fairly large number of individuals. This is difficult in jobs where there are only a small number of people recruited over time. Research on selection method validation has, therefore, focused on areas where large groups are regularly recruited, such as to the army or the civil service. The more obvious problem is the reluctance of decision-makers to agree to employ individuals who are predicted to be poor performers, just so that this can be proved!

The concurrent method of validation is sometimes used to avoid this difficulty with current employees used to validate a new selection method. The assumption behind this approach is that existing employees demonstrate variable job performance. If the new selection method can discriminate between good and poor performers, it should be able to discriminate in the same way between job applicants. In this case, the new selection method (e.g. a group exercise) is used with current employees who are scored on their performance on the exercise. This score is related to some measure of job performance, the criterion. If it is able to discriminate between good and poor performers then it is assumed to be a valid predictor and is used for selection purposes.

There are also problems with this validation process. The motivation of current employees is likely to be quite different to that of candidates, which may affect the scores. Candidates are likely to try harder than those already employed because they want the job. Also, current employees are already a restricted sample as they have been previously selected by some method. So they may, on average, be 'better' than the average candidate. More importantly, it does not prove that the differences in team-skills, as measured by the group exercise, were evident prior to employment. It might be that they were learnt by employees as a by-product of their work. If this were the case, then using this method for selection would be discriminating unnecessarily between individuals on a predictor that is not an essential prerequisite for the job.

One other issue that is particularly important when discussing issues of predictive or concurrent validity relates to the criterion or performance measure, rather than the selection method itself. This is because measuring job performance is difficult. A very common criterion measure used in validation research is supervisors' ratings of employee performance. These ratings, however, are subjective and prone to rater bias (see Chapter 11). Secondly, in terms of the focus or level, Smith (1994) argues that there are at least three levels which need to be considered: the individual job level; the group or department level; and the organization level. It may be that an individual is functioning effectively at the individual level – performing their individual tasks competently – but is not so effective at the group or organizational level, for example, because of their reluctance to share information with others. Smith (1994) argues that it is necessary to consider all three levels in developing a criterion measure of performance. Unfortunately, much research and practice does not follow this advice, but rather uses very limited measures of the criterion, namely supervisor ratings.

While it is essential to understand these issues of reliability and validity, it is also true to say that very few organizations systematically assess the reliability and validity of the selection methods they use. When psychometric tests are used there is a tendency to rely on the evidence presented in the test manual on reliability and validity based on meta-analysis research. A recent meta-analysis (Hermelin and Robertson 2001) divided different selection methods into three categories – those with high, medium and low validity. High validity methods were structured interviews and cognitive ability tests. Medium validity methods were biographical data, unstructured interviews, and integrity tests. Finally, the low validity selection methods were the personality scales measuring the 'big five' (see below).

This evidence is helpful to organizations since it clearly indicates that some selection methods have higher validity than others and that it is desirable to try and validate the selection method(s) used systematically within a given organizational context, rather than rely on intuition or secondary data. Unfortunately, the evidence also suggests that those methods with the highest validity are not the most popular. Rather, most organizations rely on the classic trio of short-listing, interviewing and references (Cook 2003; Millmore 2003).

Selection Methods

A variety of methods can be used to make selection decisions, but the first thing to note is that the interview remains the most common method, often used alone, although increasingly combined with additional methods (Shackleton and Newell 1991; see also Figure 5.2 above).

Pre-selection methods

The first stage of selection is typically based on information provided in standard application forms and CVs and the majority of candidates are selected out of the process at this stage. Biographical data (biodata) can also be used here, that is, biographical information about a person's past experiences and achievements. It is assumed that this information about a person's past behaviour can predict their future behaviour. Traditionally, this information has been used in a subjective manner (Wingrove et al. 1984). Adopting a more objective, statistical approach to this biographical information has been shown to significantly improve validity. Harvey-Cook and Taffler (2000) developed an actuarial model to predict success to entry level professional accounting positions. Using factual biographical data they developed a six variable model (which included number of A grade GCSEs, degree class, number of art or language A levels (negatively weighted), science or technology degree, head boy/girl, and independent school), which better predicted professional examination success than the methods actually being used by the accounting firms involved in the study.

This statistical approach to selection, using biodata with confirmed predictive relations to job performance can, therefore, be useful and some firms now do use common applications in this way as the first part of the selection process. Gathering biodata electronically can actually improve this early screening process (Polyhart et al. 2003). And while there have been criticisms, especially where predictive variables appear arbitrary (e.g., primogeniture as a significant predictor of US Navy diving training outcome, Helmreich et al. 1973), usually sound explanations for such findings can be found (Drakeley 1988). Once this pre-selection process has been completed, the next step is usually the interview.

Interviews

Selection interviews have had a very 'bad press' because research evidence seemed to suggest that this was a very ineffective way of making decisions. Nonetheless, interviews retain their appeal as a selection technique and virtually all employers use interviews for all categories of staff. However, as we discuss below, employers seem more aware of their limitations and are trying to use them more carefully and for some groups, such as graduates, interviews are being complemented by a variety of other selection techniques. An early study reported by Kelly and Fiske (1951) used an interview to predict the success of graduate students in psychology. The results were that neither one nor two hour interviews added to the validity of predictions made simply by using background information about the students.

Moreover, when research examined whether two or more interviewers interviewing the same candidate came to the same conclusions, the evidence was equally negative – essentially there was little consistency or reliability. However, more recently the focus has been on investigating the interview process itself to understand why the interview, at least in its typical unstructured format, is a bad predictor (see Posthuma et al. 2002).

Essentially, unstructured interviews are bad predictors because the information which is 'extracted' is different for each individual and differs between interviewers, and so comparisons between candidates cannot be reliably made. With different questions being asked of each candidate it is almost inevitable that subjective biases make the interview both unreliable and invalid. Thus, stereotyping an individual as belonging to a particular group and assuming that she/he then has all the characteristics associated with that particular 'group' is common; making decisions very quickly, within the first four minutes of the interview, based on superficial information such as physical characteristics or accent, is typical; and over-rating the importance of negative information is high. However, understanding the sources of unreliability and invalidity has also helped to develop interviews which are much less likely to suffer from these subjective biases, although these types of bias can never be totally eliminated.

Much work has been devoted to developing interview formats which minimize these subjective biases. The basic ingredient of these developments is to provide structure, so that interviews are more specifically job-related, and are standardized, so that the same topics are covered with all candidates. The best known of these structured interviews are the situational interview, the patterned interview, and the content analytical interview. In the situational interview, applicants are asked to describe what they would do in a number of hypothetical situations. This approach is based on the assumption that intentions are good predictors of behaviour (Latham et al. 1980). The situations that are used are extracted using a critical incident job analysis. The responses of the candidates are evaluated by experts using rating scales that are anchored by examples of good, average, and poor current employee behaviours. In general, situational interviews have proved to be valid (Weekley and Gier 1987). Robertson et al. (1990) provide an example of a situational interview to assess adaptability or flexibility (see Box 5.2).

Another structured approach, the patterned behavioural description interview, asks for specific examples of past behaviour (Janz et al. 1986). The approach also begins with a critical incident job analysis. Questions are then designed which ask applicants to demonstrate how they have reacted to situations with similar characteristics to these critical incidents. For example, if the critical incident analysis of a teacher's job revealed that dealing with difficult parents was an important part of the job, then an interview question might be: 'Tell me about the most difficult parent you have had to deal with in the last year.'

The content analytical interview is based on the view that talented people talk differently. The focus is on the exact content of each interviewee's responses, using a variety of questions. For example the question 'what makes you feel important?'

Box 5.2   Example of a situational interview technique

Two young people have approached the organization for finance to set up a new venture making and selling equipment to enable home-computer users to translate games easily between different models of computer. They are enthusiastic and talented but freely confess that they have no business, manufacturing or selling experience. What would you advise them?

Scale points:

Low   Contact someone else (e.g., accountant) for information on cash flows

           Tell them not to go ahead – too risky, no market

Medium   Recommend information to them

           Tell them to recruit a business person

           Tell them to get accountant to prepare cost reports

           Arrange for them to see organization's experts

           Ask them to talk more once they have thought some more about it

High   Say the organization is enthusiastic about them as customers

           Ask them about legal side of game translation

           Ask if they have a prototype

           Contact patent office

           Advise on information sources: DTI, venture capital, organization's accountants

Source: Robertson et al. (1990).

might be asked. For the interviewer, job performance categories are used to sort out the most important questions and the 'listen-fors'. Each question is an item, like a questionnaire, and is scored separately before totalling all items. Interviews are often conducted over the telephone, since it is what is said that is being listened for. Although good validity has been reported with this method (Hill and Parker 1996), it requires the interviewer to follow a script and have the interview tape-recorded. Many object to these constraints.

Research has shown that increasing the structure of the interview significantly increases predictive validity and that organizations are responding by using more structured interview approaches (Taylor et al. 2002) which has a positive effect on fairness of interview outcomes (Huffcutt and Roth 1998). The evidence suggests that there is little or no increase in validity after a certain level of structure has been achieved, a level which all three of the above methods achieve (see Huffcutt and Arthur 1994; McDaniel et al. 1994). Indeed, it has been argued that over-structuring the interview can be a problem, as the unstructured interview can serve legitimate functions which the structured interview cannot (Dipboye 1994). For example, in an unstructured interview, the interviewer can provide more realistic information about the job, with the candidate able to ask questions which relate to his or her personal needs, values, interests, goals and abilities. Through this process, the applicant and the interviewer can negotiate a mutually agreeable 'psychological contract'. Secondly, the unstructured interview can operate as a preliminary socialization tactic with the applicant learning about the culture and values of the organization (Dipboye 1997). These issues will be addressed more fully in the final section of this chapter.

While structured interviews can certainly be beneficial their usefulness will depend on the specific context. Where jobs are highly prescribed, where there is know-ledge about how work needs to be carried out and where there is clarity about what constitutes good performance, then a structured interview is likely to be appro-priate because prediction is possible and structured interviews are better predictors. However, when an organization is competing in a turbulent environment and there is considerable uncertainty about what is required of individuals, a less structured approach may be more appropriate. This does not mean abandoning structure altogether. Using job and organizational analysis as a basis for designing interview procedures and standardizing, to some extent, both the questions and the rating procedures is helpful. Moreover, in all situations, abandoning all 'slack' during the interview is unlikely to be effective because it ignores the other purposes that inter-views serve, which extend beyond assessing job competencies. As Judge and Ferris (1992: 23) argue: 'calls for structured interviews may be misplaced if the true goal, and utility, of the interview lies not in selecting the most technically qualified, but the individual most likely to fit into the organization'.

Psychological testing

Psychological testing has gained in popularity in the UK, especially for graduate and management level candidates (Shackleton and Newell 1991; IRS 1997). There has been a substantial increase in their usage and they have become an integral part of the search for greater objectivity in selection. Essentially, two types need to be distinguished: personality tests and cognitive or ability tests. Cognitive tests provide an assessment of an individual's intellectual abilities, either in terms of general intelligence (IQ, or g) or specific abilities (such as verbal, numerical, spatial abilities or abstract reasoning). Personality tests provide an assessment of an individual's general disposition to behave in a certain way in certain situations. It is important to differentiate between these two types of assessment test.

Cognitive tests

The seminal piece of work on the use of cognitive tests in selection was under-taken by Hunter and Schmidt (1990). Using meta-analysis, these researchers were able to demonstrate that although the many studies on the predictive validity of tests appeared to be inconsistent, when adjustments were made for various factors (e.g. differences in sample sizes, restrictions in the range of scores from those involved) results were in fact remarkably consistent and proved that cognitive tests were valid predictors in a wide range of job situations. In other words, general intelligence predicts at least some of the performance variation in most job situations. More-over, such tests are relatively simple to administer and score, albeit the person using such tests needs to be properly trained (see Bartram and Lindley 1994). There are two caveats to this general conclusion. First, for most jobs the range of intelli-gence of those applying for the job is likely to be very restricted. It is rare to have someone with an IQ of 90 applying for the job of a head-teacher; similarly it is probably rare for a person with an IQ of 140 to apply for the job of caretaker. The consequence of this is that a measure of cognitive ability may not differenti-ate much between the various candidates. Second, cognitive tests can be biased against certain groups. For example, it is well documented that black Americans tend to score lower than whites on tests of cognitive ability, and women tend to score higher on verbal ability than do men. This certainly raises social and ethical issues, which will need to be carefully considered when selecting particular tests.

Personality measures

In most UK selection situations, the personality measures used are of the self-report type. There is considerably more controversy over the use of personality measures, than there is over the use of cognitive tests, so much so that they have been dis-missed by some as being totally useless for selection purposes (Blinkhorn and Johnson 1990). The fact that there has been much less increase in usage of personality tests than cognitive tests over the course of the 1990s has been interpreted as a reflection of the concerns that have been raised about the validity of these tests, in com-parison to other types of test (IRS 1997: 13). Research has shown that personality measurement can be useful, but only when specific personality constructs are linked to specific job competencies (Barrick and Mount 1991; Robertson and Kinder 1993; Tett et al. 1991). Much of this work has been based on using the 'big five' personality factors of extroversion, neuroticism, conscientiousness, agreeableness, and openness. Certainly one of the problems with research on personality measure-ment has been that very different systems of personality description have been used, making it difficult to compare results. There is now a growing consensus around the five-factor model of broad traits (Goldberg 1993) and the use of Costa and McCrae's (1992) personality inventory which measures these five factors. Studies have demonstrated that these dimensions can be systematically related to different job dimensions (especially conscientiousness and integrity, Schmidt and Hunter 1998). Researchers are also beginning to explore the reasons for the links between personality traits and job performance. For example, conscientiousness is linked to a tendency to set goals which may be related to performance in jobs where there is discretion in the activities that can be undertaken; and openness to experience appears to be related to training success (Cooper and Robertson 1995).

However, it is unlikely that personality tests alone will ever be good predictors of future job behaviour. This is because job situations often present strong situational pressures which mean that differences between individuals' behaviours are minimized. Secondly, it is highly likely that the same job can be done in very different, but equally successful, ways by individuals with different personalities. This does not mean that personality measures have no place in the selection process, but it raises the question of how such measures are best used within this context. Defining a personality profile for a job and dismissing candidates who do not fit this profile is not good practice, given the limitations discussed above. On the other hand, obtaining measures of personality and then using these as the basis of discussion during an interview can be helpful. For example, an individual scoring very high on introversion applying for a sales job that involves a lot of customer contact, may be asked how she will cope with the demands of the job given her introversion. This discussion might reveal that she has developed coping mechanisms for dealing with her interpersonal shyness so that she could be very competent in the job. On the other hand, the discussion may actually make the candidate realize that she is not well suited to the job so that she withdraws her application. This should be viewed as a positive outcome if it means that an unsuitable candidate withdraws.

Issues in psychometric testing

While technical issues to do with the predictive validity of different types of psychometric test are important, there are also ethical issues raised about the use of such tests. Most importantly, individuals who have taken a test, whether cognitive or personality, have a right to the results of those tests under the code of ethics of both the British Psychological Society and the Chartered Institute of Personnel and Development. Yet Newell and Shackleton (1993) found that, especially when tests were used as part of the selection process, this did not happen in a significant minority of companies. Not only is this ethically bad practice, it also suggests that these tests are being used in ways which are unlikely to fully exploit their potential as part of the selection process, especially with respect to personality tests. The results of personality assessment can be used most effectively by discussing with the individual how, given their particular personality characteristics, they would cope with different aspects of the job and how they would fit in to the organization culture. Such a discussion, as part of an interview, allows the individual to more clearly think through their values and expectations in relation to the job and organization, so that a two-way exchange is enabled. This approach would also make it less likely that individuals would fake their answers on personality measures in a bid to present a particular self-portrait. Knowing that there is no 'right' answer and that there will be an opportunity to discuss how personality impacts on the individual's approach to work is likely to encourage more open and honest responses from candidates (see below).

Assessment centres

An Assessment Centre (AC) is not a single selection method, nor is it a place. Rather an AC refers to the utilization of a number of different selection methods over a specified period (typically 1–4 days) in order for multiple assessors to assess many candidates on a range of identified competencies or behavioural dimensions. While ACs incorporate a variety of methods, often including interviews and psychometric tests, a core element is the simulation of actual work tasks in order to observe job-related behaviours (Cooper and Robertson 1995). For managerial jobs, in-tray exercises and group decision-making exercises are particularly common, at least in ACs in the UK. The in-tray exercise provides a candidate with a range of correspondence (memos, letters, reports) and he or she is required to make decisions in order to prioritize and deal with various problems in the material, under a very tight time schedule. Such an exercise is used to assess the individual's planning and problem-solving abilities. In group decision-making exercises, individuals are put together in small groups and required to either discuss a particular issue and come to a group consensus or solve a particular problem through a group decision process. Again, problem-solving abilities may be assessed, but in addition interpersonal and leadership skills can be evaluated in these situations.

Despite growing use of ACs, especially for graduate and managerial jobs (Shackleton and Newell 1991; IRS 1997: 15), there is also increasing evidence of their limitations. Jones et al. (1991) concluded that despite the validity of different components of an AC, the overall AC validity was surprisingly low. A key problem appears to be that managers, acting as assessors, are not able to accurately assess cross-situational abilities from the different exercises. So while managers are required to rate candidates on different competencies or dimensions for each exercise, these ratings appear to be largely defined by the overall task performance of the candidate on the particular exercise, rather than by specific behaviours demonstrated during the activity (Iles 1992). Correlations between the same dimensions measured across exercises are very low, while correlations between different dimensions measured within an exercise are much higher (Robertson et al. 1987; McCredie and Shackleton 1994). When the ratings from different exercises are combined into the overall assessment rating (OAR), it appears that assessors typically do not consider the whole range of dimensions, but instead rely on only a small number, and often those dimensions which empirically have less predictive validity. Finally, a number of studies have demonstrated a low correlation between the OAR and a variety of criterion measures of on-the-job performance (Payne et al. 1992).

Despite this somewhat negative evidence there are two important points to be made. First, designing and developing an AC has the potential to improve the validity of selection, but simply putting together a series of exercises and running them over two days using a group of untrained assessors does not guarantee that decisions will be improved. For example, Gaugler et al. (1987), using meta-analysis, found that the validity of ACs improved when a larger number of exercises were included, when psychologists rather than managers acted as the assessors, when peer evaluation was included as part of the assessment process, and when the group of assessors contained a larger proportion of women.

Second, many of the problems identified with respect to ACs need to be looked at from a broader perspective than simply their criterion-related validity. A key benefit of using an AC is that it gives the potential recruit an extended opportunity to find out more about the organization. In particular, because many of the exercises are simulations of the kind of work that will be involved if the person is selected, the individual has a much better opportunity to develop realistic expectations about the job and the organization. If exercises do reflect organizational reality, not only is the organization given an opportunity to find out more about the potential recruits, but also recruits have the opportunity to find out more about the organization so that a more mutually beneficial negotiation can take place. But this requires the adoption of an exchange rather than a psychometric view of the recruitment and selection process. This is discussed next.

Recruitment and Selection: Limitations of the Psychometric Approach

The opening section of this chapter considered the importance of recruiting people who can respond to the challenges of an increasingly competitive environment. As noted earlier, adopting a more systematic approach to recruitment and selection to reduce bias and errors is useful. Yet, ironically, it could be argued that globalization and organizational requirements of flexibility, innovation and commitment make the 'best practices' advocated earlier somewhat problematic and suggest a need for an entirely new perspective on recruitment and selection.

First, considering the degree of change, organizations often now require employees to be generalists rather than specialists, able to take on a variety of different roles which require a range of skills and competencies. Even where individuals are recruited for a particular position with a specified job description, it is highly likely that the job will change. Thus, the 'best practice' prescription of doing a thorough job analysis to identify the task and the person requirements of the particular job may be difficult or inappropriate. There is not a fixed 'jigsaw hole' to fill, especially in the medium-term.

Second, alongside flexibility is the need for innovation. Identifying opportunities for change and designing creative solutions is crucial for the survival of many organizations. This creative ability is about challenging the status quo and encouraging people to think and act differently. Following 'best practice' guidelines leads to selection on the basis of whether candidates can do particular jobs efficiently and whether they fit the organizational culture. Rather than encourage innovation, traditional selection approaches may stifle creativity.

Third, increasingly organizations are operating in a global rather than a national arena. Considering the array of cross-national differences it is unlikely that organizations will be effective if they simply try to replicate their home-base operation abroad (Bartlett and Ghoshal 1989). Rather, to manage this diversity requires recruiting and selecting people with very different backgrounds and experiences at all organizational levels. However, job analysis is backward looking. If the current job-holders are all of the same race or nationality, for example, this may mean that individuals from different backgrounds will be excluded because they do not fit the existing profile of a competent employee. Alternatively, during the selection process, individuals from different nationalities may respond very differently to particular selection methods so that they are disadvantaged (Shackleton and Newell 1994), again reducing their chances of being selected.

Finally, ensuring the quality of all products and processes is now an essential prerequisite for organizations, requiring employee commitment to quality (Bolwijn and Kumpe 1990). It is very difficult, however, to assess and select for commitment because showing commitment to an organization will at least partly depend on the organization reciprocating that commitment to the individual. Employee commitment is under severe strain in an era of downsizing and short-term contracts. Consequently, recruitment and selection cannot be seen in isolation from the subsequent interactions between the individual and the organization. Emphasizing the 'right' selection decision ignores how subsequent interactions will influence how far the decision was 'right'. An exceptional individual may become demoralized by their subsequent treatment within the organization and so either leave or not contribute fully; it may be inferred – rather superficially – as a faulty selection decision.

Thus, there are problems with the traditional 'best practice' view of recruitment and selection, in particular in so far as it tends to assume that there is 'one best way' to do a particular job, as illustrated by the person specification. Instead, selection needs to be seen as part of a broader process of organizational socialization (Anderson 2001) with the psychometric properties of selection methods not the only criteria of usefulness. Recruitment and selection is about discriminating between individuals, but based on relevant and fair criteria like technical skills and attitudes, rather than irrelevant criteria like gender, race, age or disability. However, given the 'one best way' assumption, unfair discrimination and prejudice can be the result. The traditional approach to selection is likely to perpetuate the status quo. The assumption will typically be that it is necessary to find a similar shaped 'jigsaw piece' to replace that individual, which restricts certain groups who have been previously underrepresented in particular jobs, for example, black women in senior management positions (see Chapter 7).

The psychometric view of recruitment and selection also presents a very static picture of the job. It underestimates the degree of change within organizations and the situational influences on individuals. It overestimates the personal criteria which influence job performance and underestimates the role or situational demands. Thus, in many jobs role expectations are so strong that the individual has limited flexibility in how they behave. Finally, this psychometric approach assumes that it is possible to measure psychological differences between individuals in the same objective way as physical differences.

The assumptions of the traditional, psychometric, approach to recruitment and selection may therefore no longer be appropriate, at least for certain kinds of jobs, and a different approach is required. Peter Herriot (1984) has presented a very different view, arguing that it is best to see selection as a process of exchange or negotiation between two parties, the employing organization and the potential recruit. Both of these parties have a set of expectations related to their current and future needs and values. Recruitment and selection is portrayed as a series of episodes in which increasing amounts of information are exchanged to determine whether there is indeed compatibility between the organization and the individual. Negotiation is possible because neither the organization nor the individual is seen as having fixed characteristics, although the underlying values and needs of both sides are recognized to be more stable. The outcome of this process, if successful, is that a viable psychological contract is negotiated which encapsulates congruence between the expectations of both parties. However, if the process of negotiation breaks down, because the parties are unable to develop a sense of congruence, this can also be construed as positive (or in Herriot's terms, 'valid negative'). The organization avoids employing someone who will not fit the job or the organizational culture and the candidate avoids taking on a new job for which they are not suited.

Before turning to the alternative exchange view of recruitment and selection in more detail, it is important to consider the extent to which the work environment has actually changed in the twenty-first century. In terms of recruitment and selection, the traditional person-job fit approach remains dominant, even though it has some inherent limitations. More specifically, while there has been an obvious shift from manufacturing to service jobs, not all of these service jobs are for knowledge workers (see Chapter 13). Many call centre jobs require staff to perform 'emotional' rather than physical labour but their jobs, like workers on an assembly line, are still tightly controlled and monitored and they are required to perform according to predefined instructions. They are recruited based on their flexibility to deal with a variety of different people, which is seen to stem from their personality (Callaghan and Thompson 2002). So, they have to have the personality to fit the job. This indicates that they are recruited based on a set of clear criteria – a well-defined person specification – where there is little room for negotiation. Ironically, given the rigidity of the job which these employees eventually find themselves in, having to follow very scripted interactions with the customers, the flexible employees selected soon become bored with the job, so that turnover is high. However, organizations see this as the price to pay and continue to select people that fit the job requirements, albeit only temporarily. So, here is an instance where, at least in practice, the person-job fit approach continues to be used even though it is recognized that the fit will be short-lived.

The recruitment and selection process from the exchange perspective

From the exchange perspective recruitment begins with the employing organization articulating its expectations of the particular type of employee it is looking to recruit and the type of job and working environment that they will be working in. This information is then communicated to potential applicants. Importantly, negative as well as positive information about the job and organization is provided. Potential recruits can compare this information with their own personal expectations and ambitions, making it easier for individuals to decide whether or not to apply for a position. This approach to recruitment is clearly very different from the one typically found, especially for the competitive graduate market, which presents little more than a glossy, exaggerated image of both the organization and the potential career opportunities for successful candidates. Glossy recruitment brochures make it very difficult for prospective candidates to differentiate between firms, preventing informed decisions about suitable and unsuitable prospective employers.

The justification for adopting this 'glossy' approach is that each employer aims to attract the 'best' people and therefore they do not want to deter good candidates from applying by presenting more realistic information – for example, that most people will not progress to senior executive levels. But the company may fear discouraging good recruits when competitor companies are advertising seemingly limitless and swift career trajectories. It is seen to be too risky to be more realistic, even though what is really at risk is putting off those who will not fit the particular job and organizational environment.

In the traditional approach, this attempt to impress the 'best' candidates continues. The selection process is seen as a one-way process of decision making, with the organization selecting the candidate on the basis of collecting as much valid and reliable information about that person as possible. It does not see the need to reciprocate and allow candidates realistic information about the job, enabling them to make an informed decision. Even the usual final question at the interview: 'Do you have any questions?' is often treated as another opportunity for the organization to assess whether the individual can ask 'something sensible' rather than as a genuine attempt to provide the candidate with information.

The obvious problem with this traditional approach is that new employees' expectations will not match the reality of the situation they find. While it is clear that expectations are modified in the light of circumstances (Arnold 1985), there is a high turnover level arising from this approach, especially for individuals with little or no experience of employment who tend to have more unrealistic expectations (Brennan and McGeevor 1987). Adopting the exchange approach involves making the recruitment and selection process an opportunity for a genuine exchange of valid and reliable information between both parties; providing candidates with ample opportunity to understand the job and organizational culture. Recruitment methods are designed to attract candidates most suited to the job and work environment, rather than to attract the maximum number of 'good quality' applicants. Selection between candidates, if necessary, is then a process whereby more information is exchanged between the two parties in order to establish whether there is a fit between the two sets of expectations. Where the fit is found to be lacking, negotiation will take place to see if any adjustment is possible in both the individual's and the organization's expectations. Fit refers to the fit between the individual and the organization, as well as fit between the individual and the particular job.

This exchange approach also recognizes that it is not helpful to see the selection episode in isolation from subsequent interactions between the individual and the organization, especially where the individual is actually taken on as an employee. So, selecting employees who have the competencies needed, or who have the potential to develop the competencies needed, is a start not an end point of the process. Thus, evidence has demonstrated that organizational receptivity to the new employee is crucial to reducing early turnover and increasing commitment (Holton and Russell 1999). Moreover, commitment and turnover is strongly influenced by the opportunities that are provided once the person actually starts to work in the job, regardless of whether they have the competencies needed. Arnold and Mackenzie Davy (1999) found that improvements in organizational commitment were related to the extent to which graduates were able to use and develop their skills once they started work. Efforts at post-selection socialization and training are therefore as crucial to ensuring an effective selection process as is choosing valid and reliable selection methods. The actual selection decision is therefore only a single step in an entire process whereby the individual is socialized into the workplace in order to become a committed and effective employee.

Conclusion

Smith (1994) distinguished between three types of individual characteristics that relate to job performance: 'universals' which refer to characteristics that are relevant to all jobs; 'occupationals' which refer to characteristics relevant to particular jobs or occupations; and 'relationals' which refer to characteristics relevant in a particular work setting. This typology suggests that it is important to match characteristics of people with the characteristics of particular work settings, and research has indeed shown that people who 'fit' the work setting are more satisfied and committed compared to people who do not feel they fit (O'Reilly et al. 1991).

Schneider (1987) proposed his attraction–selection–attrition (ASA) model to consider the process through which this fit between personality and organizational environment is established. People with similar personalities will be attracted to particular types of organization and individuals with characteristics which are similar to those existing in the organization will be more likely to be selected. Moreover, individuals with characteristics which are different to the dominant characteristics will be more likely to leave. However, in a study of the relation between organizational climate and recruiter's perceptions of the 'ideal' personality of new recruits, Van Vianen and Kmieciak (1998) found very little evidence to support the idea that recruitment and selection created homogeneity of personality. Rather they conclude that organizational climate is mainly created by homogeneity of behaviour (especially socialization into the organization) and not homogeneity of personalities.

The key implication is that 'assessment of person–environment fit in selection should not be based primarily on personality–climate fit but on the fit between the person's needs and organizational practices' (Van Vianen and Kmieciak 1998). Such a view of recruitment and selection fits much more easily within an exchange view of the process than within the traditional psychometric view. So, both the traditional psychometric view of recruitment and selection and the exchange model emphasize 'fit' between the person and the job environment. But in the former case it is based on fixed dimensions of both the job and the person, with the organization having the sole prerogative to determine the 'fit'. From the exchange perspective 'fit' is the outcome of a process of exchange and negotiation. Moreover, in the traditional view, 'fit' is assumed between personal characteristics of the individual and the technical demands of the particular job (person–job fit). In the exchange model, 'fit' relates to the matching of expectations and needs of the individual with the values, climate and goals of the organization (person–organization fit).

The problem with the traditional approach is two-fold. First, through the recruitment and selection process messages about the organization's culture and values are inevitably communicated to candidates. However, the messages communicated are likely to be inaccurate and unrealistic so that the new employee begins with false expectations about the congruence between their own values and attitudes and those of the organization. Second, and following from the first point, where congruence between the values, goals and attributes of the individual and the organization is lacking there is likely to be lower levels of satisfaction, performance and commitment, on both sides, and higher levels of employee stress, absenteeism and turnover (Chatman 1991; Schneider 1987).

Given these problems there is now a growing recognition that increasing person–organization fit during selection can improve work-related outcomes (Bowen et al. 1991). Yet this requires a very different view of the selection process, seeing selection as an opportunity for candidates to learn about jobs and the organization, and so beginning the process of organizational socialization (Anderson and Ostroff 1997). In this sense, recruitment and selection become part of the broader process of socialization, rather than isolated episodes of choice. The criterion-related or predictive validity of recruitment and selection methods is, then, not the only, or even the most important, basis for evaluating the process (Anderson, 2001). Rather, it is necessary to consider how recruitment and selection methods influence newcomer expectations and behaviour (Iles and Mabey 1993; Robertson et al. 1991). This is why some methods, which may have limited predictive validity in the traditional sense, are nevertheless useful because they do enable candidates to develop an accurate picture of what to expect.

Allowing new employees to gain a realistic understanding of the job and organization culture and using recruitment and selection as the basis for negotiating a robust psychological contract starts the process of organizational socialization. This approach is more likely to lead to the recruitment of individuals who are willing to give long-term commitment to the organization, than is seeing recruitment and selection as a management decision-making prerogative related to a one-sided prediction of future, narrowly defined, job success.

REFERENCES AND FURTHER READING

Anderson, N. 2001: Towards a theory of socialization impact: Selection as pre-entry socialization, *International Journal of Selection and Assessment*, **9**(1/2), 84–91.

Anderson, N. and Ostroff, C. 1997: Selection as socialisation, in N. Anderson and P. Herriot (eds.), *International Handbook of Selection and Assessment*, Chichester: John Wiley and Sons Ltd.

Arnold, J. 1985: Tales of the unexpected: Surprises experienced by graduates in the early months of employment, *British Journal of Guidance and Counselling*, **13**(3), 308–19.

Arnold, J. and Mackenzie Davy, K. 1999: Graduates' work experiences as predictors of organizational commitment, intention to leave and turnover: Which experiences really matter, *Applied Psychology: An International Review*, **48**(2), 211–38.

Barber, A. 1998: *Recruiting Employees: Individual and Organizational Perspectives*, Thousand Oaks, CA: Sage.

Barrick, M.R. and Mount, M.K. 1991: The big five personality dimensions and job performance: A meta-analysis, *Personnel Psychology*, **44**, 1–26.

Bartlett, C.A. and Ghoshal, S. 1989: *Managing across Borders: The Transnational Solution*, Boston MA: Harvard Business School Press.

Bartram, D. and Lindley, P.A. 1994: *Psychological Testing: The BPS 'Level A' Open Learning Programme*, Leicester: BPS Books.

Bingham, B., Ilg, S. and Davidson, N. 2002: Great candidates fast: On-line job application and electronic processing: Washington State's new internet application system, *Public Personnel Management*, **31**(1), 53–64.

Blinkhorn, S. and Johnson, C. 1990: The insignificance of personality testing, *Nature*, **348**, 671–72.

Boam, R. and Sparrow, P. (eds.) 1992: *Designing and Achieving Competency: A Competency based Approach to Managing People and Organizations*, London: McGraw Hill.

Bolwijn, P.T. and Kumpe, T. 1990: Manufacturing in the 1990s: Productivity, flexibility, and innovation, *Long Range Planning*, **23**, 44–57.

Bowen, D.E., Ledford, G.E. and Nathan, B.R. 1991: Hiring for the organisation, not the job, *Academy of Management Executive*, **5**, 35–51.

Boyatzis, R.E. 1982: *The Competent Manager: A Model for Effective Performance*, New York: John Wiley.

Brennan, J. and McGeevor, P. 1987: *CNNA Graduates: Their Employment and their Experience after Leaving College*, London: CNAA Development Services Publication, No. 13.

Callaghan, G. and Thompson, P. 2002: 'We recruit attitude': The selection and shaping of routine call centre labour, *Journal of Management Studies*, **39**(2), 233–54.

Carlson, K., Connerley, M. and Mecham, R. 2002: Recruitment evaluation: The case for assessing the quality of applicants attracted. *Personnel Psychology*, **55**(2), 461–89.

Chatman, J.I. 1991: Matching people and organisations: Selection and socialisation in public accounting firms. *Administrative Science Quarterly*, **21**, 433–52.

Cook, M. 2003: *Personnel Selection: Adding Value through People*, 4th edn, Chichester: John Wiley.

Cooper, D. and Robertson, I.T. 1995: *The Psychology of Personnel Selection*, London: Routledge.

Costa, P.T. and McCrae, R.R. 1992: Four ways five factors are basic, *Personality and Individual Differences*, **13**, 653–65.

Crouch, C., Finegold, D. and Sako, M. 1999: *Are Skills the Answer: The Political Economy of Skill Creation in Advanced Industrial Society*, Oxford: Oxford University Press.

Czerny, A. 2004: Not so quick and easy, *People Management*, 26 February, 14–17.

Dale, M. and Iles, P. 1992: *Assessing Management Skills: A Guide to Competencies and Evaluation Techniques*, London: Kogan Page.

Decker, P.J. and Cornelius, E.T. 1979: A note on recruiting sources and job survival rates. *Journal of Applied Psychology*, **64**, 463–64.

Dipboye, R.L. 1994: Structured and unstructured selection interviews: Beyond the job-fit model, in G. Ferris (ed.), *Research in Personnel and Human Resources Management*, **12**, 79–123. Greenwich, CT: JAI Press.

Dipboye, R.L. 1997: Structured selection interviews: Why do they work? Why are they underutilized? in N. Anderson and P. Herriot (eds.), *International Handbook of Selection and Assessment*, Chichester: John Wiley & Sons Ltd.

Drakeley, R. 1988: Achievement, background and commitment: Classification of biographical data in personnel selection. Unpublished doctoral dissertation, University of London.

Farnham, D. 2000: Developing and implementing competence-based recruitment and selection in a social services department: A case study of West Sussex County Council, *The International Journal of Public Sector Management*, **13**(4), 369–82.

Fletcher, C. 1992: *Competency-based Assessment Techniques*, London: Kogan Page.

Gaugler, B., Rosenthal, D.B., Thornton, G.C. and Bentson, C. 1987: Meta-analysis of assessment center validity, *Journal of Applied Psychology*, **72**(3), 493–511.

Goldberg, L.R. 1993: The structure of phenotypic personality traits, *American Psychologist*, **48**, 26–34.

Greuter, M. and Algera, J. 1989: Criterion development and job analysis, in P. Herriot (ed.), *Assessment and Selection in Organizations*, New York: Wiley.

Grossman, R. 2000: Measuring up: Appropriate metrics help HR improve its worth, *HR Magazine*, **45**(1), 28–35.

Hacker, C. 1997: The cost of poor hiring decisions . . . and how to avoid them, *HR Focus*, **74**(10), 13–14.

Harris, L. 2000: Procedural justice and perceptions of fairness in selection practice, *International Journal of Selection and Assessment*, **8**(3), 148–58.

Harvey-Cook, J. and Taffler, R. 2000: Biodata in professional entry-level selection: Statistical scoring of common format applications, *Journal of Occupational and Organizational Psychology*, **73**, 103–18.

Helmreich, R., Bakeman, R. and Radloff, R. 1973: The life history questionnaire as a predictor of performance in Navy diver training, *Journal of Applied Psychology*, **57**(2), 148–53.

Hermelin, E. and Robertson, I. 2001: A critique and standardization of meta-analytic validity coefficients in personnel selection, *Journal of Occupational and Organizational Psychology*, **74**, 253–77.

Herriot, P. 1984: *Down from the Ivory Tower: Graduates and their Jobs*, Chichester: John Wiley & Sons Ltd.

Hill, J. and Parker, C. 1996: The salvation of the interview? Structuring interviewing, *Assessment Matters*, Spring.

Holton, E. and Russell, C. 1999: Organizational entry and exit: An exploratory longitudinal analysis of early careers, *Human Performance*, **12**(3/4), 311–42.

Huffcutt, A. and Arthur, W. 1994: Hunter and Hunter (1984) revisited: Interview validity for entry level jobs, *Journal of Applied Psychology*, **79**(2), 184–91.

Huffcutt, A.I. and Roth, P.L. 1998: Racial group differences in employment interview evaluations, *Journal of Applied Psychology*, **83**, 179–89.

Hunter, J.E. and Schmidt, F.L. 1990: *Methods of Meta-Analysis: Correcting Errors and Bias in Research Findings*, Beverly Hills, CA: Sage.

Iles, P.A. 1992: Centres of excellence? Assessment and development centres, managerial competencies and HR strategies, *British Journal of Management*, **3**(2), 79–90.

Iles, P. and Mabey, C. 1993: Managerial career development techniques: Effectiveness, acceptability and availability, *British Journal of Management*, **4**, 103–18.

IPM (Institute of Personnel Management) 1995: *The IPM Code on Recruitment*, London: IPM.

IRS (Industrial Relations Service) 1997: The state of selection: An IRS survey, *Employee Development Bulletin*, **85**, (January), 8–13.

IRS (Industrial Relations Service) 2003a: Setting the tone: Job descriptions and person specifications, *IRS Employment Review*, **776**, (May), 42–9.

IRS (Industrial Relations Service) 2003b: Sharpening up recruitment and selection with competencies, *IRS Employment Review*, **782**, (August), 42–9.

Janz, T., Hellervik, L. and Gilmore, D.C. 1986: *Behaviour Description Interviewing: New, Accurate, Cost Effective*, Boston, MA: Allyn and Bacon.

Jones, A., Herriot, P., Long, B. and Drakeley, R. 1991: Attempting to improve the validity of a well-established assessment centre, *Journal of Occupational Psychology*, **64**(1), 1–21.

Judge, T.A. and Ferris, G.A. 1992: The elusive criterion of fit in human resources staffing decisions, *Human Resource Planning*, **15**, 47–67.

Kelly, E.L. and Fiske, D.W. 1951: *The Prediction of Performance in Clinical Psychology*, Ann Arbour: University of Michigan Press.

Latham, G.P. 1989: The validity, reliability and practicality of the situational interview, in R.W. Eder and G.R. Ferris (eds.), *The Employment Interview*, Newbury: Sage.

Latham, G., Saari, L., Pursell, E. and Campion, M. 1980: The situation interview, *Journal of Applied Psychology*, **65**(4), 422–42.

Mackay, L. and Torrington, D. 1986: *The Changing Nature of Personnel Management*, London: Institute of Personnel Management.

McCormick, E.J., Jeaneret, P.R. and Mecham, R.C. 1972: A study of job characteristics and job dimensions based on the Position Analysis Questionnaire (PAQ), *Journal of Applied Psychology*, **36**, 347–68.

McCredie, H. and Shackleton, V.J. 1994: The development and interim validation of a dimensions based senior management assessment centre, *Human Resources Management Journal*, **5**, 91–101.

McDaniel, M.A., Whetzel, D.L., Schmidt, F.L. and Maurer, S.D. 1994: The validity of employment interviews: A comprehensive review and meta-analysis. *Journal of Applied Psychology*, **79**, 599–616.

Manwaring, T. 1984: The extended internal labour market, *Cambridge Journal of Economics*, **8**(2), 161–87.

Millmore, M. 2003: Just how extensive is the practice of strategic recruitment and selection? *Irish Journal of Management*, **24**(1), 87–108.

Morgenson, F.P. and Campion, M.A. 1997: Social and cognitive sources of potential inaccuracy in job analysis, *Journal of Applied Psychology*, **82**(5), 627–55.

Munro Fraser, J. 1978: *Employment Interviewing*, London: MacDonald and Evans.

Murphy, N. 2003: Making every penny count, *IRS Employment Review*, **789**, (May), 42–7.

Newell, S. and Shackleton, V.J. 1993: The use (and abuse) of psychometric tests in British industry and commerce, *Human Resource Management Journal*, **4**(1), 14–22.

O'Reilly, C.A., Chatman, J. and Caldwell, D.F. 1991: People and organisational culture: A profile comparison approach to assessing person-organisation fit, *Academy of Management Journal*, **34**, 487–516.

Payne, T., Anderson, N. and Smith, T. 1992: Assessment centres, selection systems and cost effectiveness: An evaluative case study, *Personnel Review*, **21**, 48–56.

Personnel Today. 2004: HMV goes online after successful pilot in 2003, *Personnel Today*, 13 April, 53–7.

Polyhart, R., Weekly, J., Holtz, B. and Kemp, C. 2003: Web-based and paper-and-pencil testing of applicants in a proctored setting: Are personality, biodata and situational judgement tests comparable, *Personnel Psychology*, **56**(3), 733–53.

Posthuma, R., Morgeson, F. and Campion, M. 2002: Beyond employment interview validity: A comprehensive narrative review of recent research and trends over time, *Personnel Psychology*, **55**(1), 1–53.

Premark, S.Z. and Wanous, J.P. 1985: A meta-analysis of realistic job preview experiments, *Journal of Applied Psychology*, **70**, 706–19.

Prien, K.O., Prien, E.P. and Wooten, W. 2003: Interrater reliability in job analysis: Differences in strategy and perspective, *Public Personnel Management*, **32**(1), 125–41.

Ram, M. 1994: *Managing to Survive: Working Lives in Small Firms*, Oxford: Blackwell.

Rankin, N. 2004: Agencies, employers and the new regulations, *IRS Employment Review*, **795**, (May), 45–9.

Redman, T. and Matthews, B.P. 1998: Service quality and human resource management: A review and research agenda. *Personnel Review*, **27**(1), 57–77.

Roberts, G. 1997: *Recruitment and Selection: A Competency Approach*, London: IPD.

Robertson, I.T., Gratton, L. and Rout, U. 1990: The validity of situational interviews for administrative jobs, *Journal of Organizational Behaviour*, **11**, 69–76.

Robertson, I.T., Gratton, L. and Sharpley, D. 1987: The psychometric properties and design of assessment centres: Dimensions into exercises won't go, *Journal of Occupational Psychology*, **60**, 187–95.

Robertson, I.T. and Kinder, A. 1993: Personality and job competencies: The criterion-related validity of some personality variables, *Journal of Occupational and Organizational Psychology*, **66**, 225–44.

Robertson, I.T., Iles, P., Gratton, L. and Sharpley, D.S. 1991: The psychological impact of personnel of selection procedures on candidates, *Human Relations*, **44**(9), 963–82.

Rodger, A. 1952: *The Seven Point Plan*, National Institute for Industrial Psychology, Paper No. 1.

Roethlisberger, F.J. and Dickson, W.J. 1939: *Management and the Worker*, New York: John Wiley.

Saville & Holdsworth Ltd 1995: *Work Profiling System* (WPS, updated version), London: SHL.

Schmidt, N., Gooding, R.Z., Noe, R.A. and Kirsch, M. 1984: Meta-analysis of validity studies published between 1964 and 1982 and the investigation of study characteristics, *Personnel Psychology*, **37**, 407–22.

Schmidt, F.L. and Hunter, J. 1998: The validity of selection methods in personnel psychology: Practical and theoretical implications of 85 years of research findings, *Psychological Bulletin*, **125**, 262–74.

Schneider, B. 1987: The people make the place, *Personnel Psychology*, **40**, 437–53.

Shackleton, V.J. and Newell, S. 1991: Management selection: A comparative study of methods used in top British and French companies, *Journal of Occupational Psychology*, **64**, 23–36.

Shackleton, V.J. and Newell, S. 1994: European management selection methods: A comparison of five countries, *International Journal of Selection and Assessment*, **2**, 91–102.

Smethurst, S. 2004: The allure of online, *People Management*, 20 July, 38–42.

Smith, M. 1994: A theory of the validity of predictors in selection, *Journal of Occupational and Organizational Psychology*, **76**, 13–31.

Smith, M. and Graves, C. 2002: Re-engineering recruitment to the accounting profession, *Managerial Auditing Journal*, **17**(3), 117–21.

Sparrow, P. 1997: Organisational competencies: Creating a strategic behavioural framework for selection and assessment, in N. Anderson and P. Herriot (eds.), *International Handbook of Selection and Assessment*, 543–66. Chichester: John Wiley.

Taylor, F.W. 1911: *The Principles of Scientific Management*, New York: Harper.

Taylor, P., Keelty, Y. and McDonnell, B. 2002: Evolving personnel selection practices in New Zealand organizations and recruitment firms, *New Zealand Journal of Psychology*, **31**(1), 8–18.

Tett, R.P., Jackson, D.N. and Rothstein, M. 1991: Personality measures as predictors of job performance: A meta-analytic review. *Personnel Psychology*, **44**, 703–42.

Van Vianen, A.E. and Kmieciak, Y.M. 1998: The match between recruiters' perceptions of organisational climate and personality of the ideal applicant for a managerial position, *International Journal of Selection and Assessment*, **6**, 153–64.

Watson, T. 1994: Recruitment and selection, in K. Sisson (ed.), *Personnel Management: A Comprehensive Guide to Theory and Practice in Britain*, Oxford: Basil Blackwell.

Weekley, J.A. and Gier, J.A. 1987: Reliability and validity of the situational interview for a sales position, *Journal of Applied Psychology*, **72**, 484–87.

Wilk, S. and Cappelli, P. 2003: Understanding the determinants of employer use of selection methods, *Personnel Psychology*, **56**(1), 103–22.

Williams, K. 1997: Surfing for jobs, *Management Accounting Journal*, **78**, 14–15.

Wingrove, J., Glendinning, R. and Herriot, P. 1984: Graduate pre-selection: A research note. *Journal of Occupational Psychology*, **57**, 169–71.

CHAPTER SIX

Work–Life Balance: Challenging the Overwork Culture

Janet Walsh

Work–life balance is an issue that currently has a high public profile. The publication of books such as Arlie Russell Hochschild's *Time Bind* (1997) and Madeline Bunting's *Willing Slaves* (2004) have become important reference points for discussion of the escalating demands of paid work, commonly referred to as an 'overwork culture', and its impact on home and the family. Increases in the numbers of working mothers and dual earner families, as well as lone parent households, have enhanced the pressures of managing work and family for a substantial number of employed women and men. By 2002, for instance, 58 per cent of UK mothers with children under the age of 5 worked outside the home, a rise of 10 per cent since 1990 (Dench et al. 2002). More controversially, Hochschild (1997: xxi) contends that the rise in the employment of women with children combined with the growth in lone parent families has led to a fall, on average, of 22 hours a week of time that American parents are able to spend with their children.

In the UK context the issues of overwork and work–life balance have been at the forefront of the government's employment agenda, partly due to the interest in such matters of the former Secretary of State for Trade and Industry and Minister for Women and Equality (cf. Hewitt 1993). In 2000 the Prime Minister launched the government's Work–Life Balance campaign in order to publicize the case for family friendly employment provision and to extend such policies more widely across organizations in the UK. Furthermore, new legislation, the Employment Act 2002, has given parents rights for the first time to request flexible working arrangements from their employers. Employees' legal entitlements to parental leave and the rights of part-time workers have also been strengthened. As a consequence there has been heightened pressure on employers to acknowledge the work–life balance concerns of their employees and to respond by designing policies to assist workers in their efforts to integrate the requirements of work and family.

Against the backdrop of these developments, this chapter begins by examining the context of the work–life balance debate in the UK, particularly changes in the gender pattern of employment and the evolution of the long hours work culture. It explores the concepts of work–family conflict and work–family balance and examines the causes and effects of work–family conflict on organizations and employees. The discussion then moves on to the issue of work–family policy provision. Particular attention is paid to the extent of adoption of work–family policies in the UK and the effect of such policies on employees and organizations. There is also analysis of individual measures, including flexible working, working at home and childcare assistance. Finally, the management and implementation of work–family policies is addressed and a number of key lessons for human resource managers are highlighted.

The Struggle for Work–Life Balance: Context of the Debate

Women's employment patterns and family structures

One of the most important developments in the UK labour market over the past two decades has been the dramatic increase in female employment. By 2001 more than two-thirds of women were active in the labour market compared with less than half in 1963 (Dench et al. 2002). A government estimate suggests that women will occupy roughly 82 per cent of jobs that are generated between 1998 and 2011 (DTI/HM Treasury 2003: 8). At the same time there has been an increase in the employment rate of women with dependent children from 57 per cent in 1990 to 65 per cent in 2000. Indeed, it is now claimed that children are 'a declining barrier to work' (Desai et al. 1999: 175).

The increase in female employment rates has been particularly pronounced among those women with working partners and those that are better educated. This has spearheaded major changes in family structures. An OECD study (2001) has shown that the proportion of male single breadwinner families in the UK has declined considerably since the mid-1980s, from 55 per cent of all families to 29 per cent. This reflects the increase in families with a male full-time earner and a female full- or part-time worker. High rates of female employment have important implications for men, since men are increasingly in relationships with women who are likely to be in the labour force. As Glass and Estes (1997: 290) have observed:

> Without housewives at home to attend to the organization and provision of care to children, fathers are also experiencing tensions between their work and family obligations, although not necessarily the same kind nor to the same degree as mothers.

Despite growth in the numbers of dual earner couples and some evidence that working fathers are participating more actively in parenting and housework, the gender balance in unpaid work remains unequal with women continuing to play a much greater role than men. A recent estimate suggests that full-time working mothers spend just over twice as much time on average as fathers on childcare and about twice as much time on other unpaid household work (OECD 2001: 139). Moreover, the work–life dilemmas of employees are also more extensive than simply caring for dependent children. Increasingly employees are experiencing pressures to manage care for both young children and elderly relatives, commonly referred to as the phenomenon of the 'sandwiched employee' (Lobel and Kossek 1996: 230). In addition, older workers may need to care for sick parents and/or partners.

In sum, fundamental changes in women's employment activity and the nature of family structures have heightened the complexities of the interface between work and family (Parasuraman and Greenhaus 2002). The growth in female labour force participation, especially women with dependent children, the rise of dual earner and lone parent families, as well as the increase in the number of employees with responsibilities for eldercare have greatly intensified the demands of paid work and family for significant numbers of employed women and men.

Working hours and 'face time'

The number of hours people work and the times at which they work have an important bearing on how individuals manage their work and family commitments. Hochschild (1997) has argued that parents in the United States are working longer and longer hours and are therefore increasingly caught in a 'time bind' with progressively less time for family life. Certainly the US and the UK are characterized by a higher incidence of long hours for full-time employees, particularly men. In 2001 full-time employees in the UK worked on average 44 hours a week compared to an EU average of 40 (Bishop 2004: 117). Indeed the UK appears to have the highest proportion of employees working in excess of 45 hours and over a week among EU member states.

Overtime working has become much more significant in the UK, with hours of unpaid overtime increasing especially rapidly. Table 6.1 draws on the most recent UK Workplace Employee Relations Survey (WERS), and shows that in 1998 one in eight of all employees reported that they usually worked more than 48 hours a week, including overtime hours. Long hours working was most common among managers, professional workers, and operative and assembly workers. Almost a third (32 per cent) of managers and a fifth (21 per cent) of professional workers in the UK reported usually working over 48 hours a week. While the great majority of employees engaged in operative, assembly and craft work were paid for overtime work, around two-thirds of managers and professionals did not receive either payment or time off (Cully et al. 1999: 157–8). Such employees were much more likely to cite factors associated with job commitment as the main reason for working overtime.

Table 6.1 indicates that in the majority of occupations and industries it was mainly men who worked long hours. One in five male employees worked long hours

Table 6.1 Employees working over 48 hours per week, by occupation, industry and gender

	Male % of employees	Female % of employees	All employees % of employees
Occupation			
Managers and administrators	37	21	32
Professional	24	17	21
Associate professional and			
technical	12	3	7
Clerical and secretarial	9	1	3
Craft and related	20	5	19
Personal and protective service	20	2	10
Sales	15	1	5
Plant and machine operatives	25	5	20
Other occupations	17	1	9
Industry			
Manufacturing	23	4	18
Electricity, gas and water	13	6	11
Construction	32	3	28
Wholesale and retail	18	2	9
Hotels and restaurants	19	7	12
Transport and communications	29	5	24
Financial services	22	3	10
Other business services	27	7	17
Public administration	11	3	8
Education	27	10	15
Health	13	2	4
Other community services	15	5	10
All employees	22	5	13

Base: All employees working in excess of 48 hours per week in workplaces with 25 or more employees. Figures are weighted and based on responses from 24,728 employees.

Source: Cully et al. (1999: table 7.6).

compared to only one in twenty female employees. Working fathers were also more likely to work longer hours than other men of the same age group who were not fathers (Cully et al. 1999: 154). Importantly, however, the proportion of mothers working more than 40 hours has risen dramatically, from 19 per cent in 1988 to 33 per cent in 1998 (Harkness 1999: 104). Moreover, by 1998, well over a half of full-time female employees were working unpaid overtime. At the same time fewer individuals are working the standard working week, largely a reflection of the spread of shift working, evening and weekend working. Harkness (1999: 106) estimates that in a quarter of households with children at least one parent regularly works during the evening.

It is not only the case that people have been working longer hours and at more unsociable times than in the past. Employees also feel that they are working harder. Drawing upon a series of studies of worker attitudes, Green (2001) shows that employees have consistently reported that they are working more intensively. This reflects not simply employees' willingness to exert greater effort in their jobs, but the fact that they are also 'constrained' to work hard. According to Green (2001: 66) around 40 per cent of employees in 1997 strongly agreed that they were in a job that required them to work hard, compared with less than a third in 1992. Bunting's (2004: 101) interview with a Microsoft employee provides a vivid illustration of such work pressures:

> We're a commodity, and they'll get everything out of you. If you offer Microsoft your soul and your life – and here people want to please, they need to feel valued, because Microsoft employs high achievers who want to be the top of the tree – they'll take everything that's offered. I've found people in the loo sobbing, exhausted and overstretched . . . there's tremendous pressure to perform . . .

Not surprisingly, then, increases in worker effort are associated with perceptions of greater stress. Not all work pressure can be attributed to management, however. It appears that 'fellow workers or colleagues' were an important factor contributing to increased work effort by the late 1990s (Green 2001: 69).

Why, then, have the temporal conditions of work become more intense? Many organizations operate on the basis of a social norm that presumes that an employee's presence at work, sometimes referred to as 'face time', is indicative of their commitment to the job and their productivity (Perlow 1998). Such a norm is especially prevalent in managerial work. Indeed, it has been shown that promotions at managerial level are associated with working long hours (Judge et al. 1995). Simpson (1998) has argued that in many organizations a process of 'competitive presenteeism' can occur whereby (male) managers seek to compete over who works the longest hours.

There are a number of factors, then, that create and sustain an 'overwork culture'. First, as noted above, managers play an active role in encouraging employees to work long hours. In her study of software engineers Perlow (1998: 328) observed that managers did this by *establishing work demands*, for instance arranging meetings and setting deadlines; *monitoring employees*, including inspecting their work and observing them perform tasks, and acting as *role models* by displaying the work patterns they expect their subordinates to imitate. Secondly, long working hours may reflect the contemporary dynamics of technical, professional and managerial work. In these types of knowledge-based jobs the productivity or commitment of employees is not easily assessed and therefore managers tend to rely on work hours as a convenient indicator of an employee's job performance.

Thirdly, as Simpson (1998) suggests, employees' work hours are influenced by the stance of co-workers, notably through a process of 'positional striving' that involves employees competing to keep pace with or exceed the working hours of other individuals in an organization (Eastman 1998). The outcome is that individuals work much longer hours than they desire, especially women. Moreover, an employee's 'positional striving' tends to be nullified by the competitive reactions of other individuals leading to an outcome that is less desirable overall than one in which all individuals worked fewer hours (Landers et al. 1996). A further explanation of the 'long hours' culture appears to be the material and psychological benefits that individuals can derive from working long hours. Brett and Stroh (2003) found that male managers who worked very long hours, for example 61 or more hours a week, were not only very well remunerated but the most psychologically involved and intrinsically satisfied with their work.

Finally, it has been observed that some societies, such as the United States, value long hours working more than others. Wharton and Blair-Loy's (2002: 56) cross-national study of finance professionals found that American employees were the least inclined to consider working part-time. Such reluctance to cut back on their hours, they argue, reflects 'greater individualism and a stronger equation of work with individual achievement and identity in the United States than in England and Hong Kong'. Hence, the tendency of American employees to work long hours may not simply be due to shorter holiday entitlements and a minimally regulated labour market but reflect a distinctive cultural orientation to work.

In contrast to the US, the UK's own working hours are determined partly by European regulations. In 1998 the government introduced the Working Time Regulations which sought to implement the EU Working Time Directive. This stipulated a 48-hour maximum on employees' weekly working hours, including overtime. It is important to note that employers can agree individual op-outs from the legislation. Moreover, certain categories of employees do not fall within the rubric of the 48-hour weekly limit, such as senior management and individuals who determine their own working time (Barnard et al. 2003: 225). Despite these exemptions, however, there has been a relatively steady decline in the proportion of all employees working more than 45 hours a week since the enactment of the legislation (Bishop 2004: 117). Such a trend reflects the fall in the working hours of male employees which suggests that the legislation has had some tangible, if limited, effects in this respect (Barnard et al. 2003: 229).

For those who continue to work long hours, however, it is clear that the 'overwork culture' can have detrimental effects. A review of 21 studies of the effects of hours of work on health concluded that there was a small but significant relationship between longer work hours and psychological and physical ill-health (Sparks et al. 1997). Furthermore, the well-established nature of the 'overwork culture' in many organizations has intensified the debate on the causes and effects of work–family conflict and the appropriate policy responses. It is to studies of this issue that we now turn.

Concepts and Definitions

Work–family balance or work–family integration?

Although the focus of much debate, the concept of *work–family balance* has tended to be used imprecisely. One exception is the recent study by Greenhaus et al. (2003: 513) who propose a definition of work–family balance as 'the extent to which an individual is equally engaged in – and equally satisfied with – his or her work role and family role'. 'Balance' is therefore taken to imply an equality of time, involvement and satisfaction with work and family roles. In similar vein, Clark (2001: 349, 362) defines work–family balance as 'satisfaction and good functioning at work and at home with a minimum of role conflict' but contends that such a 'synergistic' state is difficult to attain, mainly because the simultaneous combination of work and home is likely to entail some degree of role conflict. Bunting (2004: 215) too is concerned about the term's broader implications:

> what is misleading about the phrase and how it is used are the implications that 'balance' is achievable, and that it is down to the individual's personal skills – or lack of them . . . It also feminises it, so that 'work–life balance' becomes a women's issue rather than a central issue of our humanity . . .

Other researchers eschew the concept of work–life balance altogether mainly because it presumes an equality or approximate equality between an individual's experiences in the work and family spheres. Accordingly Batt and Valcour (2003: 191) propose a rather different concept, that of *work–family integration*, wherein 'employees do not experience work–family conflict and are able to integrate or successfully manage their work and family demands'.

Work–family conflict

Work–family conflict is clearly an important reference point in the debate on work and family. It is commonly defined as 'a form of interrole conflict in which the role pressures from the work and family domains are mutually incompatible in some respect' (Greenhaus and Beutell 1985: 77). In essence work–family conflict implies that time spent participating in work (or family) activities inhibits the fulfilment of obligations and responsibilities in the family (or work) sphere. The involvement of individuals in work and family activities may not necessarily be a source of conflict however. Indeed the combination of work and family roles may be beneficial for some individuals (Barnett 1998). For instance, women managers who are involved in multiple roles, such as parent, spouse and employee, appear to be satisfied with their lives in general and have a positive sense of their self-esteem and self-worth

(Ruderman et al. 2002). What appears to be important is the quality of the experience an individual has in their work and family roles. Moreover, as Barnett and Hyde (2001: 784) point out, the benefits of multiple roles depend on the number of different roles and their time requirements. If the number of roles becomes too great or the demands of one role become excessive due, for instance, to long work hours, employee well-being is likely to be negatively affected.

Certainly the research highlights that time-based pressures, such as lengthy work hours and inflexible or irregular schedules, are a major cause of conflict between an individual's work and family roles. Such factors inevitably mean that the time that an individual can devote to family activities is reduced. A number of studies have demonstrated that work time is a positive predictor of work interference with family and overall work–family conflict (Gutek et al. 1991, Major et al. 2002), although a key factor is the degree to which an individual wants to work the hours he or she works. Major et al. (2002) found that long work hours were associated with increased work–family conflict and, indirectly, with psychological distress, including increased depression and other stress-related health problems. Furthermore, the more hours a week individuals worked, the more work interference in family they reported. Particular types of employees are also more likely to experience work–family conflict. Studies have shown that employees with dependent care responsibilities, for instance young children, large families, dependent elders, are prone to higher levels of work–family conflict (Eby et al. 2005; Frone et al. 1992; Greenhaus and Beutell 1985). There is a tendency for women to experience greater work–family conflict, particularly when working longer hours (Gutek et al. 1991). In some studies work–family conflict appears to be pronounced among dual earner couples, although women typically report higher levels of work–family conflict than their male partners, especially when young children are present (Roehling et al. 2003). People's experiences of their organizations are also important. When individuals perceive that their managers are unsupportive over their efforts to balance work and family responsibilities, they perceive greater work–family conflict (Anderson et al. 2002).

The overwhelming consensus from the research on work–family conflict is that it has damaging effects on employees and their organizations. People with high levels of work–family conflict tend to be less satisfied with their jobs, careers and lives in general (Kossek and Ozeki 1998; Martins et al. 2002). Excessive work interference with family is also associated with greater stress, job burnout, increased absenteeism and higher turnover (Allen et al. 2000; Anderson et al. 2002; Greenhaus et al. 1997). There is also some evidence that an individual's commitment to the organization declines as work–family conflict increases (Allen et al. 2000; Netemeyer et al. 1996). In respect of non-work outcomes, studies suggest that work–family conflict is associated with poorer physical and psychological health as well as heavy alcohol use (Allen et al. 2000; Frone et al. 1997; Thomas and Ganster 1995).

Most research has sought to investigate how work conflicts with family. Mainly this is because people tend to perceive more work interference in family than family interference in work (Gutek et al. 1991). Nevertheless, family to work conflict – reflecting, for example, inadequate childcare arrangements – can have a harmful impact on employees leading to higher stress levels, depression and ill-health (Anderson et al. 2002; Frone et al. 1997). Family to work conflict can also damage organizational performance, primarily due to its effects on employee absenteeism, productivity and turnover (Glass and Estes 1997). In light of the negative consequences of work–family conflict it is not surprising that policies have been developed with the aim of alleviating the work–family problems of employees. The nature and effects of work–family policies are now examined.

The Nature of Work–Family Policies

What are work–family policies?

Work–family policies are generally defined as 'any benefit, working condition, or personnel policy that has been shown to . . . decrease job–family conflicts among employed parents' (Glass and Fujimoto 1995: 382). There are three types of work–family initiatives that organizations might introduce to accompany those measures required by law (Glass and Estes 1997):

- policies that respond to employees' desire for reduced working hours in order to fulfil their parental and caring responsibilities, such as part-time, term-time working and the provision of leave for vacation, illness, childbearing and family care;
- policies that enable workers to have greater flexibility or control over the scheduling of work hours and the location of work, such as flexi-time arrangements, compressed workweeks, job sharing and teleworking;
- policies and practices that provide organizational support for employees including assistance with childcare or eldercare and sick child support.

Although these initiatives may not fully eradicate employees' work–family/life pressures, they are nonetheless an essential basic requirement of any employer strategy to reduce work–family tensions and difficulties among employees and thus to facilitate a more satisfactory reconciliation of work and family life.

Employee preferences

Employers often introduce work–family policies in order to improve the recruitment and retention of staff (DTI/HM Treasury 2003). Exactly what employees expect or desire from such programmes is more difficult to ascertain, however. Individuals may have very different family needs and their requirements may change over the work–life cycle. Hence policies designed for one segment of employees may not satisfy the work–family requirements of another group, or even those of the same employees at a different point in the work–life cycle (Glass and Estes 1997). There is considerable uncertainty, then, as to how employers should respond to pressures for work–family programmes. Should employers free employees from their work demands so that they are able to care for their own children and/or elderly parents? Alternatively, should they support a shift in caregiving from individual employees to institutions such as nurseries, schools and care homes?

A recent work–life balance survey sponsored by the Department of Trade and Industry sheds some light on demand for particular initiatives (Stevens et al. 2004). This survey of around 2,000 employees conducted in 2003 indicated considerable support for flexible working arrangements, especially flexi-time (49 per cent). About one-third of employees also wanted to work reduced hours for a limited period, a compressed workweek, school term-times only or from home. Such preferences are especially salient in light of the government's legislation on flexible working. With effect from April 2003, the Employment Act 2002 gave parents of children under six or parents of disabled children under 18 a new right to request a flexible working arrangement. Under the legislation employers have a statutory requirement to consider such applications seriously, although there is scope to reject them on business grounds. Specifically, eligible employees can request:

- a change to the hours they work;
- a change to the times when they are required to work;
- to work from home.

As indicated in Box 6.1, the government envisages that flexible working can encompass a broad spectrum of arrangements (DTI 2003: 10). In addition, the legislation introduced a new entitlement to paid paternity and adoption leave and enhanced existing rights to maternity leave and maternity pay.

The Adoption of Work–Family Policies

The incidence of work–family policies in the UK

Countries differ in the ways in which they have addressed issues of work–family integration. As Bailyn (1993: 71) points out 'different countries have different social infrastructures to deal with family needs, and they are ideologically at different places concerning family roles and gender equity'. In comparison with most European countries, the UK, as well as the United States, Australia and Japan, have been characterized by few mandatory rights to family friendly working arrangements. The consequence has been relatively poor formal childcare provision and low levels of statutory maternity, paternity and parental leave (OECD 2001). In the

Box 6.1   Flexible working: DTI guidance

Annualized hours	Working time is organized on the basis of the number of hours to be worked over a year rather than a week: it is usually used to fit in with peaks and troughs of work.
Compressed hours	Individuals work their total number of agreed hours over a shorter period. For example, employees might work their full weekly hours over four rather than five days.
Flexitime	Employees can choose their actual working hours, usually outside certain agreed core times.
Homeworking	This does not have to be on a full-time basis and employees can divide their time between home and office.
Job-sharing	Typically involves two people employed on a part-time basis, but working together to cover a full-time post.
Shift working	Gives employers the scope to have their business open for longer periods than an eight-hour day.
Staggered hours	Employees start and finish their day at different times.
Term-time working	Employees can take unpaid leave of absence during the school holidays.

Source: Adapted from DTI (2003: 10).

UK, for instance, paternity leave only became a statutory right in 1999, while employee entitlements to maternity pay and leave have been among the lowest in the European Union (Hardy and Adnett 2002: 167). Much of the provision of work–family programmes in the UK has been left to firms, with a great deal of variation between employers in their degree of responsiveness. As noted earlier, however, statutory entitlements to family friendly provision have been strengthened in recent years. This reflects not only the government's own initiatives, for example on flexible working, but also the implementation of 'work–life balance' regulations from the European Union including the Parental Leave Directive, the Part-Time Work Directive, and the Working Time Regulations. While some governments, particularly in the Nordic countries, already had policies that exceeded the minimum standards set by the European Directives, others, such as the UK, have been obliged to comply with provisions enshrined in European legislation.

Although predating recent legislation, the 1998 Workplace Employee Relations Survey provides a reliable indication of the coverage of family friendly work

Table 6.2   Provision of family friendly practices for non-managerial employees

	In WERS 98 (unweighted proportion)	In the economy
Parental leave	43	34
Working from home	18	17
Term-only contracts	20	16
Working part time	58	46
Job sharing	38	28
Workplace nursery	8	3
Childcare subsidies	7	4

Source: Wood et al. (2003: table 3).

arrangements for non-managerial employees in the UK. Table 6.2 shows that there is considerable variation in the incidence of work–family provision (Wood et al. 2003). The most widely available practice is the entitlement to work part-time (58 per cent of the sample), followed by parental leave (43 per cent of the sample) and job sharing (38 per cent of the sample). What is striking is that employer provision of workplace nurseries (8 per cent of the sample) and childcare subsidies (9 per cent of the sample) is extremely rare.

Of course, firms may make overly generous estimates of their provision in order to create the impression that they are 'good employers'. Employees' perceptions of provision in their workplaces are therefore a useful corrective. WERS 98 indicates that about a half of all employees (54 per cent) reported that one or more of five different kinds of flexible and family friendly working provisions were available to them. As Table 6.3 indicates, one-third stated that they were able to work flexi-time if required, although other types of provision, including job sharing and working from home, were perceived to be far less widely available (16 per cent job sharing; 9 per cent homeworking). In line with employer responses, only a small number of employees (4 per cent) perceived that workplace nurseries and/or assistance with the cost of childcare were available to them, although parental leave was more widely reported (28 per cent).

Table 6.3 suggests that public sector and larger private sector workplaces were more likely to provide family friendly working arrangements. There were also gender differences in perceptions of provision, with women more likely than men to report that policies (except homeworking) were available. Significantly, the more highly educated the employee, the more likely they were to have access to family friendly provisions. For instance, 71 per cent of employees with postgraduate qualifications had access to one or more family friendly policies, compared with only 41 per cent of employees with no school level qualifications. Those employees who believed they had substantial control over their jobs also had greater access to one or more flexible working arrangements (Cully et al. 1999: 146). Employees

Table 6.3 Flexible and family friendly working arrangements, by gender and sector

	Sector				All employees
	Private		Public		
	Male % of employees	Female % of employees	Male % of employees	Female % of employees	% of employees
Flexi-time	24	36	37	39	32
Parental leave	21	30 ·	35	33	28
Job sharing scheme	6	15	23	34	16
Working at or from home	10	6	13	9	9
Workplace nursery/childcare subsidy	2	3	6	9	4
None of these	57	42	40	34	46

Base: All employees in workplaces with 25 or more employees.
Figures are weighted and based on responses from 25,457 employees.
Source: Cully et al. (1999: table 7.3).

(especially women) in professional and managerial positions are far more likely to receive work–family benefits than those employees in low-skilled jobs. Of course, this may reflect the fact that workers with higher levels of education are employed in larger numbers in 'family friendly' organizations. Employers may also seek to design work–family policies with these higher-level employees in mind (Cully et al. 1999: 145). In addition, such employees may be able to negotiate their own individual benefits from employers due to their advantageous employment position.

The spread of work–family policies, then, is both selective and patchy. Within this context Cully et al. (1999: 146) highlight three critical factors that affect the ability of employees to utilize work–family policies:

- the propensity of employers to offer such arrangements;
- the extent of their availability within organizations;
- the ease with which employees can access information and utilize work–family provisions.

Nevertheless, there is evidence that organizations in the UK are seeking to expand their family friendly policy provision. The government's second work–life balance survey of employers suggests that there has been a substantial increase in the number of workplaces offering paternity leave (from 18 per cent in 2000 to 35 per cent in 2002–3) and a small rise in the percentage of employers offering flexible working hours (from 62 per cent to 67 per cent) (Woodland et al. 2003). In addition, a survey of employees indicates that the utilization of flexible work arrangements, such as part-time, reduced hours and flexi-time work, has grown (Stevens et al. 2004: xvi). Despite a general increase in provision, however, few employers offer a range of flexible working time arrangements with only 9 per cent of surveyed organizations offering four or more practices (Woodland et al. 2003: 7). Furthermore, the provision of childcare by employers continues to be rare (8 per cent), as is the take-up by employees (Stevens et al. 2004: xviii).

Determinants of work–family policy provision

Organizations with a high proportion of female employees and those firms that are large in size are generally more inclined to adopt work–family policies, and to do so at an earlier stage and more extensively than other firms (Glass and Estes 1997; Osterman 1995). This may reflect the fact that firms that employ large numbers of women experience strong demand for certain types of policies, such as childcare support and flexible working, that ultimately encourages managers to adopt such policies. Institutional and societal pressures are also important influences on organizations. For instance, Goodstein (1994) found that the more widely diffused work–family practices were within an industry, the more likely that individual firms would adopt those practices. Moreover, it is generally argued that large firms, due to their greater size and prominence, are likely to feel under greater pressure to comply with institutional and societal demands for work–family policies in order to signal that they are 'good employers' (Goodstein 1994). Similarly, the research suggests that organizations that have specialized human resource departments, as well as those that are reliant on professional and technical employees, are also more likely to offer work–family policies (Osterman 1995). In a significant piece of research conducted by Milliken et al. (1998) it was found that senior human resource managers influence the availability of work–family policies. Their study indicates that organizations are more likely to offer work–family benefits when work and family issues are important to senior human resource staff and thought likely to impair organizational performance if not addressed. The collection of demographic and work–family information on employees, such as employee surveys, exit interviews, also enhanced the likelihood that an organization would respond to work–family issues. In short, human resource managers can make a difference to the availability of work–family policies. If senior human resource managers consider work–family issues to be important, then an organization is more likely to be responsive to work–family matters both with respect to policy making and implementation.

Finally, there is some evidence from the US that firms implementing high performance/high commitment work systems, characterized by employee participation and quality programmes, are more likely to adopt work–family initiatives

(Osterman 1995). A study of around 4,000 employees in 40 manufacturing plants by Berg et al. (2003) found that a high commitment work environment, comprising high performance work practices, challenging jobs and supportive supervisors, enhanced workers' ability to balance their work and family lives. More particularly, the high performance practices of participation, informal training, performance pay and promotion opportunities all positively influenced workers' perceptions that their company helped employees balance work and family demands. The character of the workplace environment may therefore have an important bearing on how employees perceive the work–family interface.

The UK

In the context of the UK Wood et al. (2003) have sought to ascertain whether workplaces have introduced family friendly policies as separate initiatives or as a 'bundle' of consistent and complementary practices. Drawing on WERS 98 they found that only one type of provision, which is associated with flexible work arrangements, could be said to constitute a coherent 'bundle' of practices. Moreover, this type of *family-oriented flexible management*, consisting of part-time work, job sharing, working from home, term-time work and parental leave, was quite distinct from the provision of childcare support (Wood et al. 2003: 244). The likelihood of firms adopting family-oriented flexible management was significantly enhanced by the following factors:

- large organizational size, notably organizations employing more than 50,000 employees;
- the presence of human resource/personnel departments;
- the provision of equal opportunity practices;
- female employees present in the workplace;
- public sector workplaces;
- the health industry;
- the financial services sector.

Interestingly, trade union representation was not associated with the incidence of either family-oriented flexible management or childcare assistance despite the fact that the TUC and individual unions have supported the expansion of work–family policy provision. Moreover, in contrast to the US research noted earlier, Wood et al. (2003) failed to find a significant link between high commitment management and the incidence of family-oriented flexible work arrangements. Indeed, in a separate study by White et al. (2003) certain 'high-performance' management practices, such as appraisals, were associated with employee perceptions of work–family imbalance. In the UK context at least high commitment work environments do not necessarily appear to further the provision of family friendly management practices.

The Effects of Work–Family Policies
on Employees and Employers

Family friendly backlash?

The rationale of work–family policies is to assist employees to balance the demands of work with those of their family commitments. There has been concern, however, that those employees who do not directly use or benefit from work–family programmes might resent such initiatives (Kossek and Nichol 1992). The notion that work–family policies are unfair and potentially discriminatory is sometimes referred to as 'family friendly backlash'. Research suggests that male employees and parents of older children have less favourable perceptions of work–family policies than do female employees and parents of younger children. Male employees, it is argued, may simply perceive that they do not need work–family policies, while parents of older children may derive fewer benefits as their children are likely to be independent (Parker and Allen 2001). Nord et al.'s (2002: 230) study of the implementation of programmes in two organizations illustrates the 'backlash' phenomenon:

> many nonusers felt their own work–nonwork conflicts and needs were neglected; non-parents observed that family-friendly programs spawned unfair burdens on those coworkers who had fewer family obligations.

Typically employees without dependants claim that they are expected to work longer hours and to travel more extensively than those employees with children. In addition, they are sometimes considered to be ineligible for work–family programmes. Significantly, around 42 per cent of employers in the government's second work–life balance survey believed that work–family/life policies were unfair on some employees (Woodland et al. 2003).

On the other hand, employees may not necessarily perceive that family friendly policies are unfair if they are unable to benefit directly as individuals. Research conducted by Grover and Crooker (1995) found that employees in organizations offering family friendly policies displayed greater organizational commitment and lower turnover intentions regardless of the extent to which individual employees personally benefited from the programmes. Why might this be the case? There is a view that family friendly policies symbolize a wider 'corporate concern' for employees thereby encouraging them to be loyal to their organization (Grover and Crooker 1995: 274). Lambert (2000: 811) also believes that work–life policies engender a 'generalized sense of obligation to the workplace'. She found that the more useful a company's work–life policies were perceived to be in terms of assisting workers and their families, the more likely individuals were to engage in organizational citizenship behaviour, including supporting co-workers with their job responsibilities, submitting suggestions for improvements and attending quality meetings. Although organizations are likely to experience positive outcomes from work–family/life policies, it is difficult to judge whether such beneficial effects can counteract the potential costs of a worker 'backlash' due to employee resentments or perceptions of inequity.

Impact on organizational performance

There is limited evidence on the impact of work–family policies on the perform-ance of firms. However, it is likely that such policies would have a positive effect on organizational performance. There has been speculation, for example, that the introduction of work–family policies is likely to enhance an organization's corpor-ate reputation. Firms should therefore be able to attract a larger, and potentially superior, pool of potential recruits who are likely to improve productivity and profits. At the same time work–life programmes should enable firms to retain well-qualified employees. It might be expected, then, that work–family programmes would engen-der greater commitment and stability among employees, thereby lowering a firm's costs and enhancing its profitability (Arthur and Cooke 2004).

A strand of research on work–family policies has sought to analyse their effects as 'bundles' of complementary human resource initiatives. Adopting a 'bundles' approach Perry-Smith and Blum (2000) found that organizations with more extensive work–family policies, including childcare provision and assistance, flex-ible scheduling, parental leave, eldercare support, experienced higher perceived organizational performance. Konrad and Mangel (2000) also demonstrate that work–life programmes have a positive influence on the (actual) productivity of firms, especially when the workforce is composed of large numbers of women and pro-fessionals. Furthermore, work–life programmes appear to improve shareholder return. An investigation of Fortune 500 companies found that announcements of work–family initiatives prompted increases in share prices which suggests that investors consider such measures to be beneficial for firms (cf. Arthur and Cooke 2004: 610). Despite the positive link between work–family policy provision and busi-ness performance, however, it is commonly observed that few companies conduct systematic evaluations of work–family initiatives. Such reluctance appears to reflect at least three factors:

- work–family programmes can sometimes affect small numbers of employees, which complicates any evaluation of their impact;
- firms often consider that it is too difficult or premature to assess the full costs of the policies;
- firms may implement a package of policies and therefore it is difficult to evalu-ate the impact of individual initiatives (Glass and Finley 2002: 329).

So far we have discussed work–family policies in general. Different types of work–family policies may have very different effects on employees, however. For instance, workplace nurseries might have the effect of increasing an employee's exposure to the organization and its work demands, while flexible work schedules could do the reverse, notably by reducing the ability of managers to directly monitor an employee's presence at work (Glass and Fujimoto 1995). Research has therefore sought to disaggregate work–family initiatives and to analyse the implications of individual programmes. Such studies are the focus of the next section.

Flexible Work, Working at Home and Childcare Support

Flexible work arrangements

Flexible work arrangements typically describe a variety of initiatives such as flexi-time, reduced hours, compressed workweeks, job sharing, and term-time working. In a review of over 30 studies, it was found that employees on flexible work schedules experienced greater satisfaction with their jobs and work schedules, were less likely to be absent and were more productive (Baltes et al. 1999). In addition, flexible schedules are associated with higher organizational commitment (Grover and Crooker 1995) and lower turnover intentions (Batt and Valcour 2003). Similarly, it appears that compressed workweeks improve employees' satisfaction with their jobs and work schedules, as well as their performance ratings (Baltes et al. 1999). Importantly, workers that are employed in organizations offering flexible work hours tend to have higher organizational commitment regardless of whether or not the employee makes use of such arrangements (Scandura and Lankau 1997). In this case flexible work hours appear to signal to employees that their organization is sensitive to work–family problems and prepared to respond to employees' needs.

A rather more controversial issue is the extent to which flexible scheduling and reduced hours enable individuals to integrate more effectively their work and family responsibilities. Research suggests that flexible schedules certainly enhance people's perceptions of control over the work–family interface. Such improved control, moreover, appears to lower people's perceptions of work–family conflict, enhances their physical and mental health and increases their job satisfaction (Thomas and Ganster 1995). Managers and professionals on reduced hour schedules in Buck et al.'s study (2000: 20) reported being happier and more satisfied with their work–home balance, as well as experiencing better relationships with their children. Higgins et al.'s (2000: 17) research also suggests that part-time work may result in less work to family conflict and greater life satisfaction for women in both higher level (professional and managerial) and lower level positions (technical, clerical, retail or production work). Part-time female employees reported some disadvantages, though, including higher workloads. Women in career positions, in particular, experienced high role overload and high family to work interference whether they worked full or part-time.

Teleworking/working at home

It is commonly presumed that working at home/teleworking is favourable for an individual's work–family balance, mainly because it can improve employees' flexibility and autonomy and reduce time spent commuting. From a work–family perspective, it is interesting to note that women do not dominate the UK teleworking workforce. About two-thirds of all teleworkers are men, and around three-quarters work in the private sector, mainly in professional, managerial and technical work (Hotopp 2002). A recent study by Hill et al. (2003) compares the effects of the virtual office, home office and traditional office on (IBM) employees' perceptions of work–life balance and family life. In this context virtual office workers had the technological capacity to work from a number of different locations, such as the home, customer work sites and shared office space. Overall, working from home was associated with significantly greater work–life balance and perceptions of success in personal-family life, largely due to the fact that home-based employees did not commute to work and were therefore able to spend more time on domestic activities. The findings were the reverse, however, for virtual office workers who reported significantly poorer work–life balance than traditional office or home office workers. This was believed to reflect the fact that they worked longer hours, which reduced their 'private' family time. Overall, however, Hill et al.'s (2003) study supports the notion that teleworking, specifically working from home, can lead to better work–life integration. In addition, working from home had a positive impact on employees' job motivation and retention. There are some negative consequences of home/teleworking for employees, however, including greater professional isolation, reduced promotional opportunities and lack of social integration (Cooper and Kurland 2002; Hill et al. 1998).

Childcare support

It might be expected that workplace nurseries, by alleviating tensions and anxieties about childcare arrangements, would have a beneficial impact on employees. Kossek and Nichol (1992) found, for instance, that users of an on-site childcare programme were significantly more likely to be positive about managing their work and family demands and were also less likely to experience childcare difficulties. Employer sponsored provision may be especially important to employees without family support who are more likely to be absent from work and to experience greater problems with care. While the use of workplace nurseries does not appear to directly enhance employees' job performance, such provision may indirectly improve workplace productivity by enabling individuals to more easily concentrate on their tasks and work activities. According to Kossek and Nichol (1992: 502) 'child care benefits may be viewed as creating a favourable climate conducive to enabling good performance'.

Certainly there is evidence that users of on-site childcare facilities have better retention rates, although not necessarily lower absenteeism (Kossek and Nichol 1992). As with performance, however, childcare support may have a positive, indirect, effect on absenteeism. Goff et al. (1990) found that the use of on-site (and off-site) childcare arrangements was related to perceptions of lower work–family conflict that were, in turn, associated with lower absenteeism. Providing information on available childcare has also been found to significantly reduce employees' intentions to leave their organization (Grover and Crooker 1995). The extent to which such research supports the provision of employer sponsored childcare facilities is less clear, however. Indeed some commentators have argued that on-site employer sponsored childcare centres may not be strictly necessary for positive worker and organizational outcomes at all (Glass and Estes 1997). What may be more important is that employees are able to access good quality childcare arrangements regardless of whether they are provided by the employer or other organizations.

Summary

So far the discussion has established that individual work–family policies, such as flexible scheduling, working from home and childcare support, not only deliver effective organizational outcomes, but also can be positive for worker well-being. Nevertheless, it is worth emphasizing that the utilization of such policies may come at a financial cost to employees. For instance, Glass (2004) found that the use of work–family policies appeared to depress the wages of women with dependent children. The 'wage penalty' was most pronounced in the case of managers and professional women working from home or on reduced hours schedules. It was much less marked when women were on either flexible schedules or had access to childcare support. Hence the research suggests that work–family policies that reduce employees' presence at work – that is, their 'face time' – are most likely to generate financial costs for employees, particularly those in higher-level positions.

Towards the Redesign of Work?

The design of work appears to be critical to the achievement of work–family balance. Research suggests that employees who have greater autonomy and influence over their work activities experience less work–family conflict and perceive greater control over the work–family interface (Thomas and Ganster 1995). In this context one influential perspective, known as the *work–family integration approach*, emphasizes that work–family initiatives, if they are to be at all effective, need to be implemented alongside complementary technologies, work systems and human resource practices (Bailyn 1993). Batt and Valcour (2003) argue, for instance, that employees' perceptions of work–family conflict, their control over the work–family interface and their turnover intentions are likely to be affected by a *combination* of policies and practices, including:

- work–family policies, such as dependent care benefits, flexible scheduling practices and supportive supervisors;
- human resource practices, including salary, job security, career development programmes and;
- work design, such as decision-making autonomy, use of flexible technology, work hours, travel demands.

More specifically, their study showed that certain aspects of work design, such as decision-making autonomy and the use of flexible technologies, improved employees' control over managing their work and family demands. In sum, the research suggests that introducing work–family policies in isolation is simply inadequate, particularly if organizations are seeking to influence employee attitudes and behaviour. Rather, employees must perceive that they have genuine flexibility and control over their work arrangements, both with respect to the timing and conditions of work.

Managing Work–Family Policies

Despite the evident benefits of family friendly programmes, employees are often reluctant to use such initiatives (Hochschild 1997). This often reflects the perception that participation in work–family programmes will jeopardize an employee's career. The second DTI employee work–life balance survey indicates that around one-half of employees believed that working reduced hours would negatively affect their career advancement. In addition, around 43 per cent reported that it would harm their job security. Two-fifths (42 per cent) of employees also thought that not working beyond their contracted hours would damage their career prospects (Stevens et al. 2004: 108).

While companies often introduce work–family initiatives in order to improve employee recruitment and retention, the entrenched nature of an 'overtime culture', and in particular the notion that productivity and commitment can be defined in terms of hours spent at the office, simply negate the logic of work–family policy provision (Lewis 1997). Moreover, although organizations might have formal work–family programmes in place, managers and supervisors play a critical role in deciding which employees are able to access such policies. Powell and Mainiero (1999) found that managers were less likely to approve requests for family friendly work arrangements if they judged that these would cause work disruptions. There was also a tendency for managers to adopt a narrow, short-term orientation in decisions about flexible work arrangements thereby neglecting the positive, long-term effects on the commitment and retention of valued employees.

Nord et al.'s (2002) investigation of family friendly programmes in two organizations showed that employees believed that the support of first-line supervisors was even more vital than that of senior management, particularly in the day-to-day implementation of policies. Indeed, employees whose supervisors are supportive of their efforts to integrate work and family are much less likely to experience work–family conflict (Batt and Valcour 2003; Thomas and Ganster 1995). These findings underscore the importance of an organizational culture that values and promotes family friendly policy provision and its implementation over the long term. Such a culture also appears to have wider implications than simply encouraging employees to participate in specific work–family initiatives. Thompson et al. (1999: 394, 409) found that a supportive work–family culture, defined as 'the shared assumptions, beliefs, and values regarding the extent to which an organization supports and values the integration of employees' work and family lives' was associated with lower work–family conflict, higher organizational commitment and lower turnover intentions. It appears therefore that the character of workplace and organizational cultures, and the degree to which they are family friendly, affect not only the take-up of work–family policies, but also employees' perceptions of their work and organizations.

Implementing work–family policies

Bailyn (1993) in her influential book *Breaking the Mold: Women, Men, and Time in the New Corporate World*, has criticized the dominant organizational responses to employees' work–family needs, first, because their aim is often to increase the availability of employees to their organizations and secondly, there is a tendency for the users of such initiatives to be stigmatized. A related concern is that traditional work–family policies often do little to fundamentally change workplace and organizational practices that impede the integration of people's work and family requirements, mainly because such programmes are disconnected from other organizational initiatives (Lobel and Kossek 1996). A major issue, then, in work–family policy research is how to change organizational cultures so that they become family friendly. Bailyn, for instance, (1993: 79–96; 105–20) advocates a radical reframing of our notions of *time, autonomy, commitment* and *equity*. This would require organizations to:

- shift the measurement of productivity/successful performance away from hours of input (time) to output or client load (results of work);
- enhance employees' discretion over the conditions of work;
- define commitment as the exercise of mutual respect and trust, and not simply the prioritization of work above all other activities;
- view equity in terms of justice and fairness in accordance with employees' diverse needs rather than the uniform requirements of a homogeneous workforce.

It is therefore proposed that organizations move beyond a piecemeal response to work–family matters based on separate, discrete initiatives, such as job sharing and flexi-time, and embrace instead comprehensive 'culture change' programmes that seek to refashion organizational norms and practices. As Bailyn (1993: 70) points out, for meaningful change to occur, work–life balance issues need to be viewed as an important strategic imperative and an integral part of organizational policy making.

Such a radical transformation of organizational practices requires changes in the orientation of senior managers and human resource practitioners. In particular, higher-level managers need to be actively committed and involved in both policy formulation and implementation. Operational changes in human resource processes and practices, such as staffing, training provision, performance management and job design, may also need to occur in order to facilitate broader shifts in the norms and values of organizations. In this context Nord et al. (2002: 236–7) propose three types of managerial interventions necessary for the successful implementation of work–life balance policies. First, human resource managers need to communicate between users of programmes and senior management, especially about how employees are experiencing policies and the ways in which relationships with clients need to be managed in order to facilitate the operation of the programmes. Secondly, support should be provided to first-line supervisors and line managers so that they are able to facilitate the implementation of family friendly work arrangements. More specifically, performance management and training systems may need to be restructured so that the productivity of employees is more accurately assessed and their contribution appropriately valued by the organization. Thirdly, task allocation, appraisals and promotions need to be managed equitably and fairly so that users and non-users of work–life programmes perceive such policies to be fair.

Despite such recommendations, however, few employers in the UK have sought to combine work–family initiatives into comprehensive programmes to meet the family needs of employees. Indeed it is claimed that most organizations view family friendly provision narrowly in terms of 'mothers and child care' (Wood et al. 2003: 248). Some commentators also consider the government's flexible working measures to be rather ineffectual, notably because employers can invoke a large number of business reasons in order to refuse employee requests (Anderson 2003). Nevertheless, there is some evidence that recent legislation has stimulated greater awareness of work–family/life issues among both employers and employees. The second DTI work–life balance survey indicated that over two-thirds of employers were aware of an employee's right to request to work flexibly, with considerable employer support for the notion of work–life balance (Woodland et al. 2003). Indeed, the majority of employers reported work–life balance practices to be cost effective with positive consequences for employee retention, motivation, commitment and employee relations. Similarly, the first DTI employee survey on flexible working found that just over half of all employees were aware of the new statutory right to request flexible working (Palmer 2004). This represented a pronounced increase in the awareness rate immediately prior to the legislation. Almost one quarter of employees with children under the age of six had requested to work flexibly, with most requests having been accepted by employers. Such findings suggest that government intervention can enhance the provision and utilization of family friendly arrangements within organizations thereby creating a more favourable climate for the consideration of work–life issues.

Summary and Conclusions

Profound changes in women's employment patterns and family structures form the backdrop to growing public concern about employees' work–life balance. As we have seen, the increase in female employment, particularly women with children, as well as the shift to dual earner and lone parent families, and the rise in elder-care responsibilities, have enhanced the pressures of managing work and family for a substantial proportion of employed women and men. At the same time organizations have become increasingly 'greedy' with respect to the temporal demands required of employees. In the UK this has meant that more employees, especially men with children, are working long hours in order to signal their commitment to their work and organizations. For managerial and professional workers such overtime is largely unpaid.

Despite some evidence that regulations on working time have led to reductions in long hours working, the 'overwork culture' is still an entrenched characteristic of many organizations in the UK. Clearly, time at work has become a convenient norm for managers in determining exactly who are the most productive and committed employees. The attitudes and behaviour of co-workers are also a key factor encouraging employees to work harder. A vicious cycle of 'competitive presenteeism' (Simpson 1998) or 'positional striving' (Eastman 1998) occurs such that working hours are progressively ratcheted upwards. Whatever its causes, it is apparent that the UK's notorious long work hours, alongside changes in workforce demography, have prompted intense debate on the causes and consequences of work–family conflict and the requirement for better work–life balance. Time-based pressures, such as long work hours and inflexible or unpredictable schedules, can lead to increased work–family conflict. Moreover, research suggests that a whole host of negative worker and organizational outcomes, including job dissatisfaction, stress, lower organizational commitment and higher turnover, are associated with work–family conflict. It is thus clear that high levels of work–family conflict can damage the performance of employees and their organizations thereby necessitating interventions from policy makers, both employers and governments.

Work–family policy making can be both a complex and contested matter, however. Employers and employees, for instance, may hold very different perspectives on the rationale and desired outcomes of such initiatives. Equally employers may favour relatively minor policy adjustments that are cheap and easy to administer, but may be reluctant to introduce more radical measures that benefit employees, such as working at home and job sharing. An additional problem is that work–family policies can generate a 'family friendly backlash' from employees who cannot access or do not need to use such programmes. Employees' perceptions of initiatives as unfair or inequitable are therefore a significant barrier to the successful operation and implementation of work–family policies. On the other hand, family friendly policies can signal to employees that organizations are aware of their work–family problems and requirements and are prepared to respond to their needs. Such 'corporate concern', it will be recalled, can have a beneficial impact on employees' perceptions of their organizations (Grover and Crooker 1995). Although the prospect of 'family friendly backlash' should not be underplayed, it appears that work–family/life programmes can generate positive organizational outcomes regardless of the extent to which individual employees personally benefit from such initiatives.

Many work–family researchers have been preoccupied with investigating the characteristics of organizations that are likely to adopt work–family policies. A series of studies highlight the role played by both personnel departments and senior human resource managers in influencing the availability of work–family policy provision. Essentially organizations are more likely to provide policies if senior human resource managers consider work–family matters to be important, especially in relation to their impact on business performance. A more controversial issue, though, is the influence of high commitment/high performance work environments. While US research suggests that high commitment work environments have a positive impact on the provision of work–family policies, as well as on the ability of workers to balance their work and family obligations, studies in the UK context have found no such effects. Furthermore, although trade unions may articulate employees' demands for work–family policies, their presence appears to have no significant impact on either the provision of childcare benefits or 'family-friendly flexible management' (Wood et al. 2003).

What is clear, however, is that work–family programmes have a positive impact on organizational performance, particularly when implemented as a 'bundle' of practices. A coherent 'business case' can therefore be made for work–family policy provision. It is also apparent that individual policy initiatives, such as flexible work arrangements, working at home and childcare support can have beneficial effects for both employers and employees, although it is certainly the case that employees suffer financial costs from using some types of initiatives (Glass 2004). Nevertheless, the introduction of separate, discrete work–family initiatives, although important, may not be sufficient to improve employees' work–life balance. The redesign of work, especially measures that are intended to enhance people's autonomy and discretion at work, appears to be a prerequisite for effective work–family integration, mainly because it assists employee control over the work–family interface (Batt and Valcour 2003). Moreover, greater decision-making autonomy needs to be complemented by other human resource processes, such as supervisors and co-workers who are prepared to facilitate the participation of employees in work–family initiatives. It is only when employees work within a genuinely 'supportive work–family culture' that utilization of work–family policies is likely to be maximized (Thompson et al. 1999).

Such observations raise issues regarding the management and implementation of work–family policies within organizations. More particularly, it suggests that work–family policies need to be integrated with wider organizational change initiatives that challenge established norms and practices, especially our notions of working time, the measurement of individual job performance and employee commitment (Bailyn 1993). Comprehensive attempts to reshape organizational cultures, inevitably involving changes in human resource processes and practices, appear to be the most promising avenue for effective, long-term work–family/life policy provision.

Of course, in the UK context only a minority of employers have sought to combine work–family/life initiatives into comprehensive programmes that require such systematic human resource policy interventions (Wood et al. 2003). In general, provision of work–family policies has been both selective and patchy. Family friendly employment arrangements are more common in public sector and large private sector workplaces. Work–family policies also appear to be targeted towards more highly educated employees and those who have significant control over their jobs. Moreover, few employers offer a variety of flexible work arrangements and the provision of childcare is rare. Within this context a crucial development is the strengthening of employees' statutory entitlements to family friendly work arrangements. The Employment Act 2002, in particular, is a significant piece of legislation, most notably its measures to improve the spread of flexible working. Although it is too early to assess the full effects of the government's legislation, there are signs that awareness of work–family policies, as well as their provision and utilization have improved. It is important, therefore, not to underplay the potential positive consequences of government intervention, especially in altering perceptions of the legitimacy of work–family policy provision. There is a possibility that recent legislation may serve to stimulate greater interest in work–family matters from employers as well as expectations from employees of more substantial employer-led policy initiatives in this area.

REFERENCES AND FURTHER READING

Allen, T.D., Herst, D.E.L., Bruck, C.S. and Sutton, M. 2000: Consequences associated with work-to-family conflict: A review and agenda for future research, *Journal of Occupational Health Psychology*, **5**(2), 278–308.

Anderson, L. 2003: Sound bite legislation: The Employment Act 2002 and new flexible working 'rights' for parents, *Industrial Law Journal*, **32**(1), 37–42.

Anderson, S.E., Coffey, B.S. and Byerly, R.T. 2002: Formal organizational initiatives and informal workplace practices: Links to work-family conflict and job-related outcomes, *Journal of Management*, **28**(6), 787–810.

Arthur, M.M. and Cooke, A. 2004: Taking stock of work-family initiatives: How announcements of 'family-friendly' human resource decisions affect shareholder value, *Industrial and Labor Relations Review*, **57**(4), 599–613.

Bailyn, L. 1993: *Breaking the Mold: Women, Men, and Time in the New Corporate World*, New York: Free Press.

Baltes, B.B., Briggs, T.E., Huff, J.W., Wright, J.A. and Neuman, G.A. 1999: Flexible and compressed workweek schedules: A meta-analysis of their effects on work-related criteria, *Journal of Applied Psychology*, **84**(4), 496–513.

Barnard, C., Deakin, S. and Hobbs, R. 2003: Opting out of the 48-hour week: Employer necessity or individual choice? An empirical study of the operation of Article 18(1)(b) of the Working Time Directive in the UK, *Industrial Law Journal*, **32**(4), 223–52.

Barnett, R.C. 1998: Toward a review and reconceptualization of the work/family literature, *Genetic, Social, and General Psychology*, **124**(2), 125–82.

Barnett, R.C. and Hyde, J.S. 2001: Women, men, work, and family: An expansionist theory, *American Psychologist*, **56**, 781–96.

Batt, R. and Valcour, M.P. 2003: Human resources practices as predictors of work-family outcomes and employee turnover, *Industrial Relations*, **42**(3), 189–220.

Berg, P., Kalleberg, A.L. and Appelbaum, E. 2003: Balancing work and family: The role of high commitment environments, *Industrial Relations*, **42**(3), 168–88.

Bishop, K. 2004: Working time patterns in the UK, France, Denmark and Sweden, *Labour Market Trends*, March, 113–22.

Brett, J.M. and Stroh, L.K. 2003: Working 61 plus hours a week: Why do managers do it?, *Journal of Applied Psychology*, **88**(1), 67–78.

Buck, M.L., Lee, M.D., MacDermid, S.M., and Smith, S. 2000: Reduced-load work and the experience of time among professionals and managers: Implications for personal and organizational life, in C.L. Cooper and D.M. Rousseau (eds.), *Trends in Organizational Behavior*, Vol. 7, New York: John Wiley & Sons Limited, 13–36.

Bunting, M. 2004: *Willing Slaves: How the Overwork Culture Is Ruling our Lives*, London: HarperCollins.

Clark, S.C. 2001: Work cultures and work/family balance, *Journal of Vocational Behavior*, **58**, 348–65.

Cooper, C.D. and Kurland, N.B. 2002: Telecommuting, professional isolation, and employee development in public and private organizations, *Journal of Organizational Behavior*, **23**, 511–32.

Cully, M., Woodland, S., O'Reilly, A. and Dix, G. 1999: *Britain at Work*, London: Routledge.

Dench, S., Aston, J., Evans, C., Meager, N., Williams, M. and Willison, R. 2002: *Key Indicators of Women's Position in Britain*. Department of Trade and Industry: Women and Equality Unit. November.

DTI (Department of Trade and Industry) 2003: *Flexible Working: The Right to Request and the Duty to Consider. A Guide for Employers and Employees*, London: DTI.

DTI/HM Treasury (Department of Trade and Industry/Her Majesty's Treasury) 2003: *Balancing Work and Family Life: Enhancing Choice and Support for Parents*, January. London: DTI/HM Treasury.

Desai, T., Gregg, P., Steer, J. and Wadsworth, J. 1999: Gender and the labour market, in P. Gregg and J. Wadsworth (eds.), *The State of Working Britain*, Manchester: Manchester University Press. 168–84.

Eastman, W. 1998: Working for position: Women, men, and managerial work hours, *Industrial Relations*, **37**(1), 51–66.

Eby, L.T., Casper, W.J., Lockwood, A., Bordeaux, C. and Brinley, A. 2005: Work and family research in IO/OB: Content analysis and review of the literature (1980–2002), *Journal of Vocational Behavior*, February, 124–97.

Frone, M.R., Russell, M. and Cooper, M.L. 1992: Antecedents and outcomes of work-family conflict: Testing a model of the work-family interface, *Journal of Applied Psychology*, **77**, 65–78.

Frone, M.R., Russell, M. and Cooper, M.L. 1997: Relation of work-family conflict to health outcomes: A four-year longitudinal study of employed parents, *Journal of Occupational and Organizational Psychology*, 70, 325–35.

Glass, J. 2004: Blessing or curse? Work-family policies and mother's wage growth over time, *Work and Occupations*, **31**(3), 367–94.

Glass, J.L. and Estes, S.B. 1997: The family responsive workplace, *Annual Review of Sociology*, **23**, 289–313.

Glass, J.L. and Finley, A. 2002: Coverage and effectiveness of family-responsive workplace policies, *Human Resource Management Review*, **12**, 313–37.

Glass, J.L. and Fujimoto, T. 1995: Employer characteristics and the provision of family responsive policies, *Work and Occupations*, **22**, 380–411.

Goff, S.J., Mount, M.K. and Jamison, R.L. 1990: Employer supported child care, work-family conflict, and absenteeism: A field study, *Personnel Psychology*, **43**(4), 793–809.

Goodstein, J.D. 1994: Institutional pressures and strategic responsiveness: Employer involvement in work-family issues, *Academy of Management Journal*, **37**, 350–82.

Green, F. 2001: It's been a hard day's night: The concentration and intensification of work in late twentieth century Britain, *British Journal of Industrial Relations*, **39**(1), 53–80.

Greenhaus, J.H. and Beutell, N.J. 1985: Sources of conflict between work and family roles, *Academy of Management Journal*, **10**, 76–88.

Greenhaus, J.H., Collins, K.M., and Shaw, J.D. 2003: The relation between work-family balance and quality of life, *Journal of Vocational Behavior*, **63**, 510–31.

Greenhaus, J.H., Collins, K.M., Singh, R. and Parasuraman, S. 1997: Work and family influences on departure from public accounting, *Journal of Vocational Behavior*, **50**, 249–70.

Grover, S.L. and Crooker, K.J. 1995: Who appreciates family-responsive human resource policies: The impact of family-friendly policies on the organizational attachment of parents and non-parents, *Personnel Psychology*, **48**, 271–88.

Gutek, B.A., Searle, S. and Klepa, L. 1991: Rational versus gender role explanations for work-family conflict, *Journal of Applied Psychology*, **76**(4), 560–8.

Hardy, S. and Adnett, N. 2002: The Parental Leave Directive: Towards a 'family-friendly' social Europe?, *European Journal of Industrial Relations*, **8**(2), 157–72.

Harkness, S. 1999: Working 9 to 5?, in P. Gregg and J. Wadsworth (eds.), *The State of Working Britain*, Manchester: Manchester University Press, 90–108.

Hewitt, P. 1993: *About Time: The Revolution in Work and Family Life*, London: IPPR/ Rivers Oram Press.

Higgins, C.A., Duxbury, L. and Johnson, K.L. 2000: Part-time work for women: Does it really help balance work and family?, *Human Resource Management*, **39**, 17–32.

Hill, E.J., Ferris, M. and Martinson, V. 2003: Does it matter where you work? A comparison of how three work venues (traditional office, virtual office, and home office) influence aspects of work and personal/family life, *Journal of Vocational Behavior*, **63**, 220–41.

Hill, E.J., Miller, B.C., Weiner, S.P. and Colihan, J. 1998: Influences of the virtual office on aspects of work and work/life balance, *Personnel Psychology*, **51**, 667–83.

Hochschild, A.R. 1997: *The Time Bind*, New York: Henry Holt & Company.

Hotopp, U. 2002: Teleworking in the UK, *Labour Market Trends*, June, 311–18.

Judge, J.A., Cable, D.M., Boudreau, J.W. and Bretz, R.D. Jr. 1995: An empirical investigation of the predictors of executive career success, *Personnel Psychology*, **48**, 485–519.

Konrad, A.M. and Mangel, R. 2000: The impact of work-life programs on firm productivity, *Strategic Management Journal*, **21**, 1225–37.

Kossek, E.E. and Nichol, V. 1992: The effects of on-site child care on employee attitudes and performance, *Personnel Psychology*, **45**, 485–509.

Kossek, E.E. and Ozeki, C. 1998: Work-family conflict, policies, and the job-life satisfaction relationship: A review and directions for organizational behavior human resources research, *Journal of Applied Psychology*, **83**(2), 139–49.

Lambert, S.J. 2000: Added benefits: The link between work-life benefits and organizational citizenship behavior, *Academy of Management Journal*, **43**(5), 801–15.

Landers, R.M., Rebitzer, R.B. and Taylor, L.J. 1996: Human resources practices and the demographic transformation of professional labor markets, in P. Osterman (ed.), *Broken Ladders: Managerial Careers in the New Economy*, New York: Oxford University Press, 215–46.

Lewis, S. 1997: Family friendly employment policies: A route to changing organizational culture or playing about at the margins?, *Gender, Work and Organization*, **4**(1), 13–23.

Lobel, S. and Kossek, E.E. 1996: Human resource strategies to support diversity in work and personal lifestyles: Beyond the 'family friendly' organization, in E.E. Kossek and S.A. Lobel (eds.), *Managing Diversity*, Oxford: Blackwell, 221–44.

Major, V.S., Klein, K.J. and Ehrhart, M.G. 2002: Work time, work interference with family, and psychological distress, *Journal of Applied Psychology*, **87**, 427–36.

Martins, L.L., Eddleston, K.A. and Veiga, J.F. 2002: Moderators of the relationship between work-family conflict and career satisfaction, *Academy of Management Journal*, **45**, 399–409.

Milliken, F.J., Martins, L.L. and Morgan, H. 1998: Explaining organizational responsiveness to work-family issues: The role of human resource executives as issue interpreters, *Academy of Management Journal*, **41**, 580–92.

Netemeyer, R.G., Boles, J.S. and McMurrian, R. 1996: Development and validation of work-family conflict and family-work conflict scales, *Journal of Applied Psychology*, **81**, 400–10.

Nord, W.R., Fox, S., Phoenix, A. and Viano, K. 2002: Real-world reactions to work-life balance programs: Lessons for effective implementation, *Organizational Dynamics*, **30**(3), 223–38.

OECD (Organization for Economic Co-operation and Development) 2001: *Employment Outlook*, Paris: OECD.

Osterman, P. 1995: Work/family programs and the employment relationship, *Administrative Science Quarterly*, **40**, 681–700.

Palmer, T. 2004: Results of the first flexible Working Employee Survey, Department of Trade and Industry Employment Relations Occasional Papers, April.

Parasuraman, S. and Greenhaus, J.H. 2002: Toward reducing some critical gaps in work-family research, *Human Resource Management Review*, **12**, 299–312.

Parker, L. and Allen, T.D. 2001: Work/family benefits: Variables related to employees' fairness perceptions, *Journal of Vocational Behavior*, **58**, 453–68.

Perlow, L.A. 1998: Boundary control: The social ordering of work and family time in a high-tech corporation, *Administrative Science Quarterly*, **43**, 328–57.

Perry-Smith, J.E. and Blum, T.C. 2000: Work-family human resource bundles and perceived organizational performance, *Academy of Management Journal*, **43**, 1107–17.

Powell, G.N. and Mainiero, L.A. 1999: Managerial decision making regarding alternative work arrangements, *Journal of Occupational and Organizational Psychology*, **72**, 41–56.

Roehling, P.V., Moen, P. and Batt, R. 2003: Spillover, in P. Moen (ed.), *It's about Time: Couples and Careers*, Ithaca: ILR Press/Cornell University Press, 101–21.

Ruderman, M.N., Ohlott, P.J., Panzer, K. and King, S.N. 2002: Benefits of multiple roles for managerial women, *Academy of Management Journal*, **45**(2), 315–30.

Scandura, T.A. and Lankau, M.J. 1997: Relationships of gender, family responsibility and flexible work hours to organizational commitment and job satisfaction, *Journal of Organizational Behavior*, **18**, 377–91.

Simpson, R. 1998: Presenteeism, power and organizational change: Long hours as a career barrier and the impact on the working lives of women managers, *British Journal of Management*, **9** (special issue), 37–50.

Sparks, K., Cooper, C., Fried, Y. and Shirom, A. 1997: The effects of hours of work on health: A meta-analytic review, *Journal of Occupational and Organizational Psychology*, **70**, 391–408.

Stevens, J., Brown, J. and Lee, C. 2004: The second work-life balance study: Results from the Employees' Survey, DTI Employment Relations Research Series No. 27.

Thomas, L.T. and Ganster, D.C. 1995: Impact of family-supportive work variables on work-family conflict and strain: A control perspective, *Journal of Applied Psychology*, **80**, 6–15.

Thompson, C.A., Beauvais, L.L. and Lyness, K.S. 1999: When work-family benefits are not enough: The influence of work-family culture on benefit utilization, organizational attachment, and work-family conflict, *Journal of Vocational Behavior*, **54**, 392–415.

Wharton, A.S. and Blair-Loy, M. 2002: The 'overtime culture' in a global corporation, *Work and Occupations*, **29**(1), 32–63.

White, M., Hill, S., McGovern, P., Mills, C. and Smeaton, D. 2003: 'High-performance' management practices, working hours and work-life balance, *British Journal of Industrial Relations*, **41**(2), 175–95.

Wood, S.J., De Menezes, L.M. and Lasaosa, A. 2003: Family-friendly management in Great Britain: Testing various perspectives, *Industrial Relations*, **42**(3), 221–50.

Woodland, S., Simmonds, N., Thornby, M., Fitzgerald, R. and McGee, A. 2003: The second work-life balance study: Results from the Employers' Survey, DTI Employment Relations Research Series, No. 22.

CHAPTER SEVEN

Walking the Talk? Equality and Diversity in Employment

Linda Dickens

Anti-discrimination legislation relating to race, sex and pay equality has been in place for over three decades; business rationales for taking action to promote equality and diversity are increasingly articulated and there has been a growth in the number of organizations with equality and diversity policies. Progress is being made within a number of organizations. At the same time, however, we have continuing discrimination in the labour market on grounds of sex, race, disability or other arbitrary factors, and a lack of equality of opportunity in employment. This raises a question over the extent to which the drivers for equality action are being experienced universally and the extent to which the rhetoric of equality is being translated into reality – whether organizations are 'walking the talk'. This chapter critically examines the factors which may encourage organizations to tackle the differential distribution of opportunities and rewards in employment, and considers the problems they face in seeking to do so.

The first section considers the nature and extent of equality action and equality policies in the context of continuing disadvantage in the labour market. The next section explores two main categories of reasons, apart from social justice considerations, why equality action might be taken: the 'business case' for equality and diversity (organizational self-interest) and legal compliance. In both areas there are recent positive developments but these potential motivating forces have not been sufficient to produce a universal adoption of equality initiatives. This unevenness of action is accounted for by considering the contingent and variable nature of business case arguments and the limitations of compliance pressures as drivers to action.

The final section addresses the issue that, where organizations have taken equality initiatives, there is often disappointment with achievements in terms of substantive outcomes. Problems in translating equality policy into practice and delivering on outcomes are examined both in terms of difficulties in implementation and weaknesses in much of the prescription. This often rests on an inadequate conceptualization of the 'problem', underplays the resistance which equality initiatives can generate, and simplifies the reasons for it. Recent developments in prescription, around culture change and mainstreaming, and a recognition of difference, potentially herald a shift of emphasis away from measures designed to help members of the disadvantaged groups progress within existing organizations towards an approach centred on changing the nature, structure and values of organizations themselves. Whether this potential is likely to be realized in practice, however, remains an open question.

Action but Continuing Employment Disadvantage

On the surface there are signs of progress towards greater equality of opportunity in employment. These include the large number of organizations declaring (in recruitment advertising and elsewhere) that they are an 'equal opportunity employer' or that they 'value diversity'; the adoption of equal opportunity policies (EOPs); the growing membership of such campaigns as Opportunity Now, Race for Opportunity, and the 'two ticks' campaign 'positive about disabled people'. Opportunity Now (formerly Opportunity 2000) is a business-led campaign launched in October 1991 to 'increase the quality and quantity of women's participation in the workforce'. Member organizations set themselves qualitative or quantitative goals, undertaking to monitor and publicize progress towards those goals. Race for Opportunity, set up in 1995 by leading UK companies, is also a business-led campaign which aims to encourage business to 'invest' in the UK's ethnic minority communities. Organizations displaying the 'two ticks' campaign logo agree, *inter alia*, to interview all disabled applicants who meet the minimum criteria for a job vacancy. Organizations belonging to such campaigns are often at the forefront of equality initiatives. Some 250 organizations have joined the Equal Pay Forum and Equality Exchanges set up by Opportunity Now and the Equal Opportunities Commission (EOC) to help employers learn from each other about equal pay.

The 1990s saw a marked increase in the proportion of organizations claiming to have an EOP but these are still far from universal, particularly in the private sector. WERS 98 found two-thirds of all workplaces (67 per cent) in the UK with 10 or more employees had some form of equal opportunities policy (Cully et al. 1999). EOPs are found most frequently in larger organizations and establishments and are more common in the public sector. This helps explain why surveys less representative of all establishments report higher incidence of equality policies and statements (for example IRS 1999). WERS data reveal that almost half of those in the private sector (43 per cent) had no EOP (Anderson et al. 2004).

The existence of an EO statement or policy (and not all organizations recognize the difference) says little about what is actually happening in the organization. Adoption of a policy may have little impact, even at the minimal level of awareness of the policy's existence (Jewson et al. 1990; Colling and Dickens 1989). Table 7.1 shows that a range of initiatives consistent with being an EO employer

Table 7.1   Equal treatment practices, by formal equal opportunities policy

	Formal equal opportunities policy % of workplaces	No policy % of workplaces
Keep employee records with ethnic origin identified	48	13
Collect statistics on posts held by men and women	43	13
Monitor promotions by gender and ethnicity	23	2
Review selection procedures to identify indirect discrimination	35	5
Review the relative pay rates of different groups	17	15
Make adjustments to accommodate disabled employees	42	16
None of these	27	67

Base: All workplaces with 25 or more employees.
Figures are weighted and based on responses from 1,906 managers.
Source: Cully et al. (1998: 13).

are more likely to be found in those organizations with a formal EOP than in those without. But among those workplaces with a formal EOP the specified practices were found only in a minority of cases. The most frequently cited was monitoring ethnic origin (48 per cent), the most infrequent (17 per cent) reviewing the pay rates of different groups. Pay is often a neglected aspect of equality policies.

As Table 7.1 shows, 27 per cent of workplaces claiming to have a formal written EOP had none of the six practices specified. This resonates with earlier surveys of self-declared EO employers which found that there may be little substance behind the declaration (e.g. EOC 1988; Hitner et al. 1981). Going no further than a declaration that they are EO employers may reflect complacency – a public declaration that there is 'no problem here'. The mere presence of ethnic minorities or women in an organization may be pointed to as evidence of no unfair discrimination or the existence of equality since many organizations fail to recognize that global numbers may mask marked disparities in distribution (Jewson et al. 1990: 11). Adopting a policy, therefore, does not necessarily indicate an intention to change the status quo but may be merely symbolic, an 'affirmation that customary behaviour conforms to the cannons of acceptability' (Young 1987: 98).

Survey and case study research often indicates a gap between policy and action. For example, research by the Commission for Racial Equality (CRE) into large private sector companies (IRS 1995) revealed nine out of ten companies (employing some 7,000 people) had policies for racial equality but only around half had implemented, or were about to implement, an action plan to realize those policies.

In the public sector, research on equal opportunities policies in NHS Trusts in the 1990s (EOR 1994) found among the 98 per cent of Trusts with a general EOP there was a wide variation in the extent to which particular policies were introduced. Monitoring by gender, ethnic origin and disability was undertaken by nine out of ten Trusts, but on job applicants only. Promotion, job termination and training were less well covered and only 30 per cent of Trusts analysed pay data by gender. Thirty-five per cent did not produce a report on the monitoring data, which raises questions as to their utility, and only a minority had set any forecasts or goals for the representation of women, ethnic minorities or people with disabilities in their workforces.

In some organizations, where the adoption of a policy is not seen as an end in itself, and equality initiatives have been taken, there have been achievements, although these may appear relatively small and the pace of progress slow. This can be seen, for example, in the Civil Service in which a 'Programme of Action' was initiated in the 1980s. The representation of women in the top three grades of the Service increased as did – slightly – the overall representation of ethnic minority staff. However, it appeared that 'ethnic minority candidates are not being recruited and promoted to more senior grade levels in the same proportions as those who are white' (EOR 1993: 9). By 1997 while women made up over half all non-industrial staff in the Civil Service they were concentrated in the three lowest grades (90 per cent compared with two-thirds of men); and although ethnic minority representation was slightly higher than in the economically active population as a whole only 10 per cent of ethnic minority civil servants were above the three lowest grades compared with over a fifth of white civil servants (EOR 1998a: 7). The most recent statistics (EOR 2003: 5) show little change in the proportion of women in junior grades although the proportion of women in the more senior grades (grades 6 and 7) increased from 19 per cent 1997 to 29.3 per cent in 2002. The proportion of ethnic minority staff increased to 7.6 per cent, although they continue to be highly concentrated in junior grades.

Equality and diversity is firmly on management agendas in a number of organizations, and a range of initiatives is being taken, with some examples of imaginative and often thoroughgoing approaches. Progress in terms of significant aggregate distributional outcomes (that is to say, changes in the representation and distribution of various disadvantaged groups within organizations and in the workforce as a whole) however, is at best slow and often difficult to identify. There clearly have been gains for some people in certain areas but this must be placed in the context of relatively little change in long-standing patterns of job segregation and pay disadvantage.

Labour market segregation and disadvantage

As Liff (2003: 429) notes there is extensive evidence that 'not only the likelihood of having a job, but also the type of jobs obtained and the benefits received, vary with different social group membership'. There are identifiable differences between different social groups in rates of labour force participation; employment and unemployment; pay and pay opportunities; who does which jobs (across occupations and sectors and at different hierarchical levels) and in working patterns and contractual status. This section sketches some of these although the availability of data for various groups varies.

While having the third highest rate of women's participation in Europe (at 70 per cent compared with 79 per cent of men in employment), the UK labour market is among the most gender segregated (Hibbert and Meager 2003: 504; Perrons and Shaw 1995) and has the fourth largest gender pay gap in Europe. Aggregate labour force statistics show patterns of continuing disadvantage for women, with vertical and horizontal job segregation and continuing inequalities in pay and conditions. The considerable growth in female labour force participation has been of a particular kind: much of it concentrated in part-time work in the service sector.

Women are more likely to work in services, and men in manufacturing and production – a gender split which has persisted throughout the 1990s despite a marked increase in women's labour market activity. Labour Force Survey (LFS) data for Winter 2004 show that over two-thirds (69 per cent) of workers in public administration, education and health and around half of those in distribution hotels and catering are women. Male employment is spread more evenly across the industrial sectors, although men constitute 90 per cent of those employed in the construction industry and 75 per cent of those in manufacturing. There is persistent occupational, as well as sector segregation with women more likely to work in administrative and secretarial, personal services and sales occupations, and men predominating in skilled trades, process, plant and machine operative occupations and in managerial occupations (Hibbert and Meager 2003). More than two-fifths (43 per cent) of women in employment work part-time compared to 9 per cent of men; two-thirds of women with children under five work part-time. They are more likely to work in occupations that are typically lower paid. Opportunities to work part-time are not spread evenly across sectors nor throughout organizational hierarchies.

Women's pay position relative to that of men has improved but women who work full-time still receive only 82p for every £1 earned by men. Women working part-time receive 40 per cent less per hour than men in full time employment – about the same as 25 years ago (EOC 2005). The gender pay gap varies by age, ethnicity and qualification. Women's earnings are closer to men's in the 16–24 age group. Earnings of those from ethnic minority groups are generally lower than those categorized as white and the gender pay gap is particularly wide for Asian groups, reflecting the low earnings of Indian, Pakistani and Bangladeshi women. Women with a degree or equivalent level qualification experience greater relative pay disadvantage compared to similar men than do those with no qualifications (Hibbert and Meager 2003).

The aggregate data available on the employment distribution and pay position of ethnic minorities (who constitute 8 per cent of the working age population) are less detailed than those available for women and there is considerable variation between ethnic groups. Surveys and analysis have revealed considerable disparities in pay and working conditions to the detriment of black men (e.g. EOC 2005; TUC 2002) and lower pay and fewer employment benefits for black and ethnic minority women when compared with white women (Bhavnani 1994: 85–91). Pirani et al. (1992: 40–1) reported that 'even when ethnic minority workers have higher education and training, their wages tend to be lower when compared with their white counterparts' and that 'ethnic minorities do not get promoted and in relative terms tend to stay on in lower grades relative to their education and qualifications'.

Analyses of Labour Force Survey and other data (Sly et al. 1998; Owen et al. 2000) reveal differences in the sectoral distribution of ethnic minority and white workers. For example, black women are more likely than women generally to work in the medical and health services, and within the Health Service black women are found in the least desirable sectors (Bhavnani 1994). Ethnic minority men are over-represented in the service sector (Owen et al. 2000). Self-employment is higher among some ethnic minorities than the corresponding white population (Moralee 1998: 125). Men from ethnic minority groups are less likely than white men to be employed as managers and administrators and more likely to be in temporary and part-time jobs than white men. Women from ethnic minorities are more likely than white women to be in temporary jobs, but are less likely to work part-time (Hibbett and Meager 2003). Most marked, however, are differences in unemployment. Unemployment rates for ethnic minority men in 2000 were twice as high as for white men and over two and half times as high for ethnic minority women compared to white women. Progress has been made since the 1980s by at least some ethnic minority groups in the labour market compared to whites (Pilkington 2001: 182–3) but disadvantage remains.

Nearly one in five people of working age in the UK have a long-term disability (Smith and Twomey 2002). Of these, 48 per cent are in paid employment compared with an economic activity rate of 81 per cent for those not disabled. The comparable figures in the mid 1990s were 40 per cent and 83 per cent (Sly 1996: 413). The unemployment rates among people with disabilities are around two and a half times those for non-disabled people. Even when levels of education and other factors were controlled, Blackaby et al. (2000) found significant differences in earnings between those with and without disabilities.

Discrimination by employers is not the whole explanation for the continuing disadvantage displayed in the survey statistics, but it is one important factor. Discrimination in employment continues to be revealed by research studies, investigations by the equality commissions and in cases brought to employment tribunals (many examples are provided in the *Annual Reports* of the Equality Commissions). Even within organizations which declare themselves to be equal opportunity employers, discrimination may continue. Bradford Metropolitan Council, for example, one of the first local authorities to declare itself an EO employer, had legal action taken against it by the CRE in 1991 for persistent discrimination. As discussed later, Ford, an organization which has long strived to be an equal opportunity employer, was threatened with a CRE investigation in 2000 following tribunal claims against it. Local government employers and civil service agencies with avowed equality policies have been found guilty of widespread gender pay discrimination (Goodwin 2003: 117).

From an outcomes-oriented perspective it would appear that too little action to promote equality and diversity has been taken or has achieved only little in practice. Reasons for this are explored later. First, consideration is given to what action is generally encouraged, based on guidance issued by the equality commissions.

Equal Opportunity Initiatives

EO initiatives concern policy and practice designed to tackle the differential distribution of opportunities, resources and rewards (jobs, wages, promotions, employment benefits) among workers, usually based on their membership of a social group. For organizations wishing to take action to address this differential distribution, there is no shortage of guidance on what to do and how to do it. Much comes from the equality commissions – the EOC, CRE and, more recently, the Disability Rights Commission (DRC) – which publish Codes of Practice to support the legislation; guidance on developing and implementing EOPs, and on particular aspects such as ethnic monitoring. The government published a code of good practice on avoiding age discrimination to encourage voluntary action in an area where it was reluctant to legislate (Loretto et al. 2000). Guidance is offered, too, by employer bodies including the Chartered Institute of Personnel and Development (e.g. a management of diversity checklist and case studies of good practice, IPD 1999), as well as by such organizations as the Employers' Forum on Age and the business-led campaigns indicated earlier. The specialist press (such as *Equal Opportunities Review*) regularly publish examples of good practice. Here we consider particularly the guidance of the EOC and CRE.

The centre-piece of the equality commissions' guidance concerns the adoption of an EOP. As described by the CRE (1984: 8), this is a policy which aims to ensure

> that no job applicant or employee receives less favourable treatment than another on racial grounds; that no applicant or employee is placed at a disadvantage by requirements or conditions which have a disproportionately adverse effect on his or her racial group and which cannot be shown to be justifiable on other than racial grounds, and that, where appropriate and where permissible under the Race Relations Act, employees of underrepresented racial groups are given training and encouragement to achieve equal opportunity within the organization.

Box 7.1 sets out the CRE's ten-point plan to help employers promote equality of opportunity in their organizations.

Box 7.1   Equal opportunities policy: ten-point plan

1. Develop an equal opportunities policy, covering recruitment, promotion and training.
2. Set an action plan, with targets.
3. Provide training for all people throughout your organization, to ensure they understand the importance of equal opportunities.
4. Assess the present position to establish your starting point, and monitor progress in achieving your objectives.
5. Review recruitment, selection, promotion, and training procedures regularly.
6. Draw up clear and justifiable job criteria, which are demonstrably objective and job-related.
7. Offer pre-employment training, where appropriate, to prepare potential job applicants for selection tests and interviews; consider positive action training to help ethnic minority employees to apply for jobs in areas where they are underrepresented.
8. Consider your organization's image: do you encourage applications from underrepresented groups and feature women, ethnic minority staff and people with disabilities in recruitment literature, or could you be seen as an employer who is indifferent to these groups?
9. Consider flexible working, career breaks, providing childcare facilities, and so on, and consider providing special equipment and assistance to help people with disabilities.
10. Develop links with local community groups, organizations and schools, in order to reach a wider pool of potential applicants.

Source: Commission for Racial Equality, www.cre.gov.uk/gdpract/eop.html

The EOC guidance is similar, presenting an EOP as ensuring that no direct or indirect discrimination operates to the detriment of women or married people in any area of employment, including access to it, and that positive action measures (encouragement to apply for jobs, single sex and 'special needs' training, childcare provision, flexible hours, return to work schemes, etc.) are introduced.

The equality commissions' advice centres on developing fair procedures and fair practice, with some 'compensatory' measures for members of disadvantaged groups. It emphasizes developing unbiased criteria and formal procedures, and guiding and training responsible staff to ensure that these are followed, with monitoring to be undertaken of process and outcomes. This forms the core of many EO initiatives.

Both the EOC and CRE have produced self-assessment standards to help employers develop equality policies, and to measure how far the organization has progressed towards being an equal opportunities employer. The CRE's *Standard for Racial Equality for Employers* (1995) has three sections. The first sets out the case for action. The second provides a checklist grouped under three headings: commitment, action and outcomes. The third section is on measuring progress in six broad areas: policy and planning, selection, developing and retaining staff, communications and corporate image, corporate citizenship, and auditing for racial equality. Five levels of achievement are detailed under each area.

These standards were designed to complement the Commission's statutory Codes of Practice, providing a managerial tool for translating the provisions of the codes into action (Ollerearnshaw and Waldeck 1995). They provided a benchmark for the Audit Commission's review of equality and diversity in local government. It found that 40 per cent of authorities had not achieved the lowest level (Audit Commission 2002).

Equality drivers and their limitations

A variety of external and internal factors can be identified which might encourage an organization to adopt the advice proffered and implement equality initiatives. These can be divided roughly into two categories: the positive pursuit of organizational benefits (the business case for equality and diversity) and penalty avoidance through legal compliance.

This is not to deny that initiatives to promote greater employment equality can arise from a sense of social justice or moral responsibility. Key individuals in an organization may be motivated by concerns for social justice. The role of John Moores in the Littlewoods Organization, which developed pioneering EO initiatives in the 1960s, has been cited as such an example (Hansard Society Commission 1990: 53). In the tougher economic conditions of the retail sector in the 1990s, however, it was the business advantages rather than the moral imperative of its equal opportunities strategies which were emphasized by the company and which were seen as more likely to engender wider managerial commitment within the organization (IPD 1999: 39). The increased attention being paid currently to the notion of corporate social responsibility may lead to a greater articulation of social justice rationales in the private sector, as well as in the public sector where they are expressed more commonly. In practice, however, social justice or altruistic considerations probably have most effective purchase when operating in combination with the organizational self-interest or compliance factors discussed below.

Although often posed as alternatives, social justice rationales for equality action may go hand in hand with business case rationales and/or compliance considerations. Liff and Dickens (2000) argue that counterposing Kantian (social justice) and utilitarian (business case) arguments poses a false dilemma in that the two can coincide in practice and be reconcilable in theory. Empirical evidence supports their view that organizations do not necessarily experience social justice and business case arguments in a polarized way. For example, a recent survey of 140 organizations (Rutherford and Ollerearnshaw 2002) found that two-thirds of public sector employers and just under a half of private sector employers taking equality action identified social justice as one of a number of drivers, although in neither sector was it the main rationale. Most surveys find multiple rationales for action being cited by employers. Similarly the distinction drawn in some literature between 'equal opportunities' (usually linked to social justice and legal compliance rationales) and 'diversity' (associated with business case rationales) is not consistently reflected in practice in the UK where the terms are often used interchangeably or together.

Organizational self-interest: the business case

The positive organizational benefits of EO always formed part of the arguments for equality action, but in the 1980s and 1990s this became the dominant mobilizing vocabulary. This was in large part a response to the economic and political environment of the time (the business case focus on economic efficiency fitting the neo-liberal market model), and an awareness that legislative levers would not be strengthened by Conservative governments pursuing a policy of deregulation. (Dickens 1999: 11–12). Emphasis on the business case for equality and diversity is now commonplace, with equality action presented as delivering win–win outcomes for individuals and organizations (e.g. EOC and CRE websites; IPD, 1996; 1999; CBI 1996; DTI n.d.).

Box 7.2 sets out the business case for racial equality as expounded by the CRE. A number of interlinked factors encouraging an interest in equality initiatives, such as indicated in Box 7.2, can be grouped under the heading of organizational self-interest: some relate mainly to competition in labour and product markets, others to improving organizational effectiveness. What they have in common is that EO is promoted as being in the best interests of the organization, providing bottom line benefits. In this section examples of how equality can contribute to business performance are given but I argue that business case arguments are contingent and variable. They will be experienced differently by (and within) different organizations and, indeed, pursuit of organizational self-interest can run counter to, rather than support, EO initiatives. Further, if the business case argument does drive an interest in promoting equality and diversity, it may encourage only a partial, selective approach.

COMPETING IN LABOUR AND PRODUCT MARKETS

At certain times labour market changes have provided an external stimulus to equality action of this organizational self-interest kind. The link to EO is that disadvantaged groups constitute an untapped or under-utilized labour supply. Both effective recruitment and the efficient use of labour require that available resources are not wasted by implicitly assuming that white, 'non-disabled' men have a monopoly

Box 7.2   The business case for racial equality

- Using people's talents to the full.
- Ensuring that selection decisions and policies are based on objective criteria, and not on unlawful discrimination, prejudice or unfair assumption.
- Becoming an 'employer of choice'.
- Getting closer to customers and understanding their needs.
- Operating internationally with success.
- Sustaining a healthy society.
- Making the company more attractive to investors.
- Making the company more attractive to customers and clients.
- Avoiding the costs of discrimination: tribunal awards; damage to morale and reputation.

Source: CRE, Racial equality means business – A standard for racial equality for employers.

of talent, or that older workers have no contribution to make, and involves identifying untapped skills within existing workforces as well as tapping into different labour market groups.

Equality action may help project the image of a 'good employer' which 'puts people first', thereby presenting the company as a quality organization in order to become an 'employer of choice', able to attract and retain quality people.

The emphasis is not only on widening and improving recruitment, but also on better retention of existing staff. In some companies, either through experiencing labour market pressure or through copying action of competitors, this has stimulated an interest in such initiatives as career breaks and more flexible working as cost effective ways of keeping valued staff. Procter and Gamble, for example, included such measures among its strategies for addressing the disproportionate loss of women from the corporate ladder despite recruiting equal numbers of male and female graduates (Rutherford and Ollerearnshaw 2002: 15). Organizational benefits which are cited as a result of supporting a better work–life balance include savings on recruitment, induction and reduced absenteeism as well as reputational advantages (e.g. Foster 2004a; IDS 2004).

The prospect of increasing market share and penetrating new markets through having a workforce more representative of a diverse customer base or better able to exploit new markets may provide a business incentive to act for some organizations. This may arise, for example, where a service sector organization is based in areas of high ethnic minority population or, more generally, developing a better understanding of diverse customer needs to deliver the required quality of service.

Examples here include British Airways, British Telecom (Dickens 1994) and Sainsburys. The supermarket group became aware of the need to achieve employee diversity as a basis on which customer diversity and satisfaction could be built (IPD 1999: 2). At the automobile manufacturer Ford, the Asian Association looks at how best to market Ford's products to the Asian community while GLOBE is undertaking a similar task involving gay, lesbian and bisexual employees (Rutherford and Ollerearnshaw 2002).

As these examples suggest certain business case arguments will have greater salience for some organizations than others. This helps account for uneven progress. For example, skill and labour shortages are not experienced in the same way everywhere. Even where they are perceived as problems, responses other than those favourable to promoting EO are possible, and are taken – for example, competing for scarce male labour through pay increases or by contracting out work rather than tapping other sources of supply. Further, the segmentation of labour markets means that the various groups are not seen by employers as interchangeable. For example, a lack of skilled (male) labour will not necessarily lead to women being seen as a potential resource where skill is itself a male gendered concept (Philips and Taylor 1980).

The appeal of particular business case arguments may vary over time as labour or product markets change, giving rise to 'fair weather' equality action (Dickens 1999: 10). The 'defusing' of the so-called demographic time-bomb in the recession of the early 1990s, for example, led to some backsliding in the detail and extent of equality provisions introduced in response to labour market pressure (for example, cutting childcare facilities) even where these had been collectively negotiated (Colling and Dickens 1998).

An organization's capacity to respond to changing labour markets in ways likely to be beneficial for EO requires an awareness of the situation, which is often lacking, and adequate qualitative human resource planning. The effective and full utilization of the labour force also calls for investment in training. As is described elsewhere in this volume, UK organizations rarely score highly in these areas. Women and ethnic minorities (particularly those working part-time) are often disadvantaged in access to training, whether provided by employing organizations or the state (Clarke 1991; Lee and Wrench 1987; Green 1991; Green and Zanchi 1997) and the training provided may reinforce rather than challenge job segregation (Cockburn 1987; Felstead 1995: 180).

IMPROVING ORGANIZATIONAL EFFECTIVENESS

Business benefits, which it is claimed accrue to EO employers through promoting equality and diversity, include an improvement in motivation and performance which, in turn, can reduce turnover levels. Such benefits are highlighted, for example, by the CIPD, drawing on reports of employer experience by Kandola and Fullerton (1994), and it notes that 'other reported benefits include better decision-making, improved teamwork, greater creativity, better customer service skills, and improved quality of output' (IPD 1996: 6). Among the reasons stated by London Underground for instituting a programme to address sexual and racial harassment were fears that it was damaging performance, contributing to high levels of sickness absenteeism and risking compromising safety (Foster 2003a: 11). Where disadvantaged groups (and/or those claiming to represent them) channel demands for social justice into industrial action (actual or potential), then EO action may be instituted in a search for better employment relations. At the BBC the business case was motivated by the perceived need for a more representative workforce to enhance diversity in programme making (Dickens 1994). This was reinforced in 2001 when diversity became a key priority of the corporation, acknowledging that, as it is funded by television licence payers, it had to reflect the interests of diverse, multicultural audiences in its output (Maxwell 2004).

The theme of gaining through a diverse workforce has been present in the US literature for a longer time than in the UK. In the USA in the late 1980s there was a move away from a concern with equal employment opportunity, seen as largely compliance based, towards valuing diversity, viewed as more in accord with organizational interests. The idea is that organizations recognize the benefits that multiculturalism can bring to them, 'including, for instance, the challenging of stereotypical opinions and traditional assumptions . . . (T)he talents and attributes of people from different backgrounds and heritages are fully valued, utilized and developed' (Greenslade 1991). This argument has particular self-interest appeal to organizations operating in a context where minority groups are important customers and in a country, like the USA, where they constitute the fastest growing segment of the population. However, the scope of diversity management in the USA widened beyond a focus on particular social groups to embrace everyone: 'to ensure that the full potential of all employees is being exploited and that barriers to their corporate development are removed' (Loden, 1998: 19). This focus is also found in the UK literature (e.g. Kandola and Fullerton 1994).

Part of the argument that EO makes good business sense is that it is cost-effective and there is evidence (for example, relating to introducing family-friendly policies) that individual initiatives can pay for themselves or even produce cost savings (e.g. Foster 2004a). Unfortunately, economic rationality does not necessarily or consistently support EO practice at the level of the individual organization. There can be cost advantages to the individual employer, for example, in the undervaluing of women's labour. It can be cheap to use ethnic origin, or other group characteristics or stereotypes, as screening devices in selection, a practice which helps reproduce patterns of gender and race segregation. Informal recruitment methods, such as word-of-mouth recruiting, often constitute indirect race and sex discrimination yet they may be attractive as cheap options for employers as well as aiding managerial control (Wood 1986; Fevre 1989; Maguire 1986). Cost advantages for employers accrue from having disadvantaged groups on the labour market who can be exploited as a cheap, numerically flexible workforce (Dex and McCulloch 1995).

Business case rationales may be problematic for EO achievement since once the debate about equality is conducted in terms of what is in the company's best interests, EO initiatives can be contested and resisted as irrelevant or marginal to the best or real interests of the organization, as defined by those currently in positions of power, or as measured in terms of short-term contribution to the bottom line (Cockburn 1989). The evidence is that narrow cost-benefit analysis, especially if undertaken by line managers operating in decentralized business units within tight financial control, may block rather than promote equality action (Dickens 1998: 33–4; Wainwright Trust 1997). Cunningham and James (2001) found that line managers often justify not employing people with disabilities on the grounds that the necessary workplace adjustments would eat into their operating budgets. In the local authority studied by Creegan et al. (2003), budgets and managerial responsibility for previously centralized activity such as equalities was decentralized, and internal trading units for human resources and training set up. In such a context, line managers did not necessarily prioritize purchasing equality advice and training from within their restricted budgets.

Because narrow cost-benefit analysis which does not take account of non-economic factors is not always likely to favour the adoption of EO measures, an appeal to 'the bottom line' may not stimulate EO action, and may even thwart it, particularly as the financial and other resource cost of thoroughgoing EOPs can be high. Although smaller organizations will face smaller costs, many of them, starting off with undeveloped personnel policies and practices and an absence of detailed personnel records, will have to bear considerable costs simply to get to first base.

Cost-effectiveness calls for long-term assessment with account being taken of less easily quantifiable gains which may be difficult to evaluate and express in financial terms. As Humphries and Rubery note (1995: 13), 'it is because the costs to firms seem immediate and palpable while the benefits are more distant and less easy to capture that individual initiatives may produce only slow and patchy changes'. Further, it is often at a level above that of the individual organization (or sub-unit) which bears the cost that the benefits of equality action may be reaped (Bruegel and Perrons 1995).

The economic business case appeal of EO also may vary depending on the competitive strategy adopted by the organization. For example, investment in EO may make more (and short-term) sense for an organization competing on quality/innovation than on cost. Different approaches to managing the employment relations (different management styles) may help explain the variable purchase of business case arguments. EO appears to fit well with the adoption of a 'soft' human resource management approach which emphasizes valuing and developing people in pursuit of organizational effectiveness. This opens the way for arguments to be made about valuing all people, and valuing diversity, thus enabling equality action to be linked to the achievement of business goals (Dickens 1998; Miller 1996: 206). Similarly EO action is argued to support initiatives such as Investors in People (IPD 1996: 1). But not all organizations are pursuing such strategies.

Business case rationales therefore can drive equality action but are likely to have uneven purchase. Further, if they do encourage action, this may be selective and partial, focused on areas where it is clear that EO and business needs do immediately coincide. Equality initiatives motivated by a search for organizational benefits can lead to the targeting of initiatives to reflect employer needs rather than the needs of the disadvantaged groups. These needs may coincide but matching is not guaranteed. It is not surprising therefore to find that a number of business needs driven initiatives, for example relating to gender equality as reported by Opportunity Now, show a greater concern with the 'glass ceiling' than the 'sticky floor' (e.g. Richards 2001) and that 'family-friendly' or work–life balance equality initiatives are often targeted within an organization rather than made universally available. As Bruegel and Perrons observe (1995: 162), 'such targeting, however understandable, will barely help to loosen the gender order'.

Organizations will vary in their appreciation of, and reaction to, various business case arguments for equality action but all organizations are subject to legal requirements outlawing discrimination. In the next section the imperative to act within the law as a driver to equality action is examined.

Acting within the law: legal compliance and penalty avoidance

There is now extensive national legislation operating in the UK within the context of European law, which has been very influential in driving and underpinning UK legislative developments (Dickens and Hall 2003). It is indisputable that the enactment of equality legislation, and key decisions by the national courts and the European Court of Justice, have provided an important stimulus to action in respect of the removal of race and sex discrimination and equal pay between men and women, and in relation to people with disability. The recent widening scope of the anti-discrimination legislation and recent amendments to tackle some inadequacies in the law and enforcement mechanisms has strengthened this driver but limitations remain. In terms of risk of legal action and the penalties for discrimination the legal compliance threat has been generally weak in the UK, and it too is variable and contingent. Furthermore, the common legal approach in the UK is to outlaw discrimination rather than impose positive duties to promote equality. This weakens its effectiveness as a driver of equality action.

Box 7.3 provides a summary overview of relevant national legislation. It merely sketches some key legal provisions and does not attempt to provide comprehensive coverage nor detail of the legislation. As Box 7.3 indicates, the major legislative focus in the UK for many years has been on sex and race discrimination and equal pay. Legal intervention in the area of disability fell far short of outlawing discrimination until the Disability Discrimination Act 1995 which, importantly, does not simply outlaw discrimination but requires employers to effect workplace adjustments to ensure those with disabilities are not disadvantaged. To comply with European law, legislation outlawing discrimination on the grounds of sexual orientation, religion or belief came into effect in the UK in 2003 and further legislation in 2006 will outlaw age discrimination. Rather than set up further separate equality commissions to cover the new areas, the government proposes a single body: the

Box 7.3   Key equality aspects of UK legislation

Equal Pay Act 1970 (amended by Equal Value (Amendment) Regulations 1983). Equal pay and other contractual conditions for men and women where engaged on same or similar work, work rated as equivalent by job evaluation, or where work is of equal value.

Sex Discrimination Act 1976, SDA 1986. Prohibits direct and indirect discrimination in all areas of employment on grounds of sex or married status. Sex may be a genuine occupational qualification (GOQ) in specified circumstances (including for reasons of authenticity, decency and privacy; delivery of a personal welfare service; certain employment in a single sex establishment). Special treatment permitted in respect of pregnancy and childbirth; and to encourage applications from, and to provide training for, under-represented sex. Discriminatory terms in collective agreement or employers' rules rendered void.

Social Security Act 1989. Equality in occupational benefit schemes (including health insurance and pensions).

Employment Rights Act 1996. Maternity rights (maternity leave, with pay; right to return after leave); time off for ante-natal care.

Race Relations Act 1976. Prohibits direct and indirect discrimination in all areas of employment on grounds of race, colour, nationality, ethnic or national origins (includes some religious groups, e.g. Sikhs and Jews). Race may be a GOQ in specified circumstances (including authenticity, delivering welfare service). Special treatment permitted to encourage applications from, and to provide training for, under-represented group. Particular action allowed by local authorities.

Race Relations Amendment Act 2000. Statutory duty on public authorities to eliminate race discrimination and promote race equality.

Part-time Workers Regulations 2000. Prevents less favourable treatment of part-time workers compared to full-time.

Fair Employment (Northern Ireland) Act 1989 (not applicable in Great Britain). Outlaws discrimination on grounds of religious belief or political opinion. Employers required to register with Fair Employment Commission, to monitor religious composition of their workforce and submit monitoring returns. Required to take 'affirmative action' where imbalances are evident, such action enforceable by the Commission.

Disability Discrimination Act 1995 (amended 2003). Prohibits discrimination and obliges employers to make reasonable adjustments to prevent any arrangements or physical features placing disabled people at a disadvantage. Amended to remove small employer exemption.

Employment Act 2002. Provisions relating to maternity, adoption and paternity leave and pay; right of parents and carers to request flexible working.

Fixed-Term Employees (Prevention of Less Favourable Treatment) Regulations 2002.

Employment Equality (Sexual Orientation) Regulations 2003. Unlawful to discriminate directly or indirectly, or to harass or victimize, on grounds of sexual orientation in employment and vocational training. Covers sexual orientation towards same sex, opposite sex or both. Sex Discrimination (Gender Reassignment) Regulations 1999 protect transsexuals. Genuine occupational requirement (GOR) provision.

Employment Equality (Religion and Belief) Regulations 2003. Outlaws discrimination, harassment and victimization on grounds of a person's religion, religious belief or similar philosophical belief. Specific exceptions provided where being of a particular religion may be a GOR for a particular type of employment.

Commission for Equality and Human Rights (CEHR) to encompass all areas, including those currently covered by the CRE, EOC and DRC (DTI 2004).

The agenda-setting role which can be played by the legal framework can be seen in the way the legislative priorities have been reflected in voluntary EO policies and initiatives. The 1998 Workplace Employee Relations Survey (WERS 98) revealed that the areas most commonly covered in EO policies are sex (in respect of which 58 per cent of all workplaces had policies) ethnic origin (58 per cent) and disability (56 per cent). Religion was covered in almost a half of all workplaces, with age and sexual orientation being covered in 41 per cent and 38 per cent. One-third of all workplaces has a policy which covers all six of these areas (Anderson et al. 2004: 56).

The influence of legislation on employer practice is also demonstrated, negatively, by the continuing incidence of age preferences in recruitment in the absence of legislation outlawing this (Worsley 1996: 18; Arrowsmith 2003). In the management interviews conducted for WERS 98 age was considered to be an important factor in recruitment in 21 per cent of workplaces, rising to one-third of those without any EO policy (Anderson et al. 2004).

The threat of numerous individual legal actions for equal pay was a tactic used by some unions to persuade employers to review grading structures in the 1990s, for example, in respect of ancillary workers in the NHS and in parts of the electricity industry (Colling and Dickens 2001: 142). The local authority single-status agreement reached in 1997 was achieved in the context of the prospect of thousands of equal value legal challenges over bonus payments and compulsory competitive tendering. This equality-informed single status framework agreement covers 1.5 million staff in local government services and provides a good example of how the incorporation of equal value considerations into job evaluation (with value being attached, for example, to caring skills and responsibility for people) could improve women's relative pay position. However, progress on fully implementing the agreement has been slow and where legal challenges have succeeded the impact appears to have been limited to the local authority concerned rather than providing a demonstration effect (Local Government Pay Commission 2003). The current wide-ranging pay and grading reform in the NHS, 'Agenda for Change', similarly seeks to establish equality proofed pay structures following some high profile and costly legal challenges (Bach and Winchester 2003).

The equality commissions have statutory investigative powers as well as a role in aiding individual complainants and in giving advice and issuing guidance on the legislative requirements and the promotion of EO. Threatened or actual investigations by the equality commissions helped stimulate progress in a number of sectors in the early days of the legislation but little use was made of their legal powers in the 1980s and 1990s. Recently, however, actual or threatened investigations have again stimulated employer action. In 2000 Ford of Britain was threatened with a CRE investigation into possible racism after a number of high profile discrimination claims. This provided a catalyst for a diversity equality assessment review undertaken jointly with the CRE, which led to thorough-going action plans. In 2002 Ford ranked fourth highest performer in Race for Opportunity's benchmarking exercise (Foster 2003b: 9). The EOC launched a formal investigation in January 2003 following allegations of widespread sexual harassment in Royal Mail. As a result the company agreed a wide-ranging action plan design to bring about a culture change in the organization (Foster 2004b).

For the most part, however, enforcement of the discrimination law rests with individuals. In the UK rights are conferred on individuals to challenge discriminatory behaviour rather than responsibilities being imposed on administrative, employing, governmental and other organizations to take action to tackle disadvantage. The emphasis is on action by 'victims' rather than action by power-wielders, an approach less likely to lead to EO action. A different approach can be found in the Race Relations Amendment Act 2000 which imposes a positive duty on various public sector employers to promote race equality in employment and service delivery (O'Cinneide 2003).

As noted in Box 7.2, the CRE includes avoiding the costs of legal action as part of the business case rationale for equality action, and publicity surrounding certain tribunal cases involving large amounts of compensation (for example, discrimination against women employed in City of London financial institutions) help draw attention to this. However, although organizations may be vulnerable to legal

Table 7.2 Discrimination claims to employment tribunals, 2002–2003

	Sex discrimination	Equal pay	Race discrimination	Disability discrimination
ACAS conciliated settlement	2,117	173	1,128	1,119
Withdrawn	3,791	484	1,059	839
Total not heard	5,908	657	2,187	1,958
% of all cases	75	57	73	79
Cases dismissed by tribunal	615	45	551	318
Cases successful at tribunal	289	47	104	90
% success rate[a]	32	51	16	22
Total cases heard	904	92	655	408
Otherwise disposed of	1,100[b]	409[b]	153	115
Total cases disposed of	7,912	1,158	2,995	2,481

[a] Proportion of heard cases which were successful at tribunal hearing.
[b] Part-time workers' pension complaints struck out for want of prosecution.

Source: ETS Annual Report.

challenge (particularly where trade unions mobilize around this) in practice the risk appears small: applications to employment tribunals remain relatively scarce and meet with limited success, as shown in Table 7.2.

As the table indicates, only a small proportion of cases are actually determined by a tribunal hearing and success rates for applicants are not very high. This is particularly and consistently so in race discrimination cases. The main remedy is a financial one. Tribunals made 98 awards in race discrimination cases in 2002–3, the median award was just below £8,000; the average award just over £27,000. In sex discrimination cases 181 awards of compensation were made by employment tribunals, the median was £5,000 and the average £8,787. Disability discrimination cases produced 80 awards with a median of £5,573 and average of £10,157. Averages are affected by some single large awards – for example, the highest race award was £814,877. Compensation awards in discrimination cases include an element for 'injury to feelings' and average awards under this head, particularly in race discrimination and sexual harassment cases, increased following two Court of Appeal decisions in 1988 which made it clear that such awards should not be nominal. Ninety-two equal pay claims were heard by tribunals in 2002–3: over half (51 per cent) were successful.

In considering why legal compliance has not produced greater change in terms of distributional outcomes, it is important to note that where discrimination is found, the emphasis in the legislation is on compensating the individual rather than requiring the employers to change their behaviour. The tribunal may make an action recommendation (for example, that an applicant discriminated against in promotion be considered for the next vacancy) but this relates to the particular case.

Compliance with the letter of the equality law does not take an organization far along the EO path. Even where pre-emptive compliance action is taken in respect of the law, therefore, little positive action is actually required from employers. Generally speaking the law requires an end to discrimination: it does not actually require that employers do anything to promote equality, at most it permits some limited 'out-reach' action such as targeting recruitment at under-represented groups. Although an EOP might be a useful defence in any legal claim against an organization, the development of such a policy is not required by law. There is no general requirement for employers to audit or monitor their workforces (although case law indicates it is advisable to do so and guidance from the equality commissions encourages this).

Importantly, apart from special provisions relating to pregnancy and maternity and the limited adjustment provisions in the Disability Discrimination Act, the legislation conceptualizes equality as treating people the same. Thus most forms of positive action to aid disadvantaged groups are actually prevented by the legislation, which is concerned with halting present discrimination but does nothing to overcome the effects of past discrimination. There is thus a tension between progressive equality and diversity policies seeking to increase representation or attainment of disadvantaged groups by positive (affirmative) action and the 'same treatment' approach of UK legislation (Barnes and Ashtiany 2003).

Although the legal requirements are limited, arguably the full potential of what compliance with the spirit of the law requires is not reflected in current practice. Potentially the concept of indirect discrimination (where apparently neutral conditions, requirements or practices have a disproportionate and adverse impact on a particular social group) is a far-reaching one, which could be utilized to throw into question much of the taken-for-granted practice in organizations and to tackle structural discrimination. But research shows a lack of understanding of the concept of indirect discrimination, and many companies which feel they have done enough to comply with the law have focused only on the more obvious direct discrimination.

Similarly, in respect of equal pay for equal value work, many organizations consider the changes they made at the time of the original equal pay legislation (which required equal pay for men and women doing the same or broadly similar jobs) to be sufficient, despite the subsequent important legislative change requiring equal pay (and other contractual conditions) where jobs are of equal value. The revised EOC Code of Practice issued in December 2003 and other publications on equal pay for work of equal value encourages and guides organizations to undertake pay system reviews and audits to reveal any gender inequality or undervaluation of work typically carried out by women in comparison with that typically undertaken by men. But this is something few employers do at present (Bevan and Thompson 1992: 5). Although there are reports of some increased activity in this area (EOR 2004b), research undertaken by the EOC found that at the end of 2003 almost half (49 per cent) of large employers surveyed had no plans to monitor the relative pay or men and women (Brett and Milsome 2004).

Explaining the Limited Impact of EO Action

The limitations of the drivers to EO action have been discussed but, separately and in combination, they have helped promote equality and diversity initiatives. Many organizations do seek to follow the steps indicated in the guidance from the equality commissions and elsewhere. And yet, as we have seen, there may be relatively little achievement in terms of distributional outcomes. In seeking to explain this relative lack of achievement when EO initiatives are taken, I look at the problems of translating EO prescription into practice, and consider the inadequacies of much prescription.

EOPs often call for the formalization of demonstrably fair procedures. However, the intention of EOPs can be neutralized through procedures being neglected or by being followed in the letter but not in the spirit. As Jenkins (1986) found in recruitment and selection, 'espoused' models (what we say we do) and 'operational' models (what we actually do) can differ considerably. Procedures operate within an organizational context and power in decision making may not be in the hands of the guardians of good practice, namely the HR department. Personnel managers (or equality officers) are often marginal to selection decisions, with real power being vested in line managers (Collinson et al. 1990; Jenkins 1986). Similarly commitment to equality at the top of an organization may not be replicated at all levels of management.

Line management is often found to be a site of resistance to equality initiatives and, therefore, the current emphasis on devolving operational personnel activities to line managers, often with greater budgetary autonomy, is not good news for equality (Dickens 1998: 34). Line managers may resist the formalization, accountability and monitoring often required by EOPs imposed by 'external' HR managers as interference with their discretion in decision making. Any change can be threatening and unwelcome but this may be exacerbated in the case of EO in that it may be seen as a challenge to personal attitudes and traditional local norms or values. EO may be experienced as criticism of those in power: managers and others can be affronted by assumptions that they discriminate.

Focusing on the reasons why prescription may be translated inadequately into practice might suggest that adequate implementation would produce desired outcomes. This is not so. Fair procedures do not necessarily produce fair (distributive justice) outcomes, as Jewson and Mason (1986) and others have argued cogently.

This is demonstrated in the area of recruitment and selection where fair procedures require the assessment of individuals against relevant, job-related criteria rather than according to their membership of a particular social group. The emphasis is on suitability criteria (skills and technical ability to do the job) rather than acceptability criteria (attitudinal, behavioural, personality factors) which tend to interact with racial stereotypes and lead to discrimination (Jenkins 1986). As Curran's (1988) work clearly demonstrates, in practice suitability and acceptability criteria may overlap. Both gender and a variety of personal attributes (social and tacit skills) in which gender (and possibly race) is embedded are regarded by many employers as specific and functional attributes and as requirements for the effective performance of particular jobs.

Implicit in much good practice equality prescription is an argument that discrimination arises from actions of prejudiced individuals, that it is irrational behaviour, indicative of poor management practice, and that it can be curbed by detailed instructions, training and policing. This neglects the fact, indicated earlier, that organizational ends can be served by not following the prescription and that, as a result, unfair discrimination can be rational and efficient for an individual and the organization.

Since there can be an organizational rationality in continuing discrimination, it becomes rational for individuals within the organization to act in ways detrimental to EO. This is not necessarily a conscious process. Where sexism and racism have become institutionalized, it is simply adherence to normal practice – 'the way things are done around here'. An organization may have adopted an EOP but individuals will respond to signals (formal and informal) about what 'really matters' in the organization and, therefore, what behaviour is likely to ensure success within it. This applies as much to those in HR management as elsewhere.

EO tends to be marginal or 'bolt-on' in organizations rather than mainstream. This problem is increasingly recognized in prescription, which advocates the mainstreaming of equality action so that, for example, 'diversity goals are written into the overall objectives of the organization and departments (for example, via business plans) and individuals (for example, through performance management system)' (IPD 1999). Mainstreaming involves ensuring that equality principles and practices are integrated into all aspects of an organization as part of everyday activities.

At present EO may be advocated as good management practice and sound business sense but unless it is a core, mainstreamed objective, priority will be given to other good management practices which serve organizational objectives and which may conflict with the tenor or requirements of EO. This can be seen in a range of current personnel developments associated with the 'human resource management' approach which, despite the rhetoric, may be at odds with the promotion of equal opportunity (Dickens 1998; Woodall 1996). Monitoring and pursuing equal pay, for example, becomes more difficult in the context of the individualization of pay systems and the spread of individual performance-related pay (Rubery 1995). The organizational pursuit of flexibility and commitment (key policy goals of the HRM model) also impacts differently on women and men (Dickens 1998) and attempts to develop and monitor EO policy are hampered by increased decentralization in organizations, an emphasis on devolution and power to the line, with management 'owning' their own decisions.

Prescriptive models often also underplay the vested interests in the status quo within organizations. Although emphasis is placed on securing the support of all employees for equality action and diversity goals, it remains the case that a key implementation problem in respect of EO 'is that support for taking action designed to improve prospects for women, ethnic minorities and the disabled must come from an overwhelmingly white, male and "non-disabled" dominant group who may well regard equal opportunities as a threat' (Lovenduski 1989: 15). The threat comes in part from the fact that white men's characteristic career paths are implicitly predicated on the existence of 'unpromotable' categories, including women and blacks (Crompton and Jones 1984: 248). EO is not necessarily the win–win game portrayed in the prescriptive literature.

The threat is not simply to career opportunities. Work is a place where identities are shaped and lived out. For men, work can be an affirmation of their masculinity: equal opportunities, the entry of women into that work, or paying women equivalent wages, can seem like an attack on that identity. Those who seek to cross gender boundaries by entering non-traditional work often find their masculinity or femininity questioned (Cockburn 1987) or find themselves subjected to harassment (Purcell 1988: 174).

Masculinity is not only shaped by work; it is shaped too by men's power over women in the home. The promotion of equality in employment can challenge this power. The potentially revolutionary nature of the demands being made under the banner of EO should not be underestimated in seeking to locate and explain resistance to it. As Cockburn (1991: 63) argues, for example, the claim for equal pay for work of equal value 'potentially undermines the whole strategy of exploiting women sex-specifically'. Of course, individual white men may not feel particularly powerful or see themselves as 'the problem'. One important criticism of racism awareness training, for example, is that it is experienced by whites as a personal attack, putting individuals in the dock on behalf of white society, and is thus resented, contributing to opposition to EOPs (see the discussion in Iles and Auluck 1989: 27–8).

But resistance to EO does not come only from white, non-disabled men. There may be resistance from within the disadvantaged groups which an EOP 'is designed to help', and this can be particularly dispiriting for those championing equality within organizations. Such resistance may arise through conflicting expectations of 'equal opportunities', a term which can mask multiple and conflicting meanings. There may be agreement at the symbolic level giving an illusion of common cause, but underlying differences in understanding and expectations can lead to feelings of betrayal (Young 1987: 4; Jewson and Mason 1986: 309).

Resistance may arise also because there are divisions between 'disadvantaged' groups. The assumption of shared interest implicit in much universalistic EO prescription is misplaced. For example, seniority rules may advantage ethnic minority men in an organization where there is low turnover, but may not be of advantage necessarily to women with interrupted employment patterns. Divisions also exist within any one disadvantaged group (for example, by race, ethnicity, sexual orientation, gender, occupational status, disability, age etc.) and, consequently, interests may differ, as may the perception of achievements or failings under equality and diversity strategies (Creegan et al. 2003).

Changing the Focus

The discussion so far indicates how problems of implementing equality initiatives and of obtaining substantive outcomes are rather more complex than suggested in much of the guidance literature and prescriptive equality models. The problems of obtaining desired substantive outcomes through procedural approaches have led some to argue for positive discrimination to effect distributional change. The 'radical' approach, outlined by Jewson and Mason (1986) in the context of a study of race discrimination, favours appointing candidates from disadvantaged groups regardless of the fact that they are 'less well qualified' in order to achieve desired outcomes in terms of proportional representation of various groups in the occupational hierarchy.

This approach, however, has been criticized (e.g. Webb and Liff 1988; Cockburn 1989) for sharing with the 'liberal' procedural approach, an acceptance of jobs and organizations as they are currently constructed. The radical approach focuses on gaining power not changing it: it is about attempting to advance disadvantaged groups within existing organizational structures whereas those organizational structures are what need to be changed to better accommodate all.

The changing perception of disability provides a useful pointer to what is required. Leach (1989: 65) noted a shift in focus from physical 'defects or deficiencies' to a recognition that most of the difficulties encountered by people with disabilities arise not from their impairment but from the systematic ignoring of their needs. Access ramps, for example, can help those with certain physical disabilities play a full part in organizational life but are necessary only because buildings have been designed with only the physically able in mind. Similarly, positive action for equality of opportunity for women and ethnic minorities at present usually consists of 'special measures' to help individuals in these groups compete for jobs designed with only white men in mind, within organizations whose norms, values and structures are similarly shaped around the traditional incumbents and power holders, again, white men.

Various 'flexibility' initiatives which recognize the current reality of women's lives, attempting to juggle waged work and domestic work, such as home-working or part-time working, are often cited as evidence of an EO approach (and are found in the CRE checklist in Box 7.1). But they may be double edged for equality in that they are seen as 'atypical' because they differ from the (male) norm. They help perpetuate the assumption that women bear (should bear) the primary responsibility for caring for children and enable women working 'atypically' to be dismissed as different, less serious or committed than male employees (Cockburn 1991: 92). Offering flexible arrangements to men as well as women is preferable to seeing them as open to women only but, without further change, this may not solve the problem. Even if career breaks, for example, are open to, and taken by, both men and women (and they rarely are) they are likely to be taken for different reasons and to be regarded differently by the organization: career enhancing if time out is taken to study, but career detracting if used for childcare, reflecting the low value currently placed on women's experience in household and family management despite the organizational, managerial and interpersonal skills involved.

Mainstreaming is potentially a move towards focusing on systems and structures which produce disadvantages, and seeking to integrate equality into them. There have been attempts at mainstreaming in the public sector (EOR 2002). However, the current focus of equality action more commonly is on helping ethnic minorities, people with disabilities and women compete 'on equal terms' with white, non-disabled men for jobs which have been shaped around the typical circumstances of white, able-bodied men, within organizations where the culture, norms, values, notions of merit, formal and informal structures all reflect the attributes, needs, work and life patterns of the typical white, non-disabled male. That is to say, there is a template for employment shaped around white, non-disabled men against which those seeking to get in and get on are measured. Rather than adopting this Procrustean approach with its focus on changing individuals to fit the template in order to obtain distributive justice, the template should be abandoned.

This argument for a different focus, for what has been called by Cockburn (1989) a 'transformative EO strategy', concerned with the nature, culture, relations and purpose of the organization, should not be taken as an argument against attempting the kind of EO initiatives indicated earlier, which, as noted, can produce gains for members of disadvantaged groups. Rather, the attempt here has been to explain why such initiatives generally fail to produce substantive change in the aggregate picture of disadvantage and discrimination, and to indicate the limitations of much current prescription. This prescription often rests on an inadequate conceptualization of the 'problem'; assumes unitary interests where divergent interests exist; pays inadequate attention to the resistance equality action generates; and simplifies the reasons for it. Furthermore, what is called for generally focuses on helping individuals from disadvantaged groups get in and get on within existing organizations, with no real challenge being mounted to the nature, structure, and values of the organizations themselves. More recent culture change approaches to EO (such as advocated by Opportunity Now) appear to represent progress here. The risk, however, is that in practice the likely focus will be the 'artefacts and creations' rather than more fundamental assertions and beliefs (Miller 1996: 207; Liff and Cameron 1997).

Potentially 'valuing diversity' contains the seeds of the required transformative approach in that it could open the way for different formal and informal organizational cultures and structures, reflective of diverse contributions, needs and attributes. At its most radical, the valuing diversity argument calls for a holistic, positive approach which recognizes and values individual and social group differences and which challenges the nature of organizations as currently constructed. Criticisms of the diversity approach can be made both empirically, in that in practice a transformational approach may not underpin the use of the label (e.g. Webb 1997) which, rather, may perpetuate existing patterns of disadvantage, and conceptually (see, for example, Lorbieki and Jack 2000, and the discussion in Kirton and Greene 2000). One criticism is that some diversity approaches, in seeking to encompass everyone, appear to involve 'dissolving' differences (Liff 1997; 1999) and to herald a move away from redressing historical group-based disadvantage towards a focus on all individuals as individuals. As Miller argues (1996: 207), this threatens to sever the link between organizational strategies and the realities of internal and external labour market disadvantage.

An individual as opposed to a social group focus is often one point of contrast made in the literature contrasting 'diversity' and 'equal opportunity' approaches (see, for example, the discussion in Torrington et al. 2002: 371) but some definitions of diversity embrace both the collectivist and individualist strand (e.g. Gagnon and Cornelius 2000: 69) and seek to build on and extend, rather than reject, aspects commonly presented as part of equal opportunity approaches. This is an area where the use of particular terms can be problematic and not necessarily illuminating as to practice.

Whatever label is used, without acknowledging through action that current organizational cultures, norms, structures, rules and notions of merit, etc. have been shaped around white, non-disabled men, and without a shift in focus away from, at best, helping people fit into jobs and organizations as presently constructed, towards changing the construction of jobs and organizations to accommodate all, achievement will always fall short of equality in employment. A focus on equality *and* diversity could help in walking the talk.

REFERENCES

Anderson, T., Millward, N. and Forth, J. 2004: *Equal Opportunities Policies and Practices at the Workplace: Secondary Analysis of WERS98*, London: DTI.

Arrowsmith, J. 2003: Theories and the practice of age discrimination: Evidence from personnel managers, *Review of Employment Topics*, **6**(1), 1–54.

Audit Commission 2002: *Equality and Diversity: Learning from Audit Inspections and Research*, London: Audit Commission.

Bach, S. and Winchester, D. 2003: Industrial relations in the public sector, in P. Edwards (ed.), *Industrial Relations*, Oxford: Blackwell.

Barnes, L. and Ashtiany, S. 2003: The diversity approach to achieving equality: Potential and pitfalls, *Industrial Law Journal*, **32**(4), 274–96.

Bevan, S. and Thompson, M. 1992: *Merit Pay, Performance Appraisal and Attitudes to Women's Work*, IMS Report No. 234, Brighton: Institute of Manpower Studies.

Bhavnani, R. 1994: *Black Women in the Labour Market*, EOC Research Series, Manchester: EOC.

Blackaby, D., Clark, K., Drinkwater, S., Leslie, D., Murphy, P. and O'Leary, N. 2000: Earnings and employment opportunities of disabled people, *Labour Market Trends*, March, 131–2.

Brett, S. and Milsome, S. 2004: *Monitoring Progress on Equal Pay Reviews*, Manchester: EOC.

Bruegel, I. and Perrons, D. 1995: Where do the costs of unequal treatment fall?, in J. Humphries and J. Rubery (eds.), *The Economics of Equal Opportunities*, Manchester: EOC.

CBI (Confederation of British Industry) 1996: *A Winning Strategy – The Business Case for Equal Opportunities*, London: CBI.

Clarke, K. 1991: *Women and Training. A Review*, Manchester: EOC.

Cockburn, C. 1987: *Two-Track Training*, Basingstoke: Macmillan Education.

Cockburn, C. 1989: Equal opportunities: The short and long agenda, *Industrial Relations Journal*, **20**(3), 213–25.

Cockburn, C. 1991: *In the Way of Women: Men's Resistance to Sex Equality in Organisations*, Basingstoke: Macmillan Education.

Colling, T. and Dickens, L. 1989: *Equality Bargaining – Why Not?* London: HMSO.

Colling, T. and Dickens, L. 1998: Selling the case for gender equality: Deregulation and equality bargaining, *British Journal of Industrial Relations*, **36**(3), 389–411.

Colling, T. and Dickens, L. 2001: Gender equality and trade unions: A new basis for mobilisation?, in M. Noon and E. Ogbonna, *Equality Diversity and Disadvantage in Employment*, Basingstoke: Palgrave.

Collinson, D., Knights, D. and Collinson, M. 1990: *Managing to Discriminate*, London: Routledge.

Copeland, L. 1988a: Valuing Diversity I, *Personnel*, June, 52–60.

Copeland, L. 1988b: Valuing Diversity II, *Personnel*, July, 44–9.

CRE (Commission for Racial Equality) 1984: *Race Relations Code of Practice*, London: CRE.

Creegan, C., Colgan, F., Charlesworth, R. and Robinson, G. 2003: Race equality policies at work, *Work Employment and Society*, **17**(4), 617–40.

Crompton, R. and Jones, G. 1984: *White Collar Proletariat: Deskilling and Gender in the Clerical Labour Process*, London: Macmillan.

Cully, M., O'Reilly, A., Millward, N., Forth, J. and Woodland, S. 1998: *The 1998 Workplace Employee Relations Survey: First Findings*, London: HMSO.

Cully, M., Woodland, S., O'Reilly, A., and Dix, G. 1999: *Britain at Work*, London: Routledge.

Cunningham, I. and James, P. 2001: Managing diversity and disability legislation: Catalysts for eradicating discrimination in the workplace?, in M. Noon and E. Ogbonna, *Equality Diversity and Disadvantage in Employment*, Basingstoke: Palgrave.

Curran, M. 1988: Gender and recruitment: People and places in the labour market, *Work, Employment and Society*, **2**(3), 335–51.

Dex, S. and McCulloch, A. 1995: *Flexible Employment in Britain: A Statistical Analysis*, EOC Discussion Series No. 15, Manchester: EOC.

Dickens, L. 1989: Women – A rediscovered resource? *Industrial Relations Journal*, **20**(3), 167–75.

Dickens, L. 1994: The business case for women's equality: Is the carrot better than the stick? *Employee Relations*, **16**(8), 5–18.

Dickens, L. 1998: What HRM means for gender equality, *Human Resource Management Journal*, **8**(1), 23–40.

Dickens, L. 1999: Beyond the business case: A three-pronged approach to equality action, *Human Resource Management Journal*, **9**(1), 9–19.

Dickens, L. and Hall, M. 2003: Labour law and industrial relations, in P. Edwards (ed.), *Industrial Relations: Theory and Practice*, Oxford: Blackwell.

DTI (Department of Trade and Industry) n.d.: *The Business Case for Diversity*, London: DTI.

DTI (Department of Trade and Industry) 2004: *Fairness for All: A New Commission for Equality and Human Rights*, Cm 6185, May, London: DTI.

EOC (Equal Opportunities Commission) 1988: *Local Authority Equal Opportunities Policies: Report of a Survey by the EOC*, Manchester: EOC.

EOC (Equal Opportunities Commission) 1990: *Equal Pay for Men and Women: Strengthening the Acts*, Manchester: EOC.

EOR 1993: Limited progress in civil service Race Action Programme, *Equal Opportunities Review*, **48**, March/April, 8–9.

EOR 1994: Equal opportunities in the health service: A survey of NHS Trusts, *Equal Opportunities Review*, **53**, January/February, 24–31.

EOR 1998a: Mainstreaming EO in the Civil Service, *Equal Opportunities Review*, **79**, May/June, 7.

EOR 1998b:Workplace Diversity – New Challenges, New Opportunities, *Equal Opportunities Review*, **78**, March/April, 18–24.

EOR 2002: Equality mainstreaming: Turning theory into practice, *Equal Opportunities Review*, **110**, October, 7–14.

EOR 2003: Latest civil service diversity data, *Equal Opportunities Review*, **121**, September, 5.

EOR 2004: Pay audits on the increase, *Equal Opportunities Review*, **128**, April, 5.

Felstead, A. 1995: The gender implications of creating a training market: Alleviating or reinforcing inequality of access, in J. Humphries and J. Rubery (eds.), *The Economics of Equal Opportunities*, Manchester: EOC.

Fevre, R. 1989: Informal practices, flexible firms and private labour markets, *Sociology*, **23**(1), 91–109.

Foster, C. 2003a: London Underground: Ending harassment, *Equal Opportunities Review*, **118**, June, 11–16.

Foster, C. 2003b: Ford: Driving diversity forward, *Equal Opportunities Review*, **116**, April, 9–15.

Foster, C. 2004a: Flexible working: Improving business performance, *Equal Opportunities Review*, **125**, January, 8–13.

Foster, C. 2004b: Royal Mail: Delivering dignity at work, *Equal Opportunities Review*, **132**, August, 8–14.

Gagnon, S. and Cornelius, N. 2000: Re-examining workplace equality: The capabilities approach, *Human Resource Management Journal*, **10**(4), 68–87.

Goodwin, K. 2003: Equal value update, *Equal Opportunities Review*, **117**, May, 8–17.

Green, F. 1991: Sex discrimination and job-related training, *British Journal of Industrial Relations*, **29**(2), 295–304.

Green, F. and Zanchi, L. 1997: Trends in the training of male and female workers in the United Kingdom, *British Journal of Industrial Relations*, **35**(4), 635–44.

Greenslade, M. 1991: Managing diversity: Lessons from the United States, *Personnel Management*, December, 28–33.

Hansard Society Commission. 1990: *Women at the Top*, London: Hansard Society for Parliamentary Government.

Hibbert, A. and Meager, N. 2003: Key indicators of women's position in Britain, *Labour Market Trends*, October, 503–11.

Hitner, T., Knights, D., Green, E. and Torrington, D. 1981: Races at work: Equal opportunity policy and practice, *Employment Gazette*, September.

Humphries, J. and Rubery, J. (eds.) 1995: *The Economics of Equal Opportunities*, Manchester: EOC.

IDS (Income Data Services) 2004: *Work Life Balance*, Study No. 768, February.

Iles, P. and Auluck, R. 1989: From racism awareness training to strategic human resource management in implementing equal opportunity, *Personnel Review*, **18**(4), 24–32.

Iles, P. and Auluck, R. 1991: The experience of black workers, in M. Davidson and J. Earnshaw (eds.), *Vulnerable Workers*, Chichester: Wiley.

IPD (Institute for Professional Development) 1996: *Managing Diversity*, London: IPD.

IPD (Institute for Professional Development) 1999: *Managing Diversity: Evidence from Case Studies*, London: IPD.

IRS (Industrial Relations Service) 1995: Implementation of racial equality policies disappointing, says CRE, *Labour Market Trends*, **578**, 2–3.

IRS (Industrial Relations Service) 1997: Historic single status deal in local government, *Employment Trends*, **639**, September, 5–10.

IRS (Industrial Relations Service) 1999: Equal opportunities: The state of play, *Employment Trends*, **691**, November, 2.

Jenkins, R. 1986: *Racism and Recruitment: Managers, Organisations and Equal Opportunity in the Labour Market*, Cambridge: Cambridge University Press.

Jewson, N. and Mason, D. 1986: The theory and practice of equal opportunities policies: Liberal and radical approaches, *Sociological Review*, **34**(2), 307–33.

Jewson, N., Mason, D., Waters, S. and Harvey, J. 1990: *Ethnic Minorities and Employment Practice: A Study of Six Organisations*, Research Paper 76, London: Employment Department.

Kandola, R. and Fullerton, J. 1994: *Managing the Mosaic: Diversity in Action*, London: IPD.

Kirton, G. and Greene, A-M. 2000: *The Dynamics of Managing Diversity: A Critical Approach*, Butterworth Heinemann.

Leach, B. 1989: Disabled people and the implementation of local authorities' equal opportunities policies, *Public Administration*, **67**, Spring, 65–93.

Lee, G. and Wrench, J. 1987: Race and gender dimensions of the youth labour market: From apprenticeship to YTS, in G. Lee and R. Loveridge (eds.), *The Manufacture of Disadvantage*, Milton Keynes: Open University Press.

Liff, S. 1997: Two routes to managing diversity: Individual differences or social group characteristics, *Employee Relations*, **19**(1), 11–26.

Liff, S. 1999: Diversity and equal opportunities: Room for a constructive compromise? *Human Resource Management Journal*, **9**(1), 65–75.

Liff, S. 2003: The industrial relations of a diverse workforce, in P. Edwards (ed.), *Industrial Relations*, Oxford: Blackwell.

Liff, S. and Cameron, I. 1997: Changing equality cultures to move beyond 'women's problems', *Gender Work and Organisation*, **4**(1), 35–46.

Liff, S. and Dickens, L. 2000: Ethics and equality: Reconciling false dilemmas, in D. Winstanley and J. Woodall (eds.), *Ethical Issues in Contemporary Human Resource Management*, Basingstoke: Macmillan.

Local Government Pay Commission 2003: Report, www.lg-pay.org.uk

Loden, M. 1998: cited in Workplace diversity – New challenges, new opportunities, *Equal Opportunities Review*, March/April, 18–24.

Lorbieki, A. and Jack, G. 2000: Critical turns in the evolution of diversity management, *British Journal of Management*, **11** (special issue), 17–31.

Loretto, W., Duncan, C. and White, P. 2000: Industrial relations codes of practice: The 1999 age discrimination code in context, *Employee Relations*, **22**(2), 146–59.

Lovenduski, J. 1989: Implementing equal opportunities in the 1980s: An overview, *Public Administration*, **67**, Spring, 7–18.

Maguire, M. 1986: Recruitment as a means of control, in K. Purcell et al. (eds.), *The Changing Experience of Employment*, Basingstoke: Macmillan Educational.

Mason, D. and Jewson, N. 1992: Race, equal opportunity policies and employment practice, *New Community*, October.

Maxwell, G. 2004: Taking the initiative in managing diversity at BBC Scotland, *Employee Relations*, **26**(2), 182–202.

Miller, D. 1996: Equality management: Towards a materialist approach, *Gender Work and Organisation*, **3**(4), 202–14.

Moralee, L. 1998: Self employment in the 1990s, *Labour Market Trends*, **106**(3), 121–30.

O'Cinneide, C. 2003: Extending positive duties across the equality grounds, *Equal Opportunities Review*, **120**, August, 12–16.

Ollerearnshaw, S. and Waldeck, R. 1995: Taking action to promote equality, *People Management*, **23**, February, 24–7.

Owen, D., Green, A., Maguire, M. and Pitcher, J. 2000: Patterns of labour market participation in ethnic minority groups, *Labour Market Trends*, November, 505.

Perrons, D. and Shaw, J. 1995: Recent changes in women's employment in Britain, in J. Shaw and D. Perrons (eds.), *Making Gender Work*, Milton Keynes: Open University Press.

Philips, A. and Taylor, B. 1980: Sex and skill: Notes towards a feminist economics, *Feminist Review*, **6**.

Pilkington, A. 2001: Beyond racial dualism: Racial disadvantage and ethnic diversity in the labour market, in M. Noon and E. Ogbonna, *Equality Diversity and Disadvantage in Employment*, Basingstoke: Palgrave.

Pirani, M., Yolles, M. and Bassa, E. 1992: Ethnic pay differentials, *New Community*, **19**(1), 31–42.

Purcell, K. 1988: Gender and the experience of employment, in D. Gallie (ed.), *Employment in Britain*, Oxford: Blackwell.

Richards, W. 2001: Evaluating equal opportunity initiatives: The case for a 'transformative' agenda, in M. Noon and E. Ogbonna, *Equality Diversity and Disadvantage in Employment*, Basingstoke: Palgrave.

Rubery, J. 1995: Performance related pay and the prospects for gender pay equity, *Journal of Management Studies*, **32**(5), 637–54.

Rutherford and Ollerearnshaw, S. 2002: Why diversity is good for business, *Equal Opportunities Review*, **110**, October, 15–16.

Sly, F. 1996. Disability and the labour market, *Labour Market Trends*, **104**(9), 413–24.

Sly, F., Thair, T. and Risdon, A. 1998: Women in the labour market: Results from the Spring 1997 Labour Force Survey, *Labour Market Trends*, **106**(3), 97–105.

Smith, A. and Twomey, B. 2002: Labour market experiences of people with disabilities, *Labour Market Trends*, August, 415.

Torrington, D., Hall, L. and Taylor, S. 2002: *Human Resource Management*, Harlow: Pearson Education.

TUC 2002: *Black Workers*, London: TUC.

Wainwright Trust. 1997: *Decentralisation and Devolution: The Impact on Equal Opportunities at Work*, Standon, Ware, Herts: The Wainwright Trust.

Webb, J. 1997: The politics of equal opportunity, *Gender, Work and Organisation*, **4**(3), 159–67.

Webb, J. and Liff, S. 1988: Play the white man: The social construction of fairness and competition in equal opportunities policies, *Sociological Review*, **36**(3), 532–51.

Wood, S. 1986: Personnel management and recruitment, *Personnel Review*, **15**(2).

Woodall, J. 1996: Human resource management: The vision of the genderblind, in B. Towers (ed.), *The Handbook of Human Resource Management*, Oxford: Blackwell.

Worsley, R. 1996: Only prejudices are old and tired, *People Management*, January, 18–23.

Young, K. 1987: The space between words: Local authorities and the concept of equal opportunities, in R. Jenkins and J. Solomos (eds.), *Racism and Equal Opportunity Policies in the 1980s*, Cambridge: Cambridge University Press.

PART III

Employee Development

CHAPTER EIGHT

Skills, Training and the Quest for the Holy Grail of Influence and Status

Ewart Keep

The chapter on training in the third edition of this volume (Keep and Rainbird 2000) focused on the concept of the learning organization (LO). The present chapter takes a somewhat different approach, with the lens of analysis focused on the role and status of training or human resource development (HRD) activity within organizations. Nevertheless, where appropriate, reference will be made to a number of common themes that span both takes on the issue, not least in terms of some of the fundamental underlying barriers and incentives that organizations and individual managers face in dealing with skills.

At the outset a word or two on nomenclature seems in order. Governments and official agencies across the UK, but particularly within England, have come to favour a terminology that revolves around learning and skills. Learning is normally taken to encompass education and training, both formal and informal, whereas training still tends to be understood as relating to formalized learning activities such as courses and structured programmes of activity under guidance from others. Unfortunately, there is a tendency for these terms to be used interchangeably, with the result that policy makers often talk about learning when what they are referring to is only the formalized area of such activity (for a fuller discussion of this issue, see Felstead et al. 2004). Underlying this problem are two competing, though often unacknowledged, concepts of learning. The first relates to learning as acquisition – of skills and qualifications gained through formalized courses. The other to learning as participation – within a particular work process and group of co-employees, through and from which learning takes place (Felstead et al. 2004).

Moreover, within the more prescriptive practitioner literature there is enthusiasm for replacing the terms 'trainer' and 'training' with the concept of 'human resource development' (HRD) (Reid and Barrington 2001). Thus HRD becomes the little brother to the wider concept of HRM (which of course is supposed to have replaced the outmoded models of industrial relations and personnel management). However, in the author's experience the term HRD has little meaning for and hold over a substantial number of those who actually work in the field, and this chapter therefore generally refers to training.

In terms of structure, the chapter opens with a brief exploration of the changing meaning of skill and of aggregate level data on patterns of training activity. It then examines the optimistic agenda for the status and position of training activity, and reviews a number of the reasons why these readings of the future may need to be qualified. The chapter then looks at the growing body of research that provides a better understanding of how and why learning occurs in the workplace and how best it can be facilitated. The implications of this research for practitioners are explored. Attention then turns to the challenges posed to company training by public policy on skills. The chapter concludes with some observations about the key issues facing those concerned with skill creation within organizations.

Training and Skills: Changing Meaning and Patterns of Provision

Nomenclature has already been highlighted as an issue in this chapter. It is particularly important in respect of the word skill, which has undergone a subtle but profound shift in meaning in recent times – some appreciation of which is important to making sense of training activity within organizations. A quarter of a century ago skill was generally taken to refer to manual dexterity (tool usage or control) and to some understanding of underpinning bodies of theory and knowledge associated with the exercise of particular trades or occupations. Since then there has been a growing prioritization of softer social skills and personal attributes (e.g. manner, deportment, appearance, dress sense, accent, ability to get on with people, and self-confidence) (Payne 1999; Grugulis et al. 2004). As one employer put it, 'we recruit attitude' (Callaghan and Thompson 2002: 240). Increasingly such attitudes and attributes are being referred to as skills (Payne 1999). This trend almost certainly reflects the massive shift in employment from manufacturing to the service sector, and from manual labour (skilled and semi-skilled) to various forms of white-collar employment.

The implications for both recruitment training are profound and cannot be discussed in detail here (see Grugulis et al. 2004 and Keep and Payne 2004 for a fuller treatment). What can be said is that some employers now view the technical skills component of work in their organizations as of secondary importance and easily trainable providing employees with the right disposition and personal characteristics are recruited (Nickson et al. 2004). In terms of soft skills themselves, employers appear to be divided on whether these are amenable to creation through training or are best acquired through the selection process (Warhurst and

Nickson 2001). The consequences of these developments are that the importance of recruitment and selection as a mode of skill acquisition may well have increased, and that at aggregate level the mix of skills that organizations' training activities are meant to be creating has shifted substantially over the years. It is likely that today there is less training in lathe operation and much more in customer care than was the case 20 years ago. Moreover, when official surveys elicit information on skills gaps within the workforce (defined as occurring when employers report some of their staff as not being fully proficient to meet their job roles), these often centre on soft skills such as problem solving, communication and customer handling (IER/IFF 2004: 75).

Outline measures of provision

This brings us to the question of what is known about employers' training activity in terms of volume, distribution, cost and focus. Only a brief overview can be presented here. The latest data on training activity comes from the 2003 National Employers Skills Survey (NESS), which covered a sample of 72,100 English establishments. For more details on training in small firms see Kitching and Blackburn (2002), and for comparisons of UK employer training activity with that of their counterparts elsewhere in Europe see Philpott (2004).

In terms of who trains, NESS suggests that 59 per cent of all establishments had provided training, with smaller establishments far less likely to provide training than their larger counterparts – 50 per cent of establishments with 1–4 employees provided training compared with 97 per cent of those with 500 or more staff (IER/IFF 2004: 21). Overall, 53 per cent of employees had received some training over the previous year. The total volume of employer provided training appears to have remained more or less constant since the late 1990s.

The distribution of training across the workforce varies greatly by sector and by occupation, with part-timers (particularly females) faring badly (Gallie et al. 1998), along with those in elementary occupations. Put simply, training incidence tends to increase with occupational status, so that professionals and managers receive the most (NSTF 2000a, b; CIPD 2002).

Employers' training provision can be broken into three main types – training to meet skill needs generated by the productive process, training to meet legislative requirements and professional or sectoral regulation (health and safety, licence to practice requirements), and participation in government supported training programmes.

On the first, NESS showed that 80 per cent of those establishments offering training provided job specific training, 53 per cent training in new technology (probably largely IT related), 51 per cent induction training for new staff, 35 per cent management training, 33 per cent supervisory training, and just 2 per cent training in a foreign language (IER/IFF 2004). What we do not know in any great detail is what the different categories of training being provided really comprise of. To take induction as an example, it is potentially a very broad category, which anecdotal evidence suggests can range from a week's formalized training courses for new staff in one major retailer, to being shown a health and safety video in another.

On the second (training to meet legislative requirements), NESS suggests that 69 per cent of establishments that train offer health and safety training. Other evidence (NSTF 2000b) suggests that the impact of health and safety and food hygiene legislation on training activity is quite considerable.

On employers' involvement in government supported training programmes, Kitching and Blackburn report that no more than 13 per cent of SMEs were engaged with any sort of government training initiative. In relation to the government's flagship programme – apprenticeships – in 2002 only 3 per cent of employers with five or more staff were involved in advanced apprenticeships and just 2 per cent with foundation apprenticeships (Brown et al. 2004: 40).

In terms of how training activity is being planned and integrated into wider business strategy, NESS shows that:

- 56 per cent of establishments had a formal business plan;
- 39 per cent had a training plan that specified the levels and types of training over the coming year (up from 24 per cent in 2001);
- 31 per cent reported having a training budget.

Overall, 'two-thirds of establishments (67 per cent) had at least one of the above plans, a fifth (21 per cent) had all of them, and a third (33 per cent) had none' (IER/IFF 2004: 20).

NESS tells us something about efforts to systematically appraise performance and skill gaps, suggesting that 75 per cent of employees had an annual performance review (which might or might not include skills and training issues). In addition, 52 per cent were subject to skills assessments that sought to identify skills gaps (IER/IFF 2004: 21).

In relation to the key issue of how much employers spend on training, there is a wide range of conflicting guestimates. Data from NESS suggests that in terms of direct costs, employers expend about £4.5 billion a year. This does not cover the wage costs of the time spent by trainees while being trained. When these are added in the authors of the NESS report (IER/IFF 2004: 21) estimate that the overall figure rises to about £14.5 billion. This contrasts quite markedly with the CIPD's estimate of no less than £35 billion (Philpott 2002: 14), and is significantly lower than the £23.5 billion figure that both the government and CBI have often quoted.

All these figures need to be treated with great caution. Case study and survey evidence suggests that the bulk of learning in the workplace is informal, uncertified, uncosted and, in many cases, unrecorded (Fuller et al. 2003; Felstead et al. 2004). At best, official data offers a very partial and incomplete view of training activity.

Training: A Glittering Future?

If the UK government and elements of the practitioner press are to be believed, now is the moment at which the era of training and the trainer (or learning facilitator) is dawning. The reasons for this optimism are as follows. First, the government, and many commentators and gurus, continue to aver that skills are *the* key to national economic success in a period of heightened globalized economic competition:

As we move into the new century, skills and learning must become the key determinants of the economic prosperity and social cohesion of our country. Knowledge and skills are now the key drivers of innovation and change. Economic performance depends increasingly on talent and creativity. (Blunkett 2000: 3)

The skills of our people are a vital national asset. Skills help businesses achieve the productivity, innovation and profitability needed to compete. They help our public services provide the quality and choice that people want . . . Sustaining a competitive, productive economy which delivers prosperity for all requires an ever growing proportion of skilled, qualified people. (foreword to DfES/DTI/HMT/DWP 2003)

In the early 1900s, businesses were founded principally on their ability to access financial capital. . . . By the mid-1900s technology was the core competence around which successful businesses were created. . . . By the early 2000s, there is a growing awareness that it is people and the inspiration, knowledge and creativity they bring that creates competitive advantage. The move from financial to technological to human capital is assuming earthquake proportions, and many commentators believe that we are witnessing a paradigm shift in the way that organizations are designed and work is created. (Gratton 2000: 28)

This suggests that training or HRD becomes the lynchpin around which revolve competitive strategy and the maintenance of competitive advantage. This view of the world is tied up with wider discourses about empowerment, knowledge workers, creativity, customization, globalization and the knowledge driven economy.

At the same time, literature aimed at training practitioners argues that as HRM has become more and more closely aligned with, and thereby able to gain influence over, business strategy, those concerned with training can join in and secure recognition and status from the organization's top decision makers through incorporation into the cadre of strategic architects who devise corporate strategy (see, for example, Garavan et al. 1995; and Mayo 2004). The director-general of the Chartered Institute of Personnel and Development (CIPD) has suggested that:

Interventions in the learning arena have got to reflect, and be reflected in, all aspects of the business. Leading trainers have been saying this for a long time, but there is now much more evidence that this is happening. (Armstrong, quoted in Manocha 2004)

Unsurprisingly, this message, with its explicit promise of power (and hence enhanced reward and career prospects) has been received enthusiastically by practitioner audiences.

If we accept these narratives, the remainder of this chapter should focus on reporting on some leading edge examples of best practice in strategic HRD and how they might be copied, and reviewing the most popular latest training techniques (coaching and e-learning for example). Perhaps sadly, the thesis concerning the centrality of skills and training is open to serious question. Like many prescriptive representations of reality, the scene painted above may be of a landscape that does not exist, certainly outside a limited sub-set of organizations. Why might this be?

Problems and Issues for Training in Organizations

Skills: best practice or 'fit'?

The original formulations of the more evangelical HRM literature suggested that the triumph of a 'one best way' model of leading edge people management practice in large multinational corporations would sweep all before it and form a universal standard and pattern applicable across the bulk of organizations (Purcell 1999). With the passing of time, and the growing realization that 'the HRM model . . . appears to be little more than a dream' (Bach and Sisson 2000: 36), the focus of attention has shifted to the issue of the degree of 'fit' between organizational strategy and HRM and HRD policies and practice. Herein lies the first major problem for more idealized views of training and the training function.

What a great deal of management research reveals is that different organizations are trying to compete in very different ways, in what are often fundamentally different markets, and that therefore the notion of a universal, best practice model is pointless. Product markets are normally segmented, with different product or service offerings appealing to different groups of consumers, often with differentiation being partly on the basis of specification and quality, and with these being reflected by price. Thus, in the market for hotel accommodation 5-star chains like the Hilton are not generally seen as being in direct competition with budget chains like the Holiday Inn (see Nickson et al. 2002). Business strategy is often a more or less explicit choice about what segment of a given market the organization wishes to compete in and how competitive advantage within that segment can best be achieved. Choices about where in the spectrum of offerings in any given product market an organization will compete are central to determining a whole range of other subordinate considerations, relating to the necessary product design and specification, production methods and technologies, and the HRM and training policies and practices that are needed to support that choice.

Research points to a link across the whole economy between what the business aims to achieve in terms of product or service specification, and the skill levels that are then needed to enable this specification to be reached (Green et al. 2003;

Mason 2004). At a more detailed level, Boxall (2003) demonstrates in relation to the service sector that a range of market segmentation approaches is available to management, and these have implications for how people are managed and trained (Batt 2000; Eaton 2000; Hunter 2000). Put briefly, the research suggests that, 'HR investments (in training, pay, career structures and staffing levels) are often greater in firms that target higher value niches' (Boxall 2003: 8). Firms in price-sensitive, mass service markets like supermarkets will see labour as a cost, will employ routinized models of work, and will have limited skill requirements from the bulk of their employees. By contrast, firms that compete in high-level business services, where differentiation of product or service is very important, will tend to embrace relatively sophisticated models of personnel management, expect employees to work with high degrees of individual discretion, and invest heavily in skill development (Boxall 2003: 13–14). Lashley's (1998) investigations in the hospitality industry also revealed a clear segmentation of offerings and a similar dispersion of resultant forms of work organization, job design, people management practices and skill requirements (see Nickson et al. 2002).

It would be unwise to assume, as UK policy makers often do, that this situation is set to change and that economic pressures are forcing all firms to think about shifting their product market strategies towards higher quality, more differentiated segments of the market. As Wilson and Hogarth's (2003) research demonstrates, in the hotels and food manufacturing sectors, there are plenty of firms that are content or resigned to competing in low margin segments with limited differentiation and relatively low specification offerings. The result is jobs for the broad mass of the workforce that are relatively lowly skilled. This was not an irrational approach on the part of these firms, many were relatively successful organizations. These findings replicate what was perhaps the key piece of data from the National Skills Task Force's entire research programme, that fully 60 per cent of firms surveyed said they had no plans to change their product market strategy and try to move into higher value added areas (NSTF 2000a: 115).

The importance of segmentation and differentiation in competitive strategy between firms within the same sector explains why so many, universalistic, one-best-way, 'best practice' models of HRM and training fail to achieve widespread adoption. For many organizations that are operating in low value added and/or mass markets, where price leadership rather than skilled employees is the key to competitive success, and where labour is thus a cost to be minimized, their prescriptions are both expensive and irrelevant. As Purcell (1999) demonstrates, rather than the universal adoption of best practice, the issue for most organizations is one of 'fit' between competitive strategy and lower order issues, such as personnel management/HRM and training.

A resource-based view of competitive advantage

Another revelation provided by management research concerns the resource-based view of the firm. The policy rhetoric points to the need for more skills across the board, and for an entire workforce that can exercise discretion and creativity in order to add value. However, the resource-based view argues that it is a 'unique set of competencies and distinctive organisational routines' (Purcell 1999: 35) that matter to competitive success, that these may be highly defused or highly concentrated, and that this will vary from case to case. For example, in a bespoke software design company the skills that determine competitive success will normally be widely dispersed across the workforce. At the other end of the spectrum, in a supermarket, the key skills in determining purchasing and supply chain management, stock keeping and logistics, marketing, pricing, store layout, and finance are located in a small core of head office employees. Store staff (even store management) have little or no input into these areas. As Purcell concludes, 'in practice the resource view will nearly always involve the identification of a core group of employees, sometimes small in number' (1999: 36).

This may mean that in some organizations the vast bulk of the workforce's opportunities for creativity and discretion in the workplace may be very limited. This is not to suggest that such staff will not need some training, merely that what they receive will tend to be narrow, generally task specific, and seen as a necessary hygiene factor rather than as the key to competitive success. The training that matters will be that of a small cadre of senior managers, and in many cases the skills that will be needed may be bought in from rivals via recruitment of high fliers from competitors. This in turn suggests that in such organizations the key developmental role will revolve around senior management development and succession planning. Interestingly, Scullion and Starkey's (2000) research in 30 large, UK-based multinationals identified the development and career management of the senior management cadre as the area where corporate HR was trying to carve out a genuinely strategic role for itself. They attribute the criticality of this group of employees to the fact that it is with them that the organization's core competences reside.

The resource-based view also again underlines why best practice models of HRM and HRD have not become widely diffused. If strategy is concerned with 'the identification and development of HR policies which are focused on some employees and not others, and which contribute to sustained competitive advantage by engendering rare and imperfectly imitable competence and routine, then questions of diffusion are largely irrelevant' (Purcell 1999: 36). Moreover, the resource-based view goes a long way towards explaining the dispersion of training opportunities across the adult workforce. The reason is simple, it is their skills that are judged to be key to delivering success rather than those of the mass of front-line and production workers.

This pattern may be being reinforced via trends in boardroom pay. In many large UK companies, the senior management team has sought to justify soaring remuneration packages and bonus payments on the basis of their unique skills held within a tight labour market for senior management expertise. In the past decade average earnings for UK employees increased by around 45 per cent, while the average earnings of lead executives in FTSE 100 companies rose by 288 per cent, that is, six times as fast (IDS 2003). This widening differential between shop floor and front-line staff pay and that in the boardroom is put down to the fact that senior management are the ones who possess the skills that make the difference to competitive performance. In these circumstances it is then difficult to be seen to admit that the skills of the mass of the workforce matter too much, in case someone asks why they are increasingly becoming relatively poorly paid.

Nesting training within business strategy

The textbook models suggest that training activity should be the outcome of a high degree of integration with the organization's strategic planning, performance management and appraisal mechanisms. Thus the HRD/training plan nests within the strategic HRM plan, which in turn nests within the higher level strategic business plan. In terms of performance management and appraisal, the ideal is for the individual worker to have his or her performance appraised, skill gaps and deficiencies identified, and then a personal development plan (PDP) formulated (usually by their line manager) to remedy these deficiencies and to develop the individual to fit their next role within the organization. This model has the benefit of neatness, but in many organizations its strictures are rarely implemented and may not be implementable.

To begin with, many organizations, particularly SMEs, appear to lack strategies in the sense of detailed, relatively stable plans that provide a context upon which subordinate elements of planning can be based. In some cases, even in large firms, a detailed, explicit business strategy may be lacking, with the business being managed through portfolio techniques, whereby the corporate centre establishes profit targets for its business units (Purcell 1989). There is no central blueprint, merely the incentive that those that do well may receive investment, while those that do not are liable to be sold.

Where strategies exist, they may be so unstable as to render meaningful planning of HRM and training issues impossible. The continuing tendency for organizations to 'fad surf', often at the whim of individual senior managers, produces waves of supposedly profound but often somewhat short-lived 'change programmes', centred on whatever happens to be the latest management fashion (Bach and Sisson 2000). In these circumstances it becomes hard to gear training to strategy, as strategy is a rapidly moving target.

The result is that over the last 20 years a series of studies have argued that training often tends to be poorly integrated into wider personnel or business planning (Coopers and Lybrand 1985; Rainbird 1994; NSTF 2000a, b; Edwards 2001). Edwards, using data from the last Workplace Employee Relations Survey (WERS), found that if we use as a measure of workplaces with a high level of training those where 60 per cent or more of the workforce had received off-the-job training in the last year, and that the average time spent per worker was two or more days, then 28 per cent of UK workplaces qualified. However, if the requirement for the training to be included in a strategic plan was added, the percentage fell to 15 per cent. As outlined above, the NESS indicated only 21 per cent of establishments had a formal business plan, a training plan and a training budget (IER/IFF 2004: 20).

Given this body of research the government's NSTF were probably correct in concluding that:

> skills tend to be a neglected issue when employers are formulating their business strategies. There must be a question therefore about whether employers properly evaluate their skill needs and, even where they attempt to do so, whether they give full consideration to these needs before they embark on a particular product market strategy. (NSTF 2000a: 19)

Or as one of Guest et al.'s respondents puts it:

> Our investment in training is actually when you add it up, pretty impressive, but it is a bit scatter-gun − it is not terribly focused and it is not linked to analysis of skills and capabilities gaps which is informed by the business planning/corporate planning process too much . . . Nobody says, well here is your PDP, we've actually worked out the skills gap in terms of what we know we need to deliver next year to meet this particular corporate goal. (Guest et al. 2001: 45−6)

The organizational salience of skill: an overview

The issues outlined above mean that there is not a universal movement towards higher skills as a key component of organizational strategy, leading to a general upskilling of the workforce. In reality, the responses of individual employers to the issue of skills will differ very significantly, both in terms of what product market strategies dictate and the degree to which there is strong articulation between product market strategy, business strategy and subordinate issues such as HRM and training.

For some, the skills of all their employees will be crucial. For others, the skills of a small minority of their staff will be important. In certain instances, skills will be of minor consequence, an issue forced upon them by the need to induct new employees and by government regulation (for example, health and safety legislation). This plainly has implications for the status and focus of training activity.

Even where the skills of a greater or lesser proportion of the workforce are important, it is perfectly possible that this will not feed through into business planning systems (if they exist) and from there into personnel and training policies and practices. This situation explains why the type, level, volume and distribution of training within and between organizations varies very considerably, and why national average figures, for example for training volume, conceal a massive range of variation between sectors, and between individual firms in each sector.

The problem for those concerned with training is that it is very hard for them to change these underlying circumstances. In some firms the wind will be blowing in its favour – product market strategies will dictate that the skills of a large pro-portion of the workforce are central to organizational performance, and there will be in place a relatively sophisticated business strategy, supported by a coherent HRM strategy within which training activity can take place. In many others, these cir-cumstances will not apply, and those concerned with training will find it hard to obtain the leverage to correct these failings and weaknesses, as they are either dictated by the organization's underlying product strategy, and/or are embodied in senior management policy and practice.

Training: A Low Status Function?

Having outlined a number of reasons why the linkages between training and busi-ness strategy may be problematic, and not always leading towards placing skills and training at the top of the senior management agenda, we now turn to a second set of issues. These are bound up with the status of the training function and its members, and with the dispersal (Auluck-Cooper 2004: 6) of the functions' roles – through outsourcing and devolution to line management.

On status, there are two competing schools of thought. One argues that enhanced strategic importance has been accompanied by increased status for HRD professionals (see, for example, Carter et al. 2002). The other suggests that training/HRD con-tinues to be a backwater within many organizations (Reid and Barrington 2001) with limited influence over the senior management team. Given that even the HRM function seems to relatively rarely be granted a seat at the boardroom table (Higginbottom 2002) it is hard to see trainers having the ear of senior manage-ment on a regular basis. It will be interesting to see what the latest version of the WERS reveals on this point, but it appears improbable, given previous trends, that the incidence of HRM and training specialists among the senior management team will have risen very sharply.

What can also be observed is that, in marked contrast to some specialisms within management (lawyers, engineers, and most especially accountants), it is open to doubt if trainers form a fully professional group. The problem is that there is no specific entry requirement in terms of qualifications. For example, a recent ana-lysis of HRD and training job advertisements in personnel and HRD magazines and on websites (Auluck-Cooper 2004), showed that 36.7 per cent of advertise-ments did not specify any minimum qualification. Of those that did require a qualification, 50.9 per cent needed a professional HR/HRD/CIPD award.

Dispersal of the function

One set of changes that has had an impact on the training function over the last decade or more has been the twin drives to devolve a much greater level of respons-ibility for the day-to-day planning and delivery of training to line managers, and the increasing recourse to outsourcing for training skills. The first of these two trends matches wider developments in HR, which have seen the role of specialist people managers as being to become consultants and facilitators, with much of the mundane detailed delivery passed to line managers. In an ideal world this is a move that makes a great deal of sense, but which has, in practice, often generated major problems, both for line managers and for trainers (see Gibb 2003 for an overview of the issues).

For line managers, the difficulties are simple – time and expertise. In many organizations, managers are faced with a multiplicity of competing calls on their time, and a reward system that usually prioritizes the achievement of a limited bundle of performance targets. Besides the day-to-day control of operations, the maximization of output and profit levels, improving product and service quality, and cost-containment exercises, managers also now find themselves responsible for appraising, rewarding, motivating, coaching and developing their staff. As Hyman and Cunningham (1998: 104) note of their case study organizations, 'whilst senior managers expected line managers to train and appraise, this was not always accompanied by either the resources, resolution or enthusiasm among line managers to ensure that it was undertaken effectively, with the result that continuing neglect of these activities was apparent in many instances'.

It is also possible to raise doubts about the ability and willingness of many managers to make the transition from some of the traditional roles of manager (spy, controller, dispenser of reward and punishment, giver of orders and arbitrator between competing claims) to the very different roles of mentor, coach, learning facilitator and 'servant of the team' (Keep and Rainbird 2000: 184–5). Besides requiring new skills sets (the time and opportunities for acquiring which may be lacking in many workplaces), much of what constitutes managerial status tends to reside with the more traditional roles that managers play in making hierarchy function in the workplace.

Taken together, pressures on time and expertise often appear to undermine the intentions of devolution to the line, with individual line managers tending to concentrate their attention on simple and more measurable goals. As research in retailing has demonstrated (Torrington and Hall 1998), the over-riding importance of tangible budgetary and performance targets meant that line managers often concentrated on the harder types of HR policy, leaving 'softer' and less tangible activities and goals to be sidelined. In any organization where staff development is not on the line manager's 'scorecard' for appraisal and reward, the danger must be that it will tend to slip off the agenda as other more important issues crowd it out.

On the other side of the equation, one of the key issues has to be the training function's ability to support this type of devolution. There is plainly the danger of tension and disagreement if trainers lack the expertise or resources to support a change of role away from training delivery to the provision of advice and consultancy to line managers. Anecdotal evidence suggests that many trainers still see themselves as deliverers and that this is the aspect of their job from which they derive both primary enjoyment and professional identity.

The other trend that has had a major impact on the shape and fortunes of the training function has been the growing enthusiasm for outsourcing large parts of its traditional activities (for example, off-the-job training courses) to external consultancies and training companies (Richbell 2001; Wustemann 2002). Again, this development mirrors wider changes within the personnel function, where in some firms an increasing volume of the 'routine' activity has been contracted out, and where in a number of instances the entire function has been outsourced, leaving a strategic contract manager as the sole in-company representative of the HR function. As ever, opinion is divided on whether contracting out represents an erosion of the training function's salience and status, or an opportunity for it to become genuinely strategic – there to advise on and design what others then deliver.

Reasons to Be Cheerful . . . ?

By this point in the chapter, readers who have a direct interest in training may be feeling somewhat depressed. However, there are some grounds for cautious optimism, at least in terms of the current potential for improving both the relevance and quality of the training and skill formation activity that is being undertaken within many organizations.

New research and theory

One reason for this is that in the last decade our understanding of how learning and skill formation occurs, and what factors within the organization will tend to help or hinder this, has grown enormously. When much of the learning organization (LO) literature was being written in the early 1990s theories of learning were largely derived from abstract psychological models that took little or no account of the organizational environment within which learning was taking place and which provided highly idealized accounts of learning activity (see Ashton 1998: 68).

Since then a range of studies have provided researchers, policy makers and practitioners with the analytical and diagnostic tools needed to gauge and understand how learning occurs in the workplace, and, even more importantly, how and in what ways it might be improved (Eraut 2000; Fevre et al. 2001; Boreham et al. 2002; Ashton 2004; Fuller and Unwin 2004; Skule 2004; and contributors to Rainbird et al. 2004). It also provides much more knowledge about how and in what ways line managers can improve or impede informal learning in the workplace (Eraut et al. 1999; Hirsch et al. 2004). Such knowledge is plainly important in a world where the devolution of many routine aspects of training activity to line managers has become the norm.

Perhaps the most important point is that this body of work offers insights that shift debate and practice away from the learning by acquisition through a formalized training courses model, towards a learning as participation model, wherein the key to more and better learning is concerned with embedding learning processes within the routine and fabric of daily activity, thereby increasing the capacity for performance enhancement that is available within the social relations of production (Felstead et al. 2004). Thus the new approach re-emphasizes the salience of social and organizational context, not least the power relationships, within which training and workplace learning activity takes place. Rather than simply look at the technical aspects of techniques for skill creation, this research tries to locate these techniques within particular productive environments and to assess the interaction between the two (Fuller et al. 2004). In making this point it has helped to counteract the tendency on the part of much of the more prescriptive practitioner-oriented literature – not least that on the learning organization – to base suggested interventions on highly idealized visions of organizations and their capacity to support and sustain skill acquisition (Brown and Keep 2003; Keep and Rainbird 2000). It also reminds us that the impact of many of the more popular formalized methods of learning is often limited, and that other approaches may be much more fruitful (CIPD 2004; Felstead et al. 2004).

The learning environment

One of the key concepts that this new body of research has thrown up is that of expansive and restrictive learning environments (Fuller and Unwin 2004). This concept grew out of research undertaken into government-sponsored apprenticeship programmes. The researchers were concerned to try and understand why completion rates for apprenticeship varied so dramatically between sectors and between firms. Were there underlying structural factors that tended to make some workplaces better able than others to support apprenticeship and work-based learning?

Fuller and Unwin's work demonstrates, drawing on detailed data from case studies, that there exists a continuum of learning environments that can be identified through reference to three 'participatory dimensions' of learning: opportunities for engagement in multiple communities of practice at and beyond the workplace; access to a multidimensional approach to the acquisition of expertise through the organization of work and job design; and the opportunity to follow knowledge-based courses and qualifications related to work. The different elements that go to make up the means of allocating an organization to a place on this continuum are illustrated in Figure 8.1.

Fuller and Unwin argue that organizations that are closer to the expansive end of the spectrum are much more likely to be able to ensure the integration of personal and organizational development for employees. Besides locating pedagogical and instructional characteristics within the context of the organization within which workplace learning is taking place, this model also provides an extremely useful diagnostic tool which allows trainers to assess where their organization stands, what

Approaches to workforce development

Expansive	Restrictive
Participation in multiple communities of practice inside and outside the workplace	Restricted participation in multiple communities of practice
Primary community of practice has shared 'participative memory': cultural inheritance of workforce development	Primary community of practice has little or no 'participative memory': no or little tradition of apprenticeship
Breadth: access to learning fostered by cross-company experiences	Narrow: access to learning restricted in terms of tasks/knowledge/location
Access to range of qualifications including knowledge-based VQ	Little or no access to qualifications
Planned time off-the-job including for knowledge-based courses and for reflection	Virtually all-on-job: limited opportunities for reflection
Gradual transition to full, rounded participation	Fast – transition as quick as possible
Vision of workplace learning: progression for career	Vision of workplace learning: static for job
Organizational recognition of, and support for career	Lack of organizational recognition of, and support for employees as learners
Workforce development is used as a vehicle for aligning the goals of developing the individual and the organizational capability	Workforce development is used to tailor individual capability to organizational need
Workforce development fosters opportunities to extend identity through boundary crossing	Workforce development limits opportunities to extend identity: little boundary crossing experienced
Reification of 'workplace curriculum' highly developed (e.g. through documents, symbols, language tools) and accessible to apprentices	Limited reification of 'workplace curriculum' patchy access to reificatory aspects of practice
Widely distributed skills	Polarized distribution of skills
Technical skills valued	Technical skills taken for granted
Knowledge and skills of whole workforce developed and valued	Knowledge and skills of key workers/groups developed and valued
Team work valued	Rigid specialist roles
Cross-boundary communication encouraged	Bounded communication
Managers as facilitators of workforce and individual development	Managers as controllers of workforce and individual development
Chances to learn new skills/jobs	Barriers to learning new skills/jobs
Innovation important	Innovation not important
Multidimensional view of expertise	Uni-dimensional top-down view of expertise

Figure 8.1 Expansive and restrictive learning environments
Source: Fuller and Unwin (2004)

is and is not possible in terms of certain approaches to learning, and what might need to change to enable different strategies to succeed.

Work organization and job design: a neglected skills issue?

The approach outlined above points to the potential importance of organizational structure, work organization and job design as issues that need to be dealt with in conjunction with training (Ashton 2004; Fuller and Unwin 2004). As many involved in training will have observed, one of the commonest grumbles from trainees is that they often find it hard to put to use what they have learned, as while their skill sets have been enhanced, the job that they are expected to do has remained static. This suggests that the current interest in learning will ultimately prove to have limited impact on performance unless and until it is matched by a parallel interest in ensuring that newly created skills can be used to productive effect within the workplace (Ashton 2004). Thus if jobs remain highly routinized and narrow, the likelihood must be that the workplace will often tend towards providing a restricted rather than expansive learning environment.

While there is little doubt that many UK workplaces have undergone profound changes over the last two decades, it is much less clear whether this reconfiguration has produced a general trend towards the kind of work organization and job design that either needs or helps create higher levels of creativity, skill and task discretion. The danger appears to be that much of the change, far from leading to a world of highly skilled, autonomous, teams of knowledge workers who self-manage themselves to high performance, has led instead to a world that is strangely familiar – one where path dependency holds sway and organizations find new ways of making their staff do more of the same old thing, harder and faster.

The research that is available certainly does not point towards a universal move towards a more empowered workforce or job design that maximizes variety, discretion and autonomy (Cully et al. 1999; Taylor 2002). Indeed some of the most worrying data generated by the second Skills Survey (Felstead et al. 2002) and associated earlier surveys related to task discretion. If control over one's job is an important aspect of what it means to be skilled, then on this measure the UK workforce has become significantly less skilled. Respondents indicated a marked decline in task discretion. For example, the proportion of workers reporting a great deal of choice over the way they do their work fell from 52 per cent in 1986 to just 39 per cent in 2001. This decline has taken place across the entire economy, but has been most marked for those in professional occupations, people who might be thought of as knowledge workers and part of the knowledge driven economy. Overall, the opportunities for displaying initiative and creativity at work appear to be shrinking rather than expanding, with an ever more highly qualified workforce able to use its skills in ever more tightly circumscribed ways. This suggests that one of the prime needs is to develop better jobs in tandem with trying to create higher levels of skill (Lloyd and Payne 2004).

The idea of creating better jobs raises a significant challenge, both for the trainers and for policy makers. Traditionally the training function has focused on skill creation, with work organization, job design and skill usage left to personnel practitioners, organizational development specialists or to production and line management. Hopefully, the growing emphasis on embedding learning within the processes and routines of work will help to widen horizons and draw training staff into debates about how work should be organized and structured.

For UK policy makers, the idea of better jobs is a strange and unfamiliar one. Work organization and job design have normally been regarded as something that lies outside public policy (except insofar as health and safety, working hours, work–life balance and family-friendly working practices impinge) and form part of the 'black box' of the productive process that reside more or less wholly within the control of the firm's management. Although there has been considerable implicit recognition that higher workforce skills ought to lead to new ways of working, it has been assumed that change will take place automatically as the invisible hands of globalization, technological change, and the labour and product markets work their inevitable, transformatory magic (DTI 2003).

As a result, external support for change has been minimal. In this area, as in so many others, the UK trails many other parts of Europe (Totterdill 1999; Ennals et al. 2001), being virtually unique in having neither a national institute or a major government programme explicitly concerned with the modernization of work organization. Moreover, experience in Norway and Finland, where national efforts along these lines are well established, suggests that promoting the desired change is an extremely lengthy and demanding process (Keep and Payne 2002; Payne 2004).

Public Policy

A final challenge facing firms comes from public policy on skills. Training is one of the areas, perhaps one of the most important, where employee relations policies within the organization interface with public policy and the aspirations of the state as embodied in central government. National skills policy now embrace a range of inter-linked economic and social goals, including competitiveness, productivity, social mobility, and social inclusion. As the then Secretary of State, David Blunkett put it:

> We must put behind us the false trade-off between economic efficiency and social justice. In tomorrow's economy there will be nothing to gain from paying people poorly, failing to provide them with the necessary skills or leaving whole communities cut off from the rest of society. (Blunkett 2001: 7)

As suggested above, the government tends to assume that universal upskilling is the order of the day. This justifies further expansion of post-compulsory education, and also efforts to encourage employers to provide more and better training to the broad mass of the adult workforce (DfES/DTI/HMT/DWP 2003). In other words, training and skills achieve a level of salience in government thinking that they may not always be accorded by employers. Moreover, the government continues to monitor progress towards upskilling of the national workforce by means of measures of formalized training, particularly achievement of qualifications, which, as discussed above, may not reflect the growing importance of informal learning in the workplace and the growing priority placed by employers on uncertified soft and social skills. This implicit tension raises a number of challenges.

Four national systems in the UK

An initial point to make is that, following devolution, the UK now has four national education and training systems, each with its own, increasingly divergent institutional and qualifications structures. This means that any organization that operates UK-wide is now, for the purposes of its interface with publicly provided vocational education and training (VET), a multinational. The majority of the comments that follow relate to the English public VET system and policies, but many of the more general points about the underlying rationale for, and purposes of, policy tend to hold true across all four administrations.

Employers 'centre stage'?

Although employers have ostensibly been allocated a pivotal role within the English training system, the nature of this primacy is fraught with contradictions, many of which have resonance with topics touched on above. To begin with the government manages the VET system and VET policy through very broad aggregate level targets for percentages of participation in VET and/or achievement of qualifications at certain levels, for given age cohorts and the workforce more generally. Informal and uncertified training usually falls off the radar of official policy.

Government targets are also predicated on a belief that the need for higher levels of skill (as proxied by qualifications) is universal – affecting the vast majority of organizations across all sectors of the economy, and right across the spectrum of occupations. In other words, the more nuanced and contingent approach outlined in the opening section of this chapter is not generally accepted, with the result that government and its agencies may be anticipating levels of investment in skills and a distribution of training opportunities across the workforce that does not match up with the product market and business objectives of individual employers.

Indeed, there are those in government who argue that rather than skill needs being determined by product market strategy, skills supply can be used as a lever to effect a fundamental change in product market strategy across the economy. For example, the Treasury has suggested:

> If, for example, the Government, employers and individuals invested in training and this had a significant impact on the skills base, then firms could begin to adopt more skill intensive (and more productive) strategies, individuals would have greater incentives to invest time and resources in training, and there could be a once and for all change in the training market. (HM Treasury 2002: 15)

Government also persists in the belief that it is possible to prove to employers that investment in training pays, and that it has a simple, direct relationship with bottom line performance. The assumption is that once such proof has been presented by public agencies to employers, firms' investment will increase. Arriving at watertight proof of this asserted relationship between skills and business performance (however measured) remains deeply problematic (Keep et al. 2002; Tamkin et al. 2004). Furthermore, as Guest et al.'s (2001) work demonstrates, even where proofs are provided by external agencies that particular employee relations policies appear to underpin better organizational performance, it is unclear what impact they might have on the investment decisions of senior management teams.

Moreover, while the government's Skills Strategy claims to put employers and their requirements centre stage in designing and managing the education and training system, in reality policy and structures are generally driven by a government agenda (Keep 2002). The main avenue for employer input into policy now rests with the new network of Sectoral Skills Councils (SSCs). These replace the old National Training Organizations (NTOs), which the government decided to abolish. Although ostensibly billed as employer-led bodies, it is worth noting that the SSCs receive their core funding from the state, are approved and licensed by the state, and have been set a number of key policy objectives by the state. How employers respond to the SSCs and how effectively the SSCs perform will represent a crucial litmus test for employer engagement with the publicly funded VET system.

Complexity and comprehensibility

A major issue for training managers and others within organizations, particularly perhaps SMEs where a specialist training function is liable to be lacking, is the comprehensibility of the VET system. As outlined above, across the UK there are now four national VET systems, each following its own trajectory of development. In England, the general direction has been one of increasing complexity. In the last few years, new government departments have joined the fray, with the Department of Trade and Industry (DTI) assuming new responsibilities for the links between skills and innovation, productivity and employee relations; and the Treasury taking the lead on target setting and efforts to improve apprenticeships and adult training. New government agencies have also entered the picture, including the Regional Development Agencies (RDAs), who are meant to be coordinating skills strategies at regional level. All have viewpoints to project, policies to launch, and interests to protect.

These developments, coupled with a long-standing tendency for both institutions and programmes within the VET system to be short-lived and unstable, raise serious issues about the comprehensibility of the system and its different elements. Even those who act as paid observers (like the author of this chapter) can no longer keep up with the rate of change and policy innovation. It is open to serious doubt whether parents, trainees, individual workers or employers can either.

Post-voluntarism?

As VET has risen up the public policy agenda in the UK, so a growing list of things employers could be doing to help the national skills effort has been formulated by policy makers. This includes, among other things, work experience for secondary school pupils, advanced and foundation apprenticeships, 'junior' apprenticeships for 14–16 year olds, involvement in designing foundation degrees and offering work placements to students, designing a new set of national occupational standards, and from these then deriving a new suite of vocational qualifications, better forecasting of skill shortages and bottlenecks, tackling problems with adult literacy and numeracy, and active involvement in the work of the new SSCs. The record under some of these headings, has, to date, been at best mixed. Of particular concern is the weak performance of government-supported apprenticeships, where outside of a few sectors, such as engineering, the quality of provision appears to be highly variable, and completion rates alarmingly low (Fuller and Unwin 2003).

In addition, the length of the list provided above points to potential tensions between what politicians and civil servants want employers to undertake and fund, and what employers might actually wish to do. As the list expands, it can be argued that these tensions will also grow. The public policy agenda therefore raises issues at a strategic level for training practitioners and organizations, not least as the government has intimated that we are now living in a 'post-voluntarist' world. The government's Skills Strategy points to this new approach:

> The 2001 Budget report set out the government's belief that, although voluntary approaches have secured increased participation in workplace training, they have not been sufficient given the scale of the problem. Addressing this problem is a priority and will require a step-change on the part of employers, individuals and the Government. The Government is therefore seeking to produce policies through this strategy which will help employers and individuals to meet their responsibilities in this area. (DfES/DTI/HMT/DWP 2003: 29)

In other words there is now the faint but growing threat that government might impose training duties on employers in order to meet public policy objectives. Implicitly, the onus is on employers to demonstrate to policy makers, using measures of performance devised almost solely by policy makers, that voluntarism can be made to work.

Conclusions

This chapter has tried to convey a number of messages. The first is that while it is easy to agree with the findings of Smith et al. (2003) concerning the importance of the integration of training and HR policy with business strategy, such linkages are highly problematic in a number of ways. Many organizations lack the kinds of explicit strategy that other, subordinate strategies can easily be linked with. Moreover, whether clear or opaque, implicit or explicit, insofar as business strategies embody a choice of product market strategy, the skill requirements they pose will vary very considerably. High quality, high value added, high specification strategies will generally demand a more skilled workforce to deliver them than those based around price leadership and mass standardization/mass customization. In addition, the skills and core organizational competences that are needed to support the product market strategy may be widely or narrowly distributed across the workforce. These points all suggest that while in some organizations training and development for the mass of the workforce will be a key element in securing and maintaining competitive advantage, in others it will be a low level activity of marginal importance, perhaps a hygiene factor.

Second, it is essential that management have a firm understanding of different training techniques. This understanding needs to be rooted in wider appreciation of how workplace learning is influenced by the environment in which it takes place. Some workplaces are configured in a manner that provides a rich and expansive learning environment, while others are not, and this will materially impact on the types, levels of intensity of learning that can and will take place therein.

Third, inculcating new skills may well be the easy part. The real difficulty, at least in some instances, is in ensuring that these skills then be used. In many workplaces it is probably the case that the existing skills of the workforce are not being used to maximum effect (Keep and Rainbird 2000). Ensuring that they are, not least through attention to work organization and job design issues, may be as important, if not sometimes more important, than devising ways of supporting further upskilling. This is new and unfamiliar territory, both for policy makers and for many trainers.

Fourth, the status of the training function is open to debate. Besides outsourcing, the issue of the devolution of responsibility for many training and development activities to line managers raises many questions for trainers and leaves them facing problems that are not necessarily of their making or within their control.

Fifth, public policy is predicated on an assumption that upskilling is required across the entire workforce, and that employers have a key role to play in securing this goal. As a result, employers are confronted with a growing list of activities that they are expected to want to become involved in and help pay for. The government's expectations may be in conflict with the skill needs and priorities that businesses perceive themselves as having. This disjuncture, coupled with a certain level of impatience by policy makers, raises the risk of outright conflict and perhaps of the potential threat of legislative intervention.

Finally, perhaps the key overall conclusion that can be drawn from the foregoing is that the role and status of training activity is tied up with wider issues about where and how people management issues figure in organizations' competitive and product market strategies. Popular models, such as the knowledge-driven economy, are misleading in that they point towards upskilling for all, and thus for a future in which skill creation becomes an extremely important activity for all employers. In some businesses and sectors this reality already exists. In many others it is a very distant prospect indeed, and likely to remain so.

Given that a glittering future for all may not be on the agenda, what is important is that those within organizations who are concerned with skills position themselves in order to exploit those opportunities that are available to them. This means forming a very clear view about what are the key skills that underpin organizational performance, and in which sections of the workforce these reside, and in being able to help create these skills. It also means having the ability to advise and support line management, and the knowledge to further understanding about the means by which the workplace can best be structured to maximize learning. This includes seeking a greater input into issues such as work organization and job design.

Overall, what may be needed is a focus that stretches far beyond traditional concerns about the delivery of training, and embraces what might be termed intermediate level organizational strategy. Whether the training function and managers more generally can and will rise to this challenge remains to be seen.

REFERENCES

Ashton, D. 1998: Skill formation: Re-directing the research agenda, in F. Coffield (ed.), *Learning at Work*, Bristol: Policy Press, 61–9.

Ashton, D. 2004: The impact of organisational structure and practices on learning in the workplace, *International Journal of Training and Development*, **8**(1), 43–53.

Auluck-Cooper, R. 2004: The Human Resource Development Function: Its status within the UK public service, paper presented to IASIA Annual Conference, Seoul, South Korea, 13–16 July.

Bach, S. and Sisson, K. 2000: Personnel management in perspective, in S. Bach and K. Sisson (eds.), *Personnel Management* (3rd edn), Oxford: Blackwell, 3–42.

Batt, R. 2000: Strategic segmentation in front-line services: matching customers, employees and human resource systems, *International Journal of Human Resource Management*, **11**(3), 540–61.

Blunkett, D. 2000: *Opportunities for All: Skills for the New Economy – Initial Response to the National Skills Task Force Final Report from the Secretary of State for Education and Employment*, Sudbury: DfEE.

Blunkett, D. 2001: *Opportunity and Skills in the Knowledge-Driven Economy – A final statement on the work of the National Skills Task Force from the Secretary of State for Education and Employment*, Sudbury: DfEE.

Boreham, N., Samurcay, R. and Fischer, M. (eds.) 2002: *Work Process Knowledge*, London: Routledge.

Boxall, P. 2003: HR strategy and competitive advantage in the service sector, *Human Resource Management Journal*, **13**(3), 5–20.

Brown, A. and Keep, E. 2003: Competing perspectives on workplace learning and the learning organisation, in B. Nyhan, M. Kelleher, P. Cressey and R. Poell (eds.), *Facing Up to the Learning Organisation Challenge: Selected European Writings, Volume 2*, Cedefop Reference series; 41–11, Luxembourg: Office for Official Publications of the European Communities, 73–91.

Brown, N., Corney, M. and Stanton, G. 2004: *Breaking out of the Silos, 14–30 Education and Skills Policy*, London: Nigel Brown Associates.

Callaghan, G. and Thompson, P. 2002: 'We recruit attitude': The selection and shaping of routine call centre labour, *Journal of Management Studies*, **39**(2), 233–54.

Carter, A., Hirsch, W. and Aston, J. 2002: *Resourcing the Training and Development Function*, Brighton: University of Sussex, Institute of Employment Studies.

CIPD (Chartered Institute of Personnel and Development) 2002: *Who Learns at Work?*, London: CIPD.

CIPD (Chartered Institute of Personnel and Development) 2004: *Training and Development 2004 – Survey Report*, London: CIPD.

Coopers and Lybrand Associates. 1985: *Challenge to Complacency: Changing Attitudes to Training*, London: Manpower Services Commission.

Cully, M., Woodward, S., O'Reilly, A. and Dix, A. 1999: *Britain at Work: As Depicted by the 1998 Workplace Employee Relations Survey*, London: Routledge.

DfES/DTI/HMT/DWP (Department for Education and Skills/Department for Trade and Industry/HM Treasury/Department for Work and Pensions) 2003: *21st Century Skills Realising our Potential – Individuals, Employers, Nation*, Cm 5810, London: The Stationery Office.

DTI (Department of Trade and Industry) 2003: *Innovation Report – Competing in the Global Economy: The Innovation Challenge*, London: DTI.

Eaton, S. 2000: Beyond unloving care: Linking human resource management and patient care quality in nursing homes, *International Journal of Human Resource Management*, **11**(3), 591–616.

Edwards, P. 2001: The puzzle of work: autonomy and commitment plus discipline and insecurity, *SKOPE Research Paper* No. 16, Coventry: University of Warwick, SKOPE.

Ennals, R., Totterdill, P. and Ford, C. 2001: The Work Organisation Foundation: A national coalition for working life and organizational competence, *Concepts and Transformation*, **6**(3), 259–73.

Eraut, M. 2000: Development of knowledge and skills at work, in F. Coffield (ed.), *Differing Visions of a Learning Society: Research Findings, Volume 1*, Bristol: The Policy Press.

Eraut, M., Alderton, J., Cole, G. and Senker, P. 1999: The impact of the manager on learning in the workplace, in F. Coffield (ed.), *Speaking Truth to Power, Research and Policy on Lifelong Learning*, Bristol: The Policy Press, 19–29.

Felstead, A., Fuller, A., Unwin, L., Ashton, D., Butler, P., Lee, T. and Walters, S. 2004: Applying the survey method to learning at work: A recent UK experiment, paper presented to the European Conference on Educational Research, Rethymnon Campus, University of Crete, Greece, 22–25 September.

Felstead, A., Gallie, D. and Green, F. 2002: *Work Skills in Britain 1986–2001*, Nottingham: DfES.

Fevre, R., Gorrard, S. and Rees, G. 2001: Necessary and unnecessary learning: The acquisition of knowledge and 'skills' inside and outside employment in South Wales in the 20th century, in F. Coffield (ed.), *The Necessity of Informal Learning*, Bristol: The Policy Press.

Fuller, A., Ashton, D., Felstead, A., Unwin, L., Walters, S. and Quinn, M. 2003: *The Impact of Informal Learning at Work on Business Productivity*, London: Department of Trade and Industry.

Fuller, A., Munro, A. and Rainbird, H. 2004: Conclusion, in H. Rainbird, A. Fuller and A. Munro (eds.), *Workplace Learning in Context*, London: Routledge, 299–306.

Fuller, A. and Unwin, L. 2003: Creating a 'modern apprenticeship': A critique of the UK's multisector, social inclusion approach, *Journal of Education and Work*, **6**(1), 5–25.

Fuller, A. and Unwin, L. 2004: Expansive learning environments: Integrating organizational and personal development, in H. Rainbird, A. Fuller and A. Munro (eds.), *Workplace Learning in Context*, London: Routledge, 126–44.

Gallie, D., White, M., Cheng, Y. and Tomlinson, M. 1998: *Restructuring the Employment Relationship*, Oxford: Oxford University Press.

Garavan, T.N., Costine, P. and Heraty, N. 1995: The emergence of strategic HRD, *Journal of European Industrial Training*, **19**(10), 4–10.

Gibb, S. 2003: Line management involvement in learning and development: Small beer or big deal? *Employee Relations*, **25**(3), 281–93.

Gratton, L. 2000: A real step change, *People Management*, **6**(6), 16 March, 27–30.

Green, F., Mayhew, K. and Molloy, E. 2003: *Employer Perspectives Survey 2002*, Nottingham: DfES.

Grugulis, I., Warhurst, C. and Keep, E. 2004: What's happening to 'skill'?, in C. Warhurst, I. Grugulis and E. Keep (eds.), *The Skills that Matter*, Basingstoke: Palgrave, 1–18.

Guest, D., King, Z., Conway, N., Michie, J. and Sheehan-Quinn, M. 2001: *Voices from the Boardroom*, London: Chartered Institute of Personnel and Development.

Higginbottom, K. 2002: HR shunned by boards, *People Management*, **8**(3), 7 February, 10.

Hirsch, W., Silverman, M., Tamkin, P. and Jackson, C. 2004: Managers as developers of others, *IES Report 407*, Sussex: Institute of Employment Studies.

HM Treasury. 2002: *Developing Workforce Skills: Piloting a New Approach*, London: HMT.

Huddleston, P. and Keep, E. 1999: What do employers want from education? A question more easily asked than answered, in J. Cramphorn (ed.), *The Role of Partnerships in Economic Regeneration and Development: An International Perspective*, Coventry: University of Warwick, Centre for Education and Industry, 38–49.

Hunter, L. 2000: What determines job quality in nursing homes?, *Industrial and Labor Relations Review*, **55**(3), 463–81.

Hyman, J. and Cunningham, I. 1998: Managers as developers: Some reflections on the contribution of empowerment in Britain, *International Journal of Training and Development*, **2**(2), 91–107.

IDS (Income Data Services) 2003: *Directors' Pay Report, 2003*. London: IDS.

IER/EFF (Institute of Employment Research/IFF Limited) 2004: *National Employers Skills Survey 2003: Key Findings*, Coventry: Learning and Skills Council.

Keep, E. 2002: The English Vocational Education and Training policy debate – Fragile 'technologies' or opening the 'black box': Two competing visions of where we go next, *Journal of Education of Work*, **15**(4), 457–79.

Keep, E., Mayhew, K. and Corney, M. 2002: Review of the evidence of the rate of return to employers of investment in training and employer training measures, *SKOPE Research Paper* No. 34, Coventry: University of Warwick, SKOPE.

Keep, E. and Payne, J. 2002: What can the UK learn from the Norwegian and Finnish experience of attempts at work re-organisation?, *SKOPE Research Paper* No. 41, Coventry: University of Warwick, SKOPE.

Keep, E. and Payne, J. 2004: 'I can't believe it's not skill': The changing meaning of skill in the UK context and some implications, in G. Hayward and S. James (eds.), *Balancing the Skills Equation*, Bristol: The Policy Press, 53–76.

Keep, E. and Rainbird, H. 2000: Towards the learning organization?, in S. Bach and K. Sisson (eds.), *Personnel Management* (3rd edn), Oxford: Blackwell, 173–94.

Kitching, J. and Blackburn, R. 2002: The nature of training and motivation to train in small firms, *DfES Research Report*, RR330, Nottingham: DfES.

Lashley, C. 1998: Matching the management of human resources to service operations, *International Journal of Contemporary Hospitality Management*, **10**(1), 24–33.

Lloyd, C. and Payne, J. 2004: Just another bandwagon: A critical look at the role of the high performance workplace as a vehicle for the UK high skills project, *SKOPE Research Paper* No. 49, Coventry: University of Warwick, SKOPE.

Manocha, R. 2004: Trainers learn rules of engagement, *People Management*, **10**(9), 6 May, 11.

Mason, G. 2004: Enterprise product strategies and employer demand for skills in Britain: Evidence from the Employers Skill Survey, *SKOPE Research Paper* No. 50, Coventry: University of Warwick, SKOPE.

Mayo, A. 2004: *Creating a Learning and Development Strategy*, London: Chartered Institute of Personnel and Development.

Nickson, D., Baum, T., Losekoot, E. and Morrison, A. 2002: *Skills, Organizational Performance and Economic Activity in the Hospitality Industry: A Literature Review*, Coventry: University of Warwick, SKOPE.

Nickson, D., Wahurst, C. and Dutton, E. 2004: Aesthetic labour and the policy-making agenda: Time for a reappraisal of skills?, *SKOPE Research Paper* No. 48, Coventry: University of Warwick, SKOPE.

NSTF (National Skills Task Force) 2000a: *Skills for All: Research Report from the National Skills Task Force*, Sudbury: DfEE.

NSTF (National Skills Task Force) 2000b: *Skills for All: Proposals for a National Skills Agenda – Final Report of the National Skills Task Force*, Sudbury: DfEE.

Payne, J. 1999: All things to all people: Changing perceptions of 'skill' among Britain's policy makers since the 1950s and their implications, *SKOPE Research Paper* No. 1, Coventry: University of Warwick, SKOPE.

Payne, J. 2004: Workplace innovation and the role of public policy: Evaluating the impact of the Finnish Workplace Development Programme: limits and possibilities, *SKOPE Research Paper* No. 46, Coventry: University of Warwick, SKOPE.

Philpott, J. 2002: *Perspectives HRH: A Work Audit*, London: Chartered Institute of Personnel and Development.

Philpott, J. 2004: Work audit: Employer training for adult workers: who are the European Champions?, *CIPD Impact*, November, 32–6.

Purcell, J. 1989: The impact of corporate strategy on human resource management, in J. Storey (ed.), *New Perspectives on Human Resource Management*, London: Routledge, 67–91.

Purcell, J. 1999: Best practice and best fit: Chimera or cul-de-sac?, *Human Resource Management Journal*, **9**(3), 26–41.

Rainbird, H. 1994: The changing role of the training function: A test for the integration of human resource and business strategies?, *Human Resource Management Journal*, **5**(1), 72–90.

Rainbird, H., Fuller, A. and Munro, A. (eds.) 2004: *Workplace Learning in Context*, London: Routledge.

Reid, M.A. and Barrington, H.A. 2001: *Training Interventions: Promoting Learning Opportunities*, London: Chartered Institute of Personnel and Development.

Richbell, S. 2001: Trends and emerging values in human resource management: The UK scene, *International Journal of Manpower*, **22**(3), 261–8.

Scullion, H. and Starkey, K. 2000: In search of the changing role of the corporate human resource function in the international firm, *International Journal of Human Resource Management*, **11**(6), 1061–81.

Skule, S. 2004: Learning conditions at work: A framework to understand and assess informal learning in the workplace, *International Journal of Training and Development*, **8**(1), 8–20.

Smith, A., Oczkowski, E., Macklin, R. and Noble, C. 2003: Organisational change and the management of training in Australian enterprises, *International Journal of Training and Development*, **7**(1), 2–15.

Tamkin, P., Giles, L., Campbell, M. and Hillage, J. 2004: Skills pay: The contribution of skills to business success, *SSDA Research Report* 5, Wath-upon-Dearne: Sector Skills Development Agency.

Taylor, R. 2002: *Britain's World of Work: Myths and Realities*, Swindon: Economic and Social Research Council.

Torrington, D. and Hall, L. 1998: Letting go or holding on: The devolution of operational personnel activities, *Human Resource Management Journal*, **8**(1), 41–55.

Totterdill, P. 1999: Britain's advantage? Work organisation, innovation and employment, Nottingham: University of Nottingham, UK Work Organisation Network (mimeo).

Warhurst, C. and Nickson, D. 2001: *Looking Good, Sounding Right*, London: Industrial Society.

Wilson, R. and Hogarth, T. (eds.) 2003: *Tackling the Low Skills Equilibrium: A Review of Issues and Some New Evidence*, London: DTI.

Wustemann, L. 2002: A pay-as-you-go personnel function, *IRS Employment Review*, 748, 25 March, 39–40.

CHAPTER NINE

Management Development and Career Management

David Guest and Zella King

For many years, the quality of management has served as a convenient scapegoat for the problems of UK industry. One widely recommended solution has been to advocate a better system of developing managers and ensuring that they have the necessary qualities or competences to affect organizational performance. A second solution has highlighted the need to ensure that processes of career management can identify and progress those most likely to make a significant contribution. This chapter discusses management development and career management, examining how far they can be expected to improve the quality, behaviour and impact of managers.

The first half of this chapter explores the role of management development, starting with an analysis of its possible contribution to resolving what is considered to be a pervasive problem of the quality of UK management. Building on some of the key analyses of this problem from the 1980s, we assess how far the problem has been addressed through management education, through the use of competences to guide management training and through the higher priority given to management development as a strategic issue within organizations. This third issue is explored through consideration of various management development activities, including organization development and the learning organization. The second half of the chapter adopts a similar perspective by exploring how far career management can help to address the problem of the quality of UK management. A short final section draws together the implications and highlights the dearth of empirical evidence to inform the analysis.

Management Development and the 'Problem' of UK Management

The problem of UK management has been defined both as a problem concerning managers and the lack of technical and managerial qualifications and skills among those in senior positions, and a problem of management, reflected in low investment, low productivity and an absence of innovation. Some observers have argued that the 'problem' of UK management can be traced back over centuries. Writers such as Corelli Barnett (1986) have noted on the one hand the disdain for work in industry among the aristocracy and the aspiring middle classes and, alongside this, a belief in the gifted amateur. The apparent UK problem has been compared against the USA, Japan and some European countries where there are different patterns of management education and development and a more successful tradition of corporate performance over a number of years. Concern about the problem of UK management came to a head in the 1980s, resulting in a series of linked reports by Constable and McCormick (1987), Handy (1987) and Mangham and Silver (1986). Their analysis highlighted the limited and generally poor quality training and development of UK managers.

The reports produced a range of recommendations which can be summarized within three main themes, each implying a rather different assumption about the 'problem' of management and about the appropriate model of management development. One core recommendation was that the UK should introduce some form of Masters in Business Administration, the MBA, to provide a more solid base of knowledge and analytic skills among managers. A second broad recommendation, which evolved into what became known as the Management Charter Initiative, was to professionalize management. A third recommendation was directed more at companies and urged them to raise their game by making management development a strategic issue. This recommendation coincided with the growing interest in human resource strategy and therefore in the role of human resource management as a basis for competitive advantage. In the context of what in the 1990s came to be known as the war for talent, there appeared to be the potential to place management development at the heart of a business strategy to compete through the effective management and development of key human resources.

Each of these approaches offers a process for improving the quality of managers in the UK. Indeed, in a review 10 years after the clutch of reports appeared, Thomson et al. (1997, 2001) were able to report substantial progress on all three fronts. However, there has been growing concern that there may have been too much focus on developing managers and not enough emphasis on improving the quality of management. This reflects a long-standing concern about the limitations of knowledge and competence when developed outside a given context. By implication, too much focus on the individual may lead to a neglect of the quality of management applied in a given organization. This has been reflected over many years in the concept of organization development (OD) with its strong connotation that learning and development is likely to be most useful if it occurs in an organizational context. In recent years, stimulated by the growth of the knowledge society, this has often been focused around the concept of the learning organization. Later we consider this perspective on management development alongside those emerging from the earlier analysis.

In summary, we have a number of different perspectives on the nature and role of contemporary management development in the UK. These are not necessarily

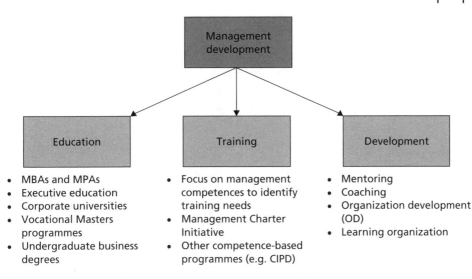

Figure 9.1 Groups of management development activities

mutually exclusive and the emphasis they receive is subject to ebb and flow, to fads and fashions and to the priorities and incentives provided by government. In the following sections, we will review each of these perspectives in a little more detail, examining what they mean for the practice of management development and appraising, where possible, any evidence about their impact. In doing so, we are developing the three main themes identified on the 1980s reports and also reflecting a distinction made by Mintzberg (2004: 198) among others between management education, management training and management development, as depicted in Figure 9.1. In the following sections, we organize our discussion around these three components, noting that all are important and arguing that the key lies in finding the right balance between them.

Management Development as Education

The reports produced in the mid 1980s bemoaned the general lack of education and more particularly business education among UK managers. During the past 20 years, much has been done to address this deficit. The most dramatic development has been the growth of Business Schools, mostly attached to universities, and the linked growth of the MBA. In 2004, there were over a hundred institutions offering MBAs to those who wish to develop their management knowledge and skills. We are also seeing a growth in the equivalent for the public sector, the Masters in Public Administration (MPA).

The MBA, with its strong educational focus, offers a platform for a management career for those who are young, and a development opportunity for those who have had significant management experience. Institutions, such as the London Business

School and the other early business schools at Manchester and Bradford, quickly established their MBA programmes and attracted talented young managers sponsored by their organizations who found that an MBA provided an effective career stepping stone. One problem that arose was that the stepping stone sometimes took the MBA graduates out of the organization that had sponsored them and into more fashionable and lucrative areas of work such as consultancy and the City. By implication, the programmes succeeded in developing talented managers and accelerated their career progress but they may also have facilitated a move out of those sectors that most needed them and into those that could most afford them.

As the number of academic institutions offering MBAs grew, they broadened their catchment. It became possible to study for an MBA without significant work experience. This inevitably results in an even stronger educational focus with little scope for direct knowledge transfer. Therefore, while it extends the education base in business and management, this type of programme may seem to offer little of direct value to organizations concerned to improve their management.

There have been a number of responses to the challenges posed by the growth of standard MBA programmes. One has been the development of the Executive MBA, often offered on a part-time basis, geared more explicitly to the experienced manager, and providing a stronger link between theory and practice. A closely related development has been the company-specific or consortium MBA in which either a single company or a set of organizations combine to collaborate with a business school to offer an MBA that provides the educational and development needs on a modular basis while retaining an emphasis on application and practice. Examples include Lancaster University's programme for British Airways and Warwick University's for a consortium including BP, the National Westminster Bank and Coopers and Lybrand. A third development, much derided in the academic community, has been the setting up of the corporate university by companies such as Motorola and McDonald's, and in the UK by BAE, Shell and Barclays Bank. Sometimes these initiatives have been little more than a re-badging of the company training and development activities with scant concern for the analytical skills and knowledge input of the typical business school programme. In a review of the growth of corporate universities, Paton et al. (2004: 105) are more positive in describing them as 'the most recent approach to providing a structure that enables important forms of work-related learning to occur within and for companies'. If this is so, it neatly reflects a counter to the concern that the MBA develops predominantly general and transferable skills.

In addition to the growth of MBAs, there has been a rapid growth of the vocational MSc in specialist areas such as finance and accounting, marketing and human resource management. These are typically directed at those who have completed their first degree and seek a semi-vocational qualification before entering employment. However, they are also attractive to managers seeking more advanced specialist knowledge and accreditation, as well as to their employers who can benefit from the application of this knowledge. Finally, within the educational context, we should note the very rapid growth of undergraduate programmes in business studies or in specialist areas such as accounting or computer science. In short, over the past 20 years, education in business and management has burgeoned.

This growth of the academic MBA has had its critics among business and management academics. A particular concern has been that there is too much emphasis on education in a narrow set of analytic skills at the expense of development in management. Perhaps the most strident recent criticism has come from Henry Mintzberg (see, for example, Mintzberg 2004, Mintzberg and Lampel 2001), one of the leading writers on management. He is particularly critical of the kind of MBA programme open to those with little or no experience as managers who are trained in a narrow form of analytic decision making that, in his view, bears little relation to the reality of management. In collaboration mainly with European colleagues, particularly from Lancaster University, he has therefore developed a distinctive MBA for experienced managers (see Mintzberg and Gosling, 2002). The aim is to get away from the specialist silos of management such as marketing, finance and strategy and away from any over-riding teaching of analytic business skills and instead to provide time to reflect on the nature of managerial work and in particular to build on a recognition that much management activity requires some integrative understanding of all of these specialist elements.

In many respects, the growth of management education through the MBA and other academic qualifications has been an undoubted success. Management has become one of the most popular subject choices for undergraduate and postgraduate study. Thousands of MBA students graduate each year in the UK. For those who study at the leading institutions, there is often an immediate return reflected in employment with a prestigious organization and a large salary increase. Yet it can only be a start; and with its focus on education rather than development, it is essentially a first step in developing managers and producing a better quality of management. The evidence from the USA indicates that an MBA is neither a necessary nor a sufficient condition for success in industry. In a polemical criticism of the MBA and of USA Business Schools more generally, Pfeffer and Fong (2002) argue that there is no link between possession of an MBA and success at the top of organizations and that the focus of elite Business Schools on research, a parallel move away from what they term 'the trade' of managing and the growing disconnect with 'management' may come to threaten their future. The challenge for business schools in the UK is to guard against this threat and to maintain their relevance by focusing a significant portion of their efforts on the *development* of managers.

Developing Managers through Training

A second stream of activity emerging from the recommendations of the reports produced in the 1980s has been designed to develop the capabilities of managers. In contrast to the MBA and its emphasis on knowledge and analysis the focus is on what a manager needs to be able to do to perform a job effectively. The underlying aim was to capture, systematize and standardize, and by implication professionalize competent management behaviour. This came to be known as the Management Charter Initiative. In the UK this focused on the consolidation of a rather traditional approach of measuring jobs and the competences required to perform them. In this context, competences refer to the things an effective manager must be able to do and the behaviours they exhibit. It might include competence in interviewing, in developing a marketing campaign or analysing complex financial data. The assumption is that within any broad class of role such as a finance manager or a human resource manager there is some kind of gradation of competences according to the level at which the job is undertaken. The aim of the initiative was to identify these competences at the various levels and then accredit those who could demonstrate that they were competent. Managers who sought these competences and did not possess them would need training and development.

This appears to be a pragmatic and highly practical approach that has the merit of covering all managers rather than the elite who tend to be the focus of much management development activity. In practice, the competences identified were often rather generic. An example reported by Salaman (2004: 63) in an educational institution is fairly typical. They had four classes of competence set out under the broad headings of interpersonal, visionary, information, and results orientation. Results orientation included motivation and drive, business awareness and technological awareness.

In considering the merits of the competency approach, there has tended to be a split in the UK academic community between organizational psychologists who place job analysis at the heart of much of their work (see, for example, Boam and Sparrow 1992; Pearn and Kandola 1988) and those adopting a more sociological frame of reference (Cockerill 1989; Reed and Anthony 1992) who are concerned about the role of competences as a control mechanism and their utility in a world of rapid organizational change and flexibility. Whatever the merits of the approach, it has proved to be highly bureaucratic and cumbersome. It is also potentially rather static and can run counter to the concerns of Mintzberg to avoid education and development within functional silos. Nevertheless, it is precisely in such areas that this approach has flourished. Therefore, students of human resource management will be familiar with the extensive and detailed set of competences provided by the Chartered Institute for Personnel and Development (CIPD) as a basis for the design of professional programmes.

The Management Charter Initiative and the focus on competences flourished for a decade, and although the use of competences has become well embedded, particularly at a national level, the movement has lost some of its impetus. It may have helped to shift the focus of management development towards a more pragmatic focus on behaviour. It may also have turned attention away from the elite or high potential managers towards middle management, a group who suffered some neglect in the 1990s during the fashion for leaner and flatter structures (Livian and Burgoyne 1997). Their potential as instigators of change has been highlighted, among others, by Kanter (1985). However, the UK version of competences is distinctly and somewhat confusingly different from the USA approach to what they term 'competencies', which focus rather more on the factors that distinguish the best from the average managers. In practice, this is something that organizations are more interested in as a basis for determining remuneration and promotion potential and identifying where they want to direct their management development efforts. At the risk of neglecting the core backbone managers in their organization, they wish to identify those with high potential and to develop them to become the top managers of the future. To achieve this, we need to focus on the third element of the 1980s reports, the need for organizations to take management development much more seriously.

The Management of Management Development

The reviews of practice in the 1980s had concluded that the treatment of management development in UK industry was very mixed, with some examples of excellence but many more of neglect. In far too many organizations, it seemed that management development was not taken seriously or even totally ignored. Indeed, Constable and McCormick (1987) estimated that in 1986, over half of the organizations in the UK made no formal provision for management training and development. There was, in effect, an apparent failure of the demand-side that needed to be remedied. Ten years on, Thomson et al. (1997, 2001) were able to report major progress. In 1996, based on a large survey including organizations of all sizes, 43 per cent had a formal written policy on management development and about the same proportion had a budget for management development activities. Across all organizations, it was claimed that the average manager spent 5.2 days a year in some kind of formal training activity. Although there had been a growth in informal and internal types of training and development, the major growth appeared to be allied to the acquisition of qualifications; and looking to the future, there was perceived to be more scope for growth in external rather than internal provision of management training and development activities. There was some indication that those organizations that had a written policy were more likely to engage in management development activities than those that did not.

One implication of the growing interest among organizations in management development is that it is viewed strategically as a source of competitive advantage. There are several possible elements to this. First, it can increase the value, competence and contribution of key human 'assets'; secondly, it can reflect part of a wider human resource strategy to develop, motivate and retain highly talented managers (Gratton et al. 1999; Lengnick-Hall and Lengnick-Hall 1988; Paauwe 2004). In the 'war for talent', the presence of an effective management development system can both attract and help to retain the most talented people. Thirdly, alongside careful succession planning and performance reviews, it can help to identify and accelerate the development of those likely to lead the organization in the short and longer-term future. However, there is still the risk that those organizations that place particular emphasis on high potential staff neglect the development of the majority of competent managers who will benefit from development and who have some potential for advancement even if they are not seen as the future leaders.

Developing managers through off-the-job activities

In many large organizations there will be formal programmes of mainly off-the-job activities that can be mapped out over a number of years with particular focus on high potential managers but also some concern for the wider management population. The aim is to prepare managers for the challenges that lie ahead, although largely focused on challenges inside the organization, rather than beyond it. The content may be general – leadership and team skills developed on an outward bound course – or highly specific – how to work with the financial system as heads of units. An important part of such activities will be the time spent networking with others on the programme. A less explicit but often important aspect may be the assessments of performance on the course made by the tutors and course directors. At more senior levels, these activities can extend to include Senior Executive Programmes at, and sometimes tailor-made by, leading business schools where a major aim is to look outside the organization for ideas and innovations. At this point, company-focused management development begins to merge with the wider approach advocated by Mintzberg.

Evidence such as the Thomson et al. (2001) survey suggests that organizations have been taking management development more seriously in the sense that they are doing more; however, there is less evidence about the impact and effectiveness of this training. One indirect source of information comes from Investors in People (IIP). This is a government-sponsored, quality assurance kitemark applied to training, development and communication activities. Over the years large numbers of organizations have attained IIP accreditation and often been re-accredited in subsequent years. This could be taken as evidence of the quality of the training and development activity and it has certainly been interpreted in this way. However, independent assessment of the IIP initiative raises some doubts. Bell et al. (2002) and Hoque (2003) have raised questions about the substance of some IIP activities and implied, to cite Hoque, that often it is 'just another plaque on the wall'.

Developing managers through mentoring and coaching

One of the long-standing concerns about all off-the-job learning and development is the problem of transfer. Can what has been learnt be applied on the job? This is a particular problem when the learning is oriented towards a future job with the scope for decay in learning before there is any scope for implementation.

One alternative is offered by mentoring or coaching activities. Mentoring is defined by Kram (1985: 2) as 'a relationship between a younger adult and an older, more experienced adult that helps the individual to navigate in the world of work'. In practice, the age differences may not be great and there are many issues about diversity, choice of mentor, the organization and the length of a mentoring relationship that have been extensively discussed (see, for example, Clutterbuck and Ragins 2002; Ragins and Scandura 1994). In Europe, more emphasis has often been given to a more developmental form of mentoring in which the process is viewed as one of helping a manager to learn and develop (Clutterbuck and Lane 2004).

Kram (1983) has described a series of typical stages in a mentoring relationship including initiation, establishment, operation and termination. Ragins et al. (2000) suggest that the success of mentoring is likely to be a function of the mentoring process, the nature of the relationship and the supportiveness of the organizational environment as key factors determining its success. These issues can be effectively addressed in formal mentoring programmes and for some managers such programmes will be necessary; however, others may prefer to find their own mentors rather more proactively and can find a more formal system inhibiting. Indeed, the challenge for organizations seeking to organize a formal mentoring system is to ensure sufficient support for it without becoming overly prescriptive and bureaucratic. The mainly US research shows greater perceived benefits from informal mentoring (Ragins and Cotton 1999; Chao et al. 1992).

Coaching potentially offers a more focused form of development. Its origins lie in sport and the performing arts and it aims to develop specific aspects of an individual's competence. It differs from mentoring in focusing much more on the current role and current performance and, unlike mentoring, the coach may be a line manager. A feature of coaching can be an emphasis on technical competence. Coaching has become more widely used for very senior executives who may benefit from an independent view on their own performance and concerns about development. It is often noted that chief executives in particular cannot easily discuss board development and succession issues, or openly reflect on poor decisions and how to learn from them. Nor can they easily expose to other managers any concerns about their own competence and development needs. An external coach or counsellor can help to address these concerns. Clearly, much depends on the quality of the coach and whether the role is primarily one of developing knowledge and skills, providing an opportunity for reflection or providing counselling about current anxieties and future developments. In practice, the boundaries between mentoring, coaching and some aspects of counselling can become blurred. Indeed, in her earlier work, Kram (1985) included both coaching and counselling in her list of mentoring functions.

Surveys of managers' experiences of management development (see, for example, Thomson et al. 2001; Newell 2004) indicate that mentoring and coaching are quite highly valued but that only about a third of organizations have some kind of formal scheme in place. A challenge for organizations is how far to formalize the process, with the attendant risks discussed above and how far to seek to embed informal mentoring as a feature of the organizational culture.

Organization development as management development

Another way of seeking to address the difficulties raised by separating learning from job activities is through a merging of organization and individual development by ensuring that much of the learning takes place in context and with a sharp eye towards action and application. The concept of organization development has been around for at least 50 years with a range of early and well-established champions such as Argyris and Schon (1978), Beckhard (1969), Bennis (1969) and Blake and Mouton (1969). Organization development has proved to be a flexible, resilient but also somewhat elusive concept, not least because it has reinvented itself under a number of labels (such as the learning organization) to suit the spirit of the times.

Organization development has been classically defined as an 'applied behavioural science discipline that seeks to improve organizations through planned, systematic, long-range efforts focused on the organization's culture and its human and social processes' (French and Bell 1990: xiv). This implies a much wider range of interventions than the conventional approaches to management development. There have been a number of systematic reviews of the many reported OD interventions (see, for example, Neuman et al. 1989; Porras and Silvers 1991) which show that structural approaches such as semi-autonomous work groups, process activities such as survey feedback and some team development activities seem to work best. Individual development and more person-centred approaches appear to have fared less well. However, many of the studies are weakly designed and there is a huge variation in the results that seems to be associated with the social and political context and the many features of organizational culture that can help to underpin or undermine such interventions.

In practice, some organization development activities may not look very different from some management development activities described above. Often there will be off-the-job courses but they can be more likely to involve a group of managers and/or staff who know and work with each other. This creates an opportunity to discuss the application of learning to the organizational context. This may be followed up by activities in the work context to facilitate application. The key focus is on processes of managing rather than the substantive content of specific functions. While the case for engaging in this type of activity can be compelling from an organizational perspective, there is a risk that the development of individuals can get lost. To address this, an appropriate combination of focus on both individual and organization is required. For the individual, this may mean additional tailored activities and planned exposure to certain kinds of experience such as working on a particular project, representing the unit at meetings or 'acting up' when the boss is absent. Or it may be facilitated through internal activities such as coaching and mentoring that we discussed above.

The Learning Organization and Leadership Development

As noted earlier, management development is somewhat susceptible to management fads and fashions. This seems to have applied in particular to two contrasting approaches that have attracted considerable attention over the past decade, namely the concept of the learning organization and the emphasis on the development of leaders. They offer a contrast because the concept of the learning organization fits well with the established notions of organization development, with the organization as the key unit of analysis but with a concern to facilitate learning embedded in context, while leadership development reflects the more individualized and elitist form of management development. Indeed, there is something of an irony in this since much of the early work on leadership focused on first line leaders (see Yukl 2002) and it is only with the elevation of the corporate leader as hero alongside a growing interest in charismatic and transformational leadership (see, for example, Bryman 1992: Conger and Kanungo 1998) that the emphasis has switched to leadership at the top of organizations.

The concept of the learning organization has its roots in the emergence of the knowledge society coupled with the importance of accepting constant change and innovation as a prerequisite for organizational survival. Zuboff (1988) has put the case powerfully:

> Learning is no longer a separate activity that occurs either before one enters the workplace or in remote classroom settings. Nor is it an activity preserved for a managerial group. The behaviors which define learning and the behaviors which define being productive are one and the same. Learning is not something that requires time out from being engaged in productive activity; learning is the heart of productive activity. To put it simply, learning is the new form of labour. (Zuboff 1988: 395)

In this context, Senge (1990), one of the best-known advocates of the learning organization, defines it as an organization

> where people continually expand their capacity to create the results they truly desire, where new and expansive patterns of thinking are nurtured, where collective action is set free, and where people are continually learning how to learn together. (Senge 1990: 3)

At the heart of the concept of the learning organization is the belief that at all levels in the organization learning should not be viewed as a set of discrete activities associated with training and development but as an on-going activity built in to the culture of the organization. Organizations must therefore develop the capacity for continuous learning. This requires a change in mind-set. Management learning and development should therefore be built in to everyday activity by ensuring that knowledge is disseminated widely within the organization and by ensuring that everyday events such as meetings are recognized as opportunities to update knowledge. By implication, a key goal of management development is to develop knowledge leaders who can effectively manage and disseminate knowledge.

While the concept of the learning organization has a contemporary feel and can be intuitively appealing to those organizations that believe they are allied to the knowledge industry, it is not always clear what steps need to be taken in practice. Writers such as Senge (1990) offer many ideas but no integrative strategy. On the other hand, Pedler et al. (1991) offer a series of steps towards becoming a learning organization. So too do Mayo and Lank (1994), while Marquardt and Reynolds (1994: 109) offer thirteen steps which they preface with the warning that 'there are no such unambiguous, easy and universally applicable steps to becoming a learning organization. If there is one principle that is obvious to learning organizations, it is that learning organizations are never fully "there", having reached perfection'.

These qualifications make it very difficult to evaluate whether any organization qualifies as a learning organization and indeed, whether the concept can really progress from an abstract notion to a realistic application. Perhaps not surprisingly, the main emphasis has often shifted to the development of knowledge systems to facilitate the flow of information rather than the more nebulous notions of organizational or indeed management learning.

The learning organization emphasizes the importance of knowledge, of being open to new ideas and of keeping up to date. In practice, this is the core of much traditional management development activity. One feature that is currently receiving more attention is the importance of taking steps to keep up to date in a context of rapidly evolving knowledge. It is reflected in the current widespread emphasis, highlighted by all professional organizations, ranging from the CIPD to the British Medical Association and the Royal Pharmaceutical Society of Great Britain, on continuing professional development. It is no longer enough to be accredited by passing examinations at the start of the career. It is now essential to demonstrate that this knowledge is regularly and appropriately updated. For example, a 2003 survey of members of the Royal Pharmaceutical Society, which is in the process of moving to compulsory continuous professional development (CPD), found that while there was only lukewarm support for the concept, perhaps because of a dislike of implied compulsion, 86 per cent had participated in some form of CPD activity in the previous 12 months. The most common activities were attending workshops, conferences and weekend schools (Guest et al. 2005).

Developing managers as leaders

The emphasis on CPD draws the focus back to the individual rather than the learning organization. This facilitates external monitoring. The individual is also very much the focus of the emphasis when the interest switches to the development of leadership. Part of this interest in the UK can be traced to the government which has been exercised by the management of change, innovation and efficiency in the public sector. They have set up bodies such as the National College for School Leadership and the Centre for Leadership in Higher Education, as well as promoting a number of leadership programmes through the Cabinet Office to develop public sector leaders (see Glatter 2004). Underpinning this is an implicit view that the public sector has much to learn from leadership in the private sector. Nevertheless in the UK private sector, interest in leadership and leadership development is also allied to a continuing concern for the quality of senior UK management and a wider debate about the need to import managers from overseas to run UK companies and to ensure that top managers are appropriately, and some would argue, disproportionately rewarded.

The pursuit of leadership development through the use of external programmes raises the question of whether leadership can be learned. Doh (2003) interviewed some of the best-known US business school experts on leadership who, perhaps not surprisingly, all agreed that aspects of leadership can be developed. They base this on the assumption that like most activities, leadership is a function of knowledge, skills and attitudes. They concede that in addition there may be some distinctive personal qualities. Nevertheless the knowledge and skill components can be learned. Much of the early leadership training and development was based on this assumption and directed at supervisors, seeking to alter their supervisory or leadership style. This is one of the few areas of development activity that was systematically evaluated, although the results were generally disappointing in revealing that even if leadership style changed, this had little impact on subordinate performance (Yukl 2002).

Mole (2004), an experienced management development manager, is much more sceptical about whether leadership can sensibly be learned outside the context in which it is applied. Although he favours exploring leadership competences, he suggests that leadership development is best advanced within the context of an OD framework. This view is developed by Antonacopoulou and Bento (2004) who, from a social constructivist perspective, are equally critical about the value of teaching leadership and advocate instead learning about leadership through experience and in particular being open to experience. The role of the person responsible for management and leadership development then faces the challenges of creating contexts for learning as a leader. Antonacopoulou and Bento build on the work of Argyris and Schon (1978) and Ferris (2002) on the use of theatre and drama to facilitate learning about leadership in a range of contexts including the classroom.

Developing managers through incidental learning

A strong case can be made for giving a high priority to management development activities that take place within the organization. The survey evidence reported by Thomson et al. (2001) and more recently, albeit with a smaller and narrower sample by Newell (2004), confirms that most managers believe that they learn primarily through work-based experience. This is particularly notable with Newell's sample since they had been participating on a distanced learning MBA programme. More specifically, they said they learned through exposure to challenging assignments and through early exposure to responsibility. Education and mentoring came some way behind these. Both surveys also raise questions about the reality of a strategic approach to management development, with many managers believing that management development is left to chance or occurs as a result of individual initiative. In the Thomson et al. study, only 37 per cent said that management development had a high profile. At the same time, Thomson et al. note that where senior management really does take responsibility and take a lead, there is more management development activity, particularly when compared to organizations where it is the responsibility of the human resource function. Not for the first time, this raises questions about the proactivity of the human resource function.

A key challenge for organizations remains how to balance the activities linked to the formal education, training and development of managers with the potentially more powerful work-based experiences. Marsick and Watkins (1990) have written extensively about the importance of informal and incidental learning. Organizations need to seek ways of turning the incidental learning into planned yet informal learning. The same issue is highlighted by Coffield (2000). To ensure scope for the informal experiences that have long been reported as the most highly valued forms of learning, senior managers have a key strategic role to play, as Schein (1992) has long argued, through their management and reinforcement of a supportive organizational culture.

Initial conclusions on management development

In his invited review of the state of UK management, Porter (Porter and Ketels 2002) commended the professionalism of UK managers, while expressing some concern about their adoption of modern management techniques. He noted that 'Problems with managerial skills in the UK seem likely to be concentrated in the lower and middle management level' (p. 37) reinforcing an issue highlighted earlier in this chapter. His analysis implies real progress over the two decades since the critical reports. There is certainly good evidence to reinforce this if we use as our measure the amount of management education and development activity. However, much of the evidence that has been collected is essentially descriptive, providing some pictures of what has been done, and of the number accredited or engaged in continuing professional development. There is a dearth of good research about the effectiveness of management development activity. We can infer impact at the company level through pragmatic evidence such as the flow of talent in the organization and indications of corporate performance benchmarked against competitors. But it is hard to argue that the results, whether positive or negative, can be attributed to management development. As noted earlier, this problem of evaluation is partly inevitable, given the future orientation of much management development activity. It is reinforced by the blurring of the boundaries between what constitutes management development, organizational learning and development and more pervasive organizational change.

The lack of an evidence base about what works leaves a vacuum which may be filled by management fads and fashions, which in turn provide plenty of scope for management as well as academic scepticism about the value of much management development activity. Yet management development is concerned with nurturing and developing the key talent in the organization. Its importance is therefore not in doubt. This appears to have a number of consequences. One is that organizations continue to engage in a range of formal management development activities, seeking reassurance for their quality partly through the quality of those who provide the development, such as academics from the leading business schools. Secondly, there is an acknowledgement that management development must remain something of an act of faith in a world where it is necessary to be a believer. Finally, it is essential to keep a close eye on the innovations in management development among competitors. In an ambiguous world where there is uncertainty about what is the right thing to do, the temptation is to engage in a form of mimetic isomorphism and follow whoever has been defined as the leader.

Career Management as a Solution to the 'Problem' of UK Management

We now move on to consider a second solution to the problem of quality of management in the UK. That solution is concerned with career management. To what extent can career management processes adopted by companies identify and progress those managers most likely to make a significant contribution, and how far can this be expected to improve the quality, behaviour and impact of managers? We have already noted that management development is future oriented; career management is even more so, since by definition it takes a long-term view of both individual and organizational needs (Schein 1978). As we shall see, this presents great challenges for implementation and evaluation.

In the wider context of policy initiatives addressed in this chapter, improving and evaluating the delivery of career management processes inevitably falls within the responsibilities of individual companies. It might be said that there is little that can be done at a public policy level, since the flow of personnel between roles within a commercial firm or a public sector organization is, ultimately, the concern of that organization, and the flow of personnel between organizations is largely a function of the labour market. It is telling that, while the Labour government's (2003) Skill Strategy explicitly recognizes the need for employers (as well as government and individuals) to invest in skill development, its consultation documents barely acknowledge the notion of skills being developed within the context of meaningful career progression. The CIPD is one of few organizations actively working to identify instances of good career management practice by employers, and to disseminate findings through its membership and the media (CIPD 2003, 2004).

However, there is considerable public interest in promoting effective career management by individuals (as opposed to employers), through a number of mechanisms. First, the professional field of vocational guidance is increasingly recognizing that effective guidance takes place throughout the course of the working life, and not just at the outset. Careers guidance is based on the predication that clarity about the future, self-insight and awareness of opportunities promote better performance within the workplace, as well as in a broader life context. Second, the Labour government's endorsement of life-long learning places a strong emphasis on self-responsibility for work-based development as a context for learning, and thereby an implicit expectation of career management by individuals, together with their employers. Third, the pipeline of self-help books concerned with career and life 'effectiveness' continues to deliver practical advice for individuals about how to manage their careers.

For the purposes of this chapter, we focus particularly on career management processes adopted by employers for their managerial employees. We do so in the belief that this, if anywhere, is where improvements in managerial performance might be achieved, but also recognizing that possibilities for improvements are inherently constrained by the extent of compatibility between individual and organizational objectives for a person's 'career'. Achieving compatibility is problematic in a context of flexible labour markets, individualized employment contracts and short-term performance targets. We focus our discussion on two issues: to what extent can career management identify and progress those managers most likely to make a significant contribution, and how far can this be expected to improve the quality, behaviour and impact of managers?

Career management as a means of enhancing managers' performance

Earlier in this chapter we reviewed the potential for management development to improve the performance of UK managers. Investment in management development by organizations is of interest in its own right, but also relevant as one of a wider set of activities concerned with managing the flow of talent and capability into, between and out of organizational roles. Management development initiatives are most likely to be effective when both the organization's long-term objectives, and the career plans of the individual concerned, are explicitly recognized and incorporated into the development activity and its transfer into a workplace context. Also, if we take the view, advanced by Gunz and Jalland (1996), that the career background of senior managers helps to shape their personal qualities and behaviour, and that these in turn affect the managerial 'rationalities' endorsed by managers lower down the organization, then career management is very clearly connected with managerial performance.

A significant challenge and risk associated with investment in future-oriented activities such as management development and career management is the uncertainty about whether such activities will pay off. This uncertainty has become all the more apparent in the light of numerous academic and popular accounts about the changing nature of work, and of work organizations, and the supposedly declining relevance of 'traditional' approaches to managing careers (e.g. Arthur et al. 1995; Bridges 1995; Brousseau et al. 1996; Cappelli 1999). Many commentators have argued that mutual investments by employer and employee in long-term, stable relationships are no longer appropriate in a world of short-term employment and transactional contracts (Rousseau 1995). Instead, employers are urged to acknowledge employees' aspirations for inter-organizational careers, to offer 'employability' in exchange for short-term commitment, to engage in explicit and ongoing negotiation with employees about their 'career' contract, and to provide opportunities for 'entrepreneurial' initiative and collective learning (Herriot and Pemberton 1996; Kanter 1989; Waterman et al. 1994).

Many accounts about the changing nature of work are based on conjecture rather than evidence. It is clear from empirical evidence that job tenure is not declining radically – indeed it is increasing for some labour market groups – and that companies have not reduced their career management solely to an 'employability' proposition (Hirsh and Jackson 1996; TUC 2000; White et al. 2004). Career management has an economic utility as a means of providing for the supply of skilled, productive, motivated labour – particularly managerial labour – and also a socio-cultural utility as a means of reproducing corporate culture through socialization and promoting shared norms (Gunz 1989; Morris and Pinnington 1998; Rosenbaum 1984). For these reasons, organizational careers are implicitly associated with performance and productivity at an organizational level (Pfeffer 1998). The virtues of an organizational career are not lost on employees either – there is some evidence that, even in an era of supposed career uncertainty, some still value the idea of a traditional career (King 2003).

Nonetheless, the uncertain context in which employment relationships are enacted does present a challenge for management development, and for the wider set of career management activities that surround it. How can employers be sure that the recipients of investment will remain within the organization long enough to realize returns on the investment? One solution, supported by principles from personnel economics and often adopted where employees receive generic skills (such as an MBA), is to require the recipients to pay for it themselves through reduced wages or some kind of financial lock-in (Becker 1962; Lazear 1998). However, since many jobs involve the development of knowledge that is largely tacit and deeply embedded in the context in which it is applied, this kind of solution is rarely straightforward.

A further challenge to both career management and management development is imposed by the delayering of managerial hierarchies and the introduction of 'flat' organization structures, since the skill gaps between one layer and another become significantly greater. For example, in case studies of four service organizations,

Grimshaw et al. (2002) found three-tiered organization structures (consisting of low-skilled assistants or operators, line managers and senior managers), which were highly dominated numerically by the bottom tier. Paradoxically, while promotion prospects for most of the bottom tier were minimal due to the relatively few promotion opportunities, the organizations nevertheless struggled to promote from within due to the huge 'promotion gap' between the bottom and middle layers, increasing the tendency to 'buy' rather than 'make' managers. Grimshaw et al.'s study addressed progression *into* the middle management tier; for those at middle and senior levels, management progression often operates within a conventional internal labour market, although Osterman (1996), Heckscher (1995) and others argue that management hierarchies have not been untouched by restructuring.

There is limited empirical evidence with which to assess whether these perceived changes in the world of work have had a wholesale effect on career management in UK organizations. Research from the 1990s indicated that, while some employers had followed fashion by experimenting with a 'self-development' or 'employability' career offering, there were considerable costs associated with this approach, including demotivation, cynicism, reduced flexibility and concerns about succession management (Gratton and Hope-Hailey 1999; Hirsh and Jackson 1996; McGovern et al. 1998). Hirsh and Jackson found that, among a sample of 15 blue chip organizations, most had withdrawn from leaving career management solely up to the employee. Other research points to the continued use of up-or-out and so-called 'meritocractic' promotion systems, at least in professional services firms (Morris and Pinnington 1998). More recently, interest has shifted to recognizing the central role of line managers in managing careers, and in enhancing their ability to do so effectively (Kidd et al. 2003; Doyle 2000). Management development is therefore not only (as we argued above) one aspect of career management for an individual manager, but also a tool by which managers may be helped in the short-term to oversee the careers of their subordinates.

The most recent survey of UK practice is the 2003 CIPD *Managing Employee Careers* survey, which reviewed current practice in 700 UK organizations. Responses were drawn from its membership, suggesting a definite bias toward large organizations, and a possible self-selection bias with respondents favourable toward career management over-represented. The survey found that almost half (48 per cent) of the organizations represented had a formal written strategy for the career management of their employees. The most commonly cited objectives for career management were growing future senior managers or leaders (cited by 52 per cent of respondents, and particularly by private sector respondents, and by medium and large organizations) and retaining key staff (cited by 50 per cent of respondents and particularly by public sector and voluntary organizations). Career management practices were suggested to cluster in five groups, which are illustrated in Figure 9.2.

Included in Figure 9.2 are activities that we referred to in the first half of this chapter, as well as a range of other activities including secondments (within or outside the organization), career breaks, developmental reviews, informal career support and advice, and the provision of career-related information and training.

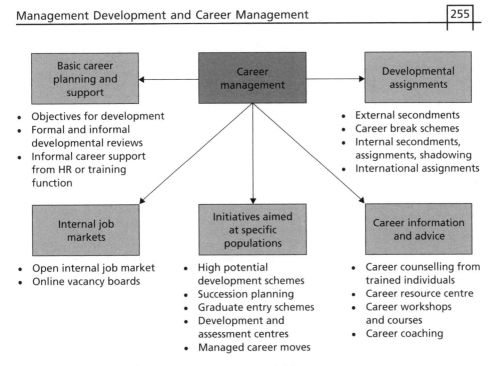

Figure 9.2 Groups of career management activities

All of these activities can be used both to deliver and to complement management development activities, and, if carefully and consistently deployed, can help the process of transferring learning from a formal context into workplace practice. Assessment centres use a variety of tools (interviews, group activities, presentations and psychometric tests) to identify candidates for management development activities. Development centres, which use the same tools as assessment centres for developmental purposes, are one means of delivering management development, although attempts to use such centres for both development and grading often provide conflicting messages to participants and dilute both objectives (Arnold 2002). Succession planning provides an overarching framework within which management development activities can be planned and executed.

Most respondents to the CIPD survey (79 per cent) agreed that career development *should* be available to all staff, but in practice the evidence suggests that only 'basic' career support activities (development reviews and information resources) and internal job markets were made widely available. Succession planning, accelerated development for high-potential staff and 'managed' careers were reserved for specific populations, such as graduate entrants, expatriate managers and future senior managers. These findings support the idea we advanced earlier – that in many organizations efforts are directed toward the careers of those with high potential, to the possible detriment of other managers who constitute the core backbone of the organization. They also suggest that, despite considerable rhetoric and case study evidence for the decline of the traditional career, many organizations still aim to manage careers in a traditional way, at least for some employee groups. Following Lepak and Snell's (1999) differentiated approach to the HR architecture, we might expect 'traditional' career management to be applied to job roles requiring context-specific knowledge that is both valuable to the organization and hard to replace.

In summary, career management processes provide a means to identify and progress those managers most likely to make a significant contribution. Some UK organizations – particularly larger and private-sector organizations such as the civil service, investment banks and professional services firms – make use of these processes, at least for future senior managers and as a means to retain key staff. For the majority of employees, and probably a significant portion of the UK's current and future managers, the expectation is one of self-responsibility for career – in terms of identifying development needs and pursuing opportunities. As Newell's (2004) research among part-time MBA students, cited earlier, revealed, this is widely recognized among managers. Whether employers choose to invest in career management depends in part on their beliefs about its ability to enhance performance – a question to which we now turn.

Evaluating Whether Career Management Enhances Managers' Performance

Throughout this chapter we have noted the future-oriented nature of management development and career management activities. Evaluating the effectiveness of career management processes in enhancing performance is difficult if not impossible – not least because of the problem of isolating the effect of such activities from other factors. Here, we offer a brief evaluation, somewhat limited by the available evidence, together with a qualitative appraisal.

It is clear from studies of large organizations that career management activities serve a purpose in developing skills and talent by channelling employees – or at least a select minority of employees – along appropriate pathways over time (e.g. Gunz 1989; Kanter 1977; Rosenbaum 1984). Scholars have offered methodologies for charting these internal labour markets (Baker et al. 1994; Vroom 1968), and have examined factors determining their existence (Baron et al. 1986; Pfeffer and Cohen 1984), but little attention has been paid to evaluating their effectiveness. This is perhaps not surprising given the difficulties discussed above, but it is regrettable, especially since contemporary proclamations about the demise of the organizational career endure despite evidence of its continued existence.

What criteria might we adopt to evaluate whether career management activities are effective? From the perspective of individual managers, we might include satisfaction with achievement, reward, grade, or recognition, or whatever subjective criteria they choose (see Sturges 1999). From an organizational perspective, we might include successful retention of key staff, and succession achieved through a strong flow of internal candidates for posts. Following the literature on HRM and performance, we might also consider the extent to which career management interventions are internally consistent with, and complemented by, a wider system of HR practices and work design which has a holistic impact on firm performance (Becker and Huselid 1998; Milgrom and Roberts 1995). Anticipating these arguments, Von Glinow et al. (1983) proposed an ambitious set of parameters for appraising the extent to which an HR system was 'career oriented'.

There have been few attempts to evaluate career management in any of these terms. One exception, focused on employees rather than managers, is a study by Noe (1996), who found no relationship between employees' ratings of career management and managers' rating of their job performance. There is some evidence that satisfaction with organizational career management reduces managers' turnover intentions (Herriot et al. 1994) and promotes loyalty and commitment among graduate employees (Sturges et al. 2000; Sturges and Guest 2001; Arnold and Mackenzie Davey, 1999). In a survey of managers and professionals, Granrose and Portwood (1987) noted that the extent of a perceived match between individual and organizational career plans increased satisfaction and reduced turnover intentions. There is a range of research on the outcomes of specific initiatives such as assessment centres, mentoring, job rotation and support for managers' non-work commitments (e.g. Arnold 2002; Campion et al. 1994; Lankau and Scandura 2002; Martins et al. 2002), and considerable interest in the effects of attempts to encourage career self-management (e.g. Anakwe et al. 2000; Kidd et al. 2003), although McGovern et al.'s (1998) study is one of few to focus specifically on managerial careers in this context.

In evaluating the impact of career management on job performance, we should also consider evidence about job performance in the absence of career opportunities. How are people affected by career plateaus or interrupted career paths? Tremblay and Roger's (2004) survey of Canadian managers found that job characteristics such as enrichment and opportunity for decision making reduce the impact of career plateauing on job satisfaction. Nachbagauer and Riedl (2002) offer similar findings from a sample of university staff and school teachers. It is clear from these studies that, consistent with a 'complementarity' approach to HRM, career management cannot be evaluated in isolation from wider aspects of work design and job content.

This last observation points to a paradox that lies at the heart of efforts by employers to manage careers of their managerial employees: effective career management depends, in part, on effective interaction between line managers and employees. Thus, middle managers are placed in a contradictory role – as both 'contract makers' with their subordinates, but also engaged as employees in a contractual exchange with senior management (Doyle 2000; Hallier and James 1997). In a context of organizational change, where renegotiations of the psychological contract are taking place, managers may be more aligned to their role as employees than their role as agents of the organization. Herriot et al. (1993) found in surveys of four organizations that managers colluded with employees in appraisals to avoid acknowledging changing career prospects. The performance of middle managers is undoubtedly affected by their ability and motivation to prioritize their managerial over their employee role – not only in discussions of subordinates' careers but also with regard to all kinds of shifting obligations. Ultimately, the objective of both management development and career management must be to tip the balance in the right direction.

Initial conclusions about career management

On balance, have 'traditional' approaches to managing the careers of managers delivered the goods in terms of enhancing managerial performance? The evidence is patchy but the answer is a resounding yes in some quarters; over three-quarters of respondents to the CIPD survey described their career management practices as 'effective' or 'very effective'. It is harder to make judgements about small UK organizations, given their diversity, but it is worth noting from the 1998 Workplace Employee Relations Survey that only 22 per cent of UK workplaces have an HR function or personnel specialist (Cully et al. 1999). More generally, as we noted at the beginning of this chapter, the quality of UK management is still deemed to be low, as vividly exemplified by Ricky Gervais's portrayal of David Brent, an incompetent, insensitive and irresponsible manager, in the hit BBC series *The Office*.

There is a disjuncture between management development as a concern for a minority occupational group, intended to reproduce the status quo, versus the need for a dynamic, adaptable approach focused on promoting flexibility and fit in the whole workforce (Wright and Snell 1998). Given the choice, most UK managers do not pursue high-performance workplaces but continue to pursue a 'low-skill, low-road' route (Guest 2001). This perhaps is one reason why 'traditional' approaches, focused only on managing the careers of elite populations, appear to have failed to deliver results in terms of wider productivity. Another reason is that most organizational career management – and the management development activities that form part of it – is focused with good reason on internal priorities, such as the development of firm-specific competences and capabilities, attracting and retaining key staff and optimizing their productivity.

Despite exhortation by academics to engage in continual renegotiations of the psychological contract, and to facilitate inter-organizational careers, the reality is that managing careers is a messy business that is laced with vested interest – both individual and organizational. The context in which careers are managed is wider than it used to be – as evidenced by increasing interest in network organizations, alliances, outsourcing and offshoring – but rather than promoting more open-ended collaborative behaviour (Miles and Snow 1996), this has the opposite effect. Employers do the best they can to retain key employees and thereby render immobile their resource-based advantage (see Barney 1991). In this context, 'traditional' approaches to managing the careers of core employees are optimal, since they promote dense social relations and unique, embedded routines (Lado and Wilson 1994), while the archetypal self-managed career (which is sometimes referred to as a 'boundaryless' career and epitomized in accounts of Silicon Valley (e.g. Saxenian 1996) is deeply threatening.

Final Thoughts

Management development and career management are widely recognized as key organizational activities that can help to deliver the high quality top managers of the future while maintaining a flow of competent and motivated people in other management roles. In their various guises, they have been seen as part of the solution to the 'problem' of UK management. This chapter has outlined and reviewed some of the perspectives on and approaches to management development and career management that might help to improve the quality of management. A review of the evidence suggests that those involved in the provision of development and career activities are broadly positive in their evaluation of these activities. However, this assessment often rests on weak foundations. While there is some limited empirical evidence about career management activities, when we consider the investment in management development, the amount of systematic evaluation remains woefully limited. Given uncertainty about what works best, it is tempting to seek out new initiatives and to be susceptible to the latest fads and fashions. For the future, there is probably more to be gained by engaging in systematic evaluation of existing approaches to provide a better understanding of the conditions under which they are likely to prove successful for all those involved.

We should note the subtext that has underpinned much of our discussion in this chapter – the significance of the individual manager or employee as an independent party, actively engaged in managing his or her development and career. Most of the interventions discussed in this chapter depend on the capacity and motivation of the individual concerned to develop and learn in a manner consistent with organizational priorities. For this reason, the 'matching' of individual with organizational needs has long been recognized as a primary objective for career management (Schein, 1978; Granrose and Portwood 1987). The reality is, however, that a career-oriented HR system (see Von Glinow et al. 1983) that is integrative but also makes provision for differentiated needs, and which is person-centred but also objective, is enormously difficult to achieve in practice. For this reason, we are far from a 'magic' solution to the problem of UK management.

REFERENCES

Anakwe, U.P., Hall, J.C. and Schor, S.M. 2000: Knowledge-related skills and effective career management, *International Journal of Manpower*, **21**(7–8), 566–79.

Antonacopoulou, E. and Bento, R. 2004: Method of 'learning leadership': Taught and experiential, in J. Storey (ed.), *Leadership in Organizations*, London: Routledge, 81–102.

Argyris, A. and Schon, D. 1978: *Organizational Learning: A Theory-Action Perspective*, Reading, MA: Addison-Wesley.

Arnold, J. 2002: Tensions between assessment, grading and development in development centres: A case study, *International Journal of Human Resource Management*, **13**(6), 975–91.

Arnold, J. and Mackenzie-Davey, K. 1999: Graduates' work experiences as predictors of organizational commitment and intention to leave, and turnover: Which experiences really matter?, *Applied Psychology: An International Review*, **48**, 211–38.

Arthur, M.B., Claman, P.H. and DeFillippi, R.J. 1995: Intelligent enterprise, intelligent careers, *Academy of Management Executive*, **9**(4), 7–22.

Baker, G., Gibbs, M. and Holmstrom, B. 1994: The internal economics of the firm: Evidence from personnel data, *Quarterly Journal of Economics*, **109**(4), 881–919.

Barnett, C. 1986: *The Audit of War*, London: Macmillan.

Barney, J. 1991: Firm resources and sustained competitive advantage, *Journal of Management*, **17**(1), 99–120.

Baron, J.M., Davis-Blake, A. and Bielby, W.T. 1986: The structure of opportunity: How promotion ladders vary within and among organizations, *Administrative Science Quarterly*, **31**, 248–73.

Becker, B.E. and Huselid, M.A. 1998: High performance work systems and firm performance: A synthesis of research and managerial implications, *Research in Personnel and Human Resource Management*, **16**, 53–101.

Becker, G.S. 1962: Investment in human capital: A theoretical analysis, *Journal of Political Economy*, **70**, 9–49.

Beckhard, R. 1969: *Organization Development: Sources, Strategies and Models*, Reading, MA: Addison-Wesley.

Bell, E., Taylor, S. and Thorpe, R. 2002: Organizational differentiation through badging: Investors in People and the value of the sign, *Journal of Management Studies*, **39**(8), 1071–85.

Bennis, W. 1969: *Organization Development: Its Nature, Origins and Prospects*, Reading, MA: Addison-Wesley.

Blake, R.R. and Mouton, J.S. 1969: *Building a Dynamic Corporation through Grid Organization Development*, Reading, MA: Addison-Wesley.

Boam, R. and Sparrow, P. (eds.) 1992: *Designing and Achieving Competency*, Maidenhead: McGraw-Hill.

Bridges, W. 1995: *Jobshift: How to Prosper in a Workplace without Jobs*, London: Brealey.

Brousseau, K.R., Driver, M.J., Eneroth, K. and Larsson, R. 1996: Career pandemonium: Realigning individuals and organizations, *Academy of Management Executive*, **10**(4), 52–66.

Bryman, A. 1992: *Charisma and Leadership in Organizations*, London: Sage.

Campion, M.A., Cheraskin, L. and Stevens, M.J. 1994: Career-related antecedents and outcomes of job rotation, *Academy of Management Journal*, **37**, 1518–42.

Cappelli, P. 1999: Career jobs *are* dead, *California Management Review*, **42**(1), 146–67.

Chao, G.T., Walz, P.M. and Gardner, P.D. 1992: Formal and informal mentorships: A comparison on mentoring functions and contrast with non-mentored counterparts, *Personnel Psychology*, **45**, 608–25.

CIPD (Chartered Institute of Personnel and Development) 2003: *Managing Employee Careers*, London: CIPD.

CIPD (Chartered Institute of Personnel and Development) 2004: *Career Management: A Guide*, London: CIPD.

Clutterbuck, D. and Lane, G. 2004: *The Situational Mentor*, Gower: Aldershot.

Clutterbuck, D. and Ragins, B.R. 2002: *Mentoring and Diversity: An International Perspective*, Oxford: Butterworth Heinemann.

Cockerill, A. 1989: The kind of competence for rapid change, *Personnel Management*, November, 52–6.

Coffield, F. (ed.) 2000: *The Necessity of Informal Learning*, Bristol: Policy Press.

Conger, J.A. and Kanungo, R.N. (eds.) 1988: *Charismatic Leadership*, San Francisco: Jossey-Bass.

Constable, J. and McCormick, R. 1987: *The Making of British Managers*, London: BIM and CBI.

Cully, M., O'Reilly, A., Woodland, S. and Dix, G. 1999: *Britain at Work: 1998 Workplace Employee Relations Survey*, London: Routledge.

Doh, J.P. 2003: Can leadership be taught? Perspectives from management educators, *Academy of Management Learning and Education*, **2**(1), 54–67.

Doyle, M. 2000: Managing careers in organizations, in A. Collin and R.A. Young (eds.), *The Future of Career*, Cambridge: Cambridge University Press, 228–42.

Ferris, W.P. (2002): Theater tools for teambuilding, *Harvard Business Review*, **80**(12), 24–5.

French, W.L. and Bell, C.H. 1990: *Organization Development: Behavioural Science Interventions for Organization Improvement*, Englewood Cliffs, NJ: Prentice-Hall.

Glatter, R. 2004: Leadership and leadership development in education, in J. Storey (ed.), *Leadership in Organizations*, London: Routledge.

Granrose, C.K. and Portwood, T.D. 1987: Matching individual career plans and organizational career management, *Academy of Management Journal*, **30**(4), 699–720.

Gratton, L. and Hope-Hailey, V. 1999: The rhetoric and reality of 'new careers', in L. Gratton, V. Hope-Hailey, P. Stiles and C. Truss (eds.), *Strategic Human Resource Management*, Oxford: Oxford University Press, 79–100.

Gratton, L., Hope-Hailey, V., Stiles, P. and Truss, C. (eds.) 1999: *Strategic Human Resource Management*, Oxford: Oxford University Press.

Grimshaw, D., Beynon, H., Rubery, J. and Ward, K. 2002: The restructuring of career paths in large service sector organizations: 'Delayering', upskilling and polarisation, *Sociological Review*, **50**(1), 89–116.

Guest, D. 2001: Industrial relations and human resource management, in J. Storey (ed.), *Human Resource Management: A Critical Text*, 2nd edn, London: Thompson Learning, 96–113.

Guest, D., Oakley, P. and Battersby, S. 2005: *The Demand for and Supply of Pharmacists*, London: Royal Pharmaceutical Society of Great Britain.

Gunz, H. 1989: *Careers and Corporate Cultures*, Oxford: Blackwell.

Gunz, H.P. and Jalland, R.M. 1996: Managerial careers and business strategies, *Academy of Management Review*, **21**, 718–56.

Hallier, J. and James, P. 1997: Middle managers and the employee psychological contract: Agency, protection and advancement, *Journal of Management Studies*, **34**, 703–28.

Handy, C. 1987: *The Making of Managers*. London: National Economic Development Organization.

Heckscher, C. 1995: *White Collar Blues: Management Loyalties in an Age of Corporate Restructuring*, New York: Basic Books.

Herriot, P., Gilbson, P., Pemberton, C. and Jackson, P.R. 1994: An empirical model of managerial careers in organizations, *British Journal of Management*, **5**, 113–21.

Herriot, P. and Pemberton, C. 1996: Contracting careers, *Human Relations*, **49**(6), 757–90.

Herriot, P., Pemberton, C. and Pinder, R. 1993: Misperceptions of managers and their bosses of each other's preferences regarding the managers' careers: A case of the blind leading the blind, *Human Resource Management Journal*, **4**(2), 39–51.

Hirsh, W. and Jackson, C. 1996: *Strategies for Career Development: Promise, Practice and Pretence*, Brighton: Institute of Employment Studies.

Hoque, K. 2003: All in all it's just another plaque on the wall: The incidence and impact of the Investors in People standard, *Journal of Management Studies*, **40**(2), 543–71.

Kanter, R.M. 1977: *Men and Women of the Corporation*, New York: Basic Books.

Kanter, R.M. 1985: *The Change Masters*, New York: Simon and Schuster.

Kanter, R.M. 1989: *When Giants Learn to Dance: Mastering the Challenges of Strategy, Management and Careers in the 1990s*, New York: Basic Books.

Kidd, J.M., Jackson, C. and Hirsh, W. 2003: The outcomes of effective career discussion at work, *Journal of Vocational Behavior*, **62**(1), 119–33.

King, Z. 2003: New or traditional careers? A study of UK graduates' preferences, *Human Resource Management Journal*, **13**(1), 5–26.

Kram, K.E. 1983: Phases of the mentoring relationship, *Academy of Management Journal*, **26**(4), 608–25.

Kram, K.E. 1985: *Mentoring at Work: Developmental Relations in Organizational Life*, Glenview, IL: Scott, Foresman.

Labour Government (Department for Education and Skills/Department for Trade and Industry/HM Treasury/Department for Work and Pensions) 2003: *21st Century Skills Realising Our Potential – Individuals, Employers, Nation*, Cm 5810, London: The Stationery Office.

Lado, A.A. and Wilson, M.C. 1994: Human-resource systems and sustained competitive advantage: A competence-based perspective, *Academy of Management Review*, **19**(4), 699–727.

Lankau, M.J. and Scandura, T.A. 2002: An investigation of personal learning in mentoring relationships: Content, antecedents, and consequences, *Academy of Management Journal*, **45**(4), 779–90.

Lazear, E.P. 1998: *Personnel Economics for Managers*, New York: John Wiley and Sons.

Lengnick-Hall, C.A. and Lengnick-Hall, M.L. 1988: Strategic HRM: A review of the literature and a proposed typology, *Academy of Management Review*, **13**, 454–70.

Lepak, D. and Snell, S. 1999: The human resource architecture: Towards a theory of human capital allocation and development, *Academy of Management Review*, **24**, 31–48.

Livian, Y-F. and Burgoyne, J.G. (eds.) 1997: *Middle Managers in Europe*, London: Routledge.

Mangham, I. and Silver, M.S. 1986: *Management Training: Context and Practice*, London: ESRC.

Marquardt, M. and Reynolds, A. 1994: *The Global Learning Organization*, Burr Ridge, IL: Irwin Professional Publishing.

Marsick, V. and Watkins, K. 1990: *Informal and Incidental Learning in the Workplace*, London: Routledge.

Martins, L.L., Eddleston, K.A. and Veiga, J.F. 2002: Moderators of the relationship between work-family conflict and career satisfaction, *Academy of Management Journal*, **45**(2), 399–409.

Mayo, A. and Lank, E. 1994: *The Power of Learning: A Guide to Gaining Competitive Advantage*, London: CIPD.

McGovern, P., Hope-Hailey, V. and Stiles, P. 1998: The managerial career after downsizing: case studies from the 'leading edge', *Work, Employment and Society*, **12**(3), 457–77.

Miles, R.E. and Snow, C.C. 1996: Twenty-first-century careers, in M.B. Arthur and D.M. Rousseau (eds.), *The Boundaryless Career: A New Employment Principle for a New Organizational Era*, Oxford: Oxford University Press, 97–115.

Milgrom, P. and Roberts, J. 1995: Complementarities and fit: Strategy, structure and organizational change in manufacturing, *Journal of Accounting and Economics*, **19**, 179–208.

Mintzberg, H. 2004: *Managers Not MBAs*, London: Prentice Hall/Financial Times.

Mintzberg, H. and Gosling, J. 2002: Educating managers beyond borders, *Academy of Management Learning and Education*, **1**(1), 64–76.

Mintzberg, H. and Lampel, J. 2001: Matter of degrees: Do MBAs make better CEOs?, *Fortune*, 19 February, 244.

Mole, G. 2004: Can leadership be taught?, in J. Storey (ed.), *Leadership in Organizations*, London: Routledge, 125–37.

Morris, T. and Pinnington, A. 1998: Promotion to partner in professional services firms, *Human Relations*, **51**, 3–24.

Nachbagauer, A.G.M. and Riedl, G. 2002: Effects of concepts of career plateaus on performance, work satisfaction and commitment, *International Journal of Manpower*, **23**(8), 716–33.

Neuman, G.A., Edwards, J.E. and Raja, N.S. 1989: Organizational development interventions: A meta-analysis of their effects on satisfaction and other attitudes, *Personnel Psychology*, **42**, 461–83.

Newell, H. 2004: *Who Will Follow the Leader? Managers' Perceptions of Management Development Activities: An International Comparison*, SKOPE Research Paper No. 51. Warwick University, Coventry.

Noe, R.A. 1996: Is career management related to employee development and performance, *Journal of Organizational Behavior*, **17**, 119–33.

Osterman, P. (ed.) 1996: *Broken Ladders: Managerial Careers in the New Economy*, Oxford: Oxford University Press.

Paauwe, J. 2004: *HRM and Performance: Achieving Long-Term Viability*, Oxford: Oxford University Press.

Paton, R., Taylor, S. and Storey, J. 2004: Corporate universities and leadership development, in J. Storey (ed.), *Leadership in Organizations*, London: Routledge, 103–24.

Pearn, M.A. and Kandola, R.S. 1988: *Job Analysis: A Practical Guide for Managers*, London: IPM.

Pedler, M., Burgoyne, J. and Boydell, T. 1991: *The Learning Company*, Maidenhead: McGraw-Hill.

Pfeffer, J. 1998: *The Human Equation*, Boston, MA: Harvard Business School Press.

Pfeffer, J. and Cohen, Y. 1984: Determinants of internal labour markets in organizations, *Administrative Science Quarterly*, **29**, 550–72.

Pfeffer, J. and Fong, C.T. 2002: The end of business schools? Less success than meets the eye, *Academy of Management Learning and Education*, **1**(1), 78–95.

Porras, J. and Silvers, R. 1991: Organizational development and transformation, *Annual Review of Psychology*, **42**, 51–78.

Porter, M.E. and Ketels, C.H.M. 2002: *UK Competitiveness: Moving to the Next Stage*, DTI Economics Paper No. 3, London: DTI.

Ragins, B.R. and Cotton, J.L. 1999: Mentor functions and outcomes: A comparison of men and women in formal and informal mentoring relationships, *Journal of Applied Psychology*, **84**, 529–50.

Ragins, B.R., Cotton, J.L. and Miller, J.S. 2000: Marginal mentoring: The effects of type of mentor, quality of relationship and program design on work and career attitudes, *Academy of Management Journal*, **43**, 1177–94.

Ragins, B.R. and Scandura, T.A. 1994: Gender differences in expected outcomes of mentoring relationships, *Academy of Management Journal*, **37**(4), 957–71.

Reed, M. and Anthony, P. 1992: Professionalizing management and managing professionalization: British management in the 1980s, *Journal of Management Studies*, **29**(5), 591–614.

Rosenbaum, J.E. 1984: *Career Mobility in a Corporate Hierarchy*, New York: Academic Press.

Rousseau, D.M. 1995: *Psychological Contracts in Organizations: Understanding Written and Unwritten Agreements*, Thousand Oaks, CA: Sage.

Salaman, G. 2004: Competences of managers, competences of leaders, in J. Storey (ed.), *Leadership in Organizations*, London: Routledge, 58–78.

Saxenian, A. 1996: 'Beyond boundaries: Open labor markets and learning in Silicon Valley, in M.B. Arthur and D.M. Rousseau (eds.), *The Boundaryless Career: A New Employment Principle for a New Organizational Era*, New York: Oxford University Press, 23–39.

Schein, E.H. 1978: *Career Dynamics: Matching Individual and Organizational Needs*, Reading, MA: Addison Wesley.

Schein, E.H. 1992: *Organizational Culture and Leadership*, 2nd edn, San Francisco: Jossey-Bass.

Senge, P. 1990: *The Fifth Discipline: The Art and Practice of the Learning Organization*, New York: Doubleday.

Storey, J. (ed.) 2004: *Leadership in Organizations*, London: Routledge.

Sturges, J. 1999: What it means to succeed: Personal conceptions of career success held by male and female managers at different ages, *British Journal of Management*, **19**, 239–52.

Sturges, J. and Guest, D. 2001: Don't leave me this way; A qualitative study of influences on the organizational commitment and turnover intentions of graduates early in their career, *British Journal of Guidance and Counselling*, **29**(4), 447–62.

Sturges, J., Guest, D. and Mackenzie-Davey, K. 2000: Who's in charge? Graduates' attitudes to and experiences of career management and their relationship with organizational commitment, *European Journal of Work and Organizational Psychology*, **9**(3), 351–70.

Thomson, A., Storey, J., Mabey, C., Gray, C., Farmer, E. and Thomson, R. 1997: *A Portrait of Management Development*, London: Institute of Management.

Thomson, A., Mabey, C., Sotey, J., Gray, C. and Iles, P. 2001: *Changing Patterns of Management Development*, Oxford: Blackwell.

Tremblay, M. and Roger, A. 2004: Career plateauing reactions: The moderating role of job scope, role ambiguity and participation among Canadian managers, *International Journal of Human Resource Management*, **15**(6), 996–1017.

TUC 2000: *The Future of Work*, London: TUC.

Von Glinow, M.A., Driver, M.J., Brousseau, K. and Prince, J.B. 1983: The design of a career oriented human resource system, *Academy of Management Review*, **8**, 23–32.

Vroom, V.H. 1968: Toward a stochastic model of managerial careers, *Administrative Science Quarterly*, **13**, 26–46.

Waterman, R.H., Waterman, B.A. and Collard, B.A. 1994: Towards a career resilient work-force, *Harvard Business Review*, July–August, 87–95.

White, M., Hill, S., Mills, C. and Smeaton, D. 2004: *Managing to Change? British Workplaces and the Future of Work*, Basingstoke: Palgrave Macmillan.

Wright, P.M. and Snell, S.A. 1998: Toward a unifying framework for exploring fit and flexibility in strategic human resource management, *Academy of Management Review*, **23**(4), 756–72.

Yukl, G. 2002: *Leadership in Organizations*, Englewood Cliffs, NJ: Prentice Hall.

Zuboff, S. 1988: *In the Age of the Smart Machine: The Future of Work and Power*, New York: Basic Books.

CHAPTER TEN

Employer and Employee Branding: HR or PR?

Martin R. Edwards

It is difficult to find a contemporary business text that does not in some way refer to the importance of corporate brands. This reflects the prevalence of branding activities in modern day organizations and the centrality of brands in the field of marketing. A relatively recent phenomenon, however, is the interest that branding is receiving within the field of human resources. In particular, there is growing interest in employer and employee branding with an emphasis on the consideration of how the company brand relates to current and potential employees. A number of recent research reports suggest that HR departments are becoming more interested in employer branding (Dell and Ainspan 2001 and IRS 2003). A survey of 138 'leading companies' indicates that as many as 40 per cent carried out some form of employer branding activities (Dell and Ainspan 2001). Employer and employee branding is now presented as an important activity that a modern HR department should focus on for the organization to be competitive and to help ensure that the HR function becomes more of a strategic force in a company's business activities (Martin and Beaumont 2003 and Ulrich and Smallwood 2003).

This interest in branding signals a different role for the HR department, one where the image of the company and what it stands for becomes more of a consideration when designing HR policies and practices. Employer branding focuses on how the company is seen by current and potential employees with the aim of 'winning the war on talent' (Ulrich 1997). This has important implications for how HR departments recruit and retain staff. Employee branding has a slightly different focus with an emphasis on ensuring that employees act in accordance with the organization's brand values, thus ensuring that customers have a consistent branded experience when interacting with a company's workforce. An organizational focus on employer and employee branding has implications for employee induction, training, development and performance management. A branding focus also has important implications for wider aspects of employee relations. The interest in employer and employee branding reflects a different direction in how employees are managed and supports recent arguments that management practice is becoming more concerned with the management of the private and personal aspects of employees (Alvesson and Wilmot 2002). Employer and employee branding focuses on winning the 'hearts and minds' of staff and ensuring that when employees come to work, they are motivated to live the organization's brand.

This chapter begins by setting out some explanations for why there has been an increasing interest in employer and employee branding. Following this, the chapter then goes on to explain what the two forms of branding involve, distinguishing between employee and employer branding. Then, how branding translates into specific HR activities is discussed followed by a consideration of the implications that this new branding emphasis has for the HR function. Finally, the chapter considers some of the potential challenges that the HR function confronts, in particular the ethical dilemmas associated with branding activities.

Explaining the Interest in Employer and Employee Branding

There are a number of reasons why both employee and employer branding has become a focus of interest for the field of HR. First, the interest in branding for the HR function can be considered to be an extension of various arguments why an organization should concentrate on brands in general. Secondly, employer and employee branding reflects an adjustment to changes in the labour market, in particular the growing interest that graduates and job applicants have in working for a company that stands for particular values. Linked to this is the suggestion that potential employees are becoming more preoccupied with working for responsible companies due to the increasing interest in corporate social responsibility. Thirdly, employer and employee branding is seen as an opportunity for the HR function to become more strategically focused; thus branding is a potential solution to the problem often identified in relation to the function, that it struggles to obtain legitimacy. Fourthly, it can be argued that the now familiar models of HRM that aim to encourage employees to be organizationally committed fit with some of the aims of employer and employee branding initiatives, in particular to ensure that employees accept and promote the values and goals of the organization. Additionally, it is argued by some authors that managers are becoming more interested in the management of identity (both organizational and employee), and the focus on employer and employee branding reflects this trend.

A fairly straightforward explanation for the interest in employee and employer branding is that in general, companies place emphasis on the importance of having a strong brand to ensure that they remain competitive in the market place; as such, the introduction of branding into the HR function is simply an extension of the dominance of corporate branding as a marketing activity. According to the marketing literature, brands help to distinguish a company from its competitors, they help to create customer loyalty and identification, they guarantee a certain level of quality and satisfaction for customers, and they help to promote the product (Hollensen 2003). Essentially, it is argued that branding helps to improve market share and to increase organizational profits (Gobe 2001).

The financial benefits of branding apply equally to employer and employee branding. In the 2003 CIPD report, *Branding and People Management*, Martin and Beaumont argue that 'branding has become the critical source of competitive advantage for many organizations' and that HR practitioners 'have much to offer in the branding process' (p. 2). They argue that employer-branding activities help to increase the quality and loyalty of staff – thus leading to better organizational performance – and employee branding bolsters an organization's brand with customers. Consequently employee and employer branding increase profits and market share.

A second reason why branding has become more of an HR activity is related to changes in what potential recruits want from an employer. Increasingly, the popular HR press discusses the presence of generation X in the job market who, it is suggested, will not work hard for a company unless they themselves believe in what it is striving to achieve. Research is presented suggesting that graduates are becoming more discerning when selecting potential employers. Turban and Greening (1996) conducted a study using graduate students who were asked to rate the corporate reputation of organizations; they also asked another group how attractive these organizations were as an employer. The study showed a highly significant positive relationship between perceptions of the reputation of organizations and how attractive these companies are as potential employers. Such research helps to explain why employer branding is becoming an important HR activity as it is seen as important to attract new recruits whose values fit those espoused in the organization's brand (Free 1999). Consequently, it is argued that the consideration of what the organization stands for, which is a key part of any branding exercise, is something that organizations need to promote in today's job market to attract and retain talented people. This is especially the case for graduate recruits, signalled by the existence of 'student brand managers' in companies such as KPMG.

The CIPD has suggested that branding activities comprise an integral component of the growing corporate social responsibility (CSR) movement. Research by Business in the Community (2003) also makes the link between corporate responsibility and internal (i.e. employee) branding by arguing that responsible business practices can be used to help enhance the employer brand resulting in organizations that are more attractive to new recruits. This report confirms that new graduates are becoming increasingly concerned about a company's values and how socially responsible they are when considering where to work. The growth in interest in CSR means that what the organization stands for, its values, and its corporate reputation image (or brand) has become of greater importance. A focus on organizational values is an inherent part of employer and employee branding activities;

as such, it is likely that organizational concerns about CSR are leading to an increased interest in employer branding.

Employer branding also represents an opportunity for the HR department to be more strategically focused and more involved in other key functions of organizations such as marketing (Martin and Beaumont 2003). This type of argument is potentially attractive to HR practitioners who have often struggled to gain legitimacy in an increasingly commercialized business context. As Legge (1978), Storey (1992), Ulrich (1997) and Caldwell (2003) have argued, there are major challenges for the HR function in terms of what its precise role is within organizations, the extent to which it is faced with role ambiguity, and the degree to which it is taken seriously as an influential and legitimate managerial force within organizations. The notion of employee or employer branding pulls the HR function into the strategic engine room of the organization, encouraging HR professionals to become Ulrich's (1997) strategic partners. It is suggested that the HR function needs to cooperate and work with the marketing function to help manage and control the organization's corporate identity and the employer brand. The management of an organization's image has traditionally been an important focus of interest for the marketing and public relations (PR) functions. The interest has tended to focus on how an organization is presented to the market place and potential customers. The increasing centrality that employer and employee branding provides for the HR department in the various processes of communication within organizations is considered by some as a positive move, one which should arguably legitimize a greater strategic role for the HR function.

A further explanation for why HR is becoming more involved in branding is the influence of HRM, in particular the emphasis on developing HR practices that ensure employees are committed to the organization. It is argued that the greater the employee's organizational commitment and identification, the greater the fusion of self and organizational interests (Meyer and Allen 1997). Numerous business arguments are presented as to why commitment and identification should be fostered (Ashforth and Mael 1989; Meyer and Allen 1997). An individual who identifies with the organization is likely to accept the goals and values of the organization, he or she is likely to want to stay with the organization, to want to 'go the extra mile' on behalf of the organization and can help 'enhance the success of firms' by engaging in 'coordinated corporate action' (Rousseau 1998: 218).

Although employer branding exercises may well be seen as more external facing to potential recruits, a key aim with both employer and employee branding is to encourage current employees to identify with the organization. The company benefits from having a strong employer brand due to increased retention of employees who enjoy 'living the brand' (Martin and Beaumont 2003) and also due to increased levels of organizational commitment when employees identify with the values that make up the organization's brand (Ind 2003). Importantly, however, the more pervasive and identifiable the values on the employer side then the greater the likelihood that the employee will identify with these values (Ashforth and Mael, 1996). An organization's values are considered important in fostering a positive corporate image and reputation. Elsbach and Glynn (1996) explicitly argue that the strategic reputation of the organization has an influence on the individual's sense of identification. Indeed they argue that the individual's organizational identification 'is embedded within their firm's strategic reputation and fostered by its reputation-building tactics'. A strong employer brand therefore fosters a positive image, identity or reputation and encourages employees to identify with the organization.

Finally, linked to the idea that employer and employee branding is in part an extension of arguments for organizational commitment and arguments for the need to consider the reputation of companies in recruitment, is the increasing interest in the management of identity at work (Alvesson and Wilmot 2002), both in terms of the management of the identity of the organization and that of employees. Ashforth and Mael (1996) discuss the importance of having an organization that has a strong, recognizable and distinctive identity. Bakan (2004: 26) suggests that branding enables corporations to humanize their image, creating a unique personality for themselves. For example, British Petroleum (BP) uses the colour green and words such as 'progressive, performance, green, innovative' to demonstrate that environmental and social responsibility is a key brand driver for BP.

Albert and Whetten (1985: 23) define organizational identity as 'the central, distinctive and enduring character of an organization' and the values of an organization are seen as a central part of this 'character'. Ashforth and Mael (1996) link this with the notion of organizational identification. The argument is presented that those organizations that have a strong identity and strong recognizable values, are likely to foster change in the individual's identity. Where an organization has clear defined values and a strong identity, the individual is more likely to be able to link aspects of their own self – such as values and goals – with those of the organization. Organizational identity 'motivates members by imparting value' (Ashforth and Mael 1996). Consequently there is a series of positive linkages between an employer brand, a strong organizational identity and employees that link some aspect of their identity to the organization.

Branding: Definitions and Human Resource Practices

As mentioned, branding has moved into the field of HR from the discipline of marketing. In principle, brands can be seen as a set of symbols which 'represent a variety of ideas and attributes' the net result of which 'is the public image, character or personality' of an organization (Hollensen 2003: 470). As such, branding activities involve constructing particular attributes (e.g. the values of an organization) that are considered to represent the image that a company wishes to communicate to potential employees, current staff and the public. Both employer and employee branding have this in common and as such they are often carried out together; they can, however, be viewed as two distinct activities.

Employer and employee branding

Employer branding (sometimes referred to as employment branding) is an activity that is often carried out by organizations in order to appear attractive to current and potential employees as a place to work. The idea of employment branding, defined by Martin and Beaumont (2003: 15) as managing a 'company's image as seen through the eyes of its associates and potential hires', emphasizes ensuring that the organization is seen as an attractive employer for both recruitment and retention purposes. Ambler and Barrow (1996: 187) define the employer brand as 'the package of financial, economic and psychological benefits provided by employment and identified with the employing company'. Employer branding involves attempting to influence how both potential and current employees perceive the organization by demonstrating why the company can be considered to be an 'employer of choice'. In doing this, the corporate brand of the organization is used to frame the employer brand, including its values, what it stands for and its mission. Importantly, the organization needs to ensure that the image presented accurately reflects its culture and working practices so as not to create unrealistic expectations with current and potential employees.

In contrast, employee branding, often referred to as internal branding, can be seen as an extension of the management of corporate culture with a particular branding slant. Harquail (2005: 4) suggests: 'Internal branding advocates a system of socialisation and communication practices intended to deliver on a brand's promise'. Through the management of an organization's values, espoused goals and mission, the culture of the organization and its branded image is being engineered and communicated internally. Importantly with employee branding, the norms, values and goals of the organization are made explicit, and are presented as an ideal that all staff should identify with to guide their work behaviour. Miles and Margold (2004: 68) define employee branding as 'the process by which employees internalize the desired brand image and are motivated to project the image to customers and other organizational constituents'. Ultimately, employee branding attempts to achieve consistency and a degree of coordination in employee actions. Free (1999) argues that managing employee brands can be seen as a 'control strategy' used to ensure that employees act in accordance with organizational requirements; as employees internalize the values and goals of the organization. Such arguments are very familiar as they are the type of arguments that have been presented by authors discussing the management of culture. The aim of cultural management programmes is to 'achieve employee commitment to those values which senior management considers conducive to improved organizational performance' (Legge 1994: 414).

Employee and internal branding attempts to develop employees, to mould them to become walking talking brand agents. Principally it involves an employer managing staff attitudes to influence how they interact with other staff and customers. With employee branding, the employee is part of the brand, they are exemplars of the brand, they have been branded.

Employee and employer branding are distinct activities due to the difference in what has been branded. With employer branding the organization is the entity being branded and prospective employees are the targeted recipients of the branding exercise. With employee branding, however, the employee is the entity that has been branded and customers are the recipients of the branding via their interactions with the workforce.

The terminology used – employee and employer branding – can be confusing because employer and employee branding activities are often complementary. Employee branding is targeted at the existing workforce, but employer branding by highlighting that the firm is an employer of choice, reinforces the employee branding message to the existing workforce. Nonetheless, it is important to note that the two activities have a different emphasis (Table 10.1).

Table 10.1 Features of employer and employee branding

	Employer branding	Employee branding
Direction of branding activities	External and internal	Internal
Branded entity	The organization	The employee
Target of branding	Current and potential employees	Customers who interact with branded employees
Roots	Personnel/HR management Marketing literature	The management of culture literature Organizational socialization literature Marketing literature
HR activities	Recruitment and selection Advertising External and internal communication Benchmarking	Induction Training and development Performance management Competency-based HR systems
Aims	To ensure the company attracts new recruits of quality and retains existing employees	Internal communications To ensure employees act 'On-brand' and share the values of the organization's brand
Intended outcomes	Winning the war for talent High quality, motivated and high performing work force Having the competitive edge	Increased employee commitment and identification Increased customer satisfaction and loyalty/identification

What does branding entail?

It is important to indicate what branding activities might involve from an HR perspective. When reviewing the branding literature, the practices that an HR department could be involved in have only recently been discussed. How does an HR function translate these branding ideas into policy and practice? There is an emerging prescriptive literature that considers these issues. Much of what is involved is related to image presentation and communication activities. Both with employer branding and employee branding an integral activity will be to establish an image of the organization and communicate this in a number of different ways to either current or potential employees.

With employer branding the key activity is demonstrating why the company should be considered an employer of choice. Actually doing this may involve a number of different steps and activities. The first step will be to clarify the employer brand. Because the branding activity needs to be linked to the corporate brand, if one exists, then the attributes of the corporate brand will need to be taken into account. If the organization does not have an existing corporate brand then the HR department will need to develop a brand from scratch that will involve identifying recognizable core values that the staff will identify with and recognize. As well as the values of the company, the HR department will have to determine what is good about working at the organization.

Identifying organizational values and what is attractive about the organization often involves surveying staff to clarify the advantages and benefits of working for that particular firm. Focus groups are frequently used at this stage to get staff to talk about the organization, in particular what attributes, characteristics and values they see as being associated with the organization. As well as consulting existing staff, it will also involve rigorous HR benchmarking to identify how the organization is different from competitors in the labour market and to establish what it offers over and above rival employers. Employer branding may also go beyond this to include introducing new benefits or terms and conditions that make it stand out from other employers. Importantly, employer branding does not just involve obtaining a static picture of the current 'package of financial, economic and psychological benefits', employer branding initiatives often involve an active construction or adjustment of the benefits provided by employment to make the organization look more attractive than its competitors in the labour market.

The organization will need to define what it stands for in terms of its values and vision and then communicate this systematically. Employer branding activities will usually include attempts to market externally and internally. Once the image or employer profile has been established, the organization will then consistently use this in its communication to both current employees and in its advertising or recruitment material. The apparent increase or interest in organizations demonstrating to current and potential employees that they are an employer of choice is reflected in the regularly published lists of 'The 100 best companies to work for'. These are published each year in many countries (e.g. in the US by Levering and Moskowitz and *Fortune* Magazine, in the UK by *The Sunday Times*). Examples of companies in the UK that have been in the top 20 for more than one year include Microsoft, Honda UK and Richer Sounds. These annually compiled lists are increasingly becoming an important index that potential employees refer to when considering whether they want to work for a particular company.

As well as being central to employer branding, a key starting point for an employee branding programme involves deciding what values legitimately reflect the organization or rather what values those in the organization should strive for. This can be a bottom-up process where the employees are asked (in focus groups, for example) or it can be driven more by the top of the organization and reflect an imposition of values on employees in order to try and encourage employees to act consistently 'on brand'. Subsequent to this, the brand of the organization is communicated consistently to employees. This process involves the communication of organizational values, a recognizable logo and more indirectly images and characteristics that reflect the characteristics of the brand. Companies such as easyJet, for example, present pictures of young people with big smiles on their faces looking very energetic. These pictures seek to give the impression of staff having fun. easyJet also show pictures of a clenched fist next to the word 'passionate'. These images conjure up impressions of the culture that characterize the company's identity (see IRS 2003).

Persistent and coherent internal communication is key in employee branding activities. Southwest Airlines, the much admired US low-cost airline, has been described as at the 'forefront of the employee branding revolution' (McDonald 2001: 57). A sophisticated programme of internal communication was introduced linked to the corporate brand notion of 'freedom'. Providing freedom to customers was a key part of the firm's corporate brand (advertised externally) and the company extended this and directed communication efforts internally with the tagline 'At Southwest freedom begins with me'. Employees were expected to take on board these principles to ensure that customers experienced the brand when interacting with staff. The firm categorized the 'employment experience' into eight freedoms: freedom to learn and grow; freedom to create financial security; freedom to make a positive difference; freedom to create and innovate; freedom to stay connected; freedom to pursue good health; freedom to travel; freedom to work hard and have fun. Southwest's 'people department' presented these freedoms to employees with a number of different media including intranet, posters and booklets. The strength of this spirit is exemplified, according to the former vice president for people, by the Southwest reservations agent who, on his own initiative, met an elderly passenger off a Southwest flight at Houston, an unfamiliar city to this passenger, and drove her to the hospital in Houston where she was due to undergo treatment for cancer (Sartain 2003: 3).

A central part of an internal branding exercise involves socialization practices where new recruits are presented with the internal value system of the organization. The socialization of new recruits starts at the beginning of the recruitment process where organizational values and norms are presented via a branded job advertisement, branded application materials (such as graduate application packs), and selection activities. Subsequently induction courses and activities are carefully designed to ensure that a consistent message is presented to employees about what the organization represents and what is expected of the employee.

Harquail (2005) suggests three main practices that are important ways to foster an employee brand. First, the most common activity is branding training where 'all employees are taught the basics of branding and market principles', where they are 'instructed on the attributes to be associated with their [the organization's] brand'. Furthermore, employees are trained in what the organization's brand stands for and how this is distinct from the brands of competitors. Another main activity involved in internal branding is a variety of communication practices. For example, 'internal corporate press and new product launches are designed not simply to inform or educate employees but also to persuade them and influence their behaviour' (p. 7). Importantly the marketing and PR functions direct their efforts internally towards employees to 'encourage on-brand behaviour'.

Thirdly, more indirectly, 'employees are branded by organizational décor that reflects the brand, such as brand consonant aesthetic schemes' (e.g. open plan spaces and décor in line with brand colours) and sophisticated employee initiatives that involve the distribution of branded 'artefacts' such as promotional materials and decorative accessories (the use of which at Domino's Pizzas is discussed by Ulrich and Smallwood 2003). Examples of such materials and accessories include corporate pens, branded stress balls, paperweights and mugs.

easyJet is an organization associated with both employee and employer branding. As part of the employee branding exercise at easyJet (whose logo is mainly of the colour orange) an 'Orange wheel' was designed and presented to current employees. They displayed a large diagram of the wheel on the wall of the company. Characteristics and values identified were presented such as 'open', 'listening loudly', 'passionate', 'up for it' and 'going the extra mile'. The wheel was a carefully designed mix of subliminal and explicit messages about the organization's character and values, which is seen as helping clarify the organization's identity for employees. Documenting and promoting the organization's values are important components of the employee socialization process. Employees 'are exposed to the values and the orange wheel from their first day in the induction process' (IRS 2003: 48).

More comprehensive internal branding activities involve the management of employee appearance. A straightforward example of this is employees wearing a uniform emblazoned with the company brand or logo. In the retail sector, Harquail (2005) highlights Gap and Abercrombie and Fitch as organizations that ensure employees wear the clothes sold by their company. Whether wearing a company uniform or (in the case of a clothing retailer) wearing clothes that are sold to customers: 'wearing the brand is supposed to make the brand's values and message salient for employees' (p. 9).

A key HR policy that is used to transmit organizational values to employees are competency frameworks. Competency frameworks are often used to help 'translate organizational expectations into employee action' (IRS 2003) and are likely to be used with both employer and employee branding activities. Indeed, competencies are a key tool that organizations use to instil consistency of behaviour and attitude across the organization, particularly the use of 'core competencies' that employees are judged against. Competency frameworks are often used during the recruitment process to select new hires. More specifically, competency-based interviews are often used to ensure that the right person with the right skills and attributes is selected. Importantly with regard to internal branding, they can be used to help select employees that may well have the appropriate person–organization fit. Competency frameworks, however, are also used in conjunction with a much wider range of HR policies and practices.

An important step in the process of internal branding is to transfer organizational values into some form of action framework. This can be achieved through the application of key values to competency frameworks (IRS 2003). An example of this is the Reuters 'FAST' forward internal branding campaign where 'F is for fast', 'A is accountable', 'S is for service' and 'T is for teamwork'. Each of these represents a key value of the organization that is then translated into a competency framework used to benchmark potential employees to determine whether they are likely to fit the brand. Additional to this, the competency framework is used in other aspects of HR practice. Reuters used the competencies and the values identified in the brand to shape and determine job descriptions and 'the language of the job description aligns itself with the four principles of the FAST initiative' (IRS 2003).

Although not often discussed in conjunction with branding activities, organizational socialization is central to the practices of employer and employee branding. As noted earlier, brand focused induction and training activities are a key part of internal branding. One of the explicit aims and objectives of induction programmes (also known as orientation programmes) is to help individuals adjust to the organization's norms. Organizational socialization can be seen as a process by which an individual employee takes on board the attitudes, behaviour and knowledge needed to participate as an employee (Van Maanen and Schein 1979). Although, a combination of self-selection and careful recruitment and selection practices might mean that when the employee arrives at the organization there is likely to be some value fit, this match will never be perfect. According to Dose (1997: 234) because there will be natural variation between the organizational values and those of new recruits: 'some amount of socialisation is in order', or using alternative terminology, some internal branding is 'in order'.

In summary, employer and employee branding activities involve a number of different HR practices that facilitate the development of organizational and employee values; practices include recruitment, selection, training, performance management and development activities. Carefully designed selection procedures not only help to ensure that a person taken on for a job has the requisite skills but that they also have the desirable psycho-social characteristics for the company; this will inevitably involve a judgment of their values and whether they fit the organization (see Chapter 5). Some organizations are explicit about this, the former vice president of people at Southwest Airlines, Sartain (2003), indicates that the company hires for attitude and fit (focusing on attributes such as energy, passion, curiosity and compassion). Subsequent to recruitment the organization encourages employees to take on board the values associated with Southwest's brand. Orientation and induction programmes are an important vehicle through which an organization helps to encourage the employee develop or acquire the values of the organization.

Remuneration systems also play a role in shaping employee values. Kessler (Chapter 12) notes the so-called 'new pay' agenda, and specifically the use of competency-based pay, which increasingly aims to reward aspects of the person and their behavioural 'traits'. Kantor (2003: 167), who discusses the growth of interest in 'total reward' strategies, makes a similar point: 'To be effective, a reward system must impact perceptions and behaviour in ways that produces desired organizational behaviours. Such arguments can be found regarding the other HR practices such as training and development, performance management practices and HR involvement in the management of culture and commitment (Legge 1994). A comprehensive employer and employee branding programme is likely to influence almost all aspects of HR activities.

Consequences of Branding

Employee value change?

An important question to ask is whether the attempted socialization fundamental to internal branding activities has a substantive effect on employee values. When engaging in employee or employer branding activities, are the intended outcomes achieved? There is little conclusive evidence because it is difficult to find out whether an organization has effectively managed the beliefs and values of its employees, but some research has looked at whether explicit socialization practices have an impact on employee values. In a study of socialization practices used at a large educational institution, Klein and Weaver (2000) found a link between attendance at an induction session/orientation training programme and the extent to which employees shared the organization's values and were affectively committed. Ashforth and Saks (1996) investigated factors influencing how recognizable and meaningful an organization's identity was to new graduates. Students from an undergraduate business programme were tracked down 4 and 10 months after they entered new jobs and the importance of deliberate institutionalized socialization practices was confirmed. They found that 'the more institutionalized the socialization tactics, the more coherent sense will be conveyed of what the organization purportedly represents' (p. 155). Additionally, the more that organizations were found to have practices in place designed to socialize employees then the more employees were found to identify with the organization after a period of orientation.

The degree to which an organization can influence employee values and the extent to which it will be able to brand employees is dependent upon how strongly employees adhere to their existing values as well as how similar these values are with those that the organization is trying to encourage. It is likely that if the individual has an existing set of work-oriented values that they believe in and the organization tries to encourage the acquisition of a quite different set of values, then this is likely to meet with some resistance. Importantly, from an individual perspective, the notion of a fit between the organizational and employee values is seen as a positive state in terms of employee well-being and is generally seen as important in a raft of work-based attitudes (O'Reilly et al. 1991). However, if there is a lack of fit, an organization may actually only be able to brand employees if they do not hold their values dear.

Kraimer's (1997) model (Figure 10.1) considers the congruence or fit between organizational and employee values and how this interacts with the strength of individual beliefs to potentially lead to a number of different employer and employee outcomes. As their typology suggests, certain factors intervene in determining what outcomes an employee and employer branding initiative is likely to have. Where the individual holds certain work oriented values dearly and these fit with the organization that they work for then employee branding is likely to lead to a strong sense of organizational identification and a greater likelihood that the employee will be willing to 'go the extra mile' for the organization. If there is a lack of fit between the employer and employee values but the employee does not have a degree of belief strength in their existing values then one would therefore expect a degree of conversion. However, it would be reasonable to expect with employee branding activities that if the values that the organization tries to encourage are too different from those that the employees hold dearly, then the lack of congruence could well lead to some serious negative effects, and ultimately some employees could leave. The Kraimer model is a useful framework to examine the likelihood of success in attempting to alter employee values.

		Weak	Strong
Work Value Congruence	**High**	Weak Effect on Attitudes Compliance Based Commitment	High Organizational Identification High OCB-Organization
	Low	Individuals Values Change to Increase Work Value Congruence	Negative External Corporate Image; Low Organizational Identification; Involvement in Non-Work Activities; High Turnover; Complaint Behaviours

Individual's Belief Strength in his/her Work Values

Figure 10.1 Individual belief strength × work value congruence: effect on outcomes

Challenges for the HR function

Despite the increased interest in employee and employer branding, it does not represent an entirely new direction for HR because it builds on the management of culture. Managing the values, beliefs and attitudes of employees or more broadly an organization's culture, is an activity HR managers, consultants and academics have discussed for many years (Legge 1994). Cultural management invariably involves addressing employee values. Over recent years the HR function has spent more time managing organizational culture, which according to Guest and King (2004: 405): has 'offered a new purpose for personnel departments. They could manage culture through a range of activities that were built on the traditions of OD.' The increased emphasis in HRM on the management of high employee commitment has meant that the HR department has become more involved in considerations relating to the management of organizational culture and the management of employee values and attitudes.

Employee branding therefore has its origins in the management of corporate culture. It is tempting to view branding as a fad that does not differ very greatly from attempts to manage employee values and attributes in which HR has been involved for some time. However, despite some similarities between the management of culture and employee branding, the explicit involvement of the HR department in activities traditionally associated with the marketing function and conversely the involvement of the marketing function in activities traditionally associated with the HR function, does indicate that employee branding represents a different challenge for the HR function.

In contrast to prescriptive accounts that suggest the involvement of the HR function in branding will lead to greater strategic involvement, there is a danger that HR branding has unintended consequences that undermine the HR function rather than bolster its influence. Employee (and internal) branding could well increase the idea of HR activities being rhetoric, thus undermining the function's legitimacy. Branding may well involve the 'new' HR function in the strategic reputation of the organization to a greater degree and this could lever the function from a more traditional position within the organization, right into the decision-making core of the company. In attempting to become more strategic, this 'new' HR department will look like it has 'learnt the rules of the game' (Legge 1978; Guest and King 2004). However, it would be reasonable to question whether or not an increase in strategic involvement through managing the organization's brand might come at a cost. These more strategic marketing activities will be pushing HR departments further away from a more 'traditional' welfare role and with this there is a danger that the HR function's involvement in the management of corporate image as well as the rhetorical devices and methods used to manage this, will actually undermine the HR department's legitimacy further (at least with employees).

Yet another challenge that could be directed at HR's involvement in employer and employee branding is that marketing and branding authors seem to view employees as a means to an end, as a device or vehicle to achieve further customer loyalty, that can be moulded to help increase customer satisfaction, loyalty and subsequently profits. The marketing and branding literature does not seem to even consider the idea that organizations might be doing something unethical when attempting employee branding. No consideration seems to be given to what this actually might mean to the individual who is being branded or that employees might actually resist being branded. When suggesting that employees should be 'on-brand', 'brand agents' or that they should have 'brand engagement' there is a danger that the HR function will appear to have scant regard for human dignity.

In a way, the expectations that employee values will in some way be changed or the values of the organization will be assimilated into the value system of the employee in order that the work force presents a consistent corporate-tied pattern of attitudes and behaviour to the customer is related to Hochschild's (1983) discussion of emotional labour. This refers to situations in which the employee's heart is managed and human feelings are commercialized or used to present a particular service image to customers, sometimes at a personal cost to the employee. Hochschild refers to this as the transmutation of an emotional system, where feelings 'fall under the sway of large organizations, social engineering and the profit motive' (p. 19). The internal branding exercise can well be considered to be a transmutation of the employee's value system. Additionally, emotional labour authors discuss the idea that when an employee smiles at a customer, it is not them smiling but the organization smiling (Bolton and Boyd 2003). These types of discussions are similar to some of the internal branding literature arguments but instead of focusing on employer encouragement of employee emotional labour, the branding literature is focusing on employer encouragement of value labour. With the emotional labour literature, discussions can be found about the commodification of employee feeling; with the internal branding literature, discussions can be found which seem to represent the commodification of employee values and attitudes. Employee values can now be seen as a commodity which the organization can utilize for the purposes of unlocking required commitment and high performance (Bunting 2004) and to ensure greater customer satisfaction and loyalty.

Doherty and Tyson (2000: 110) point out that, 'Employees are expected by their employers to act towards their customer from a set of activities and values which go beyond the range of conscious decisions and control.' Indeed it could be suggested that this emphasis on the management of organizational value systems as a means to change and manage the identity of employees could, in itself, be seen as a valueless or perhaps an unethical exercise where organizations deem it necessary to appropriate employees' private selves.

When branding writers such as Free (1999) argue that 'all staff must understand and commit personally to the brand values', it is difficult to see that there can be a happy marriage between marketing and branding activities and an ethical HR function. In calling for more management concern for the well-being of employees and more of an ethical positioning of the HR function, Doherty and Tyson (2000: 110) note that 'the responsibility for creating and sustaining the psychological state of the employee is now de facto a part of HRM' and that such a focus does not come hand in hand with an ethical approach to HR. This argument seems more than appropriate when taking into account the involvement of HR departments in employee branding exercises. Discussions around the role of HR in managing an organization's reputation and the legitimacy of the HR function to be managing, designing and presenting a value system which is to be imposed on employees, leads naturally to questioning HR's ethical status or role. Winstanley and Woodall (2000) suggest that the recent interest in the management of employee commitment and organizational culture 'raises ethical issues' and specifically that 'a desire to capture the hearts and minds in the service of corporate goals' (p. 8) has led to an increased concern with ethics in HR. They argue that such an interest leads to questions relating to what is the legitimate 'scope of employer duty of care'.

It is reasonable to ask where the boundaries lie of appropriate interference by the HR function and its representatives in what can be considered to be a personal and private aspect of employee selves. Is the management of organizational and more importantly employee value systems a step into the realm of manipulation potentially threatening employees' right to privacy and dignity? Such a point is raised by Bunting (2004: 92) who suggests that companies such as Microsoft and Asda that attempt to ensure that the corporate brand is taken on board by employees amounts to 'an unprecedented invasiveness as management practices reach after parts of the employee's personality which have hitherto been considered private'. Similar ethical questions were raised over 20 years ago in connection with the OD movement. French and Bell (1983), for example, discussed the position of OD programmes that in effect attempt to change employee attitudes or beliefs and that this might be seen as manipulative, leaving little room for human dignity.

Given the arguments presented (e.g. by the CIPD) for the branding and corporate social responsibility movement to be combined, it would be valid to question whether employee or internal branding is a socially responsible activity. Is an explicit attempt to 'engage individuals more fully' in the organization's brand while 'appropriating more of their personal selves' (Harquail 2005) socially responsible? If the HR function becomes involved in trying to manage employee values, is it the case that the function is engaging in a socially irresponsible activity? An integral part of CSR initiatives is stakeholder management (Freeman 1984). This involves a move from considering the interests of shareholders as paramount and something that should guide organizational action to the development of an awareness that there are many groups that have a 'stake' in the organization and its actions. Other groups of people will be affected by the actions, processes and success (or failure) of an organization beyond that of the shareholder group. In defining who might be considered to be stakeholders, Legge (1997: 21) suggests that 'organizations have stakeholders, that is, groups of individuals who potentially benefit from, or are harmed by, an organization's actions'. Employees can definitely be considered to be a key stakeholder in any organization.

Although some employee branding exercises may involve employees in the process of determining the organization's values, the decision to carry out employee branding will invariably be made by managers at the top of the organization and the employees will be seen as an internal target of these marketing and PR activities. It could be argued that the very nature of employee branding emasculates employees, it highlights the idea that they are a resource to be moulded and it is very unlikely that they would be treated as legitimate stakeholders. With this in mind, if viewing internal branding from a CSR lens, employee branding does not seem particularly socially responsible. In a joint publication between the CIPD and Business in the Community (2003), *Responsibility: Driving Innovation, Inspiring Employees*, an argument is presented that CSR and branding considerations are taking the management of people within organizations into a new paradigm – a paradigm where the image, or more specifically the employer brand, and the translation of corporate values to individuals becomes a central consideration of the HR department. Furthermore, recent CIPD reports (2002a and b) argue that CSR provides an opportunity for the HR department to engage in an employer branding exercise. Through various communication and HR initiatives, the employers construct or hone the image of the organization, its identity, its central recognizable values and characteristics, and (according to the CIPD) 'pitch' this to attract and retain employees. It could, however, be argued that such activities may, if anything, be ethically questionable.

Discussion: Branding and Ethical HR

The emphasis on values within organizations that employee branding brings and the move toward corporate social responsibility as a concern of HR can be seen as introducing an ethical element to people management, which until recently has not been a key focus of interest in the HR academic community (Winstanley and Woodall 2000). What the social responsibility movement does do is increase an ethical agenda in organizations that could give the HR function a greater degree of credibility, particularly as one of the potential roles of the function is to be an 'ethical ombudsman' (Winstanley and Woodall 2000). Recent work on the impact of socially responsible investment on HRM (Waring and Lewer 2004) suggests that where companies act in a socially responsible way, this will attract socially responsible investment (SRI), which will in turn put some pressure on organizations to act in a more ethical and responsible way. Importantly, Waring and Lewer argue that socially responsible companies that attract investment from SRI funds are under reputational pressure to ensure that they act ethically. The investment criteria of these SRI funds do in some way look at how organizations treat their staff. Waring and Lewer argue that the increasing emphasis of SRI and subsequently the interest in CSR will provide an 'ethical space' for the promotion of ethical people management. Importantly, SRI and CSR legitimize a discourse of ethics in HR in a language that financial directors will understand; investment in their company.

Importantly, one can legitimately question whether the emphasis of the management of employees ' "insides" – the hopes, fears and aspirations – of workers rather than their behaviours directly' (Deetz 1995: 87) is an ethical exercise. Is this HR going beyond a reasonable scope of employee management activities and is such an exercise interfering with the individual's right to privacy, dignity and self-esteem? It could be argued that employer branding, rather than bolstering an organization's socially responsible reputation, may actually conflict with the intended ethical aims of the CSR movement.

As a final point of discussion, while presenting the case for due consideration of internal social responsibility of employers, Flanders (1970) raised the problem that where an organization might attempt to act ethically or to undertake moral 'conversion' of employees, it may run the risk of being overly paternalistic. Indeed, if an organization does ordain a particular framework of ethical behaviour and attempts to lay down a model of values and beliefs that employees should accord with, this could itself be ethically problematic as it would still be using its power to impose values on people. To a degree, both CSR and related branding programmes will do this. The organization, or agents of it, will have decided upon a set of values that potentially improve its reputation either for ethical or profit reasons and will be attempting to influence (or 'cajole' as Flanders 1970 puts it) employees to encourage an integration of beliefs and attitudes ensuring value 'synergy' or congruence within the organization. Potentially, a moral conundrum exists. Because the imbalance of power in organizations favours employers, if a company tries to become ethical, this may involve attempting to change employee values and because one could argue that the employee has a right to hold their values as sacred, such an activity could indeed be unethical.

A possible counter to the argument that employee branding is unethical is that if employees volitionally accept the organization's attempt to influence the more private aspects of their selves, then employee branding is perfectly ethical (as some previously argued in relation to the OD movement). Of course, the stronger an organization's culture and the stronger its employer, internal or employee branding, the more difficult it will be for an employee to refuse to accept the values of the organization and remain in its employment. The employee does of course have a degree of choice in whether they wish to remain working for the organization, as they could always leave. In a sense this can be considered to be the ultimate defence of such initiatives; what this does assume, however, is that employees are in the fortunate position to have enough alternative employment options to freely move around organizations until they find one that has a brand that fits with their own values.

To a degree one could legitimately suggest that this emerging change in emphasis, where organizations and HR functions are getting involved in the management of the full employment experience, is actually positive for employees. Some might argue that people have a need to feel that they belong or fit in with others, as such sharing the value systems of colleagues and the organization is likely to provide a deep sense of well-being for employees. In organizations with genuinely positive concern for the well-being of employees, where employer and employee branding is carried out carefully in a reflective manner, the benefits may indeed lead to a positive employment experience for many. These are likely to be the minority of organizations, however. Assuming that employee branding does become more embedded in organizational practice, this will have implications for the majority of workers who find themselves subject to employee branding initiatives. The more such activities become the norm in organizations, the more common practice it will be for organizations to manage employee identities and values. It may result in a situation where managing the more personal aspects of employee selves is such a familiar part of what the human resource function does that the ethics of such activities are rarely questioned.

REFERENCES AND FURTHER READING

Albert, S. and Whetten, D. 1985: Organizational identity, in L.L. Cummings and B.M. Staw (eds.), *Research in Organizational Behavior, Vol. 7*, Greenwich, CT: JAI Press, 263–95.

Alvesson, M. and Wilmot, H. 2002: Identity regulation as organizational control: Producing the appropriate individual, *Journal of Management Studies*, **39**, 619–44.

Ambler, T. and Barrow, S. 1996: The employer brand, *The Journal of Brand Management*, **4**, 185–206.

Ashforth, B.E. and Mael, F.A. 1989: Social identity theory and the organization, *Academy of Management Review*, **14**, 20–39.

Ashforth, B.E. and Mael, F.A. 1996: Organizational identity and strategy as a context for the individual, in J.A.C. Baum and J.E. Dutton (eds.), *Advances in Strategic Management*, **13**, Greenwich, CT: JAI Press, 19–64,.

Ashforth, B. and Saks, A.M. 1996: Socialisation tactics: Longitudinal effects on newcomer adjustment, *Academy of Management Journal*, **39**, 149–78.

Bakan, J. 2004: *The Corporation: The Pathological Pursuit of Profit and Power*, London: Constable and Robinson.

Bolton, S.C. and Boyd, C. 2003: Trolley dolly or skilled emotion manager: Moving on from Hochschild's managed heart, *Work, Employment and Society*, **17**, 289–308.

Bunting, M. 2004: *Willing Slaves: How the Overwork Culture Is Ruling our Lives*, London: Harper Collins.

Business in the Community 2003: *Responsibility: Driving Innovation, Inspiring Employees*, FastForward Research, in association with the CIPD and Bupa; available on http://www.bitc.org.uk/resources/publications/ffwd03.html

Caldwell, R. 2003: The changing roles of personnel managers: Old ambiguities, new uncertainties, *Journal of Management Studies*, **40**, 983–1004.

CIPD Perspectives 2002: *Corporate Social Responsibility*, Autumn, London: CIPD.

CIPD Guide 2002: *Corporate Social Responsibility and HR's Role*, London: CIPD.

Deetz, S. 1995: *Transforming Communication, Transforming Business: Building Responsive and Responsible Workplaces*, New Jersey: Hampton Press Inc.

Dell, D. and Ainspan, N. 2001: *Engaging Employees through your Brand*, The Conference Board, report no. 1288, April; available at http://www.conference-board.org/publications/describe.cfm?id=461.

Doherty, N. and Tyson, S. 2000: HRM and employee well-being: Raising the ethical stakes, in D. Winstanley and J. Woodall (eds.), *Ethical Issues in Contemporary Human Resource Management*, Basingstoke: Macmillan.

Dose, J.J. 1997: Work values: An integrative framework and illustrative application to organizational socialization, *Journal of Occupational and Organizational Psychology*, **70**, 219–40.

Elsbach, K.D. and Glyn, M.A. 1996: Believing your own 'PR': Embedding identification in strategic reputation, *Advances in Strategic Management*, **13**, 65–90.

Evan, W.M. and Freeman, R.E. 1993: A stakeholder theory of the modern corporation: Kantian capitalism, in T. Beauchamp and N. Bowie (eds.), *Ethical Theory and Business*, Englewood Cliffs, NJ: Prentice Hall, 75–84.

Flanders, A. 1970: *Management and Unions: The Theory and Reform of Industrial Relations*, London: Faber.

Free, C. 1999: The internal brand, *The Journal of Brand Management*, **6**, 231–6.

Freeman, R.E. 1984: *Strategic Management: A Stakeholder Approach*, Boston: Pitman.

French, W.L. and Bell, C.H. 1983: *Organization Development: Behavioral Science Interventions for Organization Improvement*, New Delhi: Prentice-Hall, Inc.

Gobe, M. 2001: *Emotional Branding: The New Paradigm for Connecting Brands to People*, New York: Alworth Press.

Guest, D. and King, Z. 2004: Power, innovation and problem solving: The personnel manager's three steps to heaven? *Journal of Management Studies*, **41**, 367–519.

Harquail, C.V. 2005: Employees as animate artifacts: Employee branding by 'wearing the brand', in A. Rafaeli and M. Pratt (eds.), *Artifacts and Organizations*, New Jersey: Lawrence Erlbaum.

Hochschild, A.R. 1983: *The Managed Heart: Commercialization of Human Feeling*, Berkeley: University of California Press.

Hollensen, S. 2003: *Marketing Management: A Relationship Approach*. Harlow: Prentice Hall.

Ind, N. 2003: Inside out: How employees build value, *Brand Management*, **10**, 393–402.

IRS (Industrial Relations Service) 2003: Employer branding: Fad or fact? *IRS Employment Review*, **778**, 42–7.

Kantor, R. 2003: Managing global total reward, in M. Effron, R. Gandossy and M. Goldsmith (eds.), *Human Resources in the 21st Century*, New York: John Wiley and Sons, Inc.

Kessler, I. 2000: Remuneration systems, in S. Bach and K. Sisson (eds.), *Personnel Management: A Comprehensive Guide to Theory and Practice* (3rd edn), Oxford: Blackwell.

Klein, H. and Weaver, N. 2000: The effectiveness of an organizational-level orientation training program in the socialization of new hires, *Personnel Psychology*, **53**, 47–66.

Kraimer, M.L. 1997: Organizational goals and values: A socialisation model, *Human Resource Management Review*, **7**, 425–47.

Legge, K. 1978: *Power, Innovation and Problem Solving in Personnel Management*, London: McGraw-Hill.

Legge, K. 1994: Managing culture: Fact or fiction?, in K. Sisson (ed.), *Personnel Management: A Comprehensive Guide to Theory and Practice in Britain*, Oxford: Blackwell.

Legge, K. 1997: The morality of HRM, in C. Mabey (ed.), *Experiencing Human Resource Management*, London: Sage.

Legge, K. 1998: Is HRM ethical? Can HRM be ethical?, in M. Parker (ed.), *Ethics and Organizations*, London: Sage.

Maio, E. 2003: Managing brand in the new stakeholder environment, *Journal of Business Ethics*, **44**, 235–46.

Martin, G. and Beaumont, P. 2003: *Branding and People Management*, CIPD Research Report.

McDonald, D. 2001: HR earning its place at the table, *World at Work Journal*, First Quarter.

Meyer, J.P. and Allen, N.J. 1997: *Commitment in the Workplace: Theory, Research and Application*, Thousand Oaks, CA: Sage.

Miles, S.J. and Margold, G. 2004: A conceptualisation of the employee branding process, *Journal of Relationship Marketing*, **3**(2/3), 65–87.

O'Reilly, C.A. III, Chatman, J. and Caldwell, D.F. 1991: People and organizational culture: A profile comparison approach to assessing person-organization fit, *Academy of Management Journal*, **34**, 487–516.

Rokeach, M. 1968: *Beliefs, Attitudes, and Values*, San Francisco: Jossey-Bass.

Rousseau, D.M. 1998: Why workers still identify with organizations, *Journal of Organizational Behaviour*, **19**, 217–33.

Sartain, L. 2003: Getting extraordinary results from ordinary people, in M. Effron, R. Gandossy and M. Goldsmith (eds.), *Human Resources in the 21st Century*, John Wiley and Sons, Inc.

Storey, J. 1992: *Developments in the Management of Human Resources*, Oxford: Blackwell.

Turban, D.B. and Greening, D.W. 1996: Corporate social performance and organizational attractiveness to prospective employees, *Academy of Management Journal*, **40**, 658–72.

Ulrich, D. 1997: *Human Resource Champions*, Boston: Harvard University Press.

Ulrich, D. and Smallwood, N. 2003: *Why the Bottom Line Isn't*, New York: John Wiley and Sons.

Van Maanen, J. and Schein, E.H. 1979: Toward a theory of organizational socialisation, in B.M. Staw (ed.), *Research in Organizational Behavior*, **1**, Greenwich, CT: JAI Press, 209–64.

Waring, P. and Lewer, J. 2004: The impact of socially responsible investment on human resource management: A conceptual framework, *Journal of Business Ethics*, **52**, 99–108.

Winstanley, D. and Woodall, J. 2000: The ethical dimensions of human resource management, *Human Resource Management Journal*, **10**, 5–20.

PART IV

Pay and Performance

CHAPTER ELEVEN

New Directions in Performance Management

Stephen Bach

In the last decade a dominant concern of human resource practitioners and academics has been to establish the relationship between human resource management and organizational performance. The evolution of performance appraisal reflects these wider trends in personnel practice. Performance appraisal was traditionally associated with a relatively straightforward process in which a line manager met annually to review the performance of their subordinates and filled in the requisite form with little happening until the process was repeated the following year. Performance appraisal has evolved substantially, becoming more integrated into systems of performance management with far-reaching consequences for both individuals and the organizations they work for.

Employer expectations about performance requirements have increased greatly and employees are required to meet specified objectives and to demonstrate required organizational behaviours and values in achieving their targets. In these circumstances performance appraisals become far more than just an annual ritual and are viewed as a key lever to enhance organizational performance. West et al. (2002), in their study of hospitals, suggested that effective performance appraisals by providing role clarity, identifying training needs, and making staff feel valued, led to improved patient care and contributed to reductions in patient mortality. There is also a harder edge to performance appraisal with high-profile companies such as General Electric, Microsoft and McKinsey's emphasizing that measuring performance and identifying top performers has to be accompanied by systematic measures to remove consistent under-performers, termed 'C players'. It is argued in the 'War for Talent' (Michaels et al. 2001) that it is necessary to remove the bottom 10 per cent of performers annually, because they create inertia and demotivate high performers. Various euphemisms such as 'top-grading', 'bouncing' and 'ranking and yanking' are used to describe this process (Smart 1999: 61–75; Ulrich and Smallwood 2003: 90; Bunting 2004: 97).

The increased prominence of performance appraisal has, however, been accompanied by greater awareness of its limitations. Recognition that performance appraisal has often fallen short of managerial expectations has led to an emphasis on linking individual performance appraisal to corporate objectives, ensuring 'there is a clear line of sight' between organizational and individual requirements. There has also been the growth of more varied forms of feedback and broader measures of performance. A stronger emphasis on employee development is reflected in the extent to which appraisees have increased responsibility for steering performance appraisal and employers are also placing more emphasis on values, using performance appraisal to highlight the behaviours expected of staff (Armstrong and Baron 2005: 10). Alongside these developments, a more critical literature attributes the resurgent popularity of performance appraisal as part of the panoply of techniques used by employers to elicit commitment and at the same time to exercise detailed control over employee behaviour (Townley 1993; Newton and Findlay 1996).

This chapter starts by putting performance appraisal into the context of the growth in interest and coverage of systems of performance management. It proceeds to examine the forms and extent of performance appraisal and discuss the problems associated with it. It argues that the prescriptive literature concentrates on implementation problems which are viewed as remedial through proper training and communication. Radical critiques of performance appraisal, influenced by labour process and Foucauldian traditions, raise more fundamental questions about the purpose of performance appraisal, but are too one-dimensional in their assessment. The final part of the chapter examines recent attempts to overcome many of the problems of performance appraisal, focusing on the growth of 360-degree feedback. It considers also other recent trends, highlighting the impact of technology and cultural diversity on the evolution of performance management.

From Performance Appraisal to Performance Management

With the increased recognition of the problems that permeate many company appraisal schemes, there has been a shift of emphasis from performance appraisal to performance management. Reflecting the importance attached to integrating HR policies and business strategies, employers have focused on the role of performance appraisal within a broader organizational context in which appraisal is only one part, albeit the key component, of a more systematic process of performance management. The key impetus for this development has been the more competitive environment in which firms operate. This has placed a premium on firms' ability to measure and improve the performance of their staff. This pressure has not been confined to the private sector. The Labour government's emphasis on ensuring that public service employers meet a range of central government targets and demonstrate value for money has ensured a strong interest in performance management across the public sector with employees under pressure to meet a range of performance targets (see Bach 2004).

Restructuring within organizations, with an emphasis on decentralized decision making and greater responsibilities placed on line managers for staff management, has lent itself to the use of performance management systems seeking to align individual and corporate objectives. Evaluating individual performance remains the main focus of performance management systems, but it is also used to help make reward decisions especially in the private sector (IRS 2003a: 9). Moreover, many organizations have viewed the introduction of more formalized performance management as a means to facilitate cultural change and establish and evaluate staff against a set of organizational core competencies (IRS 2001).

Advocates of performance management claim that its value resides in the cycle of integrated activities, which ensure that a systematic link is established between the contribution of each employee and the overall performance of the organization. This strategic approach contrasts with the free-standing nature of performance appraisal, in which the outcomes of each individual appraisal are rarely linked to overall corporate objectives. Line managers, rather than HR specialists, have the dominant role in the design and management of the performance management process and a premium is placed on ensuring effective communication and feedback is given to employees (IRS 2003b). Armstrong and Baron (2005: 17) suggest the main value of performance management is to:

- Communicate a shared vision of the purpose and values of the organization;
- Define expectations of what must be delivered and how it should be delivered;
- Ensure that people are aware of what constitutes high performance and how they need to achieve it;
- Enhance motivation, engagement and commitment by providing a means of recognizing endeavour and achievement through feedback;
- Enable people to monitor their own performance and encourage dialogue about what needs to be done to improve performance.

The most detailed UK surveys of performance management arrangements have been undertaken for the Chartered Institute of Personnel and Development (CIPD) in 1998 and 2004 based on a sample of 562 (1998) and 506 (2004) personnel practitioner respondents (Armstrong and Baron 1998; 2005). Between 1998 and 2004 the number of organizations with a formal process of performance management increased from 69 per cent to 87 per cent, although comparison between the surveys needs to be treated with caution as the profile of respondents differed (Armstrong and Baron 1998; 2005). As important as its increased coverage was its changing character. During the 1990s there was a shift from an almost exclusive emphasis on reward driven systems, based on individual performance related pay and quantifiable objectives, towards more rounded systems of performance management with a stronger developmental focus. This was borne out by the 1998 survey results which showed that, although objective setting and annual appraisal remained the

Table 11.1 Features of performance management

Feature	Percentage
Objective setting and review	85
Annual appraisal	83
Personal development plans (PDPs)	68
Self-appraisal	45
Performance-related pay (PRP)	43
Coaching/mentoring	39
Career management	32
Competence assessment	31
Twice-yearly appraisal	24
Subordinate (180-degree) feedback	20
Continuous assessment	17
Rolling appraisal	12
360-degree feedback	11
Peer appraisal	9
Balanced scorecard	5

Source: Armstrong and Baron (1998).

dominant features of performance management, the use of personal development plans was far more prevalent than performance-related pay (see Table 11.1). Since 1998 these trends have been reinforced as organizations focus on using performance management to identify development needs rather than to drive reward policy. Consequently performance-related pay was a feature of only 31 per cent of performance management sytems in 2004 compared to 43 per cent in 1998 (Armstrong and Baron 2005: 68).

A number of other trends can be discerned over the last decade. With less emphasis placed on reward-driven performance management, the requirement to generate precise ratings has diminished; in the 1998 CIPD survey the proportion of respondents who provided an overall rating for performance had fallen since 1991 from 64 to 54 per cent (Armstrong and Baron 1998: 107). The use of rating has continued to decline with a further slight fall to 49 per cent by 2004 (Armstrong and Baron 2005: 58). Some organizations discourage managers from providing individuals with an overall rating as it is viewed as demotivating (IDS 2003: 7).

Employers have also developed more wide-ranging frameworks to assess organizational performance that extends beyond a focus on traditional financial accounting measures. Popularized by Kaplan and Norton (1996, 2001) in their 'balanced scorecard' framework, they suggested that organizations needed to establish objective measures of performance that derived from four perspectives:

- *The financial perspective*: How do we appear to our shareholders?
- *The customer perspective*: How do we appear to our customers?

- *The internal/business perspective*: What business process must we excel at?
- *The innovation and learning perspective*: How do we continue to sustain our ability to learn and grow?

According to this model organizations develop a small number of key indicators in each quadrant that reflects key performance drivers and which enables employees' individual objectives to be aligned to corporate objectives. Many large organizations including the retailer Tesco and the oil company Shell use versions of the balanced score and similar thinking informs the local government system of Comprehensive Performance Assessment (IRS 2003c). While the 'innovation and learning perspective' has a strong people management component the balanced scorecard has been criticized for paying insufficient attention to a company's human resources (Maltz et al. 2003: 189). Nonetheless many organizations, for example, the pharmaceutical company AstraZeneca, incorporate a mandatory people management objective within an individual's annual objectives (IDS 2003: 3).

This broadening of measures of organizational performance is mirrored in the requirements expected of individual employees. There has been a modification to the exclusive focus on outputs and whether individual objectives have been met by incorporating consideration of inputs and how objectives are achieved. This development signals an increasing emphasis on a shift from job-related to person-related performance criteria. As job roles evolve constantly within organizations, the person rather than the job becomes the key focus of performance management systems. Employers are therefore placing more emphasis on measuring behaviours associated with so-called 'emotional intelligence' because of the assumption that managers who exhibit characteristics such as enthusiasm, honesty, empathy and self-assurance are more effective (see Fineman 2004). At SouthWest Airlines and Yahoo!, among others, the extent to which employees are passionate, curious, motivated and compassionate are monitored carefully (Sartain 2003: 7). This change in emphasis is reflected in the widespread adoption of competency-based frameworks in which employers are not only seeking to meet short-term objectives but also to deliver long-term culture change (IDS 2003).

Finally, there is a clear trend towards increased employee ownership of the performance management process with employees assigned greater responsibility for establishing their own performance goals and for obtaining feedback on their performance. Instead of employees' being passive recipients of their line manager's appraisal they are increasingly involved via some form of self-assessment, usually see the final appraisal form, and are given the opportunity to comment on the written report. In cases in which multi-source (360 degree) feedback is utilized, employees have an integral role in the selection of individuals that will provide this feedback. This development not only reduces some of the administrative workload for line managers, but it also reflects the trend to make employees responsible for their own performance development (IRS 2001: 25; IDS 2003: 1).

These trends, which have anchored performance appraisal more firmly into a system of performance management, have recast but not eliminated many of the managerial dilemmas traditionally associated with measuring individual performance. Although Armstrong and Baron suggest that approaches to performance management became more effective during the 1990s, 37 per cent of their respondents viewed performance management as 'ineffective' or only 'slightly effective' in improving organizational performance and this figure had not altered by 2004 (Armstrong and Baron 1998: 109; 2005: 66). Consequently employers remained 'surprisingly downbeat' about the effectiveness of their performance review systems (IRS 2003a: 14). An Institute of Employment Studies survey of 926 managers in 17 public and private sector organizations, including 11 civil service departments, reported that performance review had become 'a bottleneck of stark contradictions' (Strebler et al. 2001: 54). The Institute of Employment Studies suggests these contradictions stem from three main sources.

First, the shift from performance appraisal to performance management has been associated with an increase in complexity of the systems being used. Employers have a tendency to restructure their performance management systems creating an unwieldy vehicle that is attempting to deliver too many conflicting objectives. As Strebler et al. (2001: 55) note, 'employer's eyes are bigger than their stomachs: they cannot implement what they design', with line managers unable to deliver the processes involved competently and with insufficient high quality HR support to sustain complex performance processes. A central component of this complexity is the increased use of competency-based assessment which is often difficult to use effectively. Behaviours such as 'leadership' are hard to define and this has led to considerable scepticism among managers about the value of competencies in judging performance, although they are more suited to identifying development needs (Strebler et al. 2001: 41).

Second, performance management systems that integrate individual and corporate objectives and encourage devolution to line managers have drawbacks that have not been explored in prescriptive accounts of performance management. In a context of continuous organizational restructuring and unpredictable change, aligning (and realigning) corporate and individual objectives frequently leads to the revamping of the performance management system. As a senior manager commented:

> It is clearly difficult for any system to maintain credibility when the users are regularly informed that the system is not delivering the required results and must be changed. (cited in Strebler et al. 2001: 12)

At the same time as performance management has become more complex, line managers with larger spans of control are expected to find time to provide effective feedback for staff; a task that not all line managers have been able or willing to embrace.

Finally, as employers attach more significance to the performance management process, it becomes more politicized as the consequences for individuals become more apparent; reinforcing patronage rather than meritocracy. Systems that are designed to encourage openness about development needs may in practice discourage it because of the potentially negative consequences for individual rewards. Managers, who often have doubts about the fairness or consistency of ratings within their organization, use the performance review process for their own purposes, especially if it impacts on pay. More than 90 per cent of the 926 managers surveyed had achieved an 'exceptional' or 'good/competent' rating at their previous performance review, raising questions about the rigour of performance management systems (Strebler et al. 2001: 59).

Despite these shortcomings, performance management systems are designed with the assumption that managers within organizations can establish clear unambiguous goals which can be broken down into individual components, are accepted by the individuals concerned and can be easily measured. The extent to which these assumptions are valid highlights the dilemmas associated with performance appraisal, which forms the core component of all systems of performance management.

Performance Appraisal: Policy and Practice

Concerns about performance appraisal are not new, as McGregor's (1957) 'uneasy look' at appraisal illustrates. It has only been in the last decade, however, that criticism has included a more radical tinge, challenging many of the cherished assumptions of performance appraisal. Until recently, most criticism of appraisal has come from within mainstream management writing. For McGregor (1960), with his concern for the human side of enterprise, appraisal represented a judgemental and demotivating process. Similar concerns were voiced by Deming (1982), who suggested that appraisal was 'a deadly disease', which blamed individuals for problems systemic to organizations. Margerison (1976) went as far as to predict that appraisal would 'fall apart at the seams' (cited in Gill 1977: 66) due to a combination of managerial indifference, employee ambivalence and union opposition. This theme was reiterated by Fletcher (1993), who suggested that the days of standardized appraisals were numbered. But, despite these gloomy predictions, the use of performance appraisal has flourished.

Although there is no consistent survey data that has tracked the incidence of appraisal arrangements over time, a variety of studies indicate the increased importance of appraisal schemes which are being applied to larger proportions of the workforce. In the first large-scale survey commissioned by the IPM (Gill et al. 1973), 74 per cent of respondents had an appraisal scheme in place for some of their workforce, a figure which rose to over 80 per cent by 1977 and remained at that level in 1986 (Long 1986). The authoritative 1998 Workplace Employee Relations Survey (WERS) noted that formal performance appraisals were conducted in 79 per cent of workplaces, with appraisal being slightly more common in the public sector (83 per cent) than the private sector (77 per cent). By 2004, Armstrong and Baron (2005: 67) reported that 87 per cent of respondents operated formal processes to manage performance. As significant as the widespread use of appraisal schemes has been the increased importance of performance review. A striking finding of Gallie's work is that between 1986 and 1992 the role of appraisal in determining how hard employees worked had increased substantially and had become more important than pay incentives in controlling work behaviour, the reverse of the position in 1986 (Gallie et al. 1998: 68–9). More recent data provides further support for such findings (White et al. 2003: 189). What accounts for the increased prominence of appraisal?

The purpose of appraisal

Managers are often asked why they have introduced appraisal schemes and in a recent IRS survey 89 per cent of respondents suggested it was 'to identify training/ development needs' and 82 per cent mentioned 'evaluating individual performance'. Almost a third of respondents cited 'to identify/acknowledge good performance' or 'ensure managers and staff communicate effectively' (32 per cent) with only 19 per cent identifying 'help to make reward decisions' as a reason (IRS 2003a). The responses indicate that employers have multiple objectives for appraisal systems which may account for the apparent paradox of the continuing criticism of appraisal accompanied by its increased usage. It is precisely the multiple and potentially conflicting objectives that employers seek of appraisal schemes which accounts for many of the implementation difficulties that arise for employers in their use (Beer 1981; Strebler et al. 2001).

It is often assumed that the growth of performance appraisal resulted from the extension of performance-related pay in the 1980s and 1990s. This assumption does not provide the full picture, not least because the biggest increase in the uptake of performance appraisal occurred during the 1970s. In fact, there is little evidence to suggest performance appraisal was introduced primarily to support individual performance pay. Long (1986: 15) reported that assessment of salary increases was not viewed as one of the main purposes of performance review and there had been virtually no change since 1977. For most organizations, reward policies are a less important influence on appraisal practice than broader issues of training and development (IRS 2003: 9). An Industrial Society (1997) survey reported that only 14 per cent of respondents included 'discussing performance reward' as an element of the appraisal system and only 12 per cent suggested that the main purpose of the appraisal system was 'to allocate performance increases fairly'. It is more plausible to argue that during the expansion of performance-related pay in the early 1990s, the emphasis on performance-related pay shaped the type of scheme adopted rather than being a key influence on the increasing use of performance appraisal (see Storey 1992: 107).

An important influence on the increased use of appraisal has been the commitment of successive Conservative and Labour governments to introduce private sector 'best practice' into the public sector as part of its attempt to enhance managerial authority and increase efficiency (Bach and Winchester 2003). Until the mid-1980s there had been little tradition of performance appraisal in the public services (see Long 1986: 7), reflecting the self-regulatory ethos of the professional staff which dominate the sector. The education sector is indicative of these developments, with the pre-incorporation university sector committing itself to appraisal from the mid-1980s in return for a substantial payrise (Townley 1990). In the school sector, protracted discussions led to the introduction of appraisal from the early 1990s (Healy 1997). The establishment of appraisal within the public sector initially proved contentious because employees and trade unions viewed it as a means to reinforce managerial control and ensure conformity with government priorities. Performance management has become a more accepted way of managing the workforce and has proved central to the Labour government's modernization agenda (see Newman 2001).

Historically, the main purpose of appraisal schemes has been influenced by the dominant issues in personnel management practice. Thus, in the mid-1960s, when Management by Objectives (MBO) was being forcibly advocated, appraisal practice was strongly influenced by this approach with a focus on current performance (Gill et al. 1973). Individual performance-related pay also skewed appraisal systems towards a focus on recent performance. Many organizations have become interested in defining performance against competencies and are trying to make their performance appraisal systems more forward-looking. A further stimulus for organizations to revamp their appraisal systems has arisen from the interest in gaining external accreditation, such as Investors in People. The existence of an appraisal process is central to demonstrating that training and development needs are reviewed against targets at organizational and individual level (Investors in People 1998: 26).

The main purpose of performance appraisal has continued to oscillate between a concern with short-term performance as exemplified by MBO and PRP and a more developmental orientation. Irrespective of the formal approach adopted, a common use of performance appraisal has been as a means to discipline employees despite categorical advice that appraisal should not be used for disciplinary purposes (ACAS 1996: 24). IRS (2003a: 9) found that approximately 15 per cent of respondents viewed identifying and dealing with poor performance as one main reason for introducing appraisal. In his study of trainee accountants, Grey (1994) notes that, although performance appraisal was presented as an aid for career management, in practice it was used to discipline employees and weed out poor performers in the annual 'cull'. Increased awareness of the prevalence of forms of bullying at work has been accompanied by a recognition that performance assessments which assign staff 'unsatisfactory' ratings, often without any prior warning, constitute a form of bullying behaviour (Lee 2002). The absence of a third person during appraisal interviews, in marked contrast to most selection interviews, provides greater scope for bullying behaviour than in other organizational settings.

For human resource specialists, the increased use of appraisal is welcome because the establishment of an appraisal system represents the systematic collection of information about employees which provides the bedrock of all HR practice. Unlike for line managers, who tend to view appraisal as a means to an end – whether it be to justify decisions, reward good employees or signal areas for improvement – for HR specialists appraisal is an end in itself as it provides a range of data to implement personnel policies including training and development need analysis, career planning and aspects of reward management. Appraisal data is a valuable source of information about the effectiveness of recruitment and selection and equal opportunity policies.

Who is appraised?

Performance appraisal has traditionally been associated with managerial staff. In workplaces where appraisals were conducted the 1998 WERS reported 70 per cent coverage for managers, with professional workers (69 per cent) and sales staff (64 per cent) being the other occupations most commonly subject to formal appraisal (Cully et al. 1999: 72). An important exception to this pattern of widespread managerial appraisal are board level directors. Long (1986: 9) reported that the coverage of appraisal arrangements for directors was almost half the figure for other managers. Little changed in the intervening decade with the Industrial Society (1997) noting that under half of board level directors participated in an appraisal process. This is starting to change, however, because of the increased interest in corporate governance and specifically the important role assigned to non-executive directors in the wake of US corporate scandals (Higgs 2003). The Higgs Report recommended that individual directors, including the chairman, should be evaluated annually. The board has to state in its annual report how the process was conducted and act on the results, including removing ineffective directors (Skapinker 2003). This represents a far-reaching reform of the manner in which UK boards have traditionally operated.

One of the most trumpeted developments in performance appraisal has been its extension to cover a larger proportion of the existing workforce. In addition to the large swathes of public sector professionals now covered by appraisal, its extension to semi-skilled workers has been viewed as an important initiative to develop the commitment of these workers to managerially defined patterns of behaviour. The harmonization of the conditions of employment of manual and non-manual workers, as exemplified by the 1997 single status agreement in local government, can be seen in this light. Townley (1989) put a different gloss on these developments, suggesting that in essence appraisal is being used as a more subtle form of managerial control with tighter monitoring of manual workers' performance (Townley 1989: 104–5). This argument was based on the finding by Long (1986: 9) that between 1977 and 1986 appraisal had been extended to cover more secretarial and supervisory staff and most strikingly the proportion of skilled and semi-skilled employees had increased from 2 to 24 per cent. By 1998 in those workplaces that undertook formal appraisals, more than half of clerical and craft occupations were subject to performance appraisals (Cully et al. 1999: 72).

With the changing composition of the workforce and the substantial increase in the use of part-time and fixed-term contract workers, the extent to which these groups are covered by appraisal is of increasing importance. With the trend to harmonize the working arrangements of part-time and full-timers, one could expect that the proportion of part-time workers covered by appraisal arrangements will increase. There is limited evidence on the current proportion of part-time staff covered by appraisal arrangements and without knowing their occupational composition it is difficult to assess the significance of a figure of 55 per cent inclusion (Industrial Society 1997). More starkly, only 18 per cent of workers on fixed-term contracts were covered by appraisal arrangements, which suggests that a crucial segment of many organizations' workforce remain excluded from formal performance management systems.

What is appraised?

At the core of the appraisal process is the type of performance criteria used for rating individuals. In traditional appraisal schemes, the personality traits of individuals were rated based on the 'commonsense' assumption that traits such as leadership skills and loyalty are important for effective performance. The use of personality traits was subject to extensive criticism for their subjective characteristics and because of the difficulty of isolating the particular facet of personality responsible for effective job performance. The use of trait-based methods waned over the course of the 1970s and 1980s, although this did not preclude appraisers making judgements on the basis of personality traits, even if this was justified in terms of more acceptable performance criteria (Barlow 1989). As noted earlier, since the 1990s there has been a revival of interest in assessing personality, but it has been imbued with greater authority than in the past by establishing scales to measure emotional intelligence, enabling the ambiguous to be made tangible, by a process of measurement and quantification (Fineman 2004: 721).

The dominant approach, particularly for managerial staff, continues to be the assessment of individuals against objectives established in the previous appraisal round (IDS 2003; IRS 2001). This approach is considered to allow a more objective discussion of performance and potentially allows individuals to have greater involvement in setting the performance criteria against which they will be judged. But, as Kessler (2000: 280) suggests, an array of difficulties confront managers in establishing agreed performance criteria. Especially in service industries, it may be difficult to establish tangible and quantifiable performance objectives and this difficulty may be exacerbated in politically sensitive sectors such as health and education in which the key performance criteria for staff may be contested. For other occupational groups, such as clerical staff, the scope for individual discretion may be so limited as to render the establishment of targets a futile ritual.

Lewis's (1998) study of three differing financial services organizations highlighted many of these difficulties. At the high street bank and the building society, there was considerable unease about the manner in which objectives were set. Although officially a consultative process occurred between the area and branch manager, in practice branch managers had few illusions that objectives were imposed from the centre. Managers also expressed concern about the number of key performance targets they were expected to meet – about 20 at the building society – coupled with the narrow short-term financial orientation of their targets.

A related concern is that individual's tenacious pursuit of their own performance targets may lead them to neglect other aspects of their job or to focus on achieving their objectives to the detriment of teamwork or other important aspects of organizational performance. There is a heightened danger of this occurring in a context in which managers complain that they are being pressurized to achieve harder performance targets. These concerns have led many organizations to modify their performance criteria so that managers are assessed on the manner in which they achieve their targets as well as the targets themselves (IDS 2003: 18; IRS 2001: 22).

These latter developments reflect a concern to develop performance criteria extending beyond a sole focus on objectives towards a more rounded focus on behaviour. Various dimensions of performance are linked to a series of behavioural statements and employees are assessed according to the extent to which they demonstrate these behaviours. For example, at United Distillers employees are assessed against seven management competencies: commitment to results; leadership; interpersonal effectiveness; people development; problem solving; strategic awareness and capability; and international perspective (IDS 1997: 4). At the pharmaceutical company GlaxoSmithKline, greater opportunities have been developed for production workers to take on leadership roles and emphasis has been placed on assessing and developing the necessary leadership competencies across the whole workforce (IRS 2003d: 8–11).

Appraisal under the Spotlight

The orthodox critique

Appraisal has become an integral component of managing human resources and has spread to sectors and occupational groups formerly excluded. But, despite this increased coverage, appraisal has not been immune from sustained criticism. The dominant critique of appraisal arises from within an orthodox management framework. These criticisms do not challenge the underlying managerially defined purpose of appraisal, but rather they seek to remedy the imperfections in the design and implementation of different appraisal systems.

A fundamental, and widely acknowledged problem, is that the appraisal process is used for a variety of conflicting purposes (Strebler et al. 2001; Wilson 2002). Appraisal can be used to motivate staff to improve performance by establishing

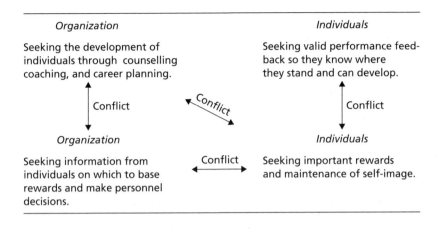

Organization   *Individuals*

Seeking the development of   Seeking valid performance feed-
individuals through counselling   back so they know where
coaching, and career planning.   they stand and can develop.

        Conflict   *Conflict*   Conflict

Organization   *Individuals*

Seeking information from   Conflict   Seeking important rewards
individuals on which to base   and maintenance of self-image.
rewards and make personnel
decisions.

Figure 11.1 Conflicts in performance appraisal
Source: Beer (1981), adapted from Porter, Lawler and Hackman (1975)

clear objectives for the future and letting them know what is expected of them. This contrasts with an appraisal process which is primarily concerned with distributing rewards based on an assessment of past performance. Finally, the appraisal process can be more geared to development with training needs identified to remedy deficiencies in performance revealed by the appraisal process. The difficulty is that, frequently, these different elements are blended together in an ill-defined manner. The appraiser is forced to adopt conflicting roles, cast as both a monitor and judge of performance, but also as an understanding counsellor (see Figure 11.1). It is generally assumed that employees are unlikely to confide their limitations and anxieties about job performance to their appraiser (Newton and Findlay 1996: 43); not least because it could directly impact on their remuneration if merit-related pay is used or at the very least indirectly hinder their promotion chances.

It is well documented that managers are reluctant to judge individuals and to assign poor ratings to them because managers are uncomfortable 'playing God' (McGregor 1957; Rowe 1964). This reluctance to transmit negative feedback to employees has been attributed to a variety of motives including: a concern that it could prove demotivating; a recognition that their own lack of support and guidance may have contributed to poor performance; and a more straightforward concern to avoid conflict (Longenecker et al. 1987). Longenecker et al.'s (1987) study of 60 senior managers found that a variety of factors, other than the subordinate's actual performance, influenced the ratings that managers allocated their subordinates (see Figure 11.2). At County Natwest human resource managers complained that 'systematic overrating of staff is an ongoing problem' (Carlton and Sloman 1992: 87). As Grint (1993: 68) points out the question of for whom this is a 'problem' does not merit discussion. Compounding the managerial problems of rater bias is the existence of the inflation of performance feedback. In other words, even when poor ratings are allocated to employees, there is a tendency for supervisors

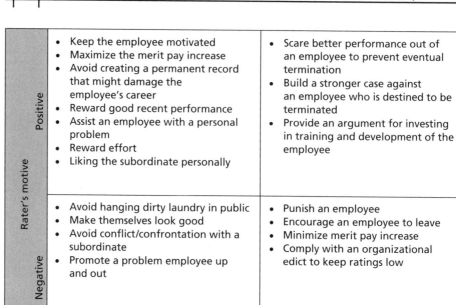

Rater's motive	Inflated ratings	Deflated ratings
Positive	• Keep the employee motivated • Maximize the merit pay increase • Avoid creating a permanent record that might damage the employee's career • Reward good recent performance • Assist an employee with a personal problem • Reward effort • Liking the subordinate personally	• Scare better performance out of an employee to prevent eventual termination • Build a stronger case against an employee who is destined to be terminated • Provide an argument for investing in training and development of the employee
Negative	• Avoid hanging dirty laundry in public • Make themselves look good • Avoid conflict/confrontation with a subordinate • Promote a problem employee up and out	• Punish an employee • Encourage an employee to leave • Minimize merit pay increase • Comply with an organizational edict to keep ratings low

Figure 11.2 A typology of rater motives and manipulative rating
Source: Adapted from Longenecker and Ludwig (1990)

to explain away lower ratings, diluting the impact of poor ratings (Waung and Highhouse 1997).

A variety of other distortions have been noted in the appraisal process which focus on the appraisal interview (Grint 1993). Given the problems of biased assessment raised in Chapter 5 in relation to the selection interview, it is not surprising that similar problems occur in appraisal interviews. There is less evidence available, however, on the outcomes of appraisal interviews compared to the numerous studies that have examined selection interviews (Fletcher 2001: 478). The first problem is the 'halo effect' distortion. This arises when one attribute of the individual is used as the basis to rate the overall performance of the person, largely irrespective of the stated criterion. A second problem relates to the reluctance of managers to be too harsh or overly lenient, which can result in an error of central tendency in which everybody is rated as average. This reluctance to differentiate between appraisees undermines the value of the appraisal process. A third problem is called 'recency bias'. Because managers rarely keep detailed notes about their appraisees, and are not very precise about rating all the behaviours they are required to judge, there is a tendency to base appraisals on the recent past, regardless of how representative it is of performance over the year. This shortcoming may be tempered by the shift within some organizations from appraisal as an annual process to a more continuous process of performance review (Armstrong and Baron 1998: 115); a trend which is particularly evident for new employees and employees whose performance is of concern (IRS 2003a: 10).

The appraisal interview is influenced also by the gender and ethnic origins of the appraisee and appraiser (Geddes and Konrad 2003). Chen and DiTomaso (1996), surveying mainly US studies, suggest that women in similar jobs to men and performing to the same level gain similar ratings. However, they contend that gender has an impact on ratings in two main ways. First, women gained better ratings when they were evaluated in 'women's jobs' and, second, cultural assumptions or implicit theories of performance criteria – that is, the choice of performance standards actually used – may be unconsciously biased towards the values of white men. Many employees, especially women, complain of a competitive masculine culture at the workplace in which long hours are equated with loyalty and commitment to the organization with detrimental implications for appraisal ratings of those workers not prepared, or able, to demonstrate this level of 'commitment' (Lewis and Taylor 1996; Simpson 1998).

In these circumstances, it is widely argued that managers lack confidence in their appraisal systems, which contributes to their ambivalent feelings about the process in which there is often a mismatch between expectations and outcomes (Box 11.1). A lack of enthusiasm among managers has been raised in many mainstream UK organizations with managers admitting that they 'go through the motions' of performance reviews because they suggested that appraisal lacked credibility (McGovern et al. 1997: 18; Storey et al. 1997: 182). Other studies have reported more positive managerial views about performance appraisal but also a recognition that with wider spans of control and increased workloads, finding time for performance appraisal is becoming more difficult (Strebler et al. 2001: 26).

One means to identify managerial commitment is to establish the percentage of appraisal forms which are completed. Few surveys pose this question. An exception is the Industrial Society's (1997: 9) survey which found that 64 per cent of

Box 11.1 People manager's views of impact of performance review processes*

76 per cent setting individual objectives improves awareness of business objectives
44 per cent has increased quality of work from direct reports
33 per cent improves the performance of my team
23 per cent enables managers to motivate staff

*Survey respondents who agreed and strongly agreed ($n = 764$).
Source: Strebler et al. (2001: 17).

organizations reported a more than two-thirds completion rate. This left 15 per cent of respondents who did not know how many appraisals were completed, 12 per cent who said that between one and two-thirds were completed, and just 4 per cent admitting that less than one-third of appraisals were completed. In the first national survey of NHS staff in 2003, 60 per cent of respondents reported having an appraisal in the previous 12 months, but in total only 36 per cent judged that they had received a well-structured appraisal (Commission for Health Improvement 2004).

Employers have adopted a variety of measures to reduce the subjectivity of the appraisal process and improve its credibility, assisted by a burgeoning applied psychology literature which has attempted to identify and eliminate 'leniency' (Kane et al. 1995; Waung and Highhouse 1997). One response, although unpopular with managers, has been to use forced distributions to prevent managerial leniency. The computer company Hewlett Packard used to use such an approach, but abandoned it because the perception among staff was that their rankings depended on the negotiation skills of their manager rather than their own performance. Instead managers are provided with guide-lines about the proportion of staff which would be expected to be in the top and bottom portions of the distribution (IDS 1997: 13). In other organizations ratings have been abandoned and more emphasis is placed on the use of portfolios of evidence to provide more objective evidence on achievement(s).

Greater recognition that the appraisal process is shaped by the behaviour of two parties has led to much greater emphasis being placed on the role of the employee in leading the performance review process (IDS 2003: 1). Self-appraisal draws on a unique source of information, providing an additional perspective on performance and involves reviewees more actively in the performance management process. Opinion is divided on the validity of self-ratings with some studies continuing to show that subjects rate themselves higher than other raters (Furnham and Stringfield 1998: 525). In addition, responses differ by gender with women tending to rate themselves less positively than do men, and are less lenient than men in their self-ratings (Fletcher 1999: 39). Company practice at firms such as Shell suggests that, rather than over-estimating their performance, staff often underestimate their abilities and that self-appraisal promotes individual responsibility and openness (IDS 1997: 6).

The most common response to problems of subjectivity and rater bias is to re-double training efforts to ensure that managers are trained in conducting appraisals, to recognize good and bad performance, and be aware of the sources of potential bias. Managers have also tried to refine their performance measurements to reduce subjectivity. Nonetheless there is often a gap between managerial and user perceptions of the performance management process. For example, in the Institute of Employment Studies research appraisees were most dissatisfied with the coaching they received from their line manager and their discussion of training needs (Strebler et al. 2001: 27). Despite some evidence that managers are concerned to rectify these deficiencies, it could be argued that in the main senior managers expend relatively little effort in making their appraisal process function effectively. This may reflect the degree to which performance appraisal is crowded out by more pressing organizational requirements. As McGovern (1997) notes, fewer than half the line managers in the seven organizations he surveyed considered successful implementation of personnel policies to be an 'important' or 'very important' factor in their own performance appraisals.

The conclusion to emerge is that within the practitioner-orientated literature there is a strong awareness of the limitations of performance appraisal and numerous suggestions on how to remedy this problem. The underlying philosophy that unites these accounts is essentially unitarist. It is assumed that employees and employers both derive equal benefits from appraisal and this is especially likely to be the case when the appraisal process is as open and objective as possible. Consequently, although appraisals can never be totally free of a subjective element, problems that arise are remedial by effective training and clear communication of the objectives and importance of the appraisal process. In short, it is the implementation of appraisal that is at fault rather than more fundamental problems associated with the assumptions that lie behind performance appraisal.

The radical critique

It is these implicit assumptions about the purpose of performance appraisal which have increasingly been questioned as a more critical literature has emerged. These perspectives, in their differing ways, are centrally concerned with the problems of management control and the contribution of performance appraisal towards ensuring that employees adhere to management objectives (Barlow 1989; Grey 1994; Healy 1997; Newton and Findlay 1996; Townley 1993). These accounts reject most of the assumptions that underpin the practitioner-orientated analysis of performance appraisal. Instead of a concern to prescribe how appraisal can operate effectively, the focus is on understanding the actual practice of appraisal within the workplace with greater emphasis on its specific context. Unitary assumptions about the benevolent purposes of appraisal are replaced by a more radical ideology concerned to examine managerial objectives, especially tighter control over behaviour and performance, the potential to individualize the employment relationship and the scope for managers to use appraisal as a veneer to legitimate informal management. Some of these authors, especially those influenced by Foucault's work, view trends in appraisal as part of a more sinister management regime to control all aspects of employee behaviour and eliminate scope for employee resistance.

A dominant thread running through these accounts is the emphasis placed on the manner in which appraisal is used to bolster managerial power and control. Barlow's (1989) study of a petrochemicals firm highlights many of the shortcomings of appraisal as perceived by line managers. But he departs from the prescriptive literature in suggesting that these 'problems' do not undermine the utility of the appraisal system to managers. Indeed, quite the reverse is true, because it allows managers discretion to promote favoured individuals but, if challenged, to legit-imize them by referring to the formal appraisal process. The spread of performance appraisal to manual workers, school teachers and university lecturers has similarly been interpreted as a means to increase managerial control over diverse occupa-tional groups formerly immune from these processes (Townley 1989, 1999; Healy 1997).

Within many of these critical accounts, there are strong leanings towards Foucault's (1981) conception of power, with appraisal used by managers as a form of disciplinary gaze (see especially Townley 1993; Grey 1994) which complement other forms of electronic and personal surveillance found in call centres and the like. The starting point for this literature is Foucault's discussion of Bentham's 'Panoptican', the model prison in which prisoners can always be observed by the prison guards, but they cannot be seen by the prisoners. Because prisoners would never know whether they were being observed, the Panoptican combines sur-veillance and discipline. For Townley (1993), the relevance to appraisal within the university sector is clear: 'Appraisal operates as a form of panoptican with its anony-mous and continuous surveillance as seen in the articulation of a monitoring role' (Townley 1993: 232). Grey (1994) pursues similar themes, suggesting that, for trainee accountants, the appraisal process is used as a form of disciplinary technology with those rated as 'satisfactory' running the risk of being summarily dismissed in the annual 'cull'.

Although these critical perspectives provide an important corrective to the prevailing prescriptive literature on appraisal, they are not beyond criticism. There is a tendency to assume that managerial intentions are necessarily translated into managerial actions, ignoring the issue of human agency (Newton and Findlay 1996). Although Healy illustrates how trade unions have collectivized some of the indi-vidualistic intentions of the appraisal, she nonetheless emphasizes the 'inevitable role of control in the system' (1997: 217). Both Barlow (1989) and Townley (1989) view the achievement of managerial objectives as straightforward, ignoring scope for employee resistance. This is curious when, as noted earlier, the management literature is replete with evidence about the ambivalent feelings of line managers towards appraisal and commentators express exasperation at the leniency shown by managers in rating employees.

Despite their limitations, these critical accounts have challenged many of the traditional assumptions about performance appraisal and helped to advance under-standing of why the anticipated benefits of appraisal do not always emerge in prac-tice. Critical perspectives highlight that it is not sufficient to assume that clearer objectives and training of appraisers will yield satisfactory results. The contested nature of appraisal, the specific managerial objectives sought, and the nature of the context in which it is applied, all have an important bearing on the impact of the appraisal process. These insights have informed many of the current develop-ments in performance appraisal.

360-degree Feedback

The adoption of multiple sources of feedback, particularly upward feedback from direct reports, has been the most trumpeted development in performance appraisal in the last few years. It has attracted positive endorsement from a range of sources. A variety of terms have been used to signify that the appraisal process is no longer the preserve of managers appraising their employees, but can incorporate performance feedback information from a variety of stakeholders in the organization, to ensure a more rounded view of overall performance is established. It is the combination of information from self-appraisal, subordinate appraisal, peer appraisal and feedback from other internal customers, with the possibility of including external suppliers and customers, which has been termed '360-degree' appraisal. The term can be misleading because the most widely adopted part of the process, and the aspect which has attracted most attention, has been the appraisal by staff of their managers, that is, 'upward' appraisal. Other sources of feedback from internal/external peers and from customers are also utilized in some organizations.

The interest in 360-degree appraisal and especially upward appraisal can be attributed to three main factors. First, changes in organizational structures with more fluid working arrangements, such as project teams, and multiple reporting lines make it inappropriate to rely solely on the judgement of one individual who may not be sufficiently close to gauge performance accurately. The emphasis on empowerment and teamwork assign greater responsibility to employees and 360-degree appraisal is a logical extension of management styles which emphasize the contribution of feedback for performance improvements and enlists employees' active participation in this process.

Second, is the belief that 360-degree appraisal overcomes many of the limitations of traditional appraisal systems. Advocates maintain that upward appraisal may provide a more accurate view of performance because direct reports are in closer contact with their manager and are more directly affected by the manager's style than the manager's superior (Ward 1997: 23). For these reasons, direct reports can observe and judge more accurately the performance of the individual manager and the extent to which the manager is adhering to, rather than paying lipservice to, the 'empowerment' philosophy which has gained ground in many organizations. Upward appraisal therefore provides a direct source of information about whether managers are able to achieve results through their people (Kettley 1997). Obtaining feedback from a number of sources provides appraisees with more information and makes it difficult for staff to ignore the results of performance feedback when it is based on more than one person's judgement.

Third, the use of 360-degree appraisal is associated strongly with the service sector and the development of a stronger more discerning customer ethic. As Chapter 13 points out, the output of service workers is often intangible and related to how customers perceive the quality of the interaction, requiring customer feedback.

360-degree feedback not only allows employees to gauge customer responses, but is also used to encourage employees to empathize and internalize customer perspectives. An IPD survey covering 51 organizations using 360-degree feedback reported that half the organizations surveyed used feedback to raise levels of customer service (cited in Armstrong and Baron 1998: 328).

Responsiveness to customer feedback has also been a central feature of the Labour government's modernization of public services which has encouraged professionals 'to be consumer focused, responding to the personalised and often strong wishes of vociferous customers' (Blair 2002: 25). In the university sector, student feedback on teaching is routinely incorporated into the performance review process and many universities have also adopted mandatory forms of peer review of teaching. 360-degree feedback has also been implemented among senior civil servants across government departments (Cabinet Office 2001).

At the end of the 1990s it was suggested that 360-degree appraisal was becoming commonplace in many UK organizations (Fletcher 1999: 39). Armstrong and Baron, however, reported that only 11 per cent of companies used this form of feedback as part of their approach to performance management, although this figure rose to 20 per cent for upward appraisal (Table 11.1). In the last few years there is little doubt that awareness of 360-degree appraisal and its usage has increased. An IRS survey of 49 employers indicated that almost half were using 360-degree appraisal (IRS 2003b: 17). As with appraisal generally it is most likely to be applied to managerial staff. These developments have been influenced by its widespread usage in the USA and facilitated by the growth of management consultants extolling the virtues of 360-degree feedback.

360-degree feedback has been used as part of the performance appraisal process to supplement traditional sources of information, but most frequently it is used for developmental purposes to enhance managers' awareness of their strengths and weaknesses. Handy et al. (1996) reported that 71 per cent of companies used feedback solely for developmental purposes, compared to 23 per cent of organizations who used feedback to support performance appraisal and only 6 per cent of companies linked the process to pay. Kettley (1997: 41–2) also found that 360-degree appraisal was most commonly used to support personal development. Many commentators suggest that when organizations shift their use of 360-degree feedback to appraise rather than develop managers, problems arise as the 360-degree process becomes entangled and confused with appraisal, undermining its usefulness as a developmental tool (De Nisi and Kluger 2000; Ghorpade 2000: 141). By contrast Bracken et al. (2001) disagree because they argue that it is only if the process is used to inform decisions that ratees and raters will engage with and benefit fully from the process. Mabey's (2001: 48) findings of 360-degree feedback at the Open University endorse such a view because he found that participants questioned the effectiveness of the process while it remained disconnected from more formal promotion and reward systems.

In the last few years there has been a significant change in perception, especially in the US literature, which has shifted from overwhelming endorsement of

360-degree feedback towards a much more questioning stance and a focus on attempts to make 360-degree feedback more effective (Bracken et al. 2001; Ghorpade 2000; Luthans and Peterson 2003). Much of the concern stemmed from a meta-analysis of the effectiveness of feedback on performance which indicated that in more than one-third of cases feedback lowered subsequent performance because negative feedback, perhaps not surprisingly, discouraged rather than motivated people to improve (Kluger and DeNisi 1996). There is also a recognition that 360-degree appraisal can generate an overwhelming amount of feedback which is difficult to make sense of. For this reason much of the 'best-practice' literature emphasizes that it is important to use expert facilitators to provide feedback and coaching with follow-up action to ensure implementation (Luthans and Peterson 2003). In many organizations, however, the emphasis is on managers taking personal responsibility for addressing shortfalls in their competencies, which may prove to be a recipe for inaction.

A prominent issue in any discussion of 360-degree appraisal is the degree to which the process is anonymous and confidential. The majority of organizations provide feedback on an anonymous basis and it is often confidential to the manager that has been rated, being used to aid that individual's self-development. Anonymity is primarily to reassure participants that there will be no repercussions as a result of their feedback and is designed to encourage honest feedback. As Ghorpade (2000: 143) points out, however, honest ratings are not necessarily accurate or valid, because of the degree to which participants' views may be distorted by organizational politics or personality differences. Moreover these types of distortions may arise because many individuals are not provided with any clear guidance about what is expected of ratee roles.

Some employers argue, therefore, that named feedback is more useful because it allows the feedback to be contextualized and related to specific situations or relationships and can reduce the scope for unconstructive personal comments. Walker and Smither (1999) found in their study of 252 managers over a 5-year period that managers who discuss the feedback with those who provided it obtained significantly better ratings than those who did not, but this does not necessarily indicate that performance improved. Irrespective of the approach taken, difficulties remain and these dilemmas are not confined to those receiving feedback. Forty-five per cent of employers using 360-degree appraisal suggested that direct reports who provide feedback felt threatened and unable to be honest and 36 per cent of employers suggested that it is threatening to participants (Handy et al. 1996).

There is a high level of consensus that this type of feedback is likely to prove most effective within relatively high trust organizations, in which managers are prepared to accept criticism and be open enough to alter their behaviour as a result of the feedback provided. As Kanouse (1998: 3) warns, multi-rater feedback can easily fail; for example, if a company is about to restructure and shed jobs, then feedback mechanisms can be viewed as a means to select employees for redundancy. 360-degree appraisal mechanisms can be subject to the same problems as arise from more traditional performance appraisal – poor communication, untrained raters and conflicting aims for the scheme (Kanouse 1998: 3).

Most of the commentary on 360-degree feedback remains positive, but some key issues are scarcely considered. In particular, it is not self-evident that these processes challenge the basic assumptions underpinning all appraisal systems as is often claimed. 360-degree appraisal shares with more traditional appraisal the assumption that performance improvements arise from measuring and rewarding the performance of individuals, but uses a different method (i.e. subordinate feedback) to measure it. Nonetheless, the focus remains on variations between *individuals* rather than examining the context in which those individuals work, which may have a greater impact on performance. 360-degree appraisal is trumpeted as 'empowering', but it does not necessarily challenge existing power relationships and behaviour within organizations. Employers decide whether to use such a system and take all the key decisions about its design and operation. Direct reports' views form only one part of managerial assessment and are used primarily for developmental rather than pay purposes. Overall, however, despite remaining doubts about 360-degree feedback, Fletcher (2001: 476) anticipates that more use will be made of 360-degree feedback as a way to measure behavioural outputs. Web-based rather than paper-based systems also enable the process to be administered more easily, encouraging increased take-up.

Summary and Conclusions

This chapter has highlighted the paradox that, although performance appraisal is being used more extensively than ever before, there is a much greater awareness of its limitations. This has encouraged considerable change in practice and an emphasis on performance appraisal giving way to more rounded forms of performance management. A summary of these trends is shown in Figure 11.3. This representation is only indicative, but the key point is that much of the shift in

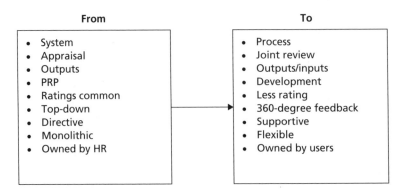

From	To
• System	• Process
• Appraisal	• Joint review
• Outputs	• Outputs/inputs
• PRP	• Development
• Ratings common	• Less rating
• Top-down	• 360-degree feedback
• Directive	• Supportive
• Monolithic	• Flexible
• Owned by HR	• Owned by users

Figure 11.3 Developments in performance management since 1991
Source: Armstrong and Baron (1998)

emphasis has drawn on the criticisms of traditional performance appraisal that have emerged not only from prescriptive literature, but also from more radical critiques of performance appraisal. These criticisms have yielded positive benefits. Not only have they revealed some of the questionable assumptions embodied in traditional appraisal practice and hastened the search for alternatives, but they have also illustrated the importance of the context in which performance appraisal is implemented. This has allowed much greater clarity in designing and implementing performance appraisal with an explicit consideration of the primary purpose of appraisal.

Since Armstrong and Baron's 1998 study of performance management two other developments have emerged which are having an impact on performance appraisal practice. The first relates to technology, and the second concerns cultural diversity. The growth of customer service work has been accompanied by more intensive computer performance monitoring which can scrutinize the time spent on various tasks, the number and length of time that a terminal is left idle, and the number of keystrokes entered. The application of technology to monitor performance is not especially novel, but these technologies have become more sophisticated and pervasive. Technological enhancement of the appraisal process itself is being more widely deployed and, as noted earlier, has contributed to the spread of 360-degree appraisal. As Miller (2003: 418) points out, intranet or internet-based software has the potential to automate some of the tedious aspects of performance appraisal by assisting raters with suggested narratives and encouraging line managers to complete a process which they are disinclined to spend much time on. Neary (2002) outlines the benefits of technologically facilitated performance management processes in TRW, a large US multinational with nearly 100,000 employees – 25,000 employee appraisal forms were lodged on the system within 6 months of its launch. The handful of 'super-users', that have access to all the company's appraisal data, are able to trawl rapidly for specific requirements (e.g. degree-level HR professionals with Chinese language), aiding performance and career management.

A second main trend is increased interest in differing perceptions and outcomes of performance appraisal between countries, related to the particular institutional context in which appraisal occurs. Such analyses draw heavily on the work of Hofstede (1980) and his dimensions of national culture. In countries with high-power distance, in which superiors and subordinates do not view themselves as equals, it is predicted that there will be a reluctance to use upward feedback or allow subordinates much input into their appraisal. Milliman et al. (2002) argue that these propositions are broadly borne out by the existing, albeit limited, research evidence of performance appraisal in countries outside of the USA and UK, with little support for subordinate input in countries such as Korea. Similar points have been highlighted in studies of Chinese and US managers in Hong Kong (Entrekin and Chung 2001). Although the work of Hofstede has been subject to extensive criticism, as Fletcher (2001: 481) highlights, it does draw attention to the fact that generalizing from US studies in other institutional contexts may be unwise.

If our knowledge and understanding of the impact performance appraisal processes in different national contexts remains sketchy, in general we have gained a much better appreciation of why performance appraisal appears to be more accepted in some organizations than others. Employer practices which genuinely sustain trust by promoting transparency and procedural fairness alongside respect for the individual are more likely to lead to appraisal systems which are accepted and valued by the workforce.

It is the sustained criticism of the imprecision and lack of objectivity of performance appraisal, and a recognition that too much weight has been attached to the annual appraisal interview, which has generated a search for more rounded forms of assessment and ones less reliant on a manager's rating of their employees. The shift towards an element of self-appraisal, the more diverse criteria used within performance management systems and the interest in 360-degree appraisal all testify to the emergence of a broader approach to performance appraisal. It appears that organizations are trying to make a virtue out of the different perspectives on performance which different stakeholders bring to the appraisal process. There are signs that these developments reflect a partial abandonment of a single 'objective' measure in favour of a more reflexive and sceptical approach which grudgingly accepts diversity. A key challenge then becomes how employers reconcile and use the diverse feedback they are receiving from a number of sources.

These developments also suggest that, while performance appraisal will remain at the heart of human resource management practice, it is likely to be increasingly facilitated by software that makes it more straightforward to draw on a wider network of performance measures from both inside and outside the organization. Some of these indicators arise from the scope to monitor performance more easily by deploying information technology. Other forms of performance information will be generated from surveillance by fellow employees, customers or mystery shoppers. These developments, while often viewed negatively within Foucauldian accounts, potentially provide opportunities for a more nuanced approach, which moves away from the rightly and increasingly much-criticized one-dimensional view of individual performance.

REFERENCES AND FURTHER READING

ACAS 1996: *Employee Appraisal*, London: ACAS.

Armstrong, M. and Baron, A. 1998: *Performance Management: The New Realities*, London: Institute of Personnel and Development.

Armstrong, M. and Baron, A. 2005: *Managing Performance: Performance Management in Action*, London: Chartered Institute of Personnel and Development.

Bach, S. 2004: *Employment Relations and the Health Service: The Management of Reforms*, London: Routledge.

Bach, S. and Winchester, D. 2003: The state: The public sector, in P.K. Edwards (ed.), *Industrial Relations*, Oxford: Blackwell.

Barlow, G. 1989: Deficiencies and the perpetuation of power: Latent functions in management appraisal, *Journal of Management Studies*, **26**(5), 499–517.

Beer, M. 1981: Performance appraisal: Dilemmas and possibilities, *Organizational Dynamics*, **9**(4), 24–37.

Bevan, S. and Thompson, M. 1992: An overview of policy and practice, in IPM, *Performance Management in the UK: An Analysis of the Issues*, London: Institute of Personnel Management.

Blair, T. 2002: *The Courage of our Convictions: Why Reform of the Public Services Is the Route to Social Justice*, London: Fabian Society.

Bracken, D., Timreck, C., Fleenor, J. and Summers, L. 2001: 360 feedback from another angle, *Human Resource Management*, **40**(1), 3–20.

Bunting, M. 2004: *Willing Slaves: How the Overwork Culture Is Ruling our Lives*, London: HarperCollins.

Cabinet Office 2001: *Getting the Best Out of 360-Degree Feedback*. www.cabinet-office.gov.uk/civilservice/scs/documents/pdf/360feedback.pdf

Carlton, I. and Sloman, M. 1992: Performance appraisal in practice, *Human Resource Management Journal*, **2**(3), 80–94.

Chen, C. and DiTomaso, N. 1996: Performance appraisal and demographic diversity, in E. Kossek and S. Label (eds.), *Managing Diversity*, Oxford: Blackwell.

Cully, M., Woodland, S., O'Reilly, A and Dix, G. 1999: *Britain at Work*, London: Routledge.

Commission for Health Improvement 2004: *NHS National Staff Survey 2003*. www.chi.gov.uk/eng/surveys/nss2003/key_findings.pdf

Deming, W.E. 1982: *Out of the Crisis: Quality Productivity and Competitive Position*, Cambridge: Cambridge University Press.

De Nisi, A. and Kluger, A. 2000: Feedback effectiveness: Can 360 degree appraisals be improved? *Academy of Management Executive*, **14**(1), 129–39.

Entrekin, L. and Chung, Y-W. 2001: Attitudes towards different sources of executive appraisal: A comparison of Hong Kong Chinese and American managers in Hong Kong, *International Journal of Human Resource Management*, **12**(6), 965–87.

Fineman, S. 2004: Getting the measure of emotion – and the cautionary tale of emotional intelligence, *Human Relations*, **57**(6), 719–40.

Fletcher, C. 1993: Appraisal: An idea whose time has gone? *Personnel Management*, **25**(9), 34–8.

Fletcher, C. 1999: The implications of research on gender differences in self-assessment and 360 degree appraisal, *Human Resource Management Journal*, **9**(1), 39–46.

Fletcher, C. 2001: Performance appraisal and management: The developing research agenda, *Journal of Occupational and Organizational Psychology*, **74**(4), 473–87.

Fletcher, C. and Williams, R. 1992: Organizational experience, in IPM, *Performance Management in the UK: An Analysis of the Issues*, London: Institute of Personnel Management.

Foucault, M. 1981: *Power/Knowledge: Selected Interviews and other Writings*, Brighton: Harvester Press.

Furnham, A. 1993: Management: Nothing to do with ability – Some of the pitfalls of employee appraisals, *Financial Times*, 23 July, 15.

Furnham, A. and Stringfield, P. 1998: Congruence in job-performance ratings: A study of 360 degree feedback examining self, manager, peers and consultant ratings, *Human Relations*, **51**(4), 517–30.

Gallie, D., White, M., Cheng, Y. and Tomlinson, M. 1998: *Restructuring the Employment Relationship*, Oxford: Oxford University Press.

Geddes, D. and Konrad, A. 2003: Demographic differences and reactions to performance feedback, *Human Relations*, **56**(12), 1485–513.

Ghorpade, J. 2000: Managing five paradoxes of 360-degree feedback, *Academy of Management Executive*, **14**(1), 140–50.

Gill, D. 1977: *Appraising Performance: Present Trends and the Next Decade*, London: Institute of Personnel Management.

Gill, D., Ungerson, B. and Thakur, M. 1973: *Performance Appraisal in Perspective: A Survey of Current Practice*, London: Institute of Personnel Management.

Grey, C. 1994: Career as a project of the self and labour process discipline, *Sociology*, **28**(2), 479–97.

Grint, K. 1993: What's wrong with performance appraisals? A critique and a suggestion, *Human Resource Management Journal*, **3**(3), 61–77.

Hall, L. and Torrington, D. 1998: *The Human Resource Function: The Dynamics of Change and Development*, London: Pitman.

Handy, L., Devine, M., and Health, L. 1996: *360 Degree Feedback: Unguided Missile or Powerful Weapon?* Ashridge: Berkhampstead.

Healy, G. 1997: The industrial relations of appraisal: The case of teachers, *Industrial Relations Journal*, **28**(3), 206–20.

Higgs, D. 2003: *Review of the Role and Effectiveness of Non-Executive Directors*, London: DTI.

Hofstede, G. 1980: *Culture's Consequences*, California: Sage Publications.

IDS (Incomes Data Services). 1997: *Performance Management*, London: IDS.

IDS (Incomes Data Services). 2003: *Performance Management*. IDS study 748, London: IDS.

IRS (Industrial Relations Services) 1994: Improving performance: A survey of appraisal arrangements. *Employment Trends*, 556, March, 5–14.

IRS (Industrial Relations Services) 2001: *Performance Management: IRS Management Review 20*, London: IRS.

IRS (Industrial Relations Services) 2003a: Time to talk – how and why employers conduct appraisals, *Employment Trends*, 769, 7 February, 8–14.

IRS (Industrial Relations Services) 2003b: Performance management: policy and practice, *Employment Trends*, 781, 1 August, 12–19.

IRS (Industrial Relations Services) 2003c: Comprehensive success, *Employment Trends*, 772, 21 March, 14–16.

IRS (Industrial Relations Services) 2003d: Developing leadership at GlaxoSmithKline, *Competency and Emotional Intelligence Quarterly*, **10**(3), 8–11.

Industrial Society. 1997: *Appraisal*. No. 37, London: Industrial Society.

Investors in People. 1998: *The Investors in People Standard*, London: Investors in People.

Kane, J., Bernardin, J., Villanova, P. and Peyrefitte, J. 1995: Stability of rater leniency: Three studies. *Academy of Management Journal*, **38**(4), 1036–51.

Kanouse, D. 1998: Why multi-rater feedback systems fail, *HRFocus*, January, 3.

Kaplan, R. and Norton, D. 1996: *The Balanced Scorecard*, Boston: Harvard Business School Press.

Kaplan, R. and Norton, D. 2001: *The Strategy-focused Organisation: How Balanced Scorecard Companies Thrive in the New Business Environment*, Boston: Harvard Business School Press.

Kessler, I. 2000: Remuneration systems, in S. Bach and K. Sisson (eds.), *Personnel Management*, 3rd edn, Oxford: Blackwell.

Kettley, P. 1997: *Personal Feedback: Cases in Point*, Sussex: Institute for Employment Studies, IES Report 326.

Kluger, A. and DeNisi, A. 1996: The effects of feedback interventions on performance, *Psychological Bulletin*, **119**, 254–84.

Legge, K. 1978: *Power, Innovation and Problem Solving in Personnel Management*, London: McGraw-Hill.

Lee, D. 2002: Gendered workplace bullying in the restructured UK civil service, *Personnel Review*, **31**(2), 205–27.

Lewis, P. 1998: Managing performance-related pay based on case study evidence from the financial services sector, *Human Resource Management Journal*, **8**(2), 66–77.

Lewis, S. and Taylor, K. 1996: Evaluating the impact of family-friendly employer policies: A case study, in S. Lewis and J. Lewis (eds.), *The Work-Family Challenge*, London: Sage.

Long, P. 1986: *Performance Appraisal Revisited*, London: Institute of Personnel Management.

Longenecker, C. and Ludwig, D. 1990: Ethical dilemmas in performance appraisal revisited, *Journal of Business Ethics*, **9**(4), 961–9.

Longenecker, C., Sims, H. and Gioia, D. 1987: Behind the mask: The politics of employee appraisal, *Academy of Management Review*, **1**(3), 183–93.

Luthans, F. and Peterson, S. 2003: 360-degree feedback with systematic coaching: Empirical analysis suggests a winning combination, *Human Resource Management*, **42**(3), 243–56.

Mabey, C. 2001: Closing the circle: Participant views of a 360 degree feedback programme, *Human Resource Management Journal*, **11**(1), 41–53.

Maltz, A., Shenhar, A. and Reilly, R. 2003: Beyond the balanced scorecard: Refining the search for organizational success measures, *Long Range Planning*, **36**(2), 187–204.

Margerison, C. 1976: A constructive approach to appraisal, *Personnel Management*, **8**(7), 30–4.

McGovern, P., Gratton, L., Hope-Hailey, V., Stiles, P. and Truss, C. 1997: Human resource management on the line, *Human Resource Management Journal*, **7**(4), 12–29.

McGregor, D. 1957: An uneasy look at performance appraisals, *Harvard Business Review*, **35**(3), 89–95.

McGregor, D. 1960: *The Human Side of Enterprise*, New York: McGraw-Hill.

McKinlay, A. and Taylor, P. 1996: Power, surveillance and resistance: Inside the factory of the future, in P. Acker, C. Smith and P. Smith (eds.), *The New Workplace and Trade Unionism*, London: Routledge.

Michaels, E., Handfield-Jones, H. and Axelrod, B. 2001: *The War for Talent*, Boston, MA: Harvard Business School Press.

Miller, J. 2003: High tech and high performance: Managing appraisal in the information age, *Journal of Labor Research*, **24**(3), 409–24.

Milliman, J., Nason, S., Zhu, C. and De Cieri, H. 2002: An exploratory assessment of the purposes of performance appraisals in North and Central America and the Pacific Rim, *Human Resource Management*, **41**(1), 87–102.

Neary, D. 2002: Creating a company-wide, on-line, performance management system: A case study at TRW Inc., *Human Resource Management*, **41**(4), 491–8.

Newman, J. 2001: *Modernising Governance: New Labour, Policy and Society*, London: Sage.

Newton, T. and Findlay, P. 1996: Playing God? The Performance of Appraisal, *Human Resource Management Journal*, **6**(3), 42–58.

Redman, T. and Snape, E. 1992: Upward and onward: Can staff appraise their managers? *Personnel Review*, **21**(7), 32–46.

Rowe, K. 1964: An appraisal of appraisal, *Journal of Management Studies*, **1**(1), 1–25.

Sartain, L. 2003: Getting extraordinary results from ordinary people, in M. Effron, R. Gandossy and M. Goldsmith (eds.), *Human Resources in the 21st Century*, Hoboken, NJ: John Wiley.

Simpson, R. 1998: Presenteeism, power and organizational change: Long hours as a career barrier and the impact on the working lives of women managers, *British Journal of Management*, **9** (Special Issue), 37–50.

Skapinker, M. 2003: Board members to face annual appraisal, *Financial Times*, 27 October, 6.

Smart, B. 1999: *Topgrading: How Leading Companies Win by Hiring, Coaching and Keeping the Best People*, Paramus, NJ: Prentice Hall Press.

Storey, J. 1992: *Developments in the Management of Human Resources*, Oxford: Blackwell.

Storey, J., Edwards, P. and Sisson, K. 1997: *Managers in the Making: Careers, Development and Control in Corporate Britain and Japan*, London: Sage.

Strebler M., Robinson, D. and Bevan, S. 2001: *Performance Review: Balancing Objectives and Content*. IES Report 370. Brighton: Institute for Employment Studies.

Thompson, P. and Ackroyd, S. 1995: All quiet on the workplace front? *Sociology*, **29**(4), 615–33.

Townley, B. 1989: Selection and appraisal – Reconstituting social relations? in J. Storey (ed.), *New Perspectives on HRM*, London: Routledge.

Townley, B. 1990: The politics of appraisal: Lessons of the introduction of appraisal into UK universities, *Human Resource Management Journal*, **1**(2), 27–44.

Townley, B. 1993: Performance appraisal and the emergence of management, *Journal of Management Studies*, **30**(2), 221–38.

Townley, B. 1999: Practical reason and performance appraisal, *Journal of Management Studies*, **36**(3), 287–306.

Ulrich, D. and Smallwood, N. 2003: *Why the Bottom Line Isn't*, New Jersey: John Wiley and Sons.

Walker, A. and Smither, G. 1999: A five year study of upward feedback: What managers do with their results matters, *Personnel Psychology*, **52**(2), 393–428.

Ward, P. 1997: *360-Degree Feedback*, London: Institute of Personnel and Development.

Waung, M. and Highhouse, S. 1997: Fear of conflict and empathic buffering: Two explanations for the inflation of performance feedback, *Organizational Behavior and Human Decision Processes*, **71**(1), 37–54.

West, M., Borrill, C., Dawson, J., Scully, J., Carter, M., Anelay, S., Patterson, M. and Waring, J. 2002: The link between the management of employees and patient mortality in acute hospitals, *International Journal of Human Resource Management*, **13**(8), 1299–310.

White, M., Hill, S., McGovern, P., Mills, C. and Smeaton, D. 2003: 'High performance' management practices, working hours and work-life balance, *British Journal of Industrial Relations*, **41**(2), 175–95.

Wilson, F. 2002: Dilemmas of appraisal, *European Management Journal*, **20**(6), 620–9.

CHAPTER TWELVE

Remuneration Systems

Ian Kessler

In general terms, remuneration refers to the way in which employees are rewarded at the workplace. These rewards can take various forms, often a broad distinction being drawn between intrinsic and extrinsic reward. Intrinsic reward is a self-generating outcome such as personal esteem and fulfilment derived from say under-taking 'interesting' or 'useful' work. Extrinsic reward is reflected in more tangible monetary and non-monetary payments in the guise of wages or fringe benefits provided by others, usually the employer. This range of available rewards is reflected in Bloom and Milkovich's (1992: 22) definition of remuneration as a 'bundle of returns offered in exchange for a cluster of employee contributions'.

As a central pillar of the employment relationship, often conceptualized as the effort–reward bargain, remuneration has attracted considerable attention. Heated debate over time and the seemingly endless search for 'new and better' ways to reward employees has essentially focused on the perennial theme of how to relate and balance the link between reward and three contingencies: job, person and per-formance (Mahoney 1989). For researchers and indeed other interested stakeholders, this theme has generated a number of questions: What approaches to reward have organizations adopted? How have particular approaches operated in practice? How 'effective' have different approaches been?

Attempts to develop analytical and theoretical frameworks to address these ques-tions have spawned an extensive research literature. This has straddled a range of social science disciplines, working on the basis of very different assumptions about the way individuals, groups, organizations and societies function. Crudely charac-terized, psychologists have focused on the effectiveness of reward, broadly defined, in terms of individual and group motivation. Behavioural psychologists have looked at the way in which certain rewards can be used to stimulate and reinforce par-ticular actions while cognitive psychologists have considered the link between motivation, reward and perceived employee needs and values (Arnold et al. 1998). Economists have more narrowly focused on pay. They have been concerned with how employers and workers have used pay in the rational pursuit of their respect-ive objectives. Employers have used pay to attract a sufficient supply of labour, while employees have been attracted to those employers paying the most competitive rates (Gerhart and Rynes 2003). In contrast, sociologists have placed more emphasis on the influence of social norms and values in shaping the selection, operation and impact of reward systems at different societal levels. They have also attached greater weight to conflict and certainly power relations in exploring these issues and explaining their outcomes.

This chapter focuses in the main on extrinsic rewards and in particular pay. It uses the three pay contingencies as a framework for evaluating the development of organizational approaches to pay. Initially, it draws upon these contingencies to identify and define pay systems and structures. It then moves to review how these approaches and the emphasis given to the link between pay and job, performance and person have been affected by three recent pressures, those linked to competition, the changing nature of the workforce and regulation. It will be argued that the impact of these pressures on approaches to pay should not be exaggerated; practice still lags behind rhetoric. However, there have been changes in the tone of debate and in practice which has seen a shift in the emphasis given to the respective pay contingencies and been reflected in a new concern with pay processes rather than narrowly conceived pay outcomes.

Definitions and Types of Reward

Pay and the job

The link between pay and job, defined as a stable configuration of organizational tasks and responsibilities, has traditionally been the building block of grading structures. The range of jobs to be found within any organization will be of differential worth to management and will therefore need to be grouped into some kind of grading hierarchy with pay determined by where exactly the individual post sits within it. As Figure 12.1 indicates, in establishing job worth, a basic distinction can be drawn between approaches which rely upon external comparisons and

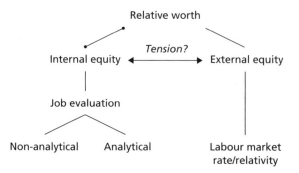

Figure 12.1 Establishing job worth

ones driven by internal organizational comparisons; in other words, job worth may be underpinned by notions of external equity or internal equity (Mahoney 1983; Evans, 2003: 420–8).

External job worth will depend on the state of the outside labour market for the posts in question. Is there a national, regional or sub-regional market for the posts? How 'tight' is labour supply in these different markets? What is the 'going rate' for similar jobs? Organizations will often seek information from a range of sources including pay surveys undertaken by consultants and pay 'clubs' which bring companies together, usually on a local basis, for this very purpose. However, the use of these sources is not always a straightforward exercise. Organizations may well design jobs in distinctive ways rendering it difficult to find comparable outside posts for benchmarking purposes.

The principal mechanism used to establish internal occupational worth is job evaluation. This process seeks to determine the relative size of jobs within the organization independent of the performance of particular individuals. The process of evaluation is not in any 'scientific' sense objective, personal judgments are inevitable. It is, however, designed to be a structured and systematic approach in that it involves the consistent application of a given set of rules. The degree of subjectivity may still vary according to the type of job evaluation technique used and in this respect the distinction between non-analytical and analytical schemes becomes crucial.

An extensive prescriptive and descriptive literature surrounds the use of both techniques (Armstrong and Baron 1995; Armstrong et al. 2004). However, in general terms, non-analytical schemes such as job ranking, paired comparisons and job classification are founded on whole job comparisons. More specifically, complete job descriptions are 'eye-balled' and compared with one another as a means of establishing relative internal worth. This is a far less formal and structured approach than that underpinning analytical job evaluation schemes and inevitably involves the exercise of high levels of personal judgment. It is a relatively low cost and quick solution to establishing job worth and may be viable in small organizations employing a limited range of clearly very different job roles. However, the value of this approach might be seen as compromised by the fact that it does not provide organizations with a defense against equal value pay claims. Depending upon their design, analytical schemes may well provide such a defence. These schemes, including factor comparison and points-factor rating, involve unpacking jobs according to their key attitudinal, behavioural and technical attributes. For instance, the Hay scheme, widely used to evaluate management grades, is based on three main factors – know-how, problem solving and accountability (Armstrong and Murlis 1991: 474). Jobs are then scored against these factors to establish relative job size. Jobs of similar size can then be bundled into the same grade.

From an organizational perspective, external or internal comparisons are not necessarily mutually exclusive approaches to determining job worth and the 'appropriate' rate of pay. The two often 'hang' together where the use of a shared job evaluation scheme by a number of organizations allows for a comparison of

rates for similarly sized jobs. Moreover, following the completion of a job evaluation exercise, an organization will have to decide how to position its pay rates
for the evaluated jobs in relation to external labour market rates. Will it be a 'high'
payer or set rates more in line with the median in the area? However, tensions may
well arise between internal and external equity where posts deemed by an internal
job evaluation exercise to be of similar size are able to attract very different rates
of pay given their relative external worth. It is a problem which organizations have
sometimes sought to deal with through the use of market supplements.

Pay, person and performance

The relationship between pay and the other two contingencies, *person and performance* has mainly been conceived in terms of pay system design. If job is the basis
for establishing the grading structure, a pay system is the mechanism used to drive
pay movements once the post and the individual employee filling it have been
placed in that structure. Pay systems have been underpinned by two basic criteria:
time and performance (Brown 1989). However, in the design of pay systems, person as a pay contingency has also touched upon time and performance to some
degree. This becomes clearer in exploring further the principles underpinning
pay systems.

Time-based pay systems reward the employee simply for the period of attendance
at the workplace. Such a system has managerial advantages such as its low cost of
administration, while employees benefit from having predictable and transparent
payouts. However, time-based pay has no incentive effect and therefore organizations need to draw upon other techniques to manage staff performance.

Time-based pay systems are often intimately related to the job with a particular
job attracting a given rate pay in the form of a daily or hourly rate, a weekly or
monthly wage or an annual salary. This job rate may be pitched at an external
market level and for workers covered by collective bargaining, unions generally
seek to ensure that this is regularly uprated to sustain a given standard of living
for the postholders.

A pay system driven by time can also come together with all three pay
contingencies – job, person and performance – where the grading structure operates
on the basis of service. Traditional grading structures have been founded on an
assumed progression up fixed incremental points to a scale maximum according
to the time served or the seniority of the person in post. The implied rationale for
this form of progression is some link between pay and the person's development in
the role. Over a number of years, the person is rewarded on the assumption that
they will acquire the skills and knowledge needed to perform the role efficiently
and effectively up to the grade maximum which is the rate of pay for doing so.

Focusing on a more direct and explicit link between pay and performance, any
attempt to develop a typology of performance pay systems must address three basic
questions: Whose performance is being assessed? How is it being measured? How

is it being rewarded? The first question encourages an interest in the unit of performance. Pay can be related to individual, group or company performance.

The second question focuses on the nature and evaluation of performance. Generally performance refers to outputs and pay can be linked to the achievement of individual or group targets and objectives. However, pay can also be linked to inputs and these are often intimately related to the person, what they, as individuals, bring to the role in terms of skill, knowledge and behaviour. It is at this point that the notions of performance and person overlap. These individual features and abilities might be seen as representing the basis for an assumed or 'promised' level performance. This link between person and performance has a long history, underpinning traditional craft-based apprenticeship schemes with their emphasis on skills acquisition. It has taken a more modern form as competence pay.

The third question concentrates on the performance-pay link. This directs attention to the distinction between a relatively fixed relationship, where a given level of output usually produces an automatic payout, and a less mechanistic link often founded on some kind of assessment of the individuals' or the groups' performance undertaken by another and requiring the exercise of judgment or discretion by this other party. This link assumes different forms in terms of how any outcome payment is related to base pay. Achieved performance may trigger a payment which becomes consolidated into base pay. However, the payment may remain unconsolidated and have to be earned anew in subsequent years. It is this unconsolidated payment which is often referred to as variable pay.

Drawing upon these dimensions a number of types of pay systems can be distinguished (Casey et al. 1991; ACAS 2003). These are presented in Figure 12.2. Three types of payment are worthy of note. First, systems may be based on some form of appraisal or assessment of the individual employee. Founded upon inputs, they are referred to as merit, skills or competency schemes. Related to individual outputs they are called individual performance-related schemes. They usually involve a payment which is integrated into base salary either in the form of a percentage increase or additional increments on a pay scale.

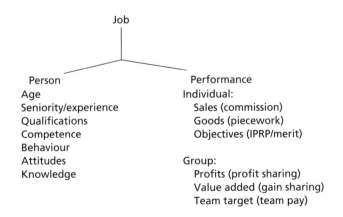

Figure 12.2 Types of payment system

The second type of pay system involves a bonus in the form of an unconsolidated payment to the individual employee. These schemes are usually founded on a relatively mechanistic relationship between pay and the individual in terms of units of production, targets or sales. They include the differing forms of piecework as well as other traditional systems such as sales commission.

The third type of system is also based on the payment of a bonus which is again usually unconsolidated and mechanistically linked to performance. In this instance, however, it is paid for the performance of a group in the form of the work team, section, department, establishment or company. Collective bonuses include Rucker and Scanlon gain sharing plans (Bowey 2000) which relate pay to changes in the sales value or the added value of a designated group within the organization. They also include profit sharing and employee share ownership schemes (Pendleton 2000), which, if approved by the Inland Revenue, qualify for certain tax benefits. The main approved scheme is the Share Incentive Plan (SIP). Introduced in the Finance Act, 2000, it is an all-employee scheme under which companies can give employees up to £1,500 worth of shares a year. Companies can then give employees up to two matching shares for each share an employee buys.

It is important to stress that organizations often seek to link pay to more than one of the three pay contingencies. For example, a fairly typical pay system provides for steady movement up a scale to a point which equates to what is seen as a competitive market rate for the job. This rate would regularly be revised to reflect any changes in external market conditions with any scope for the individual to move beyond this point being discretionary and dependent on performance. Indeed organizations may well utilize any given contingency in different ways; for instance, pay may well be related to both individual and collective performance. It is this search for what organizations and other stakeholders feel is the 'right balance' between pay and the three contingencies which provides the dynamic for pay developments. It is to these developments that attention now turns.

Competitive Pressures

Models of strategic pay

The increasing intensity of competition and the apparently relentless organizational search for 'sustained competitive advantage' has driven a range of actors with an interest in the management of the workforce to a preoccupation with the strategic use of human resources. It is the link between competition, business strategy and people management which has stimulated a raft of ideas and work around what has become labelled the 'New Pay' agenda (Schuster and Zingheim 1992) reflected in Lawler's (1995: 14) views that 'The new pay argues in favour of a pay design process that starts with business strategy and organizational change.' Clearly, the implication of such a statement is that in the past approaches to pay were somewhat detached from 'business needs'. The essence of the 'New Pay' is that pay should be integral to meeting such needs and, if used in this way, pay can become a key 'strategic lever' in improving business performance.

Attempts to consider how pay might be used in this fashion have overlapped with generic models found in the strategic human resources management (SHRM) literature. The 'universalistic' or 'best practice' SHRM model has invariably included payment systems, usually of a performance related kind, in its bundle of HR practices assumed to foster high levels of employee commitment or performance (Pfeffer 1998). However, there has not always been consistency in the types of payment systems viewed as part of this bundle; there have been debates about whether particular systems such as individual performance pay can really be viewed as likely to generate employee commitment (Wood 1996); and there has been limited evidence of a clear and unambiguous link between the payment system in these bundles and the attitudinal and behavioural changes implied.

Pay systems have also been integral to contingency models of SHRM, usually predicated on notions of vertical and horizontal 'fit'. Vertical fit implies some alignment between pay systems and strategic business objectives suggesting that the 'appropriate' pay system is dependent upon the nature of those objectives and other organizational circumstances. One of the most prominent of these conceptual models (Schuler and Jackson 1987) relates the strategic orientation of an organization, whether it seeks to compete on the basis of quality, cost or innovation, to the different behaviours required from employees and proposes that particular HR practices, including different types of reward, are best suited to generating these behaviours.

Attempts to highlight the importance of organizational contingencies as an influence on the selection of payment systems are not new. Over 30 years ago, Lupton and Gowler (1969) presented a framework highlighting the linkages between corporate pay objectives, the types of system best suited to the pursuit of those objectives and organizational circumstances in terms, say, of culture and technology. The history of such an approach and its more recent reincarnation in SHRM are a testament to the fact that in general terms it retains some plausibility. It is clear, for example, that specific pay systems, say piecework, have traditionally been prevalent in particular industries, in this case footwear and textiles, because the technology and the nature of the product lend themselves to the 'effective' use of this scheme. In both industries it is fairly straightforward to link pay to a tangible unit of output produced by the individual employee in a relatively independent way. However, a more robust testing, particularly of these more recent models, has proved difficult. Attempts to classify organizations by strategy, let alone establish whether the selection of the 'appropriate' pay systems leads to improved organizational effectiveness have been problematic.

The perceived importance of horizontal fit is based on the assumption that payment systems and other personnel practices are more likely to make an effective contribution to corporate performance where they are bundled together in mutually supportive ways. One of the most striking attempts to create this fit relates to the use of pay systems to support a development in modern job design, the emergence of team working. Team work has been presented as one of the key trends in work organization with significant implications for the way in which employees are paid. Individual performance-related pay is often criticized for undermining teamwork while team-based pay has been seen as much more attuned to the prevailing pattern of work. The use of team-based pay was given a boost, particularly in the public sector, with the Makinson Report (2001). It called for the use of unconsolidated team bonuses, seeing them as a more visible and viable form of reward than consolidated individual performance payments. In the wake of this report, team pay was introduced into the four largest civil service executive agencies, the Employment Service, the Benefits Agency, Customs and Excise and the Inland Revenue.

There is some evidence to suggest that use of team pay to support job design may have positive outcomes in terms of individual and organizational performance (Wageman 1995; Burgess et al. 2003). However, the take-up of team pay remains low with well under 20 per cent of organizations using it (CIPD 2003). Salary progressions based on team performance is even less in evidence; these findings are confirmed by other surveys (Thompson and Milsome 2001: 13). This low take-up suggests that despite some evidence of effectiveness, administrative difficulties remain in introducing team pay. It is not always easy to find a standard of team performance that can be linked to pay because teams often break up quickly and do not therefore represent a stable base for a pay. Moreover, it remains questionable whether team working in the strictest sense is as widespread as assumed (see Cully et al. 1999: 43). Team-based pay may well be rare simply because genuine forms of team working are scarce.

Interest in horizontal fit has begun to overlap somewhat with the resource-based view of management. In developing an idiosyncratic relationship between pay and complementary HR practices, which other companies cannot easily replicate, it is suggested that a pay system in its own right might 'add value' to the organization or encourages attitudes and behaviour which do so (Gerhart et al. 1996). As Cox and Purcell (1998) note, 'The real benefit in reward strategies lies in complex linkages with other human resource management policies and practices.' In this respect, attention has been drawn to the well-publicized Lincoln Electric's piecework scheme, which by virtue of its longevity has led to an employee trust in its operation, which in turn may well have contributed to it generating the 'desired' and expected organizational outcomes (Kessler 2001).

This approach suggests the importance of process in understanding the likely effects of pay. The 'best practice' and 'best fit' approaches display little attempt to consider pay processes or indeed to draw upon theories which might explain how and why particular pay systems lead to 'desired' organizational attitudes and behaviours. To suggest that the simple adoption of a particular type of pay system leads to more committed employees or behaviours in tune with a strategic orientation is to ignore completely theories from cognitive psychology. These place an emphasis on the importance of employee perception of process in explaining the impact of pay systems. For example, expectancy theory (Vroom 1964) stresses that pay is most likely to motivate when all three of the following conditions are met: that employees feel they have been set achievable objectives; that they can see a clear link between pay and the attainment of these objectives; and that they value pay. Equity theory (Adams 1965) draws attention to the relationship between motivation and whether employees feel they have been treated fairly in pay terms. Fairness is seen as residing in procedural justice, which relates to the way the payment systems operates; distributional justice which touches on pay outcomes; and interactional justice which focuses on how employees are dealt with in their contact with those managers responsible for administering pay.

What 'best practice', 'best fit' and resource based models do share is a set of assumptions rooted in economic rationality (Oliver 1997). They are primarily driven by an interest in how HR practices in general and pay practices in particular impact on business performance. Oliver (1997), however, draws attention to managements' acting in ways which have nothing to do directly with the pursuit of 'business success' but which ensures conformity with social, political and cultural expectations. It is an approach which falls within a neo-institutional sociological approach which suggests that the organization may well conform not because practices are proven to contribute to improved business performance but because they are forced or encouraged to copy what others are doing (DiMagio and Powell 1983). Few attempts have been made to apply this type of approach to the development of pay systems. However, Ahlstrand's (1990) work at Esso's Fawley plant found that productivity pay had assumed crucial symbolic significance, signalling that management was taking action to deal with a problem after any proven link between this type of pay scheme and business performance had long since disappeared. Fashions in payment systems, not least the rush towards individual performance pay in the late 1980s, might be seen in a similar light.

Rewards strategies

Emerging in the early 1990s, the 'New Pay Agenda' is no longer particularly new, but it continues to hold some allure for commentators (Reilly 2003). The need for a link between business objectives and rewards has continued as something of an orthodoxy in leading textbooks on reward. For example, Armstrong (2002a: 83) defines a reward strategy as 'a business-focused statement of the intention of the organization concerning the developments of future reward processes and practices which are aligned to the business and human resource strategies of the organization.' This emphasis reflects the fact that many large employers have reward strategies. A recent survey by the CIPD (2003) of over 500 organizations indicated that almost two-thirds had a 'strategic approach to reward'.

These strategies assume a similar form. They often combine general principles on the use of given criteria in pay determination and broad statements of intent on pay with more or less specific assertions on how pay rates will be set relative to the market. For example, British Airways 'Reward Vision' includes the use of rewards 'aligned to both individual and company performance'; rewards that 'support the delivery of BA's business strategy and plans'; rewards that 'take into account market forces and drives'; and rewards that 'help employees understand how their efforts contribute to company performance' (E Reward 2003a).

The relationship between these rather bland reward statements and the effective pursuit of business objectives is open to debate. Drawn up in such general terms, it is not difficult for an organization to rationalize any given set of pay practices in accordance with the principles and values espoused. But using a range of harder measures, there is some room for doubt as to the tangible impact of reward strategies on actual practice. First, in terms of firms taking reward strategies forward, it is noteworthy that from a list of eight companies with such strategies or philosophies, only four had an associated action plan (E Reward 2003b: 8). It is also striking that relatively few companies evaluate their payment systems once implemented with a view to establishing whether they have met their objectives (Corby et al. 2002). Second, as far as horizontal and vertical fit are concerned, a survey by the Industrial Society (1997) revealed that under half (47 per cent) of those organizations with a reward strategy felt it was efficiently linked to the HR strategy while only around a half (57 per cent) suggested that it met business needs effectively.

Finally, any evidence of the link between reward strategies, reward practice and corporate performance remains scarce. This is not to deny studies which have found a relationship between specific pay systems and tangible business outcomes. In a frequently quoted study, Lazear (1986) found a 44 per cent increase in overall productivity among 2,000 workers across a number of sites in an auto glass installation chain following the introduction of a piecework system. Moreover, studies find a small but consistently positive relationship between profit sharing schemes and various measure of business performance (Blinder 1990). In general, however, this kind of work has always struggled to control the range of variables that might affect company performance and to establish the direction of causation.

Workforce Pressures

Developments in the character of the workforce have provided a pressing and immediate impetus for change in approaches to reward. In this section a number of such developments related to diversity, industrial composition and the labour market are considered in turn.

Diversity

The workforce has become increasingly diverse in terms of gender, family circumstances, ethnicity and age. Female participation rates in the labour market have risen (Gallie 2000; Dickens et al. 2003); employment among lone parents and older people has increased (Dickens et al. 2003); and employment among a number of ethnic minority groups has also grown in recent years (Dickens et al. 2003). These developments have wide ranging implications for personnel practice (see Chapters 6 and 7). It is, however, worth briefly touching on how these social and demographic changes have had an impact on reward practices.

There have been some consequences for reward that relate to particular social groups. The most significant of these concerns older workers with pensions being thrust to the top of the reward agenda. The pensions issue has a number of different dimensions. In part, concerns have arisen over the weak performance of pension funds, not least as a result of share price fragility, and significant resulting deficits. This has led to the closure of some final salary pension schemes. A survey by consultants Mercers of more than 1,800 British company pension schemes found that the proportion of companies with final salary schemes now open to new employees had fallen from 56 per cent in 2002 to 38 per cent in 2004 (*Guardian* 2004b). This issue is also associated with high profile instances of company failure which has led to employees losing pension benefits. Estimates suggest that more than 100,000 have been detrimentally affected in this way (*The Times* 2004). It is a problem which has encouraged the Labour government to legislate, with the creation of a Pension Protection Fund. Finally, a broader public policy debate and government proposals on pension reform have been sparked by the ageing population and the need for systems that support the growing number of older people for an increasing number of years.

A more diverse workforce has encouraged some companies to review how they reward staff. The assumption underpinning this development is that different types of employee may well value different types of reward. For example, a detailed case study on the development of a new approach to rewards at Lloyds TSB notes that,

> Demographic and social changes combined to make the need for a review of reward ever more pressing . . . As the workforce became more diverse, with an array of lifestyle and family structures, the need for companies like Lloyds TSB to adopt arrangements to accommodate the requirements arising from their employee's family responsibilities was intensifying. (E-Reward 2003c)

In terms of remuneration policy and practice, this greater sensitivity to personal difference and circumstance has contributed to an interest in a 'Total Reward' approach. Such an approach is designed to incorporate as many pay and non-pay returns as possible into the remuneration package (IRS 2003a). Total rewards might be seen as responsive to diversity in broadening the basis of the remuneration package, allowing rewards to be offered which meet diverse needs including the scope to work more flexible hours and family friendly benefits such as childcare facilities and help with childcare. Lloyds TSB, for instance, offer childcare vouchers as part of their benefits package. Total Reward schemes also often provide benefits on a cafeteria basis, allowing the employee to choose from a range of options and therefore tailor packages to meet their own particular needs. As a recent report on Astra Zeneca's flexible benefits scheme noted, 'The scheme is seen as recognizing the diversity among staff by allowing individuals to choose benefits according to their life style' (*People Management* 2002).

The prescriptive rhetoric driving these approaches and the high-profile companies adopting them should not obscure relatively low take-up and associated difficulties. A CIPD (2003: 22) survey found that only 12 per cent of companies covered had 'flex plans' for all or some of their employees. The use of family-friendly benefits appears similarly limited. Thompson and Milsome (2001) note that while around two-thirds of organizations offer paternity leave, only 10 per cent have a workplace nursery, 10 per cent provide childcare subsidies and 2 per cent offer the provision of after-school care. It may well be that the low incidence of these kinds of benefits reflects the fact that from a company point of view they simply do not represent a cost-efficient means of reward. Studies suggest that employees tend to undervalue the fringe benefits they receive from a company (Thompson and Milsome 2003: 56). In the case of cafeteria benefits, the complications associated with administration are an added deterrence to their use.

Sectoral and occupational shifts

Industrial and occupational shifts have seen a move from manufacturing to service sector employment and the growing importance of non-manual jobs (Gallie 2000: 288). These changes have been reflected in a number of pay developments. They have encouraged a marked switch in the focus of policy makers and commentators. During the 1960s and 70s interest was concentrated on manual workers. Their payment systems were widely seen as ineffective and out of management control. Individual and group piecework schemes covering some six million employees were seen to have generated an instability in industrial relations which in turn was viewed as having a detrimental effect upon the UK's broader economic performance. Subsequent developments in remuneration were in large part directed towards addressing the perceived weaknesses in piecework systems.

From the 1980s and throughout the 1990s policy makers, commentators and practitioners shifted their focus of interest away from manual workers, particularly in the private manufacturing sector, towards non-manual workers, especially in the service sector. This concentration on non-manual pay was perhaps most clearly illustrated by the growing attention devoted to individual performance-related pay in the late 1980s. The third Workplace Industrial Relations Survey (Millward et al. 2000), for instance, found that between 30 and 40 per cent of establishments had merit pay for white collar staff at various levels, compared to under 20 per cent of establishments with schemes for manual staff. As Smith (1989: 61) noted in reviewing development at this time, 'The only group not experiencing the changes brought about by the reward culture are shopfloor employees.'

The second fall-out from compositional shifts in the workforce is related not only to an increased attention paid to the pay of non-manual workers but even more specifically to the greater interest shown in the pay of what have become known as 'knowledge workers' (Ledford 1995). It is not easy to 'tie down' this term. Are 'knowledge workers' to be found in particular sectors, say the 'hi-tech' sector? Do they equate with specific occupational groups, perhaps professionals or technicians? Or are they located in a given part of an organization, maybe the R&D or product development functions? Taking each of these possibilities in turn, attention has certainly been drawn to the use made of stock options as a means of rewarding employees in 'hi-tech' and start-up 'dot com' organizations. A survey of 35 UK internet companies found that two-thirds used some form of share option scheme (IRS 2001a). In the case of new companies such schemes were seen as a way of attracting staff but they were also viewed as attractive to young and 'talented staff' perhaps interested in acquiring a stake in the company.

If 'knowledge workers' are to be equated with creative and innovative workers then there is some consensus that intrinsic rather than extrinsic rewards are a better motivator (Amabile 1988). Critics of monetary incentives such Kohn (1993) have argued that in encouraging employee compliance with short-term objectives, individual performance-related pay is likely to drive out the speculation and long-term thinking associated with creative and innovative processes. How far this message has been taken on board by functions such as R&D, which might employ such workers is, however, open to question. Thompson and Heron (2002) in a survey of over 120 R&D-based firms found that considerable reliance was placed on monetary incentives for the scientists and engineers employed.

Third, recent discussion on the nature and development of payment systems can be seen as related to the shift from manufacturing to service-based employment. This has taken the form of attempts to develop pay systems which are likely to incentivize those directly working with customers and to foster employees attitudes and behaviours 'appropriate' to direct interaction with service users. In part, this has been reflected in company attempts to link aspects of variable pay to the achievement of customer satisfaction targets. For example, Sainsbury's has introduced a team bonus system using a 'mystery shopper' approach as a means of establishing whether customer service quality targets have been met (IRS 2003b) and Boots the Chemist has a quarterly bonus for retail staff related to 'customer focused' goals (Incomes Data Services (IDS) Report 2002a).

In addition, the increasing interest shown in competency-based pay might also be associated with this customer focus. One of the frequently mentioned (Kessler and Purcell 1992) managerial problems with individual performance-related pay is the 'tunnel vision' engendered by the setting of personal objectives and the tendency for employees to focus on *what* is to be achieved regardless of *how* it is achieved. Clearly, the neglect of process and a disregard for others can have detrimental consequences for service quality both in terms of dealing with internal customers or colleagues and external customers. Competency pay by rewarding behaviours and

attitudes such as co-operation, courtesy and communication is seen as a corrective to these flaws.

It is still the case that attempts to link pay solely to competence remains rare.
A recent survey of 100 organizations found that only eight had competency-based
pay in this sense (E Reward 2004). Identifying the 'right' competencies and whether
they have been achieved can be difficult (Sparrow 1996). However, the deployment of competencies in combination with individual objectives – what has become
known as 'contribution-based pay' (Brown and Armstrong 1999) – is much more
common. The same survey found that exactly a third of the organizations used
such an approach. Essex County Council is a recent example of an organization
implementing a 'contribution-based' scheme. The pay to its 9,000 employees
is linked to the achievement of around six objectives and progress in acquiring
certain competencies including those related to 'Customer/Client Orientation' (Local
Government Employers' Organization 2004).

The labour market

The state of the external labour market is crucial in driving organizational evaluation of job worth and over recent years there have been important changes in
the labour market that have affected this evaluation and had significant implications for pay practices. The UK labour market has been fairly 'tight', with unemployment at historically low levels. At the same time, recruitment and retention
difficulties and skill shortages have been particularly acute among certain occupational groups and in particular sectors (Ruiz 2004). The picture is further refined
by the fact that labour market pressures have remained somewhat uneven between
different parts of the country, continuing to be particularly acute in London and
parts of the south-east.

The perception that labour market pressures vary by region has led to public
policy pronouncements on pay determination in the public services. In the context of the government's ongoing preoccupation with the modernization of the
public services, the Chancellor in his April 2003 budget announced that 'In future,
remits for pay review bodies and for public sector workers will include a stronger
local and regional dimension' (*Society Guardian* 2003a). The proposal was met with
hostility from a range of stakeholders. The public sector unions restated their traditional support for national bargaining on grounds of 'transparency and fairness'.
However, even public sector employers were highly critical. The Local Government Employers in their evidence to the Local Government Pay Commission opposed
regional pay (*Society Guardian* 2003b). There was a feeling that the call for regional
pay was a misreading of labour market conditions with pay pressures likely to be
confined to very specific local 'hot spots' rather than equating crudely with region.
There was also a belief that the national agreements in local government and indeed
in other parts of the public services were flexible enough to respond to these local
pressures. This was borne out by an IDS survey undertaken for the unions for

their joint submission to the Local Government Pay Commission which revealed significant variation in hourly rates for similar roles in different parts of the country. Indeed, recent national agreements in the public services, in the NHS with Agenda for Change, in teaching and the university sector have included provision for recruitment and retention payments providing some scope to vary pay where local labour market conditions dictate (Bach and Winchester 2003).

A reading of the evidence from independent commentators lends some weight to this skepticism. In an implied response to the suggestion that private sector pay was more sensitive to regional factors, IDS noted that 'outside of London and the South east there is not a great deal of variation which is intrinsically regional' (IDS Report 2003a). It relates this to the fact that organizations with sites or branches across the country continue to use national structures and systems to manage pay in their different location. In some cases, such as Barclays, the system of a London allowance has been extended across much of the south, with a decreasing amount paid as the distance from central London increases. In the retail sector, a zonal pay system is most common. In Littlewoods, for example, location allowances vary according to three zonal bands (IDS Report 2003a).

Debate about regional pay has been only one response to concerns about recruitment and retention difficulties. In a number of sectors increasing sensitivity to labour market conditions has prompted activity. First, there have been some moves to increase starting or recruitment salaries as a way of attracting employees into the organization in the first place. Over recent years a national scheme of 'golden hellos' of around to £4,000–5,000 has been payable to school teachers particularly in shortage subject such as maths and science, while at local levels similar payments are being made to social workers in selected authorities (*Manchester News* 2003). In the finance sector a number of organizations are making significant increases to starting salaries for customer advisers to improve recruitment (IDS Report 2002b).

Second, and more tangibly, a number of organizations are providing employees with greater clarity when it comes to pay progression. The assumption is that employees are more likely to join and stay with an organization if they have a clear understanding of their future earnings opportunities. Such earnings opportunities are partly about the process of pay determination and it is noteworthy that some organizations have tried to introduce greater transparency into this process. Lloyds TSB, for example, removed their pay matrix which by relating pay to performance and position in the scale made pay determination somewhat opaque; Zurich Financial Services (IDS 2002c) reintroduced their scale minima for certain grades to ensure consistency and openness.

Earnings opportunities, however, are also intimately related to the scope for career progression and organizations are strengthening career pathways. White et al. (2004) found that two out of three employers in their survey had career ladders open to most employees. The development of career routes and pathways is not, however, an unproblematic process. As organizations have increasingly become flatter (Littler et al. 2003) so promotion opportunities in terms of upward movement have reduced. Indeed, research by Conyon et al. (2001) suggests that organizations which de-layer are much more likely to use performance pay than those which retain a traditional hierarchical structure.

Organizations have sought to provide career opportunities in the context of flatter structures by modifying pay and grading systems in a number of very different ways. Broad banding has broken down occupational silos and established grades which embrace a wide range of groups, so facilitating movement across the organization. It was this scope to move staff more easily around that attracted Tesco to broad banding and surveys suggest that up to a third of organizations are using such a scheme (Thompson and Milsome 2001: 11).

Another approach to developing grading structures which supports career development involves strengthening occupational silos. Often reflected in the establishment of job families, this approach provides employees with the opportunity to develop their careers and progress in pay terms by deepening their specialist skills. Job families are not particularly common, being found in only around 10 per cent of organizations. However, there are examples of this approach. British Gas has recently set up a pay structure based on job families (IDS Report 2004b). Moreover, teachers, who in the past might only have been able to progress by moving away from teaching to a headship, can now stay within teaching and move onto a higher Advanced Skills Teacher grade. Indeed, the attempt to address recruitment and retention difficulties by developing an occupationally based career route is apparent across much of the public services. Career and grading structure are being developed in local government which allow assistant and support staff to move in professional teaching and social work roles. The 'skills escalator', an essential part of the Agenda for Change agreement in the NHS, might be seen in similar terms.

The final set of consequences which derive from recent labour market conditions relate to the tension that has arisen between job and performance in pay determination. It is certainly the case that individual performance continues to be one of the main drivers of organizational pay systems. Despite the criticism heaped on such schemes from a number of quarters over the years (Kessler and Purcell 1992; Kohn 1993), the take-up of individual performance-related pay schemes remains high. A recent survey suggested that two-thirds of organizations used individual performance-related pay for their workers with take-up higher among non-manual than manual workers (E Reward 2004). However, it is equally apparent that as external labour markets have tightened, the operation of individual, and indeed collective, performance-related pay schemes has changed.

In part, this change has been manifest in a shift in managerial emphasis from performance to labour markets. An informed review of the pay scene notes that 'Benchmarking salary levels has been given more priority in the past few years as unemployment has fallen and labour markets have tightened. Simultaneously employers dissatisfied with their PRP systems have altered them to reflect more of the market influence' (IDS Report 2004a). Closely related, the shift in emphasis has also been accompanied by a 'squeeze' on performance payments. As organizations are forced to provide higher competitive pay rates, so the element of the paybill available for rewarding performance inevitably is reduced. This has been highlighted as a problem in the finance sector because 'employers are struggling to fulfil employees' expectations with pay systems which remain hybrids of market based and performance related approaches (IDS Report 2003b).

Regulatory Pressures

The regulatory framework for pay determination in the UK has changed fairly radically in recent years. This change reflects the cumulative effect of incremental developments, the recent momentum given to longstanding regulatory mechanisms and new initiatives stimulating activity for the first time. It is clear that a general weakening of the main form of voluntary regulation, collective bargaining, has continued (Cully et al. 1999: 242; Millward et al. 2000). Equally striking is the fact that even where representatives remain at workplace level their influence over aspects of pay is limited. Only a quarter of representatives negotiate on any aspects of pay. More recent developments in the public services suggest opportunities for the 'union voice' to be heard again. The pay reform programmes set out in recent agreements across the NHS, local government and higher education provide for the development of local pay systems and structures within the context of a national framework on the basis of union-management partnership principles. There is evidence to suggest that the application of these principles may be uneven within (Bach 2004) and across (Tailby et al. 2004) different parts of the public services. However, the scope for meaningful employee involvement is certainly likely to be greater here than in private sector workplaces where there are only non–union representatives (Cully et al. 1999) or no representatives at all (Brown et al. 1998).

This weakening of voluntary mechanisms for regulating pay has been accompanied by and perhaps related to the increasing importance of others means of pay regulation. These alternatives have assumed a number of forms. Codes of Practice have begun to encroach upon aspects of pay determination. For example, a recent Code of Practice has sought to guard against the development of the two-tier workforce in parts of the public services. The two-tier workforce emerged as a consequence of contracts being outsourced in public private partnerships such as under the Private Finance Initiative or after privatization. Under such arrangements in-house staff were transferred to the private sector with their pay and conditions protected by the Transfer of Undertaking (Protection of Employees) Regulations 1981. However, those workers subsequently employed were recruited on inferior employment terms. The unions have campaigned relentlessly against the two-tier workforce and in February 2003 a Code of Practice covering local government was agreed with key stakeholders. It ensures that new joiners would be offered terms and conditions which were 'no less favourable than those of transferred staff'. The government has undertaken to extend this Code to other parts of the public services.

However, the most significant alternative to voluntary pay regulation has been statutory regulation. This section focuses on three pressures for greater statutory regulation of pay, those generated by equal pay developments and by attempts to influence pay at the bottom and the top of the labour market.

Low pay

Statutory attempts to regulate low pay in the UK have a long history. The Fair Wages Resolution of the House of Commons dates back to 1891 and required contractors working on government contracts to observe terms and conditions of employment not less favourable than those in appropriate collective agreements. The Trades Board Act passed not long after, in 1909, sought to broaden and strengthen protection by setting up boards which would set minimum wage levels in particular sectors. At their peak in 1953 some 3.5 million workers were covered by 66 boards, or what became known as wages councils (Rubery and Edwards 2003). Both institutions fell victim to Thatcherite attempts to deregulate the labour market, the Fair Wages Resolution being rescinded in 1983 and all wages councils finally being wound up in 1993.

Under the first 'New Labour' administration such protection re-emerged as a public policy goal under the 'Fairness at Work Agenda'. It was given effect by the establishment of a Low Pay Commission (LPC) charged with recommending a rate for a national minimum wage (NMW). Following its report, the National Minimum Wage Act was passed in 1998 and the NMW came into effect on 1 April 1999. Achieving permanent status in 2001, the LPC has provided empirically based annual reports on the operation of the NMW which have led to further recommendations, largely accepted by the government, on up-rating and eligibility. Increasing by on average 7 per cent a year since its introduction, from October 2005 the adult rate paid to those who are 22 and above will be £5.05; a development rate for those aged between 18 and 21 will be £4.25; and recently a minimum has been introduced for 16 and 17-year-olds which stands at £3. The main means of enforcement has been through the Inland Revenue. It is an approach which by the end of 2003 had yielded almost 2,000 complaints and the recovery by the Inland Revenue of £13 million in unpaid wages (IDS Report 2003c).

Debate on the NMW has focused on its public policy objectives and its impact on various outcomes. More specifically, there has been discussion on whether it should be seen as part of an 'anti poverty agenda' or simply designed to provide a minimum protective floor, safeguarding competitiveness and ensuring limited detrimental affects on productivity, levels of employment and wage inflation (Simpson 2004).

The former anti-poverty objective has informed the approach of many unions with low paid members. UNISON, for example, has been to the fore in using the European Threshold of Decency as its baseline for establishing what constitutes low pay, a measure which yields a much higher rate than the NMW. Action in this respect has not been limited to the unions. A community action group, the East London Communities Organization, has been campaigning for a 'living wage', also well above the NMW, to be paid to catering, cleaning and security workers in a part of the capital embracing the major finance companies located in docklands. It is a campaign which has met with some success. HSBC and Barclays have agreed to pay the 'living wage' of £6.70 per hour to its cleaning staff in the area (Donovan 2004).

The government has been much more concerned with the latter objective and particularly the macroeconomic consequences of the NMW's introduction. This is reflected not least in the LPC's terms of reference. These include the need 'to monitor and evaluate the impact of the national minimum wage, with particular reference to the effect on pay, employment and competitiveness in low paying sectors and small firms.'

With the LPC supporting a range of projects, it is hardly surprising that the efforts of the research community have focused on the kinds of outcomes flagged up in its monitoring brief. The NMW has improved the pay position of a not insignificant proportion of the workforce without dramatically adverse economic consequences. The number benefiting from the NMW has gradually been calculated downwards, however, from an initial LPC estimate of 1.9 million of employees to a suggested figure of 815,000 (Dickens and Manning 2003) but this later figure still represents 3.7 per cent of the workforce. Moreover, around two-thirds of those benefiting are women, although this does not appear to have had a major effect in narrowing the gender pay gap (Robinson 2002).

Looking at outcomes and taking the three listed in the LPC terms of references – pay, employment and competitiveness – much of the initial concern about the NMW focused on 'spillover effects' in the form of employees seeking to re-establish pay differentials. There were examples of companies where this did indeed take place, particularly in the retail sector (IDS Report 2002d; 2003d). These were organizations very keen to position their pay systems and structures comfortably above the statutory rate to avoid being labelled and seen as NMW payers. In general, however, 'few spill-over effects' have been found. This finding was confirmed even in a sector, care homes, where 30 per cent of workers were directly affected by the NMW (Dickens and Manning 2003). Indeed the overall increase in the national paybill arising from the implementation of the NMW has been calculated as 0.35 per cent (LPC 2002).

Concerns about the employment effects were particularly to the fore in public policy debates on the NMW. The main rationale for the development rate was that younger workers were particularly vulnerable in this respect. In general the NMW has been found not to adversely affect employment opportunities. The LPC concluded that 'Employment growth among groups and sectors most affected by the minimum wage has generally been stronger than average', although a 'minimal negative effect' was found for younger people (LPC 2003).

Finally, while there have been plenty of threats to the competitiveness of UK firms, the NMW does not appear to have been one of them. Looking at this issue among small firms, Arrowsmith et al. (2003) explore two possible scenarios; one based on orthodox economic theory which suggests that small firms are particularly vulnerable to 'regulatory shock in harsh competitive environment' and the other on institutional theory, which implies that the NMW may actually boost efficiency and morale. They found that neither really applied. Small firms were basically 'taking the NMW in their stride', a finding they accounted for by the informality and 'indeterminacy' of pay fixing in such firms.

Top pay

The pay of those at the top of the earnings ladder in the UK has attracted considerable media attention. It is an issue which has generated heated debate among a range of stakeholders not only on grounds of fairness and equity but because it is seen to have wider implications for corporate governance. In contrast to the pay of other groups, that of executives and directors touches on questions of corporate control, decision making and crucially accountability to shareholders.

For the research community, these features have encouraged the use of principal–agent theory to explore executive compensation. In simple terms, this approach acknowledges a difference of interest between shareholders as principals and senior managers as agents and suggests the best way to optimize the performance of the senior managers is to link their pay to the performance of the firm (Jensen and Meckling 1976). There is some UK evidence to suggest a relationship between executive salaries, bonus and share options and corporate performance (McKnight and Tomkins 1999). However, this and other evidence has shown that remuneration packages are primarily determined by firm size (Reed 2000).

For policy makers and practitioners in Britain, the interest shown in senior management compensation has unfolded along two closely related but distinct lines. The first relates simply to the level of executive pay and the manner in which it is determined. The second concerns remuneration in relation to severance packages and other payments in the context of 'poor' corporate performance.

The process was 'kicked-off' by the Cadbury Report (1992) which recommended the appointment of a dedicated Remuneration Committee, made up predominantly of non-executive directors to determine senior management pay. It was, however, the Greenbury Committee (1995) and its proposed Code a few years later which provided more detailed recommendations on the make-up of the Remuneration Committee and its duties and responsibilities in relation to remuneration policy and the disclosure and approval of such policy. This was strengthened still further by the Hampel Report (1998) which drew upon both the Cadbury and Greenbury Reports to develop a Combined Code which was effectively mandatory on all UK listed companies.

Despite such action disquiet has continued not least because Pension Investment Research Consultants data reveals that median base salary for the highest paid directors among the FTSE 100 companies increased from £301,000 in 1993 to £579,000 in 2002. This is an increase of 92 per cent over a period in which inflation has risen by 25 per cent and average wages by 41 per cent (Select Committee on Trade and Industry 2003). The disquiet has been apparent among trade unions with the TUC (2002) drawing attention to these rises in executive pay in a publication entitled *Executive Excess – Time to Act*. Concerns have also been stirred up among shareholder representative bodies. For example, the Association of British Insurers (ABI) has issued guidelines on share incentive schemes and a joint statement has been issued on executive contracts and severance by the National Association of Pension Funds and the ABI.

In response, the Labour government has tightened regulatory control. The Directors' Remuneration Report Regulations 2002 introduced a new schedule into the Companies Act 1985 requiring directors of listed companies to produce a Directors' Remuneration Report. This report must include specified pieces of information and be signed off by the board of directors and certified by auditors. An ordinary resolution approving the Remuneration Report must be tabled at the annual general meeting. The resolution is only advisory and therefore lacks force. However, it has prompted some fairly high profile opposition to executive pay at AGMs; thus only 67 per cent of shareholders voted in favour of W.H. Smith's 2004 Remuneration Report which provided for a multi million pound 'golden hello' for the new chief executive; 22 per cent voted against and 11 per cent abstained (*Guardian* 2004a).

Even the tighter regulations have not quelled public concerns and these have most recently re-emerged in relation to executive severance packages. The £22 million severance package given to the outgoing chief executive of GlaxoSmithKline, Jean-Pierre Garnier, attracted particular attention. These concerns have been given an added twist by the payment of such packages when companies have apparently not been performing well. The title of the government's consultative document on this issue, '*Rewards for Failure': Directors' Remuneration – Contracts, Performance and Severance*, is indicative of the concern. At the time of writing the government had ruled out further regulation, suggesting that more time was needed to evaluate the impact of the new reporting regulations.

Equal pay

The pursuit of equal pay for women has moved rapidly up the HR agenda for a range of stakeholders. This reflects some tightening of the statutory regime on this issue and a number of judicial decisions which have sharpened its application. But there has also been some shift in political will combined with determined action by a number of interest groups. While progress by private sector employers should not be overstated, there has been a shift in the tenor and nature of the debate with the notion of internal job worth reasserting its importance relative to other pay contingencies in this context.

Highlighting some of the pressures raising the profile of the equal pay issue before moving to look at actual changes, it is clear that the statutory framework has remained firmly rooted in the Equal Pay Act 1970, as amended and extended to cover equal value claims in 1983. There has, however, been some pressure from judgments of the European Court of Justice to further 'fine-tune' this Act. The 2003 regulations amending the Act were a direct response to one such judgment. They extended the period when arrears could be received for an equal pay claim from 2 to 6 years as well as providing an opportunity to make such a claim 6 months after the end of employment rather than 6 months before it ended.

In addition, there have been tribunal and other judicial decisions which while not directly leading to changes in the regulatory regime have had major implications for its application. One such case sent 'shock waves' through the civil service when ACAS as an employer (Birmingham Employment Tribunal, 1304744/98 20.12.99) was found to be in breach of the legislation for incorporating potentially discriminatory practices from its old, time-based pay systems into its new performance-based one. More generally, various decisions, for instance in the Danfoss case (*Hanels-og Kontorfunktionaererness Forbundi Danmark v. Dansk Arbejdjivesforening, acting for Danfoss*, 1989 IRLR 532), have given added force to the importance of transparency in deciding on equal pay issues.

As well as this tightening in the substance of the statutory framework on equal pay, various parties have been prompted to take more decisive action. In large part this was stimulated by the fact that the gender pay gap had remained stubbornly wide. Although the gap between full-time male and female hourly pay has fallen significantly from 30 per cent in 1970, it remains at 18 per cent, still wider than in most European countries. The Equal Opportunities Commission (EOC), in particular, has been galvanized by this continuing gap and in 1999 it set up an employer-led Equal Pay Taskforce. It was designed to encourage employers to recognize that pay inequality was a business issue, undermining morale and threatening the recruitment and retention of a key element of the workforce. Reporting 2 years later in the publication *Just Pay*, the task group highlighted on-going pay discrimination by employers, occupational segregation and the continuing unequal impact of family responsibilities on women as the main sources of the gender pay gap.

In April 2001, added weight was given to these developments when the government set up a review headed by Denise Kingsmill, Deputy Chair of the Competition Commission, to look at ways of narrowing the pay gap. Reporting around 6 months later, it called for organizations to undertake audits to assess whether pay systems and structures were discriminatory. These were to be completed on a voluntary basis, with Kingsmill setting a target of 50 per cent of large organizations completing them before the end of 2003 and 25 per cent of all employers by the end of 2005. It was an approach the government endorsed despite calls from the unions and the EOC for the audits to be made mandatory.

Finally, the trade unions have also been stirred to determined action on equal pay. At its 2001 Congress the General, Municipal and Boilermakers (GMB) pledged to make 'equal pay central to the bargaining agenda, while in the same year the Transport and General Workers' Union (TGWU) launched its 'Pay Up' campaign and UNISON its 'Getting Equal' drive (IDS Report 2002e). The manner in which these campaigns have transferred into the collective bargaining arena is most dramatically illustrated in the local government sector. The Single Status Agreement signed in 1997 for over one and a half million manual and non-manual workers was designed to address this issue in a sector where around three-quarters of those employed are women. Central to this agreement was scope to carry out a pay and grading review using a jointly agreed 'equality proof' job evaluation scheme. Five years later and for reasons ranging from cost to intransigence on the part of both local union and management representatives, only a quarter of the local authorities had carried out such a review. Frustration at the lack of progress was one of the factors leading to a national strike in local government in July 2002. It was only resolved by setting up a Pay Commission to examine equal pay among a range of other pay issues affecting the sector.

This range of developments has had a number of consequences. It appears to have encouraged more people to make equal pay claims. Figures for 2001–2 indicated that 2,252 cases were lodged, compared to 1,288 in the preceding year (IRS 2002). But in a more general sense, it has forced a re-evaluation of the main pay contingencies and the balance between them. Equal pay, especially for work of equal value, is very much about internal job worth with job evaluation a means of establishing such worth. As such, equal pay developments represent a countervailing influence to the labour market pressures driving organization to a focus on external job worth. Certainly external job worth is 'one of the commonest' (http://eoc-law.org.uk) responses put forward by employers as a 'genuine material factor' justifying unequal pay rates. However, while this defence has been accepted in certain circumstance (*Mrs E. Rainey v Greater Glasgow Health Board*, 1987 IRLR 26, House of Lords) in others it has not (*O'Connor v The Perry Group plc*, ET 10393/94). This indicates that external market forces are not 'a blanket defence' for unequal pay.

In light of the importance of internal job work in this context, it is perhaps surprising that a significant proportion of organizations continue with pay structures which are not based on job evaluation. A recent survey (E Reward 2003d) found that exactly half of the organizations covered had never operated formal job evaluation. However, it is clear that those organizations without job evaluation tend to be small. More indicative of the impact of equal pay consideration is the fact that of those organizations with job evaluation schemes, around 80 per cent are analytical schemes and over three-quarters indicate that one of the purposes of it is to ensure the principle of equal pay for work of equal value is met.

Alongside the increased emphasis placed on internal job worth, equal pay developments are encouraging a much closer scrutiny of how the other two pay contingencies – person and performance – are being used to drive pay progression. The danger is that both might be applied in ways which discriminate against women doing similar work or work of equal value. Broad banding, in particular, has been in the 'line of fire' in this respect (Armstrong 2002b). It is an approach which can lead to people doing similar work being given very different rates of pay for reasons which may well be opaque rather than transparent and easily justified. Moreover, if employees are assimilated onto a long scale which takes many years to ascend, inequalities inherent in previous pay structures will take a long time to address. This later concern in particular is encouraging some organizations, particularly in the civil service, to abandon broad banding in favour of much shorter scales with almost guaranteed progression to the maximum (IDS Report 2002e). Warnings have also been given about performance-related pay schemes. EOC guidance on such schemes notes that because they are designed to reward individuals differently for doing the same job they may be at greater risk from equal pay claims (IDS Report 2003e). While such schemes are not ruled out, organizations have to be clear and secure in justifying the varied pay outcomes inevitably arising.

Despite these developments some question marks remain around how far equal pay concerns have penetrated organizational pay agendas and affected actual practices. Taking equal pay audits, these have been undertaken by high profile companies such as Abbey, John Lewis and British Telecom. However, more general findings suggest that Kingsmill's target of organizations completing such an audit before the end of 2003 was not achieved. A large scale survey for the EOC found that the majority of large, and two-thirds of medium-sized employers had no current plans to conduct an audit (Neathey et al. 2003).

In the public services the position is somewhat different. As the direct employer the government has been able to ensure that equal pay reviews have been conducted in the civil service, but in health and local government uncertainties remain. There is no doubt that equal pay concerns have created a momentum for change and have been central to what has been labelled the 'modernization' of pay. *Agenda for Change* states 'A member of staff's pay band (or pay range) will be determined by job weight. This meets one of the fundamental design requirements of the new pay system, which is to ensure fair pay and support the principles of equal pay for work of equal value.' The 3-year 2004 agreement in local government has set in place a timetable for achieving pay and grading reviews in local authorities by the end of 2007. However, in both the NHS and local government these pay reforms still need to be fully implemented and difficulties remain. If the new timetable for pay reform is met in local government, it will be 10 years after the single status agreement was signed. This is a testament to how difficult it is to change pay structures and provides a warning to the NHS of the potential problems ahead.

Summary and Conclusions

Over recent years, it is clear that reward policies and practices have been buffeted by a range of powerful pressures for change. In considering three sets of pressures, those related to competition, the workforce and regulation, this chapter has sought to explore the 'fallout' from this buffeting. In doing so, a number of cross-cutting patterns have emerged.

First, there has been a shift in the emphasis given to the three pay contingencies. Pay still remains closely related to person and especially performance, but there can be little doubt that recent pressures have forced organizations to concentrate on the pay–job nexus. Many of the developments outlined reflect the search for some balance between two principles which appear to stand in tension with another, external and internal job equity. As labour market pressures push external job worth to the fore in determining pay, so at the same time equal pay concerns are demanding that due weight be given to internal worth. While not easily reconciled, some organizations are seeking to deal with external labour market pressures by strengthening their internal career and grading structures. Indeed, this development resonates with the original rationale for the establishment of internal labour markets. It suggests that recruiting and retaining employees in scarce supply might be addressed by acknowledging their internal worth with the development of career and earnings opportunities. This is not a straightforward task as organizations become flatter but it is one which is attracting managerial attention.

Second, the preoccupation with the bottom line contribution made by pay practices has given way to a concern with pay processes. This is most clearly reflected in the often repeated mantra on the need for pay systems to be 'transparent, consistent and fair'. In part this focus on pay processes and these underlying principles is driven by a public policy belief that payment systems should operate in this way. Equal pay legislation has thrust process into the limelight and implicitly rejects unequal pay unless it can be proven that any difference is not related to gender. However, an interest in process also has a strong business rationale. If pay is to generate employee attitudes and behaviour which improve business performance, the way pay systems operate and treat staff becomes crucial. At the same time, 'fair' treatment, particularly in the context of very different workplace interests and values, raises crucial questions about employee voice on pay issues. Indeed, the weakening of the collective voice in pay determination and its imperfect replacement by statutory mechanisms in various guises raises very real issues about how employees can be given a meaningful involvement in pay decisions. In the absence of effective involvement, the suggestion that pay processes are 'transparent, consistent and fair' will continue to have a hollow ring.

Third, the chapter has highlighted a distinctive set of pay developments in the public services. These developments, reflected in agreements in the NHS, local government and higher education, have been taken forward under the heading of 'modernization'. Pay 'modernization' in these sub-sectors has been seen to comprise similar elements; a national framework with a pay spine at its centre; scope for constituent organizations to develop local pay and grading structures using 'equality proofed' national job evaluation schemes; opportunities for some pay flexibility to address labour market pressures and performance but with pay progression mainly based on skills acquisition and career movement. Moreover, they are explicitly designed to be taken forward on the basis of partnership principles between management and the unions, a feature which clearly modifies suggestions that the collective voice has been universally weakened. At the same time, questions remain about how effectively these pay reforms will be advanced with the protracted process of change in local government a warning to those assuming straightforward implementation.

The final pattern picks up on these implementation difficulties. The chapter has highlighted the fact that pay rhetoric continues to outpace actual change in pay practice. This is not to deny the importance of the rhetoric. For example, the 'grand' reward strategies still widely formulated provide a plausible narrative for action for internal and external organizational stakeholder and no doubt act as a stimulus for change. However, implementation of specific practices such a total reward, team pay, competence pay and broad banding continues to be patchy. Despite the pressures highlighted in this chapter, the concluding message is that changing pay structures and systems remains a complex and potentially problematic process which organizations often embark upon with some caution and trepidation.

REFERENCES

ACAS 2003: *Payment Systems*, www.acas.org.uk/publications, July.

Adams, J. 1965: Inequity in social exchange, in L. Bekowitz (ed.), *Advances in Experimental Social Psychology*, Vol. 2, New York: Academic Press.

Ahlstrand, B. 1990: *The Quest for Productivity*, Cambridge: Cambridge University Press.

Amabile, M. 1988: A model of creativity and innovation on organizations, in B.M. Staw and L.L. Cummings (eds.), *Research in Organizational Behavior*, Vol. 10, London: JAI Press Inc.

Armstrong, M. 2002a: *Employee Reward*, London: CIPD.

Armstrong, M. 2002b: What's happening to broad banding, *IDS Executive Compensation*, June, 21–3.

Armstrong, M. and Barron, A. 1995: *The Job Evaluation Handbook*, London: IPD.

Armstrong, M., Cummins, A., Hastings, S. and Wood, W. 2004: *Job Evaluation: A Guide to Achieving Equal Pay*, London: Kogan Page.

Armstrong, M. and Murlis, H. 1991: *Reward Management*, London: Kogan Page.

Arnold, J., Cooper, C. and Robertson, I. 1998: *Work Psychology*, London: Pitman.

Arrowsmith, J., Gilman, M., Edwards, P. and Ram, M. 2003: The impact of the national minimum wage in small firms, *British Journal of Industrial Relations*, **41**(3), 435–56.

Bach, S. 2004: Employee participation and union voice in the NHS, *Human Resource Management Journal*, **14**(2), 3–19.

Bach, S. and Winchester, D. 2003: Industrial relations in the public sector, in P. Edwards (ed.), *Industrial Relations; Theory and Practice*, Oxford: Blackwell.

Blinder, A. (ed.) 1990: *Paying for Productivity*, Washington: Brooking Institution.

Bloom, M. and Milkovich, G. 1992: Issues in managerial compensation research, in C. Cooper and D. Rousseau (eds.), *Trends in Organizational Behavior*, Chichester: John Wiley.

Bowey, A. 2000: Gainsharing, in R. Thorpe and G. Homan (eds.), *Strategic Reward*, Harlow: Pearson.

Brown, W. 1989: Managing remuneration, in K. Sisson (ed.), *Personnel Management in Britain*, Oxford: Blackwell.

Brown, D. and Armstrong, M. 1999: *Paying for Contribution*, London: Kogan Page.

Brown, W., Deakin, S., Hudson, M., Pratton, C. and Ryan, P. 1998: *The Individualisation of Employment Contracts in Britain*, DTI Employment Relations Series 4.

Burgess, S., Propper, C., Ratto, M. and Tominey, E. 2003: *Incentives for Public Servants: Some Evidence from the UK*, unpublished paper, Bristol University.

Casey, B. Lakey, J., Cooper, H. and Elliot, J. 1991: Payment systems: A look at current practice, *Employment Gazette*, August, 53–8.

CIPD (Chartered Institute of Personnel and Development) 2003: *Survey Report*, London: CIPD.

Conyon, M., Peck, S. and Read, L. 2001: Performance pay and corporate structure in UK firms, *European Management Journal*, **19**(1), 73–82.

Corby, S., White, G. and Stanworth, C. 2002: *Does it Work? Evaluating a New Pay System*, London: University of Greenwich.

Cox, A. and Purcell, J. 1998: Searching for leverages: Pay systems, trust, motivation and commitment in SMES, in S. Perkins and St John Sandringam (eds.), *Trust Motivation and Commitment*, Faringdon: Strategic Remuneration Centre.

Cully, M., Woodland, S., O'Reilly, A. and Dix, G. 1999: *Britain at Work*, London: Routledge.

Dickens, R., Gregg, P. and Wadsworth, J. (eds.) 2003: *The Labour Market Under New Labour*, Basingstoke: Palgrave Macmillan.

Dickens, R. and Manning, A. 2003: Minimum wage, minimum impact, in R. Dickens, P. Gregg and J. Wadsworth (eds.), *The Labour Market under New Labour*, Basingstoke: Palgrave Macmillan.

DiMagio, P. and Powell, W. 1983: The iron cage revisited: Institutional isomorphism and collective rationality in organizational fields, *American Sociological Review*, **48**, 147–60.

Donovan, P. 2004: The rise of the living wage, *People Management*, 15 July, 10:14, 14–15.

E Reward, 2003a: *A Guide to Strategic Research Reward*, Part 1, Report No. 11. www.e-reward.co.uk

E Reward, 2003b: *A Guide to Strategic Reward*, Part 2, Report No 14, www.e-reward.co.uk

E Reward, 2003c: *Pay in a High Performance Organization: A Case Study of Lloyds TSB*, Report No. 17, www.e-reward.co.uk

E Reward, 2003d: *What Is Happening in Job Evaluation: A Large Scale Survey*, Research Report. www.e-reward.co.uk

E Reward, 2004: *What Is Happening on Contingent Pay Today*, Part 1, Research Report No. 18, www.e-reward.co.uk

Evans, J. 2003: Pay, in G. Hollinshead, P. Nicholls and S. Tailby, *Employee Relations*, Harlow: Pearson.

Gallie, D. 2000: The labour force, in A. Halsey (ed.), *Twentieth Century British Social Trends*, Basingstoke: Macmillan.

Gerhart, B. and Rynes, S. 2003: *Compensation: Theory, Evidence and Strategic Implications*, London: Sage.

Gerhart, B., Trevor, C. and Graham, M. 1996: New directions in compensation research: Synergies, risk, and survival, *Research in Personnel and Human Resource Management*, **14**, 143–203.

Guardian, 2004a: Investors attack WH Smith bosses over pay, 30 January.

Guardian, 2004b: Pension crisis fails to deter leavers, 9 September.

IDS (Incomes Data Services) Report, 2002a: *Boots: Customer Reward Project Leads to Changes in Reward and Development*, **869**, November.

IDS Report, 2002b: *Pay in Banking and Finance*, **869**, November, 12–14.

IDS Report, 2002c: *Zurich Re-introducing Salary Ranges*, **853**, March.

IDS Report, 2002d: *Alldays New Pay and Benefits Package*, **852**, March.

IDS Report, 2002e: *The Equal Pay Challenge*, **856**, May, 15–18.

IDS Report, 2003a: *Regional Pay*, January, 15–16.

IDS Report, 2003b: *Markets Driving Pay in Banking*, **892**, November, 6–8.

IDS Report, 2003c: *Inland Revenue Recovers £13 million*, **891**, October, 3.

IDS Report, 2003d: *Pay in Food and Drink Manufacturing*, **883**, June, 9–12.

IDS Report, 2003e: *EOC Guidance on PRP*, **877**, March, 3–5.

IDS Report, 2004a: *Pay Trends*, **907**, June, 10–11.

IDS Report, 2004b: *Case Study*, **902**, April, 16–17.

IDS HR Studies, 2004: *Share Incentive Plans*, **781**, September.

IRS (Industrial Relations Services) 2001a: E Reward: A share of the losses? *Pay & Benefits Bulletin*, **526**, August, 2–6.

IRS 2001b: Whatever happened to team reward? *Pay & Benefits Bulletin*, **524**, July, 2–7.

IRS 2002: Chasing progress on equal pay, *Employment Review*, **774**, 19–22.

IRS 2003a: Totally rewarding, *Employment Review*, **787**, August, 34–6.

IRS 2003b: Sainsbury's bonus scheme, *Employment Review*, **748**, September.

Industrial Society 1997: *Reward Strategies*, No. 31, January. London: Industrial Society.

Jensen, M. and Meckling, W. 1976: Theory of the firm: Managerial behaviour, agency costs, ownership structure, *Journal of Financial Economics*, **3**, 305–60.

Kessler, I. 2001: Reward system choices, in J. Storey (ed.), *Human Resource Management: A Critical Text*, London: Thompson.

Kessler, I. and Purcell, J. 1992: Performance related pay: Objectives and application, *Human Resource Management Journal*, **2**(3), 34–59.

Kohn, A. 1993: Why incentive plans cannot work, *Harvard Business Review*, September–October, 54–63.

Lawler, E. 1995: The new pay: A strategic approach, *Compensation and Benefits Review*, July, 14–20.

Lazear, E. 1986: Salaries and piece rates, *Journal of Business*, **59**, 405–31.

Ledford, G. 1995: Paying for skills, knowledge, and competencies of knowledge workers, *Compensation and Benefits Review*, **27**(4), 55–63.

Littler, C., Weisner, L. and Dunford, R. 2003: The dynamics of delayering: Changing management structures in three countries, *Journal of Management Studies*, **40**(2), 225–57.

Local Government Employers' Organization, 2004: *Reviewing and Modernizing Pay Frameworks*, London: Employers' Organization.

LPC (Low Pay Commission) 2002: *The NMW: Making a Difference, Third Report*, London: HMSO.

LPC 2003: *Building on Success, Fourth Report*, London: HMSO.

Lupton, T. and Gowler, D. 1969: *Selecting a Wage Payment System*. Research Paper III. London: Engineering Employers' Federation.

Mahoney, T. 1983: Approaches to the definition of comparable worth, *Academy of Management Review*, **8**(1), 14–22.

Mahoney, T. 1989: Multiple pay contingencies: Strategic design of compensation, *Human Resource Management*, **28**(3), 337–47.

Makinson Report, 2001: *Incentives for Change*, London: HMSO.

Manchester News, 2003: Foreign staff plug gaps in care, 21 August.

McKnight, P. and Tomkins, C. 1999: Top executive pay in the United Kingdom: A corporate governance dilemma, *International Journal of Economics of Business*, **6**, 232–43.

Millward, N., Bryson, A. and Forth, J. 2000: *All Change at Work?* London: Routledge.

Neathey, F., Dench and S. Thomson, L. 2003: *Monitoring Progress towards Pay Equality*, Manchester: EOC.

Oliver, C. 1997: Sustaining competitive advantage: Combining institutional and resource based views, *Strategic Management Journal*, **18**(9), 697–713.

Pendleton, A. 2000: Profit sharing and employee share ownership, in R. Thorpe and G. Homan (eds.), *Strategic Reward*, Harlow: Pearson.

People Management 2002: Pick 'n' Mix, 7 November, 44–5.

Pfeffer, J. 1998: *The Human Equation*. Boston: HBS Press.

Pritchard, D. and Murliss, H. 1992: *Jobs, Roles and People*. Manchester: Nicholas Brealey.

Reed, H. 2000: *Corporate Governance, Board Structure and Accountability*, unpublished, ESRC Centre for Business Research University of Cambridge.

Reilly, P. 2003: New approaches in reward: Their relevance to the public sector, *Public Money and Management*, October, 245–52.

Robinson, H. 2002: Wrong side of the track? The impact of the minimum wage on gender pay gap in Britain, *Oxford Bulletin of Economic Statistics*, **64**(5), 417.

Rubery, J. and Edwards, P. 2003: Low pay and the national minimum wage, in P. Edwards (ed.), *Industrial Relations: Theory and Practice*, Oxford: Blackwell.

Ruiz, Y. 2004: Skill shortages in skilled construction and metal trade occupations, *Labour Market Trends*, March, 103–11.

Schuler, R. and Jackson, S. 1987: Linking competitive strategies with human resource management practices, *Academy of Management Review*, **1**(3), 209–13.

Schuster, J. and Zingheim, P. 1992: *The New Pay*. New York: Lexington Books.

Select Committee on Trade and Industry, 2003: *Sixteenth Report*, London: HMSO.

Simpson, B. 2004: The national minimum wage five years on: Reflections on some general issues, *Industrial Law Journal*, **33**(1), 22–41.

Smith, I. 1989: *People and Profits*, London: Croners.

Society Guardian, 2003a: Council staff threaten strike over chancellor's pay plans, 10 April.

Society Guardian, 2003b: Councils snub regional pay, 30 April.

Sparrow, P. 1996: Too good to be true? *People Management*, 5 December, 22–9.

Tailby, S., Richardson, M., Danford, A., Stewart, P. and Upchurch, M. 2004: *Partnership at Work in UK Public Services: The Employee Voice in a Local Authority and NHS Hospital Trust*, Conference Paper, Utrecht, 26–27 August.

The Times 2004: Monday threat of 1 1/2 p on tax to pay for pensions, 13 September.

Thompson, M. 1993: *Pay and Performance: The Employee Experience*, Institute of Manpower Studies, Report 258, Brighton: IMS.

Thompson, M. 1995: *Team Working and Pay*, Institute of Manpower Studies, Report 281, Brighton: IMS.

Thompson, M. and Heron, P. 2002: Reward strategies in UK R&D establishments, Unpublished paper, Oxford: Templeton.

Thompson, P. and Milsome, S. 2001: *Reward Determination in the UK*, London: CIPD.

TUC 2002: *Executive Excess: Time to Act*, London: TUC.

Vroom, V. 1964: *Work and Motivation*, Chichester: John Wiley.

Wageman, R. 1995: Interdependence and group effectiveness, *Administrative Science Quarterly*, **40**, 145–80.

White, M., Hill, S., Mills, C. and Smeaton, D. 2004: *Managing to Change? British Workplaces and the Future of Work*, Basingstoke: Palgrave Macmillan.

Wood, S. 1996: High commitment management and payment systems, *Journal of Management Studies*, **33**(1), 53–77.

CHAPTER THIRTEEN

Customer Service Work, Emotional Labour and Performance

Stephen Deery

Most British workers are employed in the service sector. Many are located in jobs that require them to interact directly with customers or clients. Whether they are nurses, financial service advisers, waiters or call centre staff their work involves a high degree of personal contact with the public and the performance of what has been termed 'emotional labour' (Hochschild 1979). They must present their emotions and manage their behaviour in such a way that both complies with the service standards of the organization and helps create a desired 'state of mind' in the service recipient. These service standards are often embodied in the rules of employment and used to judge performance (Morris and Feldman 1997).

Customer service work is quite different from manufacturing work and from jobs performed in industrial settings (Gutek 1995). The principal difference relates to the participation of the customer in the process of service work. The customer helps shape the way in which the work is performed. It is the customer whose requirements must be satisfied and whose orders must be met. In some cases the customer may act as a co-producer while in other situations they may be enlisted by the organization jointly to supervise workers and help manage the labour process (Fuller and Smith 1996). This triangular relationship between the customer, the employee and management distinguishes interactive service work from industrial production where customers are normally external to the labour process and where the dynamics of management control are more firmly located within the boundaries of the worker–management dyad. The presence of the customer in service work can result in efforts to extend management control to more aspects of the employee's behaviour at work. Because the quality of the interaction between the employee and the customer is frequently part of the service delivered, Leidner (1996) argues that there is no clear distinction between the worker, the work process and the product. As a result 'Workers' looks, words, personalities, feelings, thoughts, and attitudes may all be treated by employers as legitimate targets of intervention' (Leidner 1996: 30).

The aim of this chapter is to explore the nature of customer service work; to look at the different ways in which emotional labour can be managed by organizations and to examine how employees respond to their interactions with customers. Emotional exhaustion and stress are not uncommon features of jobs involving close customer contact. The chapter concludes by analysing the relationship between the service work labour process and employee well-being and organizational performance.

The Nature of Customer Service Work

Customer service work is performed in a diverse range of industries from hospitality and recreation to banking, retailing and professional services. The work has a number of common characteristics (Herzenberg et al. 1998; Korczynski 2002). First, it is intangible: for example, mortgage advice provided over the telephone or medical assistance supplied in a hospital cannot be touched or held. Secondly, service work is perishable. It cannot be manufactured or stored in advance. Thirdly, it is produced and consumed simultaneously. Unlike manufacturing firms, customer service organizations cannot place a quality control buffer between the production of a service and its consumption. Fourthly, service work is variable: customer demands are often idiosyncratic and service providers possess different skills, dispositions and varying levels of commitment to the customer (Peccei and Rosenthal 2001). Finally, as we have already noted, customers generally participate in the production of the service. As a consequence they can be a source of great satisfaction for the service provider or a cause of intense anxiety and stress (Macdonald and Sirianni 1996).

These characteristics have important implications for the way in which customer service work is managed. Perhaps the most significant of these relates to the scope for variability in service provision and the absence of a buffer between production and consumption. Controlling service quality is seen to be difficult because of the day-to-day variability in employee attitudes and behaviour and because services cannot be inspected after they are produced and before they are consumed (Appelbaum and Batt 1994). In response to this problem service organizations have often sought to prescribe tight rules of interaction to narrow the scope for provider-customer variability and to restrict opportunities for employee discretion in the delivery of the service.

These rules have been designed to ensure that workers act and behave in ways that are consistent with the organization's customer service objectives. Irrespective of how the worker may feel towards the customer he or she is expected to follow the organization's instructions for the performance of emotional labour. According to Wharton (1996: 92) the critical task for these workers 'is to display publicly an emotion that they may not feel privately'. They are expected to 'appear happy, nice and glad to serve the customer' in spite of any private misgivings or any different feelings they may have (Erickson and Wharton 1997: 188). This can take the form of an employee refraining from responding to abusive customers in a call centre or to a flight attendant maintaining a perpetual smile for passengers (Hochschild 1983). Some commentators have claimed that organizations demand a far greater level of personal and emotional commitment from front-line employees than they do from other types of employees:

> The assembly-line worker could openly hate his job, despise his supervisor, and even dislike his co-workers, and while this might be an unpleasant state of affairs, if he completed his assigned tasks efficiently, his attitude was his own problem. For the service worker, inhabiting the job means, at the very least, pretending to like it, and, at most, actually bringing his whole self into the job, liking it, and genuinely caring about the people with whom he interacts. (Macdonald and Sirianni 1996: 4)

The importance of the front-line worker to the success of those interactions has given rise to different types of approaches to oversee and control the service provider's encounters with customers. In some cases it has led to particularly invasive forms of workplace control. In telephone call centres, for example, computer technology is now a critical component of workplace management (Batt and Moynihan 2004). It is used to monitor the speed of work, regulate the level of downtime, and assess the quality of the interaction between the service provider and the customer. Furthermore, employees are invariably required to follow a tightly scripted dialogue with customers and conform to highly detailed instructions. This may include a fixed format for the introduction and closure of the interaction. Many call centres require their customer service representatives to follow a documented work process. Deery et al. (2002) provide an example of a call centre where all workers were directed to follow a sequence of five specified tasks: greet and build rapport with the customer; fact-find; provide solutions; close conversation; and follow (or wrap) up. These tasks had to be completed with each customer in a short and fixed time period. The close monitoring of words and manners and the limited variation that employees are often allowed in service interactions has meant that call centre workers have lost a large measure of control over their self-presentation to customers. This has left many of them with little flexibility in negotiating their interactions with customers (Wharton 1996). In her study of an Orange call centre in England Bunting (2004: 63) describes the work of one staff member:

> On Claire's computer screen, a series of little squares indicate if there are calls waiting, as well as telling her how long she has been on her current call; she usually has no more than eight seconds between calls. If a call has been difficult, there are only eight seconds in which to take a deep breath and compose her voice into the expected tone of friendliness. All the time she is managing her emotional demeanour, she's flicking through a wide range of information on the screen, which she uses to answer customer queries.

Not all service workers, however, are so constrained in their interactions with customers. Where service work requires subjective interpretation and where employees must exercise judgement to meet customer needs it is more probable that employees will be granted greater discretion and control over the conduct of their work. In these circumstances employees are more likely to be armed with information rather than instructions (Macdonald and Sirianni 1996). It is widely recognized that tight control over the labour process can deliver efficient task completion but is unlikely to elicit high-quality performance from employees. Control workers too completely, as Fuller and Smith (1996: 76) observe and management will 'extinguish exactly those sparks of worker self-direction and spontaneity' that are so critical for service quality. Customers care how services are delivered. The way in which employees display their feelings towards them can have an important effect on the perceived quality of the interaction (Ashforth and Humphrey 1993). Because the attitudes of the employee are critical to the quality of the interaction, tightly scripted dialogue and routinized responses can impair the service that is provided to the customer.

The Organization of Service Work

Herzenberg et al. (1998) have argued that there are four different ways of organizing service work. Each distinct work system is said to vary in terms of its skill requirements, the degree of autonomy that is extended to workers to perform the tasks and the extent to which the work is controlled and paced by management (see Table 13.1). They have called the first work system *tightly constrained*. Here jobs are narrowly defined, skills are low and the work is controlled and paced by a combination of technology or customer pressure. The fast pace and high stress of the job is normally accompanied by high turnover rates. Examples include many types of call centre work and fast food service. The second type of work system has been given the term *unrationalized labour-intensive*. Here skill and knowledge requirements are low; training and career advancement opportunities are limited and a good deal of learning comes from on-the-job interactions from co-workers. Herzenberg et al. (1998: 41) cite workers in such areas as childcare assistance and nursing aids as falling into this category. They contend that the market tends not to reward this type of work and that service quality often depends on individuals' socialized sense of obligation to those they service.

In the third category, the *semiautonomous* work system, workers are said to perform tasks that cannot easily be monitored or controlled. There is greater task variety and complexity and substantial firm specific skills and knowledge of the organization's products and customers. Extensive training is required and internal career ladders are provided. Examples include sales workers and flight attendants. The *high-skill autonomous* work system is the final category. This work system is built upon recognized professional qualifications and skills and formal and informal support for on-the-job learning. The work tends to be complex, non-routine and intangible and cannot be tightly supervised or easily monitored or controlled.

Table 13.1 Organizing service work

	Tightly constrained	Unrationalized labour-intensive	Semi-autonomous	High-skill autonomous
Examples	Some call centre workers, fast-food workers	Some nurses' aides, domestics	Clerical and administrative workers	Engineers, lawyers, academics
Business strategy/markets served	High volume; low cost	Low volume; low cost	Volume and quality vary	Low volume; quality often in the eye of the beholder
Task supervision	Tight	Loose	Moderate	Little
Output monitoring	Machine or technological pacing	Quantitative measurement in some cases	Quantitative measurement in some cases	Quantitative measurement rare
Formal education/ credentials	Low to moderate	Low to moderate	Moderate	High
On-the-job training	Limited	Some, informal	Limited to moderate	Substantial
Screening of job applicants	Limited	Little	Careful	Usually very careful
Internal job ladders	Limited	No	Important	Important for some workers

Source: Adapted from Herzenberg et al. (1998: 42–3).

Self-motivation is crucial and this often reflects professional commitment and craft pride. Occupations that lie within this category include lawyers, doctors and university lecturers.

The type of work system that organizations will choose to manage the labour process will depend on a number of factors. These include their business strategy and the markets that they serve – whether there is an emphasis on low cost and standardized quality or on low volume and customized service – as well as the organization's choice of technology and its history, traditions and management style. Labour market conditions and trade union policies may also influence the adoption of particular employment arrangements and work systems. A particularly important factor is the type of service provided to the customer. A tightly constrained work system may be appropriate for well-defined services such as telephone directory assistance or the serving of fast food where workers are expected to follow clearly specified processes. Leidner (1996: 29), for example, notes that at McDonald's 'Management has specified in advance almost all aspects of the work, so workers repeat a set of relatively simple tasks over and over again, with little opportunity for decision-making.' However, in the case of social work advice or hair cutting and styling the service output is more difficult to define and measure and is not as amenable to rigid process design. Under these circumstances a semi-autonomous or high-skill autonomous work system would seem more viable. Employees could appropriately tailor their services to the idiosyncratic needs of individual customers.

Encounters or relationships

Gutek (1995) has also focused on the role of the customer in helping to shape the way that service work is organized and managed. She argues that organizations can choose to structure interactions with customers as 'encounters' or 'relationships'. They can either seek to limit the contact between the service provider and the customer to an impersonal encounter whereby service providers are made functionally equivalent and are expected to complete their transactions in the minimum time possible or they can seek to develop a relationship between the service provider and the customer where personalized knowledge of the customer is emphasized and future interactions are expected. Where the service is dispensed as an encounter the organization's objective will be to maximize operational efficiency and the number of transactions handled. Where the service is structured as a relationship the organization's objective will be to maximize the repeat business of the customer by delivering a service tailored to the recipient's special needs. As Batt and Moynihan (2004: 30) note: 'The longer a client stays with one provider, the more difficult it is to shift to another provider not only because of personal relations of trust, but because of the wide variety and complexity of services that are provided.'

These different forms of interaction tend to be associated with different types of work regimes. Encounters call for little employee discretion and draw heavily on standardized and codified procedures while relationships emphasize employees' interpersonal skills and capabilities and their expertise to deal with idiosyncratic information and situation-specific needs. With organizations increasingly seeking to cut the costs of customer service there have been strong pressures to make interactions less time consuming and more standardized. However, Gutek (1995) believes that encounters have a number of major weaknesses as a means of servicing customers. First, individual service providers do not have an incentive to deliver a high-quality service as they are unlikely to have contact with the same customer again in the future. Secondly, encounters do not encourage the customer to be polite or civil and service providers may experience rude and abusive behaviour. Thirdly, in encounters problems and mistakes can be more difficult for the customer to report and to have rectified. Consequently, Gutek (1995: 68) reports that many organizations have encouraged their front-line service staff to 'make each encounter as relationship-like as possible' and to manufacture intimacy as a way of personalizing the service. She has called this form of interaction a 'pseudo-relationship'.

At Asda, one of Britain's largest supermarket chains, employees are being asked to provide 'real' smiles to customers. It has been reported that:

> Asda has mystery shoppers measuring . . . [store] warmth. They check on the friendliness of the staff, eye contact, use of the customer's name at checkout, even smiles. And says David Smith (Asda's head of human resources): 'It's got to be a real smile. We have a sense that people in the Asda family live the values. That's what makes the business go. Life is much more than what people get paid . . .'. What Asda is trying to achieve in its company culture requires employees' emotional investment. It's the first to admit it doesn't pay its 133,000 British employees particularly well; instead it lavishes them with 'Bursting with pride' and 'Thank you' certificates. (*The Observer*, 11 July 2004)

Batt (2000) has found empirical evidence of a relationship between the characteristics of customers and the organizational arrangements governing front-line service work in telephone call centres in the USA. In the case of low value customers who were supplied with a simple uniform service (as in a directory enquiry) the call centres made widespread use of technology as a control device and employees were granted little discretion over their work. They were also made subject to a highly scripted text when interacting with customers. On the other hand, high value business customers with more complex requirements were serviced by employees who had greater training, more extensive skills and wider discretion over their choice of work methods. There was very limited application of standardized processes and procedures. High-involvement human resource practices such as self-directed and problem-solving work teams were also more widely used.

It would seem therefore that where front-line service staff are dealing with customers who have complex and variable needs and are highly valued by the organization they will have less structured jobs, fewer standardized procedures and a wider scope of tasks. Consequently, it is more likely that the organization will adopt what Macdonald and Sirianni (1996: 7) have termed an 'empowerment approach' to the management of employees:

> Through careful selection, training, and motivation, employers create the kinds of people who would make decisions that management will approve . . . Rather than presenting employees with scripted patter, for example, managers will seek individuals whose personal characteristics make them more likely to interact spontaneously and perform in the manner management intends.

In a study of call centres in the banking industry Holman (2004) showed that employees who were required to demonstrate greater product knowledge and problem-solving skills with customers (such as dealing with foreign exchange enquiries or more complex mortgage requirements) were more likely to exert greater control over the timing of their work and the manner and form of their interaction with customers. They also experienced lower levels of monitoring.

However, where the yield from customers is low and a standardized and uniform service is provided it is more likely that management will use a 'production-line' approach to workforce management. The HRM practices will tend to emphasize monitoring and measurement and the training will concentrate on a knowledge of the process and the style of delivery (Gutek 1995). The aim will be to achieve high throughput and low unit costs. Monitoring will be applied to reduce variability in service delivery and constrain the time spent on each customer. Batt (2002) has suggested that high involvement employment practices such as skill enhancement and worker autonomy will normally be viewed by management as too costly to implement and generally incapable of creating a competitive edge. In order to buttress this 'production-line' approach to the labour process, management will be inclined to standardize the behaviour of the customer as a means of ensuring that the routines that they have established for the service workers are not disrupted. In her study of McDonald's, Leidner (1996: 33) shows how the company has 'minimized customers' expectations of individualized treatment while also trying to provide some semblance of personal service . . . It has greatly curtailed the unpredictability customers might bring to the work process by making sure they know how to fit into McDonald's routines.'

Forms of Management Control and HR Practice

There will be limitations on the ability of firms to standardize the behaviour of the customer and routinize the work of the service provider. Such an approach to the management of the labour process can result in job dissatisfaction and employee turnover. Moreover, it is not always possible for organizations to manufacture compliant customers and to achieve predictability in the service exchange. Customers' requirements are often fluid and uncertain. Workers require some degree of flexibility and discretion in dealing with customers. Many service organizations also face a dilemma. They want to be both cost efficient and customer orientated (viz. banks). On the one hand, they want to reduce costs per customer transaction by increasing the speed and efficiency with which they process their customers yet on the other hand, they extol the virtues of customer service and encourage their employees to be quality-orientated. Mulholland (2002) refers to this as an attempt to combine a lean production model with a soft discourse of caring and quality.

Control and commitment strategies

A combination of control and commitment strategies are most likely to be used. Quite invasive methods of overseeing and controlling customer service interactions can be mixed with teamwork for peer support and problem solving and limited levels of employee discretion and autonomy. In call centres, for example, Kinnie et al. (2000: 967) observed that high-commitment management practices as well as team competitions and games were often used 'to offset some of the worst features of call centre working'. They referred to this combination as 'fun and surveillance'.

However, the management of front-line service workers is not straightforward. The way employees are treated will affect the quality of the service that is provided. Positive expressions of emotion by employees can create favourable impressions in customers' minds while negative attitudes expressed by employees can similarly create unfavourable impressions. This has been called 'emotional contagion' (Ashkanasy and Daus 2002). The way in which employees are managed will ultimately affect the service recipient. What employees experience at work will thus be passed onto the customer (Schneider and Bowen 1993). A major problem for management therefore is 'how to direct, control, and monitor customer service interactions without disrupting them' (Macdonald and Sirianni 1996: 6). Work regimes that are too tightly specified and controlled or are too intrusive run the risk of jeopardizing the quality of the service.

In response to this dilemma most companies have sought to instil values of good customer service in their staff through normative control strategies. This may be seen as an attempt to change workers' personalities and their underlying feelings and values with the purpose of developing an internalized commitment to quality service. Thompson et al. (2001) point to the importance of recruitment in this process of control with firms focusing on personality traits and service-orientated attitudes. In their research on interactive service work in the banking industry they found that recruitment was strongly orientated towards the selection of people with certain desired social skills and attitudes rather than a particularly strong knowledge of banking. Confidence, concentration, communication skills, energy and enthusiasm were judged as highly important competencies. Bunting (2004: 68) reported that 'At the Orange call centre . . . the manager told me they never recruited someone for their technical skills. What they were looking for was a particular personality: cheerful, outgoing, flexible, good-natured, adaptable because these were the characteristics which they couldn't train.' Leidner (1996: 46), however, believes that it is difficult to make a distinction between skills and attitudes in interactive service work because 'the willingness and capacity of workers to manipulate and project their attitudes in the organization's interests are central to their competence on the job'.

Thompson et al. (2001: 936) have also observed that companies not only seek to 'recruit attitude'; they also seek to 'shape it': 'Trainees are encouraged to make the necessary changes to their "state of mind", and told that by consciously working on levels of enthusiasm they can "change themselves". They are told that sufficient concentration will improve sincerity – once rapport is built "you're there".' Korczynski et al. (2000: 676) have also noted the way in which induction and training are used to promote self-control through an identification with the customers: an active 'self-as-customer orientation'. Furthermore, they show how this form of normative control can be used as a means of obtaining acceptance of management's measurement and monitoring procedures. They found that in training sessions employees were told, for example, that the company's monitoring systems were merely created to achieve a shared objective: customer satisfaction and good service.

Different forms of management control can be used simultaneously. 'Customer control' or 'management by customers' has been identified as an important means of bolstering control of workers while at the same time allowing them to exercise some degree of autonomy and self-direction necessary to deliver quality service (Fuller and Smith 1996). Most service firms solicit customer feedback information through telephone surveys or comment cards or through the use of 'shoppers' – individuals employed by management to act anonymously as clients, guests or passengers. While pretending to be customers these 'shoppers' monitor and report on front-line staff as well as on service quality. The large US retailing firm Sears Roebuck, for example, uses a telephone survey to help evaluate its employees. The company provides a random selection of customers with a coupon worth $5 toward their next purchase if they call a toll free number and answer questions about their shopping experience and the performance of the sales employee. The employee's number is printed on the transaction coupon and the customer is required to punch it in before answering the questions. The company has stated that its goal 'is to make it possible for managers and their sales associates to have constructive dis-cussions about individual strengths and weaknesses *as seen by the customer*' (Rucci et al. 1998: 97).

The information that is collected from customers on their perceptions of service providers can have quite significant effects on the employment prospects of those workers. For example, in their study of customer-supplied information, Fuller and Smith (1996: 80) reported one manager as saying that 'the customer survey is important for monitoring workers because: "It's like a report card on individual employees"'. They also reported the case of a telephone complaint by one super-market shopper who said that: '"The blond lady in the produce department doesn't like management" (store and date identified).' Data gathered on employees from customers' observations can be used in performance reviews as well as dis-ciplinary action and placed in individuals' personnel files. Fuller and Smith (1996: 84–5) claim that the effect of these customer feedback techniques is that interactive service workers gain an 'additional boss':

> feedback from customers strengthens employers' hold over the workplace by provid-ing them with an additional source of data they can use for control, evaluation and discipline . . . Managers now have formally designated accomplices in controlling workers, insofar as they exploit customers for their observations about how service is delivered.

In interactive service work, therefore, a range of control methods ranging from simple control by managers through to normative techniques and customer feedback can be used to direct the labour process and effect service delivery. However, these different types of control systems can lead to quite dissimilar work experiences for employees.

Service Work and Worker Well-being

The performance of emotional labour can have negative consequences for workers. Where front-line staff are expected to smile and be friendly to customers and to be courteous and enthusiastic in all their service interactions it can affect their psychological well-being. Some employees find it difficult to contain their true feelings or emotions when serving customers. Consequently, when organizations require them to display emotions publicly that they may not feel privately it can lead to what Hochschild (1983: 90) has called 'emotive dissonance'. Tensions between the employees' inner feelings and the requirements of outward display can cause stress and burnout. Bunting (2004: 66) has highlighted the difficulties that some front-line service workers face:

> What all call centres drill into their employees is to 'speak as if you were smiling', and 'as if you have been waiting for this particular call'. This is a job where you're not allowed an off day – or even an off moment. If a customer is difficult or rude, the call handler must not respond aggressively. He or she certainly can't betray any irritation or frustration during the next call which is instantly routed through to them. While call handlers are expected to provide the customer with a certain pleasurable emotional exchange, they must also continually repress their own emotions to ensure a standardised service.

However, not all front-line service workers suffer negative effects from emotional labour. For some the work is tiring, stressful and emotionally exhausting. For others, however, service work provides pleasure and stimulation and a high degree of job satisfaction (Frenkel et al. 1998; Korczynski 2002). This may be due to the personality and disposition of the employee or the nature and character of the job that is performed or to the HRM practices that have been put into effect in the workplace.

HR policies and worker well-being

There is a considerable body of research to indicate that certain types of work practices and HRM policies can affect the psychological consequences of emotional labour. One of the most important would appear to be the degree of autonomy and control that interactive service workers have over their job. This is particularly salient in relation to the opportunities that employees have for self-direction in conducting their interactions with customers. In her study of banking and healthcare workers in the USA, Wharton (1993) found that workers who experienced greater job autonomy and opportunities for self-monitoring were significantly less likely to suffer from emotional exhaustion and job burnout. The research suggested that workers who were able to exercise some control over the way in which they displayed their emotions suffered less harmful consequences from interactive service work. In this sense they were better able to manage the 'potential disjunctures between work role requirements for emotion and their own feelings' (Wharton 1996: 94).

This issue lies at the heart of the problems encountered by call centre workers where employees are invariably required to follow a tightly scripted dialogue with customers which severely limits their opportunities for self-direction and their ability to exercise control over their interactions with customers. Deery et al. (2002) found that call centre workers who did not like following a conversational script with their customers were more likely to feel emotionally exhausted. There was clear evidence to indicate that the adoption of HRM policies that would have allowed employees to depart from the script and interact more naturally with their customers would have reduced anxieties and tensions associated with the work. This is consistent with other research findings. In his study of worker well-being in three call centres in the UK, Holman (2004) identified job control, task variety and monitoring as important predictors of anxiety and job satisfaction. Workers who exercised greater control over the methods they used in their work and how they talked to customers were found to be less likely to suffer from anxiety at work. Furthermore, where customer service representatives were engaged in a wider variety of tasks they enjoyed their jobs more. In this context Holman (2004: 238) observed:

> this finding suggests that excessive monitoring may have the opposite effect on performance to the one intended. Excessive monitoring, may over the long term, make employees more depressed and less active. In addition, higher levels of anxiety brought about by excessive monitoring may cause people to devote their cognitive resources to dealing with this anxiety rather than focus on providing a quality customer service.

High workloads also affect worker well-being. Burnout is more likely to occur in jobs with sustained customer contact and few opportunities for staff to vary the nature of their displayed feelings. Higher levels of interpersonal contact have consistently been linked to emotional exhaustion in a range of studies (Cordes and Dougherty 1993; Lee and Ashforth 1996). This has been identified as a common phenomenon in helping and caring professions and in customer-service occupations where the strain of frequent and often intense contact with people can result in anxiety and frustration and feelings of being used up and worn out (Maslach and Jackson 1981). In their call centre research Deery et al. (2002) identified high workload as the most important determinant of emotional exhaustion. It was noteworthy that they also found that those employees who spent longer with customers on each call experienced significantly lower levels of emotional exhaustion. In these circumstances service providers had greater opportunities to build a rapport with customers thereby making the interaction more rewarding and pleasant.

Customers and worker well-being

Invariably, front-line staff are discouraged from arguing with their customers and are expected to maintain a polite and calm demeanour in all circumstances. However, customers can be abusive and irritating and their demands may be unreasonable. For some employees customer complaints are a regular part of their work experience. This has become even more apparent over recent years with rising customer expectations about service quality often being primed by the organizations themselves. The incidence of customer abuse is said to have increased sharply because of these higher expectations. A study of service sector companies found that the primary reason for this abusive behaviour was the apparent 'insincere tone of voice from the person handling the query' (*Guardian* 1997). Indeed it has been suggested that customers are now more able to discern the difference between genuine 'quality service' and 'feigned quality service' (Taylor 1998: 87).

In order to protect themselves from abuse and ill treatment front-line employees are often encouraged to suppress their true feelings and emotionally detach themselves from hostile or difficult customers (Frenkel et al. 1998). However, this can be a difficult process for individual staff in the absence of institutionally sanctioned policies such as 'time out' to recover from customer abuse or opportunities for greater task variety. Ill treatment from customers can result in depersonalized relationships, diminished self-esteem and higher employee turnover. In the National Health Service, verbal abuse and harassment by patients and their relatives has been identified as a major cause of turnover among front-line nursing staff (Oakley et al. 2003). Macdonald and Sirianni (1996) have also argued that there is an asymmetry in the exchange of respect between customers or patients and front-line service workers. They assert that: 'the idiom of servant and master is alive and well in many kinds of service workplaces. This holds that the customer is always right and that the role of the server is to be deferent in serving, even if the customer's demands are unreasonable and demeanour abusive' (p. 16). They cite the case of clerical workers at Harvard University who were counselled to be passive and servile in the face of aggressive student behaviour: 'think of yourself as a trash can. Take everyone's little bits of anger all day, put it inside you, and at the end of the day, just pour it in the dumpster on your way out the door' (p. 17).

It is believed that women generally suffer more negative effects of emotional labour than men (Hochschild 1983). They are said to be more at risk from emotional exhaustion because they are less protected than men from poor treatment of their feelings on the job and are expected to tolerate more offensive behaviour from customers. Moreover, because they tend to have greater non-work responsibilities for the emotional well-being of others it is thought that women may find it more difficult to perform emotional labour on the job than men who often do not have a 'second shift' of emotion work at home (Wharton 1996). On the other hand, it has been suggested that women are more sociable and empathetic and have better communication skills than men (Belt et al. 1999). They are also said to be more intuitive and tolerant and have stronger teamworking skills which would imply that they would suffer less negative effects from interactive service work than men. Most empirical studies of interactive service workers, however, have found no differences between men and women in terms of the effect of emotional labour on their well-being (Holman 2004; Maslach and Jackson 1981). This has not been the case with job satisfaction. Wharton (1996) found that women who performed emotional labour were significantly more satisfied than their male counterparts. She suggests that this may reflect women's evaluations of their jobs relative to those of other women and to the fact that interactive service work is preferable to other jobs available to them. Nevertheless, she also cites evidence that women are more likely than men to value 'working with people' and to seek out roles requiring empathy and attentiveness to others, thus explaining their higher levels of satisfaction in jobs requiring emotional labour.

Job satisfaction

The discussion of emotional labour and worker well-being so far has tended to concentrate on the negative aspects of interactive service work. As we observed earlier employees can also derive great pleasure from the work. Furthermore, it can be argued that the rewards of emotional labour have been understated relative to other types of work (Korczynski 2002). Holman's (2004) research indicated that call centre workers obtained greater job satisfaction than shop floor manufacturing workers. Moreover, they reported less anxiety and depression. He asserted:

> The findings from this study go some way to challenging the stereotyped image of all call centres as 'electronic sweatshops' or 'human battery farms'. Call centre work compares favourably to shop floor manufacturing work and clerical work with regard to well-being. Indeed, at two call centres the level of well-being was equivalent to, and in many cases better than, these forms of work. (Holman 2004: 239–40)

Cross-national studies of interactive service workers conducted by Frenkel et al. (1999) also suggest quite high levels of overall job satisfaction. Wharton (1996) believes that this may be due to the fact that the work can provide important rewards that are not available in other types of jobs. There is evidence to indicate that service workers derive their greatest pleasure from 'helping people' and 'assisting others' (Frenkel et al. 1999). As Korczynski (2002: 76–7) has noted: 'Front-line workers who are empathetic to customers, who are able to help customers, who solve customer problems and who receive thanks in return are likely to see that as an intrinsically satisfying part of their job.' In some caring occupations, such as nursing, job satisfaction is closely associated with the attachment felt towards patients. Korczynski (2002: 99) reports the case of one nurse who stated: ' "I just love the close contact with the patient. I love the chance to . . . be involved in their lives".' Research suggests that if front-line service workers are encouraged by management to use their full array of skills and abilities to meet customer needs they will obtain greater job satisfaction (Deery et al. 2004). Furthermore, where service workers are given more discretion and control over their interactions with customers they will also derive greater satisfaction from their work (Holman 2004).

Personnel policies can also play a role in the job satisfaction of interactive service workers. Wharton (1996: 103) has argued that front-line service workers may find their jobs more satisfying than workers in other types of activities because their employers pay closer attention to the 'fit' between their job demands and their personal qualities. She maintains that service sector employers are particularly sensitive of the need to select staff for high-contact service roles who have strong interpersonal and 'people' skills. In this context it has been suggested that certain personality types are more likely to fit the requirements of customer service work. Outgoing or extrovert individuals are said to be better suited to this form of work because of their more sociable personalities (Rafaeli and Sutton 1987). Field research into call centres indicates that managers do seek to employ more outgoing or sociable employees who enjoy interacting with people (Belt et al. 1999; Kinnie et al. 2000). However, Deery et al. (2002) found that customer service staff in call centres who were more extrovert and had a more positive disposition towards life were significantly more likely to take time off work. They submitted that workers with high positive affectivity had higher intrinsic job expectations that were not fulfilled by the routinized nature of call centre work and that the selection of employees on the basis of those personality traits was ill conceived.

Resistance to Emotion Management

Organizational efforts to manage the emotions of employees can often spark opposition and resistance. The use of control strategies to restrict and regulate role behaviour can clash with the desire of employees to preserve their sense of self-worth and the need to defend the dignity of their work (Hodson 2001). Employees can engage in a range of activities to challenge management decision-making and resist unfair treatment and unacceptable customer behaviour. Such contests, however, are often more implicit than explicit (Macdonald and Sirianni 1996). Although collective action in the form of strikes is not uncommon among interactive service workers, resistance is more likely to be covert, individual and temporary (Sturdy and Fineman 2001).

This can take a number of different forms. Rosenthal (2004), for example, shows how workers can use management's forms of normative control – the language of customer service – and direct control – the monitoring and measurement systems

– to turn the tables on management and defend their rights and protect their interests. She argues that the espoused values of customer service invariably emphasize respect for employees, as well as for customers, and that the language of such programmes can supply workers with an effective means of enforcing standards of fair treatment. Rosenthal (2004: 612) observes that:

> management treatment of workers often is explicitly linked to worker treatment of customers. Associated human resource practices often include enhanced work discretion as well as customer service training designed to enhance the interpersonal skills of front-line workers.

She also notes how normative control can be used as a collective worker resource providing the example of a recent strike in British Telecom where the managerial language of service quality was invoked by the workers to resist pressures to increase customer throughput. In this context, Lankshear et al. (2001: 605) also found that tensions between service quality and service throughput sometimes forced managers to compromise on their quantity measures and allowed the creation of 'organizational spaces in which employees could develop and defend their own definitions of professionalism and good performance'.

Interactive service workers may confront management in other ways as well. Mulholland (2002), for example, has reported that call centre agents often challenge management's discourse about care, quality and teamwork by subjecting it to derision. She argues that 'making fun of a management style is a form of resistance' (p. 299). Sturdy and Fineman (2001) have called this resistance through distance. Employees unofficially rescript their role to 'create a degree of positive feeling, such as fun or joy. The dictates of the corporate script are actively rejected or subverted in favour of one which is more self-designed' (p. 144). By doing this they believe that employees can shield themselves from the psychological costs of engaging fully with the role. This can be done by finding weaknesses in the organization's control systems and creating free space for themselves, by ridiculing or questioning the social order or by using cynicism to create a distance between themselves and their work role. They cite the example of a flight attendant who describes her job in the following way:

> You try saying 'hello' to 300 people and sound as though you mean it towards the end. Most of us make a game of it. Someone – probably a manager – said 'This business is all about interpersonal transactions'. He was wrong. It's all about bullshit. If life is a cabaret, this is a bloody circus. (Sturdy and Fineman 2001: 146)

Some forms of resistance may be less covert and less benign. An organization's scripted conversational rules, for example, may be openly disregarded. Customer service representatives may deliberately redirect calls to other service operators in an effort to boost their productivity or they may enter misleading activity codes in the system, 'mouth words' to fictional callers to confuse supervisors or just hang up on offensive customers (Knights and McCabe 1998). Resistance can also be organized and take a collective form. Union representation has long been an embedded feature of healthcare, banking and retailing. Moreover, the more recent growth of call centres has been accompanied by an expansion of unionism and the use of industrial action to address issues including the intensification of work and the abuse of monitoring and surveillance systems (Taylor and Bain 1999; van den Broek 2004).

Resistance is not only directed towards the actions of management. Front-line service workers may also feel the need to establish a more balanced relationship with their customers and exercise a greater degree of control over their service interactions. The increasing use of 'management by customers' has given greater saliency to this struggle for control between the service provider and the service recipient (Rosenthal 2004). The tactics used by service workers to control customers can range from simply ignoring them when they are abusive or difficult to invoking the rules and routines of the organization in order to limit the duration or intensity of the exchange. Complaints to airline call centre staff about seating allocations or in-flight meals are often answered according to a scripted format which has been designed by the organization to assist service providers to respond to these commonly vexatious issues. This enables the worker to control the conversation and avoid an emotional entanglement with the customer.

Customer Service Work and Performance

There is a considerable body of HRM research that suggests that certain types of work systems and employment practices are associated with better organizational performance. Work systems that provide employees with greater discretion, more information, enhanced skills and extended opportunities for teamwork, for example, have been found to enhance organizational performance (Arthur 1994; Becker and Huselid 1998; Huselid 1995). This is particularly the case when those practices are combined or bundled together into what has been called a high-involvement or high-performance work system. Such a system is said to improve performance because it makes work more satisfying and intrinsically rewarding and thus increases workers' discretionary effort. It has been suggested that a coherent set of HR practices are needed, first, to create a motivated workforce that is willing to expend discretionary effort, secondly, to provide the necessary skills to make that effort meaningful and, thirdly, to supply the workforce with the opportunity to participate in substantive workplace decisions (Appelbaum et al. 2000).

Much of the empirical evidence on the association between high-involvement work systems and organizational performance has been based on research in manufacturing plants and on blue-collar workers. There are those, however, who have argued that the HR-performance link may be stronger in customer service settings than in manufacturing. Batt and Moynihan (2004) submit that the attitudes and motivation of workers are likely to be more important in interactive service jobs because satisfaction or dissatisfaction with work can more easily spill over into customer interactions, thereby directly affecting the quality of the service and the volume of sales. Where the behaviour of the employee is said to play such a pivotal role in shaping customers' perceptions of the quality of the interaction it has been argued that the empowerment of front-line workers will generate pro-social customer-oriented behaviour which can inspire customer satisfaction and loyalty (Liao and Chuang 2004). According to Peccei and Rosenthal (2001) empowerment is associated with training, competence and job autonomy.

Batt (2002) also believes that high-involvement practices are important for performance because they help employees develop the kind of firm-specific human capital – a detailed knowledge of the firm's products, customs and work processes – that assist them to interact more effectively with customers. A more elaborate conception of the relationship between HR practices and organizational performance in interactive services has been presented in what has been termed the 'service profit chain' (Heskett et al. 1997). According to this concept of service management, HR practices that enhance the satisfaction and competence of service workers will result in greater customer satisfaction and retention and ultimately in better performance and bigger profits. There is some empirical support for this contention.

HR practices and service performance

Research indicates that certain types of organizational and HR practices correlate strongly with customer perceptions of high quality service. These pertain, first, to the selection procedures of the organization, secondly, to the management practices that are used to motivate employees, supply them with the relevant skills and provide the organizational environment in which they can participate in decision making and, thirdly, to the development of a 'service-orientated' climate.

The first factor that has been associated with customer satisfaction and service performance relates to the personality traits and individual characteristics of employees. There is some evidence to indicate that certain types of employees may be predisposed towards providing customers with more positive service encounters and that by selecting applicants with those characteristics an organization may be able to deliver better quality service. Liao and Chuang (2004) provide some support for this argument. They found that employees in a US restaurant chain who were more conscientious and more extrovert reported higher service performance levels. They were found to be more friendly and helpful to customers and more responsive to their needs. There have also been suggestions that women may be more effective performers of emotional labour than men because they have superior 'people skills' (Wharton 1996: 107).

The second factor that has been found to shape service performance and assist employees to provide high-quality service centres on the personnel policies and practices of the organization. There is research to show that job autonomy and high-involvement work systems including employee participation and skill development and training contribute significantly to both customer-orientated employee behaviour and organizational performance. Batt (1999) found that self-managed teams were associated with higher service quality and sales per employee. Where workers were provided with greater discretion to meet customer demands they were able to offer better service quality. In a separate study she also showed that sales growth in telephone call centres was stronger in those businesses that emphasized high skills, employee participation in decision making and teamwork, and provided HR incentives such as high relative pay and employment security (Batt 2002). Most significantly, the use of such high-involvement practices was more likely to be associated with higher sales growth in those call centres that provided quite standardized services in cost-conscious markets. This implied that those practices conferred value to management because employees were better able to meet the need for a more customized service even though the interaction was seen to be relatively simple and of low value to the organization.

In their study of front-line service work in restaurants, Liao and Chuang (2004) provided further evidence that employee participation in decision making improved service performance. On the basis of their findings they claimed: 'Empowered employees can meet a wide range of customer demands and are able to share the information they collect about customer behaviors, thereby serving customers better and helping to improve service quality' (p. 45). Peccei and Rosenthal (2001) have also highlighted the importance of empowerment as a key determinant of work behaviour and performance among interactive service workers. They observed that job autonomy and the systematic provision of training in both service values and skills were positively associated with stronger customer-orientated behaviour among front-line retail workers.

HRM policies that promote organizational justice can affect both employee behaviour and customer satisfaction. Some researchers have suggested that employees will treat customers as they themselves have been treated by the organization (Masterson 2001). Thus, where organizations treat their staff fairly it could be argued that it will generate positive attitudes and behaviour which in turn will affect the attitudes and reactions of customers. In contrast, unfair acts within organizations may well diminish employees' motivation to provide high-quality customer service. In her research, Masterson (2001) provided some confirmation of the importance of organizational justice as a factor affecting both the effort and behaviour of the service provider and the reactions of the service recipient. Furthermore, HRM policies that affect worker well-being can influence performance. Singh (2000), for example, found that worker burnout was associated with the provision of lower service-quality. He observed that the principal way of reducing burnout was to introduce practices that gave workers greater task control or job autonomy. On the other hand, other HR policies may have a deleterious effect on customer service. A recent study commissioned by the Chartered Institute of Personnel and Development (CIPD) reported that the use of performance-related pay often had a negative effect on customer satisfaction and profitability (Hope 2004). The principal reason for this was that pay was frequently linked to customer throughput rather than to customer service. The study cited the case of one worker who had terminated a customer's call in the middle of a transaction because the three-minute time limit imposed by the performance-related pay system had been reached.

The development of a 'service-oriented' climate in the organization is the third factor that has been associated with enhanced service quality and higher customer satisfaction. The research indicates that if organizations are able to create an overall climate that values and rewards high quality service, employees will be more likely to deliver good service and customers will be more likely to rate that service more highly (Schneider et al. 1998). In their analysis of financial data and employee and customer service data collected from almost 600 stores of a large US retail company, Borucki and Burke (1999) found that service climate predicted employee service performance which in turn predicted store financial performance. They showed that sales staff who believed that store management both provided them with appropriate training and support and created an organizational environment that valued high-quality customer service actually delivered better service performance to the customers in the stores. This in turn was positively associated with store profitability.

The issue of service climate has also been examined within call centres. Sergeant and Frenkel (2000) found that organizational support had a positive effect on the service climate. Their research suggested that employees who received support from their immediate supervisors and from their fellow team members were more likely to be satisfied with their job and have an enhanced capacity to deliver quality service to customers. These findings complemented the research conducted by Peccei and Rosenthal (2001) on customer-oriented behaviour. They pointed to the importance of building an organizational culture in which management positively demonstrated its commitment to customer service and its support of staff in their day-to-day work. Susskind et al. (2003) also confirmed the influence of organizational support on service quality and on customer satisfaction. They found that organizations that had high standards and expectations of service delivery were better able to foster a climate of service quality. Moreover, front-line staff who received support and assistance from their co-workers and supervisors in the performance of their service-related duties were more likely to exhibit a customer-service orientation. Furthermore, in those organizations where employees reported a high level of customer orientation, the customers reported a higher level of satisfaction with the service.

Summary and Conclusion

A large proportion of the UK workforce are now employed in customer service or customer contact jobs (Korczynski 2002). Many are involved in quite routine and standardized activities where the work is governed by explicit instructions about how they must interact with customers. Others are more fortunate. Their guidelines for emotional labour are collegially determined and to a large extent they are self-supervised (Macdonald and Sirianni 1996). These types of professional employees – doctors, lawyers, academics – are, however, in a minority. Most interactive workers are closely supervised and monitored by managers or customers. Because of the absence of any buffer between the production of the service and its consumption most organizations have been anxious to limit any possible variation in the quality of the service delivered to the customer.

This has often resulted in quite invasive forms of management control. Perhaps the most obvious of these have been documented in telephone call centres (Taylor and Bain 1999). In some cases management control has been extended to nearly all areas of the workers' demeanour, self-expression and appearance (Thompson et al. 2001). This of course can stifle creativity, spontaneity and subjective judgement – qualities that are often needed if service providers are to satisfy the different needs of customers. It can also result in boredom and job dissatisfaction and in emotional exhaustion and a lack of personal accomplishment (Holman 2004). Such feelings can be transmitted to customers who may be 'infected' by the negative emotions of the service worker (Ashkanasy and Daus 2002). Dissatisfaction can also manifest itself in high employee turnover and absenteeism (Deery et al. 2002). This in turn can impair service quality and organizational performance (Batt 2002).

There is evidence to indicate that front-line service workers are treated differently when the customer is more highly valued by the organization and when their needs are seen as more complex and variable. In these circumstances jobs are often less structured, training is more extensive, emotion rules are less rigid and employees are given greater discretion over their work. Nevertheless, as a number of writers have observed, there is always a strong temptation for service organizations to pursue cost minimization strategies at the same time as they declare a desire to customize services and provide employees with specialist skills and independent discretion (Kinnie et al. 2000). In this context, Korczynski (2002) has argued that interactive service work is often infused by two contradictory and competing logics: a need to be cost efficient and a desire to be customer-orientated. Batt and Moynihan (2004) have called this a 'mass customisation' model of service delivery where firms adopt some form of standardization and rationalization along with some level of attention to service quality and the needs of individual customers. In these circumstances management control will often shift from a 'direct' or 'technical' form to a more 'normative' approach. Here the organization will cede responsibility to the worker for the management of their interactions with the customer. Frontline staff will be recruited on the basis of particular personality traits and service-orientated attitudes and training will be directed towards developing an internalised commitment to service quality. Leidner (1993: 37) has described this as 'transforming workers' characters and personalities'.

Organizational efforts to direct and control the work activities of front-line service providers can often provoke resistance. Workers may employ management's language of service quality and customer care to demand that they are treated with similar attention and respect. Managerial discourses on service quality may be used to resist organizational pressures to increase customer throughput at the expense of quality (Rosenthal 2004). In other cases workers may openly challenge or question the espoused values of the organization and subject them to ridicule in order to create a distance between themselves and their work role. Underlying this resistance is the continuous struggle by workers to establish an appropriate level of recognition and respect from both their organization and the customer for the value of their work.

Issues of recognition and respect underpin worker dignity and well-being and according to some writers provide the key to understanding why employees may be purposeful and productive or resistant and uncooperative (Hodson 2001). Research into customer service work has found that organizational practices that emphasize skill formation and employee participation in decision making do enhance motivation, effort and performance. This is most apparent when those practices are combined with high relative pay and job security as well as policies that emphasize fairness and organizational justice (Batt 2002; Masterson 2001). The creation of an internal climate of service excellence buttressed by supportive co-workers and immediate superiors also encourages customer-orientated behaviour and is associated with higher service quality. Although service work can be distinguished from manufacturing work because of the interposition of the customer in the labour process, the types of HR policies that promote both job satisfaction and organizational performance are remarkably similar in both work settings.

REFERENCES AND FURTHER READING

Appelbaum, E., Bailey, T., Berg, P. and Kalleberg, A. 2000: *Manufacturing Advantage*, Ithaca, NY: Cornell University Press.

Appelbaum, E. and Batt, R. 1994: *The New American Workplace: Transforming Work Systems in the United States*, Ithaca, NY: ILR Press.

Arthur, J. 1994: Effects of human resource systems on manufacturing performance and turnover, *Academy of Management Journal*, **37**(3), 670–87.

Ashforth, B. and Humphrey, R. 1993: Emotional labor in service roles: 'The influence of identity', *Academy of Management Journal*, **18**, 88–115.

Ashkanasy, N. and Daus, C. 2002: Emotion in the workplace: The new challenge for managers, *The Academy of Management Executive*, **16**(1), 76–86.

Bain, P. and Taylor, P. 2000: Entrapped by the 'electronic panoptican'? Worker resistance in a call centere, *New Technology, Work and Employment*, **15**(1), 2–18.

Batt, R. 1999: Work organization, technology and performance in customer service and sales, *Industrial and Labor Relations Review*, **52**(4), 539–64.

Batt, R. 2000: Strategic segmentation in front-line services: Matching customers, employees and human resource systems, *International Journal of Human Resource Management*, **11**(3), 540–61.

Batt, R. 2001: Explaining wage inequality in telecommunications services: Customer segmentation, human resource practices, and union decline, *Industrial and Labor Relations Review*, **54**(2A), 425–59.

Batt, R. 2002: Managing customer services: Human resource practices, quit rates and sales growth, *Academy of Management Journal*, **45**(3), 587–97.

Batt, R. and Moynihan, L. 2004: The viability of alternative call centre production models, in S. Deery and N. Kinnie (eds.), *Call Centres and Human Resource Management: A Cross-National Perspective*, Basingstoke: Palgrave Macmillan, 25–53.

Becker, B. and Huselid, M. 1998: High performance work systems and firm performance: A synthesis of research and managerial implications, *Research in Personnel and Human Resource Management*, **16**, 53–101.

Belt, V., Richardson, R. and Webster, J. 1999: Smiling down the phone: Women's work in telephone call centres, *Workshop on Telephone Call Centres*, London School of Economics, March.

Borucki, C.C. and Burke, M.J. 1999: An examination of service-related antecedents to retail store performance, *Journal of Organizational Behavior*, **20**, 943–62.

Bowen, D. and Lawler, E. 1992: The empowerment of service workers: What, why, how, and when, *Sloan Management Review* (Summer), 73–84.

Bunting, M. 2004: *Willing Slaves*, London: HarperCollins.

Callaghan, G. and Thompson, P. 2001: Edwards revisited: Technical control and call centres, *Economic and Industrial Democracy*, **22**(1), 13–37.

Callaghan, G. and Thompson, P. 2002: 'We recruit attitude': The selection and shaping of routine call centre labour, *Journal of Management Studies*, **39**(2), March, 233–55.

Cordes, C.L. and Dougherty, T.W. 1993: A review and integration of research on job burnout, *Academy of Management Review*, **18**(4), 621–56.

Deery, S., Iverson, R. and Walsh, J. 2002: Work relationships in telephone call centres: Understanding emotional exhaustion and employee withdrawal, *Journal of Management Studies*, **39**(4), 471–96.

Deery, S., Iverson, R. and Walsh, J. 2004: The effect of customer service encounters on job satisfaction and emotional exhaustion, in S. Deery and N. Kinnie (eds.), *Call Centres and Human Resource Management: A Cross-National Perspective*, Basingstoke: Palgrave Macmillan, 153–73.

Erickson, R.J. and Wharton, A.S. 1997: Inauthenticity and depression: Assessing the consequences of interactive service work, *Work and Occupations*, **24**(2), 188–213.

Frenkel, S., Korczynski, M., Donoghue, L. and Shire, K. 1995: Re-constituting work: Trends towards knowledge work and info-normative control, *Work, Employment and Society*, **9**(4), 773–96.

Frenkel, S., Korczynski, M., Shire, K. and Tam, M. 1998: Beyond bureaucracy? Work organization in call centres, *International Journal of Human Resource Management*, **9**(6), 957–79.

Frenkel, S., Korczynski, M., Shire, K. and Tam, M. 1999: *On the Front Line Organization of Work in the Information Economy*, Ithaca, NY: ILR Press.

Fuller, L. and Smith, V. 1996: Consumers' reports: Management by customers in a changing economy, in C.L. Macdonald and C. Sirianni (eds.), *Working in the Service Society*, Philadelphia: Temple University Press, 74–90.

Guardian. 1997: Telephone users take an even more aggressive line, 28 August.

Gutek, B. 1995: *The Dynamics of Service: Reflections on the Changing Nature of the customer/provider interface*, San Francisco: Jossey-Bass Publishers.

Herzenberg, S., Alic, J. and Wial, H. 1998: *New Rules for a New Economy*, Ithaca, NY: Cornell University Press.

Heskett, J., Sasser, W.E. and Schlesinger, L. 1997: *The Service Profit Chain: How Leading Companies Link Profit and Growth to Loyalty, Satisfaction, and Value*, New York: Free Press.

Hochschild, A. 1979: Emotion work, feeling rules, and social structure, *American Journal of Sociology*, **85**, 551–75.

Hochschild, A. 1983: *The Managed Heart: Commercialization of Human Feeling*, Berkeley: University of California Press.

Hodson, R. 2001: *Dignity at Work*, Cambridge: Cambridge University Press.

Holman, D. 2004: Employee well-being in call centres, in S. Deery and N. Kinnie (eds.), *Call Centres and Human Resource Management: A Cross-national Perspective*, Basingstoke: Palgrave Macmillan, 223–44.

Hope, K. 2004: Bonuses reward speed over service, *People Management*, 12 August.

Huselid, M. 1995: The impact of human resource management practices on turnover, productivity and corporate financial performance, *Academy of Management Journal*, **38**(3), 635–72.

Hutchinson, S., Purcell, J. and Kinnie, N. 2000: Evolving high commitment management and the case of the RAC call centre, *Human Resource Management Journal*, **10**(1), 63–78.

Kinnie, N.J., Purcell, J. and Hutchinson, S. 2000: 'Fun and surveillance': The paradox of high commitment management in call centres, *International Journal of Human Resource Management*, **11**(5), 967–85.

Knights, D. and McCabe, D. 1998: What happens when the phones go wild?: Staff, stress and spaces for escape in a BPR telephone banking work regime, *Journal of Management Studies*, **35**(2), 163–94.

Korczynski, M. 2001: The contradictions of service work: call centre as customer-oriented bureaucracy, in A. Sturdy, I. Grugulis and H. Willmott (eds.), *Customer Service*, Basingstoke: Palgrave.

Korczynski, M. 2002: *Human Resource Management in Service Work*, Basingstoke: Palgrave.

Korczynski, M., Shire, K., Frenkel, S. and Tam, M. 1996: Front line work in the 'new model service firm': Australian and Japanese comparisons, *Human Resource Management Journal*, **6**(2), 72–87.

Korczynski, M., Shire, K., Frenkel, S. and Tam, M. 2000: Service work in customer capitalism: Customers, control and contradictions, *Work, Employment and Society*, **14**(4), 669–88.

Lankshear, G., Cook, P., Mason, D., Coates, S. and Button, G. 2001: Call centre employees' responses to electronic monitoring: Some research findings, *Work, Employment and Society*, **15**(3), 595–605.

Lee, R.T. and Ashforth, B.E. 1996: A meta-analytic examination of the correlates of the three dimensions of job burnout, *Journal of Applied Psychology*, **81**(2), 123–33.

Leidner, R. 1993: *Fast Food, Fast Talk: Service Work and the Routinization of Everyday Life*, Berkeley: University of California Press.

Leidner, R. 1996: Rethinking questions of control: Lessons from McDonald's, in C.L. Macdonald and C. Sirianni (1996) (eds.), *Working in the Service Society*, Philadelphia: Temple University Press, 29–49.

Leiter, M.P. and Maslach, C. 1988: The impact of interpersonal environment on burnout and organizational commitment, *Journal of Organizational Behavior*, **9**, 297–308.

Liao, H. and Chuang, A. 2004: A multilevel investigation of factors influencing employee service performance and customer outcomes, *Academy of Management Journal*, **47**(1), 41–58.

Macdonald, C.L. and Sirianni, C. (eds.) 1996: *Working in the Service Society*, Philadelphia: Temple University Press.

Maslach, C. and Jackson, S.E. 1981: The measurement of experienced burnout, *Journal of Occupational Behavior*, **2**, 99–113.

Masterson, S.S. 2001: A trickle-down model of organizational justice: Relating employees' and customers' perceptions of and reactions to fairness, *Journal of Applied Psychology*, **86**(4), 594–604.

Morris, J. and Feldman, D. 1997: Managing emotions in the workplace, *Journal of Managerial Issues*, **9**(3), 257–74.

Mulholland, K. 2002: Gender, emotional labour and teamworking in a call centre, *Personnel Review*, **31**(3), 283–303.

Oakley, P., Guest, D. and Deery, S. 2003: Developing core practice standards to retain staff in three London Trusts, King's College London, mimeo.

Peccei, R. and Rosenthal, P. 1997: The antecedents of employee commitment to customer service: Evidence from a UK service context, *International Journal of Human Resource Management*, **8**(1), 66–86.

Peccei, R. and Rosenthal, P. 2001: Delivering customer-oriented behaviour through empowerment: An empirical test of HRM assumptions, *Journal of Management Studies*, **38**(6), 831–57.

Rafaeli, A. and Sutton, R. 1987: Expression of emotion as part of the work role, *Academy of Management Review*, **12**, 23–37.

Rosenthal, P. 2004: Management control as an employee resource: The case of front-line service workers, *Journal of Management Studies*, **41**(4), 601–22.

Rosenthal, P., Hill, S. and Peccei, R. 1997: Checking out service: Evaluating excellence, HRM and TQM in retailing, *Work, Employment and Society*, **11**(3), 481–503.

Rucci, A., Kirn, S. and Quinn, R. 1998: The employee-customer-profit chain at Sears, *Harvard Business Review*, January–February, 82–97.

Schneider, B. and Bowen, D.E. 1993: The service organization: Human resource management is crucial, *Organizational Dynamics*, **21**(4) 39–53.

Schneider, B., White, S. and Paul, M. 1998: Linking service climate and customer perceptions of service quality: Test of a causal model, *Journal of Applied Psychology*, **83**(2), 150–63.

Sergeant, A. and Frenkel, S. 2000: When do customer contact employees satisfy customers?, *Journal of Service Research*, **3**(1), 18–34.

Singh, J. 2000: Performance, productivity and quality of frontline employees in service organizations, *Journal of Marketing*, **64**, 15–34.

Sturdy, A. and Fineman, S. 2001: Struggles for the control of affect – resistance as politics and emotion, in A. Sturdy, A. Grugulis and H. Willmott (eds.), *Customer Service*, Basingstoke: Palgrave.

Susskind, A.M., Kacmar, K.M. and Borchgrevink, C.P. 2003: Customer service providers' attitudes relating to customer service and customer satisfaction in the customer-server exchange, *Journal of Applied Psychology*, **88**(1), 179–87.

Taylor, S. 1998: Emotional labour and the new workplace, in P. Thompson and C. Warhurst (eds.), *Workplaces of the Future*, London: Macmillan.

Taylor, P. and Bain, P. 1999: An 'assembly line in the head': The call centre labour process, *Industrial Relations Journal*, **30**(2), 101–17.

Thompson, P., Warhurst, C. and Callaghan, G. 2001: Ignorant theory and knowledgeable workers: interrogating the connection between knowledge, skills and services, *Journal of Management Studies*, **38**(7), 923–42.

van den Broek, D. 2004: Call to arms? Collective and individual responses to call centre labour management, in S. Deery and N. Kinnie (eds.), *Call Centres and Human Resource Management: A Cross-national Perspective*, Basingstoke: Palgrave Macmillan, 267–84.

Wharton, A. 1993: The affective consequences of service work, *Work and Occupations*, **20**, 205–32.

Wharton, A. 1996: Service with a smile: Understanding the consequences of emotional labor, in C.L. Macdonald and C. Sirianni (eds.), *Working in the Service Society*, Philadelphia: Temple University Press, 91–112.

PART V

Work Relations

CHAPTER FOURTEEN

Discipline and Attendance: A Murky Aspect of People Management

Paul Edwards

The need to dismiss employees is sometimes called the dark side of HRM, for reasons including a preference among organizations to focus on more positive-sounding areas as well as the limited attention to the issue in textbooks. Yet dismissal remains very common. More importantly the extent to which it occurs and the ways in which it is handled say a great deal about the conduct of HRM; at the extreme, a reality of assertive management may belie a rhetoric of human resource development. Dismissal is usually analysed under one of two heads: the loss of a large number of jobs as a result of a business decline or re-organization (known in the UK as redundancy); and the dismissal of an individual worker. The main legally recognized reasons for individual dismissal are:

- Lack of capability or qualifications. This includes aptitude but also physical health and is thus the heading under which someone suffering long-term illness could be dismissed; there is no necessity of attaching blame.
- Misconduct. Blame is involved here, since it covers such actions as insubordination, theft, and criminal behaviour.
- 'Some other substantial reason', which can in principle be very wide-ranging but which in practice generally involves a business re-organization and collective job losses not entailing a redundancy (Torrington et al. 2002: 235).

In this chapter, the focus is on individual rather than collective issues. Dismissal is of course the final stage of a disciplinary process that may not proceed to the ultimate step. Dismissal is therefore placed in the wider context of disciplinary rules and standards. The chapter takes the management of attendance as a key example, because absence accounts for about half of all dismissals and because the issue is a particularly sharp illustration of the 'dark side'.

'Murky' is a better label than 'dark'. The latter suggests an area of practice that is similar to other areas in terms of degree of strategic attention, HR involvement and so on, but which an organization chooses to keep hidden. The handling of discipline, however, is an area where strategic intent is often absent. It is a necessarily particularly messy area for two sets of reasons. First, it covers issues of individual personality and aptitude. It requires managers to address such issues as whether someone is 'really' ill and whether there is a case to use disciplinary sanctions for alleged misconduct. It thus entails digging into workers' motivations, and handling complex issues where facts may be unclear or disputed and where fairness and consistency can be hard to achieve. Second, it is an area where managerial policy interacts with workers' norms and expectations. Formal disciplinary rules may have little bearing on concrete practice, and managers relying on the rules may find that their actions are counterproductive.

The word 'discipline' has two different meanings. One is that of disciplinary sanctions. The other refers to a coherent and focused way of working towards a goal, as in the idea of a disciplined army, which may be underpinned by a tested body of knowledge, as with the discipline of a profession. Some HR texts cover both aspects together. For example Torrington et al. (2002) distinguish team discipline and self-discipline under the latter head. But this sense is very broad, and at its broadest it is virtually synonymous with HRM as a whole, turning on outcomes such as employee morale and on all the possible ways in which HR practice can affect these outcomes. This chapter thus adopts a more concrete focus on features to do with sanctions and penalties. It does not deal with technical questions such as the design of disciplinary procedures, for ACAS handbooks and other texts cover these admirably.

One theoretical point guides the discussion. The recent literature on self-discipline implies that managing through commitment rather than control is a novel idea, and in some accounts it suggests that control has been replaced by commitment. In fact, as earlier comments on a natural sense of duty suggest, it has always been part of discipline. An interesting discussion of the parallels between discipline in the military and employment contexts states that 'it is a pattern of behaviour which has been instilled into [the soldier or employee] so that he [or she] no longer thinks of acting otherwise' (Phelps Brown 1949: 48). The theoretical basis of this point has also been long understood. Friedman (1977) identified two broad approaches which he termed direct control (managing through tight discipline) and responsible autonomy (allowing workers discretion). Later work (Edwards 1986; Hyman 1987) established that these approaches, which Friedman tended to present as opposites, were often, indeed normally, combined.

Approaches to the management of labour entail a mix of elements rather than the development of self-contained strategies, and they are necessarily uncertain and incomplete because they try to control employees at the same time as releasing their creative potential. Self-discipline is not new, it is not necessarily in opposition to other forms of discipline and, crucially, it is still a form of control because it is part of a relationship in which managers aim to establish authority and regulate the direction of workers' efforts. Control does not necessarily mean a situation ('zero sum' in the jargon) in which workers lose in direct proportion to what managers gain. It means the way in which employees are persuaded to work under managers' authority. 'Self-discipline' is not complete freedom, nor is it merely a trick to persuade workers to work harder. It is one aspect of the way in which control has to be negotiated.

Traditional personnel management texts recognize that discipline is about more than rules and procedures. As one puts it, 'the best discipline is self-discipline, the normal human tendency to do one's share and to live up to the rules of the game' (Strauss and Sayles 1980: 218). Yet the definition by Strauss and Sayles is also too narrow in that it assumes that 'doing one's share' is uncontested. Who decides what a reasonable share is, what the rules are, and in what ways breaches of the rules are to be penalized? In any organization there will be differences on these points. A conventional view of discipline describes rules and procedures and assumes that their operation is unproblematic. Yet how people expect to behave depends as much on day-to-day understandings as on formal rules. Workplaces may have identical rule-books, but in one it may be accepted practice to leave early near holidays, in another on Fridays, in a third when a relatively lenient supervisor is in charge, and so on. What the rule is cannot be discovered from the rule-book. Day-to-day experience will create standards which may differ sharply from official rules. It is not even the case that formal rules inscribe managerial expectations while informal standards represent workers' understandings. In some workplaces, supervisors have been found to coach workers in formally illicit practices. Examples include the sales staff of a bread firm (where ways to cheat customers were taught to workers: Ditton 1979); other examples are given below. The making of rules is a process in which different levels of management may have different priorities.

The chapter has three main sections. The first examines the development of rules and procedures, thus putting current practice in context and arguing that discipline in the sense of the application of sanctions remains important. The second offers examples of how rules are created in practice, thus displaying the flexibility and negotiability of discipline. The management of attendance is addressed in the third main section.

Disciplinary Procedures and Practice

Employers have always needed to ensure the adequate performance of work tasks by their employees. Formal rules became necessary when organizations became large and bureaucratic, with the result that the employer could not oversee operations personally. Pollard (1965: 181–9) has described the disciplinary problems of the early industrial employers: the new factories demanded regular attendance and the carrying out of tasks in the prescribed fashion. Accounts of the evolution of discipline typically counterpose *coercive* and *corrective* approaches (Ashdown and Baker

1973). The former was based on strict rules and harsh punishment for their infraction, and was felt to characterize early industrial enterprises. The latter, dated variously to the rise of large organizations during the early twentieth century or to the post-1945 period, sees the goal of discipline as to induce a change of behaviour rather than simply punish mistakes. The means also shifts from arbitrary sanctions to clearly defined penalties for stated breaches of the rules. The power to discipline shifts from the supervisor to specialist managers, and formal procedures set out permitted penalties and give employees the right to appeal against sanctions. How does experience in the UK match up to such a model? There are three main considerations.

First, in terms of disciplinary systems it is clear that procedures are now extremely widespread. The 1998 Workplace Employee Relations Survey (WERS) found that 92 per cent of workplaces employing 25 or more workers had a formal disciplinary procedure, and that virtually all workplaces also allowed employees to appeal against decisions (Cully et al. 1999: 78). This proportion rose from 81 per cent in 1980 (Millward et al. 1992). Even in small businesses (stand-alone operations with between 10 and 99 employees) the proportion in 1998 was 70 per cent (Cully et al. 1999: 263). In only 8 per cent of workplaces in 1998 were supervisors given the final authority to dismiss.

Second, however, this result was not the product of a gradual realization of the values of a corrective style. Until the 1960s, around 90 per cent of British firms did not have disciplinary procedures. The Industrial Relations Act 1971 introduced provisions relating to unfair dismissal. (It is this Act that is the basis of the definitions of what constitutes fair or unfair dismissal given at the start of the chapter. Claims for unfair dismissal were to be made to Industrial Tribunals, from 1998 called Employment Tribunals.) This legislation has been widely seen as stimulating companies to reform their procedures. Employers interviewed in 1977 felt that the effect of employment protection laws had been to tighten up on recruitment and dismissal arrangements; although they claimed that management's power in discipline had been eroded, they also stressed an increase in the use of proper procedures and a decline in arbitrariness (Daniel and Stilgoe 1978: 37). A further stimulus came with the important House of Lords decision in *Polkey v A E Dayton Services Ltd* in 1987. The previous view (given clear statement in *British Labour Pump Ltd v Byrne*) was that procedural irregularities in the managerial handling of cases were to be discounted if they were likely to have made no difference to the outcome. The decision in *Polkey* overturned this approach, and established that a lack of procedural propriety would generally make it likely that a dismissal would be deemed unfair. (The legal citation for *Polkey* is [1987] ICR 142, while *Labour Pump* is [1979] IRLR 94; see IRS 1987 for discussion.)

Small firms as well as large ones were affected by this legal context. Surveys in 1978 and 2000 demonstrated a growth in awareness of individual employment rights, of which unfair dismissal protection is an important part (Clifton and Tatton-Brown 1979; Blackburn and Hart 2002). A case study investigation of 18 such firms (employing between 2 and 50 workers) found two of them clearly formalizing their procedures as a result of experience with claims taken to tribunals (Edwards et al. 2003).

Related to this point is the extent of explicit joint agreement of procedures with trade unions. One survey reported that only 38 per cent of respondents negotiated with unions representing blue-collar workers, while only 25 per cent agreed the rules with the unions (IPM 1979: 17). Procedures are likely to be agreed with unions, but in most cases this is likely to involve notification and acceptance of a procedure whose shape is set by management, and not negotiation from scratch. Relatedly, third party intervention is limited. In the UK, in contrast to the USA, independent arbitration remains rare as the final stage of a procedure. There was also a decline in the use of third parties such as ACAS as the final stage of a procedure during the 1980s (Millward et al. 1992: 194–6); more recent data are not reported. Procedures are more formal but the practice of discipline still leaves a great deal of discretion to management in deciding what is acceptable conduct and how it is to be enforced.

Third, one might expect a corrective approach to be associated with a reduction in the need to apply penalties: workers accept the rules, and only occasional punishment is needed. Yet the WERS series shows no notable trend in the use of dismissals between 1980 and 1998 or in the use of sanctions short of dismissal between 1990 and 1998. The 1998 level was 15 dismissals per 1,000 workers employed. This is arguably still a large number: on average each year three workers in every 200 can expect to lose their jobs as a result of disciplinary action. The only detailed longer-term analysis in the UK, of the railways, finds no major shift in rates of discipline over a period of about 100 years (Edwards and Whitston 1994).

A constant rate of use of sanctions could mask several things, for example declining usage for established or core workers and rising usage for new employees or 'marginal' groups. No analyses exist of such possibilities. But a key expectation is that the more 'advanced' employers will need to use penalties less than others. Yet two separate studies of the WERS series (one using the 1990 data and the other the 1998 survey) could find no association between indices of the use of HRM techniques and the use of disciplinary sanctions (Edwards 1995; Knight and Latreille 2000).

Fourth, there is substantial evidence that practice is less proceduralized than the existence of rules would suggest. Cavendish (1982: 84) reports an incident while she was working on the assembly line in a firm employing 20,000 people. A young woman was doing a particularly difficult job and expressing her dissatisfaction by working slowly. She was taken to the supervisor's office and told to work properly or hand in her resignation; she did the latter, and was thus recorded as having left voluntarily. The niceties of disciplinary procedures are a long way from a reality in which workers are weak and uncertain of their formal rights.

Survey evidence is consistent with this picture. A 1992 survey of applications to industrial tribunals found that 36 per cent of employers involved in these cases had no procedures while in a further 26 per cent a procedure existed but the case had not in fact gone through it (Tremlett and Banerji 1994: 12). These results were confirmed in the 1998 survey, which found that in over a third of cases there was no attempt of any kind to resolve the issue (DTI 2002). The latest survey results are highlighted in Box 14.1, which confirms that formal arrangements to

Box 14.1   Key results from the 2003 Survey of Employment Tribunal Applications, based on applications made in 2002–2003

- Covers applicants (i.e. people making a claim) and employers, but a matched sample was not sought.
- Applicants' mean length of service with their employer was 6 years. A quarter were members of a trade union (a proportion similar to that in the work force as a whole). More applicants were in managerial jobs than is true of the work force generally (24 per cent against 14 per cent).
- Reported use of procedures

	Percentage of	
	Applicants	Employers
Existence of written disciplinary procedure:	53	87
Where procedure existed, it was followed all the way	22	54

- Communication about the issue prior to application

	Percentage of	
	Applicants	Employers
Applicant discussed issue with employer	45	46
If discussed, formal meeting took place	57	81

- Overall, about 10 per cent of applicants and 46 per cent of employers believed that a procedure had been followed all the way, while in between a quarter (applicants) and 37 per cent (employers) of cases there was some meeting to try to resolve the issue before it was taken to a tribunal.

Source: Hayward et al. (2004).

resolve disputes remain remarkably rare. Note also that the people bringing cases cannot be characterized as atypical or misfits: on average they had worked for their employer for 6 years (the average length of stay with a single firm in the UK is about 10 years), and they were disproportionately in managerial jobs. An apt conclusion is that 'despite the existence of the ACAS Code of Practice and over twenty years of unfair dismissal law, the message is still not getting through to many employers about the necessity for the basic requirements of fairness', such as proper hearings, investigation of the facts and the opportunity for employees to state their case prior to a decision (Earnshaw et al. 1998: 15).

Very few studies have attempted to address the effects of discipline on employees. One which did found little evidence of a perception of corrective discipline. Rollinson et al. (1997: 298) found that 'for a large proportion of those formally disciplined, the process was not seen as a persuasive one designed to get them to observe rules, but as an event which gave the manager an opportunity to take retribution, or administer a deterrent to limit future transgressions'. A picture of a lack of over-all policy and of a reactive approach to particular cases is thus reinforced.

Why has discipline retained an informal character? One might expect there to be a 'disciplinary ratchet' whereby, as more firms experience tribunal cases, they learn the lesson and make their procedures work. Yet, first, the constraints that tribunals place on firms are not as large as might be thought at first sight. The key feature of UK legislation (in contrast to that of other countries such as New Zealand: Corby 2000) is that tribunals may not use their own judgement but must assess what a reasonable employer might reasonably have done in the circumstances. The test of fairness is thus at the lowest feasible boundary. Penalties on employers for unfair dismissal are also limited: the planned remedy, of reinstatement, is very rarely used and the usual sanction, compensation, is small. Pressures on employers are thus weak. Second, it is very likely that the shock of a tribunal case leads to an immediate formalization but that this effect decays quite quickly. Moreover, the shock is a particular one, for dismissal cases are different, and losing one case need have no implications for another one. This situation is very different from that in the USA, where (unionized) firms have arbitrators, who decide cases on their merits and who build up case law in a firm to which managers need to pay close attention (Haiven 1994: a comparison of the UK and Canada, with the latter in this respect being largely similar to the USA).

More recent legal changes may give a further encouragement to formalization. The Employment Relations Act 1999 made two key changes: the reduction from two years to one of the qualifying period before an employee has the right to take a case to an employment tribunal; and the right of any employee to be accompanied at a disciplinary hearing by a 'companion'. In addition, the Employment Rights (Dispute Resolution) Act 1998 gives tribunals the right to reduce an award if an employee had not used a relevant procedure and to make a supplementary award if an employer denied the employee use of the procedure. The Employment Act 2002 requires firms of all sizes to have minimum standards of disciplinary pro-cedures; the requirements were due to come into effect during 2004.

Discipline in Practice

Studies of workplace relations over many years have established some core prin-ciples about the ways in which discipline works in practice. The principles were developed in very specific contexts which may now be thought to be of only historical interest. The discussion thus elaborates the principles and explains the contexts. The second sub-section applies the principles to contemporary work organizations, arguing that their general relevance remains strong but that their detailed application reflects specific features of work organization.

Negotiation of order on the shop floor

The concept of the negotiation of order was formalized in the 1960s to refer to the many ways in which everyday practices establish norms of conduct (see Edwards 1988). Its main values include the following.

- Recognition that rules are interpreted in practice. It is not the case that there are agreed organizational rules that are fixed and clear. A classic study in an American aircraft factory found that workers used a device called a tap to force bolts into position (Bensman and Gerver 1963). The tap was formally forbidden because of the danger of weakening the airframes. Yet not only did workers use it extensively but they were also instructed in its use by supervisors. There was a well-regulated culture specifying who could use the tap (only workers with sufficient competence to deploy it 'appropriately') and when.
- Workplace negotiation is not just about workers avoiding their 'correct' duties. The point of the tap was that it eased the production process and thus helped in the securing of output targets. In another key study in an engineering factory, Roy (1954: 265) asked rhetorically, 'do we see . . . an economically "rational" management and an economically "nonrational" work group? . . . Did not work groups connive to circumvent managerial ukase in order to "get the work out"?' He found that workers bent rules, for example on the speed at which to run machines, so as to 'get the work out'. The formal rules made no sense in the light of shop floor pressures to produce.
- Enforcing formal rules may not be in management's interests. In another engineering case, Lupton (1963) discussed what the workers called 'the fiddle': a linked set of practices that they used to organize their work. Some aspects of the fiddle did not interfere with managerial needs (for example, altering the times at which work was booked as complete, in order to stabilize earnings) and others, as in the Roy case, pursued them. Lupton also stressed that tolerating the fiddle was a cheap way of gaining workers' consent, among other things tending to reduce absence and quit rates and reducing the amount of supervision and monitoring required.
- Some managerial actions are irrelevant to shop floor practice. Studying a bread factory and distribution system, Ditton (1979) found that stealing a certain amount of the product was common and that management used occasional 'purges' that had no long-term effect since the conditions promoting the stealing were unchanged. The point of the purges was to appear to be 'doing something'.
- Generalizing many of these lessons, Mars (1982) showed that fiddling had different meanings in different contexts. Three are of interest here. First, where

workers work under tight supervision in low-skill jobs, fiddles are small-scale individual means to gain a little autonomy and perhaps make some money. A key element was that many of these jobs were very low-paid, so that the need to fiddle was built into them: firms in effect created jobs in this way and in practice expected workers to fiddle while pretending that this was not so (Ditton 1977). Second, at the other end of the spectrum are workers who work in groups and have a strong sense of group identity. They practise organized fiddles, and any disciplinary crack-down would be likely to provoke strong resistance. A standard example was dockers, who not only pilfered cargo but also controlled working time; in some cases, members of a gang organized tasks so that up to half a gang might be away from work while being paid, with the other half covering their jobs. Third, between these extremes lie groups such as those studied by Ditton: they have some degree of group organization and practise fiddling opportunistically.

Further principles were identified by Gouldner (1954) in his study of a US gypsum mine and factory. He distinguished three types of bureaucratic rule.

- 'Mock' bureaucracy covers rules that are ignored by all; Gouldner's example is a no-smoking rule that management generally made no attempt to enforce.
- 'Representative' bureaucracy was exemplified by safety rules, to which management devoted considerable attention and against which workers expended few energies, the result being that safety matters were highly bureaucratized and rules were enforced.
- 'Punishment-centred' bureaucracy involves rules that are enforced by one party against another, with sanctions being imposed for disobedience, an example being the rule against absenteeism, which managers wished to enforce rigidly and which workers resented.

Breaches of different rules will be treated very differently in practice. Mock rules are ignored. Representative rules are important to all, so that a worker disobeying a safety rule is likely to be seen, by work mates as well as management, as careless and as requiring some sanction. Punishment-centred rules are imposed, and the group on whom they are imposed may well feel that they are unfair, and may react by trying to evade them, supporting those who are punished, and questioning their relevance.

Rules are not, then, all of a piece. Gouldner also stressed (1954: 205) that his types are not fixed: in an oil refinery a no-smoking rule is likely to have a representative character. He also makes an important but implicit qualification about representative bureaucracy. Safety rules can be used to control workers. For example, management introduced a rule preventing movement between parts of the factory that was justified on safety grounds and therefore hard for workers to resist, but its real purpose was to strengthen managerial control over what workers were doing. In addition, management neglected safety interests where these conflicted with the demands of production (a frequent finding: see Nichols 1997). Even 'representat-ive' rules may not serve everyone's interests, and they can be used as a cloak for other things.

Rules are thus interpreted in context. Any manager sticking to the letter of the rule book might well be surprised not merely by workers' reactions but also by line managers, who have negotiated a form of workplace equilibrium that turns on rules in practice. A more sensible approach would ask about the kind of rules in place (mock, representative, punishment-centred, or a mix) and their links to shop floor practice.

Yet the basis of these conclusions may seem to be a very particular one. Most of the studies are of male factory workers or groups such as dockers. A term in common UK use was 'custom and practice', meaning sets of understandings estab-lished through everyday activity rather than formal agreement. Several trends may appear to have rendered interest in custom and practice merely quaint. First, the relevant occupations, that of docker in particular but more generally semi-skilled jobs in manufacturing, are now much less common than they were. Second, a policy of 'management by abdication' is less feasible given heightened competitive pressures. One of the classic studies of custom and practice showed that man-agerial leniency reflected the degree of looseness in product market conditions (Brown 1973). Much less toleration would thus be expected, while trends towards per-formance measurement may have given firms the means to prescribe duties much more clearly. Third, many firms also stress worker autonomy and empowerment, which is likely to mean that surveillance through disciplinary rules loses its import-ance. These points will now be addressed.

Contemporary workplaces and patterns of discipline

A key point is that several occupations studied under the rubric of fiddles have grown, not declined, in importance. Obvious examples are the retail and hospit-ality sectors (Nolan and Wood 2003). The question then is whether changes in the management of jobs have rendered them less fiddle-prone. Mars (1982: 138–54) identified five key factors in fiddle-proneness.

1 Passing trade. The parties to a transaction meet only once and the incentive to fiddle is thus high.
2 Exploiting expertise. Workers have real or imagined skills and knowledge, of which customers are largely ignorant, garage servicing being a classic case.
3 Gatekeepers. Where gatekeepers control access to rewards, they can exploit their position most obviously by taking bribes.
4 Triadic occupations of employer, worker and customer. Employers and workers can fiddle customers by short-changing them or providing goods of lower than expected quality.

5   Special effort and skills. Where workers have autonomy in the amount of effort that they put in, they can obtain illicit rewards by bargaining informally, particularly when customers have tight deadlines.

None of these conditions is likely to have changed fundamentally. Restaurants, for example, are characterized by features 1 and 4. What may have changed are two things.

The first was identified by Mars as a secondary feature, namely, 'control systems', notably means to monitor a process and the behaviour of workers. He cited in particular electronic measurement systems, and it is likely that these have made stock control in bars and clubs easier than it was.

The second aspect is the underlying balance of the relationship between managers, workers, and customers. This has a general importance to the whole of the following discussion. As indicated at the start of the chapter, workplace relations turn on the relationship between control and autonomy. These dimensions are sometimes seen as ends of continua, but as argued elsewhere they are separate concepts (Edwards 2003, where different and rather more developed labels are used). It is possible, and arguably increasingly common, for organizations to combine autonomy in the conduct of tasks with clear performance standards for their completion; this is labelled performance management in Figure 14.1. Cases where autonomy and control are more in opposition are in the top left and bottom right areas. Finally, the area labelled 'arbitrary management power' contains cases where there is little autonomy but where clear performance standards and control systems are also largely absent. The examples from Ditton discussed above might fall here.

Such themes have been developed in relation to front-line service work by Korczynski (2002), who highlights inherent tensions between quantitative indices of performance and more subjective measures of customer satisfaction. As he points out, writers who stress unbending managerial discipline, in cases such as call centres in particular, miss the fact that service quality is important as much as quantity. Workers, moreover, report stress but also job satisfaction, and they are on occasions able to spend longer with customers than formal standards permit: in Mars's terms, worker and customer are here colluding against management.

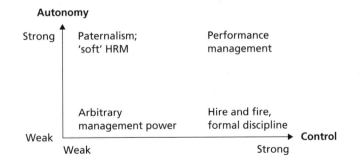

Figure 14.1 Dimensions of workplace relations

Returning then to the hospitality sector, there would appear to have been three trends. The first is the shift towards responsibility and empowerment, as described by Bowen and Lawler (1992). The second is increased performance measurement. Illustrating the above argument, Jones et al. (1997), in a study of an international hotel chain, demonstrate that the rhetoric of employee empowerment was under-pinned by a clear concern to measure and control costs, so that employee discretion was defined within clear bounds. The third, again illustrated in this study, is the influence of the customer. To some extent, the customer becomes the most powerful member of the triad, but the use of this power is also shaped by expectations generated by managers and workers: customers learn how to behave and what is expected of them (Leidner 1993).

Just what the implications are for discipline is not explicit in studies such as those just cited, but it is likely to turn on the balance of the influences mentioned. As Korczynski (2002: 90) notes, 'much of hospitality work [was] undertaken traditionally within a managerial vacuum', and he discusses the use of tipping as a way of abrogating managerial responsibility, leaving the incentive of the tip as a way for the customer to shape the interaction. Ram et al. (2001) identify, in small ethnic-minority-owned restaurants, a tacit bargain where workers are expected to work hard at busy times but are allowed leisure when custom is sparse. In such situations, discipline is likely to have its established role, with all kinds of illicit practices being tolerated but with occasional purges whenever they 'get out of hand' or a random event sparks managerial action. In rationalized fast food enterprises, by contrast, control is emphasized, and discipline is likely to be exact and efficient. In the hotel case described above, control and autonomy go together, and expectations are managed in a less rigid manner.

Wider research on front-line service workers finds that the customer is a source of frustration (demands that are hard to handle, and, in the extreme, abuse) but also satisfaction (the ability to engage in 'real' conversations, especially when work is slow, and the fact that responding to the customer may be a way of circum-venting managerial controls). As Korczynski (2002) argues, there is an inherent tension between rhetorics of customer service and those of efficiency. The implication for discipline is that a new balance of consent and control is negotiated. A good illustration is a study in two service organizations, a telephone sales office of an airline and a bank (Taylor 1997). In both cases, workers worked to performance standards which had 'hard' (measurable output) and 'soft' (personal skills) aspects. And they were evaluated by reference to the targets, through customer satisfaction surveys and by direct managerial surveillance. Yet monitoring was not simply a way of making workers work harder. As one supervisor put it:

> I'm not necessarily looking to catch them out when I observe . . . I am looking for things to praise . . . If I do tell them things, I am only trying to help. (Taylor 1997: 187)

Thus monitoring was not just about discipline as a form of control but also entailed a more disciplined and perhaps simply better approach to the task. Taylor also notes that what he terms the 'disciplinary force' (1997: 197) of revenue targets was experienced by the telephone sales staff only exceptionally, for example if sales figures were particularly low. And employees found some routes round monitoring, for example learning when the supervisor might be listening to their calls.

Illustration of this point comes from a study in six organizations including manufacturing and public services as well as private services (Collinson et al. 1998). It included a survey of employees who were asked how closely they felt that they were monitored and whether the management approach to discipline had grown more or less strict in the previous 3 years. About a quarter of the sample reported being observed or monitored 'to a great extent', but a larger proportion (43 per cent) experienced monitoring little or not at all. Over half the sample felt that discipline had grown more strict. It might be expected that monitoring and strict discipline are parts of a relatively autocratic management style and will be associated with a sceptical view of initiatives such as quality programmes. In fact, when these and other measures of attitudes to management were correlated with views of quality programmes, it was found that they were directly related to them. The authors explain this through the concept of the 'disciplined worker': the employee who accepts the discipline and purpose of a quality management system and the performance standards which go with it. It is also worth noting the parallel with Taylor's qualitative evidence: TQM does not necessarily mean that workers feel very tightly monitored on a continuing basis.

As a review of research on call centres shows, there is often acceptance of performance standards (Deery and Kinnie 2002). There are examples of cases where managements consciously adopted a tight control policy, accepting the costs of employee burnout and high quit rates. Other studies also showed a relationship between 'emotional exhaustion' and absence rates. But many firms have been found to have to balance a cost-driven approach with the demands of customer satisfaction, while low unemployment in their local labour markets is a further driver towards autonomy. In this sector, then, there appear to be a range of possible positions mainly towards the right of Figure 14.1.

Turning now to manufacturing, there are examples where traditional custom remains in play. Heyes (1997), for example, describes the practice of 'knocking' in a chemicals factory, wherein workers took it in turn to go absent with the absentee being covered by a colleague paid at premium rates. To the extent, however, that firms have shifted towards annual hours or other similar arrangements, scope for this practice will have been restricted.

In some cases, reasonably overt struggle over punishment-centred discipline has been observed. McKinlay and Taylor (1996: 288) report a study of a US-owned telecommunications company in which peer review processes were intended to develop a new and 'totalizing' discipline. Teams were supposed to practise self-discipline, but 'the lack of clear factory-wide rules quickly led to wide variations in disciplinary actions [and discipline came to be seen as] *ad hoc*, arbitrary, and distorted by personality clashes'. Teams 'gradually withdrew from their disciplinary role'.

Trends towards tighter control have been discussed in particular in relation to Japanese-owned firms. At the extreme, it was argued that such firms practised tight control through electronic surveillance of the shop floor, the implication being that rules were strictly enforced (Sewell and Wilkinson 1992). Yet other studies underline the need for managers to accommodate workers' preferences and the fact that workers could evade some demands while displaying only 'ritualized compliance' with others; these trends are interpreted through the concept of managerial 'mandate', the right to make decisions, but one qualified by workers' perceptions of fairness (Elger and Smith 1998: 192). Similarly Webb and Palmer (1998) report that workers were able to evade some organizational rules, with the tacit toleration of supervisors as long as production targets were met. Just why these different results emerge is not very clear, but they may turn on a mix of factors such as the ease of electronic monitoring and the external labour market, with situations of high unemployment being most likely to allow a harsh workplace regime.

The context of discipline thus seems to have changed. There are more organizations than in the past with explicit performance standards, and there is less space in which largely autonomous shop floor customs can emerge. Studies such as those just discussed are clear that worker autonomy remains, but also that it exists within relatively narrow limits. The implications are harder to assess. In the past, workers did not necessarily celebrate the power that they enjoyed, for it was often a negative power (the ability to frustrate some managerial goals) and it needed to be exerted to respond to what was seen as potentially unfair or incompetent management. Workers may welcome a more organized and rigorous performance management approach even if it also removes some of the space for custom and practice. Yet many other workers are still faced with harsh discipline or the need to create some shop floor rules where management operates by default. This is very clear in the case of the control of attendance.

Attendance Management: Moral Panics and Practical Vacuums

Consider the following extract from an ethnographic researcher's diary.

> Pat told me that she was 'taken upstairs' recently and told off about her poor attendance. . . . She said it was the first time in over 30 years at work that she had been told off about this and that it was unfair because people with a much worse record than her had got away with it. In the five years she had been at [the firm] Pat said every previous attendance grading had been a grade A [the top grade]. It was a story she told every new starter, and if her mates said they felt unwell Pat would always chip in that they should not take time off or they would be 'sent upstairs'.

This observation occurred, not in the 1970s, but in the mid-1990s and moreover in a Japanese-owned transplant that was highly organized in relation to many of its production processes; the case is discussed by Webb and Palmer (1998), with the above material coming from Palmer (2000). It illustrates one aspect of absence management: the lack of systematic managerial control, even in a workplace like this one where the technical control system was meticulous. Much attendance management tends to fall towards the bottom left of Figure 14.1.

The second aspect is the general recognition that attendance control is an issue for managers: 90 per cent of respondents to one of the CIPD's periodic surveys saw sickness absence as significant or very significant for their organizations (CIPD 2003). And the third is the idea of a moral panic (Cohen 1980): an over-reaction to a relatively trivial issue, which is often heightened by press coverage and the process of 'deviance amplification'. In the process, some loosely linked behaviour is identified as a concrete thing: the suffix '-ism', as in common use of 'absent-eeism', implies a self-contained and clearly defined activity driven by a shared set of beliefs among those practising it. Moral panics around absence are illustrated by press stories reporting managerial beliefs that absences are not 'genuine' (e.g. *Financial Times*, 21 October 2003) and claimed willingness of doctors to give sick notes to 'healthy' workers (*Sunday Times*, 23 November 2003). The point is driven home sharply by a report that appeared after the above remarks were drafted: a front-page story in the *Financial Times* (5 July 2004) claimed that the UK public sector 'is losing £4bn a year or more through staff sick days – equivalent to an extra 1p on income tax'. Such claims are assessed below.

The use of the idea of a moral panic has the following benefits.

- It focuses on a tendency among managers to put responsibility for attendance issues on workers, who are deemed 'irresponsible'. The issues are also often discussed as though they lie outside the organization, as where compliant doctors are blamed for certifying illnesses of dubious validity.
- It allows managers to provide hard numbers to behaviour at whose extent they can only guess. How can managers know exactly where the line between genuine and other absence should be drawn, and moreover estimate the extent of cases falling into the latter category?
- It acts as a warning in the development of attendance control policies. Managers might stop to think what the nature of a 'problem' is and how they know this before taking action.

What then is the extent of absence? Surveys of HR managers put the rate of absence attributed to sickness at about 4 per cent, or 9 days per employee per year (CIPD 2003 and 2004). Previous surveys going back to the 1980s give broadly similar numbers. Problems of low response rates and a possible tendency for reports to come from those with the best monitoring systems have led some to conclude that the data from such surveys are 'severely biased' (Barham and Leonard 2002: 184). The headline figure is, however, in line with that reported in WERS, which does not have problems of low response rates (Cully et al. 1999: 126). Absence as defined by organizations does seem to run at about 4 per cent, but any finer estimates of patterns would not be reliable. Individual employees have been asked relevant questions in the General Household Survey and the Labour Force Survey. Estimates from the latter put the average absence rate at only 2 per cent, while figures from the former indicate little overall change in absence rates since the 1970s (Barham and Leonard 2002).

Why, then, the concern? First, there are the costs of absence. Regular surveys by bodies including the CBI and the CIPD attempt to estimate these, with the CIPD figure for 2003 being £588 per employee per year. But studies over many years show that rigorous measurement remains very rare, so that these estimates are really averages of guesses. A survey of engineering firms concluded that 'much absence reporting is merely a paper exercise' (see IRS 2004: 20). A case study investigation of 13 organizations found that in only two could managers place any financial cost on absence (Bevan et al. 2004: 41). A study of seven organizations estimates that absence costs between 2 and 16 per cent of annual salary costs, with only half of this being due to the direct costs of paying absent employees; it concludes that 'even the most "leading-edge" UK employers . . . appear fundamentally ill-equipped to form a view of their sickness absence costs' (Bevan and Hayday 2001: 42). In short, there plainly are costs, but many firms do not know what they are, let alone what proportion of them might be controllable.

Second, there is evidence that patterns of absence and of underlying health are changing. A study by the Health and Safety Executive noted a growth in self-reported work-related illness, a particular rise in reports of stress, and a rapid growth in sickness absence among those with a work-related illness, which doubled in the period 1995–2002 (see IRS 2003). In the CIPD survey of 2003, just over half of respondents said that stress was a growing cause of absence. Long-term absence may thus be a growing issue.

Third, competitive pressures have been highlighted for some time (Edwards and Whitston 1993). This is coupled with the growth of 24-hour operation in many sectors, while at the same time workforce diversity means that employee expectations of working patterns are growing more varied: employers' demand for work at non-traditional times, and a non-traditional supply of labour both make 'attendance' more complex than it was in the past. Even if absence levels have not increased, the costs may be more salient, partly because organizations have less financial slack and partly because as organizations strive to be 'lean' the consequences of absence for their operations are more severe. Hence, for example, in 1998 the Cabinet Office set targets for reducing absence levels across all government bodies and produced an action checklist (Cabinet Office 1998). A feature of the Chancellor of the Exchequer's spending review of 2004 was his highlighting of the costs of sickness absence in the public sector and the announcement of a review (*Financial Times*, 13 July 2004).

Finally, there is a greater 'duty of care' that employers owe employees. This includes a safe working environment, as reflected in some court cases where the employer was alleged to be responsible for the stress suffered by an employee (Torrington et al. 2002: 517–19).

Standard good practice in attendance management is not hard to identify. It includes the following.

- Keeping records and identifying issues. As noted above, however, record-keeping appears to be limited in extent, and statistics will not identify points for action. Several organizations use triggers, such as the number of spells of absence in a year, to set off a review, but these are not necessarily applied consistently.
- The return-to-work interview. This is now standard practice, having developed during the 1980s when self-certification of short absences was introduced, with the result that firms were encouraged to review this process rather than simply rely on a doctor's note. The danger is that the activity will be merely perfunctory, and some research indicates that, with growing performance pressures, dealing with return-to-work forms is not a priority (Edwards and Whitston 1993). Case studies in seven organizations found the interview was used in only four, and then not universally (Dunn and Wilkinson 2002).
- Involvement of line managers. This is a central theme, with line managers being identified as the people who know their staff. Yet the survey of engineering firms mentioned above found that half the (personnel) respondents felt that line managers did not take responsibility for the management of long-term absence (IRS 2004). The case studies just noted found that the policy was often 'a case of "pass the baton"' (Dunn and Wilkinson 2002: 238).
- Maintain contact with long-term absentees. The difficulty here is that absentees are by definition not visible and that once they are absent for a time cover is arranged and there is no immediate pressure to maintain contact. Moreover, health problems, particularly where stress is involved, are inherently personal and difficult, and managers' inclination is likely to be to avoid these issues. Bevan et al. (2004: 23) quote a manager in a small firm as saying 'you have to be very careful what you say to people', and argue that personal relationships in such firms make it hard to 'challenge employees'. The issue is likely to be particularly salient in small firms, but is not limited to them. Dunn and Wilkinson (2002) report a general reluctance to apply formal rules and to query reasons for absence.

Good practice is one thing. Whether it works is another. Given the massive interest in attendance and the huge number of studies of its determinants, one might expect clear evidence here. Yet Wooden (1988) in reviewing relevant studies could find few that addressed the effectiveness of control measures, and was able to reach no very firm conclusions. A more recent effort systematically identified 214 apparently relevant studies, but only eight actually addressed best practice in an acceptable scientific fashion, and these eight were often old or conducted outside the UK (Spurgeon 2002). Much reported evidence in other studies was 'consensus based', that is, based on the use of some assumed good practice, rather than able to show clear effects. The indications from the eight studies were that return-to-work interviews and trigger points had no clear effect, but that attempts to improve the attendance of those with high absence levels and early contact with absentees appeared to have value.

One key feature missing from the above list of good practice is the 'attendance culture'. Long work hours, as reflected in the notion of 'presenteeism', are now a familiar issue. Just what they mean for attendance is not clear. The correlation between long hours and health, for example, seems to be rather small (Sparrow and Cooper 2003: 229–34). There are certainly some indications that workers can feel under pressure to attend work when they are ill; in one case study organization, around one-third of workers reported that they felt under pressure from management to attend when they were ill but this was rare in the other three organizations studied (Edwards and Whitston 1993).

Does this mean that attendance is either unmanageable or that it might be manageable but that we do not know how? In terms of concrete practice, it is the case that attendance is often managed poorly. The conclusion of a leading student of the subject is clear: 'most employers have only just reached base camp in their attempt to manage absence' (Stephen Bevan, quoted in IRS, 2003: 17). The study just mentioned found that, despite formal control procedures, in practice attendance was not a major issue and that it was often managed by default: no very clear policy goals were communicated to workers, and choices were left to line managers, together with occasional 'purges'. Recent case study analysis confirms that absence control is rarely a managerial priority (Bevan et al. 2004). As against this, we have the good practice recommendations but little hard evidence that they work.

Now this is only one area of HR among many where concrete evidence that a practice 'makes a difference' is weak. Demonstrating hard effects is bound to be difficult, and perhaps particularly so in this area: attendance addresses the interface between work and home and leisure, and there are many aspects of the relationship which are not amenable to managerial control. The standards of scientific evidence are important, in warning against the assumption that a given policy will necessarily work. But they can be too strict. Some policies may not directly work in achieving a stated aim, but they may well stop matters being any worse than they are. They may also be necessary but not sufficient conditions: a policy of return-to-work interviews may not in itself have much effect, but it is not necessarily useless if combined with other policies.

This may be one area, and probably not the only one, where the simple adage applies: it's not what you do, it's the way that you do it. In this case, there is nothing mysterious about the idea of regular attendance at work, and a mass of evidence suggests that most workers accept the idea. Nor is the broad principle of monitoring attendance and intervening when standards are breached likely to be controversial. Numerous reports exist of absence levels being cut through various devices including attendance bonuses (which seem to swing in and out of fashion), the encouragement of team discipline, and counselling and healthcare plans. It may not be important which particular approach is adopted, as long as there is a clear view of the issue (based on careful evidence of attendance patterns), consistency of approach, and perceived fairness.

Finally, attendance management can be about more than just attendance. The few studies of managerial policy suggest that firms tend to use attendance control to try to establish broader messages about the need for disciplined performance. The danger is that workers see this as no more than a crack-down, and possibly a merely temporary one. 'Hard' attendance policies conflict with 'soft' people development ones. With growing attention to issues of work–life balance, this situation may change. But on past experience it is likely to be only a minority of organizations that have cogent attendance policies that are applied in practice, with many others managing by default. Attendance control seems to swing from neglect to panic and crack-downs. Perhaps the most remarkable fact is that, despite cost pressures and the development of the 'lean organization', it has not become a more prominent issue on the day-to-day agenda of line and personnel managers.

Conclusions

The management of discipline and attendance has many continuities with the past. Rates of punishment seem to have changed little, there is little evidence of any shift towards a 'corrective' approach, and HRM practices seem to have no influence on the prevalence of disciplinary action. Managers are also often reluctant to manage actively issues of individual attendance and work performance, not least because these issues involve the personal circumstances of individual workers. One might expect the control of attendance to increase in importance but the evidence suggests that processes of monitoring and controlling attendance have changed little. As for workers, the desire to negotiate space in the working day remains, and the need to act on this desire is, in view of the limited take-up of high commitment strategies, likely to be widespread. Discipline is thus often handled by default, or in the terms of Figure 14.1 towards the bottom left. It need not entail a deliberately assertive management (bottom right of the figure), and we have seen, for example, that specific performance targets are used rather rarely as direct disciplinary devices. Hence the term 'murky' rather than 'dark'.

Reasons for this continuity include the following. First, accurate measurement is difficult and time-consuming. Second, cost pressures mean, ironically, that managers have less time to deal with monitoring and control than was the case in the past. Third, action can entail inquiry into workers' personal circumstances, an approach with which many managers seem to feel uncomfortable. Fourth, hard evidence on the effectiveness of control policies is lacking.

Although many broad principles have stayed the same, the terrain on which they operate has changed. Two developments may have reduced the need to give explicit attention to discipline and attendance control. The first relates to commitment. It is probably the case that the *technical* organization of work – planning, scheduling, quality control – has become more focused, as has the *social control* of this work through such things as performance management systems. Hence the arrival of the disciplined worker. But such a worker seems to exist only under conditions of reasonable job security and trust in management. In most firms, it would be rash to assume that agreement on rules and norms has broken out. The second development relates to control. Work schedules are increasingly diverse, and the workers asked to perform them have a very wide range of expectations of work. Cost pressures are often substantial. The upshot is that workers are controlled more tightly than in the past. Studies point to an increase in the use of systems of performance monitoring and to growing worker awareness of the pressure to perform, and there is clear evidence of an intensification of work effort during the 1980s and 1990s, though this levelled off during the late 1990s (Green 2001, 2003). The implication here is that managerial power has reduced the ability of workers to engage in 'undisciplined' behaviour. Yet as Green (2003: 145) concludes, a policy of work intensification is 'hardly viable as a long-term strategy for sustainable growth' and 'the limits [of the policy] may have been reached' in the UK. Firms may not be able to rely on this approach.

If managerial goals are being achieved through these means, then the vacuum in the operation of discipline and attendance control may not matter. But several considerations suggest otherwise. First, general neglect may undermine other HR policies: if the effective message is that even basic attendance is not an issue, workers may well think that other efforts to create commitment are not seriously intended. Second, we have seen in this chapter that the negotiation of rules is a continuing theme in organizations, regardless of the extent to which broad strategies of commitment or control are in place: these strategies cannot define day-to-day practice. Third, neglect followed by sudden action provoked by a particular case will create inappropriate messages. Hard cases make bad law – a point particularly salient in this area. Fourth, it is not very difficult to deal with the basics of discipline and attendance. Fifth, labour force trends may raise the importance of managing the performance of individual workers. In the recent past, firms were to some extent insulated from the issue by a rise in the numbers of people with health problems who left the work force. The figures are substantial. Among prime-age men, the rate of economic inactivity rose five-fold between the 1970s and 1990s; and over this period the proportion of inactive men reporting a limiting health problem rose from 10 per cent to 40 per cent (Faggio and Nickell 2003). To the extent that this mechanism has dried up, or even more so if there is pressure to employ formerly inactive workers, firms will find themselves managing more health problems than in the past. Add to this the general concern with stress and the issue becomes even more salient. And, finally, addressing discipline and attendance may have other benefits, notably in encouraging line managers to take the management of people more seriously than they often do.

REFERENCES

Ashdown, R.T. and Baker, K.H. 1973: *In Working Order: A Study of Industrial Discipline*, Department of Employment Manpower Papers 6, London: HMSO.

Barham, C. and Leonard, J. 2002: Trends and source of data on sickness absence, *Labour Market Trends*, **110**(4), 177–85.

Bensman, J. and Gerver, I. 1963: Crime and punishment in the factory, *American Sociological Review*, **28**(4), 588–98.

Bevan, S., Dench, S., Harper, H. and Hayday, S. 2004: *How Employers Manage Absence*, Department of Trade and Industry, Employment Relations Research Series 25. London: DTI.

Bevan, S. and Hayday, S. 2001: *Costing Sickness Absence in the UK*, Institute for Employment Research Report 382. Brighton: IES.

Blackburn, R.A. and Hart, M. 2002: *Small Firms' Awareness and Knowledge of Individual Employment Rights*, Department of Trade and Industry, Employment Relations Research Series 14, London: DTI.

Bowen, D. and Lawler, E. 1992: The empowerment of service workers. *Sloan Management Review*, **33**(1), 31–9.

Brown, W. 1973: *Piecework Bargaining*, London: Heinemann.

Cabinet Office. 1998: Managing Attendance in the Public Services. www.Cabinet-office.gov.uk.

Cavendish, R. 1982: *Women on the Line*, London: Routledge & Kegan Paul.

CIPD (Chartered Institute of Personnel and Development) 2003: *Employee Absence: A Survey of Management Policies and Practice*. www.CIPD.co.uk/surveys.

CIPD (Chartered Institute of Personnel and Development) 2004: *Employee Absence 2004: A Survey of Management Policy and Practice*. www.CIPD.co.uk/surveys.

Clifton, R. and Tatton-Brown, C. 1979: *Impact of Employment Legislation on Small Firms*, Department of Employment Research Paper 6, London: HMSO.

Cohen, S. 1980: *Folk Devils and Moral Panics*, 2nd edn, London: Martin Robertson.

Collinson, M., Rees, C. and Edwards, P. 1998: *Involving Employees in Total Quality Management*, Department of Trade and Industry, Employment Relations Research Series 1, London: DTI.

Corby, S. 2000: Unfair dismissal disputes, *Human Resource Management Journal*, **10**(1), 79–93.

Cully, M., Woodland, S., O'Reilly, A. and Dix, G. 1999: *Britain at Work, as Depicted by the 1998 Workplace Employee Relations Survey*. London: Routledge.

Daniel, W.W. and Stilgoe, E. 1978: *The Impact of Employment Protection Laws*, London: PSI.

Deery, S. and Kinnie, N. 2002: Call centres and beyond, *Human Resource Management Journal*, **12**(4), 3–13.

Ditton, J. 1977: Perks, pilferage and the fiddle, *Theory and Society*, **4**(1), 39–71.

Ditton, J. 1979: *Controlology*, London: Macmillan.

DTI (Department of Trade and Industry) 2002: *Findings from the 1998 Survey of Employment Tribunal Applications*, Department of Trade and Industry, Employment Relations Research Series 13, London: DTI.

Dunn, C. and Wilkinson, A. 2002: Wish you were here: Managing absence, *Personnel Review*, **31**(2), 228–46.

Earnshaw, J., Goodman, J., Harrison, R. and Marchington, M. 1998: *Industrial Tribunals, Workplace Disciplinary Procedures and Employment Practice*, Department of Trade and Industry, Employment Relations Research Series 2. London: DTI.

Edwards, P.K. 1986: *Conflict at Work*, Oxford: Blackwell.

Edwards, P.K. 1988: Patterns of conflict and accommodation, in D. Gallie (ed.), *Employment in Britain*, Oxford: Blackwell.

Edwards, P.K. 1995: HRM, union voice and the use of discipline: An analysis of WIRS, *Industrial Relations Journal*, **26**(3), 204–20.

Edwards, P.K. 2003: The employment relationship and the field of industrial relations, in P.K. Edwards (ed.), *Industrial Relations*, 2nd edn, Oxford: Blackwell.

Edwards, P.K., Ram, M. and Black, J. 2003: *The Impact of Employment Legislation on Small Firms*, Department of Trade and Industry, Employment Relations Research Series 20, London: DTI.

Edwards, P.K. and Whitston, C. 1993: *Attending to Work*, Oxford: Blackwell.

Edwards, P.K. and Whitston, C. 1994: Disciplinary practice: A study of the railways in Britain, 1860–1988, *Work, Employment and Society*, **8**(3), 317–38.

Elger, T. and Smith, C. 1998: Exit, voice and 'mandate': Managerial strategies and labour practices of Japanese firms in Britain, *British Journal of Industrial Relations*, **36**(2), 185–208.

Faggio, G. and Nickell, S. 2003: The rise of inactivity among adult men, in R. Dickens, P. Gregg and J. Wadsworth (eds.), *The Labour Market under New Labour*, Basingstoke: Palgrave.

Friedman, A.L. 1977: *Industry and Labour*, London: Macmillan.

Gouldner, A.W. 1954: *Patterns of Industrial Bureaucracy*, New York: Free Press.

Green, F. 2001: It's been a hard day's night, *British Journal of Industrial Relations*, **39**(1), 53–80.

Green, F. 2003: The demands of work, in R. Dickens, P. Gregg and J. Wadsworth (eds.), *The Labour Market under New Labour*, Basingstoke: Palgrave.

Haiven, L. 1994: Workplace discipline in international comparative perspective, in J. Bélanger, L. Haiven and P. Edwards (eds.), *Workplace Industrial Relations and the Global Challenge*, Ithaca: ILR Press.

Hayward, B., Peters, M., Rousseau, N. and Seeds, N. 2004: *Findings from the Survey of Employment Tribunal Applications 2003*, Department of Trade and Industry, Employment Relations Research Series 33, London: DTI.

Heyes, J. 1997: Annualised hours and the knock, *Work, Employment and Society*, **11**(1), 65–82.

Hyman, R. 1987: Strategy or structure: Capital, labour and control, *Work, Employment and Society*, **1**(1), 25–56.

IPM (Institute of Personnel Management) 1979: *Disciplinary Procedures and Practice*, London: IPM.

IRS (Industrial Relations Services) 1987: Lords overrule labour pump, *IRS Industrial Relations Legal Information Bulletin*, **343**, 13–15.

IRS (Industrial Relations Services) 2003: Work-related absences are growing longer, *IRS Employment Review*, **784**, 17–20.

IRS (Industrial Relations Services) 2004: Managing long-term absence and rehabilitation: Part 1, *IRS Employment Review*, **794**, 18–24.

Jones, C., Nickson, D. and Taylor, G. 1997: Whatever it takes, *Work, Employment and Society*, **11**(3), 541–54.

Knight, K.G. and Latreille, P.L. 2000: Discipline, dismissals and complaints to employment tribunals, *British Journal of Industrial Relations*, **38**(4), 533–56.

Korczynski, M. 2002: *Human Resource Management in Service Work*, Basingstoke: Palgrave.

Leidner, R. 1993: *Fast Food, Fast Talk*, Berkeley: University of California Press.

Lupton, T. 1963: *On the Shop Floor*, Oxford: Pergamon.

Mars, G. 1982: *Cheats at Work*, London: Counterpoint.

McKinlay, A., and Taylor, P. 1996: Power, surveillance and resistance, in P. Ackers, C. Smith and P. Smith (eds.), *The New Workplace and Trade Unionism*, London: Routledge.

Millward, N., Stevens, M., Smart, D. and Hawes, W.R. 1992: *Workplace Industrial Relations in Transition*, Aldershot: Dartmouth.

Nichols T. 1997: *The Sociology of Industrial Injury*, London: Mansell.

Nolan, P. and Wood, S. 2003: Mapping the future of work, *British Journal of Industrial Relations*, **41**(2), 165–74.

Palmer, G. 2000: Embeddedness and Workplace Relations, PhD thesis, University of Warwick.

Phelps Brown, E.H. 1949: Morale, military and industrial, *Economic Journal*, **59**(1), 40–55.

Pollard, S. 1965: *The Genesis of Modern Management*, London: Arnold.

Ram, M., Abbas, T., Sanghera, B., Barlow, G. and Jones, T. 2001: 'Apprentice entrepreneurs': Ethnic minority workers in the independent restaurant sector, *Work, Employment and Society*, **15**(2), 353–72.

Rollinson, D., Handley, J., Hook, C. and Foot, M. 1997: The disciplinary experience and its effects on behaviour, *Work, Employment and Society*, **11**(2), 283–311.

Roy, D. 1954: Efficiency and 'the fix': Informal intergroup relations in a piecework machine shop, *American Journal of Sociology*, **60**(2), 255–66.

Sewell, G. and Wilkinson, B. 1992: Someone to watch over me, *Sociology*, **26**(2), 271–90.

Sparrow, P.R. and Cooper, C.L. 2003: *The Employment Relationship*, London: Butterworth Heinemann.

Spurgeon, A. 2002: *Managing Attendance at Work*, Institute of Occupational Health, University of Birmingham. www.BOHRF.org.uk.

Strauss, G., and Sayles, L.R. 1980: *Personnel*, 4th edn, Englewood Cliffs, NJ: Prentice-Hall.

Taylor, S. 1997: 'Empowerment' or 'degradation': Total quality management and the service sector, in R.K. Brown (ed.), *The Changing Shape of Work*, Basingstoke: Macmillan.

Torrington, D., Hall, L., and Taylor, S. 2002: *Human Resource Management*, 5th edn, London: Financial Times/Prentice Hall.

Tremlett, N. and Banerji, N. 1994: *The 1992 Survey of Industrial Tribunal Applications*, Employment Department Research Series 22, London: Employment Department.

Turnbull, P., and Wass, V. 1994: The greatest game no more: Redundant dockers and the demise of dock work, *Work, Employment and Society*, **8**(4), 487–506.

Webb, M. and Palmer, G. 1998: Evading surveillance and making time, *British Journal of Industrial Relations*, **36**(4), 611–27.

Wooden, M. 1988: *The Management of Labour Absence*, National Institute of Labour Studies, Flinders University, Working Paper 97.

CHAPTER FIFTEEN

Direct Participation and Involvement

Mick Marchington and Adrian Wilkinson

In its various guises, the topic of employee participation and involvement has been a recurring theme in UK industrial relations and personnel management. Different periods have embraced new forms of participation which have sometimes replaced, and at other times existed alongside, those which already existed. The wider political and economic environment has had a key influence in facilitating particular forms. In the 1970s, for example, developments centred on notions of power sharing through industrial democracy and representative participation through trade unions. The decline in union membership and influence and changes in public policy both conspired to move industrial democracy off the domestic agenda during the 1980s and 1990s, but the potential impact of the Information and Consultation Directive in the UK has led to renewed debate (Gollan 2002; Gospel and Willman 2003; Sisson 2002).

In any event the last 20 years has witnessed growing managerial interest in participation, specifically in the area of employee involvement (EI). Recent EI initiatives have been management-sponsored and, not surprisingly, have reflected a management agenda concerned primarily with employee motivation and commitment to organizational objectives. EI has focused on direct participation by and with small groups and individuals, it is concerned with information sharing at work-group level, and it has tended not to include worker input into high level decision making. As such, direct participation is fundamentally different from industrial democracy and representative participation schemes (Wilkinson 2002). In this chapter, we analyse EI and direct participation.

One of the major factors shaping direct participation within organizations is competition and product market change in the private sector. The public sector has also been subjected to such forces, arising from deregulation and commercialization and linked to notions of customer choice. Secondly, government policy has set the scene for wider changes in management approaches, and in particular the free market stance advocated by successive governments has lifted restrictions on employers in order to encourage 'enterprise'. This fits well with political changes in North America, although it has remained at odds with European developments that seek a more uniform social framework. Thirdly, in addition to shifts in the structure of employment in the UK away from manufacturing to services, which have impacted on EI, there have also been changes in patterns of employment and the increased use of contracting. In these situations, where the employer is 'elusive' and there is no simple relationship between a single employer and its employees, it is difficult to devise appropriate systems of participation which apply to workers on different contracts of employment (e.g. agency workers) (see Marchington et al. 2004).

While each of these factors is important in shaping the environment within which direct participation operates, we also need to examine how these macro level changes interact with developments at organizational level where business decisions are made. An important influence here has been the 'ideas brokers' – consultants and popular management writers – who offer their interpretation of the changing global market and put forward new normative recipes. For example, organizations were encouraged to be flexible, innovative and responsive, rather than seeking economies of scale through mass production (Piore and Sabel 1983). More recently the knowledge economy also provided impetus for involvement in decision making (Scarborough 2003), which has been viewed as a positive development for employers *and* employees. As Poole et al. (2000: 497) note, 'increased competition' and concerns about economic performance have made the achievement of 'rights-based' employee participation more remote whilst encouraging the development of EI as a route to better 'market performance'.

This has clear implications for the management of employment and direct participation. Compliance, hierarchy and following rules are seen as supposedly less appropriate for employees who are expected to work beyond contract, exercise their initiative and embrace teamworking. As Walton (1985: 76) put it, managers have now 'begun to see that workers respond best – and most creatively – not when they are tightly controlled by management, placed in narrowly defined jobs, and treated like an unwelcome necessity, but instead when they are given broader responsibilities, encouraged to contribute, and helped to take satisfaction from their work'. Similarly, best practice HRM or high commitment management (Huselid 1995; Becker and Huselid 1998; Wright and Gardner 2003) have both emphasized the importance of employee involvement by drawing on an array of sophisticated statistical evidence. These results have been mirrored by some UK research (Patterson et al. 1997; Wood 1999; Department of Trade and Industry 2002). A wide variety of labels has been attached to these direct participation initiatives: high performance work design (Buchanan 1987), lean production (Womack et al. 1990), high involvement work systems (Edwards and Wright 2001), teamworking (Mueller 1994), self-managed teams (Pfeffer 1998) and high performance HRM (Ramsay et al. 2000). Of course, there is a danger that these initiatives are viewed solely in a positive and upbeat manner, so ignoring the more contested and mundane nature of participation. For example, rather than leading to autonomy and self-management, empowerment may merely produce greater work intensification, increased stress levels and redundancies.

This introduction sets the scene for the remainder of the chapter. First, we review briefly the dynamics of participation, focusing in particular on cycles and waves as competing explanations of how and why participation has varied in extensiveness and importance over time. Second, we analyse four separate categories of direct participation, considering in each case some of the major characteristics and problems associated with these schemes, and we then review the different meanings and interpretation of EI in general. Finally, we evaluate the role of direct participation in general, picking up on a number of key themes and issues.

The Dynamics of Participation

Employee participation and involvement are somewhat elastic terms with considerable width in the range of definitions given by authors (see for example Poole 1986; Bar-Haim 2002). As Heller et al. (1998: 15) note:

> Definitions of participation abound. Some authors insist that participation must be a group process, involving groups of employees and their boss; others stress delegation, the process by which the *individual* employee is given greater freedom to make decisions on his or her own. Some restrict the term 'participation' to formal institutions, such as works councils; other definitions embrace 'informal participation', the day-to-day relations between supervisors and subordinates in which subordinates are allowed substantial input into work decisions. Finally, there are those who stress participation as a *process* and those who are concerned with participation as a *result*.

It is helpful if the terms can be deconstructed according to degree, form, level and range of subject matter. Taking the first of these, *degree* indicates the extent to which employees are able to influence decisions about various aspects of management – whether they are simply informed of changes, consulted or actually make decisions. The escalator of participation (see Figure 15.1) illustrates this; it implies a progression upwards rather than simply a move from zero participation to workers' control. Secondly, there is the *level* at which participation takes place; task, departmental, establishment, or corporate. The *range* of subject matter is the third dimension, ranging from the relatively trivial – such as canteen food – to more strategic concerns relating, for example, to investment strategies. Fourthly, there is the *form* that participation takes. Indirect participation is where employees are involved through their representatives, usually elected from the wider group (see Chapter 16). Financial participation relates to schemes such as profit sharing or gainsharing whereby employees participate directly in the commercial success or failure of the organization, usually linking a proportion of financial reward to corporate or establishment performance. Direct participation and involvement, the subject of this chapter, is concerned with face-to-face or written communications between managers and subordinates that involves individuals rather than representatives. This is referred to as 'on-line' participation (Appelbaum and Batt 1995)

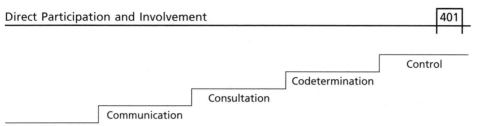

Figure 15.1 The escalator of participation

where workers make decisions as part of their daily job responsibilities as distinct from 'off-line' participation where workers make suggestions through a formal scheme. In our view empowerment relates to all aspects of direct participation given it covers a very broad range of initiatives (Wilkinson 2002; Psoinos and Smithson 2002; Wall et al. 2004).

There have been various attempts to trace the dynamics of participation, of which the cycles of control thesis (Ramsay 1977) is the best known. This argued that we have seen four broad cycles of interest in participation over the last 100 years, starting with profit sharing in the late nineteenth century. The second and third related to consultative arrangements between management and workers and included the Whitley Committees during and just after the First World War, and the Joint Production and Advisory Committees (JPACs) of the 1940s. In the 1960s and 1970s, attention changed to new forms of participation in the shape of productivity bargaining and worker directors. The reason for this waxing and waning of interest is simple according to Ramsay. Employers are attracted to the notion of participation only if their authority is under threat from below and, by appearing to share some elements of control, they are able to regain it. Once the threat from labour has abated, management lose interest in participation and allow schemes to fade into more trivial forms or to vanish altogether. Ramsay later updated and refined the cycles thesis in the context of early 1980s Thatcherite industrial relations, arguing that the potential for industrial democracy had been 'swept under the carpet' through the new managerial offensive. He concluded (1983: 219) that the cycles analysis had been more dramatically vindicated than could readily have been imagined in the mid-1970s.

The 'cycles' theory appeared plausible as an explanation for some developments in participation but it has been criticized as a general all-encompassing explanatory theory (Ackers et al. 1992). First, it is essentially rooted in manufacturing and public sector workplaces and has less relevance where trade unions are weaker. Secondly, looking principally at extensiveness and interest, it fails to take into account how schemes are actually used at the workplace and assumes that participation has a single, universal meaning. Thirdly, it assumes labour relations are of paramount importance to employers and that control over the labour process is one of their principal objectives. Fourthly, it fails to explain more recent developments in direct participation (Geary 2003; Wilkinson et al. 2004) where we have witnessed a huge array of initiatives in a climate where, according to Ramsay, one would expect decline (Marchington 2004).

An alternative thesis has been advanced by the authors, termed the 'waves' analysis. The argument here is that a single all-embracing explanation of change is inappropriate, and that participation might be driven by a variety of motives. For example, developments in profit sharing in the 1980s were facilitated by politically driven legal changes which could be seen as a mechanism to improve recruitment and retention. Similarly, some employers introduce participation for moral, religious or philosophical reasons, and the early profit-sharing schemes were implemented by owners who held religious-paternalist views. Once the analysis is broadened to allow for pressures other than from organized labour, we can look more closely at the role managers play. A central component of the waves analysis is that internal managerial relations helps to explain the ebb and flow of participation initiatives and the shape of EI in organizations varies significantly over time, and can be characterized in terms of wave patterns. These are subject to a range of forces, one of the most important being the career aspirations and mobility of managers, and conflicts between different functions and levels in the organizational hierarchy. The impetus behind many participation schemes is the career aspirations of managers in various functions, and the dynamics of participation is related to the progression of these people, internal political rivalries within management, and supervisory problems in sustaining the schemes. In other words, patterns of EI in particular workplaces owe as much to relations *within* management, as they do to relations between managers and workers (Marchington et al. 1993).

The detailed and longitudinal case studies on which the waves metaphor was based demonstrated clearly that, irrespective of broader developments, the dynamics of participation at workplace level was highly uneven. Some patterns did emerge, due largely to organizational factors such as the age and size of establishments, their sector and degree of centralized decision making – as well as trade union power – but processes were seen as critically important. Interestingly, subsequent case study research by the same team (Marchington et al. 2001) has confirmed the unevenness of developments, and that schemes recently introduced into one workplace may have been terminated in another. Additionally, so called new developments – such as partnership – have become more extensive, but in some cases they have been operating for years under different labels (Ackers et al. 2004). A key point to emerge from the waves concept is that, valuable though broad brush and macro level theories are, much more attention needs to be focused on the intricacies of workplace relations and the motives of all parties in order to analyse the dynamics of participation.

Direct Participation in Practice

Over the last 20 years, direct participation has become more extensive in the UK while indirect participation has declined (Millward and Stevens 1986: 165). Over the course of the 1990s direct participation became much more apparent together with the concomitant decline in indirect participation (Millward et al. 1992: 175–6; 2000: 117–37). The 1998 Workplace Employee Relations Survey (WERS) confirmed the continuation of these trends reporting that four of the top five 'new management practices and employee involvement schemes' were forms of direct participation. These were: teamworking (65 per cent of all workplaces employing 25 or more people); team briefing (61 per cent); staff attitude survey in the last 5 years (45 per cent); and problem-solving groups such as quality circles (42 per cent). The only other aspect of direct participation in the 16 practices identified was regular meetings of the entire workforce which, at 37 per cent, was rather more extensive than the existence of a joint consultative committee or an employee share ownership scheme for non-managerial employees. While noting this increase in the use of direct participation, we should also be alert to limitations due to definitions and survey design, a point to which we return later. In the case of teamworking, for example, though present in 65 per cent of workplaces, in just 5 per cent of these did it take the form of autonomous work groups in which team members were given responsibility for their task, jointly decided how work was to be done or appointed their own leader (Cully et al. 1998).

Nevertheless, direct participation has been a major growth area in employment relations, coinciding with (and perhaps related to) reductions in collective bargaining scope and coverage in the last 20 years. Bryson (2000) notes that between 1984 and 1998 representative structures halved while direct voice channels went up threefold. Similar tendencies are evident across much of the rest of Europe; for example, 80 per cent of workplaces now have some form of direct participation (Gill and Krieger 1999; Sisson et al. 1997). Even in the countries of southern Europe with the lowest coverage (Spain and Portugal), over 60 per cent of workplaces surveyed reported the existence of direct participation. The picture in North America and Australasia (Poole et al. 2000) also appears similar, although Lawler et al. (2001) note that the utilization of EI practices in the USA has levelled off more recently.

Regardless of growth, there are major problems with the terminology which is used to describe direct participation and the range of practices which appear to be subsumed under its banner. The definitions may be as broad and all-inclusive as 'any form of delegation to or consultation with employees', or as narrow as a 'formal, ongoing structure of direct communications' such as through team briefing. As Gallie et al. (2001: 7) note, the literature on participation has rarely distinguished between the different forms that employee involvement in decision making could take. Consequently, it is difficult to make precise comparisons about the extent of change over time, and there are dangers that generalizations are made when in fact different practices are being compared. For this reason, it is worthwhile to outline briefly the range of practices which are included under the title of 'direct participation'. Drawing upon previous categorizations by the authors (Marchington et al. 1992) we employ a simple four-fold schema: downward communications; upward problem solving; task participation; teamworking and self-management. These are differentiated in terms of direction of communication (up, down or lateral), level and scope of subject matter (company-wide, departmental or work group), regularity of involvement (continuing or scheduled at set times) and centrality to the work process (on-line or bolted-on). This schema is discussed briefly below.

Downward communications represents the most dilute form of direct participation, to some extent because of the direction of the communication but also due to the fact that it is typically bolted-on to the work process rather than forming part of everyday life. It takes a number of forms in practice – ranging from formalized written documents to all employees, through to face-to-face interactions between line managers and their staff – although it has a common purpose to inform and 'educate' employees about managerial actions and intentions. This can be viewed as nothing more than a mechanism to convey information about a particular issue (e.g., a new order, a change to car parking arrangements or a reminder about work standards), although alternatively it could be interpreted as an instrument to reinforce management prerogatives and shape employee expectations. More extensive and open communications are often seen as an important precursor to 'fuller' employee involvement. In the sense that information is rarely neutral however, messages may have a more insidious intent and/or consequences (Tebbutt and Marchington 1997).

In the past, many workers only discovered what was happening at their place of work through reports in local or regional newspapers, the grapevine or the trade union branch. The fact that managements now appear more committed to disseminating information within their organizations, is reflective of more general changes and expectations in society. In part, these developments have been stimulated by a desire to ensure that employees receive information direct from management, but also by a feeling that there is a potential link between information disclosure and higher levels of employee commitment to and identification with organizational goals (Marchington et al. 2001).

The principles behind face-to-face communications systems are simple. They rely on bringing small 'natural' groups of staff together at predetermined times (say, once a month) to hear about new developments direct from their line manager who is responsible for conveying relevant information, as well as using the briefing session to help build teams. Information is cascaded down the organizational hierarchy, with the original core message being adapted to suit specific audiences. Although briefings themselves are intended as one-way, downward communications, there is often provision for feedback up the line management chain in order to clarify issues and ensure that senior managers are aware of workers' feelings. Although there is widespread support for team briefings in principle, in practice they can run into a number of problems – such as line managers not being able to communicate effectively, the information lacking relevance or not being timely, and trade unions seeing briefing as a device to undermine or marginalize their role.

Upward problem solving incorporates a range of techniques designed to tap into employee knowledge and ideas, typically through individual suggestions or through ad hoc or semi-permanent groups brought together for the specific purpose of resolving problems or generating ideas. As with downward communications, these schemes tend to be 'bolted-on' rather than integral to the work process. These types of scheme have also grown considerably in extensiveness and importance since the 1980s, and are central to notions of 'soft' human resource management (Storey 2001) and so-called 'bundles' of best practice (Guest et al. 2003). These practices are predicated on assumptions that employees are a major source of competitive advantage whose ideas have been ignored in the past. These practices are designed to increase the stock of ideas available to management and increase co-operation at work, encouraging the acceptance of change. Although clearly offering a greater degree of participation than downward communications, they are also seen by critics as problematic precisely because they encourage employees to collaborate with management in helping to resolve work-related problems.

There are basically two different types of upward problem solving technique. The first is suggestion schemes – which have a long pedigree in the United Kingdom – where employees receive financial rewards for their suggestions provided they do not relate to their own work area. These schemes are a relatively marginal form of employee involvement, but they also have the potential to create bad feelings as well as good, especially if the employee making the suggestion feels that her/his idea merits a higher reward. Moreover, there is a danger that paying for suggestions merely encourages an instrumental approach to work.

Problem-solving groups and quality circles constitute the second type in this category of upward communications. These consist of small groups of employees who meet voluntarily on a regular basis to identify, analyse and solve quality and work-related problems. A typical circle would comprise about ten people, drawn either from the same group or from a range of different work areas who meet under the guidance of a leader, with assistance from one or more facilitators. As with other aspects of direct participation, problem-solving groups are designed to achieve explicit production or service goals (such as productivity improvements or zero defects) as well as enhance employee morale and commitment.

Task-based participation represents the third category, differing from the first two in being integral to the job and forming a part of everyday working life. As with certain aspects of upward problem solving, the practices included under this heading have a much longer history, especially under the guise of Quality of Work Life Programmes in the USA and Sweden in the 1960s and 1970s (Heller et al. 1998). Delayering, devolution and the removal of demarcations have increased pressure on employees to take responsibility for a greater range of tasks than under previous organizational structures, potentially encouraging empowerment. However, as with employee involvement generally, task-based participation illustrates elements of both 'soft' and 'hard' human resource management, regarding employees not only as resourceful humans but also workers as a cost that has to be minimized.

Task-based participation can occur both horizontally and vertically. The former is where workers undertake a variety of tasks at the same skill level, something which has now become a common feature in many workplaces. The range of tasks may be relatively small and require little additional training or skills acquisition, especially on assembly lines where each individual task can be learned without much difficulty. While offering a way in which to alleviate boredom, in terms of employee involvement, the improvements may be minimal; as Herzberg (1972: 118) famously wrote, when 'adding another meaningless task to the existing one, the arithmetic is adding zero to zero'. Vertical task-based participation comprises two different forms. Employees may be trained to undertake tasks at a higher skill level or they may be given some managerial and supervisory responsibilities, such as taking over the planning and design of work as well as its execution. At one level, this is a genuine attempt to give non-managerial employees greater discretion over how their own work is organized. On the other hand, devolving responsibility may increase stress levels and have a detrimental effect on workers' home and family lives as well as their health (Hochschild 1997).

The final category is *teamworking and self-management*, both of which have been central to recent discussions about direct participation as well as forming part of the 'best practice' human resource management bundle. As with many 'new' initiatives, one of the problems in attempting to analyse teamworking is the breadth and inconsistency in definition. Drawing on a range of definitions (Banker et al. 1996; Cordery 2003; Thompson and Wallace 1996), teamworking and self-management are seen to incorporate the following sorts of elements: responsibility for a complete task; working without direct supervision; discretion over work methods and time; encouragement for team members to organize and multi-skill; influence over recruitment to the team. Clearly, teamworking is more far-reaching than other forms of direct participation due to its centrality to work processes and the level and scope of subject matter which can be under the influence or control of employees. In theory, increasing team autonomy may improve collective motivation (Cordery 2003: 109) but it may also enable learning and knowledge-based action in furtherance of improved task performance (Parker et al. 2001).

Because of this, some analysts regard self-managing teams as the ultimate in direct participation, but others see this as merely increasing the pressure on workers to perform, exposing them to the vagaries of their team-mates and to interpersonal tensions. Barker (1993: 408) suggests that self-managing teams produce 'a form of control more powerful, less apparent and more difficult to resist than that of the former bureaucracy'. Under a teamworking regime, pressure for performance comes from peers rather than from managers, and while some would see this as liberating and genuinely positive, others would view it as management control at its most subversive and effective because workers take over responsibility for peer surveillance.

So far, we have considered the dynamics of direct participation and the various forms it takes in practice. In the remainder of the chapter, we focus on three major themes and issues in direct participation: meanings and interpretation; impact and performance; line managers and trade unions.

Meanings and Interpretation

The terminology employed in analyses of direct participation is often vague and imprecise, making it difficult to draw meaningful comparisons between findings. On some occasions, the same term is used for quite different practices; for example, a daily team briefing just before a shift commences may be quite different from one which is held on a quarterly basis. The latter could be seen as a bolted-on off-line activity which involves little in terms of time and has minimal impact on daily work, while the former is far more significant in relation to everyday work activities. Moreover, the *way* in which direct participation is introduced can be as significant as the form of participation chosen, and clearly this may affect the perceptions of prospective participants. Analysis based on survey data which is abstracted from organizational context can gloss over the real meaning and interpretation of these processes (Marchington et al. 1994), so it is important to ensure that direct participation is analysed in the context of organizational policies (see also Foster and Hoggett 1999).

Survey questions about extensiveness (or absence and presence) tell us nothing about the degree to which schemes are embedded within a workplace or an organization. A particular technique may have been in operation for many years but be marginal to everything that occurs at the workplace; for example, a briefing group may only give workers information they already know or are not interested in. Moreover, if more than one scheme is in operation, it is not possible to work out which has the greater influence or importance in the organization, nor can we assess how different stakeholders feel about participation at work.

There is a clear polarization in much of the writing on direct participation. On the one hand, prescriptive writers see it as something of a panacea (working smarter) which offers benefits to all (Byham 1991; Foy 1994), part of the re-enchantment of work and the gradual democratization of the workplace. On the other hand, direct participation can be regarded as wholly exploitative (working harder), with benefits accruing only to employers (Sewell and Wilkinson 1992). Thus, rather than employees being allocated greater power to do things, being entrusted with authority and achieving higher levels of control over their work, it is argued that any increase in authority is heavily circumscribed within the confines of managerial control systems. Delbridge (2003: 34) comments that while the prospect for meaningful involvement in decision making is a central component in the rhetoric of lean manufacturing, in reality managers do not provide the opportunity for workers to secure any form of autonomy.

Instead of employees being granted greater autonomy and discretion, as the proponents would argue, delegation of responsibility merely reinforces authority and disciplinary control through more sophisticated means, e.g. electronic surveillance. Under this regime, 'space' is reduced and workers find it difficult to maintain any room for non-productive or idle time or to hide work away for 'rainy days'. Performance is analysed by breaking down the work process into constituent parts, with performance that deviates from set targets being rendered transparent and subject to discipline. Actions which appear to empower employees may actually be disempowering as workers collaborate in their own exploitation. Equally, while empowerment may lead to a lowering of informal and interpersonal barriers between managers and non-managerial staff, this does not impact on formal hierarchies or management prerogatives (Wilkinson and Willmott 1994). Rather than gaining greater

Table 15.1 Contrasting meanings of participation

Bouquets	Brickbats
Education	Indoctrination
Empowerment	Emasculation
Liberating	Controlling
Delayering	Intensification
Teamwork	Peer group pressure
Responsibility	Surveillance
Post-Fordism	Neo-Fordism
Blame-free culture	Identification of errors
Commitment	Compliance

Source: Wilkinson et al. (1997).

power, workers assume higher levels of accountability and responsibility, and can be more easily blamed when things go wrong. Table 15.1 summarizes these contrasting views.

While those who regard participation as 'management by stress' (Parker and Slaughter 1993) have undoubtedly extended our understanding, their analyses lack sophistication. As with those who celebrate participation, the critics have been far too eager to accept its rhetoric at face value (Edwards et al. 1998; Wilkinson et al. 1997; Collinson et al. 1998), and their analysis is not so much wrong as partial. Many of the critical reviews can be seen as mirror images of the prescriptive management literature that assumes workers are malleable and passive recipients of whatever management desires. Research findings are often polarized into a simple evaluation of participation as *either* increased work effort and intensification *or* more job satisfaction – with no allowance for the fact that much depends on context and processes (Edwards and Wright 1998). There is evidence that the two can occur simultaneously as workers gain improvements and increased job satisfaction while also working harder to meet defined performance standards (Cappelli et al. 1997; Geary 2003; Wilkinson et al. 1997).

Geary and Dobbins' (2001: 19) study of teamworking showed how work was reorganized and managerial authority was reasserted, but not in a crude manner where management's power was used merely to intensify workers' efforts. New work patterns were established, some of which were helpful to employees (and were welcomed) while others imposed new demands and intensified effort. But the balance of costs and benefits 'was not simply six of one and half a dozen of the other'. Employees' responses were influenced by, and connected to, their expectations and prior experiences, as well as to payment levels and management style. It was found that teamwork could bring out autonomy *and* responsibility, albeit within clearly defined parameters that granted discretion to develop working practices which did not interfere with management's prerogatives.

Moreover, it is insulting to regard workers as cultural dupes or 'docile bodies' who are won over by managerial ideas and practices (Guest 1999). It may be difficult for workers to disagree with certain discourses in principle – for example, the idea of improving quality – but once the initiative has been implemented there is ample opportunity to contest decisions and shape events. As McKinlay and Taylor (1997: 282) point out, it is misleading to view participation as 'a form of self-subordination so complete, so seamless that it stifles any dissent' and it certainly overstates management power. Consequently, it is unlikely that senior management's interpretation of empowerment is adopted without challenge or modification by other actors. Thompson and Ackroyd (1995: 633) argue that, 'innovatory employee practices and informal organization will continue to subvert managerial regimes'. There is little doubt therefore that, despite the explosion of managerial initiatives designed to elicit greater effort and commitment, their success is far from guaranteed.

Impact and Performance

Evaluating the impact of direct participation on performance is tricky for a number of reasons. First, there is a range of measures which can be used to evaluate success – such as increases in productivity, improved employee attitudes, or changes in the balance of power – that depend on the standpoint of the observer. In most estimates of EI, however, workers' needs are typically subordinate to production or service goals. Secondly, given that direct participation is only one factor among many that can affect performance, it is difficult to disentangle the impact of direct participation from that of other variables – such as a change in technology, shifts in the external labour market or even exchange rate fluctuations. Thirdly, even when authors do find a significant association between direct participation and performance, it is very difficult to determine the direction of causality. It could be argued that superior organizational performance contributes to positive employee attitudes rather than the conventional view that direct participation causes employees to be more satisfied or to work harder and more effectively. In short, the view that direct participation is connected with high levels of commitment and organizational performance is predicated upon a series of assumptions, none of which can be taken for granted.

A number of senior managers and consultants (Wickens 1987; Morton 1994) have made grand claims about the benefits of participation to the business. The organizations in the Cunningham et al. (1996: 152) study reported benefits in terms of cost savings, improvements in quality and increased employee commitment. Psoinos and Smithson (2002: 145) note that 'people see the adoption of empowerment as rather successful although clearly the measurement of such schemes is difficult'. However, it is difficult to specify the precise contribution of direct participation given that this does not take place in isolation but is part of a wider set of organizational and human resource changes. Indeed, research on high performance work teams has identified the context in which they operate as critical to success. Other studies have shown how work redesign is linked to more participative decision making, innovative rewards and systematic career planning and development (Buchanan 1994). Similarly, work on best practice HRM also points to the import-ance of interlocking practices which support and reinforce each other. As Pfeffer (1994: 31) notes, 'it is important to recognise that the practices are interrelated – it is difficult to do one thing by itself with much positive result'.

There is an impressive amount of data illustrating the importance of integrating different EI practices, both on a cross-sectoral basis and in particular industries such as vehicles (Adler 1993; MacDuffie 1995), steel (Arthur 1994), and apparel plants (Appelbaum et al. 2000). Ichniowski et al. (1996: 299) conclude that a 'collage of evidence suggests that innovative workplace practices can increase performance, primarily through the use of systems of related practices that enhance worker parti-cipation, make work design less rigid and decentralise managerial tasks'. Various studies (Applebaum et al. 2000; Brown and Appleyard 2001; Guest et al. 2003; Ichniowski et al. 1996; Marchington 2004) have suggested that individual work practices have little effect on their own but the utilization of a coherent and integrated system of EI can lead to improvements in performance and worker out-comes. Various studies link levels of job satisfaction and commitment to employee perceptions of the opportunity to participate (Appelbaum et al. 2000) and the depth and breadth of EI as a whole (Cox et al. 2003). This is then supposed to translate into performance as a result of more efficient work processes and better motivation – referred to respectively as cognitive and motivational models (Vandenberg et al. 1999). Freeman and Rogers (1999) report that 79 per cent of non-managerial parti-cipants in employee involvement programmes report having 'personally benefited from [their] involvement in the program by getting more influence on how [their] job is done'. In other words, it has been argued that a combination of related EI and HR practices can have beneficial outcomes for workers and organizational performance alike.

However, there are a number of reasons to adopt a less optimistic interpreta-tion of such studies. As Whitfield and Poole (1997: 757) point out there are unre-solved issues of causality, problems of the narrow base of the research work undertaken, concerns that much of the data is self-reported by management, as well as doubts about the measures of performance that are used. Even if the data indicates a causal link, we lack understanding of the processes involved and the mechanisms by which practices translate into desired outcomes. Wall et al. (2004: 34) agree that while recent studies 'provide encouraging evidence' of the link between HRM and per-formance they are not a sound basis for causal inference nor do they establish whether or not empowerment is a key ingredient'. As Boxall and Purcell (2003: 171) note, in relation to voice:

> the problems of evaluation are threefold. First, given the very wide range of schemes, it is impossible to take a unified approach boiled down to one question. Second, while one can measure the existence of a structure, mechanism or arrangement, one

cannot impute that these lead to certain behaviours. We know that the crucial variable is how, and to what extent, line managers support and activate employee involvement as a process . . . Third, the idea of a bundle of HR practices is that it is a
combination of mutually supportive practices which appear to have performance outcomes where these are appropriate to firm strategy . . . Thus it becomes hard to sort
out individual policies.

The impact of direct participation on employee attitudes and commitment appears
to be influenced by a number of factors, not least the type of scheme which is
introduced. In general terms, the more comprehensive and participative the scheme
the greater the impact, in terms of its effects on employee behaviour; depending
on one's standpoint, this could be seen as good or bad for workers.

Studies by the authors (Marchington et al. 1992, 1994, 2001) have suggested
that three sets of factors are important irrespective of the specific schemes that
are implemented. These are workers' prior experiences of participation and work
in general, management's approaches to employee relations, and the recent and
projected performance of the organization. Inevitably, these can be interrelated.
Prior experience of participation mean that there may be occasions when similar
types of scheme are perceived in quite different ways by workers. For example,
members of staff with relatively little experience of participation are more likely to
welcome any initiative that gives them some opportunity to become involved, no
matter how limited. On the other hand, employees who work for organizations with
a long history of EI may well react negatively to schemes which offer them less than
they are accustomed to. Experience of participation may also generate a desire for
more – the so-called 'taste for power' hypothesis (Drago and Wooden 1991). However,
prior experience is only one factor and much depends on how workers interpret
management's approach to employee relations in general as well as to the specific
schemes which are being operated. For example, at each of the organizations
studied by Marchington et al. (1994: 888), 'employees were less positive about EI
where they saw a tightening-up of management styles on the factory floor or in
the office'. Conversely, where direct participation was one component in a bundle
of human resource policies which were delivered by senior managers who were
trusted, employees tended to view schemes in a much more positive light. Of course,
it is much easier for management to maintain a consultative style in an environment where competitive and employment prospects are rosy in comparison to where
the future looks bleak or redundancies have recently taken place. Not surprisingly,
workers are likely to be sceptical if schemes do not offer long-term employment
security even if they may make work more interesting and enjoyable.

Empowerment is a central issue in considerations of direct participation, but
much depends on what one means by the term. There is overwhelming evidence
that empowerment has not been associated with a significant shift in the locus of
power (Harley 1999) and it has even been referred to as 'mythical' (Sewell 2001).
There is no doubt that participation schemes are located within a strict management agenda that is largely confined to operational issues and does not extend to

significant power sharing or involvement in higher level decision making (Edwards et al. 1998; Rees 1998; Wilkinson et al. 2004). However, since neither those implementing schemes intend them to produce radical changes nor those whose working lives it affects expect this, it is hardly surprising to find the balance of power does not shift or that direct participation fails to resolve contradictions within the employment relationship. It is perhaps too easy to compare some naive vision of empowerment with the mundane reality, and then dismiss initiatives as either a conspiratorial management trap, or too inconsequential to be worthy of further analysis. If 'full participation' (Pateman 1970) is not on offer, does that mean we should dismiss partial participation as small beer? Drago and Wooden (1991) suggest that direct, lower-level participation is introduced to deflect employee interest away from higher level managerial issues. However, a more pragmatic line is arguably more useful. Workers may favour the removal of what are sometimes referred to as 'sand in shoe' irritation (Morton 1994) – for example, 'over-the-shoulder supervision' – and welcome the opportunity to allocate work among themselves and also to address work-related problems. This may not be earth shattering, but in a working environment where there is little opportunity to exercise discretion, it may improve working lives. Even where workers are well aware of the underlying managerial motivations for direct participation, they may still be well-disposed to the initiative. It is also clear that opportunities for empowerment relate to the knowledge requirements of work; if these are low there is little scope for knowledge development and fewer opportunities for empowerment (Wall et al. 2004).

The Role of Line Managers and Trade Unions

The prescriptive literature suggests an optimistic scenario in which line managers who develop participation move from being holders of expert power to facilitators (or from 'cops to coaches') and hence take on new skills and responsibilities. However, this picture contrasts with research investigating the reactions of line managers and supervisors to direct participation (Klein 1984; Denham et al. 1997; Marchington et al. 2001), some of which indicates they find participative management a burden.

First, it is suggested that line managers do not believe in the principles underlying direct participation, especially for more far-reaching schemes. Attempts to involve and empower workers are often regarded as 'soft management' or pandering to the workers, as opposed to a more traditional view that 'a branding iron is a more suitable instrument to work with than any concept of employee involvement' (Wilkinson et al. 1993: 32). This illustrates succinctly the gap between the values of senior management and those of line managers and supervisors. Secondly, while some line managers may see the value of direct participation in principle, they have concerns as to its actual operation in the context of current organizational structures and support mechanisms. This is due to conflict between participative practices – such as briefing and quality circles – and business goals such as meeting production targets or minimizing queue lengths. In this context, employee relations considerations are typically regarded as secondary to production or service goals. The failure to reward line managers for meeting EI goals, and in some cases their lack of skill in implementing EI methods due to lack of training, in itself provides telling insights about the relative importance senior managers attach to direct participation (Fenton-O'Creevy 2001). Thirdly, line managers are anxious about their own futures, whether or not they will continue to have jobs, and if so the extent to which these will differ dramatically from current activities. A paradox of change operates here. Jobs at the interface between managers and managed are likely to alter most, but equally supervisors are required to play a critical change agent role in relation to direct participation. Given a mix of disbelief and agnosticism in their views, and a lack of skills and confidence in their ability, in addition to uncertainty as to the value which senior management attaches to direct participation, it is hardly surprising that problems occur. According to Fenton-O'Creevy (2001: 37):

> It is not middle management attitudes that are the barrier to successful employee involvement implementation. Rather, we should look more closely at constraints on management behaviour and the web of managerial relationships within organisations . . . Are performance management systems working against the goals of employee involvement? Are middle managers' roles structured so that they have no time to develop and involve subordinates?

It is clear that senior managers have failed to provide appropriate support structures and have tended to blame line managers instead (Edwards and Wright 1998). If experience of EI is necessary, managers could be recruited from or seconded to other organizations with a participative culture (Fenton-O'Creevy 2001). Nevertheless, there are some signs of cultural change. In the organizations analysed by Wilkinson et al. (2004), the past decade had seen the departure of less participative managers through restructuring and the extended use of new technology and electronic forms of employee voice that allowed workers to more easily bypass middle managers.

The relationship between direct participation and trade unions is complex. A variety of outcomes are possible, ranging from compatibility or even synergy, through to tension and competition between management and union representatives to secure influence. Alternatively, the relationship may be relatively unaffected with direct participation and trade unions co-existing because they are seen to operate in quite separate zones. It has been common to suggest that there are 'a priori' reasons why direct participation may marginalize unions; for example Beale (1994: 120) suggests that participation schemes represent 'a significant challenge to the traditional influence of trade unions in the workplace. Employee involvement can offer an alternative source of information, ideas and interpretation of workplace experiences, an alternative to that provided by the union'. There are examples where managers have introduced a barrage of direct communications aimed directly at employees with the objective of marginalizing trade unions. This also

makes it more difficult for union representatives to challenge management's interpretation of issues. Some unions opposed team briefings for fear that they would
seriously challenge the union's own channels of workplace communication and
the authority of workplace representatives (Beale 2003: 86). In practice, however,
union representatives can discredit and exploit team briefing to their advantage.

There are other examples where employers have not implemented direct participation with the explicit aim of undermining unions, although a consequence of
managerial action has been to marginalize the union (Marchington et al. 2001).
A more open approach to employee relations, which includes a package of direct
participation measures, could help to erode distrust, leading employees to identify
more with their employer, and hence diminish the role of the union. In situations
where unions lack membership or recognition, it is possible that a substitution effect
takes place in that direct participation fills in the gaps otherwise occupied by trade
unions.

There are also situations where a degree of complementarity can exist between
union organization and at least some parts of the direct participation mix. In one
of the chemical firms studied by Marchington et al. (2001), part of the process of
change included a wide-ranging involvement exercise in which senior managers
made extensive efforts to maintain an open, sharing relationship with the senior
stewards. The latter were aware of the potential dangers of being 'incorporated'
into management, but saw their involvement in the change programme as essential for the future well-being of their members and the company. In this context
union representatives were happy for team briefing to be introduced as a vehicle
for establishing better internal communications.

Yet another scenario is where direct participation and unions run in parallel, with
no obvious or overt relationship between them, in a 'dual' approach to the management of employment (Storey 1992: 258). In these cases, union representatives may
take an agnostic view of direct participation, regarding them as largely irrelevant
to the union's role and unlikely to affect collective bargaining. Indeed, it is difficult
for stewards to argue against direct participation which is designed to improve communications, largely because problems relating to breakdowns in information flow
are regularly pointed out as a major concern by employees and unions in attitude
surveys. Finally, trade unions can also limit the development of direct participation.
This situation occurs where employees are suspicious of management intentions
in a context of low-trust relations, but also where unions retain the influence and
ability to mobilize collective resistance (Beale 2003).

Conclusions

A major theme running through this chapter has been that it is simplistic either
to celebrate direct participation as a panacea for organizational ills or equally to
dismiss it because it has failed to transform the employment relationship. To

celebrate direct participation as empowerment is to ignore the major operational and human obstacles to its implementation whereas to dismiss participation because it does not fundamentally challenge existing relations between capital and labour is to overstate its potential contribution. Indeed, as we have argued elsewhere (Wilkinson et al. 1997) management initiatives are probably more limited than the enthusiasts claim, but more constructive than the critics admit. So much depends on the context in which direct participation is introduced – the competitive situation, management style, employee expectations, and other human resource practices – as well as on the types of schemes themselves.

Much of the literature assumes a simple differentiation between management and employee perspectives and fails to acknowledge that there are widely differing sets of actors in the workplace – differentiated by function, level in the organizational hierarchy, geographical location, previous educational and work experiences, for example – with different views and ambitions. Direct participation is notable for its diversity and variety in practice, for the use by management of both direct and indirect participation, and for several different types of each form being used at the same workplace. On some occasions, there appears to be a cohesive and systematic rationale behind the participation mix whereas in others it is the result of competing initiatives driven by different departments, functions or individuals. Accordingly, schemes may overlap with and directly contradict each other, and reflect the quite diverse perceptions of different groups of managers. Although, in the context of direct participation, 'more' certainly does not mean 'better', attempts to develop works councils in organizations which already have well-established schemes of direct participation might be more meaningful given that they focus on quite different sets of issues and operate at different levels in the hierarchy.

Indeed it could be argued that a combination of direct and indirect participation can produce high performance (Sako 1998) and that employee representatives may well act as agents of change (Sisson et al. 1997: 204). Moreover, as Wood and Fenton-O'Creevy (1999: 45) argue, exclusive reliance on direct involvement can lead to lower levels of overall employee involvement and poorer productivity. They suggest that managers should 'stop thinking in either/or terms: union versus non-union methods, or direct versus indirect'. Genuine employee voice is unlikely to occur with direct participation alone and the absence of representative participation can have detrimental effects on employee influence (Millward et al. 2000: 137).

A paradox of new management techniques is that while they require employee commitment and high trust relations to make them work effectively, simultaneously they may erode any basis for such relations. This takes us back to the critical issue of context: individuals empowered to make decisions may be unwilling to use their discretion if they feel continually under the watchful eye of 'Big Brother'. This is perhaps most obvious in the public sector where 'technologies of distrust' (Miller 1997) may undermine professional judgement, or at least place such judgement under the gaze of rational (accounting) expertise. Not only might such approaches fail to deliver what is expected, they may also lead to unintended consequences as workers subvert the system and undermine management. Indeed, there is evidence that while management might define direct participation in a particular and narrow way, workers might use the discourse of empowerment and quality to bring managers into line with their own expectations (Rosenthal et al. 1997; Wilkinson et al. 1997).

In our chapter in the previous edition we suggested that most UK employers have implemented direct participation in a half-hearted and partial way, adopting techniques in an ad hoc and piecemeal manner, thus falling short of the holistic, integrated approach which research suggests is required to make EI work effectively. Faddism and fashion in management approaches has been noted by a number of writers (e.g. Collins 2000; Gill and Whittle 1993; Hilmer and Donaldson 1996; Micklethwait and Woolridge 1996), and we ourselves have written about this in the area of participation (Marchington et al. 1993). Work by Staw and Epstein (2000) shows why fashion takes hold. Their study found no evidence of economic or efficiency benefits, but they did report 'reputational effects' from participation, as organizations were seen as more innovative and having better management. Since there is a relatively low technical base to participation initiatives, compared with information technology or new product design for example, it has been easy for managers to introduce new practices without extensive professional training. Accordingly, acting as a champion for teamworking, for example, might offer managers a cheap and easy 'solution' to problems as well as a route to enhance their own promotion prospects. There is little doubt that the prescriptive literature underestimates the difficulties in implementing direct participation as well as the costs involved, often ignoring requirements for training, for new reward systems, and for integration. It could be argued, therefore, that many of the problems with participation are less to do with the concept itself and rather more due to short-sighted or misguided attempts at implementation.

However, in more recent work, we noticed many of the techniques examined in the early 1990s have been replaced or recast, and sometimes fused into a more all-embracing voice mechanism (Ackers et al. 2004; Wilkinson et al. 2004). There appeared to be less ad hocery and fragmentation and more evidence that schemes are now better integrated with each other, in particular with other forms of upward problem-solving and collective representation. In addition, senior managers now appear to see greater value in working with trade unions and sharing information with union representatives at earlier stages in the process. We know that participation waxes and wanes over time, taking on different forms at different times, and often with several schemes operating alongside each other at the same workplace. But participation itself is more of a constant. Willman et al. (2002) point out that the proportion of all establishments in the WERS choosing to have some form of voice remains pretty stable over time; for example in 1984, 84 per cent had some form of voice, and by 1998, this had dropped by just 2 per cent.

For most commentators, the Information and Consultation Directive has focused attention on representative participation, so what does this mean for the future of direct participation? We know there is little switching from indirect to direct participation or vice versa, so those organizations which have direct participation alone will probably need to adopt a dual track approach. Professional bodies such as the Chartered Institute of Personnel and Development (CIPD) have argued that it is crucial that direct participation is not neglected in the process of developing representative structures (Emmott 2003) and point to how the combination of direct and indirect consultative arrangements has the potential to improve organizational performance (Beaumont and Hunter 2003). This raises the issue of how the two interact and much depends on management motivation. Representative participation may be introduced only as a bureaucratic requirement with purely ceremonial adoption or it could be used to do something rather ambitious in developing employee voice. Gollan (2005) argues that a mechanism solely for communication may not be enough and that voice – a right to be heard and have a say over workplace issues – may be an essential component of worker satisfaction and commitment.

Critics have tended to focus on the problems with participation, in particular that schemes seem to have a limited shelf-life, in order to argue that it is destined to fail due to an inability to resolve contradictions inherent in the employment relationship. We would not disagree with the conclusion that direct participation is unlikely to transform employment relations and that problems are bound to arise once schemes lose their initial appeal, especially if they have been implemented in a faddish and non-integrative manner. Hill's (1991) optimistic view that initiatives such as total quality management (TQM) may 'institutionalise participation' has not been achieved. On the other hand, it is important to note that managements return repeatedly to the idea of participation as part of their search for more effective ways to run organizations. This suggests that direct participation does have something of value for employers and employees, even if it does not remove problems at work. Much also depends on how practices fit with strategy, and the use of direct participation as part of a high commitment philosophy may yield better results. As Boxall and Purcell (2003: 182) argue:

> Few voice systems and positive union-management relations will exist, or exist for long, unless they are valued in their own right as legitimate and morally necessary activities irrespective of the performance outcomes. They have to have social legitimacy.

Given the recent obsession with finding how HRM can lead to improved performance, this is a timely and useful reminder that participation is a complex and multi-faceted phenomenon that illustrates the contractions of the employment relationship.

REFERENCES

Ackers, P., Marchington, M., Wilkinson, A. and Goodman, J. 1992: The use of cycles? Explaining employee involvement in the 1990s, *Industrial Relations Journal*, **23**(4), 268–83.

Ackers, P., Marchington, M., Wilkinson, A. and Dundon, T. 2004: Partnership and voice, with or without trade unions: Changing UK management approaches to organizational participation, in M. Stuart and M. Martinez Lucio (eds.), *Partnership and Modernisation in Employment Relations*, London: Routledge.

Adler, P. 1993: Time and motion regained, *Harvard Business Review* (January–February), 97–108.

Appelbaum, E., Bailey, T., Berg, P. and Kallenberg, A. 2000: *Manufacturing Advantage: Why High-Performance Work Systems Pay Off*, Ithaca, NY: ILR Press.

Appelbaum, E. and Batt, R. 1995: Worker participation in diverse settings: Does the form affect the outcome, and, if so, who benefits? *British Journal of Industrial Relations*, **33**(3), 353–78.

Arthur, J. 1994: Effects of human resource systems on manufacturing performance and turnover, *Academy of Management Journal*, **37**, 670–87.

Banker, R., Field, J., Schroeder, R. and Sinha, K. 1996: Impact of work teams on manufacturing performance: A longitudinal field study, *Academy of Management Journal*, **39**(4), 867–90.

Bar-Haim, A. 2002: *Participation Programs in Work Organizations, Past, Present, and Scenarios for the Future*, London: Quorum Books.

Barker, J. 1993: Tightening the iron cage: Concertive control in self-managing teams, *Administrative Science Quarterly*, **30**, 408–37.

Beale, D. 1994: *Driven by Nissan? A Critical Guide to New Management Techniques*, London: Lawrence and Wishart.

Beale, D. 2003: Engaged in battle: Exploring the sources of workplace union militancy at Royal Mail, *Industrial Relations Journal*, **34**(1), 82–95.

Beaumont, P. and Hunter, L. 2003: Information and consultation, *Compliance and Performance*, London: CIPD.

Becker, B.E. and Huselid, M.A. 1998: High performance work systems and firm performance synthesis of research and managerial implications, in G.R. Ferris (ed.), *Research in Personnel and Human Resources*, Vol. 16, Stamford, CT: JAI Press.

Bougen, P., Ogden, S. and Outram, Q. 1988: Profit sharing and the cycle of control, *Sociology*, **22**(4), 607–29.

Boxall, P. and Purcell, J. 2003: *Strategy and Human Resource Management*, London: Palgrave.

Brannen, P. 1983: *Authority and Participation in Industry*, London: Batsford.

Brown, C. and Appleyard, M. 2001: Employment practices and semiconductor manufacturing performance, *Industrial Relations*, **46**(3), 436–71.

Bryson, A. 2000: Have British workers lost their voice, or have they gained a new one?, Policy Studies Institute, mimeo, July.

Buchanan, D. 1987: Job enrichment is dead: Long live high performance work design, *Personnel Management*, May, 40–3.

Buchanan, D. 1994: Principles and practices in work design, in K. Sisson (ed.), *Personnel Management*, Oxford: Blackwell.

Byham, W. 1991: *Zapp! The Lightning of Empowerment*, London: Century Business.

Cappelli, P., Bassi, L., Katz, H., Knoke, D., Osterman, P. and Useem, M. 1997: *Change at Work*, Oxford: Oxford University Press.

Collins, D. 2000: *Management Fads and Buzzwords: Critical-Practical Perspectives*, London: Routledge.

Collinson, M., Rees, C., Edwards, P. and Inness, L. 1998: *Involvement but no Empowerment: A Case Study Analysis of Quality Management and Employee Relations*, London: Employment Relations Research, Series No. 1.

Cordery, J. 2003: Team work, in D. Holman, T.D. Wall, C.W. Clegg, P. Sparrow and A. Howard (eds.), *The New Workplace: A Guide to the Human Impact of Modern Working Practices*, Chichester: John Wiley.

Cox, A., Zagelmeyer, S. and Marchington, M. 2003: The embeddedness of employee involvement and participation and its impact on employee outcomes – an analysis of WERS 1998, paper presented at the European Group for Organizational Studies, Copenhagen.

Cully, M., O'Reilly, A., Millward, N., Forth, J., Woodland, S., Dix, G. and Bryson, A. 1998: *The 1998 Workplace Employee Relations Survey: First Findings*. Department of Trade and Industry, London: HMSO.

Cunningham, I., Hyman, J. and Baldry, C. 1996: Empowerment: The power to do what? *Industrial Relations Journal*, **27**(2), 143–54.

Delbridge, R. 2003: Workers under lean management, in D. Holman, T.D. Wall, C.W. Clegg, P. Sparrow and A. Howard (eds.), *The New Workplace: A Guide to the Human Impact of Modern Working Practices*, Chichester: John Wiley.

Denham, N., Ackers, P. and Travers, C. 1997: Doing yourself out of a job? How middle managers cope with empowerment. *Employee Relations*, **19**(2), 147–59.

Department of Trade and Industry 1998: *Fairness at Work*, London: DTI.

Department of Trade and Industry 2002: The role of employee involvement in a modern economy high performance workplace: A discussion paper, DTI, London.

Drago, R. and Wooden, M. 1991: The determinants of participatory management, *British Journal of Industrial Relations*, **29**(2), 177–204.

Edwards, P., Collinson, M. and Rees, C. 1998: The determinants of employee responses to total quality management, *Organization Studies*, **19**(3), 449–75.

Edwards, P. and Wright, M. 1998: HRM and commitment: A case study of teamworking, in P. Sparrow and M. Marchington (eds.), *HRM: The New Agenda*, London: Pitman.

Edwards, P.K. and Wright, M. 2001: High-involvement work systems and performance outcomes, *International Journal of Human Resource Management*, **12**(4), 568–85.

Edwards, P. and Collinson, M. 2002: Empowerment and managerial labor strategies, *Work and Occupations*, **29**(3), 272–99.

Emmott, M. 2003: Response to the DTI (October), *High Performance Workplaces: Informing and Consulting Employees*, London: CIPD.

Ewing, K. 2003: Industrial relations and law, in P. Ackers and A. Wilkinson (eds.), *Understanding Work and Employment Relations: Industrial Relations in Transition*, Oxford: Oxford University Press.

Fenton-O'Creevy, M. 1998: Employee involvement and the middle manager: Evidence from a survey of organisations, *Journal of Organizational Behaviour*, **19**(10), 67–84.

Fenton-O'Creevy, M. 2001: Employee involvement and the middle manager: Saboteur or scapegoat? *Human Resource Management Journal*, **11**(1), 24–40.

Foster, D. and Hoggett, P. 1999: Change in the Benefits Agency: Empowering the exhausted worker? *Work, Employment and Society*, **13**(1), 19–39.

Foy, N. 1994: *Empowering People at Work*, London: Gower.

Freeman, R. and Rogers, J. 1999: *What Workers Want*, Ithaca, NY: Cornell University Press.

Gallie, D., Felsted, A. and Green, F. 2001: Changing patterns of employee involvement, ESRC Skills, Knowledge and Organizational Performance (SKOPE) Working Paper.

Geary, J. 2003: New forms of work organizations: Still limited, still controlled, but still welcome? in P. Edwards (ed.), *Industrial Relations: Theory and Practice in Britain*, 2nd edn, Oxford: Blackwell.

Geary, J. and Dobbins, A. 2001: Teamworking: A new dynamic in the pursuit of management control, *Human Resource Management Journal*, **11**(1), 3–23.

Gill, C. and Krieger, H. 1999: Direct and representative participation in Europe: Recent survey evidence, *International Journal of Human Resource Management*, **10**(1), 572–91.

Gill, J. and Whittle, S. 1993: Management by panacea: Accounting for transience, *Journal of Management Studies*, **30**(2), 281–95.

Gollan, P. 2002: So what's the news? Management strategies towards non-union employee representation at News International, *Industrial Relations Journal*, **33**(4), 316–31.

Gollan, P. 2005: Silent voices: Representation at the Eurotunnel Call Centre, *Personnel Review*, **34**(4), forthcoming.

Gospel, H. and Willman, P. 2003: High performance workplaces: The role of employee involvement in a modern economy. Evidence of the EU Directive Establishing a General Framework for Informing and Consulting Employees, Centre for Economic Performance, London.

Guest, D. 1999: Human resource management: The workers' verdict, *Human Resource Management Journal*, **9**(3), 5–25.

Guest, D., Michie, J., Conway, N. and Sheehan, M. 2003: Human resource management and corporate performance in the UK, *British Journal of Industrial Relations*, **41**(2), 291–314.

Hardy, C. and Leibo-O'Sullivan, S. 1998: The power behind empowerment: Implications for research and practice, *Human Relations*, **5**(4), 451–83.

Harley, B. 1999: The myth of empowerment: Work organisations, hierarchy, and employee autonomy, *Work, Employment and Society*, **13**(1), 41–66.

Heller, F., Pusiæ, E., Strauss, G. and Wilpert, B. 1998: *Organizational Participation, Myth and Reality*, Oxford: Oxford University Press.

Herzberg, F. 1972: One more time: How do you motivate employees?, in L. Davis and J. Taylor (eds.), *Design of Jobs*, London: Penguin.

Hill, S. 1991: Why quality circles failed but total quality might succeed, *British Journal of Industrial Relations*, **29**(4), 541–69.

Hilmer, F.G. and Donaldson, L. 1996: *Management Redeemed: Debunking the Fads that Undermine our Corporations*, New York: The Free Press.

Hochschild, A. 1997: *The Time Bind: When Work Becomes Home and Home Becomes Work*, New York: Metropolitan Books.

Huselid, M. 1995: The impact of human resource management practices on turnover, production and corporate financial performance, *Academy of Management Journal*, **38**(3), 635–72.

Ichniowski, C., Kochan, T., Levine, D., Olsen, C. and Strauss, G. 1996: What works at work: Overview and assessment, *Industrial Relations*, **35**(3), 299–333.

Klein, J. 1984: Why supervisors resist employee involvement, *Harvard Business Review*, **84**(5) 87–95.

Kochan, T., Katz, H. and Mckenzie, R. 1986: *The Transformation of American Industrial Relations*, New York: Basic Books.

Lawler, E., Mohrman, S. and Benson, G. 2001: *Organizing for High Performance: The CEO Report on Employee Involvement, TQM, Re-engineering, and Knowledge Management in Fortune 1000 Companies*, San Francisco, CA: Jossey-Bass.

MacDuffie, J.P. 1995: Human resource bundles and manufacturing performance: Organizational logic and flexible production systems in the world auto industry, *Industrial and Labour Relations Review*, **48**, 197–221.

Marchington, M. 1980: *Responses to Participation at Work*, Farnborough: Gower.

Marchington, M. 2004: Employee involvement: Patterns and explanations, in B. Harley, J. Hyman and P. Thompson (eds.), *Essays in Honour of Harvie Ramsay: Participation and Democracy at Work*, London: Palgrave.

Marchington, M., Goodman, J., Wilkinson, A. and Ackers, P. 1992: New developments in employee involvement, Employment Department Research Paper No. 2.

Marchington, M., Wilkinson, A., Ackers, P. and Goodman, J. 1993: The influence of managerial relations on waves of employee involvement, *British Journal of Industrial Relations*, **31**(4), 553–76.

Marchington, M., Wilkinson, A., Ackers, P. and Goodman, J. 1994: Understanding the meaning of participation: Views from the workplace, *Human Relations*, **47**(8), 867–94.

Marchington, M., Wilkinson, A., Ackers, P. and Dundon, T. 2001: *Management Choice and Employee Voice*, London: Chartered Institute of Personnel and Development.

Marchington, M., Grimshaw, D., Rubery, J. and Willmott, H. (eds.) 2004: *Fragmenting Work: Blurring Organizational Boundaries and Disordering Hierarchies*, Oxford: Oxford University Press.

McKinlay, A. and Taylor, P. 1997: Through the looking glass: Foucault and the politics of production, in A. McKinlay and P. Taylor (eds.), *Foucault, Management and Organizational Theory*, London: Sage.

Micklethwait, J. and Woolridge, A. 1996: *The Witch Doctors: What the Management Gurus are Saying, Why it Matters and How to Make Sense of it*, London: Heinemann.

Miller, P. 1997: Dilemmas of accountability: The limits of accounting, in P. Hirst and S. Khilnani (eds.), *Reinventing Democracy*, Oxford: Blackwell.

Millward, N. and Stevens, M. 1986: *British Workplace Industrial Relations, 1980–1984*, Aldershot: Gower.

Millward, N., Stevens, M., Smart, D. and Hawes, W. 1992: *Workplace Industrial Relations in Transition*, Aldershot: Dartmouth.

Millward, N., Bryson, A. and Forth, J. 2000: *All Change at Work?*, London: Routledge.

Morton, C. 1994: *Becoming World Class*, London: Macmillan.

Mueller, F. 1994: Teams between hierarchy and commitment: Change strategies and their internal environment, *Journal of Management Studies*, **31**(3), 383–403.

Parker, M. and Slaughter, J. 1993: Should the labour movement buy TQM?, *Journal of Organizational Change Management*, **6**(4) 43–56.

Parker, S.K., Wall, T.D. and Cordery, J. 2001: Future work design research and practice: Towards an elaborated model of work design, *Journal of Occupational and Organizational Psychology*, **74**, 413–40.

Pateman, C. 1970: *Participation and Democratic Theory*, Cambridge: Cambridge University Press.

Patterson, M., West, M., Lawthorn, R. and Nickell, S. 1997: *Impact of People Management Practices on Business Performance*, London: IPD Report No. 22.

Pfeffer, J. 1994: *Competitive Advantage through People*, Boston MA: Harvard Business School Press.

Pfeffer, J. 1998: *The Human Equation: Building Profits by Putting People First*, Boston, MA: Harvard Business School Press.

Piore, M. and Sabel, C. 1983: *The Second Industrial Divide*, New York: Basic Books.

Poole, M. 1986: *Towards a New Industrial Democracy: Workers Participation in Industry*, London: Routledge and Kegan Paul.

Poole, M., Lansbury, R. and Wailes, N. 2000: A comparative analysis of developments in industrial democracy, *Industrial Relations*, **40**(3), 490–525.

Psoinos, A. and Smithson, S. 2002: Employee empowerment in manufacturing: A study of organisations in the UK, *New Technology, Work and Employment*, **17**(2), 132–48.

Ramsay, H. 1977: Cycles of control: Workers' participation in sociological and historical perspective, *Sociology*, **11**(3), 481–506.

Ramsay, H. 1983: Evolution or cycle? Worker participation in the 1970s and 1980s, in C. Crouch and F. Heller (eds.), *Organizational Democracy and Political Processes*, London: John Wiley and Sons.

Ramsay, H., Scholarios, D. and Harley, B. 2000: Employees and high-performance work systems: Treating inside the black box, *British Journal of Industrial Relations*, **38**(4), 501–31.

Rees, C. 1998: Empowerment through quality management: Employee accounts from inside a bank, a hotel and two factories, in C. Mabey, D. Skinner and T. Clark (eds.), *Experiencing Human Resource Management*, London: Sage.

Rosenthal, P., Hill, S. and Peccei, R. 1997: Checking out service: Evaluating excellence, HRM and TQM in retailing, *Work, Employment and Society*, **11**(3), 481–503.

Sako, M. 1998: The nature and impact of employee 'voice' in the European car components industry, *Human Resource Management Journal*, **8**(2), 5–18.

Scarborough, H. 2003: Knowledge management, in D. Holman, T.D. Wall, C.W. Clegg, P. Sparrow and A. Howard (eds.), *The New Workplace: A Guide to the Human Impact of Modern Working Practices*, Chichester: John Wiley.

Sewell, G. 2001: What goes around, comes around, inventing a mythology of teamwork and empowerment, *The Journal of Applied Behavioural Science*, **37**(1), 70–89.

Sewell, G. and Wilkinson, B. 1992: Empowerment or emasculation? Shopfloor surveillance in a total quality organisation, in P. Blyton and P. Turnbull (eds.), *Reassessing Human Resource Management*, London: Sage.

Sisson, K. 2002: The Information and Consultative Directive: Unnecessary 'regulation' or an opportunity to promote 'partnership'?, Warwick Papers in Industrial Relations No. 67.

Sisson, K., Ulrich, P., Chouraqui, A. and Frohlich, D. 1997: *New Forms in Work Organisation: Can Europe Realise its Potential?*, Dublin: European Foundation for the Improvement of Living and Working Conditions.

Smith, C., Child, J. and Rowlinson, M. 1990: *Reshaping Work: The Cadbury Experience*, Cambridge: Cambridge University Press.

Staw, B. and Epstein, S. 2000: What bandwagons bring: Effects of popular management techniques on corporate performance, reputation and CEO pay, *Administrative Science Quarterly*, **45**, 523–56.

Storey, J. 1992: *Developments in the Management of Human Resources*, Oxford: Blackwell.

Storey, J. 2001: *HRM: A Critical Text*, London: Routledge.

Tebbutt, M. and Marchington, M. 1997: Look before you speak: Gossip and the insecure workplace, *Work Employment and Society*, **11**(4), 713–35.

Thompson, P. and Ackroyd, S. 1995: All quiet on the workplace front: A critique of recent trends in British industrial sociology, *Sociology*, **29**(4), 615–35.

Thompson, P. and Wallace, T. 1996: Redesigning production through teamworking: Case studies from the Volvo Truck Corporation, *International Journal of Operations and Production Management*, **16**(2), 103–18.

Townley, B. 1989: Communications, in K. Sisson (ed.), *Personnel Management in Britain*, 1st edn, Oxford: Blackwell.

Vandenberg, R., Richardson, H. and Eastman, L. 1999: The impact of high involvement work practices on organizational effectiveness: a second-order latent variable approach, *Group and Organization Management*, **24**(3), 300–39.

Wall, T.D., Wood, S.J. and Leach, D. 2004: Empowerment and performance, in C. Cooper and I. Robertson (eds.), *International Review of Industrial and Organizational Psychology, Vol. 19*, London: John Wiley.

Walton, R. 1985: From control to commitment in the workplace, *Harvard Business Review*, March–April, 77–84.

Whitfield, K. and Poole, M. 1997: Organising employment for high performance, *Organization Studies*, **18**(5), 745–64.

Wickens, P. 1987: *The Road to Nissan*, London: Macmillan.

Wilkinson, A. 2002: Empowerment, in M. Poole and M. Warner (eds.), *International Encyclopaedia of Business and Management Handbook of Human Resource Management*, London: ITB Press, 507–17.

Wilkinson, A., Marchington, M., Goodman, J. and Ackers, P. 1992: Total quality management and employee involvement, *Human Resource Management Journal*, **2**(4), 1–20.

Wilkinson, A., Marchington, M. and Goodman, J. 1993: Refashioning industrial relations: The experience of a chemical company over the last decade, *Personnel Review*, **22**(2), 22–38.

Wilkinson, A. and Willmott, H. 1994: Total quality: Asking critical questions, *Academy of Management Review*, **20**(4), 789–91.

Wilkinson, A., Godfrey, G. and Marchington, M. 1997: Bouquets, brickbats and blinkers: Total quality management and employee involvement in practice, *Organization Studies*, **18**(5), 799–820.

Wilkinson, A., Redman, T., Snape, E. and Marchington, M. 1998: *Managing with Total Quality Management: Theory and Practice*, London: Macmillan.

Wilkinson, A., Dundon, T., Marchington, M. and Ackers, P. 2004: Changing patterns of employee voice, *Journal of Industrial Relations*, **16**(3), 297–321.

Willman, P., Bryson, A. and Gomez, R. 2002: Why do voice regimes differ?, mimeo, Centre for Economic Performance, London School of Economics.

Womack, J., Jones, D. and Roos, D. 1990: *The Machine that Changed the World*, New York: Rawson Associates.

Wood, S. 1999: Human resource management and performance, *International Journal of Management Reviews*, **1**(4), 367–413.

Wood, S. and Fenton-O'Creevy, M. 1999: Channel hopping, *People Management*, 25 November.

Wright, P.M. and Gardner, T.M. 2003: The human resource-firm performance relationship: Methodological and theoretical challenges, in D. Holman, T.D. Wall, C.W. Clegg, P. Sparrow and A. Howard (eds.), *The New Workplace: A Guide to the Human Impact of Modern Working Practices*, Chichester: John Wiley.

CHAPTER SIXTEEN

Management and Trade Unions: Partnership at Work?

Stephanie Tailby and David Winchester

This chapter explores the changing pattern of union–management relations in the UK in recent years. The first section outlines various dimensions of trade union membership decline and organizational weakness that emerged after the election of the first of four consecutive Conservative governments in 1979. It reviews the extensive literature that explores the causes of trade union decline, especially changes in workforce composition, macroeconomic conditions, and the policies of government, employers and trade unions, before and after the election of a 'new' Labour government in 1997. It also briefly discusses the nature of the *representation gap* in employment relations, and various meanings attached to the concept of *employee voice*.

The second section explores the significance of 'partnership at work' for the relationship between management and trade unions. It discusses the contested meanings of the idea of 'social partnership' in Europe, and the more limited notion of 'partnership agreements' at enterprise and workplace levels in the UK. The emergence of such agreements is located in the specific political context of the mid-1990s, and the assessment of their impact draws on the findings of the extensive volume of case study and survey research published in the last few years.

The third section focuses on the impact of the legislation on trade union recognition that came into effect in 2000, and the political debate and policy developments that preceded the transposition of the European Union Directive on Information and Consultation of Employees into UK employment law with effect from April 2005. The consequences of these statutory innovations are uncertain, but the inevitable interaction between them will influence the pattern of employment relations generally, and the nature and forms of workplace representation in particular, over the next decade. The fourth and final section outlines a brief evaluation of the current state and future prospects of union–management relations.

Union Membership Decline and Workplace Organization

Over the last 50 years, aggregate trade union membership in the UK has fluctuated considerably. Between 1948 and 1965, there was a modest increase in membership from 9.1 to 9.7 million, although union density (that is, membership as a proportion of all civilian employees) declined from 46 to 43 per cent. Trade union membership increased rapidly from 1965, reaching 12.6 million members and a union density of 56 per cent in 1979. Thereafter membership fell in each year until 1998. This was 'the longest period of continuous annual membership decline since 1892, when records were first compiled. The membership gains secured between 1965 and 1979 were lost in half the time it had taken to achieve them' (Waddington 2003a: 219), and aggregate trade union density fell below 30 per cent.

The decline in union membership was arrested at the end of the 1990s, and although small increases have been recorded in some years since then, they have arisen mainly from the growth in public sector employment. In the autumn of 2003, the number of employees who were members of trade unions was 7 million, and union density was 29.3 per cent. These aggregate data, however, conceal significant differences in union density between industrial and occupational groups. For example, in 2003, union density was 59 per cent in the public sector and 18 per cent in the private sector. Within the private sector, union density in the electricity, gas and water supply industries was close to 50 per cent, whereas in the wholesale and retail trade it was less than 12 per cent, and in hotels and restaurants, only just above 5 per cent. In occupational terms, professional and associate professional and technical occupations had union densities close to 50 per cent, while union density in sales and customer service occupations was less than 13 per cent (Palmer et al. 2004).

The decline in trade union membership since the 1980s is closely related to changes in the coverage of collective bargaining. When the first of a series of Workplace Industrial Relations Surveys (now the Workplace Employee Relations Survey – WERS) was conducted in 1980, collective bargaining between employers and trade unions was the dominant method of pay determination in the UK. Over the last two decades, the surveys have tracked the diminishing importance of collective bargaining. The authors of the 1990 survey described the decline in the coverage of collective bargaining, from 71 per cent in 1984 to 54 per cent in 1990, as 'one of the most dramatic changes in the character of British industrial relations' (Millward et al. 1992: 93). The 1998 survey found that the proportion of employees covered by collective bargaining had fallen further to 40 per cent (Millward et al. 2000: 197), and Labour Force Survey (LFS) data showed that in 2003 collective agreements affected the pay of only 36 per cent of all employees; 72 per cent in the public sector, and 22 per cent in the private sector (Palmer et al. 2004: 35).

Over the past two decades, a number of explanations have been advanced on the causes of trade union membership decline (Blyton and Turnbull 2004). In many accounts, changes in the economic context, and structural shifts in the composition of industry and employment, are viewed as one of the explanations of union membership decline. In addition, most analysis also focuses on the changing policies of governments, employers and managers, trade union leaders and activists, and the attitudes of employees (union members and potential members). As Waddington (2003a: 219) argues, 'there is a complex web of inter-relationships between these explanations, which precludes the identification of their individual effects'.

Explanations of union membership decline

Most accounts of union decline since the 1980s explore the changing structure of industry and composition of employment. The contraction of manufacturing employment, and the concentration of employment growth in the service sector – often in smaller workplaces, with high levels of female, part-time employment – contributed to the decline of trade union membership (Millward et al. 1992: 356). It has been estimated that changes in the composition of employment may have accounted for more than 25 per cent of the decline in union membership in the 1980s (Waddington 2003a: 221). There is a broad consensus, however, that 'compositional effects' offer only a partial explanation of trade union weakness (Metcalf 2004: 4).

Many of the 'adverse' trends in employment pre-dated the 1980s, and union density rose more rapidly among women than among men in the 1970s when strong rates of union recruitment among white-collar workers narrowed the gap with manual union density. In explaining why trade unions have found it so difficult to recruit in 'non-traditional' areas, research findings suggest that the resistance of employers, as well as the limitations of union recruitment campaigns, were important. Moreover, the evening out of earlier variations in union density – between production and service industries, male and female employees, manual and white-collar workers – in the last two decades has arisen because union density declined most rapidly in some of the former heartlands of trade unions (Cully and Woodland 1998: 357). By 2003, union density in manufacturing was 26 per cent – below the whole economy average of 29 per cent – and close to union density in financial services (Palmer et al. 2004: 17).

The second set of explanations of union decline focus on macroeconomic conditions. It has been conventional wisdom since the 1960s that low inflation and rising real wages reduce the incentive of employees to join trade unions, while high and rising levels of unemployment strengthen the ability of employers to resist unionization. Some accounts attributed union membership decline in the 1980s largely to the impact of such cyclical factors and, in support of this view, the rate of decline was much greater during the recessions of the early 1980s and early 1990s (Waddington 2003a). Yet the impact of macroeconomic conditions is less clear-cut in later periods. Metcalf (2004: 5) argues that as the level of unemployment fell more or less continuously since 1993, and with no appreciable positive impact on union membership or density, the 'cyclical factors' thesis 'no longer stands up to scrutiny'.

The third broad explanation of trade union decline explores changes in government policies, especially relating to employment legislation. Conservative governments – in office between 1979 and 1997 – sought explicitly to undermine trade union influence in the workplace, and to exclude it altogether from national political representation. The latter was achieved by dismantling the tripartite institutions created in the 1960s and 1970s that gave trade unions a voice – however small – in some areas of policy-making. Conservative governments also sought to reduce the role of the state in economic activity through a radical restructuring of the public sector. In combination, the privatization of most of the nationalized industries and public utilities, compulsory competitive tendering and tight public expenditure limits, reduced employment and eroded union organization in parts of the public services.

New employment legislation also created problems for many trade unions. Between 1980 and 1993, Conservative governments enacted nine pieces of legislation designed to undermine aspects of trade union organization. The statutory union recognition procedure of the 1970s was repealed, and the 'closed shop' was progressively outlawed. The scope for trade unions to engage in lawful industrial action was restricted to trade disputes between employees and their immediate employer, held after new – and increasingly onerous – statutory balloting requirements had been fulfilled. Freeman and Pelletier (1990) attributed a large part of the decline in union membership in the 1980s directly to the impact of this legislation. This analysis has been questioned, however, by some commentators who argued that it is difficult to estimate the specific effects of the union legislation in isolation from other aspects of the wide-ranging attack on organized labour by governments (e.g. Waddington 2003a: 221).

The fourth factor that contributed to trade union weakness concerned the attitudes and policies of employers; especially their influence on the inclination of employees to seek union membership. Bain and Price (1983) described a 'virtuous circle' of union growth in which:

> The greater the degree of recognition which employers confer upon unions the less likely employees are to jeopardize their jobs and career prospects by being union members, the more easily they can reconcile union membership with 'loyalty' to the company, and, most important, the more effectively unions can participate in the process of job regulation and thereby offer employees services and benefits which will encourage them to become and to remain union members. (p. 18)

The analysis of Bain and Price focused on the period of strong union membership growth in the 1960s and 1970s, when the extension and scope of union recognition appeared to have embedded trade unions more deeply in the management process than ever before. In contrast, the economic, political and legal environment of the 1980s and 1990s provided the incentive and opportunity for employers to review their approach to employment relations. Firms in many industries faced greater product market competition arising, for example, from increasing globalization and market liberalization in the European Union, and financial and industry deregulation in the UK. Alongside mass unemployment and hostile legislation, these pressures placed the trade unions on the defensive, and created the opportunity for employers to review their policies. It is widely accepted that changes in the policies and practices of employers contributed to a 'vicious circle' of trade union membership decline in the 1980s and 1990s. Whether this represented an opportunistic shift in HR and employment practices, or a long-term hardening of employers' attitudes against unions and traditional forms of joint regulation, was not clear (Terry 2003a).

The Workplace Employee Relations Surveys (WERS) found a significant decline in the proportion of workplaces where managers recognized trade unions as bargaining agents. Between 1984 and 1990, the proportion declined from 66 to 53 per cent, and by 1998, declined further to 42 per cent of the workplaces surveyed. The decline was almost wholly 'a private sector phenomenon' (Millward et al. 2000: 97). While trade unions were recognized in 87 per cent of public sector workplaces in 1998, union recognition in private sector workplaces declined from 50 per cent in 1980 to 25 per cent over the next 8 years. The authors of the 1998 survey identified the persistently lower rate of recognition among new workplaces as the principal factor fuelling the continuing decline in trade union recognition (Millward et al. 2000: 136).

The 'age of workplace' effect outweighed compositional effects (that is, workplace size, industry location, the composition of the workforce and so on). The evidence that newer workplaces were less likely to have union recognition than longer-established ones offered support for the belief that a hardening of employers' attitudes had taken place against trade unions and collective bargaining. Given the relationship between union recognition and union membership, the failure of unions to secure recognition among new workplaces was, for Disney et al. (1998: 17), the key factor underpinning union membership decline, and one that might be cumulative in its effects. The increasing demands of trade unions for the re-introduction of statutory union recognition procedures in the 1990s were therefore not surprising.

Examples of de-recognition of trade unions partly contributed to the overall decline in union recognition after the mid-1980s. Its incidence increased in the late 1980s and early 1990s, but it remained a relatively rare phenomenon in most industries (Gall and McKay 1999; Millward et al. 2000: 136). De-recognition of unions can take a number of different forms. The first two WERS surveys found that the scope of collective bargaining had, on average, been narrowed in workplaces with recognized unions. Although there appeared to be no general continuation of this trend in the 1990s, the case study research of Brown et al. (1998: iii) suggested that, in some companies, the scope of bargaining had been so reduced as to amount to 'implicit or partial de-recognition'.

The termination of industry-wide bargaining arrangements by e[...]
last two decades can also be viewed as the *de facto* de-recognition [...]
recognition lapsed at many workplaces or was not renewed (Millv[...]
99). The demise of multi-employer bargaining in private manufactu[...]
reduced the proportion of employees whose pay was affected by coll[...]
More employers opted to set pay without reference to trade unions o[...] [...]
bargaining, an approach already dominant in the private services by the early 1980s
(Millward et al. 2000: 221).

Finally, the analysis of union membership decline – and the prospects for trade
union revitalization – has focused on the attitudes of employees. The research has
produced sharply contrasting interpretations: some accounts suggest there has been
a falling away of employee interest in trade union membership; while others highlight a 'frustrated demand' for union representation. The analysis of the 1998 WERS
data by Millward et al. (2000: 107–8, 150–1) supported the first of these two interpretations; union membership density had declined in many workplaces where unions
were recognized. This could be explained partly by the legal restrictions on the
'closed shop' and other government policies that dissuaded managements from encouraging trade union membership. The decline that occurred in the 1990s, however,
appeared to be unrelated to the degree of support that (managers reported) was
offered for union membership. Yet the analysis does not establish that employees
have lost their 'appetite' for trade union membership and representation. It may
be the case that unions were perceived to be too weak to deliver the benefits that
formerly accrued from membership.

In the light of the above developments, many commentators have drawn attention to the growing *representation gap* in UK workplaces. Heery et al. (2004) argue
that the right of workers to participate in aspects of enterprise governance has
been frustrated by the decline of traditional forms of employee representation at
work; that is, effective trade union organization in support of joint regulation through
consultation and collective bargaining. The 1998 WERS found that half of all the
workplaces surveyed had no 'union presence', and the proportion rose to three-
quarters in the private sector. Moreover, such workplaces were much less likely
than those with recognized trade unions to have in place any other mechanisms
for consulting with employees on a collective basis (Cully et al. 1999: 109). Towers
(1997) viewed the representation gap as a frustrated demand for union representation, implying there were many workers who would join a trade union if one
were accessible at their place of work. The analysis of employee survey data by
Metcalf (2004: 9–10) attempts to quantify this. It estimates that among employees
who are non-union members in the 'unorganized' sector of the economy (not
covered by collective agreements), around 2.8 million would welcome a union,
or would be likely to join if one were available.

Alongside discussion of the representation gap, the concept of *employee voice* has
attracted attention in the HRM literature in recent years. Dundon et al. (2004:
1149) argue that this interest has arisen 'both from those seeking higher levels of
organizational performance and from those desiring better systems of employee
representation'. Different types of employee voice mechanisms have been advocated

as the means of achieving one or other of these objectives, or the means through which they can be reconciled. As the following sections on partnership at work, and statutory procedures for union recognition and information and consultation indicate, the evolution of different forms of employee voice may have a significant impact on the future pattern of union–management relations.

Partnership at Work

The concept of partnership has been widely discussed by academics, policy makers and practitioners over the last decade. The relative weakness of trade unions at the workplace and in the political arena, encouraged the TUC to champion a partnership approach in management–union relations from the early 1990s. Before and after its election in 1997, the Labour government also supported the idea of partnership as part of its desire to redefine its relationship with trade unions, and develop positive relations with the business community. Throughout this period, the Involvement and Participation Association (IPA) actively campaigned for various forms of partnership at work, based on its long-standing commitment to co-operation at work. Each of these parties identified the idea of partnership, co-operation, and mutual gains as the prerequisite for meeting the challenge of more intense international competition. They held rather different views, however, on the desirability of different forms of partnership: for example, which parties should be involved; at which levels should partnership arrangements operate; and in which ways could potential 'mutual gains' be achieved?

This section has three main parts. The first explores two important sets of ideas that influenced the academic and policy debates on partnership in the UK: the attraction of the *European social model* for trade unions; and the US literature on the *high performance workplace* and *mutual gains enterprise*. The second part analyses the political dimension of the partnership debate in the UK. This focuses on the ways in which the Labour government associated partnership with the reform and modernization employment relations, and the TUC's definition and advocacy of the main principles of partnership. The third part explores the extensive literature on the impact of partnership agreements. This focuses on the distribution of costs and benefits among the main parties (employees, trade unions, managers and employers), and the variation in outcomes in different organizational and sectoral settings.

Trade unions and the European social model

Trade union leaders in the UK developed a more positive attitude towards economic and political integration in Europe from the end of the 1980s, especially in relation to the social dimension of EU policies. The involvement of unions and employers' associations in the formulation and implementation of social policies at national and EU levels contrasted sharply with the political exclusion of unions from policy making in the UK.

Although there was considerable diversity in the systems of employment relations among EU member states, it was possible to identify the outlines of a *European social model* with the following features: trade unions were accepted as legitimate social partners; the collective regulation of employment relations strongly influenced individual employment contracts; and a general framework for employee representation was supported by legislation or agreements between federations of trade unions and employers.

In combination, these features of the social model in Europe became increasingly attractive to UK trade union leaders. In the context of the growing representation gap in the UK, they could not fail to notice that in France, a country with low and declining union membership density, industry-wide collective agreements could be extended to cover all employees. The main union confederations also obtained the majority of votes in elections for representatives of works committees (*comités d'entreprise*), and they participated in dozens of public bodies. Moreover, in other countries (e.g. Germany and the Netherlands) the idea of *social partnership* had strong institutional and legal support. Dialogue between the social partners on economic and social policies took place in national forums, in industry-wide collective bargaining, and in works councils at enterprise and workplace levels.

The notion of social partnership in Germany was closely associated with the dual structure of interest representation: that is, the formal and legal separation of sector-wide collective bargaining (between trade unions and employers' associations), and the system of works councils. In the latter, the law provided rights to information, consultation and co-determination on a wide range of specified issues. These rights were accompanied by the legal obligation of works council members to work with management 'in a spirit of mutual trust for the good of the employees and of the establishment', and 'activities that interfere with operations or imperil the peace of the establishment' were prohibited.

The widely admired 'German model' of social partnership depended for its success not only on its institutional and legal foundations, but also on the strong preference for compromise in a political system in which coalition politics was the norm. The economic context was also crucial: collaborative industrial relations and the foundation for mutual gains between the social partners were developed within the framework of a successful Keynesian welfare state (Hyman 2005: 261). Since the mid-1970s, and especially in the last 15 years following German reunification, weak economic conditions have eroded many aspects of the German model, including the previously optimistic view of social partnership. More generally, many features of the European social model have been threatened by low economic growth, persistently high levels of unemployment, and increasing competition from low cost countries in recent years. Although trade union leaders in the UK express a strong commitment to the European social model, their interest seems to lie mainly in pressurizing the UK government to implement EU-initiated employment rights in a less grudging and minimalist manner. Also, the debate on 'partnership' in the UK has focused mainly on company and work-place employment relations, rather than wider conceptions of social partnership. In this respect, it has drawn on a second source of inspiration, one that focuses on North American academic studies of the *high performance workplace* and the *mutual gains enterprise*.

The mutual gains enterprise

Partnership has been a prominent theme in much of the US management science literature on the 'high performance workplace' (e.g. Applebaum and Batt 1994; Applebaum et al. 2000). This proposes that 'new' management practices achieve organizational performance outcomes that are superior to more traditional work and employment relations practices, and that they do so by motivating employees to contribute their knowledge, skills and discretionary effort. In other words, higher worker performance is enlisted through management practices that are believed to improve employees' job satisfaction and material rewards, rather than exacted through a 'command and control' regime. In his critical review of the literature, Godard (2004: 351) categorizes the practices associated with what he calls the 'high perform-ance paradigm' as of two types: alternative work practices, and high-commitment human resource management techniques. The former include alternative job design practices, such as work teams (autonomous or otherwise), and formal employee participation (via structured two-way communications, quality circles, and con-tinuous improvement schemes). The latter include practices such as sophisticated selection and training, behaviour-based appraisal and advancement criteria, single status policies, contingent pay systems, and job security provisions.

The 'high performance workplace' literature proposes that the grouping of such practices achieves 'win–win' outcomes, or mutual gains: more satisfying and well-paid work for employees; and improvements in productivity, competitiveness and profitability for employers. Furthermore, it argues that their implementation creates opportunities for trade union revitalization. The theory, summarized by Godard (2004: 349) is that unions can 'discard their traditional, adversarial role in favour of a new, partnership one', and some accounts stress the critical contribu-tion that a reformed industrial relations regime can make to the success of the high performance practices. In their 'mutual gains enterprise' thesis, Kochan and Osterman (1994: 46) argued that to achieve and sustain competitive advantage from such a strategy required 'the strong support of multiple stakeholders in an organiza-tion'. Employees were more likely to commit to organizational objectives where they felt they had independent representation at work and the means of airing conflicts openly and achieving their resolution (p. 51). And the involvement of employees and their representatives in management decision-making helped to create high-trust relations, and to sustain a virtuous circle of management commit-ment to the 'high road' of securing competitive advantage from human resources, and employee commitment to organizational aims.

Kochan and Osterman thus argued that 'the active partnership of union representatives' could be a 'powerful force for sustaining commitment to workplace innovations' (p. 145). They believed that it was the quality of the employer–worker representative relationship, rather than the form of worker representation, that was all-important, and identified much of merit in the European system of works councils (p. 167). Other contributors to the 'high performance paradigm' have insisted that the employee voice mechanism should be union representation, although they have prescribed similarly restricted options for union representatives; to 'force or foster' innovation in the direction of the high performance workplace (e.g. Frost 2000). This is on the assumption that the new management practices achieve benefits for employees, as well as employers. Many evaluations of relevant survey and case study data, however, have concluded that the evidence for this is 'mixed at best' (White et al. 2003: 178; Godard 2004; Danford et al. 2004), and have reported negative consequences for employees, including work intensification, work-related stress and a poorer work–life balance.

The politics of partnership

The idea of partnership formed part of the manifesto of the 'new' Labour Party prior to its general election success in May 1997. In advocating a 'third way' in economic management, it sought to redress some of the economic and social costs of the policies pursued by four Conservative Party governments, and to redefine its relationship with trade unions and the business community. The economic priorities of the government soon became clear: the Bank of England was given independence to set interest rates and control inflation; growth in public expenditure was limited to the modest plans of the previous government for 2 years; and a series of welfare-to work measures were introduced to reduce the previously high levels of unemployment.

The Labour government reiterated the commitment of its Conservative predecessors to labour-market flexibility, and insisted that it would not repeal or amend most of the legislation covering trade unions and industrial conflict passed in the 1980s. Crucially, however, it ended the UK opt-out from the Social Protocol attached to the Treaty on European Union, thus limiting its capacity to resist new EU-initiated employment rights. A number of individual and collective employment rights were outlined in the 1998 *Fairness at Work* White Paper, in the foreword to which Tony Blair argued that the government wanted to 'replace the notion of conflict between employers and employees with the promotion of partnership'. New employment legislation was implemented in a series of measures, of which the 1999 Employment Relations Act was the most significant. The government thus introduced a modest re-regulation of the labour market, and increased the social legitimacy of trade unions and collectivism. As Howell (2004: 2) has argued, the government's preference, however, was for 'a system of industrial relations relying more heavily on the regulation of the labour-market via individual legal rights, enforceable through courts and state agencies, than on collective bargaining'.

The new individual employment rights included a national minimum wage, increased holiday entitlement for several million employees, the partial regulation of working-time, a reduction in the length of service required to qualify for unfair dismissal protection, and a number of 'family-friendly' provisions arising from EU Directives. Labour ministers justified these measures in terms of their contribution to economic efficiency, rather than social justice considerations alone. Similarly, the introduction of new collective employment rights was defended on the basis of the contribution that a (consensual) 'union voice' in the workplace can make to competitiveness. In its first term in office, the implementation of the statutory union recognition procedure was one of few innovations covering collective employment rights.

After its re-election in 2001, the Labour government was able to celebrate the apparent success of its economic policies. The UK economy benefited from historically low levels of inflation and interest rates and, in comparison with the three largest EU member states, had consistently higher levels of economic growth, and much lower unemployment and budget deficits. These achievements, however, did not prevent the strong opposition of trade union leaders to many government policies. Their criticism focused on two main issues: the unwillingness of the government 'to embrace aspects of the European social model, in an attempt to maintain relations with employers'; and the 'contested nature of the reform of public services' (Waddington 2003b: 336). On the former issue, trade unions criticized the way in which the government initially opposed – and thereafter sought to minimize – the regulatory impact of EU Directives (e.g. on information and consultation, working-time, and workers on fixed-term contracts). The latter issue, the government's strategy for the reform of public services, dominated political debate throughout its second period in office.

The main focus of trade union opposition were government plans for a greater private sector involvement in the funding, management or delivery of public services, but it also reflected disappointment with the achievements of the 1997–2001 government. The very limited increases in public expenditure in this period exposed problems in the delivery and quality of services. Moreover, as pay settlements were on average below those in the private sector, recruitment and retention problems intensified among core groups (e.g. nurses and teachers), and there was clear evidence of increasing workloads, stress and declining staff morale. Alongside the harsh public criticism of government ministers, however, the leaders of most public service unions were willing to participate in lengthy negotiations on the reform and modernization of pay structures and systems. The *Agenda for Change* negotiations in the National Health Service, and the 'workforce re-modelling' agreement, designed to deal with the excessive workload of schoolteachers, were later viewed as positive examples of partnership between government, employers and trade unions. These agreements were facilitated partly by the commitment of substantially higher levels of public expenditure between 2001 and 2004.

This *dirigisme* in the public sector contrasts with government policies for the private sector. The aim of the government to reduce the productivity gap with other leading economies has not been achieved. The DTI's 1998 competitiveness White Paper, *Building the knowledge-driven economy*, argued that firms needed to compete on the basis of workforce knowledge, skills and creativity, rather than on low wages and weak skills. An interventionist approach to assist the 're-profiling' was rejected, however, in favour of measures to 'make markets work better', coupled with state assistance in skills provision and employment legislation hailed as supportive of 'modern employee relations practices, built on a spirit of partnership in the workplace' (cited in Lloyd 1999).

The Labour government sought to 'modernize' employment relations on the basis of partnership, without identifying trade unions – or the collective representation of employees – as central to this aim. It provided some incentives for employers to reconstruct their relations with trade unions. A *Partnership at Work Fund* was launched in 1998 with a £5 million budget to 'promote the best of modern partnership policies and to stimulate many more innovative partnerships at work' (Arrowsmith 2002; see also Terry 2003c). Otherwise it has been left to third parties, especially the TUC and the IPA, to advocate the benefits of working in partnership with trade unions, or arrangements that included a collective, non-union employee voice, in the private sector. As noted above, the government has been more interventionist in strongly unionized public services with national systems pay determination. Labour ministers have used these structures to negotiate national 'framework agreements' on pay and grading reforms designed to facilitate the reform of work organization at local level (Tailby et al. 2004).

TUC partnership principles

The TUC's interest in partnership arose from its potential to renew and extend trade union influence in the workplace and with government. It has advocated a partnership approach in employment relations since the early 1990s, as a viable strategic choice for trade unions in an inhospitable environment. Its proposals can be read as an attempt to 'define a role for trade unionism which balances its central concern to represent employees' interests with a productivist appeal to employers and government' (Claydon 1998: 180). Thus the proposals are viewed as a recognition of the defensiveness of trade unions, and an attempt to construct a strategy that is more proactive than appeals for union moderation, or the 'new realism' in union aims and methods, in the 1980s (Ackers and Payne 1998).

TUC publications on partnership highlight the value-added contribution that a consensus-seeking trade unionism can make as the champion of the 'high road' to competition based on better work and employment relations practices (TUC 2002). Six partnership principles are presented as 'vital preconditions for a new accord between unions and employers' (Stuart and Martinez Lucio 2005: 10–11). These define the need for 'a common understanding of market imperatives' but also the 'centrality of voice mechanisms, job security and investments in the quality of employees' working conditions to sustainable and effective partnerships'. As such, they represent 'an attempt to marry efficiency issues with social ones'. The principles (adapted from TUC 2001) are as follows:

- *Commitment to the success of the enterprise.* Effective partnerships are built on a shared understanding and commitment to the organization's business goals and its success.
- *Recognizing legitimate interests.* 'Genuine partnerships' will recognize that the partners will at times have differences of interest and priorities, and will have in place arrangements to resolve these in an atmosphere of trust and respect.
- *Commitment to employment security.* 'Good partnerships' will address employment flexibility although ensure it is not earned at the expense of employees' security.
- *Focus on the quality of working life.* Effective partnerships should broaden the employment and organizational issues tackled by unions and employers, so that these lead to improvements in terms and conditions, including employees' personal development, and employee participation in decisions about their work.
- *Transparency.* Meaningful partnerships are based on a real sharing of information about business plans at an early stage and genuine consultations with unions and staff.
- *Adding value.* The hallmark of an effective partnership is that it taps into sources of motivation, commitment or resources not encouraged by previous arrangements.

The TUC developed these principles to create a legitimate trade union presence in the partnership 'industry' that boomed after the 1997 general election (Stuart and Martinez Lucio 2005; Terry 2003c). Its Partnership Institute, established in 2001, provides consultancy and advisory services to unions and employers, in a manner similar to that of the IPA. The latter espouses a conception of 'workplace partnership' that is in some ways similar to that of the TUC, although it regards workers' representative participation in management decision making as the most critical issue, rather than their representation in dealings with management via an independent 'union voice'. In the period before the 1997 general election, TUC and IPA proposals envisaged a 'social partnership' operating at national, enterprise and workplace levels. The TUC's aspirations for 'political inclusion', however, were largely disappointed in the new government's first term of office. A dilute form of tripartism nevertheless emerged in the government's efforts to fulfil its preelection commitments to the trade union movement on employment law, while maintaining its image of being more 'distanced' from unions (Howell 2004). Some new bodies were formed in the process; most notably, the Low Pay Commission included trade union and employer representatives.

The Confederation of British Industry (CBI) and the Chartered Institute of Personnel and Development (CIPD) have endorsed the philosophy of partnership. Given that its appeal has been expressed mainly in terms of the potential for mutual gains arising from collaborative employment relations, if would be surprising if this were not the case. Employers have nonetheless opposed the extension of individual and collective employment rights on the grounds that it imposes too much 'red tape', or increases the potential influence of unions. Moreover, the CBI has made it clear that their definition of partnership is not restricted to arrangements in which trade unions are the 'employee voice channel' or, indeed, in which there is any means for the expression of a collective employee voice at all (Waddington 2003a).

The TUC estimates 'that about eighty partnership agreements adhered to the six principles' by the end of 2002 (Waddington 2003b: 347). An unknown number of other collective agreements had the title 'partnership agreement', but this may have reflected 'the political climate rather than the content of the agreement', or the aim of employers to reach voluntary agreements before the statutory recognition procedure came into effect (Waddington 2003a: 236) The available evidence suggests that typically, employers have initiated, or have been the main proponents of partnership agreements. Thus it is relevant to consider the business case for partnership, and to note that the issue has been central in the heated academic debate on the philosophy and its practice.

Partnership in Practice: Debates, Issues and Evidence

Partnership has been discussed in the academic literature and by policy makers as a shift away from adversarial, zero–sum industrial relations and towards long–term relationships of mutuality and trust, that facilitate a process of reciprocal exchange and mutual gains (flexibility for employment security; employee commitment and contribution for greater 'employee voice'). Despite the strong support of the TUC, the concept of partnership has been controversial within the trade union movement, and in the academic industrial relations community. The central issue in dispute is whether the perceived benefits of mutual gains are realizable, or whether partnership in practice operates to distribute costs and benefits unevenly. Much of the academic debate focuses on partnership as a trade union revitalization strategy. What do unions gain or risk by embracing the philosophy? Does it enhance their representative capacity or diminish it?

Most of the early contributions to the debate were highly polarized in their views. Ackers and Payne (1998) presented one of the most optimistic interpretations. This was based on an assessment of the 'enlightened self interest' of employers in reconstructing collective employment relations to achieve their business objectives. It also explored the potential impact of the government's employment legislation; and the opportunities that the rhetoric of partnership presented for the trade unions. It argued that HRM initiatives, and the use of direct employee involvement to bypass trade unions, achieved only limited success in enlisting employee commitment in the 1980s. For some firms at least, there was a business interest in developing channels for representative employee participation and courting trade union assistance as the means of 'making employee involvement work' – that is, securing legitimacy for its objectives (p. 531). The ambiguous meaning of partnership provide the scope for the unions to engage with, and capture it. They could 'play back the rhetoric of employee involvement' and by 'championing universal worker rights and more extensive forms of worker participation . . . regain their institutional presence' at the workplace and beyond (p. 529).

Critics emphasized that the business interest in partnership derives from the imperative for firms to extract 'discretionary effort' from labour, as the means of surviving inter-firm competition, and sustaining and raising profitability (Kelly 1996, 2005; Taylor and Ramsay 1998; Danford et al. 2004). They argued that the idea that weakened trade unions could rebuild their representative capacity by working in partnership with management was fatally flawed. A more likely prospect was union co-optation in the management of change that would undermine union influence in the workplace by extending management criteria for 'flexible' working. This was because partnership proposed 'joint problem solving' in place of collective bargaining. Workers gained consultation rights while management strengthened its prerogative in decision-making. Partnership threatened worker solidarity by developing individualized employee involvement in the workplace. It undermined union organizing because the emphasis was on the commonality of worker-management interests, rather than the means of articulating workers' shared grievances.

A wide range of intermediary positions has now been inserted in the debate. There are sceptics and agnostics as well as advocates and critics of 'partnership at work' (Johnstone et al. 2004). Stuart and Martinez Lucio (2005) have sought to shift 'the stalemate' of the partnership debate by conceptualizing partnership as a process that, rather than having predetermined outcomes, is shaped by distinct and sometimes contradictory forces: economic and organizational factors, trade union engagement factors and the political and regulatory context. Some researchers have pragmatically examined the organizational contexts in which employers have championed partnership or have encouraged union overtures, and assessed whether the balance of risks and gains for the unions is more favourable in some circumstances than others (e.g. Oxenbridge and Brown 2005).

It is not easy to evaluate the voluminous literature on partnership. Researchers have explored different types of partnership arrangements (from formal, written agreements to informal understandings) in a number of industry sectors with very different product- and labour-market conditions and diverse industrial relations traditions. They have employed a variety of research methodologies, in terms of theoretical perspective and research design; including survey-based research, and single, multiple or 'paired comparison' case studies. They have also focused on different research informants. Many studies are based on the perceptions of managers and trade union officials or workplace representatives. Relatively few have questioned employees directly about their experiences and perceptions, even though partnership ostensibly is about 'employee voice'. Notwithstanding this diversity, some patterns emerge in the findings. Perhaps the most interesting is the widespread conclusion that partnership presents high risks, rather than clear opportunities, for trade unions.

Union–management partnership agreements were pioneered from the early 1990s (e.g. Blue Circle, Hyder, Rover), when they were mostly concentrated in manufacturing and the privatized utilities, and were typically stimulated by business crisis or corporate restructuring initiatives. They might be thought of as a 'productivity coalition' forged from a mutual interest in survival, although some were 'coerced' in the sense that employers had contemplated union de-recognition before opting for a partnership deal (Heery 2002). The industry spread of partnership became more diverse from the second half of the 1990s, to include some high profile agreements in the financial services and retail sector, and in the public services where managers were expected to achieve performance targets, and the reform of work and employment practices.

Oxenbridge and Brown's (2005) study of eleven 'partnership orientated' companies in production and private services suggests the types of circumstances in which employers have sought formal partnership agreements or less formal 'partnership relationships' with trade unions. They include company financial problems, to manage workplace change initiatives and implement quality-based methods, to secure the harmonization of terms and conditions (e.g. after corporate mergers or takeovers), and in the case of two outsourcing organizations, to support efforts to gain public service contracts. The production sector firms had 'long-standing, sometimes adversarial relationships with unions' which had become partnership relationships typically because of some sort of 'critical incident', for example financial crisis stemming from competitiveness difficulties. Among the production and service sector organizations management's interest in partnership reflected a 'willingness to involve trade unions in implementing far-reaching, often difficult organizational changes' (p. 88). It was union assistance in managing the initiatives that for managers was their greatest gain from partnership. But mutuality in the relationship was less evident. Two types of partnerships were observed; those 'nurturing' and 'containing' collective bargaining in the production and service contexts respectively. And the 'co-operative relations' with the unions in the former did not deter managers from 'seeking greater control over communication structures and trying to shift worker loyalty away from the unions' (p. 98).

Guest and Peccei's (2001: 231) survey among 54 IPA member organizations found that in these apparently favourable settings, the mutuality presumed to be at the centre of partnership was somewhat unbalanced. Levels of direct employee participation in work decisions and representative participation in wider organizational policy was generally low. Ackers et al. (2005) revisited in 2001 seven organizations among 25 studied in earlier research on worker representation. They found a more coherent approach towards employee involvement and some renewed management interest in schemes for workers' representative participation. While the former could undermine union representation and influence in the workplace, the unions' involvement in the latter was conditional on their contribution to organizational objectives; their ability to deliver workforce co-operation with change. Managers sponsored whatever arrangements contributed to these ends, and appeared least likely to be tolerant of strong and independent trade unions:

> employers may develop effective (in their eyes) non-union forms of partnership, where unions are either too weak or too adversarial to deliver employee consent. From the perspective of UK managers, the prospects for unions in the workplace will depend on their willingness and ability to contribute towards partnership between employees and employers. And rarely will the unions be the exclusive channel for achieving this. (Ackers et al. 2005: 23)

Thus in the firms studied there was evidence that managers were shifting away from the '1980s dualism of parallel union and EI channels, either by drawing the unions into closer partnerships or by marginalizing it, even in strongly unionized companies' (Ackers et al. 2005: 41).

Wills (2004) considers the tensions that can arise for trade unions responding to partnership initiatives in her study of the Barclays partnership agreement with Unifi. This arose after industrial action in 1997 that suggested the union's relative strength. Through the partnership, the union gained greater involvement in management (in joint working parties) and an extension of its recognition within the bank that included workplace representation rights. It recorded membership increases. However, the union's ability to sustain members' confidence in its autonomy and legitimacy was strained by the terms of its partnership with management. It was required to take the business case into account in talks with the employer, and 'co-own' agreed policies. Joint working with management tended to distance it from policy formulation with members, and some of the joint union-management policies presented were unacceptable to its members. The union received management information but had to respect confidentiality, limiting the scope to formulate policy with members. The bank scrutinized the union's communications with its members, and this requirement for joint communications restricted the ability to show independence or the union's role in securing any improvements in terms and conditions. Oxenbridge and Brown's (2005) study of nine organizations with formal or informal partnerships with trade unions (some 'robust', some 'weak') identifies similar tensions for the unions. Representatives' closer involvement with management tended to isolate them from members, not least because of the requirement to treat the management information received as confidential (see also Johnstone et al. 2004).

What do employees risk or gain from partnership? Guest and Peccei (2001) surmised that there were employee benefits, in terms of a 'better psychological contract and greater voice', although as they point out this assessment was made indirectly, through the survey of employee representatives. And they concluded from their research that overall, partnership achieved a 'constrained mutuality', with the balance of advantage accruing to management.

The analysis of the principles that are endorsed and of the practices that are in place indicates that greater emphasis is placed on employee contribution than on promotion of employee welfare and rights and independent representation. (Guest and Peccei 2001: 231)

Kelly (2005) compared the employment and wage outcomes in partnership and non-partnership organizations, and found little support for the 'mutual gains' thesis. There was no evidence that workers were better-paid or secured better terms and conditions (working hours, annual holiday leave) in partnership firms, and their employment security seemed worse than in the non-partnership organizations, at least in industries that were retrenching. The research of Danford et al. (2004; see also Tailby et al. 2004) focused explicitly on employees' experiences of partnership, using interview and survey methods, and explored each of the aspects of work and employment identified by the TUC's partnership principles. In the aerospace case studies – environments that in principle model the 'high performance workplace' – the reported accounts were of work intensification and increased employment insecurity, each contributing to stress and an impaired quality of working life. In place of an enhanced 'voice' in the workplace, employees reported an experience of 'communication without dialogue, consultation without influence'.

Legislation and Employee Representation

There is little evidence to support the view that workplace partnership agreements have significantly altered the climate of management–union relations in the UK, or achieved the potential mutual gains identified by its more optimistic advocates. Given the very limited diffusion of partnership agreements, it follows also that they have done little to reduce the workplace representation gap. As was discussed earlier, there has been a serious decline in the proportion of workplaces with union recognition, and in the strength of union organization in those with recognition. The 1998 WERS survey found that no union representatives were present in a quarter of the workplaces where unions were recognized, and that consultation had been substituted for negotiation in many of them. In the light of this and other evidence, Terry (2003b) argued that the effectiveness of employee representation in the future would depend largely on the impact of legislation.

This section first explores the early experience of the statutory trade union recognition procedures of the Employment Relations Act 1999 that came into effect in June 2000. It then examines the potential impact of the Information and Consultation of Employees Regulations that transposed into UK law the 2002 EU Directive (2002/14/EC), with effect from April 2005 in undertakings with more than 150 employees. The analysis focuses on the policies of trade unions and employers, and their attempts to influence government on the content of both statutory procedures. In particular, it considers whether the impact of the two legal innovations is likely to be mutually reinforcing in assisting trade unions to reduce

the representation gap, or whether employers might use the provisions of the information and consultation legislation to undermine further the fragility of single-
channel trade union workplace representation.

The impact of the union recognition legislation

Employers' associations opposed the reintroduction of a statutory trade union recognition procedure. The CBI lobbied government ministers on the details of the
law, but despite its successful exercise in 'damage limitation', it continued to express
misgivings about the potential impact of the law. TUC leaders welcomed the
legislation, but criticized several aspects of the statutory procedure: it excluded undertakings with fewer than 21 employees; and it required a majority of employees
voting in secret ballots (and at least 40 per cent of those eligible to vote) to win
recognition. The general secretary of the TUC argued that the main effect of the
law would be to encourage more voluntary recognition agreements, arguing that
'only a small minority of employers were now hostile to unions in principle; most
recognize that modern unions want partnership, not needless conflict' (cited in
Hall 2000). The expectation that legislation would increase the number of voluntary agreements was soon confirmed. In 1999, the year before the statutory procedure took effect, an estimated 267 new recognition agreements were concluded,
almost three times the number signed annually in the three previous years. In 2001,
the number increased to 470, and then fell to 305 new agreements in 2002. This
trend had been predicted: unions focused their initial campaigns on 'easy wins', and
later had to confront employers who were more resistant to union recognition.
Fewer than 50 of the 775 agreements reached in this 2-year period, however, were
concluded after a ballot ordered by the Central Arbitration Committee (CAC) under
the statutory procedure.

The research of Oxenbridge et al. (2003: 324–5), based on case studies in
60 companies in 1999–2000, confirmed the widespread assumption that 'voluntary
agreements were preferred by both parties because they allowed them to manage
the process', rather than have an agreement imposed under the statutory procedure. In the case study companies with recognition agreements, 'managers reported
union–employer relationships to be very positive', but in organizations where union
recognition was a contentious issue, a substantial proportion of managers expressed
anti-union sentiments and pursued union avoidance strategies. The research also
found that the practical effect of trade union recognition was variable: in some of
the case studies the scope of bargaining – especially over pay – was very limited;
and in others, managers had developed more extensive consultative arrangements,
either to pre-empt trade union recognition, or to co-opt unions 'into managing
the process of organizational change'.

Some of these findings were replicated in the research of Moore et al. (2004),
based on an analysis of more than 200 recognition agreements concluded between
1998 and 2002, and nine organizational case studies based on interviews conducted

in early 2004. This research also identified variations in the scope of collective bargaining. Its limitations arose either from the assertion of employers' prerogative, or from the limited aspirations or experience of union representatives. The case studies also found that the parties often held different views on the distinction between negotiation and consultation, especially if they were constrained by policies set by higher levels of management. In some cases a dual channel of communication had emerged to represent non-union (as well as trade union) members and, in anticipation of legislation on employee rights to information and consultation, some employers believed that they might later be able to supersede union recognition (p. 82). In contrast to the earlier research of Oxenbridge et al., however, the case studies of Moore et al. found that bargaining over annual pay increases was central to the new bargaining relationships.

A third study by Gall (2004), focused on the resistance of employers to trade union recognition. Based on a wide range of research methods – including survey data, interviews with union officials, and CAC cases – the findings explored the variety of ways in which employers sought to avoid trade union recognition by 'substitution' or more overt forms of suppression. The former included the provision of consultative forums, the resolution of grievances, and the pursuit of single-union agreements with compliant unions to prevent recognition claims from more appropriate or forceful ones. The latter, more aggressive form of resistance, especially prevalent in new or small firms, and those with low profit margins, covered a wide range of tactics. These included the threatened or actual dismissal of union members, propaganda highlighting the dangers posed by unions, and delays in responding to union requests for meetings or for on-site access to its members and potential members. These tactics often undermined or deterred union recognition claims, although the research concluded that only a minority of employers pursued this approach.

Legislation on information and consultation of employees

Since the mid-1970s employers in the UK have faced legal obligations, emanating mainly from EU Directives, to inform and consult with employees on specific issues, such as redundancies and business transfers. An important ruling of the European Court of Justice in 1994 affirmed that the obligation of employers to consult with employee representatives on such issues applied in organizations with or without recognized trade unions. Subsequently the UK government introduced information and consultation regulations relating to aspects of health and safety, working-time agreements and parental leave. As Hall and Terry (2004: 208–9) argue, these piecemeal developments challenged the traditional 'voluntarist' policy that employee representation should not be regulated by law, and that 'recognized trade unions constituted the "single channel" through which collective employment rights have been applied'. The adoption of the EU Directive on information and consultation of employees in national undertakings in March 2002, however, potentially signalled a more decisive break with past practice. As one of the few member states without 'general, permanent and statutory' information and consultation systems, the UK was able to phase in the implementation of its regulations: they will apply to undertakings with at least 150 employees from April 2005; those with at least 100 from April 2007; and those with at least 50 from April 2008.

The government – under strong pressure from employers' organizations – had previously opposed the draft Directive. In the absence of sufficient support from other member states to prevent its adoption, the government sought to inject a strong degree of flexibility in the way in which it would be implemented. The CBI praised the government for negotiating 'the least damaging deal available', while stating that it still opposed 'EU intervention in national rules on employee involvement as a matter of principle' (Anon. 2002). The CBI participated in the tripartite discussions with the TUC and government ministers that shaped a consultation document on the implementation of the Directive, and a set of draft Regulations in July 2003. A year later, the government published a revised draft of the Regulations and guidance on their implementation. The main provisions are outlined in Box 16.1.

The 'good practice advice' published by the Advisory, Conciliation and Arbitration Service (ACAS 2004) emphasizes the flexibility available to employers in complying with the information and consultation Regulations. It notes that 'employers need not do anything unless employees trigger a request for negotiations', and that pre-existing agreements may be retained if they are written, cover all employees, have been approved by employees, and set out how information and consultation is to be provided for employees or their representatives. The ACAS advice also draws attention to a statement made by the Secretary of State on the draft Regulations: namely, that the aim was to encourage people 'to develop their own arrangements tailored to their particular circumstances, through voluntary agreements'.

It is difficult to assess the potential consequences of this legislation, not least because its implementation in undertakings with between 50 and 100 employees will not take effect until April 2008. As Hall and Terry (2004) suggest, however, it may be helpful to explore the impact of the earlier issue-specific legal regulation of information and consultation, and to review the research evidence on the incidence and characteristics of existing systems of employee consultation, especially in non-union firms. The current attitudes and policies of employers and trade union officials, may also provide some insight into the likely impact of the new legislation.

Hall and Edwards (1999) found that the election of employee representatives for consultation on proposed redundancies in non-union firms was sometimes problematic. Even after more detailed regulations and guidance on elections had been introduced – and extended to include workforce agreements on working time and parental leave – the difficulties persisted. More generally, the research did not find that the statutory right for consultation on redundancies had encouraged more vigorous attempts to strengthen union organization, or to increase union influence within non-union workplaces (Hall and Edwards 1999: 211).

Box 16.1 The main provisions of the information and consultation regulations

- The regulations apply to all public and private undertakings which carry out an 'economic activity' whether or not operating for profit
- The legislation is triggered when a valid employee request (supported by at least 10 per cent of employees) is made to negotiate an Information and Consultation (I&C) agreement, or an employer starts the process
- The agreement must set out how the employer will inform and consult employees or their representatives on an ongoing basis. More detailed issues such as method, subject matter, frequency and timing of information and consultation arrangements will be for the parties to decide
- Pre-existing agreements which have workforce support may be retained
- Disputes arising from the process of negotiation, or complaints of failure to abide by agreements, should be resolved by the Central Arbitration Committee
- Where the parties fail to negotiate an agreement, *Standard I&C Provisions* will be applied, including the following:
  - Employee representatives should be elected
  - Information should be provided on recent and probable development of the activities and economic situation of the undertaking
  - Information and consultation on the situation, structure and probable development of employment within the undertaking, and on anticipatory measures envisaged where there is a threat to employment
  - Information and consultation with a view to reaching agreement on decisions likely to lead to substantial changes in work organization or in contractual relations
  - Employers may, on confidentiality grounds, restrict information provided to employee representatives in the legitimate interests of the undertaking

Source: Adapted from DTI (2004).

Much more research has focused on the impact of the Regulations introduced in response to the European Works Councils (EWCs) Directive of the EU in 1999. Hall and Terry (2004) argue that the research 'presents a mixed picture'. Some survey evidence found that the initial fears of UK managers were often assuaged;

a majority of respondents reported that EWCs could be useful in presenting management views to employees and hearing the voice of employees. In other surveys, managers were critical of the financial costs incurred, and anxious that EWCs raised employee expectations and increased bureaucracy. Case study research focused on the employee side found that UK workforce representatives often played a less important role in EWC meetings than their foreign counterparts: they had little or no experience of the kind of consultation with senior management typical of works councils in many countries; and they had only limited resources and support at workplace level. Some of these findings offer clues on the potential impact of the new legislation, although the experience of large, transnational companies may have limited relevance for managers and union representatives in many UK undertakings and establishments.

The statutory provisions on information and consultation will have an impact on both unionized and non-union undertakings. In the case of the former, few organizations have 100 per cent union membership or collective bargaining arrangements covering all employees; indeed, in many organizations strongly unionized occupational groups can be found alongside other groups with weak or non-existent union organization. Thus, many managers will have to decide whether to develop integrated or parallel systems of employee representation, and whether they want separate or integrated structures covering consultation and negotiation. Hall and Terry (2004) suggest that there is likely to be a growth in the number of hybrid systems, and that the new legislation may test the degree of commitment that managers have for trade union-based collective bargaining. The impact of the legislation, however, will be greater in organizations with no union recognition, because 'the overwhelming preference among non-union employers is *not* to create any formal indirect structure of employee representation' (Hall and Terry 2004: 214).

The 1998 WERS survey found that under a half of all workplaces reported that they had no trade union presence, and only 11 per cent of these had any system of non-union representation. In many cases, employee representatives were volunteers or were appointed by managers, rather than elected by employees. There is evidence that the minority of employers that have introduced non-union forms of representation were often motivated by the desire to prevent union recognition, but case studies have found that some employers created representative participation for other reasons: for example, to rationalize information and communication systems, or to seek improvements in enterprise performance (Hall and Terry 2004: 216).

Non-union organizations cannot, of course, be viewed as a homogeneous group. Managers in many small and medium-sized firms have no interest in employee participation, have few formal procedures for regulating employment relations, and invest little in human resource management skills. In contrast, some non-union organizations have developed sophisticated human resource management strategies in which employee consultation and involvement play a significant part. These and other differences in management strategy are likely to produce wide variations in the way in which organizations respond to the legislation on information and consultation of employees.

Trade union leaders and activists have had to reconsider their traditional attitudes towards the statutory regulation of employee consultation. Their commitment to the principle of 'voluntary' employment relations has been gradually eroded over the last two decades, but until fairly recently, many remained suspicious of statutory intervention in the sphere of employee representation. The legislation on information and consultation clearly poses a threat to the survival of a single-channel of trade union representation in some unionized workplaces. The involvement of TUC leaders in the consultation process that shaped the details of the legislation was designed partly to minimize this threat. Some union leaders nonetheless recognize that employee rights to information and consultation may provide opportunities to establish a presence in non-union workplaces, and to increase the scope of bargaining in some unionized workplaces.

Conclusions and Prospects

An assessment of the state of management–union relations in the UK at the end of 2004 might offer the following brief comments. First, even though trade unions have actively pursued a number of important reforms over the last decade, as yet they have been unable to increase union membership density, or the strength of workplace union organization, much beyond the historically low levels reached in the mid-1990s. Second, even though opinions differ on the extent to which employees recognize the benefits of trade union membership, it is clear that the majority of employers – especially in small and medium-sized workplaces – have little interest in recognizing trade unions and engaging in meaningful negotiations on pay, hours and other conditions of employment. Relatively few employers have sought partnership agreements with unions, although the research evidence shows that they often deliver more substantial benefit to employers than to their employees and trade unions.

The prospects for union renewal, and a large part of the HR agenda for change, may be shaped by employment legislation much more decisively than in the past. At the time of writing, it is difficult to predict the impact of the forthcoming and staged implementation of the information and consultation regulations, and the recent amendments to the law on trade union recognition. On both issues, it is likely that a form of 'legislatively-prompted voluntarism' will occur: that is, employers and/or trade unions seek voluntary agreements to avoid being subject to statutory enforcement procedures (see Hall 2003). In practice, this means that employers will decide whether or not to inform their employees of their new rights, and employees in unionized and non-union workplaces will have to take the initiative in finding colleagues willing to become representatives.

It is possible to predict more confidently that employers' representatives will continue to oppose the further extension of individual and collective employment rights, although managers in the UK still face fewer legal constraints on their decision-making than their counterparts in most other EU member states, and on average, achieve lower levels of productivity than in other major European economies. Trade unions will also continue to criticize the limits of existing UK legislation. Information and consultation rights will still be denied to a quarter of the workforce when the regulations apply to undertakings with between 50 and 100 employees in 2008, just as more than 5 million workers currently are denied access to the statutory trade union recognition procedure because they are in workplaces employing fewer than 21 people.

REFERENCES AND FURTHER READING

ACAS 2004: Information and consultation: Good practice advice: http://www.acas.org.uk/info_consult/goodpractice.html

Ackers, P. and Payne, J. 1998: British trade unions and social partnership: rhetoric, reality and strategy, *International Journal of Human Resource Management*, **9**(3), 529–49.

Ackers, P., Marchington, M., Wilkinson, A. and Dundon, T. 2005: Partnership and voice, with or without trade unions: changing UK management approaches to organizational participation, in M. Stuart and M. Martinez Lucio (eds.), *Partnership and Modernisation in Employment Relations*, London: Routledge.

Anon. 2002: UK reaction to agreement on EU Employee Consultation Directive, *European Industrial Relations Observatory*: http://www.eiro.eurofound.eu.int/2002/01/inbrief/uk0201116n.html

Applebaum, E. and Batt, R. 1994: *The New American Workplace*, Ithaca, NY: ILR Press.

Applebaum, E., Bailey, T., Berg, P. and Kalleberg, A. 2000: *Manufacturing Advantage: Why High-performance Work Systems Pay Off*, Ithaca, NY: Cornell University Press.

Arrowsmith, J. 2002: Partnership 'alive and well', *European Industrial Relations Observatory*: http://www.eiro.eurofound.eu.int/2002/05/feature/uk0205103f.html

Bain, G.S. and Price, R. 1983: Union growth: Dimensions, determinants and destiny, in G.S. Bain (ed.), *Industrial Relations in Britain*, Oxford: Blackwell.

Blyton, P. and Turnbull, P. 2004: *The Dynamics of Employee Relations*, 3rd edn, Basingstoke: Palgrave Macmillan.

Brown, W., Deakin, S., Hudson, M., Pratten, C. and Ryan, P. 1998: *The Individualisation of Employment Contracts in Britain*, Department of Trade and Industry, Employment Relations Research Series 4, London: HMSO.

Charlwood, A. 2004: The new generation of trade union leaders and prospects for union revitalization, *British Journal of Industrial Relations*, **42**(2), 379–97.

Claydon, T. 1996: Union derecognition: A re-examination, in I. Beardwell (ed.), *Contemporary Industrial Relations: A Critical Analysis*, Oxford: Oxford University Press.

Claydon, T. 1998: Problematising partnership: The prospects for a co-operative bargaining agenda, in P. Sparrow and M. Marchington (eds.), *Human Resource Management: The New Agenda*, London: Financial Times/Pitman.

Cully, M. and Woodland, S. 1998: Trade union membership and recognition 1996–97: An analysis of data from the certification officer and the LFS, *Labour Market Trends*, July, 353–64.

DTI (Department of Trade and Industry) 1998: *Fairness at Work*, DTI White Paper, Cm 3968, London: Stationery Office.

DTI (Department of Trade and Industry) 2004: Informing and Consulting Employees: Summary Guidance to the New Legislation: http://www.dti.gov.uk/er/consultation/brief_guide.doc

Danford, A., Richardson, M., Stewart, P., Tailby, S. and Upchurch, M. 2004: High performance work systems and workplace partnership, *New Technology, Work and Employment*, **19**(1), 14–29.

Disney, R., Gosling, A., Machin, S. and McCrae, J. 1998: *The Dynamics of Union Membership in Britain*, Employment Relations Research Series, Research Report 3, London: Department of Trade and Industry.

Dundon, T., Wilkinson, A., Marchington, M. and Ackers, P. 2004: The meaning and purpose of employee voice, *International Journal of Human Resource Management*, **15**(6), 1149–70.

Freeman, R. and Pelletier, J. 1990: The impact of industrial relations legislation on British union density, *British Journal of Industrial Relations*, **28**(2), 141–64.

Frost, A. 2000: Explaining variation in workplace restructuring: the role of local union capabilities, *Industrial and Labor Relations Review*, **53**, 559–78.

Gall, G. 2004: British employer resistance to trade union recognition, *Human Resource Management Journal*, **14**(2), 36–53.

Gall, G. and McKay, S. 1999: Developments in union recognition and derecognition in Britain, 1994–98, *British Journal of Industrial Relations*, **37**(4), 601–14.

Godard, J. 2004: A critical assessment of the high-performance paradigm, *British Journal of Industrial Relations*, **42**(2), 349–78.

Guest, D. and Peccei, R. 2001: Partnership at work: Mutuality and the balance of advantage, *British Journal of Industrial Relations*, **39**(2), 207–36.

Hall, M. 2000: Statutory trade union recognition procedure comes into force, *European Industrial Relations Observatory*: http://www.eiro.eurofound.eu.int/2000/07/feature/uk/0007183f.html

Hall, M. 2003: Draft information and consultation legislation published, *European Industrial Relations Observatory*: http://www.eiro.eurofound.eu/int/2003/07/feature/uk0307106f.html

Hall, M. and Edwards, P. 1999: Reforming the statutory redundancy consultation procedure. *Industrial Law Journal*, **28**(4), 283–302.

Hall, M. and Terry, M. 2004: The emerging system of statutory worker representation, in G. Healey, E. Heery, P. Taylor and W. Brown (eds.), *The Future of Worker Representation*, Basingstoke: Palgrave Macmillan.

Heery, E. 2002: Partnership versus organising: Alternative futures for British trade unionism, *Industrial Relations Journal*, **33**(1), 20–35.

Heery, E., Healy, G. and Taylor, P. 2004: Representation at work: Themes and issues, in G. Healy, E. Heery, P. Taylor and W. Brown (eds.), *The Future of Worker Representation*, Basingstoke: Palgrave Macmillan.

Howell, C. 2004: Is there a third way for industrial relations?, *British Journal of Industrial Relations*, **42**(1), 1–22.

Hyman, R. 2005: Whose (social) partnership?, in M. Stuart and M. Martinez Lucio (eds.), *Partnership and Modernisation in Employment Relations*, London: Routledge.

Johnstone, S., Wilkinson, A. and Ackers, P. 2004: Partnership paradoxes: A case study of an engineering company, *Employee Relations*, **26**(4), 353–76.

Kelly, J. 1996: Union militancy and social partnership, in P. Ackers, C. Smith and P. Smith (eds.), *The New Workplace and Trade Unionism*, London: Routledge.

Kelly, J. 2005: Social partnership agreements in Britain, in M. Stuart and M. Martinez Lucio (eds.), *Partnership and Modernisation in Employment Relations*, London: Routledge.

Kochan, T. and Osterman, P. 1994: *The Mutual Gains Enterprise*, Boston: Harvard Business School Press.

Lloyd, C. 1999: Productivity, competitiveness and the knowledge-driven economy: A new agenda?, *European Industrial Relations Observatory*: http://www.eiro.eurofound.eu.int/1999/02/feature/uk9902182f.html

Metcalf, D. 2004: British unions: Resurgence or perdition?, CEP Working Paper, No. 1347, London School of Economics.

Millward, N., Stevens, M., Smart, D. and Hawes, W.R. 1992: *Workplace Industrial Relations in Transition*, Aldershot: Dartmouth.

Millward, N., Bryson, A. and Forth, J. 2000: *All Change at Work*, London: Routledge.

Moore, S. 2004: Union mobilization and employer counter-mobilization in the statutory recognition process. In J. Kelly and P. Willman (eds.), *Union Organization and Activity*, London: Routledge.

Moore, S., McKay, S. and Bewley, H. 2004: *The Contents of New Voluntary Trade Union Recognition Agreements 1998–2002: Volume 1 – An Analysis of New Agreements and Case Studies*, Employment Relations Research Series No. 26. London: Department of Trade and Industry.

Oxenbridge, S. and Brown, W. 2005: Developing partnership relationships: A case of leveraging power, in M. Stuart and M. Martinez Lucio (eds.), *Partnership and Modernisation in Employment Relations*, London: Routledge.

Oxenbridge, S., Brown, W., Deakin, S. and Pratten, C. 2003: Initial responses to the statutory recognition provisions of the Employment Relations Act 1999, *British Journal of Industrial Relations*, **41**(2), 315–34.

Palmer, T., Grainger, H. and Fitzner, G. 2004: *Trade Union Membership 2003*, London: Department of Trade and Industry. Available at www.dti.gov.uk/er/inform.htm

Stuart, M. and Martinez Lucio, M. (eds.) 2005: *Partnership and Modernisation in Employment Relations*, London: Routledge.

Tailby, S., Richardson, M., Stewart, P., Danford, A. and Upchurch, M. 2004: Partnership at work and worker participation: An NHS case study, *Industrial Relations Journal*, **35**(5), 403–18.

Taylor, P. and Ramsay, H. 1998: Unions, partnership and HRM: Sleeping with the enemy?, *International Journal of Employment Studies*, **6**(2), 115–43.

Terry, M. 2003a: Partnership and the future of trade unions in the UK, *Economic and Industrial Democracy*, **24**(4), 485–508.

Terry, M. 2003b: Employee representation: Shop stewards and the new legal framework, in P. Edwards (ed.), *Industrial Relations: Theory and Practice*, 2nd edn, Oxford: Blackwell.

Terry, M. 2003c: Can 'partnership' reverse the decline of British trade unions? *Work, Employment and Society*, **17**(3), 459–72.

Towers, B. 1997: *The Representation Gap: Change and Reform in the British and American Workplace*, Oxford: Oxford University Press.

TUC, 2001: *Partners for Progress: Winning at Work*, London: Trades Union Congress.

TUC, 2002: *Submission on the Government's discussion document, High Performance Workplaces*, London: Trades Union Congress.

Waddington, J. 2003a: Trade union organization, in P. Edwards (ed.), *Industrial Relations: Theory and Practice*, 2nd edn, Oxford: Blackwell.

Waddington, J. 2003b: Heightening tension in relations between trade unions and the Labour Government in 2002, *British Journal of Industrial Relations*, **41**(2), 335–58.

White, M., Hill, S., McGovern. P., Mills, C. and Smeaton, D. 2003: 'High-performance' management practices, working hours and work–life balance, *British Journal of Industrial Relations*, **41**(2), 175–95.

Wills, J. 2004: Trade unionism and partnership in practice: Evidence from the Barclays-Unifi agreement. *Industrial Relations Journal*, **35**(4), 329–43.

Index